Webster's New World™
SECRETARIAL HANDBOOK

Fourth Edition

**Prepared under the editorial supervision
of In Plain English, Inc.**

Prentice Hall

New York • London • Toronto • Sydney • Tokyo • Singapore

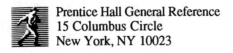

Prentice Hall General Reference
15 Columbus Circle
New York, NY 10023

This new and revised edition of *Webster's New
World™ Secretarial Handbook* includes some material
previously published in *The New World Secretarial
Handbook*, copyright © 1968 by Simon & Schuster,
Inc., and the revised edition copyright © 1974
by Simon & Schuster, Inc.

Materials from *Essentials of Grammar and Style* copyright © 1966
by John I. McCollum is used by permission of the author.

A Webster's New World™ Book

*Dictionary Editorial Offices: New World Dictionaries,
850 Euclid Ave., Cleveland, Ohio 44114*

Library of Congress Cataloging-in-Publication Data

Webster's New World secretarial handbook / prepared under the
supervision of In Plain English, Inc.—4th ed.
    p. cm.
Includes index.
1. Office practice—Handbook, manuals, etc.
2. Secretaries—handbooks, manuals, etc.
I. In Plain English, Inc.
651.3'741'—dc20   89-5698
                                   CIP
ISBN (cloth) 0-13-949256-9
ISBN (paper) 0-671-86471-8

Manufactured in the United States of America

10

Contributors

Susan C. Bauer, Associate Professor, Office Management, *State University Agricultural and Technical College,* Farmingdale, New York

Jeanette L. Bely, Ph.D., F.I.B.A., Professor of Education, *Bernard M. Baruch College of the City University of New York*

Murray Bromberg, Director, Supercenter, Council of Supervisors and Administrators, *The New York Board of Education,* and the *City University of New York*

Linda A. Bruce, President, *New York City chapter of Professional Secretaries International,* New York; Office Manager/Executive Secretary, *American Academy,* Rome, New York

Lois M. Burns, Assistant Professor, Department of Secretarial Science, *New York City Technical College,* Brooklyn, New York

William W. Cook, J.D., Director of Development, *Husson College,* Bangor, Maine

Rose A. Doherty, M.A., Instructor, Business Communications Department, *Katharine Gibbs School,* Boston, Massachusetts

Julie Eichenberger, M.Ed., former Instructor, *Long Island Business Institute,* Commack, New York

Joyce Gold, Adjunct Professor of English, *Fairleigh Dickinson University,* Rutherford, New Jersey; former Instructor, Business Communications Department, *Katharine Gibbs Secretarial School,* New York City

Charlotte B. Holmquest, M.Ed., Business Teacher, *Seabrook Intermediate School,* Seabrook, Texas

Audrey Katz, Legal Secretary

Milton Katz, Adjunct Assistant Professor, English Department, *State University Agricultural and Technical College,* Farmingdale, New York

Ruth Kimball Kent, M.A., Associate Editor (retired), Dictionary Division, *Simon and Schuster*

Doreen La Blanc, Assistant Professor, *Bronx Community College of the City University of New York,* Bronx, New York

John I. McCollum, Ph.D., Professor (retired), Department of English, *University of Miami,* Coral Gables, Florida

James C. Matthews, Associate Professor, Department of Secretarial Sciences, *New York City Technical College,* Brooklyn, New York

Ardis Morton, President, *National Association of Educational Office Personnel;* Secretary, Office of Human Relations, *Fairfax County Schools,* Connecticut

Emojean G. Novotny, B.S., Director, Secretarial Science Division, *Dyke College,* Cleveland, Ohio

Barry Persky, Chair, Education Department, *Walden University,* Minneapolis, Minnesota; Adjunct Assistant Professor, *Brooklyn College,* Brooklyn, New York

Naomi Platt, Ed.D., Professor and Director of GED Support Centers, *Kingsborough Community College,* Brooklyn, New York

Warren T. Schimmel, President, *The Berkeley School of Westchester,* White Plains, New York

Abba Spero, Ph.D., Associate Professor, Accounting, *Cleveland State University*

Contents

The Secretary Today

What It Means to Be a Professional Secretary

by Lois M. Burns

The secretary is a professional—not only because of the knowledge and preparation necessary for the job but also because being a professional implies competence, pride in one's work, and a dedication to excellence. The secretary is a professional with each of these qualities. Moreover, the secretary is an important member of the management team, responsible not only for carrying out the executive's wishes but also for helping to maintain a well-organized and efficient office.

The word *secretary* comes from the Latin *secretarius,* meaning "confidential employee." The secretary of today is still an employee who is privy to confidential information. In that respect, the job has not changed. However, the tools of the trade have changed over the years.

Office automation and machine dictation have revolutionized the type of work that the secretary does, and changes are expected to continue. The changes that will take place in the future are impossible to predict, but the professional secretary—also sometimes known as the administrative assistant, administrative secretary, private secretary, or several other titles—will be able to learn and adapt to each new challenging environment.

ENTERING AND SUCCEEDING IN
THE PROFESSION

The relative ease with which a person can enter the secretarial profession is a plus. A high school education; typing, shorthand, machine transcription, and filing skills; and knowledge of office procedures, word processing and computer equipment, and software packages will enable one to advance along a career path. A post-secondary education is an additional asset.

The secretary entering the work force is faced with a multitude of possible job situations. Although the conditions under which a secretary works are fairly standard throughout the economy, a choice can certainly be made about location, the size of the company, and the company's services or products. Each and every area of the economy needs the expertise of a secretary, and the professional secretary has only to choose the field most interesting to him or her and the one in which career goals can be furthered. Weekly pay and fringe benefits are as important as ever, but today's secretary is also concerned with the possibilities for professional growth within a company.

Secretaries are professionals with career goals. Most large organizations have a human resources department that is concerned with the professional growth and development of their employees. By providing training and educational opportunities for employees from date of hire until retirement, these organizations are able to enhance the effectiveness of their operations and to enrich the lives of their employees.

Specialized training is a matter of professional survival in a world where the methods of handling information are changing rapidly. The secretary will be increasingly involved with office automation and needs to be familiar with the concept and the technology. The responsibilities of the secretary are multifunctional: typing/keyboarding; transcribing; processing mail; telephoning; scheduling appointments; greeting visitors; composing and editing documents; researching; coordinating meetings, conferences, and teleconferences; making travel arrangements; handling reprographics; and organizing time and work. Supervisor and management education and advanced technical and professional education are available to those who are interested in moving ahead in the organization. The director of education at a nationwide insurance company states that one of the great benefits of a well-developed education and training program is that people on the secretarial level can move into supervisory, administrative, and managerial positions if they have the desire and the ability to do so.

Secretaries are encouraged to develop career paths and life plans just as executives do. The secretary's projected work life is just as long as the executive's. These years will be more pleasant if the individual takes steps to examine what kind of job will be the most personally satisfying now and in the future. This kind of examination also benefits the organization, because it keeps personnel from changing companies when a change in work responsibility would be more satisfying.

Many organizations also encourage secretaries to avail themselves of outside educational opportunities through financial support. Frequently these outside courses must be job related or related to a degree which the company agrees would benefit the employee and employer. Sometimes, however, these courses are promoted for the personal enrichment of the employee. All of these personnel-development efforts increase the secretary's satisfaction with the job and the employer.

PROFESSIONAL DEVELOPMENT

Participation in professional organizations is one way a secretary can grow professionally. Organizations offer the opportunity to network with other professionals and promote personal development by providing information, contacts, and support. Several professional organizations sponsor annual conventions, local conferences, seminars, and courses to enhance secretarial performance.

The following organizations provide many opportunities for service, educational, and professional growth: Professional Secretaries International (PSI), the Association of Information Systems Professionals (AISP), the American Association for Medical Assistants (AAMA), the American Association for Medical Transcription (AAMT), and the National Association of Legal Secretaries (International). Several of these organizations sponsor certification programs.

Professional Secretaries International (PSI) fosters an awareness of professional pride and the maintenance of high standards by promulgating the following definition:

> A secretary shall be defined as an executive assistant who possesses a mastery of office skills, demonstrates the ability to assume responsibility without direct supervision, exercises initiative and judgment, and makes decisions within the scope of assigned authority.

The importance of an organization like PSI cannot be overemphasized. All professional people take pride in their affiliation with organizations that attest to the importance of their field. Lawyers have bar associations; doctors have the American Medical Association; teachers have national educational organizations. In each of these groups the purpose is to set standards for the profession and to honor those who meet the standards. Professional Secretaries International awards the title of Certified Professional Secretary (CPS) to those who have passed a comprehensive two-day, six-part examination. The title of Certified Professional Secretary brings respect from peers and superiors.

The examination that the aspiring secretary must take calls upon knowledge that has been gained through education and work experience. Office administration and communication, office technology, accounting, economics and management, business law, and behavioral science in business are the areas covered by the test. For one who has not yet become a Certified Professional Secretary, membership in PSI and participation in the local chapter's activities will bring a sense of the importance of a secretary's job to the functioning of society and will introduce the secretary to others who have similar professional goals.

Additional information may be obtained from Professional Secretaries International, 301 East Armour Boulevard, Kansas City, MO 64111-1299.

THE TOOLS OF THE PROFESSION

Keyboarding, shorthand, transcription, filing, office procedures, and knowledge of word processing systems and equipment are the skills for which the secretary was hired. However, the ability to use the language and a commitment to professionalism will earn respect and promotions.

Language

The raw material to which the secretary applies these skills is the English language. A command of and a respect for the English language, both in writing and in speaking, are essential. A good dictionary, a thesaurus, and a grammar book must be kept handy for immediate checking of spelling, end-of-line division, usage, and sentence construction. In the automated office, equipment may have a built-in spell checker or a software program with a dictionary or grammar component. Work still has to be proofread, however, because the equipment and programs cannot distinguish between homonyms, nor can they determine if the transcript omitted a word. Letters, whether the secretary composes them or transcribes them, represent the company, the employer, and the professional secretary. The recipient of a letter must never get the impression that any one of the three is less than first rate. Most executives have a good speaking command of the language. This asset is often one of the reasons why an individual reaches a top management position. However, it is the secretary's responsibility to check details of grammar, spelling, and punctuation. An employer with an excellent command of English presents a double challenge to the secretary. Transcribed letters must be absolutely perfect, and letters composed for the executive must match them in composition, tone, and clarity.

The secretary may occasionally be the final check on grammar. An executive may have been hired for an area of technical expertise, not language ability. In this case the secretary will be responsible for editing all of the written communications from the office. The executive and the secretary in this situation must realize their mutual dependence and work to turn out superior written material. Correcting a dangling participle or making the verb and subject agree will demonstrate to the executive that the secretary is a professional with extremely valuable skills.

Professional Reading

Trade journals are published for each area of the economy and for each profession. By reading these publications, the secretary demonstrates professional concern and also learns new ideas and new vocabulary that may soon find its way into transcription. The competent secretary does not have to read these magazines from cover to cover but will develop a system for skimming, using the table of contents as a guide, to stay abreast of developments.

Numerous magazines and professional journals pertaining to the secretarial profession and business management and organization are available. These periodicals will help the secretary cope with difficult situations by discussions of how others solved similar problems and will alert the secretary to new products, procedures, and equipment for the office.

Reading magazines such as *The Secretary, Fortune, Business Week, Forbes, Today's Office,* and *Office Administration and Automation* is part of the commitment to professional excellence.

Information Processing

The combination of word processing and microcomputer systems has revolutionized the way secretaries work and process information. More and more offices have acquired the most sophisticated technological equipment, and the secretary needs only the ability and the desire to grow and change with each new development or modification.

Such systems provide an automated information center that upgrades the quality of hard copy materials while improving office efficiency by increasing the speed with which the material is produced. Today's businesses must deal with more written information than ever before, and they must transmit that information quickly and accurately. The secretary who puts the material into the system is irreplaceable, but the system can perform at speeds that a typist would find impossible. Material for bulk mailing and form letters can be keyboarded in a much shorter time by the equipment. Having an executive decide to insert three paragraphs on page 60 of a 200-page document no longer means that the entire document must be re-keyboarded. The material to be inserted is keyboarded into the machine, and the finished document is produced, often in seconds. Complete documents of hundreds of pages can be sent from one office to another in minutes, rather than days. And, by using satellite communication, a subsidiary company's entire monthly report can be transmitted to the home office half a continent away in 30 seconds.

New vocabulary and procedures must be learned to use the information processing equipment. The competent secretary will not only learn how to respond to the instructions of the system but will also make every effort to understand how the system works and how best to make use of the various options offered. Entirely new systems of office management have resulted with the installation of word processing systems, word processors, microcomputers, and numerous software programs.

The future is unlimited for the secretary who takes advantage of all training opportunities and remains open and flexible to the changes that will certainly develop in the industry.

A Professional Manner

The secretary is classified as a white-collar, rather than a blue-collar, worker because neither work clothes nor protective clothing are required in the office. However, the secretary should view clothing as a uniform that fits the image of the office and thus advances the secretary's career goals along with the purpose of the office. If there is no declared dress code, clues about formality should be taken from the other employees in the office. If the men always wear conservative business suits and the women are always dressed in conservatively tailored clothing, striking a blow for individuality in dress will do nothing for one's personal goals. If the office is very informal, the secretary who wishes to be noticed and moved ahead will wear clothing that is just a shade more formal and more professional. The goal is not to alienate other workers but to make oneself stand out as the secretary who takes work seriously. When the executive office has an opening, the secretary who has demonstrated the most personal polish, in addition to superb skills, is the one who will be chosen.

A proper office manner should be cultivated by the secretary, and this manner should be based on the fact that the executive and the secretary are expected to work as a team. The secretary should follow the lead of the executive in office style. Whether working for an individual, a pair of executives, or a whole department, the secretary's duty is to help fulfill the executive job responsibilities. Therefore, assignments that appear in the job description (if there is one) are done conscientiously, and those chores that do not appear but that need to be done in order to free the executive from routine tasks will be done by the professional secretary without grumbling.

Much has been written about people moving ahead in careers because of the mentor/protégé system whereby a seasoned hand in the business takes on the education of someone younger who has promise. Although the superior may be grooming someone for a place on the management level, the secretary can also be a protégé who moves upward in salary and responsibility with the boss or with the boss's blessing.

As part of the team, the professional secretary protects the employer. He or she does not contribute information to office gossip but does report any rumor that may be helpful to the superior, first qualifying the information as gossip. Also, the professional does not spend company time on personal phone calls, in clock watching, or in being late.

THE COMPETENT SECRETARY

The secretary plans not only a career path but also short- and long-range work for the company. Short-range planning enables the secretary to do each day those things that must be done. For example, a routine is established whereby the secretary's and the employer's desks are ready for work at the beginning of each day. Standard procedures for handling mail, for advising the executive of telephone calls, and for handling dictation and transcription are set up, but this schedule does not lead to inflexibility. The competent secretary is capable of taking any kind of interruption in stride. When the emergency or interruption has been dealt with, the work routine is resumed at the point of interruption. Long-range planning makes it possible for the secretary to concentrate on low-priority projects at a slow time of the year and also makes it possible for the executive to call on secretarial aid at times when the work flow is heavy.

Effective Use of Time

The secretary's time is a valuable and perishable commodity. All duties are performed as quickly as possible so that the unexpected may be dealt with. A sense of the relative urgency of activities is developed with experience, so that it is possible to distinguish the important from the trivial. A long-distance caller does not distract the secretary from the necessity to transcribe an urgent letter. The unexpected visitor is started on his or her way courteously and firmly, rather than being allowed to waste company time.

Business calls are evaluated for length, and they are not continued beyond the time that is absolutely essential for courtesy and the exchange of information. The secretary should structure the business call in the form of a business letter. It should be planned ahead and should have a beginning, middle, and end. If one is making a call, a clear statement of purpose should open, followed by details, questions, or whatever the call must accomplish. The call should be completed by thanking the person on the other end, stating the action you or your boss expect to be taken, or getting a firm commitment for future action or the time of a return call. Remember that this is a business call and avoid those verbal ticks like "you know" and slang that would be appropriate in a personal call.

Responsibility and Follow-Up

By carefully following through on any tasks assigned, the secretary demonstrates a sense of responsibility every day. When the employer is out, the secretary displays professionalism by making sure that the office is covered at all times, especially when the workday begins in the morning. Every experienced secretary knows that this is when the problems start.

Take, for example, a situation in which the executive and the secretary are the only ones who know all aspects of a given situation. When the boss is away, something that vitally affects that matter happens. The competent secretary is present and immediately gets in touch with the employer so that the appropriate course of action can be decided and so that the secretary can set the wheels in motion.

Relationship with Executive

The personal relationship between the executive and the secretary will vary according to the people involved and the formality of the company. The secretary should always remember that the relationship is a business arrangement and that the structure of any organization makes the executive more important than the secretary. Without the executive to set the overall objective and to plan for action to attain that objective, the secretary's job would not exist. Nevertheless, the indispensable contribution of the secretary to the execution of the executive's work should be a source of professional pride.

The executive may ask the secretary to explain a matter, but the secretary does not have the right to call upon the executive to justify decisions. However, when a good working relationship exists, office authority is not a source of discontent because both the secretary and the executive realize that they are there to make that office run at peak efficiency.

No job is without its dull routines as well as its stimulating aspect. No employer is without faults. There may be times when you consider your employer unreasonable. You may be asked to do chores that you consider demeaning or outside your province or job description. Decide how intrusive these jobs are, and discuss the matter with your employer. Perhaps the duties can be added to your job description. Otherwise, see if you can arrange for the writing of a job description if there is none.

Appropriate Behavior

Personal life must be separated from professional life in dealing with all office personnel. It is very possible to work well with people one does not like at all; likewise, it is possible to work professionally with people who are personal friends. Personal problems should not be brought into the office. However, worries about sickness at home, financial problems, and domestic difficulties do affect the quality of work, and the professional will do everything possible to keep the level of professional performance high. The fact that a doctor has personal troubles is not an acceptable excuse for a faulty diagnosis of a patient. One expects the doctor to perform well, and the executive has the right to expect the secretary to remain competent despite difficulties. People, however, are not machines and are not expected to behave as such. When overwhelming problems are present, the supervisor should be told before one's work is held up for censure.

Professional behavior as part of a team determines the relationships with the rest of the organization. In dealing with other members of the group, the secretary should make it clear that those others are viewed as the experts in their jobs. The professional secretary is courteous to everyone regardless of the individual's position on the company ladder. The order-processing clerk, the shipping clerk, the receptionist, the typist, and the file clerk will be much more helpful to the secretary/executive team if this attitude of professionalism is maintained.

Alertness to Mistakes

The secretary must be very honest in all relationships within the company. Blame must be accepted if a mistake has been made. Everyone makes mistakes, and the good secretary will do everything possible to avoid them. The need to make use of other people's expertise must be recognized, and the secretary should help others in the office in an effort to foster a spirit of helpfulness to insure that good work is turned out. For example, even if a secretary's typing can be called excellent, proofreading of important documents should be done by two people. The secretary should therefore try to make arrangements to proofread material with a co-worker.

Alertness to the mistakes of others so that the mistakes may be corrected is characteristic of the competent secretary. Especially if work is done under pressure, people have a tendency not to check a figure, proofread a page, or make certain that a statement conforms to policy. The secretary must check and double-check to avoid errors that, more than simply being embarrassing, might affect important decisions adversely.

Level of Authority

Differentiating between the executive's requests and the secretary's requests is necessary. In the first instance, the secretary has a lot of authority; in the second instance, there is much less. If the executive needs the report by 4 P.M., the department responsible will recognize that the effort and expense are inconsequential compared to the importance of meeting the deadline. However, the secretary must not push co-workers unless the pressure is justified. Everyone has a schedule to which he or she must adhere. Remember to respect the importance and the schedules of other people's work. Never claim authority for yourself when you are passing on the executive's wishes. "Professor Brown would like all class schedules completed by Friday" will get a better response than "I would like all class schedules completed by Friday." Even with suggestions the same rule is followed. A suggested course is far more likely to be implemented if put forward as the boss's idea, particularly if it involves difficulty.

Accurate Record-Keeping

The secretary's filing system gets the same careful attention given to other duties. The employer must have an accurate record of what has happened in the past in order to take future action. For highly confidential matters or the employer's personal correspondence, a system consistent with filing rules but responsive to the needs of the office should be set up. If the company has a central files department, the secretary works closely with the assigned file clerk, whose expertise should be recognized.

Filing is a historical recording of events that have occurred in a given aspect of company development. Filing requires intelligence, an intimate knowledge of the subject matter, and an organized method of recording. The secretary should work with the file clerk. All material should be carefully marked to indicate whether there has been any previous correspondence on the subject. If the previous reference could not be easily identified by the file clerk, a notation indicating the subject with which it should be filed is a courtesy that will save time, prevent confusion, and contribute to a helpful attitude in the office, which will be to everyone's benefit. If a subject is especially important or unusually complicated, an exchange of ideas may enable the file clerk to set up the file intelligently. A sense of history on the part of the secretary and the file clerk will enable them to build up a file coherently, so that a person reading it will be able to determine the sequence of events and the actions taken. When the secretary recognizes the complexity of the file clerk's job, the employer will get the file or information sought, not an excuse.

Today, many firms have word processing and computer equipment and documents are stored on disks and automatically filed in the system.

SECRETARIAL SPECIALTIES

A competent secretary may work in one particular type of office and become familiar with the equipment, vocabulary, procedures, and duties specific to that type of office. In some cases, specific training is required. A few secretarial specialties are discussed here and a more detailed discussion of some of the more common ones is provided later in the book in the major section titled "For the Specialized Secretary."

The Executive Secretary

The executive secretary or the administrative assistant is more than just a secretary or an assistant to an executive. In some companies and organizations, the terms seem to be interchangeable; in other companies, one is placed above the other on the organizational ladder. Whether one uses the term executive secretary or administrative assistant, in terms of responsibility, knowledge of the company's business, judgment, and experience, this person is an executive. The executive secretary (the term we shall use in this discussion) may indeed employ a secretary or a whole staff. Making decisions that affect an important segment of the company's operations and, in some cases, taking charge of business while the executive is absent brings the executive secretary financial and personal rewards. But these benefits are earned. At this highest level of secretarial authority, the responsibilities are such that the greatest possible effort to check procedures and avoid errors is essential. Planning, discretion, knowledge, accuracy, efficiency, and dependability are watchwords of the job. The executive secretary has top skills and keeps them serviceable. Technical skills and knowledge of the latest automated equipment are essential.

Confidence of the executive's staff is built slowly and carefully. These are the people who have the responsibility to carry out the objectives of the company or department. The executive secretary's duty is to screen demands on the executive's time, not to make the executive as unapproachable as Presidents of the United States have sometimes been made by their staffs.

Decisions must be made promptly; action must be taken swiftly. Anything that slows that action is detrimental to the overall operation of the company. When a member of the staff has to see the boss, it may be because that person faces some decision beyond the scope of his or her particular authority. It may seem a simple matter to give notice that the subordinate has to see the executive, but what if the secretary has six or seven calls from different staff members? Who sees the executive first, who next, and who not at all? It is up to the secretary to win the confidence of each member of the staff so that person will be absolutely honest as to the urgency of any particular request. Each has to know that if the employee says, "I must have it five minutes before noon," he or she will have it if it is humanly possible, and that if the employee says, "Tomorrow will be fine," he or she will see the executive tomorrow without any further reminders to the secretary. In such circumstances, maximum use is made of everyone's time. The secretary can work out an orderly plan with the executive to conserve time. The subordinate can attend to other projects without wasting time calling back or attempting to waylay the executive in the hall. In this cooperative atmosphere, everyone realizes that the short-term advantage would not be worth the risk of losing the secretary's confidence.

The secretary must always be aware of being a representative of the executive, and while the staff is subordinate to the executive, the staff is not subordinate to the secretary. As the subordinates' confidence grows, they will ask advice or opinions on how the boss would like something done. The secretary has a responsibility to give accurate advice and to state only opinions that truly represent the executive's feelings. If the secretary's personal opinion is given, the subordinate may be misled as to the executive's actual sentiments on the matter.

The executive secretary cannot play favorites. The executive must view operations as a whole and must be able to depend upon the secretary to reflect this accurately in dealings with subordinates. It is important that each staff member be recognized as an integral part of the team and as making a contribution to the company. Each employee wants the good opinion of the boss, and perhaps even without consciously recognizing it, the secretary's reaction to an employee may be interpreted as a reflection of the boss's opinion. The secretary must remember that a personality trait that is unattractive to the secretary may be exactly the trait that makes the subordinate effective in a particular function. The subordinate who insists upon "dotting every i and crossing every t" may be far more effective in controlling costs than the easygoing, affable staff member who has difficulty in keeping even a personal expense account within proper bounds. The boss may have a higher opinion of the former than of the latter, and a secretary's favoring of the affable over the precise subordinate might be doing an injustice to both individuals and to the executive. By dampening the enthusiasm of one and giving a false sense of confidence to the other, the executive is misrepresented and the company's objectives may be impeded.

The job of executive secretary or administrative assistant is challenging and rewarding and a lot of hard work. Intelligence, interest, dedication, plus experience and training are essential for success.

The Legal Secretary

Accuracy and speed are the hallmarks of the legal secretary in the one-lawyer office or the large firm with a national reputation. The work of a law office is exacting; an inaccurate record can be extremely expensive to the firm. Terminology is precise. Since many legal procedures have to follow an initial action in exact sequence, timing and organization are essential.

Typing/keyboarding, shorthand, transcription skills, and a knowledge of legal documents and legal terminology are important. Verbal and writing ability are essential because the legal secretary's work is very exacting. The work is also highly varied and involves extensive contact with clients. The legal secretary must, of course, refrain from answering legal questions.

Word-processing systems and microcomputers have been added to most law offices to aid in the preparation of legal documents. The secretary who wishes to remain in the field should take advantage of every opportunity to learn the newest automated equipment.

The legal secretary's job is not easy, because there is a lot of pressure and there usually are long hours of work. However, it is one of the most lucrative jobs in the secretarial field. The fringe benefits are generally excellent, and the vacation periods are usually generous.

Certification. The legal secretary may become a certified professional legal secretary. The Certified Professional Legal Secretary designation is the only certification program for legal secretaries providing a standard measurement of legal secretarial knowledge and skills.

Any person who has had five years' experience as a legal secretary and who meets the other application requirements may sit for a rigorous two-day examination. A partial waiver of the five-year experience requirement may be granted if the applicant has a bachelor's or associate's degree. Seven areas of legal secretarial practice and procedures are included in the examination: written communication skills and knowledge; ethics; legal secretarial procedures; legal secretarial accounting; exercise of judgment; legal secretarial skills; and legal terminology, techniques, and procedures.

For additional information contact the National Association of Legal Secretaries, 2250 East 73 Street, Suite 550, Tulsa, OK 74136, or telephone (918) 493-3540.

For a more detailed discussion of the requirements and duties of a legal secretary, see Chapter 18, "Legal Secretary."

The Medical Secretary

Medical secretaries may be employed in a physician's office, medical clinic, hospital, public health facility, health maintenance organization, nursing home, research center, foundation, laboratory, insurance company, pharmaceutical company, government-related health service agency, private agency, publishing company, medical department of a business organization, business that manufactures medical supplies and equipment, or medical transcription service company. Each job requires keyboarding skills, machine transcription, and a knowledge of word processing, computers, and software programs in addition to familiarity with medical terminology.

The medical secretary may need to know how to perform certain medical tasks, how to complete insurance claim forms, how to take a patient's medical history, how to handle the doctor's billings, and how to perform other clerical duties peculiar to a doctor's office. In addition, the secretary may need to deal with people who are ill, a task requiring patience, sympathy, and tact.

Regardless of the setting—a one-doctor office or a large facility— the medical secretary must observe medical ethics. Cases should not be discussed except in the context of office business, and no comments or questions regarding a patient's condition or ailments should be made in the presence of other persons.

The professional medical assistant enjoys an enviable professional status. The medical assistant is eligible to join the American Association of Medical Assistants (AAMA) and can apply for certification. The AAMA offers a certifying examination, the successful completion of which leads to a certificate and recognition as a Certified Medical Assistant-Administrative (CMA-A) or a Certified Medical Assistant-Clinical (CMA-C) or both. The examination is given in January and June of each year at designated centers throughout the United States. As of 1988, revalidation every five years is mandatory, and it can be accomplished through continuing education units (CEUs) or reexamination.

The AAMA provides members the opportunity of attending local, state, and regional meetings and a national convention where one can participate in workshops, learn of educational advances in the field, visit exhibits, hear prominent speakers, and establish a networking system with other medical assistants. The Association publishes a bimonthly journal, *The Professional Medical Assistant.*

For more information contact the American Association of Medical Assistants, 20 North Wacker, Suite 1575, Chicago, IL 60606.

The American Association for Medical Transcription (AAMT) member has the opportunity to attend local, state, and regional meetings and a national convention where one can participate in workshops, learn of educational advances in the field, visit exhibits, hear prominent speakers, and establish a networking system with other medical transcriptionists. The Association publishes a professional journal four times a year, the *Journal of the AAMT,* and publishes a newsletter six times a year, the *AAMT Newsletter.*

The AAMT offers a certifying examination, with successful completion leading to a certificate and recognition as a Certified Medical Transcriptionist (CMT). The examination is given on the last Saturday in April and a specialty examination on the first Saturday in November at various locations throughout the United States. Certification by examination is valid for three years and may be renewed by paying the annual continuing education assessment fee and earning a minimum of 30 continuing education credits in each three-year period of certification, or achieving a passing score on the certification examination every three years. Of the 30 continuing education units, at least 20 must be in the medical science category. A CMT must continue upgrading skills through attending the Association's lectures and obtaining continuing education units (CEUs).

Additional information may be obtained from the American Association for Medical Transcription, P.O. Box 6187, Modesto, CA 95355, or by telephoning (800) 982-2182.

The Technical Secretary

The growth of research, both governmental and private, and the explosion of knowledge have created the need for secretaries with the ability to deal with technical terms and symbols. Typing, editing, and proofreading are necessary skills for all secretaries, but technical secretaries must possess the highest level of skills. The ability to accurately type information that can be understood only by the researchers is essential, and the ability to proofread material that makes little or no sense to someone who is not technically trained in the field is indispensable.

The technical secretary must also recognize that the scientists and researchers have been hired for their technical competence, not their writing skill, and frequently the secretary will need to edit material to make it grammatically correct and smooth flowing. This task calls for much tact, patience, and humility in the face of material that is written in English but is often incomprehensible to the layperson. However, for the secretary with the ability to deal with mathematical equations, Greek letters, and so forth, advancement to the level of technical aide and research assistant is possible.

The technical secretary's job is demanding and exacting and

requires specialized skills. A strong background in mathematics, science, and technical terminology is a definite asset. The remuneration and benefits in these situations are usually quite good.

The Educational Secretary

The opportunities for secretaries in educational institutions from the preschool to the graduate level are as varied as the institutions themselves. The secretary in the elementary school may occasionally have to comfort a sick child who is waiting to go home or help a parent deal with the multiple forms that educational systems require. In higher education the secretary may be assigned to a specific academic or administrative area. The educational secretary meets school visitors and has close contact with students, teachers, and parents.

The duties of the secretary vary from school to school and often depend on its size. In a small school the secretary may have to handle student records, transcripts of grades, orders for materials and supplies, personnel records, the scheduling of facilities, and many other tasks. In larger institutions the secretary may be assigned just one of these duties or may be responsible for a specific department.

The minimum education requirement for an educational secretary varies. In some institutions a high school education is sufficient, whereas in others, especially colleges and universities, some type of college experience or a degree is required.

The National Association of Educational Office Personnel is the professional organization for secretaries in this field.

See also Chapter 21, "Educational Secretary."

The Secretary in Advertising, Radio and Television, Journalism, and the Arts

The skills required for these jobs are the same as for a job in any business, but the amount of contact with interesting personalities, public figures, and the public is increased. When dealing with public personalities, the secretary must be able to maintain a professional manner. If the employer does not wish to talk to a local public figure or a network newsperson, the secretary must be firm and diplomatic. Jobs in these fields require the ability to deal with people whose job it is to manipulate responses.

The professional secretary will decide just what kind of job will give the most satisfaction and the kind of atmosphere that will be pleasant. Will the high-pressure atmosphere of an advertising agency or television station make you nervous or will it challenge you? The fact that you are contributing to the success of a gallery or a museum may be the kind of reward that means the most to you. The excitement of putting any kind of publication "to bed" may be just what you want. Remember to take extras, such as house seats for a play, into consideration when you are considering a career.

The Secretary in Government

The federal government is the largest employer in the United States and should not be overlooked by the professional secretary. In order to become eligible for most governmental positions, the secretary must take a written civil service examination. Promotions are usually made from within based on availability and the demonstrated skill and industry of the applicant. Government positions offer annual salary increments, job security, and retirement systems.

There are also employment opportunities for secretaries in foreign countries. The Department of State has Foreign Service offices in over 300 cities worldwide.

Other jobs are also available in the public sector. State, county, and municipal governments, plus the many quasi-governmental agencies, all have need of skilled secretaries.

The secretary who is interested in public service should contact the Office of Personnel Management in the region in which he or she wishes to obtain employment.

The Secretary in Travel

Excitement and adventure are the fruits of secretarial work in the travel industry. Airlines, resorts, and travel agencies often offer free or reduced rates in transportation, hotel accommodations, and tours to their employees.

However, one does not get all this just for the asking. The job requires hard work. One must have a sincere liking for and a desire to help people. You are helping them to spend the money for which they have often worked hard all year. Also, you must deal with harried offices that may have to get an executive to Europe as quickly as possible.

A secretary in the travel industry must know geography well, be able to read different companies' timetables, plan itineraries, and make reservations through a computer. In short, you must know how to do everything and anything that will contribute to the comfort and enjoyment of your company's customers. Above all, you must be accurate. The pleasure of a vacation or a business opportunity can be lost by a single error.

Each year the volume of business and pleasure travel exceeds the previous year's. A person with the right combination or interest in people and ability to deal with details will find a bright future as a secretary in the travel field.

SPECIAL EMPLOYMENT SITUATIONS

Most secretaries are employed on a full-time basis in a particular office. However, there are available certain other types of employment situations, among them temporary work and part-time work.

The Temporary Secretary

Temporary employment services throughout the country fulfill a need for both employers and employees. The secretary who works on a temporary basis fills in vacancies created by vacations, illness, sudden resignations, or other situations including short-term openings during peak workload periods.

Secretaries take on temporary employment for a number of reasons. Some use temporary employment as an opportunity to explore different industries, organizations, and working conditions so as to determine a preference and a career path. For others, family obligations or other responsibilities make a permanent position inconvenient and a temporary situation ideal. A temporary position also permits a flexible schedule and a choice of job locations, and these considerations may be important to someone pursuing further education or an avocation.

Agencies that engage temporary employees prefer secretaries who have had experience so that they will be able to go into an office and immediately assume the responsibilities of the job. Temporary secretaries must be flexible, confident, and adaptable.

The pay in temporary work is slightly lower in many cases than that of permanent workers who have the same job skills and responsibilities. Fringe benefits are becoming more available to temporary workers. Some agencies that place temporary secretaries in offices now offer group life and medical insurance, paid holidays, paid vacations, referral bonuses, seniority or longevity bonuses, profit sharing, scholarships, and training on word processors, computers, and related office equipment.

The Part-time Secretary

Doctors, educational institutions, small businesses, and, to a growing extent, large corporations often need part-time secretaries. The individual or firm may require only a few hours of work each day or only a few days per week. In other situations, a few weeks or a few months of the year may be required. Some companies are now willing to divide a full-time job between two part-time secretaries; two secretaries, in other words, share one full-time job. Part-time work enables the secretary to maintain skills while freeing the individual for other responsibilities or interests.

THE SECRETARY'S DAY

Job descriptions by their nature make the task of organizing the workday a bit easier, but if your job does not have a formal description of duties, organization is the word to keep in mind. Not only must the secretary's desk be organized but also the work that flows across the executive's desk must be ordered. Decisions about what is important must be made constantly, since most secretaries will have more work to do in one day than can be reasonably accomplished. The principle to be used to help one decide what is most important is the principle that keeps the executive and the secretary working together as a team.

The interests of the superior must come first, and the good secretary will be sure to perform tasks that the executive wants completed quickly and thoroughly. Deadlines between the secretary and the executive in the office may be missed because of extraordinary circumstances, but if your boss misses a deadline with higher company executives because your work was not completed on time, do not expect to have an excuse accepted.

Prepare the afternoon before. The schedule for each day begins the afternoon before when the secretary goes through the tickler or follow-up folder to determine exactly what must be done the next day. The follow-up file should be set up in whatever way the secretary finds most convenient. If the office operates on a yearly schedule with certain meetings, promotions, and correspondence scheduled for the same time each year, the secretary may wish to have monthly files with notations about the amount of time it took to plan last year's fall sales meeting and the list of tasks to be performed in connection with that meeting. In an office that does not have this repetitive schedule, the secretary may use a desk calendar to keep track of letters to be answered, telephone calls that must be made, shipments expected, and so forth. The secretary should make a list of the items that must be taken care of the next day and a list of appointments for the executive, along with pertinent information and the materials that should be prepared. To conclude the day, the equipment should be turned off and covered and the desk cleared so that the maintenance staff will be able to work.

Prompt morning start. The office must be ready to function at whatever time it opens, and the secretary should be at work in the office, not returning from the washroom or talking in the next office. Certain jobs must be performed each day, and the secretary taking over an office would be wise to make a list of these in the order in which they should be done until the routine becomes second nature.

After opening the mail and putting the most important item on top, the trusted secretary may be required to call certain items to the executive's attention. This practice, however, should be begun only when permission has been given. The executive may ask that some of the journals and newspapers the office receives be skimmed and that pertinent articles, notices of new products, promotions, and so forth be marked for special notice.

Mail must be moved quickly from the secretary's desk to the appropriate correspondent; rerouting is done immediately. If some of the letters can be answered by the secretary, the executive may return them with notations about content. This letter-writing and typing task will then be completed as soon as possible.

Priority of duties. The previous afternoon the secretary should have made a list of tasks for the following day by using the techniques of time management. Tasks fall into three categories: those that must be done immediately, those that may be done, and those that may be put off. Just as the executive has a list of appointments, the secretary should have a list of tasks and some notation after each entry to indicate its relative importance. All necessary items can be given an A or 1; the tasks that should be done when there is time, a B or 2; and the tasks that can be left until a slack period, a C or 3. The mental exercise of deciding which items are the most important is the first step in getting the day's work finished. The trap of putting down jobs which are part of the daily routine or filling the list from the third category must be avoided. Putting down small jobs just for the satisfaction of crossing them out is a dangerous game to play. The executive will not want to hear that all of the filing is up-to-date and that the invitation for the annual office party has been sent to the printers if the report that was due in the president's office at 11 A.M. has not been typed.

Importance of the memo pad. The duties of a secretary are as varied as are jobs and employers. But in any situation it is safe to assume that the secretary is responsible for handling the mail, making calls and answering the telephone, taking and transcribing dictation, following up orders and work in progress, and organizing office work. More often than not, the secretary must keep track of the employer's appointments and maintain a filing system—all in addition to the specifics of the job.

How can one keep all of these duties in mind? The experienced secretary knows that it is impossible. Everything must be written down on the memo pad that is at hand at all times. Every request, every assignment, every message is noted. Nothing is left to memory or chance. The secretary's work procedure depends upon the nature of the job and the size of the company. Some offices have established routines; some employers will specify the methods they prefer; sometimes a departing secretary will train an incoming one. The basic tools of organization are a memo pad, a calendar, an appointment book, and a telephone-address book or file.

The memo pad will function as an added memory bank. Notations are made from each phone call, each request for an answer, each new assignment. By writing the information down, the secretary is freed from the need to keep small pieces of information in a mental notebook. Also, by writing all information down, the secretary is able to resume work at the point of interruption.

Keeping an appointment book. The appointment book is one of the most important records in the office. There are various methods of recording and following up appointments, but essential to each is the appointment book. In automated offices, there is an electronic calendar.

In some offices the book is kept on the executive's desk. The secretary must maintain an accurate duplicate appointment book so that both members of the office know how each day is to be spent. In other offices the executive assigns the appointment book to the secretary, who makes all of the appointments. To examine the book, the executive will have to go to the secretary's desk and read it there or temporarily remove it.

Before making appointments, the secretary must be familiar with office procedure. Such matters as availability of executives, availability of conference rooms for meetings, daily arrival and departure times, and average schedules and length of conferences affect the making of appointments.

The appointment should be entered under the day and the hour agreed upon by the person requesting it and the secretary. The entry includes the names of the persons concerned, some notation of the topic to be discussed, and any other pertinent information. The secretary uses these notes to produce needed documents for the executive to read before the meeting. If the material is complex, the secretary may give it to the executive days ahead of time when the work flow is slow. On the day of the appointment the secretary follows through to be sure that there is no misunderstanding and to be sure that the appropriate materials and notes are on the executive's desk. If the appointment is canceled, arrangements for a new appointment should be made immediately.

Developing familiarity with sources of information. The secretary who can find not only the names of those whom the employer must reach most frequently but also the names, addresses, and phone numbers for services, emergencies, and sources of information is a valuable asset to the office and is rewarded as such. Many secretaries in education and research organizations will keep a separate file of reference books or sources with notations about the contents and the call letters if they are in the public or the company library. The secretary would do well to become familiar with the area's Yellow Pages and with the various sources of information listed in the section on reference materials in this volume.

Time- and Work-Saving Units

Time is one of a businessperson's most precious commodities. The secretary who learns to organize work and plan time wisely will save minutes out of every hour, hours out of every week. This free time will be used by the professional to expand knowledge and expertise.

Here are a few time- and work-saving suggestions:

1. *Make efficient use of your desk.* Keep the surface clear of everything except your immediate work so you will not have to search through piles of other material when you want page 2. Form the habit of using filing folders for anything of a temporary nature—work in progress, incoming or outgoing communications, work being held for additional information— and keep these folders in the file drawer of your desk where they are instantly accessible but not in the way.

2. *Plan your time; never waste it.* When work is slow, plan ahead. Do what can be done to relieve the workload at peak periods. Try to learn more about your company's operations. Consider what you can do to make your part of it run more smoothly. Become familiar with reference materials; learn how to use the reference books your boss consults frequently. The next time you may be able to find that chart or graph that is badly needed. Bring the address book up-to-date. Get to know the filing system.

3. *Learn to schedule your time realistically.* It may take you an hour to type that stack of letters, provided that you are not interrupted; but you will be. The telephone will ring, your employer will call upon you to take care of something urgent, and people will stop at your desk to ask questions. That one

hour may become two or three hours. If you learn to expect interruptions, you will not be flustered by them or lose time trying to pick up where you left off. Interruptions are part of your work and require a place in your schedule.

4. *Be part of the team.* When the workload is heavy, when your employers and other members of the staff are up against a deadline to get a job done, be willing to pitch in and help even if it is a little after closing time. Your ability to function as a professional will be remembered when you have a favor to ask and when you wish a promotion.

THE FUTURE

The need for skilled secretaries will continue to grow. The secretary of today and the future may be entering the field from high school, vocational school, or college; may be returning to work after many years of child-rearing; or may be making a midlife career change. What all these secretaries have in common is their professionalism and their recognition of the importance of the work they do. The secretary of today and the future recognizes that a life's work deserves to be planned, and the professional secretary chooses a career path carefully. The professional secretary who will assume an important place in business and society will need to be able to respond to the concept and technology of information processing, possess decision-making ability and human relations skills, and be adaptable to learning new skills in a rapidly changing office environment. Secretaries can expect to take more responsibility as the more repetitive aspects of their jobs are automated.

Office Equipment and Supplies

by Susan C. Bauer

> *Vendors*
> - *Supplies*
>   *Paper*
>   *Envelopes*
>   *Erasers, Correction Tabs, Correction Fluid*
> - *Storage*
> - *Inventory*

The office has changed more in the 1970s and 1980s than it did in all the decades following the invention of the typewriter and telephone over 100 years ago. The revolution began with the invention of the Selectric typewriter by IBM in 1961 and continues today with little sign of slowing down.

Today's secretary has a wide range of equipment available to make the job easier—from electronic typewriters to voice mail. Technology has had an impact on office work at all levels. Executives are using keyboards in the form of personal or professional computers both in the office and at home.

New technology has also created new supplies, such as paper for the copier and printer, ribbons, toner, diskettes, and software. In a small company, the secretary usually has full responsibility for ordering and monitoring supply levels and arranging for equipment repair and/ or replacement. In a large organization, the secretary or administrative assistant generally orders items needed for the department from a central supply officer.

It is important that the secretary have up-to-date knowledge of equipment and supplies so that he or she may choose those that best meet the needs of the office. This chapter discusses both equipment and supplies.

WORD PROCESSING EQUIPMENT

Word processing is the automated production of documents and correspondence using electronic equipment for preparation, editing, storage, reproduction, and sometimes distribution.

A variety of equipment is available for word processing ranging from simple electronic typewriters to personal computers using sophisticated software to on-line computers. There is a type of equipment to fit every need.

This section briefly discusses electronic typewriters and dedicated word processing systems. A major section on computers follows. In more and more offices computers are used for word processing—and

Figure 2-1. Electronic typewriter. (Courtesy Panasonic Company.)

a host of other tasks, such as accounting, payroll, inventory control, and order processing.

Electronic Typewriters

As microcomputer technology became more sophisticated and less expensive, features once available only on dedicated text-editing equipment were combined with improved typewriter technology, and the electronic typewriter was born. This combination brought automatic features to those who had low-volume production and editing needs.

Electronic typewriters are more reliable than mechanical typewriters because they have fewer moving parts to wear out or malfunction. They are especially suited to jobs requiring small-to-moderate amounts of text with little revision required, such as letters, memos, envelopes, and labels. (See Figure 2-1.)

Electronic typewriters may or may not have displays. This optional feature ranges from a one-line window to an add-on partial page display. Many models may also be upgraded by adding a disk drive; this is particularly useful as volume grows and memory needs increase.

Other features commonly found on electronic typewriters are

automatic carrier return
automatic centering
automatic indent
automatic underscoring
column layout
multiple pitch
insert and delete
bold print
decimal tab.

Some equipment models in this category can be used as letter quality printers for personal computers. The main drawback to this is that the machine cannot be used as a typewriter and as a printer at the same time.

Dedicated Word Processing Systems

The original dedicated word processing systems were designed for high-volume production and heavy editing. Text was recorded on floppy disks or on a shared hard disk. At first, the price of these systems was high, and they were often placed in centralized word processing centers to ensure their full utilization.

In addition to the features listed under electronic typewriters, dedicated word processors include:

automatic search and replace
automatic page numbering
automatic widow/orphan adjust
block move and copy
document assembly/merge
document copy and move
document statistics
dual column print
global hyphenation, global search and replace
glossary/programmable keys
headers and footers
math functions
pagination and repagination
sort
spell check

A large number of dedicated word processing machines are still used in business today mainly because when they were purchased they provided the best solution to the document processing problem. Today's equipment is generally part of an office information system or is connected to a local area network (LAN) to allow communication with other types of equipment. As this equipment is replaced, a personal computer is usually chosen to take its place.

Shared Word Processing Systems

Word processing systems can be shared. Shared systems fall into two categories: shared logic systems and shared resource systems.

Shared logic system. In a shared logic system, numerous terminals are connected to a single central processing unit (CPU). Text is entered at the terminal, but the actual processing takes place at the CPU. The terminal is called a "dumb" terminal. There is one drawback to this type of system: if there is a problem with the CPU, the entire system can be down. However, a problem with an individual terminal does not affect the rest of the system.

Shared resource system. In a shared resource system, the individual terminals operate independently of one another but share some peripheral device such as a printer, intelligent copier/duplicator, or optical character reader.

COMPUTERS

The impact of the computer on business has been growing by leaps and bounds since its introduction to the office after World War II. The first computers were very expensive, took up a great deal of room, and could handle relatively small amounts of information by today's standards. Today, computers come in a wide range of capabilities, speeds, sizes, and prices. They are common in all types of businesses, used for word processing and many other functions.

This section briefly describes the main types of computers and then concentrates on the personal computer, the type found in most offices.

Types of Computers

There are several categories of computers: mainframe, minicomputers, microcomputers, and laptop computers.

Mainframe Computers

The mainframe is a large-volume computer capable of processing millions of instructions in minutes. This capability enables several users to run different programs at the same time. One of the main advantages of this type of system is its ability to manipulate large data bases.

When a mainframe is already in place, a word processing package can be added to it. This type of installation can be a cost-effective method of making word processing available. The communications system already exists and the need for purchasing and tracking multiple copies of software is eliminated. Additional terminals can be added to meet the needs of the users. Since all users are linked to the mainframe, documents can be distributed electronically through the computer network.

More and more software originally written for microcomputers has been adapted for use on mainframes, thus allowing the user to perform tasks without the aid of a programmer.

Minicomputers

Minicomputers are general purpose systems. Sometimes it is difficult to distinguish between a minicomputer and a mainframe because of the wide range of sizes, costs, and functions available for both types of systems; in other words, it is often difficult to distinguish a large minicomputer from a small mainframe.

Minicomputers are frequently used at the department level to perform functions such as accounting or word processing as well as to share peripheral devices, while the mainframe handles corporate applications. Because minicomputers are often selected to meet the needs of small-to-medium-size businesses, they are sometimes referred to as small business computers.

Microcomputers

Microcomputers are also known as *personal computers* (*PCs*) and *desktop computers*. They make up the fastest-growing category of computer, widely used in schools, homes, and businesses. (See Figure 2-2.)

Microcomputers are named for the microprocessor chips that function as the brains of the equipment. Originally developed for personal or home use, they have been continually upgraded in terms of processing speed and memory. Software packages are available in the areas of word processing, spreadsheets, data base management, graphics, communications, calendaring, and spell checking. In addition, there is a wide range of personal application software, including organizers, time managers, financial planners, portfolio managers, and games—to name just a few.

Figure 2-2. Personal computer. (Courtesy Zenith Electronics Corporation.)

Laptop Computers

A laptop computer is just that—a computer small enough to put on your lap or carry in a briefcase. Laptops provide a wide range of computing power, with some rivaling the power of desktop computers. Laptops may include a backlit screen, floppy disk drive, internal hard disk drive, separate numerical keypad, or other features. Some are convertible, meaning that they can be used with the monitor and printer of a compatible PC. (See Figure 2-3.)

A laptop computer allows the executive to communicate with the office while traveling—almost to take the office on a trip. The laptop user can key in trip reports, place orders, retrieve information and electronic mail, and perform other tasks.

Parts of the Personal/Desktop Computer

The personal or desktop computer (PC) system is the type found in most offices. The basic system consists of a monitor, processing unit (CPU), disk drive, keyboard, and printer. This equipment is called the

Figure 2-3. Laptop computer. (Courtesy Zenith Electronics Corporation.)

hardware of the system. The *software* is the instructions and programs used to run the system. The software needed for particular applications as well as the specifications for the output determine the type of equipment needed for processing and printing.

Before purchasing a personal computer, answer several questions. What applications will the computer be expected to perform? What software is available for these applications? What type of hardware (equipment) is needed? What type of output is required—letter quality printouts, graphics, charts, or what? Only after these questions have been analyzed should a system be purchased. A system can be purchased piece by piece from several vendors, or all components can be purchased from a single vendor or as a package from a single supplier.

Monitor

The monitor, or cathode ray tube (CRT), is a screen that lets you see the information and instructions you are giving to the computer as well as the results of the computer's work. Monitors come in several sizes; the most common is a partial-page display that displays approximately 25 lines of text.

The choice of a monitor largely depends on how you plan to use your PC. Is the main use for the production of text? Is it for calculations and spreadsheets? Graphics? If you plan to use your PC primarily for word processing, a monochrome monitor that displays in white, green, or amber on a dark background should be adequate. The characters should be clear and flicker-free. Contrast and intensity of display should be adjustable. (If graphics are needed, a color monitor may be needed.)

Central Processing Unit (CPU)

The processing unit or system unit is where the work of the PC is actually performed. It controls all devices connected to it—disk drives, printer, monitor, etc. The brains of the system are in the microprocessor chips. The early PCs had a maximum random access memory (RAM) of 64K, or 64,000 characters. As more powerful chips were designed, memory went to 256K and today may be as much as 640K, or 640,000 characters, ten times the original amount.

As the processing capabilities of the computer increased, it became possible to provide the user with on-screen help, thus making the equipment and software "user friendly." The increased memory also led to the development of new software with enhanced features.

Disks

The original personal computers used floppy disks to store information. As the amount of information grew, the management of floppies, as these disks came to be known, became a tremendous job. Hard disks capable of storing more data then became available and with them tape drives to back up the hard disks. Hard disks not only store data but also store programs. Stored on disks, programs become readily accessible and the constant shuffling of disks is eliminated. Data can also be accessed faster on hard disks than on floppies.

Data that is confidential should be protected. A codeword can be used to limit access to the hard disk on which the data is stored, or the information should be stored on a floppy disk and the floppy stored in a secure place.

Printers and Related Equipment

There are two major categories of printers: impact printers and nonimpact printers. In addition, there are devices for specific applications, such as graphics, and numerous accessories that can be used with computer printers.

Impact Printers

Impact printers actually strike the ribbon, creating a character on the page. They can be very noisy and usually require an acoustic shield or cover. Since they print a character at a time, impact printers are also called *serial printers*.

The impact printers associated with word processing equipment and desktop computers are the letter quality printer and the matrix printer.

Letter quality printers. A letter quality printer produces a document that has the quality of an original typed on an electric typewriter. A carbon ribbon is usually used. A letter quality printer is more expensive than a matrix printer.

Although some electronic typewriters and some older word processing models use the familiar "golf ball"-type element, most of the equipment used today uses the daisy wheel. Daisy wheels are available in plastic or metal and come in various styles and pitches. Special wheels containing special symbols or characters are available. Daisy wheel printers are usually bidirectional, printing when moving in either direction. Bidirectional printers have an output speed ranging from 350 to 700 words per minute.

Matrix printers. A matrix printer strikes the ribbon with a series of tiny pins arranged in the shape of the character to be printed. The characters are made up of tiny dots.

Matrix printers are faster and less expensive than daisy wheel and solid character printers. They are a good choice for computer output when the emphasis is on information and not on the quality of the output. They are used to print charts and graphs, in data processing, and for rough drafts in word processing as well as for graphics.

A high-end matrix printer referred to as *near-letter-quality (NLQ)* is available. In this machine, the print head makes several passes over the same line, each time striking at a slightly different location so that characters appear to be solid as opposed to a series of dots.

Nonimpact Printers

Nonimpact printers do not print characters by using a device that strikes the paper. Rather, the characters are created through the use of light or by spraying ink on a page. Because of this, nonimpact printers are noiseless and well suited to the office environment. Their main disadvantage is that they cannot make carbons.

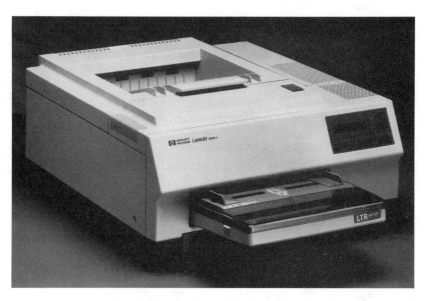

Figure 2-4. Laser printer. (HP LaserJet Series II printer.)

There are three main types of nonimpact printers: ink jet printers, intelligent printer/copiers, and laser printers.

Ink jet printers. Ink jet printers spray ink onto the paper in the shape of the character intended. The print quality is excellent. Printer speeds range from 1,100 to 2,200 words a minute. Paper and envelopes can be fed automatically. Ink jet printers that can print graphics in color and mix colors are also available.

Laser printers. The original laser printers were used with mainframe computers and cost several thousand dollars. Small desktop laser printers are now available for use with personal computers. (See Figure 2-4.)

Laser printers use a laser beam to form images on a light-sensitive drum. These images are transferred onto paper a page at a time. The machines print at a rate of 6 to 8 pages per minute for desktops to over 1,000 pages a minute for high-volume equipment. Copies are of the highest quality with some approaching typeset quality, and the printers are so quiet that you hardly know that they are working. Since they print the entire page at one time, laser printers are also referred to as *page printers*. These features make them ideal for the office.

Laser printers are not only capable of printing in a variety of fonts and colors on the same page, but they can also produce forms, letterheads, and signatures. The speed, quality output, and ability to be shared with several computers make laser printers an attractive choice—even considering that they are more expensive than other printers. The boom in desktop publishing can be attributed to the advent of the desktop laser printer.

Many office automation experts think that the laser printer will be the predominant type of equipment for producing letter-quality documents in the future.

Intelligent printer/copiers. Intelligent printers combine the technology of the microprocessor, the laser, and the photocopier. They print a page at a time at a rate of 50 to 100 pages per minute. A microprocessor allows them to accept text, graphics, and instructions from computers, word processors, or magnetic media and produce hard copy directly from the digitized information received. Because these machines combine features associated with both printers and photocopiers, such as two-sided copies, collating and stapling, reduction and enlargement, copy interrupt, and automatic document feed, they are also referred to as printer/copiers.

Intelligent printer/copiers can also handle the production of copies from originals.

The price of these machines seems high initially. However, the machines can be shared by many users directly through communications or indirectly as a high-volume copier in a reprographics center.

Plotters

A plotter is used to print graphics. A movable arm with a pen or pens moves across the page or transparency and draws curved lines, three-dimensional figures, bar charts, graphs, etc., according to instructions from the computer.

Some plotters are capable of adding text labels to the charts produced. Plotters are often used in engineering applications such as preparing blueprints and schematics. Business applications include sales projections and presentation graphics. Plotters produce better graphics than most other printers. The main differences between the lower and higher end devices are speed and ease of use. There is little difference in quality.

Printer Accessories

A number of hardware devices are available for printers in the area of document handling and noise control.

Forms tractor. A forms tractor is a sprocket device attached to the printer that automatically feeds continuous forms and stationery through the printer and advances to the next item to be printed. This device allows for unattended printing once the job is started.

Sheet feeder. A sheet feeder automatically feeds individual sheets of paper into the printer and advances them to a preselected line. A page is ejected when finished. Some sheet feeders have multiple paper trays to allow for letterhead and second sheets. A sheet feeder is a necessity where a large volume of merged letters or multipage documents are produced.

Envelope feeder. An envelope feeder works in the same way as the sheet feeder but feeds envelopes instead of sheets of paper.

Wide carriage printer. This device allows for use of stationery wider than the standard $8\frac{1}{2}'' \times 11''$ size.

Burster. A burster separates originals and copies of multipart forms.

Sound cover. A sound cover fits over the top of an impact printer to absorb noise. The top opens for easy access to the printer. Models to fit over printers with forms tractor and sheet feeder attachments are available.

Computer-Related Equipment

There are several devices and systems often used with computers. Among these are optical character recognition (OCR) scanners and local area networks (LANs).

OCR Scanner

The optical character reader is a computer device that can read text in a variety of typefaces and styles. The copy is stored on magnetic media and at the same time is reproduced immediately on a cathode ray tube for correction and revision. New OCR equipment does not have the rigid requirements of earlier models. Photographs, drawings, and charts can now be scanned for use in desktop publishing or electronic filing. Accuracy is excellent with approximately one error in every 300,000 characters.

The use of OCR equipment saves rekeying of information already in typed or printed form. It can also be used to bridge the gap between noncompatible pieces of equipment. Information from one type of equipment is printed out as hard copy and then scanned into the other system. The decline in price and improvement in the accuracy of OCR equipment combined with its new use in desktop publishing has led to increased interest in OCR.

Local Area Networks

A local area network (LAN) allows several computers to be tied together in order to share files, programs, and peripheral devices within a building, department, campus, or other limited geographic area. The LAN can carry voice, data, text, and images. LANs allow communication with mainframes and other LANs and, in general, bridge the gap between different types of equipment and operating systems.

Components. LANs have the following components:

hardware—computers and peripheral devices

interface—device that connects each device to the network

central computer—computer that contains the network software, hardware, and operating system

file server—system that controls the access of various computers to central files stored on the disk

cables—wires that connect the network components

Configurations for information exchange. There are three basic configurations or topologies for information exchange on the network. These are the ring, the bus, and the star. The choice of configuration depends on the size and communications needs of the network.

In the *star configuration*, the individual devices are all connected to a central switching station or computer in a pattern resembling the spokes of a wheel connected at the hub.

In the *ring configuration* all devices are connected in a closed loop or circle and information is passed along the loop until it reaches the receiver.

The *bus configuration* has all devices connected to the main line so that additions can easily be made at the end of the network without interruption.

Computer Software

A very large number of programs are available for use with personal computers. We shall briefly discuss the ones most frequently used in business—the ones a secretary would be most likely to use.

Word Processing

Word processing is the largest single PC application. As PCs became more powerful, it was only natural to look to the PC to take on word processing functions. The cost of dedicated word processing systems was decreasing, but these systems were generally bulky pieces of equipment, limited in their capabilities and inefficient in functions such as math and sorting.

One of the first word processing programs was *Wordstar*, a code-intensive package. Then came *Multimate*, which gained in popularity because of the similarity of its menu format to *Wang*, the leader in dedicated word processing at the time.

As the number of word processing packages started to increase, competition led to the development of more and more sophisticated packages that then exceeded the capabilities of the dedicated machines. Functions that were sold as separate packages, such as mail merge, were incorporated into basic word processing packages. One of the greatest benefits of PC word processing is that information from a data base or spreadsheet can be incorporated into a text document without rekeying. In addition, since many executives use a PC for electronic mail or to draft correspondence and reports, executive or professional word processing packages were developed.

Today, many word processing packages are available, ranging from inexpensive ones with very basic functions to those costing $400 to $600 or more and containing sophisticated features.

Data Base Management

Data base management software programs are used to enter, organize, store, and retrieve data. These programs organize data in a manner similar to a filing cabinet. Data is first organized into files relating to a particular subject, such as customer lists, accounts receivable, employees, and inventory. Within the file are individual records. These records could be compared to the folders in the file cabinet. Specific information in each file is broken down and contained in fields. An employee file might have fields such as last name, first name, date of birth, address, department, date of hire, and position.

The data base software directs the computer to search the files and assemble specific information from the records into a report form that can be used by managers to make informed decisions. Knowing what type of information will be needed aids in the structure of the data base so that retrieval will be efficient.

Spreadsheets

The development of the electronic spreadsheet was the fuel that sent PC sales skyrocketing. Spreadsheets arrange information in columns and rows. The intersection of a column and row is called a *cell*. Text, mathematical formulas, and values are placed in the cells. The beauty of the spreadsheet is that if a value or formula is changed, everything affected by that change is automatically recalculated. The format for a spreadsheet can be saved so that new information need only be entered into it. A year-to-date report, for example, only requires taking the last report and adding the current month's figures. The spreadsheet will recalculate the rest automatically.

Add-on packages have been developed to give additional functions to spreadsheet information. A word processing add-on linking a table in a document to a spreadsheet will update the information in the document to reflect changes made to the spreadsheet. Graphic add-ons allow the user to display the spreadsheet information using a variety of graphs. The benefit is that the user does not have to exit the spreadsheet to utilize the add-on.

Graphics

Graphics packages enable the user to take information from a spreadsheet and display it as a pie, bar, or line graph or as a chart. This saves the executive much time in reading through figures to find the specific information needed for analysis and decision-making. Similar charts produced by hand would take hours. Charts can also be used to show trends or comparisons. Graphics produced by computer can be converted into slides or printed out as hard copy. If color is required for printed charts, special equipment is required.

Communications

Communications software allows the PC to talk to other PCs, mainframes, facsimile machines, telex machines, public and commercial data bases, etc. Such software requires a modem and connection to telephone lines. Those using terminals that are connected to the mainframe will need to consult with their computer staff to find out what commands are necessary to communicate, since the software will be on the mainframe. The communications software handles logging on and off the communications network, dialing, saving messages, and sending or receiving information from a central computer.

Integrated Packages

An integrated package is one with different programs that can work together. All the programs in the package use similar menus and commands for ease of use, and the user can move from one application to another as needed. If, for example, you were preparing a sales report, the graphics program would be used to display the sales information as a chart, the word processing program would be used to add the text portion of the report, and the communications program would be used to distribute the report electronically. Many integrated packages allow information from several documents to be displayed at once by dividing the screen into several parts called *windows* or by overlapping documents as they are brought to the screen.

Integrated packages allow the user to keep working without having to stop and exit and enter new programs. However, some programs in integrated packages may not meet specialized applications since they may lack some of the features of a dedicated package. Integrated packages also take up a large amount of computer memory.

Desktop Publishing

Desktop publishing is used to create newsletters, manuals, forms, reports, proposals, flyers, etc. The development of page layout software and the availability of affordable easy-to-use laser printers are responsible for the growth in this area. Using a page layout program, the user can program text to flow around graphics according to the instructions given. Different type styles or fonts can be used in several sizes. A scanner can be used to convert pictures and drawings into electronic images. Once this is done, the images can be made larger or smaller or can be otherwise modified. More control of a job is obtained since work does not have to be sent out to achieve professional quality. A setup for desktop publishing generally requires a PC, preferably an Apple Macintosh or IBM XT or AT compatible, with at least 640K memory, a 20-megabyte hard disk, a graphics monitor, a laser printer, and desktop publishing software.

A wide variety of desktop publishing software exists. In some the capabilities are limited to a few different type fonts and the ability to mix text and line art and produce multi-column formats; these programs work best with short, preferably one-page, documents. More sophisticated packages include those whose strength is multi-page documents and whose end product is ready for typeset output. Templates, which are predesigned formats, have made it possible to create professional-looking pages without design training.

DICTATION EQUIPMENT AND METHODS

In some offices, the executive dictates to a secretary who takes shorthand, or, in an emergency, to a typist at a typewriter. Dictation may also be taken by machine shorthand, as legal testimony in a courtroom. Traditionally, the courtroom stenographer goes to the typewriter to spend many hours transcribing such testimony into typescript, but the shorthand machine is now compatible with some computers. Thus with the proper equipment, the computer can be programmed to transcribe machine shorthand.

In the modern business world, the executive is increasingly more apt to dictate into an electronic or portable battery-operated dictation unit or into a central recorder for which a microphone or telephone is used. In either of these cases, if the equipment is fitted with a phone-in adapter, up to 30 minutes of dictation can be recorded when the executive telephones from a remote location. Most of these recorders are now voice-activated, so that when the speaker pauses, the tape or other medium stops until the voice resumes.

All dictation machines allow the dictator to make simple corrections without going over the entire letter or report and also allow the user to give special instructions to the transcriber.

Equipment and Supplies

There are several types of dictation equipment available. (See Figures 2-5 and 2-6.)

Cassettes and Disks

Cassettes are a commonly used dictation medium. The small metal or plastic cartridges contain magnetic tape that winds from one reel to a second. *Minicassettes* and *microcassettes* are smaller than the standard cassette and fit into correspondingly smaller units. They were specifically developed to be used for dictation. There are also *magnetic disks,* looking like small records but without grooves, and *magnetic belts* that fit over a pair of rollers in a dictation unit. These tapes, disks, and belts are all reusable. They should be considered semipermanent. They may be stored for some time but will eventually deteriorate.

Endless (Continuous) Loop Recorder

Another type of dictation equipment is the endless (or continuous) loop recorder. It resembles the reel-to-reel tape recorder. The tape fits within a case called a *tank.* The tape is erased as the material is transcribed and is then ready for reuse.

Other Types of Equipment

To be used for permanent records, and therefore not erasable or reusable, are various media including some that use a plastic belt that is inscribed or embossed with visible grooves.

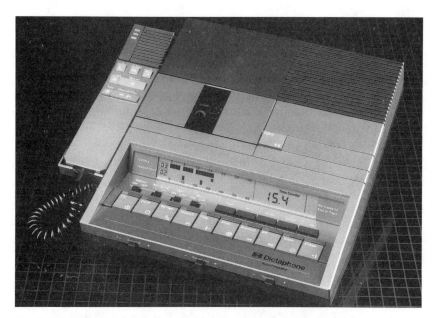

Figure 2-5. Desk dictation equipment. (Courtesy Dictaphone Corporation.)

Figure 2-6. Portable dictation equipment. (Courtesy Dictaphone Corporation.)

Dictation and the Word Processing Center

The use of word processing centers in many companies has affected the use and methods of dictation. An executive may gain access to the company's word processing center in any of a number of ways for dictating. In one type of setup, the dictator uses the central equipment by dialing any telephone within the company. In another system, the dictator's unit is connected to the system by a push-button phone. The central recorder can be accessed by use of any push-button phone whether it is inside or outside the company. In a third type of connection, the dictator has a private wire, and he or she uses a handset or microphone that is wired to the recorders in the company's word processing center. All of these methods are called *on-line* systems because they are connected by wire or phone to the recorder. (In contrast, a portable dictating machine or one that is an independent unit within the dictator's office is characterized as *off-line*.)

Advantages of Machine Dictation

The advantages of machine dictation over in-person dictation are varied. It is faster for the executive to dictate into a machine than directly to the secretary—and it is faster for the secretary to transcribe from the spoken word than from notes, handwritten copy, or shorthand. A distinct advantage is that the secretary does not need to be present. At the time the executive is dictating, the secretary can be typing or doing other important office work.

When it comes time to transcribe the dictation, the transcription can be done by other office workers beside the secretary if this should be more convenient; the process is no longer limited to the one person who can decipher the executive's handwriting or the secretary's shorthand notes.

REPROGRAPHICS

Reprographics is the technology for making copies. Other commonly used terms are copy processing and image processing.

A wide variety of equipment for making copies is available. The choice of which process to use depends on the quality and quantity of copies needed, cost, and the time factor involved. Large organizations frequently have their own copy or reprographics departments where large jobs may be handled using expensive high-speed equipment that otherwise would not be feasible. Offset duplicating and phototypesetting are usually handled by this department.

Carbon Paper

In spite of the advent of a great variety of copying methods for business letters and documents, carbon paper remains a commonly used and convenient method of making copies. Only one person and one machine is involved. The secretary stays in one place. The copies are produced on lighter-weight paper than is needed for other copying methods, so that a minimum amount of filing space is necessary for storage. And the method is, in any specific instance, the fastest copying method, for the original and its copy or copies are produced simultaneously.

Photocopiers

The photocopier is perhaps the most commonly used office machine for reproducing documents. After a document is printed, additional copies are generally photocopied unless multiple originals are needed. This frees the printer for additional jobs. A photocopier reproduces material quickly, gives an exact copy, maintains the same quality of reproduction throughout the run, and demands no prior preparation. Its speed and convenience is matched only by its cost, which is much higher than any other method in use today.

This expensive reproduction method costs from twice to fifteen times as much per page as other methods available. It is also subject to much misuse within the office. To prevent these abuses, many "copy control systems" have been worked out in various offices. Some office managers discover that the number of copies made in the office is suddenly reduced by a tenth to as much as half when a control system is put into effect.

For some copier models, toner cartridges are available in several colors. This type of equipment will produce the entire document in one color. Copiers are available that can produce full-color copies of originals. The number of full-color copiers is expected to increase with the demand for color graphics.

Special Features

Many features are available on photocopiers as options or as standard features on high-volume machines.

Reduction and enlargement. A machine with this feature can reduce large computer printouts, drawings, or other documents by 30%, 50%, or another percentage to allow, say, a large document to fit on an $8\frac{1}{2}'' \times 11''$ page. Small items may be enlarged to show detail or to make details more easily visible.

Automatic document feed. This device feeds pages to be copied one at a time and ejects them after copies are made.

Sorter or collator. With a sorter or collator, each copy is directed to a separate bin. At the end of the job, collated sets are removed from the bins.

Stapling. Some high-volume machines have the ability to staple collated sets.

Multiple paper trays. Trays are available in several sizes (for example, $8\frac{1}{2}'' \times 11''$ and $8\frac{1}{2}'' \times 14''$) so that when a different size of paper is needed, one tray can quickly be removed and replaced with the tray containing paper of the desired size. In some models the trays can be changed simply by pushing a button on the machine.

Duplexing. Duplexing is copying both sides of the paper. This process saves filing space as well as paper.

Categories of Copiers

Photocopiers are divided into three categories according to their copy volume. These are low, medium, and high volume. A company may have several different types of copiers depending on its needs.

Low-volume copiers. These copiers are also called *convenience copiers* because they are usually located close to the people who need them. Low-volume copiers are the least expensive type of photocopier. They make within a range of 2,000 to 20,000 copies per month at speeds of approximately 10 to 20 copies per minute. Some models are small enough to fit on a desktop; others come with their own stand, which can also be used to store paper and supplies.

Low-volume copiers are usually slow and meant for small jobs. This type of copier is suitable for a small department or situation where most jobs are only a few pages in length. Few special features are available.

Among the recent additions to the copier market are *personal copiers.* They are available with black, green, brown, and red color toner cartridges and have different features depending on the model. *Hand-held copiers* that can copy only a portion of a page at a time are also available.

Medium-volume copiers. Copiers in this category produce between 20,000 and 50,000 copies per month at speeds of 20 to 50 copies per minute. A large organization may have these copiers at several locations throughout the firm to handle large jobs and those requiring special features, such as automatic feed and sorting. Making five copies of a 50-page report is a time-consuming task if done on a copier without automatic document feed, duplexing, and sorting capabilities. Although special features add to the initial cost of copier equipment, the soft dollar saving in labor can well exceed the hard dollar cost of the purchase in a short time.

High-volume copiers. High-volume copiers can produce between 50,000 and 100,000 copies per month at speeds of 50 to 100 copies per minute. A high-volume copier is either an intelligent printer/copier (described in the section on printers) or a dumb printer/copier. The main difference is that the dumb printer/copier can only duplicate material. It cannot merge information such as text and graphics or handle communications, because it lacks a microprocessor.

Stencil Duplicating

A stencil is a waxed sheet of somewhat fibrous paper. The stencil is prepared by writing or drawing with a stylus, by typing with the ribbon inoperative, or by a mechanical or electronic printer. The wax coating is perforated by the typebars, stylus, or other means, and the ink flows through the openings to produce an exact reproduction on the highly absorbent paper. Ink is available in several colors.

An electronic stencil maker that scans original documents to produce a stencil is available. Thus a document can be created using word processing or desktop publishing and a stencil master easily prepared for duplication.

Stencils, or mimeos, are used most often for runs of 25 to 2,500 copies. Most stencil machines will handle anything from $3'' \times 5''$ cards to a sheet of $14'' \times 18''$ stock and can print from 60 to 150 copies per minute. Stencil duplicating is low in cost and can produce large quantities of good-quality copies, and it is still frequently used by schools, churches, and organizations.

Spirit Duplicating

In this method of reproduction, spirit masters are prepared by typing or drawing on a glazed paper that is backed by a special carbon paper. The spirit duplicator is the most economical process for duplicating up to 250 or 300 copies.

Master units come in several colors, and a single master may be made in two or more colors by inserting patches of the alternate carbon sheet in the areas where the different colors are to appear. Also available are masters that can be prepared by placing the original between the sheets of the spirit master and running through a thermofax machine. Because of its simplicity and low cost, this method is popular for internal use in schools and small organizations.

Offset Printing

Offset is designed for high-quality, long-run production. The initial cost for an office offset machine is high, but the resulting pieces of printing are nearly professional.

The principle used in offset (lithography) is that oil and water do not mix. Oil-based ink in an ink-water mixture is transferred only to the image area of the master, while the water is attracted to the nonimage area. The master used for offset printing may be paper, metal, or plastic (electrostatic). The paper master will produce from 25 to 3,000 copies, the plastic up to 5,000 copies, and the aluminum up to 50,000 clear copies.

The secretary who runs an offset machine will need special training. Time necessary to set up the operations and clean up afterward is greater than that needed for other office copying devices. However, if high-quality reproduction of photographic (halftone) work is desired, the offset machine is available to the modern office.

Phototypesetting

Phototypesetting is a photographic printing process in which each character is formed on photosensitive paper or film at high speeds. This film is then developed and proofread for errors or omissions. Material can be directly input through the phototypesetting equipment or prepared on a word processor or personal computer and sent to the phototypesetter through communications or on compatible media. Special printing codes can be inserted as the text is being prepared or by the printer when the material is sent in on media. Material can be kept in memory or on magnetic media for future use. Material produced using desktop publishing can also be prepared so that camera-ready copy is delivered to the printer. Keying the copy in-house gives more control over the job and can save a great deal of time and money.

Phototypesetting produces documents of the highest quality. A wide variety of type sizes and fonts are available. In addition, one typeset page can be the equivalent of two typed pages. Documents prepared using this process include books, newspapers, brochures, promotional materials, etc.

OTHER ELECTRIC/ELECTRONIC EQUIPMENT

Electric equipment includes some items that have been common in offices for many years, plus newer inventions that have been welcomed with pleasure. Some ensure greater accuracy; others bring relief from onerous chores.

Electronic Copy Board

The electronic copy board is a tool for those who participate in meetings where ideas are generated, comments solicited, diagrams or charts prepared, or items need to be written down and distributed. With the touch of a button, copies are produced of whatever is on the copy board at the time. Participants at a meeting can leave with information in hand instead of waiting for it to be distributed.

Facsimile Machine

A device that received limited acceptance after its initial introduction is the facsimile or *fax* machine. A document is placed in the machine and it is scanned and sent over telephone lines to a fax machine. Some machines can send and receive information automatically. Text, drawings, pictures, charts, signatures, logos, etc. can all be read by this equipment. The transmission speed and quality of the copy received has been greatly improved while the size and cost of these machines has decreased. Some of today's facsimile machines can also be used as copiers. Others can transmit and receive information directly from a personal computer. For these reasons, facsimile equipment is enjoying renewed popularity. (See Figures 2-7 and 2-8.)

Automatic Electric Copyholder

The automatic electric copyholder is a boon for typists who handle either manuscript or tabular material. It is operated by a foot pedal or hand switch that allows a line guide to advance down copy as the typist progresses. If needed, the movement may be reversed, so that an up-or-down movement may alternate. A variable feature allows the guide to move from one side to the other. The copyholder fastens to the typewriter or stands independently and is generally made in four sizes to accommodate letter size, legal size, or two sizes of ledger paper.

A simpler nonelectric copyholder is also available. The line guide is simply moved by hand as the typist proceeds through the copy.

Electric Paper Shredder

The electric paper shredder has provided needed security in a great many offices that handle sensitive material. It comes in a great many different models and is usually selected according to the volume of paper that it must handle. The smaller paper shredders are desk-top, while large free-standing units can handle up to 140,000 sheets of paper an hour.

Other Electric Devices

Various machines that help in the handling of paper are of great utility in the modern office. If the volume of mail is great, the electric *letter*

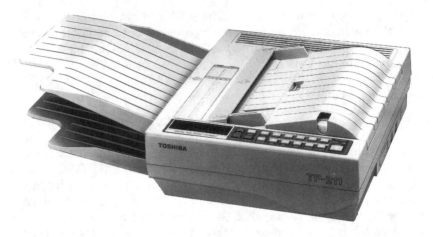

Figure 2-7. Fax unit. (Courtesy Toshiba America Corporation.)

Figure 2-8. Fax unit with telephone. (Courtesy Toshiba America Corporation.)

opener is helpful. The electric *collator* is extensively used in offices where related material that runs to many pages is regularly produced. A manual *paper cutter* is fine in the smaller office, but an electric counterpart may be imperative in the larger concern. In an office that turns out a regular newsletter or ongoing reports, the electric *paper folder* and the *saddle stitcher* or stapler get much use. If such reports or letters are regularly kept in ringed binders, an electric *paper punch* can be utilized.

Then there is, of course, the electric *pencil sharpener*, especially valuable in an office where much pencil work is done.

SELECTION OF OFFICE EQUIPMENT

The selection of office equipment involves a great deal more than product demonstrations and price comparisons. An assessment of organizational plans and needs must be made. In a large organization, the secretary's involvement will likely be concerned with the type of work done, ease of use of equipment or software, special features required, and what is presently being done and what needs to be done that cannot be done at the current time. On the other hand, a small company may have the secretary directly participate in the process of equipment selection, since the secretary is probably the person most knowledgeable about what is needed.

Only a few of the major considerations will be discussed here, since an entire chapter could be written on this subject. The discussion will center on the purchase of a single PC and software, but the basic factors discussed apply to the purchase of any major office equipment.

Among the factors to be considered in the purchase and selection of office equipment are a careful analysis of needs, the possibility of demonstration and follow-up support, cost, and choice of vendor.

Needs Analysis

Before any personal computer—or any major office equipment—is purchased, an analysis of the office or company needs must be made. This analysis should include consideration of the expected applications of the new equipment, the users of the equipment and the ease of use, and the versatility and upgradeability of the equipment as well as the documentation, instruction, and support services available for it.

Applications

When considering the purchase of a personal computer, generally software applications should be addressed first. What do you want the computer to do? Word processing? Spreadsheets? Data base management? Graphics? Desktop publishing?

Once the general applications have been determined, specifics need to be examined. What word processing features are required? What is the maximum size of the spreadsheet? Can spreadsheets be linked together so changes on one are reflected on the other? What types of graphics are required? What are the limitations on bar, pie, and line graphs? Can your desktop publishing software import documents prepared in the word processing package used? Can imported text be edited in desktop publishing or only in word processing? Does it support multipage documents? Samples of actual or anticipated applications should be carefully analyzed to determine the features needed.

Users

Who will use the equipment? Do the users require a dedicated piece of equipment or can it be shared by a department? Do users require information from the mainframe, outside data bases, etc.? Was the equipment purchased to run a particular application? If the equipment is purchased primarily for word processing, each secretary might require one. In an accounting or financial area each user would probably require a personal unit.

Versatility and Upgradeability

A major concern when purchasing equipment and software is the continual advances in technology. While one should purchase based on the needs of the present and foreseeable future, one does not want to overbuy. The cost of technology keeps going down, and it may cost less to upgrade later. If software upgrades are being planned, will they be compatible with earlier releases? Will new applications packages require upgrading of operating system software? Are there sufficient expansion slots for communications, second printer, etc.?

Ease of Use

For users who have operated other office automation equipment—for example, a dedicated word processor—the transition to using word processing software on a PC will be easier than for someone making the change from an electric typewriter to a PC.

The advances in technology have made more on-screen help available to the users. Some types of equipment use icons or pictures to represent the task to be performed. The pointer is moved to the desired icon—for example, a file drawer to represent filing—by moving a control called a mouse and pressing a button to execute the task. Other types of equipment allow choices to be made by touching the screen or by using a light pen or probe to make the selection. Integrated software contributes to ease of use because of the similarity of instructions from application to application.

Consideration should also be given to the user's comfort. Most equipment is modular so that it can be arranged to the user's comfort. The brightness and contrast levels can be controlled by the user, and antiglare attachments are available. A vast array of adjustable furniture is available for the physical comfort of those using the equipment.

Documentation and Support

Documentation and support are primary areas of concern, especially for a novice. Equipment should come with detailed set-up instructions. Software may have a tutorial diskette to acquaint new users with the package. The instruction manual should be well organized and clearly written for the users—not for programmers or technicians.

Templates that fit over the keyboard and list the functions performed by various keys or combinations are of great help to the user. There is also an extensive selection of "how to" books on computers, operating systems, and software packages.

Do the equipment manufacturer and software developer have a toll-free number to answer questions about the workings of hardware or software, at least for the initial one-to-three-month period? In general, the level of support provided will be greater for a large company buying in quantity. And, a computer store will be able to provide more guidance than a mail-order house.

Vendors who provide training generally train an agreed-upon number of employees to use the equipment. After initial training, there is a fee for each additional person trained. Some types of training usually need to be provided on large systems for newly hired, upgraded, and transferred personnel. An in-house training department might be appropriate for a large corporation. A smaller company might bring a trainer in-house and individual users may have to attend a seminar or course or purchase an audiovisual training package.

What will happen when there is a problem with the functioning of equipment? Is a maintenance contract available through the vendor? Is the repair provided by the vendor or is it contracted to third parties? If the equipment is purchased from a computer store, does it have to be brought in for repair? Is a substitute available while the equipment is being repaired? These are all questions that should be answered before a purchase is made.

Software vs. Hardware Considerations

Once the appropriate software has been selected to do the job, other considerations need to be addressed. How much on-line storage is needed? With the abundance of software available, what software should be on-line? How many disks does the package have? How lengthy are the documents, spreadsheets, data bases, etc.? Answers to these questions will aid in determining the size of hard disk and processing speed required. The more software stored on the system, the less room for manipulation and processing of data.

Is security an issue? If using a hard disk, how will the information be protected? How many levels of security are available? Where will the backup copies be stored, and how often will they be updated? Will confidential documents be communicated electronically? In a single computer operation, the entire computer may be locked or confidential documents transferred to tape or disk and stored in a safe.

If expansion is planned, is a site license available for software selected? Can software be purchased in a version that will run on a network? Can equipment be upgraded easily?

These are only a few of the questions that should be asked before any computer system is purchased. Similar detailed questions should be considered before the selection of any other type of office equipment.

Demonstration

A vendor demonstration will highlight the good features of the equipment or software. There are a few points to remember, however. Since demonstrations are done by experienced personnel who know the product well, features that may be difficult to use look like they are very simple. Features that are important to you might not even be part of the demonstration. Make sure the product demonstration is done with the applications you need in mind.

Again, let's use the purchase of a PC and software as an example. After the choice of software has been narrowed down to one or two that seem to fit the requirements of the office, actual applications using the software should be tried. Assemble several jobs that are representative of the applications needed and that contain any special features that might be required. These applications should be tried by a person who will use the software on the job and is familiar with the company needs.

If possible, the software should be demonstrated on the type of equipment it will be used on. The same software can run at speeds that differ according to the equipment. Printers should also be tried.

Cost

Equipment can vary in cost for a number of reasons. Mail order houses, which have low overhead costs, generally offer lower prices than do computer stores. Equivalent equipment, or "clones," of well-known brands made by different manufacturers are also usually less expensive. And, finally, the price per unit is usually lower when items are purchased in quantity.

Vendors

After the choice of which type of equipment or software is to be purchased is made, a decision must be made regarding the vendor from whom it may be purchased. The preceding paragraph on costs mentions a few factors to be considered in choosing a vendor. With regard to equipment in particular, if a substantial investment is being made, will the vendor still be in business to honor commitments next year? Next month? Has the vendor's product line kept up with technological advances? Does the vendor enjoy a good reputation in the area?

SUPPLIES

Paper

A great many varieties of paper have been developed and perfected by the paper mills of today. The factors that the secretary must consider in choosing paper are (1) size, (2) type according to its intended use, (3) weight, (4) material from which it is made, and (5) finish and color.

Size

The standard paper size for ordinary office use is $8\frac{1}{2}'' \times 11''$. The longer sheet used in the law office varies in different parts of the country. In some sections legal paper (also called "cap size" or "legal cap") is $8\frac{1}{2}'' \times 13''$, while in others it is $8\frac{1}{2}'' \times 14''$.

Some offices also keep on hand the $7\frac{1}{8}'' \times 10\frac{3}{8}''$ size sheet called "Monarch" for formal correspondence and the $5\frac{1}{2}'' \times 8''$ size called the "half-sheet."

Type

The type of paper selected is directly related to its intended use.

Typewriter paper. The best-known kind of typewriter paper is "bond paper." It was given this name because it was originally developed for the printing of bonds and other important documents. Typewriter papers have a dull, very smooth finish. The paper absorbs ink and is generally nonsmearing. When selecting typewriter paper, the secretary will pay attention to its degree of whiteness, its weight, its strength, and the kind of crispness ("crackle") usually associated with bond paper.

Second sheets. The most common use for second sheets is for carbon copies. This "onionskin" paper is available in the same qualities as is bond paper. The secretary may keep on hand two or three kinds of second sheets. The better quality, perhaps with a cockle finish, will be used for carbon copies to be sent to others, while the cheaper, lighter second sheet is used for the copy to be retained in the company files.

The kind of second sheet called "manifold" is dull on one side so that it won't slip in the typewriter but is glazed on the other side so that it will be easy to file. The second sheets come in various colors so that the copies in the files can be easily color coded. Weight of second sheets is an important consideration. If the secretary needs to make several carbon copies of the same letter, the lightweight 9-lb. onionskin will make the clearest copies. It also occupies less room in the files.

Some second sheets have "COPY" printed in large red letters down one side, or diagonally or horizontally across the sheet. This feature may be desirable for instant identification.

Xerographic papers. This kind of paper has a smooth, hard finish and is carefully cut to exact dimensions, generally either the regular $8\frac{1}{2}'' \times 11''$ letter size or the legal size used in a particular area. The exact cutting and the hard finish ensure that the paper feeds into the copying machine without jamming. The secretary may find it unwise to try to substitute another paper in the machine.

Xerographic paper must also be selected for the kind of machine in which it is used, depending on whether the copier uses a liquid toner process or a dry toner.

Duplicator paper. Duplicator papers are specially crafted to exert the least amount of wear on the duplicating master. They are to be used with spirit or gelatin (hektograph) machines. These papers are somewhat limp and soft and have a surface that is rougher than a xerographic paper but smoother than mimeograph paper.

Mimeograph paper. This bulky paper has a somewhat rough finish, a quality which allows the paper to absorb ink through the stencil rapidly so that the image is not offset to the following sheet; nor is the image blurred or feathered as it is reproduced. Opacity is another important factor; being completely opaque allows the sheet to be printed on both sides.

Scratch paper. Most offices want to keep on hand some kind of inexpensive paper for rough drafts or for handwritten drafts of letters, reports, or any kind of written composition. Many executives are happy with the "legal pad," the familiar lined, yellow sheets in legal size. If material is drafted in rough form on the typewriter, an inexpensive typewriter paper will serve. The secretary may also find it useful to keep a variety of notepads in the stock of supplies.

Weight

The "basis weight" of paper refers to the weight in pounds of 500 sheets (a ream) of the paper cut to 17″ × 22″ size. (The terms "basic weight" or "substance" are sometimes used.) When cut to the standard size of $8\frac{1}{2}″ \times 11″$, the basis weight shown on the box will be the weight of the ream from which the paper was cut. The most widely used office papers today range from a very lightweight $7\frac{1}{2}$ lb. (onionskin) to a very heavy-weight 24 lb. The most commonly used office paper is 16 lb. The law office may make use of the heavy 20-lb., or even 24-lb. substance paper for important documents.

Paper is usually sold by the ream. It is also available in 80-sheet, 100-sheet, or 250-sheet packages, but these sizes are not economical for the business office.

Material

The best bond papers are the cotton fiber (or "rag content") papers. The 100% cotton fiber is called "parchment deed" and is used for documents, insurance policies, or the like, or for papers that are to constitute permanent records. Another heavy paper is called "vellum." This was originally lambskin, calfskin, or kidskin but is now just an unusually strong paper. A 75% cotton fiber paper may be used for legal papers. It stands repeated folding well. The 50% and 25% cotton fiber papers have qualities of toughness and permanence to a lesser degree but are excellent papers and much used. The 25% cotton fiber is the most commonly used paper for letterheads.

Some paper companies have the year of manufacture coded into the watermark of the 100% or 75% cotton fiber paper. This is an important feature for legal use.

Office papers are also made from wood-pulp chemical fibers or from combinations of chemical and cotton fibers. The most common of these is the chemical fiber sulphite, which is less expensive than rag content and is suitable for many office needs.

Finish

The finish most suitable for the kinds of writing and typing done in the business office is the customary smooth finish. However, a favorite in good-quality typing paper and onionskin is a finish known as "cockle." The surface of this finish has a puckery or ripply appearance that is distinctive and elegant.

Another finish is that of the so-called "erasable" papers. During the manufacturing process special coating is put on this paper that keeps the ink from penetrating it to any great extent. Thus the paper is very easy to erase, often with only a pencil eraser, while the ink is still wet. Once the ink has dried, the image is fairly permanent. This paper is often recommended for beginning typists, although they may become discouraged by smudging. Erasable paper is not to be used for documents that are to be kept on file indefinitely.

White is, of course, the common color for typing papers. However, there are degrees of whiteness, and the executive may prefer one type or brand of paper over another. Off-white papers are sometimes used for less formal correspondence.

Envelopes

The quality of the paper used for envelopes should match exactly that used for the letterhead. Envelopes are designated by numbers according to size. The following list shows the names of the letterheads and the envelope numbers that can be used for the different sizes of letterhead sheets.

Letterhead	Envelope Number	Envelope Size
Standard	$6\frac{3}{4}$	$3\frac{5}{8}'' \times 6\frac{1}{2}''$
	9	$3\frac{7}{8}'' \times 8\frac{7}{8}''$
	10	$4\frac{1}{8}'' \times 9\frac{1}{2}''$
Half sheet	$6\frac{3}{4}$	$3\frac{5}{8}'' \times 6\frac{1}{2}''$
Monarch or Executive	7	$4'' \times 7\frac{1}{2}''$

Erasers, Correction Tabs, Correction Fluid

Erasers come in many types and are of little use if not suited to the writing surface on which they are used. The general rule is to use a hard eraser on hard paper and soft eraser for soft paper. The hard eraser used on soft paper will tear it; and the soft eraser used on hard paper will not do the work.

The *rubber eraser* is the soft, all-purpose eraser found at the end of a pencil. The word "rubber" came from the fact that this substance was found to be valuable for rubbing away pencil marks when it was first discovered by the Western world. The rubber eraser comes in small rectangular or square blocks or in pencil-like sticks.

A *kneaded eraser,* as found in art shops, may prove to be handy in an office. It is not abrasive, can be shaped to any desired form, and works well on pencil, chalk, and charcoal. It is also useful for cleaning typewriter keys or the keys on an adding machine.

The pencil-shaped *typewriter eraser* is highly abrasive. It is invaluable for typed work but must not be used on soft or thin paper. The brush is needed to whisk eraser dust away. The chief advantage of this eraser is that it may be sharpened to a point to erase a very small area. The *paper-wrapped eraser* is of similar substance and also may be sharpened to a point. The paper is peeled away to expose more erasing edge as needed. It has no brush. The chief disadvantage to each of these is the eraser dust that tends to fall downward into the typing mechanism. If it is possible to push the typewriter carriage over far enough so that the eraser dust falls outside of the typebar area, this should be done.

It is important to remember that erasers should be clean when they are applied to the paper to avoid smudging. A piece of emery board taped to the side of the typewriter or kept elsewhere on the desk may be used to clean an eraser quickly.

Correction fluid is not desirable or permissible in every typing situation. It may crack and flake off an erasable-finish or a cockle-finish paper. If the liquid is not carefully dabbed on any paper it may blend with the ink and result in a streaked, grayish patch. The ink may "bleed through" with age, and the correction fluid itself may rub off on documents that must stand a great deal of handling. Correction fluid is totally unacceptable in legal typing or in copy that is to be fed into a scanner for reproduction on a cathode-ray tube (CRT) prior to being set in type. The scanner "sees through" the correction and comes to a halt.

Another useful typing correction method for the secretary is provided by *correction tabs.* These are small patches (usually $2\frac{1}{2}''$ × $1\frac{1}{4}''$) of coated papers or film to be inserted between the typed sheets and the typewriter ribbon.

The corrections made with these tabs may show up too plainly on some kinds of paper but blend into others in a satisfactory manner. Then too, if the paper has slipped down slightly, the tops of the incorrectly typed characters may still show. Trial and error is the key. Correction tabs may be a convenience, but they cannot work magic.

Correction tabs are available in white or various colors. Be sure to purchase the kind needed for your particular typewriter ribbon. A different kind of tab must be used for polyethylene (carbon) ribbon than that used for the conventional nylon, silk, or cotton ribbon.

Correction tabs come in cheaper or better quality; it is worthwhile to study the various kinds. A different tab is needed for carbon copies.

To use correction tabs, backspace to the letter or letters that were typed incorrectly, and place the correction tab over the error and on each carbon copy with coated side down. Retype using exactly the same type characters as the ones that are wrong. Remove correction tab or tabs, again backspace, and type in the correct characters.

Also available for "correctable film" ribbons are special "lift-off" tabs that literally take the typed character off the paper. Corrections made by this method are rarely discernible. Most modern electric and electronic typewriters have such correction tapes as part of the machine.

STORAGE

Office supplies in storage should be arranged according to age, with the oldest stock in front for immediate use. Only one box of a single item should be opened at a time. Like items may be stacked one in front of the other on shelves. Unlike items should be kept separate to ensure that no stock is concealed from sight and forgotten. Shelves, boxes, and packages should be plainly marked to show contents and date of purchase. It is important to store supplies so that humidity and temperature are as close to ideal as possible.

INVENTORY

The secretary who has the obligation to look after office supplies will do well to keep a running record of what supplies are on hand and the frequency with which each separate item needs to be reordered. A workable method is to place on the calendar or tickler file a reminder at the beginning of each month to check all or some of the office supplies. A yearly inventory is time-consuming; an ongoing monthly account is generally better.

A card record should be kept for each item. This record should include name of supplier, name of salesperson, quantities usually purchased, sizes, colors, and other details. The cards may be filed alphabetically by supplier, item, or category. They may be used as inventory records, showing the quantities coming in, the quantities distributed, and the minimum quantity to be kept in stock. As the record approaches the minimum, the item should be added to an order list or immediately placed on order. The minimum order should be of a quantity large enough that the stock is never exhausted and yet does not result in an overload of the item, for paper, typing ribbons, and certain other supplies deteriorate with age.

The following list of common office supplies is categorized. It includes items already discussed in detail and then goes on to include other basic materials that the secretary will need to list on the inventory record.

Paper and Filing Products

typing paper
carbon paper or carbon sets
scratch pads and paper
memo pads
dictation notebooks
telephone message pads
3″ × 5″ cards
4″ × 6″ cards
card files
business envelopes
manila envelopes
padded envelopes
mailing tape
address labels
postage stamps

manila or plastic file folders
  (color coded as needed)
hanging file folders
file folder tabs and labels
alphabetized dividers
file baskets, trays, and stacks
transparent tape
bookmarks
calendars
planning diaries
binders
looseleaf covers and fillers
telex paper (in rolls)
paper for calculating machines

WP/PC Supplies

WP/PC ribbons
typewriter erasers
correction fluid (with thinner)
  (white and color as needed)
correction tabs (white and
  color as needed)

type cleaning brushes
exchangeable type elements
typewriter covers
typewriter "anchor" pads
copy-holders
diskettes

Duplicating and Dictating Supplies

stencil and/or mimeograph
  masters
microfilm
microfiche film
microfiche index

cassette tapes
tape storage unit
tape demagnetizer
tape splicer
copier toner

Desk Supplies

staplers, staples, staple removers
pen and pencil holders
rulers
paper clips
rubber bands
magnifying glasses
scissors
pushpins
book holders
bookends

ashtrays
letter openers
tape dispensers
fineline, broad-nib, or felt-tip pens
writing and marking pencils
erasers
rubber stamps, including date stamp
ink pads for rubber stamps

Miscellaneous

postal scales
first aid kit
fire extinguisher
keys
batteries

globe
maps
easels
planning boards

Desk Reference Sources

desk dictionary
secretarial handbook
current office supply catalog
style manual
almanac
chart for current postal rates
current telephone directory
telex directory, if needed

international area code booklet, if needed
office address and/or telephone directory (booklet, sheet, or rotary file)
ZIP Code directory

Office Correspondence

3

Word Processing and Typing Techniques

by Doreen LaBlanc

Continuing office innovations have brought significant changes in the way that responsibilities are executed and duties performed in the modern office. Since the 1960s many office activities have been automated. The typewriter has been one of the fastest-changing pieces of equipment in the office. The use of word/information technology has increased productivity, expedited work flow, improved quality, and controlled the ever-increasing volume of correspondence that needs to be processed expeditiously.

This rapid growth and development has increased the qualifications for office personnel. A secretary must possess not only the basics (human relations skills, language arts skills, and high performance skills) but also the ability to integrate these skills with the new office technology—namely, electronic typewriters, dedicated word processors, and microprocessors with short- and long-term memory. The secretary must be familiar with the most commonly used types of equipment and with the variety of methods by which tasks can be completed on the equipment.

This chapter discusses word processing equipment and its use to perform a variety of tasks as well as techniques basic to all typing/word processing activities.

WORD PROCESSING EQUIPMENT

Word/information processing is the automated production of documents and correspondence using electronic equipment. It includes the traditional processing of alphabetic information as well as data, voice, and image (graphic) information through a cycle of input (keyboarding), processing (editing), outputting (printing), distribution/communication (mailing/calling), and storage and retrieval (filing). All documents processed in the office go through all or part of this cycle.

Several types of word processing equipment are available, and changes are still occurring in the field. As advances have been made in word processing equipment, so too have changes been made in the grandfather of word processors—the electric typewriter.

Once a very simple machine, the electric typewriter is now dressed up with many optional features to speed up the typing process and meet specific requirements. New models include features such as automatic feeders and automatic correction keys with lift-off or cover-up correction tape. Many offices continue to use electric typewriters because of their simplicity and durability. Others, usually small and medium-sized offices, are replacing them with electronic typewriters.

An electronic typewriter may be considered a low-level word processor. Other levels include dedicated word processors and sophisticated microprocessor (computer) units. How you view the word/information processor affects your mastery of its functions and capabilities. Although word/information processing is a way to simplify typing, it should not be viewed as straight typing but rather as a way of incorporating and completing many tasks in one operation. You can type a document only once; then change words, sentences, and paragraphs effortlessly; and, within a minimum of time, produce an error-free document for distribution and storage in a compact form—all in one integrated process.

Electronic Typewriter

The electronic typewriter is similar in appearance to the electric typewriter, but it has a memory, a limited visual display screen, and automated features with special keys. It is ideal for handling memos, letters, reports, proposals, invoices, and various short documents that need limited revisions. Its low cost and ease of use coupled with its ability to increase office efficiency and productivity make it increasingly popular for today's small and medium-size offices.

Memory

Memory takes the risks out of processing documents: a perfect document is always at your fingertips. The electronic typewriter has both internal and external memory.

Internal memory. The internal memory can store phrases (date-lines, standard complimentary closings, signature lines, line lengths, and tab settings) or information for later retrieval or printing. An electronic typewriter's internal memory capacity is anywhere from a few hundred to 64,000 (64K) characters. Capacity can be increased by simply adding a microchip to the existing memory.

The internal memory is sometimes referred to as the *temporary*, or *working*, *memory*. If the typewriter is turned off, the information is automatically deleted from memory if it has not been stored.

External memory. External memory requires some form of magnetic media, usually disks/diskettes. Some disks can provide additional memory capacity ranging up to 300,000 characters.

Visual Display

Another important feature of the electronic typewriter is its ability to display the characters being input on a thin window or small screen built into the typewriter. Depending on its size, the display window may show from 16 characters up to 10 lines of text.

Automatic Special Features

Most electronic typewriters have a number of special features that make typing easier. Among these features are centering, underscoring, column alignment, hyphenation, block indentation, right margin justification, automatic pagination, search and replace, and text repositioning. To perform these basic operations, you simply depress a "code button" and an alphabetic/numeric key that has the particular function you wish identified on the face of it.

Dedicated Word Processor

The middle, or intermediate, level word/information processor is the dedicated word processor—a machine that does word processing exclusively.

The dedicated word processor is designed for higher volume and heavier editing than is the electronic typewriter. It is also designed to do more sophisticated applications, such as electronic mail, calendaring, list processing, security, records processing, math, the design of forms, split-screen editing, and integration.

Microprocessor Word/Information Systems

Today more and more word processing is done using a computer. In fact, word processing is the largest single application of personal computers today. A computer (microprocessor) word processor is multifunctional and extended. In addition to all the basic and advanced features found on electronic typewriters and dedicated word processors, the computer word processor uses software programs for word processing, data base management, spreadsheets, graphics, and other applications. One great benefit of computer word processing is that information from a spreadsheet or data base can be incorporated into a text document without rekeying.

Parts of Word/Information Processors

The components of a word/information processor are an expanded keyboard, a visual display terminal, a central processing unit (CPU), and a printer.

Keyboard. The keyboard contains alpha/numeric, format, editing (also known as functional), directional and locational, calculator, and command keys.

Display terminal. The visual display terminal consists of a cathode ray tube (CRT), similar to the tube used in a television, that displays text—from a few lines up to a full page.

Central processing unit (CPU). The central processing unit is the logic or heart of the system, controlling all of its operations. It contains permanent memory and runs or executes the instructions given to the processor.

Printer. The printer is the device that produces a document on paper—a hard copy—exactly as it was input.

MORE ABOUT MEMORY

Memory is probably the single most important feature distinguishing word processors from earlier typewriters. There are two basic types of memory associated with word processing units: permanent memory and temporary memory.

Permanent Memory

Permanent memory is a combination of the set of instructions that enables the word processor to act when entered from the keyboard and the instructions given to the word processor when manufactured.

When a central processing unit takes instructions from the permanent memory, the process is called *reading*. The permanent memory is called *read-only memory*, or ROM. The larger the capacity of the ROM section in the CPU, the more special and automatic functions the word processor can be instructed or programmed to perform. And it is permanent—if the processor is turned off, the contents of the permanent memory remain and will be there when the unit is turned on again.

Temporary Memory

The temporary memory, also called the *buffer memory* or *working memory*, is quite different from the permanent memory. The temporary memory holds the automatic feature instructions and characters given it via the keyboard.

When the central processing unit takes information from the keyboard into its temporary memory, the process is called *writing*. The temporary memory is also called *random access memory*, or RAM. This term is used because the central processing unit can access information in its temporary memory in any order.

SEQUENCE OF WORD PROCESSING ACTIVITIES

Information processing consists of a sequence of activities: inputting, processing, outputting, distribution or communication, and storage and retrieval.

Stage One—Inputting

The first stage in word/information processing is inputting—keyboard-ing. Information is transferred electronically from the input device to the memory until the unit is instructed to process the information. The data may be held in temporary memory to be revised or printed immediately, or it can be stored on external media—disks—for retrieval at a later date.

Menu

When first turned on, the word processor provides a list, known as a *menu*. The various activities that can be performed on the word processor, each with a specific code number or letter, are listed on the menu. A typical word processor menu may list the following:

1. Edit Old Document
2. Create New Document
3. Print Document
4. Special Print Functions
5. Document Index
6. Document Filing
7. Telecommunications
8. Other Functions (Wang OIS)

To choose an activity, you press one key or, in most cases, a combination of keys.

Types of Keys

In addition to the usual letter and numeral keys of a standard keyboard, there are several special keys on most word/information processor keyboards.

Cursor key. A cursor is a spot of light, which may blink, that identifies the position in the text at which you are working.

Directional keys. Directional keys are keys used to move the cursor up, down, left, and right.

Operation keys. Operation keys are used to send keyboarded information to the storage unit or to retrieve information from storage for viewing on the screen. An operation key is also used to instruct the printer to print a hard copy.

Function keys. Function keys instruct the processor to perform certain functions, such as insert or delete, automatically. These keys eliminate much of the repetitive, tedious, and time-consuming tasks once performed on a typewriter.

Format keys. Format keys are used to direct the overall placement or layout of the information in a document. Format keys can be used for several functions, including

formatting—adjusting for proper length of typed line, tab position, spacing, centering, and indentations

word wraparound—automatically moving words to the next line when the right-hand margin is reached without the use of the return key except when making a new paragraph

centering—establishing the center of a horizontal line of text based on line length or the number of characters keyed in a line. (Left and right margin settings are set before printout.)

underscoring—automatic underlining of text and data

scrolling—moving text forward, backward, left, or right, depending on the size of the video display terminal

indenting—automatic indenting of blocks of information by establishing a temporary left or right margin

bold printing—emphasizing a word or portion of text by printing bolder (darker)

hyphenating—automatically allowing for a uniform right margin by identifying words that will go beyond the desired position or that may need hyphenation

Prompts

Throughout the inputting stage, as various commands are given to the word processor, the unit may display questions or an explanation of steps that must be completed before progressing to another activity. These questions or messages are called *prompts*.

Stage Two—Processing, Correcting, and Editing

The second stage of word processing is processing, correcting, and editing. It is during this stage that you decide whether to print a draft (because revisions are expected) or a final copy or to store the document for future use.

Features for Correcting Errors

As you proofread the document, make any necessary corrections or changes. There are several special features to help in correcting and editing.

Backspace strikeover. When an incorrect key is depressed, backspace and strikeover with the correct character.

Delete. Move the cursor to the first character, word, line, paragraph, or any portion of the text in the document that needs to be deleted and depress one or a combination of delete keys. Characters may highlight to make you more aware of what you are deleting so that you do not destroy needed information.

Insert. Place the cursor under the character where the insertion should be made and keyboard the new character(s), spaces, words, paragraphs, or pages.

Move/Copy. Text can be moved or copied from one position in the document to another paragraph or page simply by identifying the text, indicating its new position, and depressing the move or copy key.

Required space. A space that is necessary to retain information as a unit, such as a date, name, or amount, can be made simply by pressing the appropriate keys.

Search and replace. A word or group of words in the text may be automatically located and replaced either entirely throughout the document or in selected places.

Special Programs for Editing and Correcting

Programs that automatically check spelling and grammar are available for word/information processors. The entire document is scanned and misspelled words are highlighted. Then, the program may make the correction automatically or you may use a dictionary and correct the error yourself.

With the calculator keypad, you can add, subtract, multiply, and divide horizontal and vertical columns, align numbers, and determine percentages.

Stage Three—Outputting

The third stage is outputting—usually in the form of a printed copy. Once a document has been formatted, input, and processed, it is ready for printing.

If you are using a dedicated word processor, you may need to complete a print summary screen before printing begins, indicating the number of originals needed, the typeface desired (elite, pica, proportional), right justification, merging information, and whether the copy is to be output on continuous form sheets or individual sheets. If you are using a computer (microprocessor), you will have provided most of this information during initial inputting. You can then select the keys necessary to direct the document to the printer. The printer will output all the documents based on the input instructions.

Stage Four—Distribution or Communication

It is essential that the information be distributed or communicated to the appropriate people. Today distribution options vary considerably and include interoffice mail, use of the postal services, electronic mail, and various express services.

Stage Five—Storage and Retrieval

The fifth stage of processing documents is storage and retrieval. Once a document has been input, processed, output, and distributed, it must be saved. This includes saving not only the keyboarding of the document itself but also all the additional instructions given to the word/information processor during the inputting and revision stages. It may be wise to store a long document several times during the inputting stage to avoid loss of information because of interruptions during the day.

A primary concern is which type of storage is best suited to office needs—some form of magnetic media, such as microfilm, microfiche, diskette, or hard disk; or hard copy, such as a carbon or photocopy. If media are used, it is often a good idea to keep a backup (second copy) because a diskette may become damaged and, if that happens, the central processing unit will not be able to store or retrieve any information from it.

Some offices that store hard copies have established a centralized filing center to have better control of paper flow. All copies, except a limited number that must be kept in the individual office, are directed to one central location for filing.

BASIC SKILLS AND TECHNIQUES IN TYPING/WORD PROCESSING

Typing/Keyboarding Techniques

Many of the techniques used in typing are also applicable for keyboarding, and many secretaries who first learned to type quickly transfer their skills to keyboarding on sophisticated word processors.

Typing

In the beginning speed can be achieved by a rapid, quick-finger release of the typewriter keys. The fingers should be well curved so that they strike the center portion of the keys and eliminate excess hand and finger motions. It is important to develop an even stroking rhythm regardless of the difficulty of the combination of the letters to be typed. A strong, steady pace can be achieved by practicing words frequently used in the area of specialization (legal, medical, or technical, etc.), thereby improving not only speed but also familiarity with the terminology.

Along with a steady, stroking motion of the keys and pacing, total concentration on the material being typed will ensure control and speed and thus result in higher productivity and longer endurance.

Body position and comfort are also important. Most secretaries work best with the feet flat on the floor; the desk at a proper and comfortable height to achieve a 90-degree elbow angle; the chair back against the small of the back; and the copy being typed positioned within a reasonable distance for easy reading.

Keyboarding

With the advent of automated office equipment, a few adjustments had to be made to adapt to the new enhanced keyboards and video display terminals.

Because of their greater sensitivity, electronic typewriter and word processor keys must be struck with an even lighter touch than that used on electric typewriters. A heavy strike may cause a string of characters to appear on the screen. The soft, quick stroking needed is called *ballistic stroking*.

Adaptations are also necessary when using a video display terminal. If the document is at the same level as the screen, the eyes do not have to move upwards and downwards, eye strain is reduced, and productivity is increased.

Proofreading

Whether done on an electric typewriter, an electronic typewriter, or a sophisticated computer word processor, documents must be proofread. Detecting errors in documents before removing the paper from the electric typewriter and other more sophisticated units is just as important today as it was many years ago. The ability to proofread well requires a critical eye for detail and good judgment.

Proofreading can be considered in terms of the three major types of errors most often committed.

Formatting errors. Check length of line of type, indentations, centering, date line, inside address position, salutation and closing position, signature line, title, references, enclosures, and postscripts.

Data. Check specific data—for example, time, amounts of money, phone numbers, column figures, and other figures.

General content. Check for transposition of characters or words, spacing, repeated characters or words, substitutions, omissions, grammar, punctuation, and information displaced from one line to another.

Making Corrections on the Electric Typewriter

Errors that you have just made can be corrected in several ways. Some of the ways depend on the features of the specific typewriter being used.

On machines with self-correcting feature. If you are using a typewriter that has a self-correcting feature, correcting an error is a very simple process. When you make an error, backspace to the point where the error was made by using the special error correction key (or word erase key). In the process, the self-correcting ribbon on the typewriter lifts off or covers up the error. Then you type the correct character(s).

Using correction paper. A special paper coated with a chalklike chemical can be used to correct errors. Backspace to locate the error, place the coated side of the paper over the error, and retype the incorrect character. The chalklike substance covers up the incorrect character. Then, backspace so that you are positioned on the now-empty space, and type the correct letter.

Using liquid correction fluid. Liquid correction fluid is a thin paintlike substance that allows you to cover an error to conceal it. Simply brush the fluid over the error, allow the fluid to dry, and then type the correct character.

Making Copies

With the development of improved photocopying machines and the decrease in their prices, many offices prefer to retain photocopies of documents rather than onionskin (carbon) copies. If, however, an onionskin copy of a document is needed, use of "one-time carbon packets" is convenient. Such a packet has a lightweight carbon paper attached to a sheet of onionskin paper. You simply place that packet behind the original being typed. If you make an error, you can use a pencil eraser to correct the error on the second sheet. However, if you are using word/information processing equipment, you must use the delete or insert method to correct the error and then insert a new original and carbon packet to reproduce the document. As the name indicates, the carbon paper in these packets is used only once.

FUTURE TRENDS

In spite of the tremendous changes taking place in word/information processing technology, word processing is expected to be the nucleus of office automation for the foreseeable future. The electronic typewriter will continue to enjoy rising popularity, especially in small or medium-sized offices, because of its capabilities and low cost. The use of dedicated word processors will probably decline, following the trend of the past several years, as more and more offices use microprocessors. In the late 1980s approximately 48% of offices used microprocessors for word processing, and word processing software has grown to become a powerful tool for a variety of applications.

4

Dictation and Transcription

by Lois M. Burns

- *Types of Dictation*
    In-Person Dictation
    Machine Dictation
    Telephone Dictation
- *Transcription*
- *Rough Drafts*
- *Envelopes and Mailing Instructions*
- *Signature and Follow-up*

For many years secretaries took dictation; typed letters, memos, and reports; answered the telephone; and maintained filing systems. Today, secretaries still do many of these same things, but electronic technology has made office work much easier. Offices now use electronic typewriters, word processors, computers, and various types of dictation equipment and telephone hookups. The technology for processing, storing, and communicating information is changing rapidly. Much less time is spent on routine tasks, such as correcting errors and retyping, and greater efficiency has been the result.

The basic secretarial skills of dictation, transcription, keyboarding, and communication are still very much in demand. Shorthand dictation is generally requested at 80 to 100 words a minute, and typing speeds range from 60 to 80 words a minute. However, today's secretary must be able to adapt to the ever-changing technology and to transfer skills to the new office equipment and job requirements. For example, approximately 60% of offices now use machine dictation and transcription on word processors.

This chapter discusses the types of dictation, transcription, rough drafts, and final mailing and follow-up procedures for both a conventional and an electronic office.

TYPES OF DICTATION

In some offices an executive dictates to a secretary who takes shorthand. However, in many modern offices, the executive is more likely to dictate into a dictation unit or into a central recorder via a microphone or telephone. Regardless of the equipment used, it is the secretary's responsibility to listen carefully and transcribe the dictated material accurately and in the format desired.

In-Person Dictation

In an office in which in-person dictation is used, the secretary must be prepared at all times to take the executive's dictation and process it. Efficiency is improved if the tools and materials needed for dictation are kept ready, a dictation routine is established, and special signals are used to draw attention to urgent matters or items that need special attention.

Tools

The tools and materials needed for efficient in-person dictation are:

1. A spiral-bound notebook, with a rubber band around the used portion. If dictation is taken from more than one executive, it might be well to have a separate notebook for each, to avoid confusion when transcribing. The first date of dictation should be entered on the front binder and the final date entered when the book has been filled. The dictator's initials can be shown on the cover also. The filled notebooks should be filed in the event there is a question later about a dictated item. The length of time such notebooks are kept will depend upon the policy of the employer.

2. A pen (ballpoint, felt-tip, or whatever is preferred by the secretary); one or two sharpened lead pencils; and a colored pencil, usually red. Notes written in ink are easier to read when transcribing than those written in pencil. The lead pencils are used if the pen runs dry; the colored pencil is for special notations.

3. A folder for correspondence and other reference materials.
4. A supply of paper clips, either along the binder of the notebook or clipped to the edge of the folder. These may be used for clipping memos of special instructions or small notes to the pages of the notebook.
5. A pocket-sized calendar, taped to the binder of the notebook or to the front of the correspondence folder. The calendar will be used to check days and dates in the dictated material.

A Dictation Routine

Before dictation begins, enter the date in red pencil at the bottom of the first page to be used that day.

With the permission of the executive, place all dictation materials on a corner of the desk rather than in the lap. (Long periods of dictation can be difficult and very tiring if the secretary has to juggle papers, files, and other materials in the lap or retrieve them from the floor.) The executive's appointment calendar should be close at hand for checking dates so that conflicts in scheduled meetings, travel arrangements, etc., are avoided.

The executive should indicate the number of copies required for each dictated item and, following the dictation, give all related correspondence to the secretary. The secretary may then number the correspondence to agree with the number in the shorthand notebook, place the correspondence in the appropriate folder, and later use it to check names, addresses, quoted dates, calculations, and other data prior to transcribing.

Many secretaries use only the left-hand column of the notebook, reserving the right-hand side for corrections, insertions, special instructions, and so on. (Left-handed secretaries reverse this procedure.)

If the dictation becomes too rapid, the secretary should signal the dictator, reading back the last few words taken down. To avoid breaking the dictator's train of thought, the secretary should wait until the end of a sentence or paragraph before interrupting. (The new secretary may be reluctant to interrupt during dictation, but the executive will usually realize a "breaking-in" period is to be expected and will make allowances.)

The secretary should feel free to ask that unusual names or terms be spelled out and then write them in longhand. This can be done at the end of the dictation.

If the dictation is interrupted by a phone call or a visitor, the secretary should use this time to read back over the shorthand notes, inserting punctuation, checking dates on the calendar, or filling in words that may have been missed. If the interruption is extended, the secretary should quietly gather up the materials and return to her or his desk to prepare for transcribing, returning to the executive's office when called.

Special Dictation Signals

The secretary is wise to use special signals to indicate rush or priority items, special instructions, missing items, or other items that need special attention. The following are guidelines used by many experienced secretaries.

- Write the word "RUSH" in red pencil to call attention to urgent letters. It is also a good idea to fold the lower left-hand edge diagonally until the page protrudes one-half inch beyond the edge of the notebook as a signal that this is a priority item.
- Draw a rough box around special instructions and notations of attachments or enclosures to alert you when you are transcribing.
- Leave a blank space in the notes for material to be entered later, such as a date, a name, or other information to be provided by the executive (or secretary), which might not have been available during the dictation period.
- Use a caret or star for small insertions and a circled capital A, B, and so on for longer insertions.
- Use a crosshatch to indicate the end of each dictated item.
- Use standard symbols commonly used by secretaries to indicate special typing or printing instructions—for example, a wavy line under the notes to indicate underscoring; two lines to indicate all capitals; three lines to indicate both underscoring and all capitals. (Note that these are not the standard proofreading symbols used in publishing and many other fields.)
- Draw one or two diagonal lines through the notes after they have been transcribed.

Machine Dictation

Many executives use dictating machines to record some or all of their dictation, since they are able to dictate when no one is available to take notes. This method provides a great deal of flexibility for the dictator, who can dictate while commuting to work, on a business trip, or after working hours.

Types of Dictating Machines

There are several types of dictation/transcription machines available. Desk-top dictation machines are used primarily by executives who

Fig. 4-1. Central dictation system. (Courtesy Sony Corporation of America.)

dictate frequently. Portable dictation machines, which record on minicassettes, are becoming very popular because they are small and lightweight, operate on batteries, and provide a great deal of flexibility for the dictator. With centralized dictation systems, originators call a central recording device to dictate, and a supervisor assigns dictation transcription to an operator. (See Figure 4-1.)

Dictating to a Machine

With all types of dictation units, the dictator speaks into a microphone (or telephone) and the words are recorded on cassette (or minicassette). The dictator must speak distinctly, spell any unusual words, and record the punctuation, capitalization, and paragraphs. For the transcriber's guidance, the number of required copies and other instructions should be dictated at the beginning.

Transcribing from a Machine

The transcriber must learn to adjust the speed, volume, and tone controls of the machine as well as the start, stop, and repeat mechanisms. The machine may be equipped with either a hand or foot control for starting and stopping and a reverse control to replay the dictation when necessary. Some machines are also equipped with an *indicator*, or *index slip*, which enables the transcriber to determine easily the length of letters, corrections, or special instructions. Some machines feature electronic scanners that allow the transcriber to scan the dictation for any special instructions the originator/dictator may have included.

The beginning transcriber usually starts the transcribing machine, listens to a few words or a phrase, stops the machine, types the words or phrases, and then repeats the process—start, listen, stop, type. The goal of a good machine transcriber is to keep moving with very few interruptions in the typing process.

The transcriber should be careful not to erase any dictation while transcribing and should be sure that all items are transcribed before returning the cassette (which can be reused) to the dictator's machine.

Material transcribed from a dictation unit should be proofread and handled in the same manner as shorthand transcription.

Telephone Dictation

Executives who travel may frequently call and dictate letters, conference notes, instructions, and other messages to the secretary by telephone. The notes, especially names, dates, and figures, should be read back to the dictator before the conversation is terminated.

A *teleconference* is a meeting using electronic technology so that several people in different locations can participate by using telephones and linking computers to communicate and to present and discuss documents. Another advance, *video teleconferencing*, allows the participants to see one another on a screen as they meet.

The secretary may be asked to monitor an important phone call or teleconference to provide a record of what was discussed. A transcribed summary of what was said is usually sufficient and should be typed immediately while the conversation is still fresh in the secretary's mind.

TRANSCRIPTION

Before transcribing anything, whether it be shorthand or machine dictation, the secretary should establish priorities for the work to be done. Items may be sorted into stacks to be:

1. handled at once. (This may be a mailgram, a phone call, or a letter to be typed, signed, and mailed immediately.)

2. transcribed before the day is over.
3. transmitted to others for handling.
4. handled by the secretary, but under no deadline.
5. placed in the tickler file for follow-up.
6. filed.
7. discarded.

After the sorting has been completed, the secretary should proceed according to the priorities set.

Becoming Familiar with Standard Formats

Many companies have a standard format for correspondence and intracorporate memos and a different style for letters to customers or clients. The secretary should be familiar with these formats and follow them when transcribing. If there is no company standard, the secretary should use the style preferred by the executive or a style that is generally accepted in an up-to-date style manual.

Checking Notes and Other References

If the secretary has taken in-person dictation, he or she should read through the notes, inserting punctuation where necessary, paragraphing where necessary (if not dictated), checking the calendar for possible conflicts in days and times of meetings or appointments, correcting errors in grammar and facts, restructuring poor sentences, and so forth. Many executives rely on their secretaries to make whatever changes are necessary. However, if the secretary notices that a change in fact is necessary, he or she should mention it to the executive. And, if the executive wants the material transcribed exactly as dictated, the secretary should do so.

A dictionary and a current secretarial handbook should be on every secretary's desk so that he or she may check the spelling of unfamiliar words and place names, rules of punctuation, the division of words at the end of a line, and so forth. (One new feature of *Webster's New World Dictionary, Third College Edition* is a unique system of end-of-line hyphenation.)

Transcribing and Preparing the Final Copies

With experience, the secretary can easily determine the length of a letter to be transcribed and the margins to be set on the typewriter. It is necessary to take into consideration the size of the shorthand notes or the length of the dictation on the machine as well as the type style (pica, elite, and/or proportional spacing) of the typewriter. It may occasionally be necessary to type a rough draft when material not dictated, such as a list of names or a statistical tabulation, is to be inserted.

In a traditional office, the transcriptionist sets the margins, tab stops, and line spacing, and proofreads and edits the documents at the typewriter. Minor mistakes may be corrected with correction tape or correction fluid. More substantial errors may require retyping one or more pages. Today's transcriptionist may occasionally use a carbon packet for copies; however, photocopies and hard-copy originals are more commonly used.

If the transcription process is interrupted, the secretary should put a small check mark in the shorthand notes to indicate the place to resume typing.

In the word processing or electronic office, margins, tabs, and line spacing can be adjusted or changed automatically. Editing tasks such as adding or deleting words, lines, or paragraphs can be accomplished without retyping whole pages. Equipment may have a built-in spell checker or a software program with a dictionary or grammar checking component. The work still should be proofread, however, because the equipment and programs cannot distinguish between homonyms, nor can they determine if the transcript omits a word. The final transcript will be a clean, neat, original document with no trace of revisions.

With modern electronic equipment, the secretary can merge various pieces of information into one document. If you are sending the same letter to several different people, once you have typed the letter, you can merge it with a file that contains a list of names, addresses, and salutations. The computer will then print the same letter with the appropriate inside addresses and salutations.

ROUGH DRAFTS

The executive may request that the secretary type a rough draft of a letter, report, speech, or legal document. This should be done on inexpensive paper. A rough draft of a letter may be single spaced and corrections made in the margins. Speeches and reports should be double or triple spaced, leaving room for editorial changes. Rough drafts are retained until the final draft is approved.

On occasion the secretary may deem it advisable to type a rough draft of a letter without being asked, if experience dictates the probability of a rewrite. It could be diplomatically explained that the rough draft was for the secretary's own guidance in layout or because the shorthand notes were not clear. This will give the executive an opportunity to review the material before the final transcription and to make any changes desired.

Offices equipped with electronic typewriters, word processors, or computers enable secretaries to draft all items, make corrections, or rearrange paragraphs and then push a button to produce a final copy with centered headings, justified margins, and different type styles within the document. These machines are excellent timesavers for secretaries who type manuscripts, technical materials, routine specialized documents, or correspondence for executives who habitually make many changes in their dictation.

ENVELOPES AND
MAILING INSTRUCTIONS

Envelopes for letters should be typed as soon as the letter is transcribed. A method preferred by many executives is to place the letter and the enclosures, if any, under the flap of the envelope with the addressed side of the envelope on top. This same procedure may be used with those copies that are to be sent to another party.

Because of the extended use of automated equipment the Postal Service has made available a leaflet entitled "Secretarial Addressing for Automation" (Notice 23-B), which may be obtained from customer-service representatives and postmasters. Some suggestions included are:

1. The address area should be in block form with all of the lines forming a uniform left margin. It should be four inches from the left edge of the envelope and on the fourteenth line down from the top edge of the envelope. No print should appear to the right or below it.

2. Mail addressed to occupants of multi-unit buildings should include the number of the apartment, room, suite, or other unit. The unit number should appear immediately after the street address on the same line—never above, below, or in front of the street address.

3. Street addresses or box numbers should be placed on the line immediately above the city, state, and ZIP Code. When indicating a box number at a particular station, the box number should precede the station name. Correct spelling of street names is essential, since some machines match the names in the address to those like it on the machine's memory.

4. City, state, and ZIP Code should appear in that sequence on the bottom line of the address block. Two-letter state abbrevi-

ations and nine-digit zip codes should be used. Automatic sorting equipment is instructed to look for this information in that position. Mail presorted by ZIP Codes bypasses many processing steps in the post office and can get to its destination quicker.

5. Type addresses in upper-case letters without punctuation:

> GENERAL XYZ CORP
> ATTENTION SALES DEPT
> 1000 MAIN ST
> PO BOX 23302 CENTRAL STATION
> DALLAS TX 75223-1234

It should be noted that this style of addressing envelopes is not mandatory and the secretary should consult with the executive before adopting it.

Special mailing instructions should be typed in all capital letters five or six spaces below the area where the postage will be placed, or special labels may be used if available.

If a letter states or implies that materials are to be sent separately, the material should be prepared, placed in an envelope or mailing container, and a mailing label typed. If the mailing is to be taken care of by a different person or by another department, the secretary should make a note to check and determine that the mailing was actually done.

SIGNATURE AND FOLLOW-UP

After the dictation has been transcribed and proofread and the envelopes and enclosures have been prepared, the secretary should review his or her notebook to be sure that no items or special instructions have been overlooked.

The secretary should then note any pertinent dates or reminders on the calendar and place follow-up items in the tickler file. The executive's appointment calendar should also be posted, if this was not done during the in-person dictation period.

The completed correspondence should be put in a folder marked "For Your Signature" and placed on the executive's desk. Rush items should be taken in to the executive immediately. Others may be accumulated and presented to the executive later in the day, but be sure to allow sufficient time for the letters to be signed and mailed on schedule.

Some executives prefer to sign each piece of mail personally. Others authorize their secretaries to sign for them. If authorized to sign, the secretary should place his or her initials after the dictator's/originator's signature, unless otherwise instructed.

5

Business Letter Format

by Lois M. Burns

Letters leaving a business office are, in a very real sense, ambassadors of good will. The impression an individual letter creates may mean the difference between the gain or loss of a prospective customer, a client, or an influential friend for your company. This impression depends as much on the appearance of the letter as on its tone or contents.

This chapter discusses different letter styles, the basic parts of a business letter and other parts that may be included, and rules for spacing with punctuation marks and division of words.

LETTER STYLES

It has often been said that an ideal letter should resemble a picture in an appropriate frame, but this is not always practical today because of the many different letterhead styles. Letters must be arranged and typed according to the style of the letterhead as well as the letter style the company has chosen. Most organizations have a procedural manual for their employees giving the letter style and explaining how they want the various parts of the business letter typed.

In the following pages, only modern letter styles and their variations will be illustrated.

Block Style (Letter 1)

The block style letter, also called a *full block style* letter, is typed with all lines beginning at the left margin. Paragraphs are not indented. This type of letter is easy to type because there are no tabular stops. The more tab stops there are in a letter, the longer it takes to type, and the greater the chance of typist errors.

Modified Block Style (Letters 2, 3)

The modified block style letter places the dateline, the complimentary close, and the sender's name and title in the center of the page. Paragraphs may be indented, or they may begin at the left margin. (The recent trend is not to indent unless a very short letter is double-spaced.)

Simplified Letter Style (Letter 4)

The simplified letter style, also known as the *AMS* (Administrative Management Society) letter, is the most modern letter style. This style eliminates the salutation and the complimentary close. A subject line typed on the third line below the inside address in all capital letters replaces the salutation. All lines begin at the left margin. The sender's name and title are typed in all capital letters three lines below the body of the letter. This style of letter eliminates salutation problems (whether to use Miss, Ms., Mrs., Gentlemen, or Ladies and Gentlemen) and increases the productivity of the typist.

SUPER COMMUNICATIONS COMPANY

2504 Mill Road / Richmond, VA 23230-1609 / (804) 555-9857

Date   September 11, 19__   (operate return 4 times)

Inside address   MRI Media Research, Inc.
Attention line   Attention Communications Division
                     25 Main Street
                     Buffalo, NY 14222-5147 (DS)

Salutation   Gentlemen (DS)

Body of   Enclosed find Survey Form MR43 that you have requested
letter   from us. We have studied the results of your letter
                     survey and are considering using this style for business
                     letters. Let us go over each element. (DS)

                     This letter is typed in "block style." All lines begin
                     at the left margin. The salutation and complimentary
                     close are used. (DS)

                     The style is flexible. Some executives prefer to use
                     the conventional marks of punctuation. More often, the
                     colon after the salutation and the comma after the
                     complimentary close are omitted. This punctuation style
                     is known as "open punctuation."

                     You will see that the company name is given before the
                     signature of the writer of the letter. It is typed in
                     all capital letters. The typed signature follows the
                     space for the written signature. Below or following the
                     typed signature is the title of the writer. (DS)

Complimentary   Sincerely yours (DS)
close
Company name   SUPER COMMUNICATIONS COMPANY   (operate return 4 times)

                     Joan R. Starr

Writer's name   Ms. Joan R. Starr
Title   Public Relations Director (DS)

Typist's initials ms (DS)

Enclosure   Enclosure (DS)

Copy notation   pc Thomas Smith

Letter 1: Block style, open punctuation

FERRIS INTERNATIONAL CORPORATION

308 Fifth Avenue / New York, NY 10001-4596 / (212) 789-1234

Date   October 3, 19__   (operate return 4 times)

Inside address   Mr. William Sommers
                        Vice President
                        United Books International
                        909 Fifth Avenue
                        New York, NY 10001-4596 (DS)

Salutation   Dear Mr. Sommers: (DS)

**Subject line
centered**   SUBJECT: The Modified Block Style Letter (DS)

**Body of
letter**   This letter is typed in modified block style with
                        indented paragraphs. Mixed punctuation is used in the
                        opening and closing lines. This punctuation style calls
                        for a colon after the salutation and a comma after the
                        complimentary close. (DS)

                            In contrast to the block style letter, the date,
                        complimentary close, typed signature line, and title
                        line have been moved to the center point. All other
                        lines begin at the left margin. These modifications of
                        the block style letter give this letter its name--
                        modified block. (DS)

                            If a subject line is used, it may be centered over
                        the body of the letter a double space below the
                        salutation, or it may begin at the left margin. (DS)

**Complimentary
close**   Sincerely,   (operate return 4 times)

                                            David C. Cannava

**Writer's name
Title**   David C. Cannava
                                            Director (DS)

Typist's initials   lb

Letter 2: Modified block style, indented paragraphs, mixed punctuation

FERRIS INTERNATIONAL CORPORATION

308 Fifth Avenue / New York, NY 10001-4596 / (212) 789-1234

Date   October 3, 19__   (operate return 4 times)

Inside address   Mr. William Sommers
                        Vice President
                        United Books International
                        909 Fifth Avenue
                        New York, NY 10001-4596 (DS)

Salutation   Dear Mr. Sommers: (DS)

Subject line   SUBJECT: The Modified Block Style Letter (DS)

Body of   This letter is typed in modified block style with
letter   blocked paragraphs. Mixed punctuation is used in the
                        opening and closing lines. This punctuation style calls
                        for a colon after the salutation and a comma after the
                        complimentary close. (DS)

                        In contrast to the block style letter, the date,
                        complimentary close, typed signature line, and title
                        line have been moved to the center point. All other
                        lines begin at the left margin. These modifications of
                        the block style letter give this letter its name--
                        modified block. (DS)

                        If a subject line is used, it begins at the left margin
                        or is centered over the body of the letter a double
                        space below the salutation. (DS)

Complimentary   Sincerely,   (operate return 4 times)
close

                                                  David C. Cannava

Writer's name   David C. Cannava
Title   Director (DS)

Typist's initials   lb

Letter 3: Modified block style, blocked paragraphs, mixed punctuation

Date	October 3, 19__
Inside address	Ms. Joan Donner One Main Street Cleveland, OH 44224-5429 (TS)
Subject line	SIMPLIFIED STYLE LETTER (TS)
Body of letter	This letter is typed in the simplified style that is recommended by the Administrative Management Society (AMS). It is typed in block form with all lines beginning at the left margin. Note that there is no salutation and no complimentary close. This feature saves the typist time not only in typing, but sometimes in trying to determine what title is proper for a salutation. (DS) A subject line is typed in ALL CAPS a triple space below the inside address; the first line of the body is typed a triple space below the subject line. Note the word "subject" is omitted. (DS) The writer's name and title are typed in ALL CAPS four lines below the last line of the body of the letter. (DS) The reference initials of the typist are typed a double space below the writer's name.
Writer's name **Title**	*Joseph H. Feng* JOSEPH H. FENG ASSISTANT MANAGER (DS)
Typist's initials	rm

Letter 4: Simplified Style

BUSINESS LETTER PUNCTUATION

There are two punctuation styles for business letters. In *mixed punctuation style,* a colon is placed after the salutation and a comma is placed after the complimentary close. In *open punctuation style,* no punctuation is used after the salutation or the complimentary close.

BASIC PARTS OF A BUSINESS LETTER

Letterhead

Most business letters are typed on printed letterhead. The format of the letterhead differs with each firm, but the contents of the letterhead are fairly standard: the company name, the street address, the name of the city and state, and the ZIP code. Other elements that may appear in the letterhead are the telephone number (with area code) of the firm and the names and titles of the corporate officers.

Dateline

The dateline begins on about the third line below the company letterhead or on line 14, whichever is more eye-appealing for letter placement. The dateline consists of the month, the day, and the year.

The month is always spelled in full. The date and the year are given as numerals, and the date is followed by a comma.

Preferred style	October 3, 1988
Military style	3 October 1988
Unacceptable styles	October 3rd, 1988
	Oct. 3, 1988

In the block style letter (Letter 1) and the simplified style letter (Letter 4), the date is typed at the left margin. In the modified block style (Letters 2 and 3), the date begins at the center.

Inside Address

A complete inside address is very important to ensure not only that the letter is directed to the correct person but also that accurate files may be established. The inside address may be typed anywhere from three to twelve lines below the date line, depending on the length of the letter (see placement chart on page 96). It is typed at the left margin for all letter styles.

The inside address should include the following elements: person's name, person's title, name of company or organization, street address, city name, state name, and ZIP Code. If a company or organization is being addressed, or a person at a company or organization, the inside address should be typed exactly as it appears in the addressee's letterhead.

If you are unable to determine a specific person's name, then you may use an *attention line* with a business title. In this way, the letter will be directed to the proper person. The attention line is the second line of the inside address.

If the address includes an apartment number or room number, type these elements on the same line as the street. State names should be abbreviated in the address according to the two-letter state abbreviations. The nine-digit ZIP Code is typed one or two spaces after the state abbreviation.

Mr. John Alexander, President ABZ Company 1234 East Sixth Street, Room 1410 Buffalo, NY 14222-5147	The ABZ Company Attention Sales Manager 1234 East Sixth Street Buffalo, NY 14222-5147
Mr. John Alexander National Sales Manager ABZ Company P.O. Box 1614 Buffalo, NY 14222-5147	Mr. John Alexander 666 Fifth Avenue, Apt. 4D Buffalo, NY 14222-5147

General guidelines to follow when typing the inside address:

1. Type names as they appear in the letterhead; always check the spelling of all proper names by referring to your files.
2. The number (#) symbol is not necessary when typing the house number, room number, or post office box number. House numbers, with the exception of one, are typed in figures.

   One East Sixth Street

   2 East Sixth Street

3. When street names are numbers, write out names below ten and use figures for names above ten.
4. When figures are used in street addresses, it is not necessary to use endings such as st, d, nd, or rd after the numbered street name.

   1234 East 12 Street

5. Type the city name, state name, and ZIP Code on the same line.

6. Type the city name in full, followed by a comma, and then the two-letter state abbreviation.

7. Type the ZIP Code one or two spaces after the two-letter state abbreviation. There is no punctuation after the state abbreviation.

Salutation

The salutation is typed two lines below the last line of the inside address. The salutation is omitted in the simplified letter. In all other letter styles, the salutation is typed starting at the left margin and followed by a colon if mixed punctuation is used.

Capitalization of salutations. Capitalize the first word, the title, and any noun in the salutation:

Dear Mr. Jones
My dear Professor Clark
Dear Mrs. Morgan
Your Excellency

Abbreviations in salutations. Mr., Ms., Mrs., Messrs., and Dr. are abbreviated. Write out other titles such as Captain, Professor, Father, Reverend, etc.

Forms of salutations. For the forms of salutations to use in addressing church or government officials, judges, doctors, etc., see Chapter 15, "Forms of Address."

When an organization is composed of men and women, the salutation used is still Gentlemen if the correspondence is addressed to a company. Although this style is frowned upon by some groups, it is still used simply because a more acceptable salutation has not yet evolved.

Table 5.1 provides guidelines for salutations when a letter is addressed to a firm or an individual.

Body of the Letter

The part of the letter containing the message is known as the "body." It is typed a double space below the salutation or a double space below the subject line. The paragraphs should be blocked or indented depending upon the letter style that is used. The paragraphs are single-spaced. Occasionally short letters are typed in double space.

Whether the lines are single-spaced or double-spaced, use only double spacing between paragraphs.

The body of the simplified letter style is typed on the third line below the subject line.

TABLE 5.1

Guidelines for Salutations

Addressee	Salutation
Firm's name	Gentlemen
Firm's name and an attention line is used	Gentlemen
Married woman, a widow, or a divorced woman who uses the title Mrs.	Dear Mrs. Jones
Unmarried woman	Dear Miss Jones
	Dear Ms. Jones
Unknown whether woman is married or single	Dear Ms. Jones
Group (composed of men and women)	Ladies and Gentlemen
Married couple	Dear Mr. and Mrs. Jones
Man and a woman	Dear Mr. Jones and Mrs. Black
	Dear Sir and Madam

Letter Placement Guide

Type of Letter	Words in Body	Line Width	Spaces Pica	Spaces Elite	Set Margins Pica	Set Margins Elite
Short letters	Under 100 words	4″	40	48	22–62	27–75
Medium letters	100 to 200 words	5″	50	60	17–67	21–81
Long letters	200 to 300 words	6″	60	72	12–72	15–87

The date is placed on line 14 on plain paper. When printed letterheads are used, the date is placed on the third line under the letterhead. However, if the letterhead is short (5 to 9 lines deep), bring date to line 14 for better placement.

Type of Letter	Words in Body	Lines from Date to Inside Address
Short letters	0–50	12
	51–75	11
	76–100	10
Medium letters	101–125	9
	126–150	8
	151–175	7
	176–200	6
Long letters	201–225	5
	226–250	4
	251–300	3

At least a triple line space must be kept between date, or last line in return address, and the inside address.

Raise the inside address one line for each extra line of introductory or closing material:

1. Five-line inside address
2. Subject line
3. Postscript
4. Enclosure line
5. Copy notation line (one line for each name)
   cc—carbon copy; pc—photocopy; c—copy

Tabulated matter in body of the letter. Tabulated matter in the body of a letter is indented at least five spaces from both the left- and right-hand margins.

Enumerated paragraphs. Enumerated paragraphs are also indented five spaces from both the right- and left-hand margins. These paragraphs begin with a number followed by a period. Two spaces after the period, begin typing the paragraph. Single-space each enumerated paragraph but double-space between the enumerated paragraphs. (If each enumerated paragraph contains only one line, you may single-space between paragraphs.)

1. _____
   _____

2. _____
   _____

Complimentary Closing

The complimentary closing is typed two lines below the last line of the body of the letter.

Capitalize only the first word in the complimentary closing. Follow the complimentary closing by a comma, unless open punctuation is used. If open punctuation is used, no punctuation is needed.

Placement of complimentary closing. The placement of the complimentary closing depends upon which letter style is used. (See Letters 1–3.)

Degrees of formality. As with the salutation, there are also degrees of formality recognized in complimentary closings.

1. Formal tone: Yours truly, Yours very truly, Very truly yours.
2. More formal tone: Respectfully yours, Yours respectfully, Very respectfully yours, Yours very respectfully.
3. Less formal and more personal tone: Sincerely, Cordially, Sincerely yours, Cordially yours, Yours sincerely.

Typewritten Signature and Title

When a company name appears as part of the signature, it is typed in all capitals a double space below the complimentary closing. The typewritten signature is then typed on the fourth line below the company name or the complimentary closing. The penned signature is placed in the intervening space. If a letter is unusually short, place the typed signature on the sixth or eighth line below the company name or complimentary closing. If the writer's handwriting is unusually large, the signature may be typed from five to eight lines below the company name or complimentary closing.

The writer's title may appear on the same line with the typed signature or on the line below the typed signature, whichever gives a better balance to the page.

Yours very truly,

Clarence Brown

Clarence Brown, Manager

Yours very truly,

Clarence Brown

Clarence Brown
Manager

In the simplified letter style, beginning at the left margin, type the writer's name and title on the fifth line below the body of the letter in all capital letters, or the name on the fifth line and the title on the sixth line. (See Letter 4.)

Joseph H. Feng

JOSEPH H. FENG
ASSISTANT MANAGER

Division or department. Frequently a division or department is used in the closing lines of a letter; it is typed below the typed signature and title.

Very truly yours,

R. M. Brown

R. M. Brown, Supervisor
Plastics Division

More than one signature. When a letter requires two signatures, you may use either of the following forms:

Sincerely yours,

Jane R. Jones

Ms. Jane R. Jones
District Manager

Milton Trout

Milton Trout
General Manager

OR

Sincerely yours,

Jane R. Jones

Ms. Jane R. Jones
District Manager

Milton Trout

Milton Trout
General Manager

Signature for the employer. If, as a secretary, you are required to sign a letter for your employer, you may use either one of the following forms:

Sincerely yours,   Sincerely yours,

Myrna Lane   *Myrna Lane*

Secretary to Ms. Jones   Ms. Myrna Lane
                                                Secretary to Ms. Jones

Signing someone else's name. When signing someone else's name, it is not necessary to write "per" or "by." Simply sign the individual's name and then your initials.

If your employer has a facsimile signature, use it.

When the individual signing a letter for another person is not the person's secretary, use either one of these forms:

Sincerely yours,   Sincerely yours,

Milton Trout (L.W.)   *Milton Trout (L.W.)*

For Milton Trout   Milton Trout
General Manager   General Manager

Academic, military, and professional titles. These titles should appear in the typewritten signatures as given below.

Yours truly,   Yours truly,

Grace Johnson   *James Simpson*

Ms. Grace Johnson, C.P.S.   James Simpson, M.D.

Yours truly,   Yours truly,

Laura Wilson   *Leonard J. Richardson*

Laura Willson, Ph.D.   Leonard J. Richardson
Professor of Humanities   Colonel, USAF

The salutations in replies to each of these would be, respectively, Dear Ms. Johnson, Dear Dr. Simpson, Dear Professor Willson, and Dear Colonel Richardson.

Courtesy titles. When a first name could be a man's or a woman's name, or initials are used, the courtesy title of Mr. should be used.

Sincerely,

Dale Harrington

Mr. Dale Harrington

Sincerely yours,

D. K. Harrington

Mr. D. K. Harrington

It is customary for a woman to include her courtesy title (Ms., Miss, Mrs.) in her signature. If she does not, she presents a problem to the person replying to her letter. Without a signature that lets respondents know what title the woman prefers, they have little choice than to use Ms., even though they risk offending some women who object to this title.

Sincerely yours,

Francine Booth

Mrs. Francine Booth

Yours truly,

Sincerely,

Francine Booth

Miss Francine Booth

Ms. Francine Booth

If the writer is a single woman and wants to be recognized as being single, she should use Miss. If a woman is married and does not feel that her married status is relevant, she may use Ms. or Miss.

If a married woman prefers to be addressed by her husband's given name, then she should use the format:

Yours very truly,

Mrs. Paul A. Booth

Mrs. Paul A. Booth

A divorced woman may use any courtesy title she wishes regardless of whether she has resumed her maiden name or retained her married surname.

Reference Initials

All typed business letters should contain identifying initials. Today, most firms prefer only the typist's reference initials. Occasionally there are two sets of initials: the first set representing the author of the written document and the second set, the typist. If both sets of initials are used, the first set is typed in capital letters and the second set in lower case with either a slash or a colon separating the sets.

Reference initials are typed at the left margin a double space below the typewritten signature and title. Illustrations are as follows:

JRJ:lm   JRJ (author of document) and lm (typist)

JRJ/lm   JRJ (author of document) and lm (typist)

lm   (typist's initials only)

Occasionally an executive will type his or her own business letter. When this is done, the executive may repeat his or her initials (RK:rk) to indicate that a typist was not involved.

OTHER ELEMENTS IN A BUSINESS LETTER

In addition to the standard parts in all business letters, other elements are sometimes included.

Attention Line

The writer may wish to direct the letter to a particular person or department within the firm. When the inside address is directed to a firm name and the writer wishes a certain person or specific department to also be aware of the contents of the letter, an attention line should be used.

The attention line is typed after the company name and before the company address in the inside address. The word *attention* must appear; however, no punctuation is necessary after it.

ACE Recruitment International
Attention Mr. Samuel Jones
8225 Dunwoody Place
Atlanta, GA 30339-7329

Subject Line

When a subject line is used, it should be typed a double space below the salutation. The subject line may be typed starting at the left margin, centered, or indented five spaces, depending on the style of the letter. The word *Subject* may precede the subject line. It may be typed in all caps, or it may be typed in initial caps. Today many businesses prefer to type the subject line in all caps, without the word *Subject* preceding it.

If the simplified letter style is used, the subject line should replace the salutation and be typed on the third line below the last line of the inside address. The subject line should be typed at the left margin in all capitals. The word *Subject* does not precede the subject line.

Reply Reference Notation

Place the notation as you would a subject line. The word *Reference* or *Re* followed by a colon and two spaces may be shown before the notation.

Enclosure Notation

Whenever an item is to be enclosed with a letter, this should be indicated on the letter by typing an enclosure notation two lines below the reference initials at the left margin. This tells the recipient to check the envelope or package for additional items.

When more than one item is enclosed, any one of the following forms may be used:

> Enclosures 2
> Enclosures (2)
> Enc. 2

Important enclosures should be listed:

> Enclosure: check

> Enclosures:
>   check
>   contract

> Enclosures:
>   1. check
>   2. contract

Copy Notation

A record of every written communication that leaves the office must be prepared and filed. Carbon copies or photocopies may be used.

When a carbon is prepared for the information of a person other than the addressee of the letter, the notation *cc* followed by the name of the person receiving the copy is typed at the left margin, a double space below the reference initials or enclosure notation. If more than one person is to receive a copy, the names should be listed either in order of importance in the company or in alphabetical order. Common examples follow.

ms   ms

Enclosure   cc   Raymond Smith

cc: Raymond Smith
      Albert Wayne

Some organizations keep a record of their correspondence by preparing a photocopy of outgoing communications. The following notations may be used:

pc: Rosemarie Sweeting   pc   Rosemarie Sweeting

Other organizations make no distinction as to the type of copy made and use the following notations:

c: Sandra Delgado   c   Sandra Delgado

Blind Copies

There are instances when it is necessary to send a copy of a letter to one or more persons without the knowledge of the addressee. This is known as a blind copy (*bc*). To make this special notation, remove the original letter and any other copies on which the *bc* should not appear. Then type the *bc* notation on each of the remaining copies at the bottom of the letter at the left margin. Make sure the firm's file copy shows all the *bc* notations. The letters *bcc* indicate blind carbon copy.

Postscript

A postscript is often used to emphasize a special point by setting it apart from the rest of the letter or to relay a personal message to the recipient of the letter. A postscript should be typed as a single-spaced paragraph a double space below the last notation. The letters *PS* are not necessary. Indent the paragraph if the paragraphs of the letter are indented.

Mailing Notation

Any special mailing notation (AIRMAIL, SPECIAL DELIVERY, REGISTERED, CERTIFIED, EXPRESS MAIL) should be typed midway between the date and the inside address. It should appear in all capital letters at the left margin.

MULTIPLE-PAGE LETTERS

When a letter consists of more than one page, the second page and successive pages are typed on plain paper of the same size, color, and

COMMUNICATIONS ASSOCIATES

385 Pennsylvania Avenue, NW / Washington, DC 20001-1438 /
1-800-432-5739

Date	October 7, 19__ (DS)
Mailing notation	REGISTERED (DS)
Inside address **Attention line**	Data Information Corporation Attention Purchasing Director 1945 West Parnell Road Jackson, MS 49201-1638 (DS)
Salutation	Ladies and Gentlemen (DS)
Subject line or **reply reference**	SPECIAL FEATURES IN BUSINESS LETTERS (DS)
Body of **letter**	We are delighted to enclose a copy of our latest booklet, SPECIAL FEATURES IN BUSINESS LETTERS. This booklet highlights many of the special features used in today's business letters. (DS) The special features presented in this letter are: mailing notation, attention line, subject line, company name in closing, enclosure notation, copy notation, and postscript. (DS) Most letters will not include all these special features; however, one should understand these features and know how and when to apply them. (DS)
Complimentary **close**	Sincerely (DS)
Company name	COMMUNICATIONS ASSOCIATES (operate return 4 times)
	Louise Rouse
Writer's name **Title**	Ms. Louise Rouse Communications Specialist (DS)
Typist's initials	lb (DS)
Enclosure	Enclosure (DS)
Copy notation	pc Diane Varadi (DS)
Postscript	Additional free copies of the booklet are available.

Letter 5: Block style, open punctuation, special features

quality as the letterhead. If possible, leave at least two lines of a paragraph at the bottom of the page and carry at least two lines to the next page. Do not end a page with a divided word.

Each successive page requires a *heading*. The heading consists of the name of the addressee, the page number of the letter, and the date, typed on the seventh line from the top edge of the paper. Triple-space after the heading and continue typing the remainder of the letter. Use the same side margins as for the first page.

There are two formats for headings for the second and subsequent pages of multiple-page letters: block style and horizontal style.

The block style heading is typed at the left margin:

Miss Jane R. Smith
Page 2
October 7, 19--

In the horizontal style, the name of the addressee is typed at the left margin, the page number is centered, and the dateline ends at the right margin:

Miss Jane R. Smith   2   October 7, 19--

ENVELOPES

There are several guidelines that should be observed when typing business envelopes because the post office optical character readers are programmed to scan a specific area of the envelope. The address must be completely within the read zone, blocked and single-spaced. Two-letter state abbreviations must be used. Nine-digit ZIP Codes should be used. Apartment and room numbers should follow the street address on the same line. The U.S. Postal Service prefers the use of all capital letters and no punctuation in envelope addresses.

The two standard-sized envelopes are:

No. 6¾ Envelope measures $6\frac{1}{2} \times 3\frac{5}{8}''$
No. 10 Envelope measures $9\frac{1}{2} \times 4\frac{1}{8}''$

On a small envelope (No. 6¾) the address should start on line 12 from the top edge of the envelope and two and a half inches from the left edge of the envelope. On a large envelope (No. 10) the address should start on line 14 from the top edge and four inches from the left edge.

Special notations to the addressee (CONFIDENTIAL, HOLD FOR ARRIVAL, PERSONAL) are typed in all capitals about three lines below the return address.

Special mailing notations (AIRMAIL, SPECIAL DELIVERY, REGISTERED, CERTIFIED) are typed below the stamp (about line nine) to end five to six spaces from the right edge of the envelope; these notations are typed in all capitals.

The return address should start on the second line down from the top edge of the envelope and three spaces in from the left edge of the envelope.

ADDRESSING NO. 6¾ ENVELOPE FOR OPTICAL CHARACTER READER
(Preferred by U.S. Postal Service)

```
L M SMITH
245 MAIN STREET
GLENDALE NY  11385-7342


HOLD FOR ARRIVAL




            MS ROBERTA ROGERS
            987 KINGSTON DRIVE  APT 7
            DES MOINES IA  50310-3636
```

ADDRESSING NO. 10 ENVELOPE FOR OPTICAL CHARACTER READER
(Preferred by U.S. Postal Service)

L M SMITH
245 MAIN STREET
GLENDALE NY 11385-7342

REGISTERED

DATA INFORMATION CORPORATION
ATTENTION PURCHASING DIRECTOR
1945 WEST PARNELL ROAD
JACKSON, MS 49201-1638

TRADITIONAL METHOD FOR ADDRESSING NO. 6¾ ENVELOPE

```
Mr. L. M. Smith
245 Main Street
Glendale, NY  11385-7342


HOLD FOR ARRIVAL




                    Ms. Roberta Rogers
                    987 Kingston Drive  Apt. 7
                    Des Moines, IA  50310-3636
```

SPACING USED WITH PUNCTUATION MARKS

Period. Space twice after a period at the end of a sentence, after a term used as a subhead at the beginning of a line, or after a number as used in enumeration of items. Space once after the period following an abbreviation or following an initial.

Comma. Space once after a comma.

Question mark. Space twice after a question mark at the end of a sentence, once after a question mark within a sentence.

Exclamation point. Space twice after an exclamation point at the end of a sentence, once after an exclamation point within a sentence.

Semicolon. Space once after a semicolon.

Colon. Space twice after a colon. Exception: leave no space after the colon used in expressions of time (as 7:25).

Quotation marks. No space is left between the quotation marks and the material they enclose. When typing a list or quoting lines of

TRADITIONAL METHOD FOR ADDRESSING NO. 10 ENVELOPE

```
Mr. L. M. Smith
245 Main Street
Glendale, NY  11385-7342


                                  REGISTERED


                    Data Information Corporation
                    Attention Purchasing Director
                    1945 West Parnell Road
                    Jackson, MS 49201-1638
```

poetry, leave the first quotation mark to the left of all the items or lines, so that the first words line up at the left. At the end of such material, the closing quotation marks come after the period (or closing word if no period is used) on the last line.

Double quotation marks. For a quotation within a quotation, single quotation marks are used. No space in typing is left between the single and double quotation marks.

Parentheses. If the material in parentheses falls within a sentence, leave one space before the opening parenthesis, two spaces when the material in parentheses follows a sentence, and no space after the opening parenthesis. The closing parenthesis requires no space before it, one space after it when the material in parentheses falls within a sentence, and two spaces when the material in parentheses constitutes a complete sentence and is followed by another sentence outside the parentheses.

Apostrophe. No space is left after an apostrophe within a word; one space is left after an apostrophe at the end of a word within a sentence.

Asterisk. The asterisk, used to refer a reader to a footnote, is typed immediately after a word or a punctuation mark with no space before it. In the footnote itself, one space is left after the asterisk.

Diagonal. No space precedes or follows the diagonal, sometimes called the slash mark or virgule.

Dash. No space is used before or after a dash made up of two hyphens (or the longer dash on a typewriter with this character on one of its keys). The dash should never be used at the beginning of a line.

RULES FOR THE DIVISION OF WORDS

1. Avoid excessive word division.
2. Do not divide a word that contains only one syllable.
   Examples: brought, freight, friend
3. Divide only between syllables.
   Examples: ac knowl edg ment, har mo nize, tab u la tor
4. Do not divide a word unless it has at least six letters.
   Examples: ask ing, fil ter, man tel
5. Do not divide one or two letters from the remainder of a word.
   Examples: against, agen da
6. Do not divide a word immediately before a one-letter syllable.
   Examples: co ag u late, o bit u ar y, spec u late
   If the one-letter syllable is part of a common suffix, such as *able* or *ible*, carry the suffix over to the next line (reli-able, convert-ible, etc.).

7. If a consonant is doubled where syllables join, generally divide the word between the consonants.
   Examples: admis sion, confer ring, sug gestion

8. If a suffix has been added to a root word that ends in a doubled letter, ordinarily divide before the suffix.
   This rule could be considered an exception to the one preceding. A word such as *telling* is made up of the root *tell* and the suffix *ing*. It would logically be divided after the second *l*. Here are several other words that would be governed by this rule:
   cross ing, drill ing, fall ing, miss ing, ebb ing, stuff ing

9. Divide a hyphenated word only at the hyphen.
   Examples: self- explanatory, non- participatory

10. Do not end more than two consecutive lines with a hyphen. Also, try to avoid dividing the first line of a paragraph.

11. Avoid the division of names. Proper nouns should be divided only when absolutely necessary. It is generally better to leave a line slightly short than to break a word such as Prendergast or Massachusetts. Divide proper noun groups so that they can be read with ease. The name Donald S. Crenshaw might be typed with Donald S. at the end of one line and Crenshaw at the start of the next.

12. DO NOT DIVIDE THE LAST WORD OF A PARAGRAPH OR THE LAST WORD ON A PAGE.

13. Do not divide the following units:
    June 23, 1988
    8 percent
    12 pounds
    8:22 a.m.

Special Report Format

by James C. Matthews, Ed.D.

In addition to letters, other types of reports frequently have to be prepared by secretaries. The preparation may include dictation; transcription; typing or word processing; preparation and inclusion of charts, tables, and other visual aids; and other tasks to ensure that the final report is accurate and attractive. This chapter discusses the secretary's role in the preparation of business reports, office memorandums, minutes of a meeting or conference, news releases, copy for publication, technical reports, and legal documents.

BUSINESS REPORTS

A business report is a lengthy in-depth communication, with facts and ideas, to workers in a company. Reports can appear in several forms, and there is no authoritative list of all types of reports. Reports may be catalogical, analytical, or compartmentalized. The procedures described in this chapter put the elements together to produce an effective, quality report. Some reports are typeset and include artwork (as an annual report to stockholders or to a board of directors). Others are typewritten or word processed with unjustified or justified margins. Since reports are more in-depth than letters and memorandums, more time and effort is required. If possible, all reports should be keyed using a text-editing package. Storage and retrieval allows for easier final editing.

Types of Business Reports

There are several types of business reports, including corporate reports, executive summaries, and abstracts. The secretary must know how to format each element.

Corporate Report

This category includes memorandum reports, letter reports, and megareports (very lengthy, complex reports containing hundreds of pages). A corporate report might introduce and analyze a specific problem, discuss it, and provide impetus for its resolution. The content may be technical or general. The secretary may have responsibility for the production of the entire report, including careful proofreading, checking for accuracy, duplication, binding, collating, and distribution.

Executive Summary

An executive summary is a brief description and summation of a report's contents. Significant data are summarized. A summary of this type is used for problem solving and covers the problem, how it should be solved, and what the benefits are. Usually detailed data are not given. The summary may be part of a longer report.

Abstract

An abstract, like an executive summary, is a brief description or overview of the contents of a report. There are two types of abstracts: informative and descriptive. An *informative abstract* is a summary, an internal discussion. A *descriptive abstract* lists the elements covered in a complete report without stating the supporting data; it is an external discussion or framework.

Format and Preparation

Careful formatting and preparation of a business report is a must. Whether you cut and paste, type straight, or use a word processing or software package, you must be consistent in form, type style and fonts, and so forth to produce a quality document. Before beginning preparation of the report, the secretary must give thought to the paper, type style, and format as well as the special features of the report and the care and use of the equipment to be used in preparing the report.

Paper

In typing reports use a good quality of paper, usually $8\frac{1}{2}'' \times 11''$, and use a black ribbon. Use white paper with rag content. The higher the rag content of paper, the longer its life. A watermark imprinted on rag-content paper tells the brand of paper and the percentage of cotton fiber in it. The right side of the paper shows a readable watermark. Use either 16-, 20-, or 24-pound paper. Type on the face of the paper showing the readable watermark.

Since multiple originals can be generated by automatic text-editing equipment and many offices use photocopies to produce quality copies, carbons may not be necessary. Should you have to make carbons, find out the number of carbon copies required. Carbon copies that are to be widely circulated should be on heavier paper, for readability is a factor in obtaining acceptance of a report. Chemically treated carbons may be obtained for multicopying (six or more). Paper used for duplicates has a right and a wrong side. If you are duplicating the report, make certain that you place it on the right side of the paper for best results.

Executive Summary

Simulations and models for strategic planning are being used by business and industry more and more. Strategic planning concerns itself with business decision-making and problem-solving. Some questions addressed are:

- What should a company be doing?
- What are our service fields?
- What are our strengths and weaknesses?
- How can we achieve maximum production in meeting our goals?

To answer many of these questions and their subsets, we must have a strategic plan through a model or a simulation. A model is a representation of reality, and a simulation is an exercise conducted on the model to find out what would result if specified conditions occurred. At times, the specified conditions may be assumed.

In the mid-1980s, approximately 70% of the Fortune 500 companies used strategic planning techniques to forge their companies toward high levels of productivity and output. Strategic planning works. The simulation used is of greatest interest to strategic planners primarily due to the findings and results from one time period to determine what will happen in the next time period.

Recommendation: Hire a consulting firm to develop a strategic plan for the early 1990s to Year 2000.

Example of an *Executive Summary.*

Type Style

Pica type (pitch 10) is preferred for reports because its larger size makes it easier to read than elite type (pitch 12). As for design, the conventional roman type is still the most widely acceptable. It is the standard style on the modern typewriter. A variation such as the square-serif roman may be available. Then again, a sturdy, modern sans-serif design is clean, easy to read, and makes single-spaced or tightly packed data appear less crowded. Neither script nor italic type is suitable for reports. However, italic type may be used to highlight certain words in the text of a report. Certain text-editing packages and some electric typewriters have this capability. If italic type is not available, italicized words are typed underscored. The underscoring equals and should be interpreted as the word(s) being in italics. In all cases the style must be good letter quality. Some dot-matrix printers are letter or near-letter print quality.

Format

The format, or arrangement and layout of material, in a report can vary in indentations, footnoting or citations, page numbering, spacing, etc. The secretary may be required to follow a certain format or have a preference for a certain style, but the format must be consistent throughout the report. Because of the increased use of text-editing equipment in the automated office, several software formatting packages can be obtained to assist with technical, detailed formatting projects. However, some caution is to be taken. Familiarity with the operation of automated equipment and its interface with commercial software packages is necessary to do the job effectively.

   Format ruler. The format ruler, sometimes called a *word processing ruler* or *forms ruler,* is a handy tool used for checking margins, spacing, and counting the number of lines of a document. On a display terminal, it can be used to check vertical and horizontal spacing, centering, and so forth. The format ruler is usually 12, 15, or 18 inches in length and contains a centering scale, pitch 10 and 12 scales, lines of text, metric calculations, and so forth.

   The format ruler is particularly useful if, for example, you are asked to produce an exact copy of a letter (or other document) with identical measurements. To find out the pitch, you would use the ruler to verify the spacing by placing a given line on the pitch-10 or pitch-12 scale. Exact placement would indicate the type style in which the letter was originally keyed. If line 12 is to be transposed to line 20, the number of lines scale could easily guide you to the appropriate

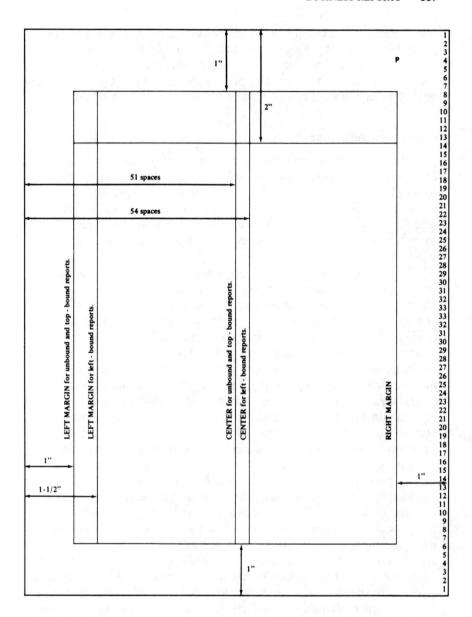

Sample of a Report Typing Guide: This typing guide can be used for a report that is to be top-, left-, or unbound. All pages of the report must follow the same guide. A format ruler may be equally useful in calculations of certain measurement.

line without the necessity of manually counting. This is most appropriate for stored text in a database file. The cursor should also be used to locate line 20. The cursor movement (vertical and horizontal) is correlated with the line count. By placing the format rule on the screen, quick line adjustments can be made without working from a hard copy.

Other Preparatory Tasks

Choice of appropriate software. If you will be using a computer or sophisticated word processor and a text-editing or similar software package, check beforehand that the features in the software package meet the needs of your company or the particular types of business reports you will be creating. If, for example, you will frequently want to use underscoring or superscripts, be sure that the software package you will use has these features.

Thousands of pre-packaged applications programs are available for personal computers to help produce quality documents. A microcomputer can handle alphanumeric or graphic information for text editing, depending on the type of program run on it. Dozens of text-editing programs are available, including, but not limited to, Multimate, Multimate Advantage, Word Perfect, Word Star, and Microsoft Word. Auxiliary features include dictionaries, spelling verification and grammar and math checkers, storing, list processing (mailing, inventory), a glossary, selective and global searches, style guides (*APA, Chicago Manual of Style*), a thesaurus, graphics (pie, line, bar, and graph charts), forms format (résumé), and graphic and text combinations (desktop publishing or electronic publishing, film, and blueprints).

Best-selling types of business software are listed periodically in two service publications: *PC World* (Subscriber Services, P.O. Box 55029, Boulder, CO 80322-5029) and *Administrative Management* (The Automated Office, Ltd., 1123 Broadway, New York, NY 10010). When using electronic equipment to produce a business report, you might use a combination and/or integration of these various applications. Of special interest to the secretary is *The Secretary,* the professional publication of Professional Secretaries International (PSI) (301 East Armour Boulevard, Kansas City, MO 64111-1299). This magazine highlights new technologies affecting the modern-day secretary and discusses change as well as implementation of effective production measures.

Developing familiarity with electronic editing and printing. Many word processors and text-editing software programs used with personal computers have an automatic wraparound feature by which a long word keyed in near the right margin is carried to the beginning of the next line, triggered by a space before and after. If the program does have this feature, the secretary should check the right margin to be sure that too much white space is not left. Depending on the appearance, the secretary might want to impose hyphens and divide words in order to achieve evenly worded lines and an evenly formatted right margin. For example, with automatic wraparound the word *acknowledgment,* if keyed near the right margin, would automatically be wrapped around to the following line unless the secretary decided for appropriate word division and keys in the hyphen so that it became "acknowl-edgment" on two lines. In these cases, it is important to remember to delete the hyphen because later insertions, deletions, or other changes to the middle of a line may move the word where the hyphen would be inappropriate.

Extra care must be taken when editing documents on a screen. Adjust the contrast, clarity, and color. Use the cursor (pointer) to proofread from line to line or paragraph to paragraph. Check the printout for accuracy, since at times the text appearing on the screen may not be replicated on the hard copy due to slippage or movement in the printwheel or other part of the printer. With automatic typewriters and word processors, data are recorded by magnetic cards, disks, memory, or computer storage; with personal computers, by floppy and hard disks. Errors are corrected by backspacing and rekeying the correct character over the error. Once the correction has been made, the file must be updated to eliminate the original error.

The secretary should also make sure that the printwheel is clean, the ribbon fresh, and the printer producing evenly dark copy. An impression adjustment may be necessary.

Parts of a Business Report

The business report may include, along with the main body, all or some of the following: letter or memorandum of transmittal, title page, preface, table of contents, list of tables and/or figures, bibliography, appendix, and index. The secretary needs to know how to handle each of these elements and how to put them together. Secretaries play an important role in getting a report accepted. A report is much more likely to be looked upon with favor when it is properly formatted, well arranged, and easy to read.

Letter or Memorandum of Transmittal

A letter of transmittal is used to introduce the reader to the report. The content of the letter should tell the reader what the topic of the report is, why it was written, how it was compiled, who worked on it, and what major findings or conclusions resulted from the research.

The letter of transmittal appears directly after the title page, and it may be typed in any acceptable business letter or memorandum format.

Title Page

The title page will usually contain the name or title of the report, the name and title of the person or organization for whom it was written, the name and title of the person or group who wrote it, and the date it was submitted. The title page may also include more information if necessary.

Type the main title in all capital letters approximately two inches from the top of the page. Type the date two inches from the bottom of the page. Space the other information equally between the top and bottom margins, typed in lower-case letters with the first letter of each main word capitalized. Center each line horizontally.

There are various formats for title pages. For an acceptable style, see the illustration on page 121.

Preface

The preface, also called the *foreword,* is optional. It allows the writer to give a personal message to the reader. The author may, for example, provide special information not necessarily appearing in the body of the report (methods used, points of emphasis, pragmatic considerations, reasons for treatment of content).

Table of Contents

The table of contents is one of the last things prepared. It should be typed after all pages of the report are completed and numbered. The table of contents lists in order the numbers and titles of the sections or chapters in the report and the pages on which they begin. It should not be confused with the index, which is arranged alphabetically and includes more items.

Type the heading, TABLE OF CONTENTS, in all capital letters centered two inches from the top edge of the paper. Type "Page" a triple space below the heading, pivoted from the right margin.

Begin typing the contents a double space below "Page" at the left margin. Use the same margins that you use in typing the body of the report.

Use all capital letters in typing those entries of the contents page that refer to the major sections of the report. Those sections of lesser importance should be indented under their main heading, listed in the

INTRODUCING INFORMATION PROCESSING INTO THE BUSINESS CURRICULUM

AT ST. ANN'S TECHNICAL COLLEGE

The Effect of Change

The State University of New York Program in Office Management

by

Technical Consultants, Inc.

August 16, 19__

Sample title page.

same sequence as they appear in the report, and typed in capital and lower-case letters. Leaders should be used to guide the reader's eye across the page from a content's entry to the page number.

See page 123 for a sample of a TABLE OF CONTENTS.

List of Tables or Figures

When a report contains several tables and/or figures, separate lists of these enclosures should be included after the table of contents. Type the lists in a format similar to that of the table of contents. Should a report contain both tables and figures, the list of tables precedes the list of figures. In the separate lists, number each title or figure, and give the full caption or title of each. Type each list on a separate page.

Body of the Report

Use a report or manuscript typing guide for setting up reports. These may be purchased or you may design your own.

Margins. Margins for reports and manuscripts are a minimum of one inch; however, many authors prefer one and one-fourth inches. When the report is to be bound on the left side, allow for the binding by making the left margin one and one-half inches wide. This makes the center point of the writing line three spaces to the right of the present center; if you are centering lines at 51, you will now center them at 54. You can accomplish the same result by merely moving the paper one-fourth inch to the left of the spot where you normally keep it.

The top margin on the first page should be at least two inches; on the other pages, it should be one inch. If the report is to be bound at the top, allow an additional half inch for this. Keep the bottom margins at least one inch deep; in some cases you may want to make them as much as one and one-half inches deep.

Spacing. Usually reports are double-spaced, and the first line of each paragraph is indented five spaces. The number of spaces paragraphs are indented may be eight or ten, but paragraph indentions are always used.

When quotations are of three lines or more, indent the quoted material five spaces from the left and right margins or indent it the same number of spaces from these margins as you indent the paragraphs. Indent the first line of the quotation to show a paragraph indention. Copy the indented quotation in single spacing and omit the quotation marks. The indention tells the reader that the material is quoted.

If listings are included in your report, single-space them. Center

TABLE OF CONTENTS

Sample table of contents.

the College, considering the above circumstances, was most
understandable. It was and is a risky undertaking at this period
of time when college enrollment is declining.

Population Under Investigation

The population under investigation for this study is the
administration of the College, the Business and Economics
Division, the Secretarial Administration Department, the students
enrolled in the secretarial program, the surrounding business
community, and the certificated and classified staff of San
Bernardino Valley College.

Definition of Terms

Mag Card II Typewriter. Paula Cecil states in her word
processing textbook:

> In April 1973 IBM introduced the use of "memory" in
> word processing typewriters with its new Mag Card II.
> Previously, recording of typing had been made directly onto
> the magnetic tape. But on the Mag Card II the recording is
> made "in memory" from which it can be played back. If the
> operator wants to store the recording on a card, a button is
> depressed which records all information that was typed into
> memory.[4]

Memory Typewriter. In the same textbook Ms. Cecil describes
the Memory typewriter:

> In March 1974, another member of the IBM family was
> introduced: the Memory Typewriter. This unit has all the
> features of the Mag Card II except the use of cards, thereby
> eliminating long storage and merging applications. The
> Memory Typewriter has a 50-page memory storage and a 4000-
> character-per-page capacity for revising, which means a
> total memory capacity of 200,000 characters. This unit is
> sold mainly to small offices for production of regular
> correspondence, some stored letters or paragraphs, and
> short-turnaround revisions.[5]

[4]Paula B. Cecil, Word Processing in the Modern Office (Menlo
Park, California: Cummings Publishing Co., 1976), pp. 85-86.

[5]Ibid., p. 87.

Sample of a page from the body of a report.

the items on the page. If the length of items varies, select the longest one to be centered and line up the others with it. If your listings contain widely separated columns, use leaders to assist the eye in reading the material. Make these leaders by alternating periods with spaces. Note whether the periods fall on the odd or even spaces in the first line, and then match the location of the periods accordingly in succeeding lines.

Allow at least two lines of a paragraph to appear at the bottom and top of each page, adjusting the bottom margin, if necessary, to accommodate the ending and beginning lines. Avoid single lines that carry over to end a paragraph at the top of a new page. Avoid dividing the last word on a page.

White space. As you prepare each page of the business report, avoid leaving excessive space without type. This distracts the reader and takes away from the appearance, organization, and format of the page. If white space is necessary before and after an illustration, artwork, or visual, leave not more than two inches. This applies to tables and figures; if they are typed and follow the text, allow at least triple linear spacing before and after. If reductions are necessary because of width, length, or both, make them; however, these reductions should fit within the margins.

Tables, Figures, Illustrations

The placement of tables, figures, and illustrations in the body of the business report is very important and must be carefully done. Each visual (whether a table, figure, or other type of illustration) must have its own identification number (Table 1, Table 2, and so forth; Figure 1, Figure 2, and so forth). Tables may present quantitative or qualitative data. The data should be arranged so that the significance of different items is obvious at a glance. Allow ample spacing between rows and columns; here, white space helps create order to the data being displayed. Turning a report sideways to read a table or study a figure is often an inconvenience to the reader. If possible, reduce the visual so that it conforms to the margins. Remember, reducing the width of a visual reduces the length by the same percentages; for example, reducing a visual's width by 77% simultaneously reduces its length by 77%. The same applies for enlargements.

Headings

The main heading is centered in all capital letters at the beginning of the report. No other heading should be typed in all capital letters. If the report has a subheading (secondary heading that explains or amplifies the main heading), separate it from the main heading with a double space, then triple-space before beginning the body of the report. The subheading should be centered and the main word or words capitalized.

First-order side headings are preceded by a triple space and followed by a double space. Side headings should be typed at the left margin, underlined with main words capitalized, and have no terminal period (or other terminal punctuation).

Second-order side headings or paragraph headings are preceded by a double space. They are indented to the paragraph point (usually only the first word is capitalized), underlined, and followed by a period. Begin typing the paragraph on the same line as the heading.

Footnotes

Footnotes usually fall at the bottom or end of the page where the reference is made. The secretary must plan the page so that there is sufficient space for the footnotes.

Footnotes have a number of purposes: they may confirm or add meaning to the author's statements; they may refer to other parts of the report that have a bearing on the topic discussed; they may make acknowledgments; or they sometimes make additional explanations of the content or terms used.

Footnotes are identified in the text by raised figures called *super-scripts*. The superscript is typed one-half space above the line of writing immediately after the word or statement to which the footnote applies. To type this superscript, engage the automatic line spacer and roll the paper down about one-half of the line. Type the figure and put the line spacer lever back in typing position. Touch the platen knob gently, and the paper will resume its former position. It is more convenient to use the automatic line-spacer lever (sometimes called "line finder" or "ratchet release lever") than to use the variable spacer on the platen knob, because the former will automatically bring the platen back to its original line of writing. Most modern electric typewriters and word processing equipment have a special superscript (and subscript) key so manual paper adjustment is not necessary.

Some software packages have a footnote feature that makes the spacing and arrangement of footnotes fast and easy. Use a format ruler to check calculations whether you are using a preprogrammed package, checking the screen, or working from rough draft copy.

Footnotes may be numbered in one of two ways: consecutively throughout the article or chapter, or consecutively on each page, beginning with the number 1 for each new page. Be uniform in numbering the references. In rough-draft work and thesis work, it simplifies the typing if footnotes are numbered consecutively on each page. Then if there is an addition, deletion, or correction, subsequent footnotes need not be renumbered.

When you use footnotes, type the reference figure in the text following the passage to which the footnote refers. Type the footnote on the same page on which the reference figure following the passage appears. Type footnotes to end one inch from the bottom edge of the page. Use the page-end indicator on your typewriter or a guide sheet to determine where to begin the footnote in order to have this one-inch margin. Usually you are safe if you allow three or four lines for each footnote.

After you type the last line of the text before the footnote, single-space and type a horizontal underscore line one and one-half to two inches long, starting at the left margin and extending the line toward the center. Type the footnote a double space below this line. Precede the footnote with the corresponding reference number raised about one-half space above the line. Start the footnote at the paragraph indention. The second line of the footnote should begin at the left margin. Footnote entries should be single-spaced with a double space between each footnote.

For a footnote that refers to published material, give the same information that is given in a bibliographical reference plus the page number of the cited material. The examples given below follow the *Chicago Manual of Style*.

> *Example of a footnote: book with two authors.*
>
> _____
>
> [3] Rosemary T. Fruehling and Constance K. Weaver, *Electronic Office Procedures* (New York: McGraw-Hill Book Company, 1987), p. 29.
>
> *Example of a footnote: magazine article.*
>
> _____
>
> [4] Stephen McMillen, "Secretarial Development: The Other Side of the Coin," *The Secretary*, (June/July, 1987), p. 26.

If two or more footnotes are identical, you do not need to retype the details. Use one of the following abbreviations for Latin phrases:

Ibid., meaning "in the same place." Use *Ibid.* when referring to the word cited in the immediately preceding footnote, without an intervening footnote. This abbreviation may be used several times in succession.

Example:

---

⁵ *Ibid.* (Use when the reference is identical to the one in the preceding footnote.)

⁶ *Ibid.*, p. 35. (Use when the reference is identical to the one in the preceding footnote but on a different page.)

loc. cit., meaning "in the place cited." Use *loc cit.* with nonconsecutive footnotes that refer to the same material, the same work, and the same page or pages. Repeat the author's name before *loc cit.*

op. cit., meaning "in the work cited." Use *op cit.* with nonconsecutive footnotes that refer to the same work but different pages. Repeat the author's last name.

Example:

---

⁸ Walshe, *loc. cit.*

⁹ Baker, *op. cit.*, p. 77.

Notes or Endnotes

These are writer's comments appearing at the bottom of a page or at the end of a report. They may be writer's identification notes, content footnotes, or copyright permission footnotes. If there is a single author's note on a page, an asterisk (*) may be used, not a number. The asterisk in the text with a note at the bottom of the page is called a *natural footnote*. You must leave a one-inch bottom margin. At times, especially in technical reports, notes and endnotes are lengthy. Remember, a one-inch bottom margin must be left below the notes.

Header/Footer

A *header* is a line or two at the top of each page in the report or at the top of the first page of the report that contains identifying information. Usually, the header contains the topic or subtopic in that particular section of the report. It may also identify a specific section of the report by number.

With a top margin of one inch (6 lines), start on line 7. It is acceptable to use line 2 or 3 for the header. The header should not be more than two lines long.

```
             TypeRight Software 1.1
             Chapter 1.3: Compatibility    HEADER

      The program design of major software is copyrighted.
   Moreover, some programs are compatible with major manufac-
   turers' equipment.  However, caution must be taken as to
```

A *footer*, located at the bottom of a page, is also identifying information. Generally, it contains the date of the report, page number, and other data. The footer may also note the coding or file number assigned in the database if text-editing equipment is being used.

Note that the types of identifying information included in headers and footers vary from one company to another. The examples given are typical; however, always follow company procedures.

```
Recommendation:   Specifications must be drafted by the end
                  of the third quarter.  The feasibility study
                  will cost $30,000.
September 1, 1988                      Coding  23    FOOTER
```

Bibliography

A bibliography includes the references used in the preparation of the report. Arrange it alphabetically by names of authors. When listing books, copy the information from the title page, rather than from the outside cover. When listing references from periodicals, take the title from the article itself.

Depending on the content of some reports and the company's policy, items in the bibliography may be numbered in order of their appearance in the report. Sometimes you may be asked to use abbreviated (shortened) forms of citations in your draft copy and complete forms in the final copy.

Each reference lists the surname of the author, followed by given name or initials; the title of the work; the publisher; the place of publication; and the date of publication. When using references from periodicals, one may include such identifying information as volume and page numbers. Observe these rules:

Underscore the titles of books and magazines.

Enclose the titles of magazine articles in quotation marks.

Type the author's initials after the surname. If some references use a full name and others only initials, be consistent, particularly when the references come close together. Usually it is better to use the full name.

If the author has written some books alone and collaborated with other authors on some materials, list first those books the author wrote alone.

If the publication has more than three authors, list the publication under the name of the first mentioned author and then use the words "and others" or *et al.*

If the publication is out of print, indicate this in parentheses following the reference.

Volume numbers of periodicals are written with Arabic numerals.

To make the author's name stand out, type the first line of the entry at the left margin and indent all other lines.

If there are many sources of reference material, classify them according to books, periodicals, pamphlets, or other documents.

When two or more books by the same author are listed in succession, instead of retyping the author's name each time, simply use a solid line of five underscores followed by a comma.

Example:

Popyk, Marilyn K., *Word Processing: Essential Concepts*, New York: McGraw-Hill Book Company, 1983.

_____, *Word Processing and Information Systems: A Practical Approach to Concepts*, New York: McGraw-Hill Book Company, 1986.

B I B L I O G R A P H Y

Books

Fruehling, Rosemary T., and Weaver, Constance K. Electronic
    Office Procedures. New York: McGraw-Hill Book Co., 1987.
    544 pp.

Keene, Michael L. Effective Professional Writing. Lexington,
    MS: D.C. Heath and Co., 1987. 450 pp.

Popyk, Marilyn K. Word Processing and Information Systems: A
    Practical Approach to Concepts. New York: McGraw-Hill Book
    Co., 1983. 336 pp.

Journals

Hart, M.B. "Status of OS in 29 Texas Companies (With
    Implications for OS Curricula)," Office Systems Research
    Journal. (1986).

McEntee, A. "Determining Core Competencies Necessary for Success
    in the Automated Office," Journal of the Business Education
    Association of New York. (1985).

Munter, M. "Using the Computer in Business Communication
    Courses," The Journal of Business Communication. (1986).

Unpublished Work

Xavier, Chris. "Office Needs" (Assessment Criteria, Star
    Associations, 1988), "Mimeographed."

Sample bibliography page.

References. Only citations used or referred to in the report are listed in the bibliography. Some reports provide a listing of suggested or recommended readings. These are separate from the bibliography and should be noted as such. In other words, the suggested or recommended readings (books, magazines, films, etc.) are neither cited nor used in the preparation of the report; they are intended for further study or review only.

There are a number of style manuals that can be used in preparing a bibliography (or other part of a report). Whatever manual you choose, use it properly: consistency, clarity, and common sense must prevail.

List of Style Manuals*

General

> *The APA Style Sheet*
> *The Chicago Manual of Style*
> Kate Turabian's *A Manual for Writers of Term Papers, Theses, and Dissertations*
> *The MLA Handbook*
> The US Government Printing Office's *Style Manual*

Technical

> The American Psychological Association's *Publication Manual*
> The American Institute of Physics' *Style Manual*
> Harvard Law Review's *A Uniform System of Citation*
> The American Institute of Industrial Engineers' *The Complete Guide for Writing Technical Articles*

---

* "Publication style" means the way references appear on printed pages of a journal in final form. "Manuscript-submission style" means the way references appear in the original manuscript as submitted by the writer (author). Note that the two styles are very different. Many journals print bibliographic references as footnotes; however, most such journals also require that references appearing in the manuscript be in end-note form (a separate page at the end of the report).

Appendix

Material supportive to the report should be placed in a supplementary section called an appendix. It should follow the bibliography. Examples of items placed in the appendix are copies of questionnaires, maps, lists, tables, sample forms and letters, and detailed summaries of data. Because of electronic (desktop) publishing, visuals, tables, graphics, and other inserts may be reduced and incorporated in the body of a report. This procedure saves the reader from turning back and forth to refer to cited items.

The appendix may be preceded by an introductory page entitled APPENDIX, typed in all capital letters and centered both horizontally and vertically. This page may also include a list of the items included

Appendix C[*]

Manual of Operations

---

[*]This manual has internal pagination.

Sample appendix page.

in the appendix. If this is used, both the title and the listing are centered vertically, or the title may be typed two inches from the top of the paper with the listing beginning a triple space below the title. When more than one item is appended, each item should be numbered or lettered and placed under a separate heading, such as Appendix A, Appendix B, etc.

Should the style manual you are using specify that appendices be lettered and you have more than 27 appendices, begin the 28th by doubling the letter as AA, BB, CC, and so forth. If an attachment has internal pagination, indicate the pagination by using an asterisk superior to the appendix letter followed by a note at the bottom. (See example on page 133.)

If an appendix is rather lengthy and bulky, label it "Enclosure" and attach it after the last appendix. If there is only one appendix, no letter or number is necessary. The word Appendix is sufficient. Triple-space and begin the text of that single appendix.

Index

An index is a listing of subjects, their subsets, and cross-referenced, correlated subjects citing key words in the body of the report.

It may be necessary to prepare an index as well as a table of contents for some reports. Be sure the index is typed in alphabetical order. Put the entries first on 3″ × 5″ cards and then arrange them alphabetically. Then type the index from the cards.

However, index cards are awkward to handle in bulk form. If you have access to a personal computer, word processor, or electronic typewriter, use an electronic filing procedure. Create a database and print a hard copy when needed. Electronic keying allows quick additions, deletions, and insertions. By creating a database, you eliminate misfiling and loss of cards. By the same measure, always keep a backup disk of all your keyed documents.

Final Tasks

After the draft of a report has been completed and corrected and all lists, tables, charts, and visuals inserted in their proper places, the secretary must prepare the report in its final form.

First, the pages must be numbered. Number the pages in the body of the report with Arabic numbers and those in the preliminary section (for example, the Table of Contents or List of Tables) with small Roman numerals.

If the report is unbound or bound at the left, the page number of the first page (if numbered) is centered one-half inch (3 lines) from the bottom of the page. Other pages of the report are numbered in the upper right corner on line four, with the number ending flush with the right margin. Begin the first line of typing on line seven; this will leave a one-inch top margin for the body of the report. Usually, if a manuscript is bound at the top, it is numbered at the bottom, centered on the third line from the bottom of the page.

In the preliminary section, count the title page as "i" but do not type the numeral. Number the remaining preliminary pages with small Roman numerals (ii, iii, iv, v, vi, etc.) centered on the third line from the bottom of the page.

Most text-editing software packages have a feature for automatic pagination and repagination. For originally keyed data, automatic paging is done. When new pages or text are inserted that will expand the contents of a page, the secretary need only program the feature and all of the pages will automatically be repaginated. However, always remember to update the file to show all corrections and adjustments. Some advanced software packages will even automatically repaginate footnotes, notes, and endnotes.

OFFICE MEMORANDUMS

An office memorandum, almost universally referred to as *memo,* is basically a letter between company employees and is less formal than a traditional letter. It may be short or long, single or multipage. The secretary may compose memos as well as type them for executives.

Like all other office communications, memorandums transmit information and provide a record that information was transmitted. Office memorandums are used for several purposes: a) for messages that are complicated; b) to avoid making unnecessary telephone calls for business that may not be urgent; and c) when a record is needed. They not only avoid situations that may be misunderstood but also protect people by having a written record. Usually, office memorandums are brief and direct. However, there are exceptions depending upon the nature, purpose, and scope of the subject discussed and the writer's purpose and intent.

The plural form of memorandum may be either *memorandums* (add "s") or *memoranda* (add "a"; Latin form). However, when composing or writing, be consistent and use only one form for the plural. Also, when typing from an originator's draft copy, always check for consistency in spelling.

Types of Memos

Interoffice Memorandum

The interoffice memorandum is an in-house communication and is sent to a person in your own firm or department within one location; in other words, it is confined. Forms vary widely from company to company. However, all the principles of writing and business correspondence apply to memorandums as they do to letters.

Intraoffice Memorandum

The intraoffice memorandum is used within the same company between offices in different buildings or locations. For example, Company A may have two offices in New York City and one in Westchester County. Thus, the written communication is external; that is, it is not distributed in one location but must be transmitted elsewhere.

Parts of a Memo

All memorandums, whether printed or not, are composed of similar elements (parts). However, format may differ. These elements include to/from, date, subject, body, and end references (*i.e.*, reference initials, distribution of copies, etc.). There may be slight differences in heading and closing information or in the order of the elements, especially if the forms are printed.

To/From

The "To/From" section may be reversed. Some feel that using "to" first is more courteous to the reader. However, follow the company preferences. Personal titles (Mr., Mrs., Ms., Miss) should be omitted, but you may use professional titles such as Prof., Dr., etc.

Usually, there is a name and a title in both the "To" and "From" sections, as:

TO: Horace Denize, Executive Director
FROM: Julia Brown, Chairperson, Board of Directors

There is no salutation, complimentary close, or signature. However, the person who is sending the memorandum may initial it between the name and title or at the end of the "From" line.

Date

Follow a standard format. Do not use shortcuts. Type the date as:

September 29, 19-- or 9/29/--

Interoffice Communication

TO: Horace Denize, Executive Director

FROM: Julia Brown, Chairperson, Board of Directors

DATE: October 15, 19__

SUBJECT: Organizational Meeting

A Board of Directors meeting has been scheduled for Wednesday, October 30, 19__, in Conference Room A, East Building.

The agenda will include:

* Approval of Minutes
* Report for the Chairperson
* Discussion of Goals
* New Business

Since this is the first meeting, your attendance is necessary. Please bring business report No. 23-A, located in the central database file.

JB/TS 8.8a

Distribution:

Jerome L. Abrams
Bennette Von Brun
Josephine D'Allo
Maye Santiago
Norman Zapper

Sample interoffice memo.

When using the numeric form, proofread carefully to be sure that numbers are not transposed.

Subject

The "Subject" lines provides a short description of what the memorandum is about. It focuses attention and may serve as a subject category for filing and retrieval. It should be brief and to the point. Delete unnecessary words.

Body

This section contains the main idea and purpose of the memorandum. If there are enumerations, use an acceptable format, as: 1), 2) or a), b), etc.

Some special typing symbols may be used before the enumeration to capture the reader's attention. These include dashes (—) and bullets (•). (To make a bullet, type an "o" and darken with a black pen.)

- Call Mr. Gomez and make an appointment.
- Cancel the Simmons' contract (No. 23-A).
- Print out file #23.A-9 (4.1).

This technique calls immediate attention to enumerations and enhances the appearance. Numbering and/or lettering the items or points also makes it easier for the reader to follow the sequential development of ideas and comments.

Reference Information

Several types of reference information may be located at the end of a memorandum. These include reference initials, copy notations, enclosures, filing code, and word processing code. Reference initials may be typed in lower- or uppercase:

je or JE or E (transcriber)
JM:JE or jm:je (dictator and transcriber)

At times, the composer or originator of a document may be someone other than the executive or principal. If this is the case, use:

MC:CH:MI (Executive, composer or originator, transcriber)

Word/Information Processing Codes

Many documents are electronically memorized and processed. For ease of retrieval in these cases, codes are necessary:

MJ/e 8.8
MJ/CH 8.8a

A colon (:) may be substituted for the slash (/). The code 8.8 may represent month, day, disk number, or another meaning such as file No. 8.8. Since such codes are not standardized, the secretary or executive should create one. If using electronic equipment (personal computer, word processor), keep a hard copy of the index for easy referral.

Copies/Distribution

This is the final section of the memorandum and alphabetically lists the names of those who were sent copies. The list may be ordered by seniority or by rank. Follow the company policy and check with your superior. The omission of a name may be an oversight, or it may be deliberate.

With electronic mail and other automated communications, copies may be sent electronically through a network to various terminals. If this procedure is used, the usual distribution lists should be keyed in a database. The receipt of a transmission can easily be acknowledged by return transmission; a reply can also be keyed. If electronic messages are stored, keep an index. These data can then serve as boilerplates and standard paragraphs that can be inserted in other future memorandums without rekeying.

Memo Paper

Memorandums are often typed on plain paper or on printed forms that contain standard parts. If plain paper is used for one or more pages, use quality paper. If the memorandum is short, use a half sheet. If a preprinted form is used, align typing evenly with the printed headings.

Memo Format

The format of a memo—margins, paragraphs, special features, tabulation stops—should be uniform. Use the format procedures adopted by your company, and collect samples for a reference file.

Margins

Margins may vary. However, for plain paper, leave one-inch side margins and a one-and-one-half-inch top margin. Begin on line 10 (9 lines = $1\frac{1}{2}''$). Leave sufficient space at the bottom. If you are using text-editing equipment, an appropriate form may be keyed in and retrieved, thus eliminating the need for rekeying format instructions. In other words, the format would be set—similar to a standardized preset formatting software package.

For printed forms, the left margin should begin evenly with the "to/from" element printed on the form.

Spacing

Whether using typed or preprinted forms, begin typing two or three spaces from the colon. Triple-space between the subject line and the beginning of the text. Single-space the content of each paragraph, but double-space between paragraphs.

Tabulations in Body

Tabulation represents the keying of columns of information. It is used to present complex information in isolated, but related, columns for easier reading, comprehension, and comparison. Detailed, technical materials should be arranged logically to allow for comprehension. If space allows when keying long or multipage memorandums, use ruled columns to enhance the tabulated data. Single-space the text of columns and have equal horizontal spacing before and after the tabulated material.

MINUTES OF A MEETING

The executive may ask the secretary to take minutes at a formal or informal meeting. *Minutes* is a term used to describe an official record of the proceedings of a meeting. Keeping minutes of meetings is always advisable. Although the minutes may not be disseminated, they should be filed in case they are needed at a later date.

Types of Meetings

There are basically two types of meetings: formal and informal. A *formal meeting* is a preplanned, structured meeting, such as an annual conference or convention and its workshops and symposia. Usually, there is a prepared agenda. An *informal meeting* may be short and announced only a short time before it is held; it is usually held on company premises. To inform staff members of a quickly scheduled meeting, the secretary may use electronic calendaring, if available, or the telephone. Always confirm by sending a follow-up note.

Another type of meeting—a *teleconference*—has been made possible by modern technology. In a teleconference, two or more persons in different geographic locations communicate electronically (audio, video, computer). It is effective for informal meetings and serves as an adjunct to more formal, structured meetings. By using audio, video, and/or computer equipment, including the *electronic blackboard*, meetings can be held simultaneously or on a delayed basis with several groups participating in various locations. Everything in a teleconference is taped.

The minutes of a teleconference can be completed from the recorded media. This allows the secretary time to devote to other duties. The minutes, when completed, can be distributed electronically.

Preliminary Duties

Preliminary duties before a formal meeting may include reserving the meeting room, sending pertinent materials, preparing mailing lists, making calendar notations, preparing an agenda (the order of business), and handling last-minute details, such as supply and equipment needs (e.g., overhead projector or VDT). If you plan to take shorthand notes at the meeting, be sure you have sufficient notebooks, pencils, and other supplies. If you plan to record the meeting, check reel-to-reel or cassette recorders to ensure the equipment is operating and that you have sufficient supplies.

Some companies employ technical assistants to be available during electronic transmissions if needed. At a computer conference, the secretary may be asked to keyboard messages and retrieve stored data. These types of conferences should be planned in advance.

Preparing the Minutes

The most important phase of preparing minutes is the accurate recording and reporting of the actions taken. The record should report what was said. At times, it is difficult to report what is done. For informal meetings, the minutes are compact and simple; for formal meetings, the minutes are complex. If you find that grouping the minutes around a central theme is clearer, do so. On the other hand, the executive may prefer chronological order.

Corporate minutes (official minutes of a formal nature) must be prepared in the order of occurrence, showing details and the exact wording of motions, resolutions, and so forth. By law, corporations are required to keep minutes of stockholders' and directors' meetings. These minutes are legal records and should be protected from tampering.

When preparing corporate minutes, use watermarked paper, and place the finalized minutes in keylock binders. Any corrections resulting from a subsequent meeting should be written. Incorrect portions are ruled out in *ink* and initialed in the margin. The official secretary of

```
            MEETING OF THE EXECUTIVE COMMITTEE
                     April 2, 19__
```

ATTENDANCE

The weekly meeting of the executive committee was held in the office of Cortez Diaz, first Vice President of Operations, at 10 a.m. on April 2, 19__. Mr. Diaz presided. Present were James Madison, Frederick McAllison, Yolanda Smith, Anne Marie Johnson, and Lewis Smith. Patricia Mendea was absent.

ITEMS COVERED

1. Contract No. 23-a.1 was approved in the amount of $125,000,000.

2. Yolanda Smith gave an update report on Contract No. 24. Further information is to be presented at the May 21 meeting.

3. Anne Marie Johnson reviewed the service budget for the first quarter. Recommendations were made. A feasibility study is to be conducted for implementation of an improved MIS.

4. Lewis Smith presented the proposed budget for the Xavius Project, a government grant. A draft copy of his recommendations will be distributed before the May 21 meeting. This item will be discussed and voted upon at the May 21 meeting.

ADJOURNMENT

The meeting was adjourned at 12 noon.

James Madison
_____
James Madison, Recorder

Sample minutes of a weekly committee meeting.

```
                    MEETING OF THE EXECUTIVE COMMITTEE

                            April 2, 19__


                                 AGENDA


        1.   Review and vote for Contract No. 23-a.1.

        2.   Update report on Contract No. 24.

        3.   Report on service project for the first quarter.

        4.   Proposed budget for Xavius Project, a government grant.

        5.   New business.
```

Sample agenda.

the corporation has responsibility for the completeness and accuracy of corporate minutes, but the secretary may have to type and prepare them.

Format of Minutes

Follow these suggestions in preparing minutes:

1. Use plain white paper (watermarked for official corporate stockholders' and directors' meetings).
2. Center and capitalize the title. Example:

   MEETING OF THE EXECUTIVE COMMITTEE

3. Double-space the text. Allow a one-and-one-half-inch left margin, a one-inch right margin, and a generous top margin. The left margin should allow for hole-punching or binding. Be consistent.

4. Indent five to ten spaces.
5. List the name of the presiding officer and the recorder. The recorder should sign.
6. Follow the agenda's subject headings as closely as possible.
7. List absences and indicate quorums.
8. Follow the company's policy on capitalization of words such as *committee*, *department*, etc.
9. Paginate at the bottom consecutively.
10. If a formal resolution, motion, or vote is passed, record it word for word. Persist in making sure the wording is exact.
11. Record the time of adjournment.
12. Use businesslike language. Avoid descriptive adjectives, such as *outstanding*.
13. List and summarize the gist of what was said.
14. Transcribe minutes while they are still fresh in your mind.
15. Prepare a rough draft for approval before finalizing. To avoid rekeying, electronically key and store, if possible.

Resolutions

A resolution is a formal statement of a decision voted (an expressed opinion or will of those voting). After a resolution is drafted and finalized, it is the secretary's responsibility to have it signed, distributed, and incorporated in the minutes. Areas of concern may include but not be limited to expressions of recognized achievements, stated objectives, sympathy, and so forth. Each paragraph in a resolution begins with WHEREAS or RESOLVED in solid capital letters or underlined.

NEWS RELEASES

News releases are typed double-spaced on $8\frac{1}{2}''$ × $11''$ plain paper or on a special news-release form. Side margins should be generous, at least one and one-half inches or wider, to give the editor room for notations. Try to limit the release to one page.

The editor likes to see identifying information at the top of the sheet. This information should include the date and the name, address, and telephone number of the person to whom requests may be made for more information.

```
                        RESOLUTION
                 Adopted December 29, 19__


WHEREAS, JoAnne Logan has been a member of the consultant firm of
    Kelaher & Kelaher, Inc., for the past fifteen years and has
    contributed significantly to the professional prestige of
    this company; and

WHEREAS, Mrs. Logan is retiring; therefore, be it

RESOLVED, that the members of this company go on record as
    expressing their deep appreciation of Mrs. Logan's
    professional service throughout the years and that they wish
    her well in her retirement; and be it

RESOLVED FURTHER, that our Secretary send a copy of this
    resolution to the Chairperson of the Board of Directors.



                                      Lillian Marti


    Judy Martinez
_____           _____
Judy Martinez, Secretary          Lillian Marti, President
```

Sample resolution.

The article itself starts with an indented date line consisting of the name of the city and the date. The city name is typed in all capital letters; the date is typed in capital and lower-case letters and is followed by a dash. The name of the state is given only if the city is not well known or if there is likely to be a doubt as to the identity of the city.

If the news release runs to more than one page, end each page with a complete paragraph and put the word MORE at the bottom, centered or at the right side of the page. Continuation pages should be numbered and have a brief caption typed flush with the left margin near the top of the page. Copy is often divided so that it can be given to different typesetters. MORE tells the typesetters that there are more pages. End the news release with a concluding centered symbol such as ####, –0–, –end–, or (END).

The following is a sample of a news release heading.

```
N E W S   R E L E A S E     From Sandra Demous
                            Free Press
                            500 South Broadway
                            Los Angeles, California 90055
                            Telephone (213) 666-5555

                            Release July 30, 19--


            CENTERED TITLE OF A NEWS RELEASE

        LOS ANGELES, July 30--continue typing the news

    release with double spacing in report form.
```

```
        This is an example of the bottom of a page of a news release

    that is continued to the next page.

                                                           MORE
```

```
        This is an example of the last page or end of a news release

    with one of the concluding symbols.

                        #  #  #  #  #  #
```

COPY FOR PUBLICATION

Typing/Keying

When the copy is to be printed, keep the typewritten lines six inches long and use double spacing. Avoid dividing words at the ends of lines as much as possible. Type headings in the position they will occupy on the printed page and be consistent in style. Type on one side of the paper; make side margins at least one inch wide. Keep the pages equal in length. Do not staple pages together.

Proofreading

Proofread the material. It is a good idea to lay the material aside before giving it a final check. The second reading may reveal errors overlooked the first time. Two heads are better than one for proofreading. When working with an assistant, the typist should follow the original and the assistant the final copy. The secretary is really a stand-in reader. It is the secretary's job to find those errors so elementary that they escape the author's attention.

Another method for proofreading is to read aloud. When reading copy aloud if you have missed a word, it is quickly obvious to the ear. If you have keyed copy on a word processor, you may print a copy and have a second person proofread it.

Correcting Copy

Use proofreading marks in making corrections. Short corrections can be made by crossing out the incorrect word and writing the correction over it. If the correction is lengthy, type it on a separate sheet of paper, which should then be attached to the original. If a whole paragraph needs correction, you may find it convenient to type the correction on a separate sheet and staple, tape, or glue it over the original. Use rubber cement for gluing. (Rubber cement allows for easy removal without tearing, which becomes a problem when using tape.)

The best time to number the pages of the manuscript is after the whole job has been typed and all corrections have been made. Pages are numbered consecutively, and the page number usually appears in the upper right-hand corner of each page, indented one inch from the right edge, on line four from the top of the page.

Artwork

Identify all artwork either by number or by some other system of labeling, and keep a list. If you use numbers, make certain that the numbering agrees with the order in which the items will appear in the finished job. Type the identification line on a separate label and attach it to the back of the illustration.

Avoid writing on photographs with either pen or pencil, because the marks may break the finish on the photograph and show in the reproduction. If writing is absolutely necessary, use special nonrepro-ducing pens and pencils, which may be obtained from an art shop or stationery store.

Depending on the quality and sensitivity of the artwork, you may have to place onionskin paper or thin art paper over it. This protects the artwork and prevents running of colors, lines, etc.

Layout

The printer will advise on the layout and will make a dummy if it is part of your agreement. A dummy is a set of blank sheets, cut and folded to the size and shape of the finished job. The dummy indicates the location of any artwork.

Estimating Length

Often it is necessary to tell the printer the approximate length of the material. Select three or four lines of the copy and count the number of words in these lines. From this count determine the average number of words per line. Now count the number of lines on the page and multiply this by the number of words in each line. Suppose in four lines you count 44 words. This means that you have an average of 11 words to each line. If there are 27 lines on your page, 27 times 11 gives you 297 words, or nearly 300 words to the page. A report, then, of ten full pages would be about 3,000 words.

Galley Proofs

The printer returns the original manuscript with two or more copies, or proofs, set in the typeface selected. Compare the printer's copy, word for word, with the original. Again, it is always better if two people work together. Careful checking saves time and money, because the printer charges an extra fee for changes.

Reading these proofs, the galley proofs, is the next major step. This reading gives you the opportunity not only to detect and call attention to errors made by the printer but also to make any last-minute alterations you may find desirable. However, if your revisions deviate much from the original, you pay a heavy penalty in time rates. Changes in the galley proof become very costly. Read material through for continuity in thought. Some of the things to watch for in checking are:

spelling and punctuation errors
inconsistencies in style, spelling, or paragraphing

transposition of letters and lines

errors in page numbers

continuity from page to page and line to line (Does the last word on a page make sense with the top of the next page?)

omissions.

If your employer frequently publishes manuscripts, keep a record of each manuscript on a 3" × 5" card or some other memory device. Record such facts as the title, the date the manuscript was submitted to the printer, how many pages it contained, and the number of illustrations or visuals included. Create a file for each manuscript to keep track of detailed supportive data.

Desktop Publishing

Desktop publishing, also called *electronic publishing*, is a new technology. It refers to a personal computer-based system or dedicated word processor that runs page composition. It is possible to include graphics and multiple type styles and fonts similar to a typeset page. A laser printer is used for the highest quality.

Desktop publishing software is appropriate for newspapers, advertising materials, and columns of text with limited length and complexity. The visual image on the screen gives you an idea of what the printed page, including graphics and other visuals, will look like.

TECHNICAL REPORTS

The typing done for engineers, chemists, mathematicians, scientists, and other professionals is often referred to as "technical typing." The material often involves equation typing. In such work accuracy is extremely important, much more important than speed. Because you are typing symbols in patterns, spacing both horizontally and vertically becomes a consideration that may require some experimentation and technical knowledge. Use of a format or word processing ruler may help in decision-making of such calculations as insertions of visuals, equations, charts, etc.

Equations generally include raised and lowered symbols. Those symbols written above the regular line of writing are called superscripts; those written below, subscripts. It is essential, therefore, that technical reports be typed in double spacing to allow room for writing these subscripts and superscripts. Most modern electric typewriters and word processing equipment have special superscript and subscript keys.

Typewriters can also have special keys with mathematical symbols and Greek letters. If you are operating a typewriter that utilizes an element, you may purchase a special element called the "universal symbol element." This element has the mathematical symbols and the letters of the Greek alphabet used frequently in equation typing.

For the larger symbols you will want a template. This is a small plastic rectangular guide that resembles the letter guides for stencil work, except that it provides outlines of symbols used in scientific reports. You trace the stencil symbol with a sharp-pointed pencil.

Always leave a space before and after the arithmetical operational symbols: $=$, $+$, $-$, $\div$, and $\times$. However, if the symbol is used adjectively, as -3, there should be no space between the minus sign and the 3.

Multiplication is expressed by using the "$\times$" or a centered period $(4 \cdot 6)$ or by parentheses enclosing an expression to be multiplied. Often the multiplication sign is omitted and the letters are typed together, as ab. Thus, in the equation $7ad(s - y) = mx,$ there is no space between d and the opening parenthesis, but there is a space before and after the equal sign and the minus sign.

Type fractions as follows: If the equation is short, the fraction may be part of the running text and is typed in the shilling style, which looks like this: 4/5. If you use mixed numbers, put a space between the whole number and the shilling fraction; for example, 43 5/6.

Equations are numbered consecutively throughout a report to make it easy to refer to any equation in the text. Each equation number is put in parentheses at the right margin. Set a tab stop for this location. Arrange the tab setting so that the closing parenthesis will be just inside of the right margin of your page. When making reference to these equation numbers, abbreviate equation to "Eq." Your reference will look like this: (Eq. 5).

Usually punctuation is not used with equations. If your author requests punctuation in equations, then observe these rules:

Consider each equation as a clause of a complex sentence and follow it with either a comma or semicolon.

If the equation concludes the sentence, a period follows it.

If you have a series of equations, introduce them by a colon in the line preceding the equations.

Sometimes equations are too long for one line and must be placed on several lines. Break them before the equal sign when possible. Before any one of the operational signs ($+$, $-$, $\times$, $\div$) is another good place to divide an equation. You may also divide it between fractions or after brackets and parentheses. Do not put part of an equation on one page and the rest of it on the next page.

Some authors help their typists to read the symbols in an equation by writing all lower-case symbols and printing upper-case symbols. Why not suggest this to the author of the report? You will also find it helpful to draft all the equations in the report before typing. Let the author check your arrangement of the equations. If the author has no objection, then you are ready to do the finished report and can proceed with confidence that the material is arranged in the very best form.

Hints for Typing Symbols

If the typewriter does not have special keys for the symbols you need to make, you may try to produce the symbols by using other keys showing similar symbols or a combination of keys. For example, to make the symbol for inches or seconds, type double quotation marks; to make the symbol for feet, type a single quotation mark or an apostrophe.

If a symbol cannot be made on the typewriter, use a black pen and insert the symbol by hand. Be sure that the ink matches the color of the printwheel or the typewriter ribbon. Practice writing the symbol several times on a separate sheet of paper before writing it on the original and final form.

Common Business Symbols

Symbol	Meaning	Examples
´ or `	accent	Buenos días, Genève
& (ampersand)	and	Meyers & Jones
*	asterisk	*Note (used as a footnote symbol)
@	at, each	@ $2.45
[ ]	brackets	[Diskette 45]
¢	cents	30¢
°	degrees	45°F
/	diagonal/slash	either/or; and/or; 1/2
$	dollars	$85.00
'	feet; minutes	7'
"	inches; seconds	7"
#	number	#1 (before a numeral)
%	percent	99.99%
#	pound	45# (after a numeral)
/S/	signed	In legal documents, used before copied signature: /S/

LEGAL DOCUMENTS

Even though you may not be employed in a law office, at times you may find it necessary to type a legal document or, at least, to complete a printed legal form. Accuracy is essential, because a changed word or a correction may affect the validity of the paper. If you have any doubt about making a correction, consult your supervisor. When changes must be made in a document after it has been signed, all changes must be initialed by the signers. In some instances, erasures or corrections are not acceptable; the document with a correction would not be legally binding.

Most legal documents are typed on "legal cap" paper. This paper is stronger than regular stationery and is usually slightly larger, measuring $8\frac{1}{2}'' \times 13''$ or $8\frac{1}{2}'' \times 14''$. It has a double-ruled line $1\frac{1}{4}$ inches from the left edge of the paper and a single-ruled line one-half inch from the right edge. Not all legal documents are put on these ruled sheets. Many wills, for example, are written on plain sheets of paper.

To avoid crowding the information in the document, type it double-spaced and use generous side margins (at least two spaces within the rulings). If your paper has no rulings, use a $1\frac{1}{2}$-inch left margin and a one-half-inch right margin. Start the first line of each page two inches from the top edge and end each page within an inch of the bottom. Indent all paragraphs ten spaces, and use only one side of the paper. Never end a page with the first line of a paragraph or begin a page with the last line of a paragraph. At least two lines of the document must appear on the page that is to have the signature.

Spell out sums of money and repeat them in figures enclosed within parentheses. Dates may be either spelled out or written in figures but not both ways.

The first page is usually not numbered, except on a will. Numbers of subsequent pages are centered between the margins, three blank lines from the bottom of the page. Type a hyphen before and another after the page number.

Use the underscore for signature lines. The signature lines for the principal signers start at the center of the page and extend toward the right margin. The signature lines for witnesses begin at the left margin and extend toward the center. Lines should be at least three spaces apart. Lightly pencil the respective initials at the beginnings of the signature lines to guide the signers. If you prefer, use the small "x" to mark the spot where the parties are to sign.

Type the introductory and closing phrases in all capitals. Put either a comma or a colon after the phrases, depending on how the phrase is used.

Some of these phrases are:

> KNOW ALL MEN BY THESE PRESENTS, that . . .
> IN WITNESS WHEREOF, the parties . . .
> THIS AGREEMENT, made June . . .
> WHEREIN IT IS MUTUALLY AGREED AS FOLLOWS: 1.
>   At that . . .

File copies can be made on onionskin paper. If carbon copies are to be signed, make the copies on the same quality of paper that you use for the original.

Most legal documents have cover sheets or binders, called "legal backs." These are endorsed with a brief description of the document. To prepare the binder, lay it on the desk and bring the bottom edge up to within one inch of the top; crease. Bring the creased end up to approximately one inch from the top and fold again. Open this fold and insert the binder in the typewriter. Do not type beyond the crease. After typing the endorsement, turn the top edge of the backing sheet down, crease it, and insert the document in the crease. Staple it in place. Fold the document to fit the creases in the binder.

Legal Binder: folded and endorsed (*left*), and flat with document in place.

Software for Legal Documents

Because of the universal format of legal documents, several standard-ized software packages are available for basic contracts, wills, court orders, deeds, codicils, affidavits, and powers of attorney. Preprinted legal forms for several common documents are also available from stationery stores that supply legal offices. These are called *legal forms* or *law blanks*.

Most law offices today are equipped with automated text-editing equipment. A significant portion of many legal documents consists of standard paragraphs that have been court-tested. These paragraphs can be keyed in once (or be part of a software package) and serve as *boiler plates* that can be retrieved automatically each time needed. Since typographical errors and corrections are critical places in a legal document and can disqualify a document for court purposes, these boiler plates are very helpful. They provide error-free typing. All the secretary has to do is fill in the variables.

Lawyers often generate documents that have been created before. When merged with new or edited text, the final document is unique when seen as a whole. Computer networks have been set up to serve law offices by providing indexes for legal material, including opinions, reviews, cases, and decisions. In many cases, the linkage with the network is a community word processor, terminal, or personal computer.

For processing legal documents, useful word processing features include automatic page numbering; line numbering facility; specialized spell-check dictionaries; redlining and strikeout; document assembly; merging; automatic table of authorities and contents; automatic in-dexing; outlining; columnized documents; file-find commands; header/ footer controls; and automatic math calculations.

There are also several useful primary text-editing techniques. In a technique known as *macros,* memorized keystroke sequences are used to automate groups of keystrokes for names, terms, and sequences used frequently. (For example, the memorized sequence TWIC may automatically automate all the keystrokes needed for the frequently used phrase "To Whom It May Concern.") In *merging* techniques, fill-ins are used as variables in standard documents; in *segment retrieval*, standard paragraphs or parts of paragraphs are used to create documents in leases and contracts. And, finally, any variety of these techniques may be used together in a *combination.*

HANDLING NUMBERS IN REPORTS

There is no uniform or simple style for typing numerals, and the rules established by a variety of style manuals can sometimes be perplexing.

The following list provides some generally accepted basic rules.

Use figures for	*Use words for*
Exact numbers above ten *35 club members*	Exact numbers, ten and below *mail five boxes*
Amounts of money *$29.95; $46; 9 cents*	Round or approximate numbers *four hundred people*
Percentages *6 percent*	Beginning of sentences *Fourteen years*
Dimensions, measurements, etc. *15 feet; size 9;* *4½ acres*	Names of centuries and decades *the sixteenth century* *the Roaring Twenties*
Exact age *11 years, 4 months, 2 days*	Approximate age *seventeen years old*
Time with A.M. or P.M. *4 P.M.*	Time with "o'clock" *four o'clock*
Street names above ten *14 West 24 Street*	Street names ten and below *Fifth Avenue*
Word "number" followed by figure *No. 4*	Numbered sessions of Congress *Seventy-eighth Congress*
House or building numbers *47 Genesee Street*	Fractions standing alone *send one-half of the order*
Dates *July 4, 1976* *5th of May*	Two numbers coming together *six 4-inch bolts* *210 six-pound crates*
Plurals of numbers *16's or 16s*	Mixed numbers *six and three-fourths*
Large even amounts *15 million dollars*	Smaller amounts in round numbers *fourteen hundred copies*

Some additional guidelines for handling numbers in reports:

- Spell numbers from one to ten. However, if a sentence contains a series of numbers over ten, use numbers.

  > The team won 24 games in 1986, 21 games in 1987, and 10 games in 1988.

  > The group consisted of two group leaders, one recorder, and three secretaries for each of the projects.

- If a number begins a sentence, use the word form.

  > Ten thousand students were present at the conference.

- Except in legal documents, type amounts of money in figures.

Use ciphers after the decimal point when fractional amounts appear in the same context.

> The book was $19.51 with tax, but the magazine was only $5.00.

> The magazine was only $5.

- Use a hyphen to represent the word *to*.

> 1974-1988.

- When a sum of money is used as an adjective, spell it out and hyphenate.

> He bought a twenty-dollar pen.

- Use figures for federal, state, and interstate highways.

> U.S. Route 67 (or U.S. 67)

> New York State Throughway 37

> Interstate 68 (or I-68)

VISUAL AIDS

Visuals are any display materials in business reports or other reports that make them clearer and more attractive. Visuals may be inserted in the text, in which case they often have a great impact on the reader, or, if they are lengthy, they may be placed in the appendices of a report.

The secretary should develop knowhow about when and where to use visuals. In general, visuals are used to:

- enhance a page
- clarify text
- emphasize a specific point or purpose
- motivate and arouse interest
- illustrate a point in greater detail
- explain or simplify technical material.

Kinds of Visuals

The type of visual to use depends on the intended purpose of the visual, the audience, the subject, the type of paper to be used, and the printing process to be used for reproduction.

Basically there are two types of visuals: pictorial and numerical or other data. Pictorials include photographs, figures, and illustrations. Numerical data include tables, charts, and graphs.

Preparation of Visuals

Visuals may be prepared in several ways with automated equipment or with simple cut-and-paste techniques. With the increased use of automated equipment, many firms have established a separate unit or department to handle the work involving the production of different types of visuals. Some other firms contract the preparation of visuals to a professional service outside the firm. In these situations, the secretary's main responsibility becomes formatting. However, in some businesses visual preparation is still the secretary's responsibility.

Secretaries who do not have access to a sophisticated word processor or personal computer may have to use the cut-and-paste method and produce a mechanical which is then copied on the appropriate paper and serves as an original to be reproduced. This technique allows for reduction or enlargement of the visual so that the final version conforms to the page size and format of the report.

For pictorial visuals, draw—or hire an artist to draw—the desired likenesses and images. Sometimes a standard template can be used to draw or copy the image (see Figure 6-1). Alternatively, cut out the image and paste it on paper, photocopy it, or trace and generate it on a computer. When inserting visuals in the text, be sure that all lines are properly balanced, that the visual is crisp and defined, that all photographs are sharply focused, and, if the visual is not an original, that proper credit is given.

Numerical or other data visuals are easier to produce. Use numerical visuals when you wish to make comparisons and contrasts more vivid and when you want to pinpoint a detail clearly. For graphs, be sure to:

- list the scale used and indicate where zero is
- use an acceptable range of precision
- check that the graph reads left to right and bottom to top.

Formatting of Visuals

Once the visuals—whether pictorial or numerical—are prepared, it is usually the secretary's responsibility to format them in the report. Mainly, format preparation involves the reduction, enlargement, and placement of visuals in the text. Care must be taken at all times to ensure quality, error-free reproduction.

Loose Material

Most visuals must be attached to paper. Use rubber cement or liquid or stick glue that will not tear the paper if the visual has to be removed.

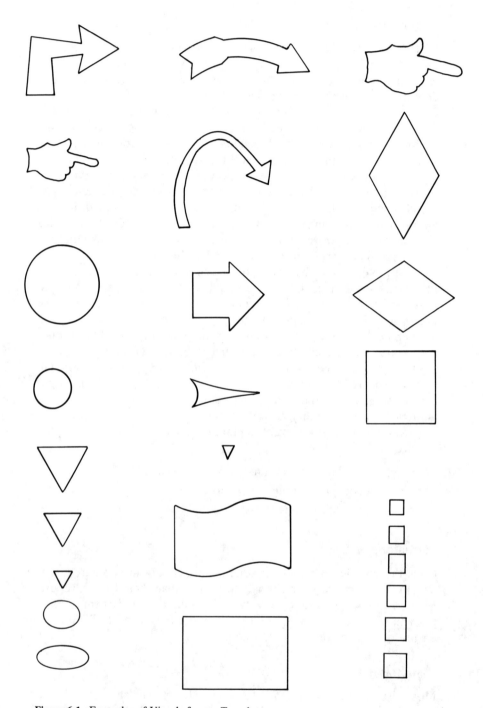

Figure 6-1. Examples of Visuals from a Template.

Make sure that extraneous lines from the edge of the attached material do not appear in the copy to be reproduced. Such lines may be covered with tape or white-out liquid.

Reduction/Enlargement

If a visual is too large (too wide, too long, or both), reduce it to fit within the page format designed. Special reprographics equipment is available for reductions in a variety of percentages: 77%, 74%, 66%, 50%, 25%, and smaller. Conversely, visuals may be cut and then enlarged to show specific points more clearly. A well-equipped photo-copy shop or department can provide a variety of enlargement and reduction services.

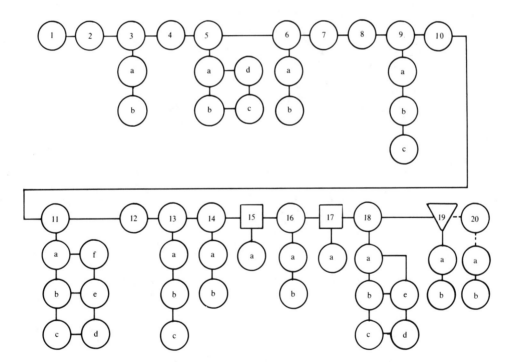

Figure 6-2. Example of a Reduced Visual.

Placement

Avoid inserting visuals in such a way that they can be read only by turning the report. Always try to make the visual conform to the normal page of a report. If this is not possible and the visual must be inserted sideways, be sure that the heading of the visual is placed at the binding or spine (left side) of the report.

Figure 6-2 shows a typical visual—a process flow chart. The circles were drawn using a template. Then the illustration was enlarged. After the enlargement, the numbers and letters were typed and the connecting lines drawn using a black pen and a ruler. The visual was then reduced by 64% so that it would fit within the margins of a $8\frac{1}{2}''$ × 11″ sheet of paper. The final reduction was cut and pasted and then recopied.

7

Communications Techniques

by James C. Matthews, Ed.D.

Assembling Data for Outgoing Calls
Telephone Services
Telephone Record Keeping
Special Telephone Equipment and Systems
Telephone Answering Services
Telephone Answering Devices

Effective and efficient communication is an essential for any business and is required of all employees. Some basic methods of communication have remained largely unchanged; others have changed greatly with technological developments and increasing sophistication. The secretary must be familiar with all communications techniques and how and when to use them. This chapter briefly discusses the major communications techniques: mail, telegrams, cables, radio messages, and the telephone.

THE OFFICE MAIL

The processing and handling of mail constitutes the most important method of communication between a company and its contacts in the business world. The way in which mail is handled by the secretary affects every phase of a company and its external and internal procedures of information processing. A secretary who can effectively deal with office mail is indeed a valuable asset to an employer.

Update on the U.S. Postal System

For the distribution of mail outside of the office, the U.S. Postal Service is still the oldest, most widespread, and cheapest way. In April 1988, massive changes and updates in the postal system occurred, including an increase in the cost of postage. Many of the changes have affected procedures as well as the handling of mail in general. Guidelines are still being released. For a current ready reference for those changes in effect as of April 1988, write for a copy of:

> POSTAL BULLETIN (Special Bulletin)
> PB 21666—March 25, 1988

The address is:

> U.S. Postal Service
> Washington, DC 20260-1571

This special bulletin contains the new rates, fees, and classifications as well as some changes in regulations necessary to implement them; all relate to the domestic rates and fees for various classes, services, and mail classifications. The bulletin also includes *interim* international rates and fees. Future issues will include notices of the adoption of final international rates and fees. This and related postal bulletins will serve to guide you in the handling of office mail via the U.S. Postal Service.

Electronic Mail Transmission

Electronic mail is the popular term for many of the new forms of communication that use computer and telecommunications technology. Also sometimes called *electronic data communication,* it is the non-interactive communication of text, data, voice, and image messages between a sender and a recipient using system links.

There are two advantages to electronic mail. One is the high speed with which large amounts of data can be sent from one place to another. The second is that data can be distributed to a specific location and stored in electronic form until it is needed by the recipient.

Electronic mail is rapidly becoming an indispensable tool in communications. Not only do companies use electronic mail for in-house communication but also for many employees who work at home from computer work stations and terminals. With the use of public access networks, such as Tymnet, Telenet, and other digital systems, it is possible to link host computer facilities simply, through a local phone call from almost anywhere in the world.

Electronic mail is implemented with several different technologies, among them facsimile transmission, telex, communicating word processors, microcomputers and other computer-based networks, electronic document distribution systems, and voice technologies. We shall discuss briefly a few of these means.

Telecommunications is the process of transmitting information over a distance, or "at a distance," by electromagnetic or electrical systems. (The prefix *tele* is derived from a Greek root meaning "at a distance.") Telecommunicated information may be in several forms, including voice, data, image, or message. The transmission systems include telephone lines, cables, microwaves, satellite transmission, and light beams.

Message systems. Message systems send information in data form. Telegrams and teletypewriter messages transmitted through systems such as TWX and Telex are examples of message systems. These systems, which the secretary may use frequently, provide for faster transmission of information than does the postal system.

INTELPOST Service Destinations

Argentina	Greece
Australia	Guernsey
Bahamas	Iceland
Belgium	Ireland
Brazil	Isle of Man
Canada	Israel
Channel Islands (includes Guernsey,	Hong Kong
Jersey, and the Isle of Man)	Japan
China, People's Republic of (Service	Jersey
to Beijing, Guangzhou, Shanghai,	Korea, Republic of
Shenzhen, and Zhuhai)	Liechtenstein
Cyprus	Luxembourg
Denmark	Macao
Egypt	Malaysia
England	Monaco
Finland	Netherlands (Holland)
France (includes Corsica,	Northern Ireland
Guadeloupe, Martinique, Fr.	Norway
Guiana, Reunion, St. Pierre, and	Papua, New Guinea
Miquelon)	Portugal
Germany, Federal Republic of	Qatar
Great Britain (includes England,	Scotland
Northern Ireland, Scotland, Wales,	Singapore
and Channel Islands)	Sweden
	Switzerland
	Wales

International electronic postal service. Various networks and services are available for rapid telecommunications. The secretary in an automated office should be familiar with the various network services, know which is best suited for particular purposes, and be able to use them. One such service is the International Electronic Postal Service, usually known as INTELPOST.

INTELPOST is a computerized network designed for high acceleration of information. The service links the United States, Canada, and Europe. Messages are transmitted by satellites, which use electronic and microwave technology. Documents such as charts, graphs, and photographs, as well as any type of printed text, can be transmitted.

Facsimile Transmission

Facsimile transmission is perhaps the oldest form of electronic mail— and also a rapidly advancing telecommunications technology. Often

TABLE 7.1

Facsimile Standards

Group	Minutes per page	Technology
1	6	low resolution; analog*
2	2–3	low resolution; mostly analog
3	fraction of a minute	higher resolution; digital**

* conversion to electric signals
** conversion to binary signals

known as *fax,* facsimile transmission is a proven method for sending information in the form of image replication (facsimile). It is flexible, inexpensive, and easy to do. Fax machines are now in many business offices and all secretaries should know how to use them effectively.

A fax unit can send a variety of documents—photographs, diagrams, drawings, statistical information, and handwritten or typewritten language messages—to any location that has a telephone line. The telephone line is the connection; without the telephone the system cannot work. The distance between two fax units is irrelevant. Information can be sent to another office in the same building or across the continent.

Fax units can store and forward information. They also have delay features that permit automatic dialing of one or more stations so that unattended transmission to multiple locations is possible on a 24-hour basis.

In 1980 the Consultative Committee on International Telephone & Telegraph (CCITT) set facsimile standards and groupings. The groupings refer to the amount of time it takes to send or receive a standard message over the telephone.

Incoming Mail

A new secretary may find a well-established system of handling mail within an organization. Changes may need to be suggested tactfully. The size of the organization has a great bearing on the system that evolves. In a small office one person may sort and open all mail except that marked "Personal" or "Confidential." (Letters so marked are delivered unopened to the person to whom they are addressed.) A large organization usually has a mailing department, where both incoming and outgoing mail are handled according to a fixed system. In an office where the secretary is assigned the responsibility for opening the mail for the employer, a routine procedure will permit rapid handling of each day's mail.

Necessary Supplies

The secretary will need supplies to open the mail. The following items and others you will need on your desk or work station should be placed there *before* the mail is processed. You may arrange the items in a circular fashion or another configuration for convenient and easy access. The suggested items are:

envelope opener
stapler or clips
date or time stamp
routing slips
transparent tape
pencils/pens (at least two different colors)
memo pad
mail register or log, if needed
staple remover

If electric equipment, such as a mail opener or time stamp, is available, use it. It will save two-thirds of the time as compared to manual equipment.

Opening the Mail

The mail should be opened as soon as it is delivered to the secretary's desk, and an orderly procedure should be followed to ensure that nothing is misplaced or lost, that time is not wasted, and that the executive receives the information needed.

Opening the envelopes. All envelopes should be opened before the contents are removed from any of them. To ensure that the contents will not be torn while the letter is being opened, tap the envelope firmly on the edge of the desk so that the contents will slip away from the top. Slit the upper edge of the envelope with a letter opener. If the contents of a letter are cut by the opener, use transparent tape to paste the parts together.

Checking the contents. After removing the contents of an envelope, check the letter for a return address. If there is none, staple the envelope containing the return address to the contents. (Caution: If the contents include a punched card, use a paper clip for fastening rather than a staple.) The envelope should also be retained if the signature on the letter is not easily distinguishable.

Another check should be made to determine that all enclosures stipulated in the letter are accounted for. If not, a notation should be made immediately on the face of the letter, indicating what is missing.

Even though annotating a letter is one of the procedures encouraged, some companies do not like correspondence marked up, especially legal or business firms that might have to submit a piece of correspondence as evidence in a court of law. Always follow company policy. Some companies prefer that you place a buck slip (adhesive) with the notation on the face of the letter. In theory, it serves the same purpose.

Dating the mail. It is always wise to affix each day's date on incoming mail. The easiest procedure is to use a rubber stamp. Such a procedure is helpful if the letter has arrived too late to meet a deadline requested, has been in transit longer than it should have been, or is undated. In either of the latter two cases, it is well to staple the envelope to the letter in addition to dating the letter. This will give evidence of the date of mailing as well as the date of receipt.

Envelopes. Generally the envelope may be destroyed after it has been ascertained that everything has been removed and that there are no problems concerned with the names, addresses, or dates. However, in certain situations, especially legal matters, envelopes sometimes serve as evidence of date and time received (from the precanceled postage stamp). In such situations, envelopes may be kept and clipped or stapled to the back of the letter.

Preparation of Mail for Employer

In order to save the employer's time, the efficient secretary should take the time to prepare the mail. This involves two basic steps.

1. Read each letter, underlining important points that will aid you and your employer in answering the letter. Underline only those things that are of significance, such as publications, dates, and names of people.
2. Make annotations on each letter. This involves writing notes in the margins. Generally, annotations fall into three categories, namely, a note indicating:
   a. Action required by the letter—date of appointment for correspondent, reservations for a trip the employer may have to make as a result of the correspondence, etc.
   b. Procedures to be followed. These may depend upon former correspondence with the same person or related correspondence, which will have to be sought in the files.
   c. The priority the letter should receive, symbolized by a code. In an agreement with the employer a given place on each letter should be established for this code. For example, a red number may be written in the upper left corner. Such a

code might be:

Code 1. Mail and reports with high priority and requiring a decision. These should be answered the same day they are received. (It is assumed that personal or confidential mail is delivered unopened to the addressee as soon as it arrives on the secretary's desk.)

Code 2. Mail for which additional information must be procured and for which answering may have to be deferred for a day or two while data are being collected. *All mail should be answered within 48 hours of receipt*, except under very unusual circumstances.

Code 3. Routine mail that the secretary may be able to handle. Many employers want to see all mail; it is wise to determine an employer's preference in this regard. After the relationship is well established, many secretaries have their employers' permission to reply to routine letters. In such instances it is usually good procedure to supply the employer with carbons of the letters sent and the original letter.

Code 4. Letters that require notations but no reply.

As the secretary reads and annotates the mail, it becomes a simple matter to encode and sort the mail as it is prepared for the employer. A fifth or even a sixth category may be added as needed. Usually important reports require a special category, while weekly, monthly, or semimonthly periodicals may require no encoding. Most employers prefer to examine the periodicals before they are made available to others in the office.

Preparing supplementary material. As the letters are being annotated, an efficient secretary will also make a list of files or pieces of correspondence and other information to be looked up before presenting the correspondence to the employer.

Some employers wish to see the mail as soon as it has been opened. In that case the secretary may bring the mail in as soon as it has been annotated. While the mail is being read, the secretary may take the compiled list and seek the necessary files, reports, and other information for acting upon the urgent mail. To keep all papers pertaining to each piece of correspondence together, use file folders or small clips.

Arranging the mail. After the sorting process has been completed, the secretary may arrange the mail either in one pile with the high-priority mail on top or in any other arrangement that has been agreed upon. Whenever the mail is placed on the desk of the employer, some provision should be made to prevent others from reading the top letter. Some secretaries simply place the top letter face down.

Absence of the employer. When the employer is away from the office, letters requiring immediate replies may be handled in either of two ways. First, if a decision must be made immediately, it may be necessary to give the mail to the person in charge during the employer's absence. Second, if the employer will be in the office within a day or two and the decision can wait, the secretary should write the sender immediately and explain when a reply may be expected and the reason for the delay.

The efficient secretary to whom the employer has entrusted routine correspondence will maintain a file of materials handled during an absence of the employer. The folder should be readily at hand upon the employer's return.

Outgoing Mail

If the secretary is responsible for the preparation of outgoing mail, as the case may well be in a firm too small to have a separate mailing and shipping department, time and expense can be saved by learning about the various postal and shipping services available and the general regulations and normal charges pertinent to these services. It is important to be alert to frequent changes.

An accurate scale for weighing postal matter is a worthwhile piece of office equipment. It saves time and eliminates guesswork.

Sources of Mail Information

To obtain correct information on postal procedures and rates, which are subject to change, consult the local postal authorities. From them, or from the Superintendent of Documents, Government Printing Office, Washington, DC 20402, may be obtained a number of useful pamphlets which are periodically brought up to date. These are some of them:

Mailers Guide
Packaging Pointers
Domestic Postage Rates, Fees, and Information
How To Prepare Second- and Third-Class Mailings
Mailing Permits
International Postage Rates and Fees

Some of the information in these pamphlets is taken from the *Postal Manual*, which contains complete data on postal regulations and procedures. Chapters 1 and 2 of this manual, which deal with domestic postal service and international mail, respectively, may be purchased separately.

A monthly publication called *Memo to Mailers* is available to business mailers without charge. It tells of rate and classification changes, along with other news of postal matters. Address:

> MEMO TO MAILERS
> U.S. Postal Service
> Post Office Box 999
> Springfield, VA 22150-0999

Stamps, Stamped Envelopes, and Postal Cards

Postage stamps may be purchased in several forms—single stamps, sheets, books, and coils—and denominations for both regular mail and overseas airmail. For the coil form, inexpensive dispensers are available at the post office. Stamped envelopes are also sold at the post office; these may be obtained in two standard sizes. Postal cards are available with the stamp printed on the address side; they come in single or double (reply) forms, with or without postage on the reply half.

Precanceled and meter stamps are two means of reducing the time and cost of mail handling. In order to use precanceled stamps (i.e., stamps canceled before mailing), a special permit must be obtained from the post office. For regulations applying to precanceled stamps, consult the *Postal Manual* or the local postal authorities.

Postage may be paid by printing meter stamps with a postage meter. Postage meters hasten the purchase, control, and attachment of postage and therefore facilitate mailing. Postage-meter machines may be leased from authorized manufacturers. Again, the *Postal Manual* or the local postal authorities should be consulted for regulations governing the leasing, use, and licensing of postal meters and also their manufacture and distribution.

Zip Codes and Two-Letter State Abbreviations

The U.S. Postal Service uses a set of two-letter abbreviations, to be followed by the ZIP Code, for all of the states and possessions of the United States. Although traditional abbreviations, such as Calif. for California and Mich. for Michigan, are still used, the Postal Service suggests the use of these two-letter abbreviations with ZIP Codes. Nine-digit ZIP Codes are now used.

The U.S. Postal Service relies heavily on ZIP Codes in the processing of mail. While some letters (at this writing) are still delivered even if the ZIP Code is not used, they may be delayed by lack of the number code. On the other hand, the Postal Service will not accept quantity mailings of letters, circulars, brochures, catalogs, etc., unless the pieces to be mailed are ZIP Coded and sorted by the code.

AK	Alaska	IL	Illinois	ND	North	RI	Rhode Island
AL	Alabama	IN	Indiana		Dakota	SC	South
AR	Arkansas	KS	Kansas	NE	Nebraska		Carolina
AZ	Arizona	KY	Kentucky	NH	New	SD	South
CA	California	LA	Louisiana		Hampshire		Dakota
CO	Colorado	MA	Massachusetts	NJ	New Jersey	TN	Tennessee
CT	Connecticut	MD	Maryland	NM	New Mexico	TX	Texas
DC	District of	ME	Maine	NV	Nevada	UT	Utah
	Columbia	MI	Michigan	NY	New York	VA	Virginia
DE	Delaware	MN	Minnesota	OH	Ohio	VI	Virgin Islands
FL	Florida	MO	Missouri	OK	Oklahoma	VT	Vermont
GA	Georgia	MS	Mississippi	OR	Oregon	WA	Washington
HI	Hawaii	MT	Montana	PA	Pennsylvania	WI	Wisconsin
IA	Iowa	NC	North	PR	Puerto	WV	West Virginia
ID	Idaho		Carolina		Rico	WY	Wyoming

ZIP stands for Zoning Improvement Plan. The ZIP Code itself is a designation by numbers that expedites mail deliveries by cutting down on the steps required to move a letter from sender to addressee. The digits identify state, city, and post office, enabling most efficient use of air, highway, and rail transportation of the letter or parcel.

The *National ZIP Code and Post Office Directory* is available from the Information Service, U.S. Postal Service, Washington, DC 20260, or at any post office or branch. Having the latest ZIP Code directory is important, for over a thousand ZIP Codes change each year. The *National ZIP Code and Post Office Directory* is printed by the Government Printing Office and is exchangeable free of charge each year for the annually revised edition. ZIP Code manuals printed by private companies must be paid for anew each time an updated printing is desired.

Because of the many changes in ZIP Codes, even the latest printing of such a handbook may not provide the secretary with the one needed. In that case, local post offices generally have a separate department for this and a ZIP Code can easily be ascertained by telephone.

Your local telephone directory will usually show local ZIP Codes.

Coding for Mail to Canada

Canada uses a different coding system (called *National Postal Code*) to speed mail deliveries. The following two-letter abbreviations are recommended for use with this code:

AB	Alberta	NT	Northwest Territories
BC	British Columbia	ON	Ontario
LB	Labrador	PE	Prince Edward Island
MB	Manitoba	PQ	Quebec
NB	New Brunswick	SK	Saskatchewan
NF	Newfoundland	YT	Yukon Territory
NS	Nova Scotia		

Business offices that send a large amount of mail to Canada can write to the following address for Postal Code information:

Mail Collection & Delivery Branch
Postal Coding Division
Canada Post
Ottawa, Ontario K1A 0B1
Canada

Classes of Mail

There are six classes of domestic mail, and these will be discussed in detail. Postal regulations and rates change quite frequently. Those who are responsible for mailing packages and parcels, or large quantities of advertising material, or cards or letters of unusual size, will want to acquire a copy of the appropriate *Leonard's Guide* for their city, available by mail; write to 2121 Shermer Road, Northbrook, Illinois 60062.

Private, commercial "mail" services are now established, providing an alternative to the U.S. Postal System, which has had problems in effecting speedy delivery. Often such services operate only within a metropolitan area, but a few nationwide services also exist. All of these will be listed in the Yellow Pages, generally under "Delivery Services." There, too, will be found a listing of companies that will pick up mail and deliver it to the post office for speedier handling or will make pickups of mail directed to a box number at a post office.

First class: all handwritten or typewritten material and all material sealed against postal inspection.

Priority mail: any mailable matter that requires the speediest transportation and expeditious handling, weighing up to 2 pounds.

Second class: newspapers and periodicals.

Third class: circulars, books, catalogs, and other printed matter, and merchandise not included in first or second class, weighing less than 16 ounces.

Fourth class: all mailable matter not included in first, second, or third class, weighing one pound or more, but no more than 40 pounds, and not exceeding 84 inches in combined length and girth (in some circumstances, 70 pounds and 100 inches).

Express mail: guaranteed fast, reliable overnight delivery, on a money-back basis, of mail and packages.

First-Class Mail

The rate for first-class mail is determined by weight (the ounce or fraction thereof), without regard to the distance the article is to travel.

Address. Instructions for typing envelopes are given in Chapter 5. To ensure prompt delivery, observe these precautions regarding the address:

Write the address clearly and legibly if it cannot be typewritten.

Mail addressed for delivery through a city-delivery post office must include the street and street number, or post-office box number, or general delivery, or rural or star route designation. Mail for patrons on a rural route may be addressed to street names and numbers, provided that this type of address has been approved by the post office. The rural route number or the words "Rural Delivery" should be used in such addresses. Most patrons on rural routes have been assigned box numbers and this number should be included with the address.

Be sure that all mail bears the name and address of the sender, either in the upper left corner or on the back flap.

Include the nine-digit ZIP Code on all mail.

Remember that mail pieces bearing more than one street address, or the name of more than one city or town in the return address or in the recipient's address, are not acceptable for mailing.

Some firms use both a post office box number and the street address. The U.S. Postal Service will deliver the item to the address immediately above the city-state-ZIP Code line. Therefore, if the company wants addressees to know its street address, yet prefers to have mail directed to its post office box, the box number will come next to last in its return address or letterhead. The secretary should be sure to address the envelope for return mail with the elements in the order shown. For the secretary's own company, such preferred order should be carefully specified when ordering letterheads, envelopes, or other company paper bearing an address.

	The BCX Company	The BCX Company
	200 Main Street	P.O. Box 800456
Mail will be delivered →	P.O. Box 800456 ⟶	200 Main Street
	Small Town, NJ 06780-1243	Small Town, NJ 06780-1243

USPS-enhanced box numbers. The USPS has developed a new program for expediting and ensuring the delivery of mail to post office box numbers. The new system requires an adjustment of a post office box number to ensure the uniqueness of the number and decrease the likelihood of confusion. Before the new program was instituted, a box number was not unique because the same number could exist in a number of other post offices in the same borough, county, or locale. Therefore, mail containing a correct box number but an incorrect ZIP Code or no ZIP Code at all was difficult—if not impossible—to deliver to the correct box.

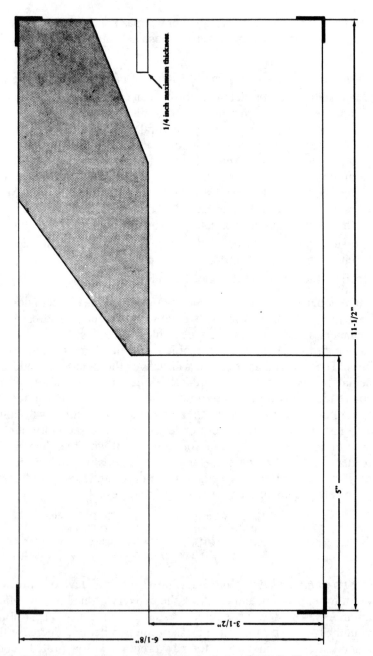

Figure 7-1. Dimensional Standards Template for Letter-size Mail. The full-size template with measurements shown is to be used for first-class mail of one ounce or less or third-class mail of two ounces or less. When the piece to be mailed is aligned with the lower left-hand corner, the tip of the upper right-hand corner must touch the shaded area, to be mailed at regular postage.

In the new system a prefix has been added to all post office box numbers. All box numbers now have been expanded to six digits or more. The first two digits are the last two digits of the five-digit ZIP Code. The last four digits are the current box number; if the box number has fewer than four digits, at least one zero precedes the box number.

Old	*New*
XYZ Company	XYZ Company
Post Office Box 22	Post Office Box 180022
Brooklyn, NY 11218-0006	Brooklyn, NY 11218-0006

Bar-coded envelopes. Specially printed bar-coded envelopes or labels, for which the originator has paid the postage, may be distributed for business reply mail or forwarding mail that is to be returned to the originator.

The location of the bar code must be on the address side of the mailpiece and within a clear space called the "bar code read area." This area extends $\frac{5}{8}$ inch from the bottom and at least $4\frac{1}{2}$ inches from the right edge of the mailpiece. Within the read area, the left-most bar of the bar code must be located between $3\frac{1}{4}$ and 4 inches from the right edge of the mailpiece. The bottom of the bars must be positioned $\frac{1}{4}$ inch (plus or minus $\frac{1}{16}$ inch) from the bottom edge of the mailpiece. The bar code must be completely contained within the solid rectangle as shown in Figure 7-2. There should be typewritten or handwritten items on either side of the mailpiece or at the bottom. Mailpiece refers to envelopes, cartons, labels, and adhesive items.

These bar codes are read by optical character recognition (OCR) readers. In other words, the bars are scanned. Characters are converted into signals and are recorded and/or interpreted as to meaning and destination of the mailpiece. The OCR scanner allows reduced input time, increased accuracy, and faster output. Special print shops and the post office branch offices provide envelopes at cost; however, the forms of imprint must conform to the requirement of the U.S. Postal Service.

Envelope size. All envelopes differing widely from the standard sizes should be marked "FIRST CLASS." A rubber stamp is often used for this purpose, although it is not essential. First-class mail that weighs one ounce or less and exceeds $6\frac{1}{8}$ inches in height, $11\frac{1}{2}$ inches in length, and $\frac{1}{4}$ inch in thickness, and whose length is less than 1.3 times the height or more than 2.5 times the height, is considered nonstandard mail. The secretary should call the post office to determine the rate for an outsized piece of mail or should alert the company mail department that a nonstandard piece of mail is going out.

Certain minimum standards went into effect April 3, 1988, and mail not meeting these standards will be refused. Mail must be at least

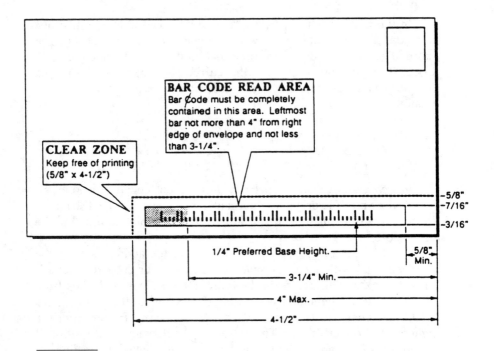

Source: Special Postal Bulletin, U.S. Postal Service.

Figure 7-2. Barcoded Envelope. The envelope typing format remains the same. Do not write or type in the left and right margins. Nothing should appear below the bar codes or bottom margin of the mailpiece.

.007 inch thick, that is, about the thickness of a postcard. Mail that is $\frac{1}{4}$ inch thick or less must measure at least $3\frac{1}{2}$ inches in height, be at least 5 inches in length, and be rectangular in shape.

Postcards. Government-printed postal cards measure $3\frac{1}{2}'' \times 5\frac{1}{2}''$, while commercial postcards are $4'' \times 6''$ or slightly larger. In order to be mailed at the postcard rate, which is lower than the first-class letter rate, cards cannot be larger than $4\frac{1}{4}'' \times 6''$. A larger card must bear the first-class letter postage. Cards less than $3\frac{1}{2}'' \times 5''$ are not acceptable for mailing. Cards must be at least .007 inch thick but not over .0095 inch.

Double postal cards are two attached cards, one of which is to be detached by the receiver and returned through the mail as a reply. The reply portion does not have to bear postage when originally mailed. Double cards must have the address of the reply portion on the inside.

Business-reply mail. Specially printed business-reply cards, envelopes, cartons, and labels may be distributed so that they can be returned to the original mailer without prepayment of postage. A permit must be obtained from the local postmaster in order to distribute such mail. Postage is collected on each piece of business-reply mail at the time it is delivered to the original mailer. The rates are the regular postage rates, plus an additional fee. No special services may be included in these rates.

No limitation is made on the quantity of business-reply mail, but it cannot be sent to any foreign country except to U.S. military post offices overseas.

The forms of imprint and address for business-reply mail must conform to the requirements of the Postal Service. One standard format is shown in Figure 7-3.

Priority Mail

Mailable matter that weighs more than 12 ounces and is to be sent by the fastest means of transportation with the most expeditious handling may be sent by priority mail. Matter cannot exceed 70 pounds in weight nor 100 inches in length and girth combined.

Special envelopes or stickers should be used to clearly identify the package or envelope as priority mail. To ensure proper handling,

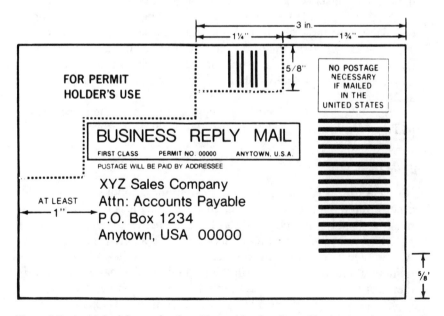

Figure 7-3. A standard format for the address side of a piece of business-reply mail.

the identification "PRIORITY MAIL" should be clearly marked in large letters on all sides.

Second-Class Mail

The category of second-class mail includes newspapers and other periodical publications. The secretary may be concerned with the mailing of such matter if the company puts out a newsletter regularly. Special rates apply, according to the nature of the publication, the frequency of publication, and so on.

Publications issued by, and in the interest of, nonprofit organizations and associations, such as religious, educational, scientific, philanthropic, agricultural, labor, and fraternal groups, are categorized for mailing under a special-rate structure.

Because of the variation and specialization of postal regulations in this category, the secretary to whom the responsibility of handling this kind of mail is assigned should get specific information from the post office on the particulars applying to the publication with which the office is concerned. However, these few general observations on the wrapping or covering of second-class matter may be useful.

Preparation for mailing. Second-class mail must be prepared so that it can be easily examined. Even if envelopes, wrappers, or other covers are sealed, the use of second-class postage rates indicates that the sender consents to postal inspection of the contents.

Sealed or unsealed envelopes used as wrappers and sealed wrappers or covers must indicate, in the upper right corner, the "second-class" status, acknowledging the post office's right of examination. The upper left corner must have the name of the publication and the mailing address to which undeliverable copies or change-of-address notices are to be sent.

Special instructions must be followed for sorting the pieces before mailing. These are available through the local post office.

Third-Class Mail

All pieces in the third-class category—circulars, books, catalogs, and other printed matter, and merchandise weighing less than 16 ounces—must be legibly marked "THIRD CLASS" whether they are sealed or not. They may be mailed and charged by the single piece or in bulk. All the pieces in a bulk mailing must be identical in size, weight, and number of enclosures, although the printed textual matter need not be identical. Special rates are available for nonprofit organizations.

A single piece of third-class mail is considered nonstandard if it weighs 2 ounces or less and exceeds a height of 6⅛ inches, a length of 11½ inches, or a thickness of ¼ inch and is less than 1.3 times or more than 2.5 times the height. An additional charge will be made for such mail.

Preparation for mailing. Third-class mail must be prepared by the sender so that it can be easily examined. It need not be marked "May Be Opened for Postal Inspection," for this is implied in the sending of mail under this class.

Mailers must sort the mail and place each piece with the address side up and in the same position; the pieces should then be tied, lengthwise and crosswise, into packages, with twine strong enough to withstand handling in processing and shipping. The "Bulk Mail" labels should be large enough to cover the top piece of exposed mail and should be attached so that they will not slide out from under the twine. Mailers should follow special instructions from the post office. Wrapping, in general, should be handled as for parcel post (see below).

Writing permitted. Other than the address, the only writing permitted on the wrapper of third-class mail is in the form of instructions, such as "Printed Matter"; "Photograph—DO NOT BEND"; or "Do Not Open until Christmas."

Enclosures. With catalogs or booklets, one order form, a business-reply card or envelope, and one circular concerning the product being sent may be enclosed.

A letter may also be enclosed in the package if separate first-class postage is paid for the letter in addition to the third-class rate for the package and if the wrapper is marked "Letter Enclosed."

Fourth-Class Mail

Domestic parcel post makes up most of the fourth-class mail, but the classification also includes bound printed matter and the "special fourth-class rate" for books, 16-millimeter films (or films with less width), sound recordings, manuscripts, and a special library rate. Fourth-class mail includes merchandise, mailable live animals, and all other matter not included in first, second, or third class.

Parcel post service is provided for packages weighing one pound or more. In the conterminous United States, packages mailed from larger post offices are limited to 35 pounds and 84 inches in length and girth combined. However, parcels mailed from smaller offices and any office in Hawaii or Alaska are accepted up to 70 pounds and 100 inches. Rates are determined by weight (fractions of a pound are computed as a full pound) and by distance or zone. To find out which zone the place of destination is in, and also to learn of weight and size limitations on parcels, consult an updated edition of *Leonard's Guide* or the official zone chart furnished by your local post office. The zones are measured as follows:

- Local Zone (within delivery limits of local post office)
- Zone 1—Within the same sectional center area
- Zone 2—Up to 150 miles
- Zone 3—Up to 300 miles
- Zone 4—Up to 600 miles
- Zone 5—Up to 1,000 miles
- Zone 6—Up to 1,400 miles
- Zone 7—Up to 1,800 miles
- Zone 8—Beyond 1,800 miles

Note: These data represent pieces weighing up to 35 pounds.

Special fourth-class rates apply to books, library materials, educational materials, and some advertising matter. Educational materials include 16-millimeter films and 16-millimeter film catalogs (except films and catalogs mailed to commercial theaters); printed music; printed objective-test materials; sound recordings and magnetic tapes; manuscripts of books, periodical articles, and music; printed educational reference charts processed for preservation; and loose-leaf pages and their binders, consisting of medical information for distribution to doctors, hospitals, medical schools, and medical students. The outside of packages containing books or educational materials must be labeled "SPECIAL FOURTH-CLASS RATE: BOOK (or FILM, etc.)." To classify as a book to be mailed at the special fourth-class rate, it must have 24 pages or more, at least 22 of which are printed, consisting wholly of reading matter.

Wrapping and cushioning. Two or more packages may be mailed as a single parcel if they are about the same size or shape or if they are parts of one article. They must be securely wrapped or fastened together and must not, together, exceed the fourth-class weight and size limits.

Packages may be excluded from the mail unless they are wrapped in such a way as to ensure safe transport. A package sealed with masking tape or transparent adhesive tape is not acceptable for mailing. Special wrappers and envelopes in a variety of sizes are now available from the post office at cost. These wrappers and envelopes are manufactured to meet the packaging requirements of the U.S. Postal Service. The package to be mailed is simply inserted in an appropriate envelope or wrapper, and a label is prepared and affixed thereon.

Containers in which the goods are to be shipped should be strong enough to retain the contents and protect them from the weight of other parcels with which they will be transported.

Corrugated cardboard may be used to protect contents. Cellulose materials, plastic bits, cotton, shredded paper, or tissue paper may be used for lighter items. Special wrappers and envelopes with cushioning interiors may be purchased from the post office at cost.

Nonfragile materials may be wrapped in heavy paper and sealed securely with tape. Thin paper bags are not acceptable. Articles that are self-contained may be mailed without outside packaging or wrapping. However, the post office is not responsible if the surface or finish of the article becomes marred or damaged. A cardboard carton in good condition may be wrapped and sealed with reinforced kraft paper tape or nylon filament tape. Avoid using twine if possible.

Addressing and mailing instructions. All parcel-post packages should be delivered to the post office and not deposited in mailboxes. The following rules should be followed in addressing and labeling the package.

1. The return address of the sender must be shown on the face of each package. If the addresses of the sender and the addressee are close together, label the return address "from" and the addressee's "to." It is always wise to include inside each package the name and address of the sender as well as of the addressee.

   Addresses should always be written with ink or an indelible marking pencil or typewritten on a label that is affixed to the package. Tied-on tags should be used only with packages too small to contain the complete address. Do not repeat the address on the back of the package.

2. Special inscriptions, such as "Merry Christmas," "Do Not Open until Christmas," or "Happy Birthday," may be written on the wrapper.

3. Packages containing fragile articles such as glassware, china, jewelry, and so forth, must be labeled "FRAGILE."

4. Products that may decay quickly, such as fresh meat or fresh produce, must be labeled "PERISHABLE."

5. The label "DO NOT BEND" may be used only when the contents are fully protected with fiberboard or corrugated cardboard.

Enclosures. Only certain types of handwritten and typewritten materials may be included in parcel-post packages. Invoices and customers' orders may be enclosed with the merchandise stipulated thereon. A letter may be enclosed, provided that the wrapper is marked

"Letter Enclosed" or "First-class Enclosure" immediately below the place for postage. Separate first-class postage is charged for such an enclosure in addition to the fourth-class charge for the parcel.

Special handling. To ensure that a parcel-post package receives the fastest possible handling and transportation, the special-handling service may be used, for an additional fee. It does not include special-delivery service. Priority mail or express mail can be used for parcels going over long distances when faster delivery of the parcel is desired.

Express Mail

Express mail is a service provided by the postal system that guarantees overnight domestic delivery of mail. This service was implemented because of a continuing demand for speedier delivery of mail. Various private carriers also provide this service.

Under express mail, there are four offerings:

1. *Express Mail,* which allows for delivery the next day.
2. *Express Mail Custom Designed Service,* which provides for special shipments for customers who make regularly scheduled shipments on a routine basis.
3. *Express Mail Same Day Airport Service,* which provides service between major airports; for this service, the customer takes the mail to the airport.
4. *Express Mail International Service,* which provides service to different countries. A service agreement is required for this service. Check for countries providing this special international service.

Printed Matter

Books and catalogs of 24 or more bound pages (at least 22 of which are printed) and weighing less than 16 ounces apiece are considered third-class mail. Other material that may be mailed at the third-class rate includes circulars and other printed matter, such as proof sheets, corrected proof sheets with related manuscript copy, and bills or statements of account produced by any photographic or mechanical process.

All other matter wholly or partly in writing, except authorized additions to second-, third-, and fourth-class mail, should be sent as first-class mail.

Bulk Mailing

Items that are to be mailed at the special bulk-mailing rate should be enclosed in mail sacks or other suitable containers and separated

TABLE 7.2

Express Mail Rates and Fees*

Postage Rate Unit (Lbs.)	Same Day Airport Service	Custom Designed	Next Day & Second Day PO to Addressee	Next Day & Second Day PO to PO	Postage Rate Unit (Lbs.)	Same Day Airport Service	Custom Designed	Next Day & Second Day PO to Addressee	Next Day & Second Day PO to PO
½ . . $8.35	$ 7.75	$ 8.75	$ 8.50	36 . . 33.60	51.00	52.00	49.85
1 . . . 9.70	11.00	12.00	9.85	37 . . 34.25	52.10	53.10	50.95
2 . . . 9.70	11.00	12.00	9.85	38 . . 34.95	53.15	54.15	52.00
3 . . 12.40	14.25	15.25	13.10	39 . . 35.60	54.25	55.25	53.10
4 . . 12.40	14.25	15.25	13.10	40 . . 36.25	55.35	56.35	54.20
5 . . 12.40	14.25	15.25	13.10	41 . . 36.95	56.45	57.45	55,30
6 . . 13.60	16.75	17.75	15.60	42 . . 37.60	57.50	58.50	56.35
7 . . 14.25	17.45	18.45	16.30	43 . . 38.25	58.60	59.60	57.45
8 . . 14.95	18.15	19.15	17.00	44 . . 38.95	59.70	60.70	58.55
9 . . 15.60	18.85	19.85	17.70	45 . . 39.60	60.80	61.80	59.65
10 . . 16.25	19.55	20.55	18.40	46 . . 40.25	61.85	62.85	60.70
11 . . 16.95	20.25	21.25	19.10	47 . . 40.95	62.95	63.95	61.80
12 . . 17.60	20.95	21.95	19.80	48 . . 41.60	64.05	65.05	62.90
13 . . 18.25	21.65	22.65	20.50	49 . . 42.25	65.15	66.15	64.00
14 . . 18.95	22.35	23.35	21.20	50 . . 42.95	66.20	67.20	65.05
15 . . 19.60	23.05	24.05	21.90	51 . . 43.60	67.30	68.30	66.15
16 . . 20.25	24.10	25.10	22.95	52 . . 44.25	68.40	69.40	67.25
17 . . 20.95	25.45	26.45	24.30	53 . . 44.95	69.55	70.55	68.40
18 . . 21.60	26.80	27.80	25.65	54 . . 45.60	70.55	71.55	69.40
19 . . 22.25	28.20	29.20	27.05	55 . . 46.30	71.65	72.65	70.50
20 . . 22.95	29.55	30.55	28.40	56 . . 46.95	72.80	73.80	71.65
21 . . 23.60	30.90	31.90	29.75	57 . . 47.60	73.90	74.90	72.75
22 . . 24.25	32.30	33.30	31.15	58 . . 48.30	74.90	75.90	73.75
23 . . 24.95	33.65	34.65	32.50	59 . . 48.95	76.05	77.05	74.90
24 . . 25.60	35.00	36.00	33.85	60 . . 49.60	77.15	78.15	76.00
25 . . 26.25	36.40	37.40	35.25	61 . . 50.30	78.25	79.25	77.10
26 . . 26.95	37.75	38.75	36.60	62 . . 50.95	79.35	80.35	78.20
27 . . 27.60	39.10	40.10	37.95	63 . . 51.60	80.40	81.40	79.25
28 . . 28.25	40.45	41.45	39.30	64 . . 52.30	81.50	82.50	80.35
29 . . 28.95	41.85	42.85	40.70	65 . . 52.95	82.60	83.60	81.45
30 . . 29.60	43.20	44.20	42.05	66 . . 53.60	83.70	84.70	82.55
31 . . 30.25	44.55	45.55	43.40	67 . . 54.30	84.75	85.75	83.60
32 . . 30.95	45.95	46.95	44.80	68 . . 54.95	85.85	86.85	84.70
33 . . 31.60	47.30	48.30	46.15	69 . . 55.60	86.95	87.95	85.80
34 . . 32.25	48.65	49.65	47.50	70 . . 56.30	88.05	89.05	86.90
35 . . 32.95	49.90	50.90	48.75				

Note: Add: $4.00 for each pickup stop. $4.00 for each Custom Designed delivery stop.

Source: Special Postal Bulletin, U.S. Postal Service.

Express Mail International Service Destinations

Argentina	Italy
Australia	Japan
Austria	Jordan
Bahamas	Korea, Republic of
Bahrain	Kuwait
Bangladesh	Luxembourg
Barbados	Macao
Belgium	Malaysia
Bermuda	Mali
Brazil	Mexico
Burkina Faso	Netherlands (Holland)
Canada	Netherlands Antilles
Cayman Islands	New Zealand
Chad	Niger
Chile	Nigeria
China, People's Republic of	Norway
Colombia	Oman
Côte d'Ivoire (Ivory Coast)	Pakistan
Cyprus	Panama
Denmark	Portugal
Djibouti	Qatar
Egypt	Saudi Arabia
Finland	Senegal
France	Singapore
Germany, Federal Republic of	South Africa, Republic of
Great Britain and Northern	Spain
Ireland	Sweden
Greece	Switzerland
Guyana	Taiwan
Hong Kong	Thailand
Hungary	Tunisia
Iceland	Turkey
India	United Arab Emirates
Indonesia	Uruguay
Ireland	Venezuela
Israel	

---

according to ZIP Code area. The containers must be taken to the post office.

If the third-class rate is to be used, postage is computed by rates per pound on the entire mailing at one time. An annual bulk-mailing fee must be paid at or before the first mailing of each calendar year. In addition, a postage permit is required. Under this permit, which may be obtained from the post office for a fee, mail must be prepaid.

If an imprint is used instead of precanceled stamps or meter stamps, the permit imprint may be made by printing press, hand stamp, lithograph, mimeograph, multigraph, addressograph, or a similar device. It may not be typewritten or hand-drawn. The style must conform to the specifications set forth by the United States Postal Service. Each imprint must show the name of the post office and the permit number. The fourth-class bulk rate may be used if at least 300 separately addressed pieces are involved and if they are identical in weight.

Bulky mail, called *slugs,* usually is marked *Hand Stamp* in large red letters. This stamp alerts the handler not to place the bag in canceling machines, which may cause serious damage to the machine and to the contents of the mail piece because of its bulky nature.

Airmail

Airmail is no longer specified as such within the 50 states of the United States, as all first-class mail with a destination more than a certain number of miles away is routinely transported by air. Airmail service is also available for some parcels and for overseas mail. The word "AIRMAIL" should appear on all sides of such a parcel. An adhesive label for this purpose is available without charge at the post office. The return address of the sender must be shown on the address side of each air parcel.

International Mail

International mail is mail sent between countries. Certain articles of a dangerous or objectionable nature are generally prohibited in the international mail: poisons, narcotics, intoxicating liquors, most live animals, explosive or flammable articles, obscene or libelous matter, and so on. In addition to these, each country generally prohibits or restricts the importation of various other articles. Such information may be obtained at the post office, provided the country named has made its restrictions known to the post office.

A person or company that wishes to prepay a reply letter from another country may do so by sending the correspondent one or more international reply coupons, which may be purchased at U.S. post offices. To avoid delay and inconvenience, postage on all foreign mail should be prepaid according to weight.

Forwarding foreign mail. Mail arriving in this country from a foreign country may be forwarded to any destination within the United States without additional postage.

Mail may not be forwarded to another foreign country without rewrapping, procuring a customs declaration, and affixing new postage.

U.S. mail to be forwarded to a destination outside the country should always have any additional postage affixed before leaving the United States, because some countries charge double postage for mail arriving with postage due.

International postal union mail. International mail is divided into two general categories: International Postal Union mail and parcel post. Postal union mail includes two classes of matter:

1. LC mail (letters and cards): letters, letter packages, Aerogrammes (air letters), postcards, and postal cards.
2. AO mail (other articles): printed matter, samples, commercial papers, matter for the blind, and small packets.

The special postal services that apply to Postal Union mail are registration with a standard limited indemnity, insurance (though not to all countries), and special delivery in most countries. Consult the post office for details, including what marking the mail should bear.

For all postal union mail, the address on all articles must be legible and complete, showing the street name and house number or the post-office box number, the name of the post office, the province (if known), and the country (on the last line). If the item is addressed in a foreign language, the name of the post office, province, and country must also be shown in English. The sender's name and address should be shown in the upper left corner of the address side.

All Postal Union articles except letters and letter packages are required to be left unsealed, even if registered.

Mailers must endorse the envelopes or wrappers of all Postal Union articles except letters and postcards to show the classification under which they are being mailed; for example, "Printed Matter," or "Printed Matter—Books." The words "Letter (Lettre)" should be written on the address side of letters or letter packages which, because of their size or manner of preparation, may be mistaken for mail of another classification.

In addition, airmail articles should be plainly endorsed "Par Avion" or have such a label affixed; articles intended for special delivery should be marked boldly as "Express" or "Special Delivery."

International parcel post. Parcel-post packages that exceed certain size limitations are not accepted for mailing to foreign countries. Consult the post office about these and other restrictions.

If the addressee has left a forwarding address, a package will be delivered and the addressee will be charged additional postage, depending upon the weight of the package and the distance forwarded. If there is no forwarding address, the package will be returned to the sender, and a charge will be made for the return postage.

Special Postal Services

Insurance. To assure the sender that payment may be obtained for loss of, rifling of, or damage to domestic mail, insurance is available. The fee, which is charged in addition to the regular postage, is based on assessed value. By paying an additional charge, the sender is assured that an insured package will be delivered only to the addressee. (See Figure 7-4.)

Third-class and parcel-post mail may be insured up to $500. Insurance may be obtained for merchandise mailed at priority or first-class rates. The post office generally obtains a receipt of delivery from the addressee for all articles that are insured for more than $15. Insured mail may contain incidental first-class enclosures, so long as they are noted on the face of the package and paid for at the first-class rate. The mail must bear the complete names and addresses of sender and addressee. Articles not sufficiently well packed and wrapped to withstand normal handling are not acceptable for insurance.

Collect on delivery. A patron can mail an article that has not been paid for and have the price and the cost of the postage collected from the addressee when the article is delivered. Collect-on-delivery service may be used for merchandise sent by parcel-post, first-class, or third-class mail, and the article may be sent as registered mail. Collection is made for the cost of the merchandise and postage, plus the C.O.D. fee; the merchandise cost is returned to the sender by postal money order. The fees include insurance against loss or damage of the merchandise and are limited to a maximum valuation of $400; fees vary according to the amount to be collected.

Registered mail. Additional protection for valuable pieces; irreplaceable articles, regardless of value; and all items valued up to $25,000 may be obtained by using registered mail. This service gives the sender evidence of mailing and delivery and provides security; the mail is controlled throughout the postal system. (See Figure 7-5.)

The sender is required by law to tell the postal clerk or, if the sender is a company, to enter on the company mailing bill the full value of mail presented for registry. Table 7.3 provides a guide to the required declaration of values of various types of valuable mail.

Only first-class and priority mail may be registered. C.O.D. parcels may be registered, but they will be accepted only at the rate for first-class mail. The registry fees are in addition to postage and include insurance protection up to $25,000 for domestic mail only. In the registry of international mail, the indemnity varies according to the country of the addressee.

Special delivery. Immediate delivery at the address of the recipient during prescribed hours and within certain distance limits may be

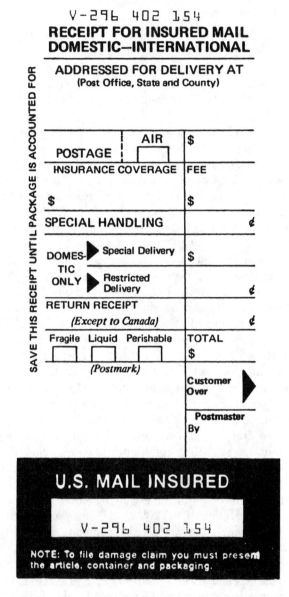

Figure 7-4. Receipt form for insured mail—domestic and international.

Source: U.S. Postal Service.

REGISTERED NO.   POSTMARK OF

Reg. Fee $	Special Delivery $	
Handling Charge $	Return Receipt $	
Postage $	Restricted Delivery $	
Received by	☐ Intl	

Post Office Completion

All Entries MUST be in Ball Point or Typed

Customer must declare Full value $

☐ With Postal Insurance   ☐ Without Postal Insurance
$25,000 Domestic Ins. Limit

Customer Completion *(Please Print)*

FROM

ZIP CODE

TO

ZIP CODE

PS FORM **3806**   RECEIPT FOR REGISTERED MAIL   *(Customer Copy)*
July 1983

(See Information on Reverse)

Save This Receipt For Registered Mail Claims & Inquiries

DECLARATION OF VALUE—Mailers are required to declare the FULL value at the time of mailing on all registered mail articles, whether insurance is desired or not. Failure to declare full value may invalidate any claim.

INSURANCE—Domestic Postal insurance may be purchased by paying the appropriate fee. Domestic insurance on registered mail is limited to the lesser of (1) the value of the article at the time of mailing or the cost or replacement if lost or totally damaged, or (2) the cost of repairs. An article may also be sent by registered mail without postal insurance by paying the appropriate fee. No indemnity will be paid for articles mailed without Postal insurance coverage. Consult your postmaster for additional details of insurance limits and coverage for domestic and international registered mail.

FILING CLAIMS—Claim must be filed within 1 year from the date of mailing. Present this receipt and submit evidence of value, cost of repairs, or cost of duplication. The contents and packing must be presented when filing a claim for damage or loss of contents.

INTERNATIONAL REGISTERED MAIL—Indemnity coverage for International Registered Mail is limited. Consult postmaster for maximum indemnity limits.

PS Form **3806,** July 1983 (Reverse Part 1)

Figure 7-5. Receipt form for registered mail (front and reverse).

Source: U.S. Postal Service.

TABLE 7.3

Declaration of Value for Different Types of Mail

Kind of Mail	Value to be Declared

Negotiable instruments
  Instruments payable to bearer and
    matured interest coupons
	Market value

Nonnegotiable instruments
  All registered bonds, warehouse
    receipts, checks, drafts, deeds, wills,
    abstracts, and similar documents
  Certificates of stock, including those
    endorsed in blank
	No value or replacement cost
	  if postal insurance
	  coverage is desired

Money	Full value
Jewelry, gems, precious metals	Market value or cost
Merchandise	Market value or cost

assured by payment of a special-delivery fee. Payment of this fee does not insure the safety of delivery or provide for payment of indemnity; therefore, money or other valuables sent special delivery should be registered also. Insured, certified, and C.O.D. mail may be sent special delivery.

Fees for special-delivery mail sent by regular first class are based on weight. For all other classes of mail, fixed special-delivery fees apply. Special-delivery fees must be paid in addition to regular postage.

Special handling. Special-handling service is available on third- and fourth-class mail only, including insured and C.O.D. mail. It provides preferential handling in transportation but does not provide special delivery. Special-handling parcels are delivered as regular parcel post is delivered. The special-handling fee, which is based upon weight, must be paid on all parcels that require special care, such as baby chicks and packaged bees.

Certified mail. Certified-mail service provides a receipt for the person mailing the item and a record of the delivery of the item from the post office from which it is delivered. No record is kept at the post office at which it is mailed. Certified mail is handled in the ordinary mails and is not covered by insurance. If the matter mailed has no intrinsic value, but the sender wishes to be sure that it has been sent to the correct point of receipt, this service is worthwhile. (See Figure 7-6.)

Any item on which first-class or priority postage has been paid will be accepted as certified mail. This matter may be sent special delivery if the required postage is also paid. An additional fee is involved if delivery is restricted (i.e., delivery only to the person named in the address) or if a return receipt is requested.

P 873 881 888

RECEIPT FOR CERTIFIED MAIL

NO INSURANCE COVERAGE PROVIDED
NOT FOR INTERNATIONAL MAIL

(See Reverse)

Sent to	
Street and No.	
P.O., State and ZIP Code	.
Postage	$
Certified Fee	
Special Delivery Fee	
Restricted Delivery Fee	
Return Receipt showing to whom and Date Delivered	
Return Receipt showing to whom, Date, and Address of Delivery	
TOTAL Postage and Fees	$
Postmark or Date	

PS Form 3800, June 1985

Fold at line over top of envelope to the right of the return address.

CERTIFIED

P 873 881 888

MAIL

Figure 7-6. Receipt form for certified mail.

Source: U.S. Postal Service.

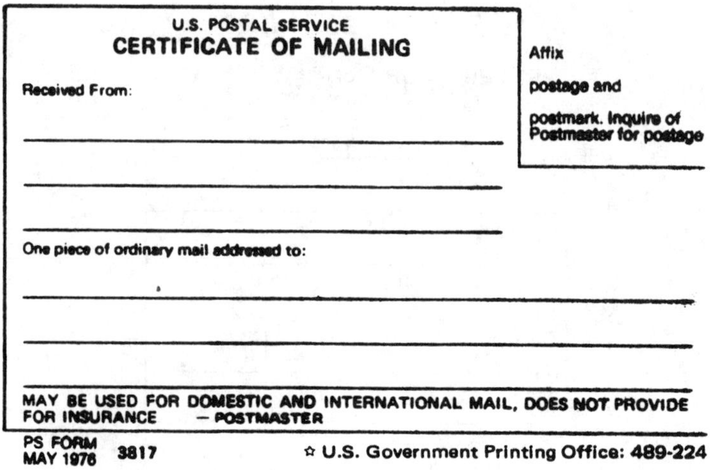

U.S. POSTAL SERVICE

CERTIFICATE OF MAILING

Received From:

One piece of ordinary mail addressed to:

MAY BE USED FOR DOMESTIC AND INTERNATIONAL MAIL, DOES NOT PROVIDE FOR INSURANCE — POSTMASTER

Affix postage and postmark. Inquire of Postmaster for postage

PS FORM MAY 1976 3817 ☆ U.S. Government Printing Office: 489-224

Figure 7-7. Certificate of mailing.

Source: U.S. Postal Service.

Certificates of mailing. At a fee somewhat lower than that for certified mail, certificates of mailing furnish evidence of mailing only. No receipt is obtained upon delivery of mail to the addressee. The fee does not insure the article against loss or damage. (See Figure 7-7.)

Return receipt. For mail that is registered, certified, insured, or sent C.O.D. or by express mail, the sender may wish to have evidence that the mail was received. When such proof of delivery is desired, a return receipt should be requested at the time of mailing. It identifies the article by number, the signer, and the date of delivery. Evidence of the exact address of delivery may also be requested. Restricted delivery service may be requested if the sender wants the mail to be delivered only to the addressee or to a particular individual authorized in writing to receive the mail of the addressee. Each of these services requires an additional fee as well as the regular postage. (See Figure 7-8.)

Money orders. A practical and safe method of sending money through the mail is by postal money order. The fees vary according to the amount sent and also according to whether the order is domestic or international. There is usually no limitation on the number of orders that can be purchased at one time. Lost or stolen money orders can be replaced and copies of payments can be obtained for two years after date of payment.

SENDER: Complete items 1 and 2 when additional services are desired, and complete items 3 and 4.
Put your address in the "RETURN TO" Space on the reverse side. Failure to do this will prevent this card from being returned to you. <u>The return receipt fee will provide you the name of the person delivered to and the date of delivery.</u> For additional fees the following services are available. Consult postmaster for fees and check box(es) for additional service(s) requested.
1. ☐ Show to whom delivered, date, and addressee's address.   2. ☐ Restricted Delivery
    (Extra charge)   *(Extra charge)*

3. Article Addressed to:	4. Article Number
	Type of Service: ☐ Registered ☐ Insured ☐ Certified ☐ COD ☐ Express Mail ☐ Return Receipt for Merchandise
	Always obtain signature of addressee or agent and <u>DATE DELIVERED</u>.
5. Signature — Address X	8. Addressee's Address *(ONLY if requested and fee paid)*
6. Signature — Agent X	
7. Date of Delivery	

PS Form **3811**, Mar. 1988   ★ U.S.G.P.O. 1988-212-865   **DOMESTIC RETURN RECEIPT**

Figure 7-8. Domestic Return Receipt.

Source: U.S. Postal Service.

Other Postal Services

The U.S. Postal Service also offers a variety of supplemental services to insure that the mail reaches its destination. Among others, these include: New Address Verification Cards (Figure 7-9); Change of Address Requests for correspondents, publishers, and businesses (Figure 7-10); and a consumer service card for identifying specific mailing problems (Figure 7-11).

Other Instructions about Mail

Recall of mail. At times it is desirable to recall a piece of mail that has already been taken to a post office or dropped into a mailbox. In such instances the sender must go to the post office and complete a written application and present a similar envelope or wrapper to identify the piece of mail being recalled.

Change of address. Prior to moving, each individual or firm should

---

Fold and Tear on Perforated Line Before Mailing

NEW ADDRESS VERIFICATION CARD

Check yellow forwarding labels on your mail when you arrive at your new address. If your name or new address information on the lable is incorrect, please send the following information to your Postmaster at the City/State/ZIP Code of your former address. Please print or type clearly.

YOUR NAME _____

ADDRESS OF YOUR FORMER RESIDENCE:

Apt./Suite/P.O. Box/R.D. No. _____

No. and Street_____

City, State, ZIP Code _____

INFORMATION SHOWN ON FORWARDING LABEL:

Your Name _____

Apt./Suite/P.O. Box/R.D. No. _____

No. and Street_____

City, State, ZIP Code _____

CORRECT NEW ADDRESS:

Your Name _____

Apt./Suite/P.O. Box/R.D. No. _____

No. and Street_____

City, State, ZIP Code _____

DATE   **SIGNATURE**

PS Form 3575A June 1985   Signature & title of person authorizing address change. (DO NOT print or type)

Figure 7-9. Form for new address verification card.

Source: U.S. Postal Service.

procure from the post office and complete the official U.S. Postal Service change-of-address form. Change-of-address cards are available in quantity, so that all correspondents and publishers of periodicals regularly received may be notified of the new address and the date of its effect. If possible, it is wise to notify the publishers of periodicals six or eight weeks before the move takes place, so that magazines and newspapers are not sent to the old address.

Undeliverable mail. First-class mail that bears no return address cannot be returned to the sender in the event that it is undeliverable. Therefore, it is imperative that all mail have a return address typed or written on it.

Franked mail. The federal government uses "franked" mail—that is, mail sent free of postage. The franked envelope may be used only for surface mail; it may not be used for overseas airmail unless the airmail postage is affixed. There is a federal penalty for misuse of franked mail. A franked piece of mail must have a facsimile or real

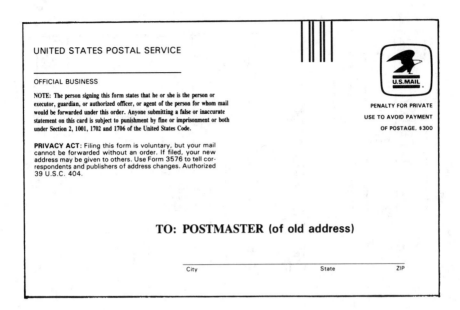

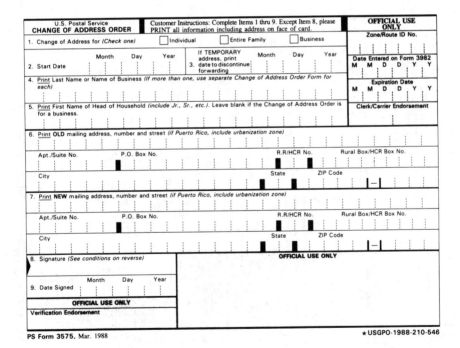

Figure 7-10. Form for a change of address request (front and reverse).

Source: U.S. Postal Service.

1 PRINT FIRMLY — 2 REMOVE TOP COPY FOR CUSTOMER RECORD (do not separate remaining copies) — 3 FILL IN ADDRESS BLANK ON BACK OF LAST CARD — 4 MAIL (postage free)

U.S. POSTAL SERVICE CONSUMER SERVICE CARD

Name	Date *(Mo., Day, Yr.)*	No. K 1 359 983	
Address *(Apt./Suite No., No. and Street, City)*	State	ZIP Code	Customer Phone *(8 a.m.-5 p.m.)*

Is This

☐ Information Request ☐ Suggestion ☐ Problem ☐ Compliment

Did It Involve	**If This Is A Problem With A Specific Mailing, Please Complete The Following:** Was It	Was Mailing	**This Section Is For USPS Use Only**
Delay	Letter	First-Class	Recording Employee Name
Nonreceipt	Package	Special Delivery	Date Customer Contacted
Damage	Newspaper/ Magazine	Certified	Customer Contacted By
Misdelivery	Advertisement	Registered	USPS Action
Improperly Returned	Electronic Transmission	Insured	
Change of Address		Express Mail	
Vending Equipment		Other	
Window Services			
Personnel			
Other			

Please Give Essential Facts *(If this involves a change of address problem, please include previous address.)*

PS Form **4314-C,** Mar. 1984 — THANK YOU. You will be contacted soon by your Post Office. — **CUSTOMER COPY - 1**

Figure 7-11. Form for consumer service (card). ***Source:*** U.S. Postal Service.

signature of the sender appearing in the place of the stamp. The words *Official Business* must appear on the address side.

The authorized use of franked mail is limited to certain categories: members and members-elect of Congress, resident commissioners, the Secretary of the Senate, the Sergeant at Arms of the Senate, and the Vice President of the United States.

Penalty mail. Mail pieces falling in this category are also official and free. Penalty mail is used for official government correspondence. The correspondence is enclosed in penalty envelopes or under penalty labels specifically marked *Official Business—Penalty for Private Use.* In some cases, the amount of the penalty may be printed.

Free mail. Mail pieces falling in this category are sent without postage by the general public, such as census mail and absentee ballot envelopes from members of the armed forces and military personnel of the U.S.

Unmailable items. The following items may not be sent through the U.S. mails. In fact, penalties are imposed on the mailers of these items.

Meat and meat-food products without certificate of inspection

Plants and plant products not accompanied by required certificate; certain plants are prohibited from shipment into certain states by quarantine order (Before attempting to mail plants, consult a postal authority)

Poisons, except those for scientific use and those sent to licensed dealers

Intoxicating liquors

Narcotics and other controlled substances as defined by federal regulations

Explosive, flammable, corrosive, or toxic substances

Live animals, except tiny ones that need no care, as bees, earthworms, or day-old chicks

Poisonous reptiles and insects and all kinds of snakes

Foul-smelling articles

Dangerous mechanical devices or machines

Sharp-pointed or sharp-edged tools insufficiently protected

Firearms capable of being concealed on the person (with exceptions)

Radioactive material, unless special permission is granted and special packaging and labeling requirements are met

Matter tending to incite arson, murder, assassination, insurrection, or treason

Indecent matter, written or other

Defamatory, dunning, or threatening matter on post cards or on the outside of any piece of mail.

Endless-chain enterprises, or fraudulent matter

Mail opened by mistake. At times mail is delivered to the wrong address and opened by mistake. When this happens, the person who opens it should simply reseal the envelope with tape and write "Opened by Mistake." The mail should then be dropped into a mailbox or handed to the mail carrier.

Express

Most things that can be transported can be sent by express, but nothing irreplaceable should be sent by this means. Valuable papers, such as bonds, can be sent by express, provided that they can be replaced. Certain items are barred from express shipments, such as those containing acids or corrosives, antiques, artworks, coins, explosives, gems or jewelry, or uncrated household goods. Consult the nearest express agency office for other specific limitations.

Preparation for shipment. The following information must be given to the express company before a shipment can be made:

Consignee's name and local address

Value of shipment

Number of pieces of shipment and type of container

Weight

Description of articles shipped

Shipper's name and address

Information regarding payment.

The address of the shipper and the consignee should both be written on the packing slip and also enclosed in the package.

Domestic Air Express

Air express is available for those cities having airports. The service is extended to the areas surrounding such cities, but an additional charge is made to "off-line" points outside the area served by the airport. The nearest express office should be queried as to the exact points to which delivery is made without additional charge.

Many airlines accept small packages and envelopes for airport-to-airport delivery; the item will be held for pickup at the luggage-return area or at the air express office.

Package Express by Bus

Bus lines offer package express within the United States and Canada. Consult them for information on rates, requirements, and restrictions, and for up-to-date schedules.

Prohibited articles. The following articles are not accepted for shipment by bus:

Acids or corrosive substances

Alcoholic beverages and liquors

Animals, live, including birds and reptiles

Articles packed in wet ice or water

Batteries, electric-storage, wet

Dangerous articles, including ammunition, explosives, and flammable materials

Fluorescent signs

Gases in cylinders

Jewelry, when the declared value is more than $50

Materials having a disgreeable odor

Money

Neon signs or bent neon tubing

Wild game, killed

X-ray tubes

SUMMARY*

Changes to Domestic Rates, Fees, and Classifications

A. **General.**
There will be changes to the following rates, fees, and classifications:
1. First-Class Mail (excluding Priority Mail)
2. First-Class Nonstandard Surcharge
3. Express Mail Service
4. Second-Class Mail
5. Third-Class Mail
6. Fourth-Class Mail, including parcel post, bound printed matter, special fourth-class and library rates
7. Second-Class Application Fees
8. Permit Imprint Fee
9. On-Site Meter Setting Fees
10. Stamped Envelopes
11. Special Services:
    a. Registered Mail
    b. Certified Mail
    c. Insured Mail
    d. COD
    e. Special Delivery
    f. Special Handling
    g. Parcel Airlift
    h. Business Reply Mail
    i. Merchandise Return (decrease)
    j. Certificates of Mailing (bulk mailings only)
    k. Return Receipts
    l. Restricted Delivery
    m. Money Orders
    n. ZIP-Coding of Mailing Lists
    o. Post Office Box and Caller Service Fees
    p. Return Receipt for Merchandise (new service)
12. Annual Fees:
    a. Annual Presort Fee (First-Class)
    b. Annual Bulk Mailing Fee (Third-Class)
    c. Annual Presorted Special Fourth-Class Mailing Fee
    d. Annual Business Reply Mail Permit Renewal Fee
    e. Annual Business Reply Mail Permit and Accounting Fee
    f. Annual Merchandise Return Service Permit Fee
    NOTE: In addition to increases for these annual fees, the payment structure has changed from once each calendar year to an annual basis.

B. **First-Class Mail.**
   1. **General.**
      All rates, except Priority Mail, will change.
      NOTE: All rates in the Domestic Mail Manual (DMM) are now expressed in dollars (as opposed to being expressed in cents). Do NOT move the decimal two places to the left before computing postage.

---

* *Source:*   Special Postal Bulletin, U.S. Postal Service, March 1988.

2. **Single Piece Rate First-Class Mail (Other than Cards).**

   There is a change in the rate structure. These rates will apply only to pieces weighing **11 ounces or less.**

3. **Presorted First-Class Rate.**

   There is a change in the rate structure. See Exhibit 310.

4. **ZIP + 4 Presort Rate.**

   The tolerance for the placement of the bar code in the bar code clear zone, for those wishing to bar code as an option in a ZIP + 4 Presort mailing, has been relaxed.

5. **ZIP + 4 Barcoded Rate.**

   The new ZIP + 4 Barcoded rate is established. See DMM 325.

6. **Carrier Route First-Class Rate.**

   There is a change in the rate structure. See Exhibit 310.

7. **Priority Mail Nomenclature.**

   The name "Zone Rate (Priority) First-Class Mail" is changed to "Priority Mail." Priority Mail rates will now apply to all single-piece First-Class pieces weighing **more than 11 ounces.** (Pieces at lower weights may also be mailed at Priority Mail rates at the mailer's option.)

8. **Nonstandard Surcharge.**

   A lower surcharge of $0.05 per piece has been established for nonstandard pieces mailed at the Presorted First-Class and Carrier Route First-Class rates. The surcharge remains at $0.10 for nonstand-ard-sized pieces at the single-piece rates.

C. **Express Mail.**

   1. **General.**

      All rates change.

   2. **Rate Structure Changes.**

      a. A new lower letter rate for up to $\frac{1}{2}$ pound is now available for all service options. The Post Office to Addressee letter rate is $8.75.

      b. Zones are eliminated for all weights.

      c. Custom Designed Service rates are lowered.

   3. **Pickup Service.**

      On-call pickup service may be provided in addition to scheduled pickup at designated postal facilities. A new pickup fee of $4.00 per stop is available for all service options.

   4. **Second-Day Service Added.**

      Express Mail Second-Day Service is added to resolve off-net problems.

   5. **Noon Delivery.**

      Postage return guarantee is extended to include noon delivery within the major market network.

D. **Second-Class Mail.**

   1. **General.**

      All rates change.

      NOTE: All rates in the DMM are now expressed in dollars (as opposed to being expressed in cents). To compute second-class postage, multiply the applicable postage (which is in dollars) times the appropriate number of pounds or pieces. DO NOT move the decimal two places to the left before computing postage.

   2. **Rate Structure Change.**

      The outside county per-piece discount for the nonadvertising portion of publications (the nonadvertising adjustment) is increased for regular-rate and science-of-agriculture rate publications, and a non-advertising adjustment is added for special nonprofit and classroom rate publications.

3. **Mailing Statement Submission for Combined Mailings.**

   For mailings that include more than one second-class publication and/or edition, separate mailing statements will be required for each publication and/or edition in the mailing. See 468.4.

4. **Computation of Nonsubscriber Copy Limits.**

   Effective January 1, 1989, the 10-percent limits on (a) the number of nonsubscriber copies eligible for preferred rates and (b) the number of nonsubscriber/nonrequester copies eligible for subscriber/requester rates without being commingled with subscriber or requester copies will be applied to the number of copies, as opposed to the weight of copies, mailed to subscribers/requesters during the calendar year.

E. **Third-Class Mail.**

1. **General.**

   All rates change.

   NOTE: All rates in the DMM are now expressed in dollars (as opposed to being expressed in cents). To compute postage DO NOT move the decimal two places to the left before computing postage.

2. **Sorting Requirements for 5-Digit Presort Level Rate.**

   Third-class 5-digit presort level rate sorting requirements are revised to eliminate the requirement that there be at least 10 pounds or 50 pieces for any 5-digit ZIP Code separation in nonunique 3-digit sacks. Packages of 10 or more pieces to a 5-digit ZIP Code in a 3-digit sack will qualify for this rate in accordance with 667.42.

3. **New Basic ZIP + 4 Rate.**

   A new basic ZIP + 4 rate is established. See DMM 622.14 and 662.4.

4. **New 5-Digit ZIP + 4 Rate.**

   A new 5-digit ZIP + 4 rate is established. See DMM 622.15 and 662.5.

5. **New ZIP + 4 Barcoded Rate.**

   A new ZIP + 4 barcoded rate is established. See DMM 622.16 and 662.6.

6. **Required Marking for Special Bulk Third-Class Rates.**

   The option to show the marking "Nonprofit" instead of "Nonprofit Org." on pieces mailed by organizations authorized the special bulk third-class rates has been added to DMM 662.2b.

F. **Fourth-Class Mail.**

1. **General.**

   All rates change.

   NOTE: All rates in the DMM are now expressed in dollars (as opposed to being expressed in cents). DO NOT move the decimal two places to the left before computing postage.

G. **Special Services.**

1. **General.**

   All fees are increased except for: a) Merchandise Return Service fees (which are reduced); b) Money Order Fees (see also change noted in item 5); c) corrections to mailing lists (including lists corrected in conjunction with sequencing of address cards); and d) address changes provided to election boards and registration commissions.

2. **New Business Reply Mail Discount Category (BRMAS).**

A new discount category is available for ZIP + 4 prebarcoded business reply mail paid for through a business reply account (requires payment of a permit and accounting fee). See 917.14, 917.213, 917.343a, 917.525, 917.528, and 917.6.

3. **Merchandise Return Service.**

Temporary changes adding registry service and special handling as service options in conjunction with merchandise return service are made permanent.

4. **Insured Mail.**

The fee structure is changed. A $0.70 fee will insure items valued at $50 or less.

5. **Money Orders.**

The upper dollar-value limit for the first category of money order fees changes from $25 to $35.

6. **New Return Receipt for Merchandise Service.**

A new return receipt service, that may be obtained without any other special service, is added for merchandise mailed at Priority Mail, third-class, and fourth-class parcel post rates.

7. **On-site meter setting fees.**

The fee structure has changed. See DMM 144.351.

8. **Business Reply Mail.**

The accounting fee has been combined with the permit/renewal fee.

H. **Stamped Envelopes.**

1. **Sizes.**

Additional sizes are added to all product lines.

2. **New Double Window Envelopes.**

3. **Envelopes in "Household Quantities."**

Printed envelopes (both regular and window) will be available in quantities of 50. A double window envelope will also be available in quantities of 50.

I. **Annual Fees.**

1. **General.**

All annual fees increase.

2. **Fee Payment Structure.**

The fee payment structure for all annual fees changes from once each calendar year to once each year effective with the month and day of payment. The following fees are affected by this change:

a. Annual Presort Fee (First-Class).

b. Annual Bulk Mailing Fee (Third-Class).

c. Annual Presorted Special Fourth-Class Mailing Fee.

d. Annual Business Reply Mail Permit Renewal Fee.

e. Annual Business Reply Mail Permit and Accounting Fee.

f. Annual Merchandise Return Service Permit Fee.

J. **Mailing Statements.**

Forms 3541, 3541-A, 3602, 3602-PC, and 3605 will be amended to accommodate the new rates and rate structures. The **Postal Bulletin** of March 31, 1988 includes samples of these new forms and examples of how to modify current mailing statements while the new forms are being distributed.

TELEGRAMS

A telegram is a message sent via a Telex network to someone without a Telex-receiving piece of equipment. The intermediary connection is Western Union, which receives the message by telephone or Telex. After the message is received, Western Union calls the recipient, reads the text, and sends a printed copy, if requested.

The Telex network spans the globe. There are approximately 190,000 users in North America and 1.7 million worldwide. As the descendant of the Morse Code telegraph, it uses a standard keyboard printer, such as teletype or teleprinter, connection with a telephone system, and a printer at the receiving end.

In 1981, the U.S. Government deregulated the industry. Now Western Union can connect you directly to an overseas number, and other private companies, called International Records Carriers (IRCs), may also forward messages through their domestic networks and offer many of the services available through Western Union. Refer to the companies listed in Figure 7-12. The IRCs have approximately 41,000 total subscribers; and a directory listing, combining Telex subscribers of IRCs, may be obtained from:

> US Telecommunications Subscribers
> 250 Hudson Street, 14th Floor
> New York, NY 10013

Western Union also has a directory that lists Western Union subscribers only.

All networks *interconnect*, allowing a message to be sent regardless of the network affiliation. In other words, Telex is a direct-dial subscriber-to-subscriber service for record and data communications made available by Western Union within the United States and, through connections with other carriers, to Canada, to Mexico, and to most overseas countries. A subscriber to this Western Union service is provided with a console-mounted teleprinter, supplemented with dial and automatic answer-back equipment. Connection with another subscriber in the United States, Canada, or Mexico is established within eight seconds by dialing the distant subscriber's station number. The automatic answer-back feature enables the subscriber to confirm the correctness of the connection established, thus permitting transmission even though the called subscriber's station is unattended.

There is a fixed monthly service charge, plus a charge for the amount of actual time used during the connection of each telex call. There is no minimum period charged for on telex calls to stations in the United States, Canada, and Mexico. For subscribers desiring to prepare their communications in advance, and thereby keep their telex

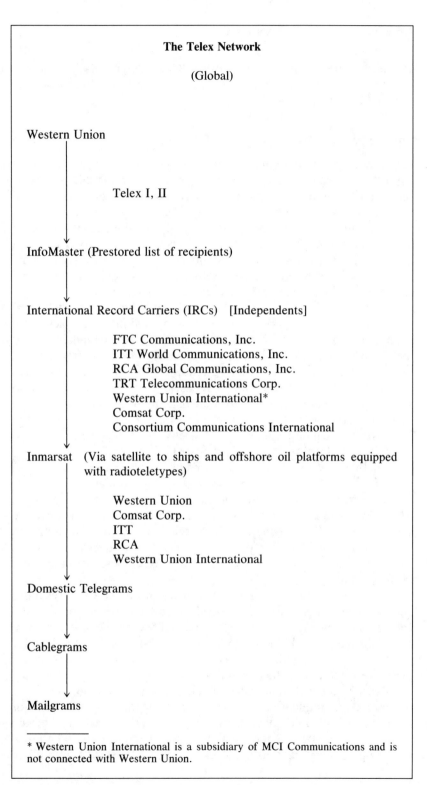

Figure 7-12. The global telex network.

call usage time to a minimum, Western Union offers, at an additional charge, alternate equipment that enables the subscriber to prepare and transmit perforated tape.

Advantages and Disadvantages of Telegrams

A telegram, or cable, comes instantly to mind when speed is of vital importance in sending a written message locally or abroad. However, sending a telegram does not necessarily mean that the message will be delivered within minutes or hours. There are different classes of service, some of which are considerably faster than others. Often a phone call is not only much faster but also less expensive. Even an overseas call may cost only a little more than a brief cable, and if the message can be delivered verbally rather than in writing, the additional expense may be justified by speed and certainty of receipt.

A key question, then, is whether the message *must* be delivered in print on paper with a record of when sent (and in some cases when received). Many companies and organizations understandably insist that such information as prices and specifications be submitted in a form that can be kept by them as a record—if not in letter form, then by telegram, cable, or telex. In such cases, however, the person who sends the telegram *must specify* that it actually be delivered to the recipient; otherwise, the message will simply be telephoned by the local Western Union to the recipient. Delivery of the printed message will follow by local mail only if requested.

Another key question is whether one message to one person is involved, or whether the same message will go to many people—for example, to all the men and women on a large sales force, or to all the dealers who sell a particular product. Western Union has effective systems for wide distribution of a specific message, including a comparatively inexpensive overnight service. The overnight service can be used to ensure quick delivery of important messages in all parts of the country.

If a response is desired, it is advisable to specify how that response should be sent. For example, a travel agency may be asked to send a cable requesting a hotel room, with a cabled response of confirmation. But if the agent sends the cable by reduced-rate night service, and if the hotel responds similarly by delayed service, the exchange of cables may take three days rather than a few hours.

Because the rates and rules of telegraph, cable, radio, and other means change frequently, no attempt will be made to specify costs or to provide detailed instructions as to the number of words transmitted at various base rates. Where such details appear, they are to be taken as examples rather than as specifics. The local Western Union office will provide the latest printed material on request (along with blank forms).

It is important to note the domestic telegrams cannot be considered cost effective. They are expensive. A message should be sent via a long-distance telephone line if possible. But telegram messages are sometimes required in certain business situations. Telegram notification is at times required in legal matters, legal contracts, and so forth.

Time of day. The time of day at which a telegram is sent is of vital importance. When a New York business office closes, a Chicago (Central Time) office has one hour left in the business day; a Denver (Mountain Time) office, two more hours; and a San Francisco (Pacific Time) office, three more hours. At 4:45 P.M. in New York there is time left to complete a pending deal in Chicago, thereby perhaps saving the company dollars that a day's delay may cost. (See Chapter 25.)

Classes of Service

Full-rate telegram (speed service). There is no special indication needed for sending a full-rate telegram. If the sender does not specify otherwise, the telegraph message will be sent as a full-rate telegram. The characteristics of this class of service are as follows:

15 words to start with

Additional words charged at low extra-word rate

Address and signature not charged

Immediate transmission and delivery

May be sent in plain language or code

Faster type of message service available for sending and telephone delivery 24 hours a day, 7 days a week.

Mailgram. This service can be used when a low-cost, high-impact message is desirable. These messages are sent over Western Union's microwave and satellite networks to the addressee's post office and delivered by letter carrier with the next day's mail. The characteristics are:

100 words to start with

Additional charge for extra words

Name, address, and signature included in word count

Delivery guarantees not made by Western Union

Messages received before 7 P.M. destination time are generally delivered the next postal service day

Messages received after 7 P.M. may not be delivered until the second postal service day.

Night letter (NL). A night letter may be sent at any time up to 2 A.M. for delivery no later than 2 P.M. of the next business day. On weekends or holidays deliveries are made to business offices when open, and other disposition will be made if instructions from the addressee are on file or if the sender specifically requests it. Deliveries are made to residences on any day. The minimum rate is for 100 words. Additional words are counted individually.

Selecting the Class of Service

Full-rate telegrams usually provide the most efficient service. Night letters are less expensive and are used when the speed of delivery is not an important consideration. They can be used effectively to send information on which action is not required until the following morning or messages going out late in the business day.

When speed of service is important, a choice must be made between a full-rate telegram, a Mailgram, or an overnight telegram. For messages of less than 15 words, the full-rate telegram is most efficient. For messages of over 15 words, it is generally less expensive to select an overnight telegram or the Mailgram, which is by far the least expensive.

Code words as well as plain language may be sent in full-rate messages, Mailgrams, and night letters at the prevailing rates.

Preparing the Telegraph Message

Even if the message will be transmitted by telephone, it is helpful for the secretary to type the message on one of the telegraph blanks provided by Western Union. The file copies will then most closely resemble the recipient's message. Complete the blank as follows:

In the box at the upper right, indicate the class of service to be used, such as an overnight telegram, so that this fact may be checked against the bill from Western Union.

Always date the message. In business, questions often arise as to when a message was sent and when it was received.

Type in double space, using capital letters so that you will see the message as it will appear on the telegram itself.

Type the full name and address of the recipient. Use as many words in the address as are necessary to indicate the exact location of the addressee. When sending a telegram to a person in a large office building, be sure to include either the name of the company or the room number of the office, or both.

Include the ZIP Code on Mailgrams, as these messages are delivered by the U.S. Postal Service. The ZIP Code should also be included on full-rate telegrams or night letters for quick transmission to branch offices.

Designate states by using the two-letter Postal Service abbreviations, without periods.

A well-written telephone message is concise. Because the charges are based upon the number of words sent, each word in the message should convey meaning, and no word necessary to the meaning should be omitted.

Use nouns and verbs freely to convey the message. Often prepositions, pronouns, adjectives, and adverbs may be omitted without affecting the meaning of the message.

Omit salutations and complimentary closings.

Do not divide words at the end of the line.

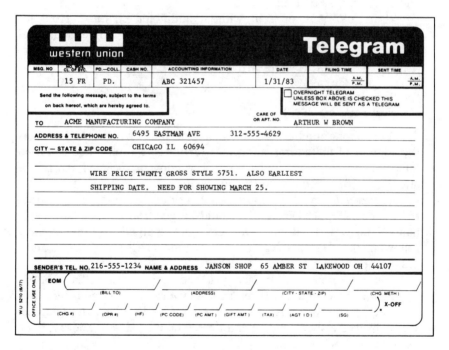

Figure 7-13. Western Union telegram form correctly filled out.

Calculating Telegraph Costs

To calculate in advance the cost of telegraph messages, the secretary must have the rate sheets, which can be obtained from Western Union. Because rates are subject to change, it is important to check with the telegraph company to be sure that the rate sheets on file in the office are up to date.

The telegraph company charges nothing for the name and address of the addressee, unless more than one one name is given (for example, "Henry Adams or Jeffrey Rose"). In this case, a charge is made for the alternate name.

The full name and address should be used, as:

Laura Allen Room 304
Todd Leather Company
1616 West Berk Street
New York, NY 10003

"Mrs.," "Ms.," or "Miss" is generally used to signify that the recipient is a woman, although the use of a title is tending to decline in the business world. "Mr." is not used in telegrams unless no first name or initial is given. The titles "Dr.," "Rev.," "Major," "Hon.," and so forth may be used.

"Care of" may be sent without additional charge. "Hold for Arrival," followed by the time or a date, may be sent without additional charge:

Leon P. Adams, Hold for Arrival, 6 PM
    (or May 15)
Summit Hotel
New York, NY 10002

A telephone number may be sent free of charge when it accompanies the address of the addressee. The receiving telegraph office will then telephone the message and later mail a copy of the message to the addressee, if the request for this is made.

Report delivery. If a report of delivery of the message is desired, the words "Report Delivery" should be given after the addressee's name. The words "Report Delivery" are charged for. Immediately following delivery, a telegram is sent (and charged to) the sender, indicating the time and date of delivery.

Two addresses may be given, if necessary, with a charge made for the alternate address. If report of delivery is to be requested, this may include (at an extra charge) the address to which the telegram was delivered as well as date and time. The inclusion of address must be requested in this case.

Personal delivery only. The notation "Personal delivery only" may be stipulated if the sender wishes to ensure that delivery of the message will be made only to the addressee.

"Will call" should be given immediately after the name in the address if someone is going to call at the telegraph office for a given message. The message is held at the central telegraph station, but it can be quickly transmitted if it is called for at any branch office.

"Do not phone" may be given in the address at no extra charge.

Messenger delivery is available only to certain destinations, and the secretary will determine from Western Union whether the service can be requested in a particular instance. An additional charge is made for messenger delivery.

Message to a passenger on a ship in port. Messages may be transmitted to ships at sea or to ships arriving in port and delivered to passengers. Give full details:

Name of passenger	Viola Acierno, passenger
Name of steamship line	Woodson Line
Name of ship and stateroom number (if known)	SS Calgary, Stateroom B202
Time of sailing and pier	4 PM sailing, Pier 97
Departure port	New York, NY 10004

Word Count

Any word listed in a standard dictionary as one word will be counted as one word; this includes hyphenated words (as *self-defense*). That rule can be applied to all telegraphic messages. Nondictionary words or expressions are counted as one word for every five letters.

An abbreviation of five letters or less is counted as one word, provided it is written with no spacing: "COD" or "C.O.D."; "AM" or "A.M."

Geographical names are counted according to the number of words as normally written:

New York City, 3 words	NYC, 1 word
St. Augustine, 2 words	
United States, 2 words	US, 1 word
North Carolina, 2 words	NC, 1 word

Proper names are counted by the number of words and initials they contain:

Van de Perle, 3 words
Vanderbilt, 1 word
P. Conners, 2 words

Each initial in a name is counted as a separate word:

A. F. Miller, 3 words
Sara B. Wolf, 3 words

A surname prefix, such as "Mac" in MacDougall, is not counted as a separate word when it is written without separation by a space. However, the "De" in De Berendinis is counted as a separate word because of the space.

Punctuation. Punctuation marks are free. Punctuation marks such as the period, comma, colon, semicolon, dash, hyphen, decimal point, parentheses, question mark, quotation marks, and apostrophe are neither counted nor charged for. On the other hand, an apostrophe used in a figure group to designate "feet" or a quotation mark used to designate "inches" is counted as a chargeable character.

All words are counted: "stop," "comma," and "quote" are charged for as words when they are spelled out.

Figures and characters. Figures are counted as one word for a group of five figures or less:

67,383 = 1 word
1,343,682 = 2 words
1-12-65 = 1 word

Figures that are written out are counted as they are written:

thirty-six, 2 words
one hundred five, 3 words

Signs such as #, $, &, and the / (diagonal) for fractions are counted and charged for in figure groups, but the diagonal counts as a separate word in expressions such as "and/or":

#22 (3 characters), 1 word
$36.42 (5 characters), 1 word
2 1/2 (transmitted 2½), 1 word
and/or, 3 words
12/2/68 (7 characters), 2 words

The symbols ¢ and @ cannot be transmitted and should be written out. The percent sign, %, is transmitted as 0/0 and counts as three characters.

Signatures. Only one individual's name is carried without extra charge, but a title, a department name, or the name of a firm added to an individual's name will be carried without charge:

Ruth M. Henderson, Treasurer
Ruth M. Henderson, Credit Department
Ruth M. Henderson, Woodrow Lumber Company

When an individual's name is followed by a title and a firm name, the title is charged for. "Sales Manager" would be charged for in the following example:

| Ruth M. Henderson, Sales Manager
| Woodrow Lumber Company

Telephoning a Telegram

Messages are now most often telephoned to a Western Union office and charged either to the monthly telephone bill or to a credit-card account. The person answering at Western Union will take any message given. Simply give the following information:

| Calling telephone number (for billing purposes)
| Class of service
| Addressee's name and address
| Message
| Sender's name and address

When dictating a message over the telephone, spell each difficult word.

Means of Transmitting Messages

The secretary may have several choices as to how the domestic telegram may be filed with the telegraph company.

Desk-Fax. The Desk-Fax is a unit of facsimile equipment. The sender may either write or type the message and place it around the drum of the Desk-Fax. Inside the machine an electric eye scans the telegraph message and automatically sends an exact reproduction of it directly to the Western Union office in the area.

As discussed earlier (see the section on "Facsimile"), fax machines are now standard automated equipment in many offices to send messages and other illustrations (charts, graphs, etc.) outside of the office.

Private-wire system. Regardless of size or complexity, the function of any private-wire system furnished and maintained by Western Union is to provide instantaneous, continuous communication between stations on the system.

The simplest private-wire system is a two-point channel with a teleprinter at each end that both sends and receives messages. These machines may be on two different floors of the same building or hundreds of miles apart, perhaps connecting the company with a branch office or a correspondent.

Large private-wire systems may be thought of as roughly resembling a huge wagon wheel in their physical layout. Around the rim of the wheel are the stations that send and receive messages. These stations are linked to each other by a switching center at the wheel's hub. In addition, if there is a large volume of communications between two points on the rim, these points can also be connected with each other by direct circuits as well as to the switching center at the hub. A major advantage of such a system is that it permits a message to be routed instantly from any station on the system to any or all of the other stations through the central switching station at the hub. Just as in the case of simple two-point circuits, the extensive private-wire systems are engineered to provide two-way record communication between any two stations on the system.

Because of such technological advancements as integrated data processing (IDP) and electronic computers, greater importance has developed upon high-speed, reliable communications. Through private-wire systems it is possible to provide sufficient volumes of data at a centralized processing center to utilize the full potential benefits to be derived from a computer installation. Private-wire systems are engineered to handle either administrative messages or bits of data in machine language over the same system with equal facility.

Receiving Telegrams and Cablegrams

A message of such urgency that the sender selected telegraphic service should be delivered immediately to the addressee. In cases when the addressee is not in the office, the message may be read by the secretary or some other person given the responsibility of attending to urgent messages.

Code messages. If a code word is included in a message, the meaning of the word should be written above it before the message is passed along to the person for whom it was intended. Should a major part of the message be in code, the decoded message should be typed on a separate sheet and attached to the original message.

Copies. When a copy of a telegraphic message is desired, a facsimile may be made on any photographic duplicator.

Special Service—Teletex

An additional service available to Western Union telex subscribers, Teletex, permits the subscriber to send messages to nonsubscribers in major cities in the United States, Canada, and West Germany. The telex subscriber dials and transmits the message to the destination telegraph office, where delivery is made to the addressee. A flat-rate fee is made for each message, plus the time used for transmission.

Teletex is not a physical network, but rather a standard that involves a high transmission speed through whatever connections that exist.

Teletex's text (the message) allows lowercase letters, and the text looks like a standard business letter. The process interconnects with the Telex network (see Figure 7-12).

This service is not to be confused with Teletext, a system that involves transmission of text to home television sets and other receiving stations.

Other Services Offered

Wirefax. A public facsimile service between major cities provides direct transmission of letters, drawings, or any graphic materials.

Teletypewriter exchange service (TWX). Subscribed to by many companies for direct subscriber-to-subscriber transmission of telegraph messages, TWX service is made possible by the installation in the subscriber's office of a Teletype machine that can be connected by wire to Teletype machines of other TWX subscribers within the United States. A monthly rental is made for the equipment, and the subscriber is billed for each three-minute period of usage, with an additional charge made for each additional minute or fraction of a minute of usage. TWX service is also available to Canadian subscribers, the basic charge being for one minute.

Personal opinion message (POM) service. A special service offering reduced rates permits the sending of telegraph messages expressing the sender's views on current issues to the President of the United States, the Vice President, senators, and congressmen in Washington, or to the governor, lieutenant governor, and legislators at a state capital.

Speedata. At the point of origin, data on sales, payrolls, and inventory are sent on regular telegraph forms and converted to punched tape before being delivered to the recipient. The customer may select the speed of service desired and send data as a full-rate telegram or a night letter.

Telegraphic money orders. Money may be sent quickly and safely as day money orders, which are delivered within five hours during the open hours of the destination office or as overnight money orders that are delivered before 2 P.M. the following day. Money-order payments in foreign countries are usually made in the currency of the country of destination and are subject to prevailing exchange rates. In addition to the charges for a message to the destination city, a money-order fee applies, depending on the amount of money transmitted.

To send money by telegraph, complete a telegraphic money-order form, giving the name and address of the recipient, any message, and the sender's name and address; then deliver the money and the completed form to the telegraph office.

At the destination, the telegraph office will deliver a money-order draft or notify the recipient by telephone that the money may be called for at the telegraph office. Before a money-order draft can be cashed, the person is asked to present evidence of identity.

Special greetings. Suggested texts for greeting messages are available at the telegraph office, or the sender may compose an original message. Appropriate telegraph blanks are available for all major holidays and other occasions.

CABLES AND RELATED SERVICES

A cable, also called a *cablegram,* is a message sent overseas; it is an international telegram. Cablegrams can be sent by Telex, Western Union, or an IRC service. They are handled at the receiving end in whatever manner is standard in the receiving country.

Technological improvements in communications have resulted in increased speed and capacity, as well as in reduction of costs for sending cablegrams. The use of sophisticated computers now permits automatic electronic handling of messages through high-frequency radio channels, submarine cable, or radio satellite. In addition to cablegrams, there are two other services: telex and leased-channel service.

Cablegram

Cablegrams may be written in any language that can be expressed in roman letters or in secret language. A minimum charge is based on seven words, including the address and signature. Twenty-four-hour service is available for rapid transmission of messages. Each secret-language, nondictionary word is counted at the rate of five characters, or a fraction of five characters, to the word.

Special Cablegram Services

There are several special services available for users of cable.

Cable code address. A company that sends a volume of cable messages will find it economical to register a cable code address of its choice at any Western Union office. Such an address enables a company to economize on words in the signature of a message, thus reducing the cost.

Prepaid messages. A sender of a cablegram may wish to prepay the charges for a reply to the original message. When this is done, the indicator "RP" (reply paid) and figures showing the amount prepaid are inserted before the addressee's name.

Forwarding messages. Cablegrams may be forwarded to an addressee who has left the place to which the message was addressed. If the sender wishes to assure delivery in such cases, the indicator "FS" is placed before the addressee's name. A charge is made for the additional word.

Delivery after business hours. If the sender wishes to be assured that the message will be delivered by the foreign telegraph office after the close of the regular business day, the word "NUIT" should be indicated before the addressee's name. An additional charge is made for the one word. (For time differences in various parts of the world, see Chapter 25.)

Report of time delivery. When the sender wishes to receive a report as to the time of delivery of the cable, the indicator "PC" should be inserted before the addressee's name. The cost is for one word plus a six-word reply. Note that the indicator "PC" *does not* mean personal computer.

Sending International Messages

ITT World Communications, Inc. issues periodically revised rate folders, which serve as a handy reference for sending international telegraph and telex messages to virtually all parts of the world. Free copies may be obtained from ITT World Communications, Inc., 67 Broad Street, New York, New York 10004, Telephone: 1-212-425-9050.

Collect messages may not be used for foreign countries except for Canada and Mexico.

Basic Regulations

Each word of the address, text, and signature is counted and charged for.

Each plain-language, standard dictionary word is counted at the rate of 15 characters, or a fraction of 15 characters, to the word.

Figures, letters, signs, or combinations of them are counted as five characters per word.

If the name of a place is a compound word (e.g., Stratford-on-Avon), the name of destination point is joined and counted as one word, regardless of length.

In figure or letter groups, each punctuation mark is counted as one character.

Examples	No. of characters	Words charged
15,545	6	2
6,121	5	1
127,545	7	2

Punctuation marks used in conjunction with words are counted as one word each and transmitted only on special request of the sender. Exceptions are the two signs forming the parentheses ( ) and quotation marks (" " or ' '), which are counted as one word.

Examples	Words charged
( )	1
" "	1
' '	1

Those punctuation marks and signs acceptable for transmission upon the sender's recommendation are:

period (.)
comma (,)
colon (:)
division sign (÷)
question mark (?)
apostrophe or feet or minutes (')
inches or seconds (")
hyphen, dash, or subtraction sign (-)
diagonal (/)

Word count. In addition to the above, charges are based on the number of words in a message. Charges per word can be more than 30¢. If you regularly use cablegrams, it is important that you understand word-count rules. Basically, as a rule, any word in the English language that can be found in a dictionary is counted as one word. The minimum number of words is 15.

Code words (5 letters), combinations of letters and numbers, numbers by themselves, and every space all equal one word:

De La Cruz	=	counted as three words
DeLaCruz	=	counted as one word

With certain exceptions, some punctuation marks can be used, but they are counted as one word. To save money, short words may be counted together:

tobe (instead of "to be")

Caution: Such combinations count as code words; thus, the five-letter rule applies.

Characters and special symbols ($, #, &, %, ¢) should *not* be used in cablegrams because they are not used overseas. One-word cable addresses can be found on the company letterhead. Using them is cost effective. As a reference, one-word cable addresses may be found in the annually updated *Marconi's International Register*. Check local general and business library indices.

Letter Telegram

LT = letter. If LT is the first word, the message becomes a letter telegram and costs 50 percent less. Some countries will not accept letter telegrams and codes (code words) therein. The minimum length for an LT is 22 words. Verify these details with the carrier *before* you send the cablegram.

Similar Services

In addition to cablegram, two other services are available: telex and leased-channel service.

Telex

Telex service is available for overseas written communications over Western Union telex or TWX. The service is offered by ITT World Communications, Inc., RCA Communications, Inc., and Western Union International, Inc. To communicate with firms having telex equipment in their offices overseas, the procedure is to call the Telex Center of any one of the three international carriers, identify yourself and give the area code for the country being called, plus the telex number of the correspondent.

By means of Data Telex, it is now possible to send some 1,500 words per minute over special broad-band channels of the international carriers for the transmission of intelligence of any type. To take advantage of this high-speed service, special computers and data equipment must be installed at both ends of these circuits in the carrier's and the correspondents' offices. The rates for Data Telex service, where it is available, carry a minimum charge for each connection. Special arrangements must be made with the international carriers, as this service is limited and must be scheduled in advance.

Leased-Channel Service

Through one of the major companies providing international communication service, leased-channel service provides instantaneous two-way radio communication 24 hours a day for firms whose volume of international messages warrants it. Service may be leased for a month or longer.

The company renting the service may transmit quickly and effi-

Courtesy: Trans-Lux Corporation.

Telex Teleprinter 16K: The Trans-Lux TLT/16K teleprinter is quiet, easy to use, and built for heavy-duty action every day. It can be connected to such domestic and international telex networks as Western Union, RCA, and ITT. The 16K TLT has an electronic memory and uses impact paper.

ciently messages that otherwise would be handled by cable, airmail, or telephone.

RADIO MESSAGES

Shore-to-ship communication either way is possible via radio marine service. Radio messages fall in the category of international communication, and in many respects, such messages are treated as telegrams and cablegrams.

Satellite Communications Network

Because of rapid advances in satellite communications and microwave technology, the transmission of television broadcasts, computer data, facsimiles, telephone calls, and radio messages by telegrams and cablegrams is possible from shore to ship. In the mid-1980s, more than 20 communications satellites were orbiting the earth.

Microwave communications are sent by transmission towers located on the ground (shore); signals are relayed from tower to tower via each tower's antenna. Shore signals are picked up by satellites orbiting about 23,000 miles above the earth. Signals, digital or otherwise, then are relayed to ships at sea.

Radio communications make possible instantaneous oral exchanges between two receiving units. The system is bilateral; the major emphasis is that communication is instantaneous. However, distance is a prime factor. A ship radiogram is used for messages to and from ships at sea and serves as an international service.

Overseas telegrams and cablegrams are sent by underwater cables or by satellites. Telex (TWX) provides communications networks to send messages between ships and shore by radio.

INMARSAT, one of Telex's maritime satellite services, can be used to send messages via satellite service to ships, offshore barges, and oil platforms with radioteletypes. Western Union, Comsat Corp., ITT, RCA, and Western Union International provide this service. Consult your Telex directory for specific instructions.

Sending a Radio Message

When you wish to send a message, contact your local operator and ask for the marine operator. Ships in port, near a coastal city, or at sea can be reached through the marine operator. The marine operator initiates a shortwave radio link to the ship's radio room. The INMARSAT procedure can be used for international calls; however, the ship must be properly equipped. You should provide the following information:

1. What ocean the ship is in
2. The ship's telephone number

INMARSAT calls cost about $10 per minute. If a satellite connection is involved, there will be additional cost. The international access code is 011. Ocean codes are:

Atlantic	871
Pacific	872
Indian	873

When calling, follow this procedure:

- Dial the international access code (011).
- Dial the ocean code.
- Dial the ship's seven-digit number.
- Press the # button if you have a pushbutton telephone.

Only full-rate telegraphic service is available from the United States to ships anywhere in the world. Plain or secret language or a combination of both may be used. Plain-language words are counted at 15 characters to the word; secret-language words are counted at five characters to the word. Addresses and signatures are charged for.

When preparing messages, write "INTL" above the name and address to stipulate "international message." The address must include the name of passenger, name of ship, ship's general location, and radio station.

Marine Radio stations are written as one word, such as SANFRAN-CISCORADIO or KEYWESTRADIO:

> INTL
> William Alberts
> SS United States
> North Atlantic
> Newyorkradio

When speed is a primary factor, messages may be filed directly with the coast station serving the general vicinity of the ship. If the sender is not familiar with the coast station, the message may be telephoned or filed TWX by indication CHATHAMRADIO for ships in the Atlantic Ocean and SANFRANCISCORADIO for ships in the Pacific Ocean.

THE TELEPHONE

Despite the vast number of devices, methods, and alternatives for communicating information, the telephone remains the most popular means of communication. It allows for communication between two or more persons, and it is the key instrument in initiating telecommunications networks worldwide.

Since the telephone is such an important communication device, it is essential that the secretary use it to its maximum effectiveness and be familiar with its peripheral equipment.

Telephone Techniques

The secretary is expected to be knowledgeable in the use of the telephone. It is also important to keep up with the constantly expanding and changing services available from the telephone company, as well as the many and varied pieces of equipment that can add to the efficient operation of the business office. The telephone is the most frequently used audio-communication medium in the business world. The dependence upon this instrument has grown so that currently over 900 million telephone calls are made daily.

The reputation and good will of the employer and the firm may depend upon the secretary's approach and skill in using the telephone. Although most people in our society begin to use the telephone in early childhood, perhaps the majority of them still need to be trained in proper telephone techniques. An impressive way to point out defects in techniques, and one that results in a rapid and desirable change, is to make a recording or tape of a telephone conversation. Such a recording emphasizes the faults in telephone techniques and vividly points out areas needing improvement. Many organizations, even though they are efficiently organized, lose customers, money, and good will simply because employees answering calls are incoherent, curt, or impolite.

Speaking Clearly and Pleasantly

The caller at the other end of the phone cannot see the person who is talking. This should be remembered at all times, for it means that the caller has no visual image on which to base impressions. The telephone caller's attention is focused entirely upon the audio impressions coming over the wires. If these sounds are jarring or unpleasant, a busy executive may quickly lose patience and discontinue association with the firm in question. On the other hand, a pleasant and understanding voice coming over an inanimate instrument can accomplish wonders. The power of the spoken word can and does exert a great impact upon the listener.

The telephone is not a nuisance instrument designed to interrupt the secretary in the midst of some important or complicated task. It is, rather, a vital business communication facility that assists the employee in carrying out duties and responsibilities owed to the employer.

In order to enhance one's telephone personality, it is necessary to inject variety and flexibility into the voice, so as to convey mood and attitude in telephone conversations. These qualities can be obtained through pitch, inflection, and emphasis. The development of these qualities is individual. A high-pitched voice may convey an impression of childishness and immaturity or of impatience and irritability. On the other hand, a voice that is well modulated carries the impression of culture and polish. "Pitch" in speaking, like "pitch" in music, refers to the key in which one speaks. Everyone has a range of tone within which a pleasant speaking voice is possible, and it can be consciously controlled. Each person must be conscious of his or her own range and practice utilizing it effectively. An individual is said to speak in a "modulated" voice when the pitch is in the lower half of the possible range. This tonal range carries best and is easiest to hear over the telephone.

In cultivating an interesting individual telephone personality, voice development alone is insufficient; it is essential also that the speaker enunciate clearly and distinctly. A garbled and indistinct speech pattern will annoy the listener who cannot understand what is being said. Do not be afraid to move the lips. One cannot form rounded vowel sounds or distinct consonants unless the lips accomplish their function. It is not necessary to exaggerate or to become stilted; clear enunciation and pronunciation should be made a part of the secretary's natural, daily speech pattern, because it is just as important in face-to-face conversations as in telephone conversations. Above all, be sure that your voice reflects your personality, that it transmits alertness and pleasantness, and that it is natural, distinct, and expressive, and neither too loud nor too soft. Avoid repetitious, mechanical words and phrases, and try to enunciate in a manner that is neither too fast nor too slow.

Answering Promptly

Answering a business telephone call is similar to welcoming a visitor. Therefore, it is essential that each call be greeted by a prompt, effective, and pleasing answer.

The telephone should be placed on the secretary's desk so that it is readily accessible. A pad and pencil or pen should be kept handy in order to jot down necessary information. These should not be used for doodling when speaking on the phone; this habit distracts the secretary from the business at hand and interferes with giving the caller undivided attention.

When the telephone rings, answer it promptly—at the first ring, if possible. Try not to put incoming calls immediately on "hold"; many callers find this practice infuriating. If it becomes increasingly necessary to do this, the employer should be alerted. It may be desirable to install another telephone line and to hire another person, if only for the busiest hours of the day, to help handle incoming calls.

If the secretary finds it necessary to leave the desk, arrangements should be made to have someone else answer the telephone and take the messages during that interval. The instrument should not be left unattended. An unanswered telephone becomes an instrument of failure—failure to the company because of the loss of customers and failure of the individuals responsible. It is well to inform the person who covers the telephone why the secretary will be away from the desk and for how long. Armed with this information, the one who answers the telephone can be more helpful to the caller.

This courtesy, of course, should be extended in both directions. Each secretary should reciprocally cover the calls of colleagues when it becomes necessary for them to be away from their desks so that telephones are never unattended for any period of time.

In many businesses, if the telephone is unattended, an answering unit is used. This machine will record a message after a "beep" usually preceded by a message.

Identifying Who Is Answering

For efficiency, the office should be identified immediately when the phone is answered. The secretary's name may also be given. It is correct to say, "Mr. Wright's office; Miss Dubrowski speaking," or the firm name may be used, as, "Smith and Grey; this is Mr. Lopez." The identification formula depends upon the size and structure of the organization. When the telephone is answered in this fashion, the caller is assured that the proper office has been reached. Avoid answering the business telephone by saying, "Hello." Using this form of greeting is much like saying, "Guess who this is," and is unbusinesslike. Business people have no time to play guessing games, and this form of address can become irritating, particularly if it is necessary to call the office frequently.

In answering calls for others, identify yourself and the office of the person whose calls are being taken. For example, "Miss Jones' office; Mr. Liska speaking." Unless this is done, the caller will not know whether the right person has been reached at all. If the caller expects to hear the voice of Miss Jones' secretary, he or she may be taken aback when an unfamiliar voice comes over the wire. The fact that the correct office has been reached is made clear at once.

Identifying Who Is Calling

The wise secretary develops a keen ear and learns to recognize the voices of important or frequent callers. However, a word of caution. Do not become too sure of an infallible ear, for voices may sound different over the telephone. If the voice is known beyond a doubt, use the caller's name when speaking. If the voice has been identified correctly, the caller will be pleased to be recognized and addressed by name. Then speak *to the person* at the other end of the wire, not *at the telephone*. If the secretary was incorrect in identifying the voice before divulging any information, little harm was done, since the caller will make the correction. Apologize tactfully and take up the business at hand. However, when the name of the caller is not revealed and/or the nature of the business is not identified, the secretary's skill at diplomacy comes into play. Many executives prefer their secretaries to screen incoming calls. This must be done with tact and discretion. In some cases the executive will speak with anyone who calls but would like to know beforehand who is calling and the nature of the business. It is the secretary's duty to obtain this information before transferring the call to the executive. Curtness and rudeness must be avoided in doing so. It is correct to say, for example, "May I tell Mr. Brown who is calling?" or "Mrs. Winslow is talking on another line. Would you care to wait, or may I have her call you? I believe her other call may take some time." or "Mr. Zobkiw is in conference. May I help you?" Be sincere and courteous in your explanation, but do not divulge information unnecessarily. Your goal is simply to find out tactfully who is calling if you can.

Screening Calls

Although some executives answer the telephone themselves, many depend upon their secretaries to answer all incoming calls. The secretary must, therefore, be familiar with the executive's preferences. It is important to learn which calls the secretary is expected to handle, which are to be referred to the executive, and which should be transferred to someone else. Consequently, the secretary must classify telephone callers accurately and quickly. Every call is important. Enough information must be ascertained to classify the call. A caller cannot be allowed to get to the end of a long inquiry before being referred to the proper person. In order to forestall this, the secretary may make a discreet vocal sound that may cause the caller to pause slightly so that the secretary may say, "Mr. Chan in the shipping department should be able to help you with this. Please let me transfer your call to him."

Handling the Call

Generally the calls that can be handled by the secretary are as follows:

Requests for information. The secretary can handle this type of call if the information is not confidential and if there is no doubt concerning the facts. Sometimes it may be necessary to check with the employer before imparting information. If any complications arise, it is always wiser to turn the call over to the executive. In certain situations, the secretary may ask for a letter of request and, upon its receipt and approval, respond.

Requests for appointments. The secretary is sometimes authorized to make appointments for the employer. However, both the executive's and the secretary's diary should be checked before any appointments are made in order to avoid conflicts. If the employer is out of the office, the appointment should be verified immediately upon return. Commitments could easily have been made about which the executive had either forgotten to inform the secretary or the opportunity had not yet arisen to have had them entered in the desk calendars.

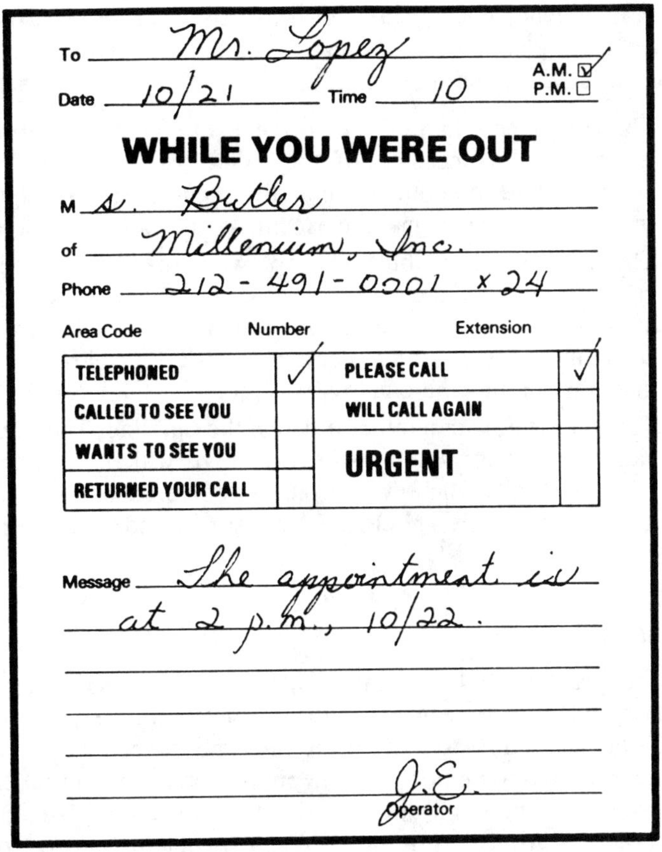

To _____ *Mr. Lopez* _____

Date _____ *10/21* _____ Time _____ *10* _____ A.M. ☑ P.M. ☐

WHILE YOU WERE OUT

M _____ *s. Butler* _____

of _____ *Millenium, Inc.* _____

Phone _____ *212 - 491 - 0001   X 24* _____

Area Code   Number   Extension

TELEPHONED	✓	PLEASE CALL	✓
CALLED TO SEE YOU		WILL CALL AGAIN	
WANTS TO SEE YOU		**URGENT**	
RETURNED YOUR CALL			

Message _____ *The appointment is* _____
at 2 p.m., 10/22.

J.E.
Operator

Figure 7-14. Telephone message slip.

Receiving information. Often the secretary can conserve the employer's time by taking down telephone information. If the message is taken in shorthand, this must be transcribed as soon as possible and placed on the employer's desk.

Transferring calls. If the call cannot be handled by the secretary or the employer, it should be transferred to the office that can give the caller the information sought. This should be done only with the caller's permission, however. If transferral is refused, obtain the information and call back. If the caller agrees to a transfer, make sure that the right office is reached before hanging up and give the person in that office sufficient information so that the caller will not need to repeat it.

In taking calls from persons who wish to speak to the executive directly, the secretary must know how to handle the following situations tactfully, discreetly, and diplomatically.

1. The employer is in and free. The executive is informed of who is calling. On occasion, if the caller is well known to the employer and someone to whom the executive talks frequently, the secretary may signal the executive to pick up the telephone.
2. The employer is in but does not want to be disturbed. The caller is told that the executive is engaged at the moment and asks whether a message may be taken. If the caller insists on speaking to the executive personally, ask if a call back may be made as soon as the employer is free.
3. The employer is in another office in the building. The secretary should ascertain whether the executive will be available for telephone calls when away from the office. Generally only the most urgent calls should be transferred under such circumstances.

Taking Messages

It is good practice to keep a written record of all incoming calls, particularly when the executive is away from the office. In recording the call, the secretary should indicate the time the call was received; the name, business affiliation, and telephone number of the caller; and the message. The note may be signed with the secretary's initials. If the message is from an out-of-town caller, the area code or the telephone operator's number should also be recorded, so that the executive can return the call in a short time and without confusion. It is best when taking a message to read it back to the caller in order to avoid errors or misunderstandings. Messages should always be taken verbatim. Be patient and pleasant but persistent. Ask the caller to spell out both first and last names if necessary. If numbers are involved, repeat the sequence for verification. Taking a telephone message accurately often saves calling back to check information. Then again, if a message is completely garbled, it may be impossible to call back and a valuable contact could be forever lost.

When a call is taken, the "phone message" slip should be placed on the executive's desk immediately. The secretary will also anticipate the executive's needs by attaching to the slips any material (possibly annotated) that may be necessary for reference in order to conclude the transaction successfully—back correspondence, a bill, price lists, or whatever may assist the executive in handling the call intelligently.

To be able to handle the incoming calls more efficiently, the secretary should know where the executive will be when away from the office, whether urgent messages can be relayed, and the expected time of return to the office.

Also, in taking calls for other persons in the office, as suggested above, it is helpful if one can state when the person called will return or whether the call can be transferred somewhere else. It is best to offer whatever information possible; otherwise the caller may get the impression of being put off with an excuse. Be courteous, and use discretion in explaining an absence from the office. It is less offensive to say, "Miss Jones is away from her desk just now. May I have her call you, or would you prefer to leave a message?" than to say bluntly, "She's out," or "This is her coffee break," or "I don't know where she is." The secretary must always use tact in dealing with callers, whether it be for one's own executive or for another secretary whose calls are being taken.

Taking Action

The secretary should promise the caller some definite action and see to it that the promise is kept. If the caller is told that the executive will call back, then this information must be conveyed to the employer so that the call can be made. A broken promise can result in a canceled order or a lost customer, and it may take many months to regain lost good will.

On some calls that the secretary can handle, more information may be needed than is within immediate reach. Therefore, it may become necessary to leave the telephone to look up the necessary information and to inform the caller of this fact and of the length of time it may take to obtain the material. Offer the caller a choice of waiting or of being called back. The customer should never be left waiting for an unreasonable amount of time at the other end of the wire. If a promise is made to call back with the needed information, this promise must be honored.

If the caller is waiting to speak to the executive, the secretary should reassure the caller periodically that the call will be connected as soon as the employer is free. Otherwise the caller will be uncertain as to whether the call is still connected, and a minute's silent delay will seem like a half-hour's wait. When the secretary is ready to transfer the call, thank the customer for waiting.

Completing the Incoming Call

At the completion of the call, indicate readiness to terminate the conversation by summing up the details. Use the caller's name when saying a pleasant "Goodbye." It is courteous to wait for the caller to terminate the call first; the secretary who is too hasty in hanging up the receiver may cost the firm money. The impression may be given that the caller's business is of little importance to the organization because the call is cut short. Permitting the caller to say "Goodbye" first also allows time for last-minute orders or special instructions. The receiver should be replaced gently in its cradle, for the pleasantest "Goodbye" can be spoiled by the jarring sound of a receiver dropped into position. It is like slamming the door after a visitor. The abruptness may not be intentional, but the effect is the same. Do not hang up until your caller has done so first.

Limiting Personal Calls

Because of the secretary's status and the prestige of that position, an example should be set for the office personnel by refraining from making and accepting personal calls during business hours except those that stay strictly within the rules set by the employer. The policy of the company or executive should be determined by the secretary at the very beginning of employment.

Telephone Dictation

Frequently the secretary is called upon to take dictation over the telephone. For this reason a shorthand notebook and pen should be placed near the telephone and ready for use. The caller is always informed of the fact that the conversation will be taken by the secretary. The secretary picks up the receiver and indicates readiness to record the proceedings. In the case of telephone dictation, unlike dictation taken at the employer's desk, the dictator cannot tell whether the secretary is getting all the information. Therefore it is necessary for the secretary to repeat the material phrase by phrase as it is taken down in shorthand. This informs the dictator as to the rate of dictation, clarity of reception, and errors in grammar or facts. Corrections can then be made immediately instead of waiting until the end of the dictation, which may lead to confusion. If the dictation is too fast, it is best to indicate this immediately. It is a good practice to read back the notes at the termination of the dictation to ensure that the correct information was received and recorded and to correct any misinterpretations. The notes should be transcribed as soon as possible, and a copy should be sent to the telephone dictator. Of course, if the transcription equipment being used is of the type that can be utilized for recording telephoned dictation, the caller will be able to complete the dictation far more rapidly.

Telephone Reference Materials

The efficient secretary must be aware of the available sources of information that will be of help in placing a call expeditiously, skillfully, and economically. Directories and booklets published by the telephone company provide much information. A desk file for frequently used numbers should also be maintained. In the modern automated office, a secretary with a computer terminal at his or her desk may create a database for telephone reference materials and retrieve information from it in a matter of seconds.

Telephone Directories

Telephone directories contain three general sections—the introductory pages, the alphabetical listing of subscribers (which may be divided into subsections), and the classified section, familiarly known as "the Yellow Pages." In many areas of the country, all three sections appear in one volume of the telephone directory. However, in metropolitan areas where the listings are voluminous, the classified section is a separate book.

The introductory section gives instructions on what numbers to call in various types of emergencies, where to place service calls, how to ask for directory assistance, how to make mobile and marine calls, and the different types of calls that can be made. It lists area codes for faster calling and sample rates for long-distance and person-to-person calls. It explains how to make collect calls; how to call overseas; how to call the telephone company's business office and the operators who handle customer information; where to pay bills and transact business in person; and what modern telephone services are available to the customer. A map illustrates area code zones.

The subscriber section lists in alphabetical sequence the names, addresses, and telephone numbers of all the telephone subscribers in a locality, borough, town, village, city, or county. Sometimes the kind of business or the occupation of a subscriber is also shown. In some large directories, business, professional, and organizational listings are given in a separate section from that for residences. Government offices may also be listed in still another section.

At the top outside corner of each page guide, names, or "telltales," indicate the first and last listings on the page for quick location of the page on which a particular name appears. If a name might be spelled in several ways, a cross-reference spelling directs the user to additional listings. The divisions, departments, or branch offices of an organization with separate telephone listings are usually indented under the firm name. Alternate call listings can likewise be found in the telephone directory. These listings indicate telephone numbers to be called when no one answers the regular numbers. Governmental agencies and state, county, and municipal offices are shown with major headings for the principal listing and indented entries for subordinate departments and divisions.

The local alphabetical and classified directories are usually distributed to all subscribers. Out-of-town directories may be purchased by calling the telephone business office.

Street-Address Directories

In some cities, street-address directories are available and may be rented from the telephone company. These directories list telephone numbers according to the alphabetical and numerical arrangements of streets in that city. They are of special value and usefulness to credit and collection agencies and for companies or organizations who desire to make up mailing lists.

Desk Telephone Files

For efficiency and expediency, a desk telephone file of numbers and area codes should be compiled. This list consists of

1. business numbers the employer calls frequently and, possibly, taxi, railroad-terminal, and airline numbers
2. emergency numbers for ambulance service, fire department, police department, and so on
3. personal numbers of the employer's family
4. extension numbers in other offices
5. frequently called long-distance numbers, with notations indicating the difference in time zones.

Unlisted numbers should be added to this list, with an identifying mark indicating the nature of such a number. Unlisted numbers are never revealed without specific instructions from the executive to do so. They were given to the employer for personal use, and this fact should be respected.

It is a good idea when compiling a desk telephone list to make it as informative as possible. The secretary should identify individual names by noting title and company affiliation in addition to the address and telephone number and area code. In entering the name, address, and telephone number of an organization, also indicate the name and title or department of the person or persons with whom the secretary or the employer talks most frequently.

The placement of the desk telephone list depends upon its size. If quite short, it may be taped neatly to the top or the slide panel of the desk; if long, it may be kept in a book or on a rotary file attached to or near the telephone.

Database Files

Because electronic communication is used in today's automated office, you may have access to or use a terminal at your desk or workstation. To automate telephonic communications, create databases for telephone reference materials and desk telephone files. Then, you can easily retrieve complete citations for easy reference as well as make changes and additions within seconds. The advantage is that you don't have to handle a book and check via a system to find the data needed. You simply key the data to initiate retrieval. Such databases help speed up directory assistance inquiries. Instead of paging through phone books, operators input a name, and a list of possibilities appears on the screen. Through scrolling, the desired number, if listed, is revealed.

Assembling Data for Outgoing Calls

In order to place outgoing calls quickly for the employer, the secretary should master all the telephone techniques that enable one to do this skillfully. Be absolutely certain of the telephone number before calling. It will save time, trouble, and irritation if the number is checked with the desk list, telephone directory, or correspondence file before calling.

Then assemble all the information that may be necessary to conduct the business transaction when the call is put through. It may be necessary to obtain materials from the files to refresh the executive's memory on previous business or other information that will be of help in making a successful call. All pertinent material should be placed on the executive's desk before the call is made.

It is also a good practice to be sure the executive will be free and available to take the call as soon as it goes through. No one likes to be called and then find that it is necessary to wait because the caller is talking on another line or is otherwise not ready to take the call immediately. Delay may not only lower the prestige of the company and the executive and cause annoyance but also prove costly to the firm making the call.

The question frequently arises as to which executive should answer first. Courtesy prescribes that the caller should be on the line, ready to talk, when the person called is put on the line by his or her own secretary, particularly if the person called outranks the caller. The secretary should put the executive on the line immediately, if possible. This can be done readily if the secretary identifies the employer when the call is answered. The secretary at the other end will then be able to transfer the call to the person called without delay or immediately inform the caller of how to reach that individual.

Telephone Services

In addition to business calls within the local community or surrounding areas, it frequently becomes necessary to place calls to more distant points. The ability to handle long-distance calls capably will enhance the secretary's value to the employer.

Toll Calls

Long-distance calls are those made from one town or city to another town or city outside of a local calling area. A charge is made for such calls in addition to the charge for the regular telephone service. The amount of the charge depends upon the distance, the type of service requested, the time of day or night the call is made, and the time taken for the conversation.

There are two classes of long-distance calls—station-to-station and person-to-person.

Station-to-station calls. Any state in the United States can be reached by direct dialing today. The telephone directory carries a listing of cities and states and their area codes. In order to place a call to any of these localities, dial "1" first, the area code second, and then the local telephone number of the individual. If the city or town is not listed at the front of the telephone directory, refer to the area code directory; then call the directory assistance operator in that area and give the name and address of the party you want to reach.

A station-to-station call is made to a particular telephone number, and the caller speaks to anyone who answers the telephone. Therefore, if someone answers the ring, the individual making the call is charged for it, and the charges start as soon as the call is answered. However, this type of call is less costly, is more frequently made, and is usually faster than the person-to-person call.

Person-to-person calls. To place a person-to-person call, the secretary dials zero, the three-digit area code, and then the telephone number; at this point the operator intercepts and the secretary gives the name of the individual being called. When the call is put through, the person called may not be present or available to take the call. Then a decision may have to be made as to whether someone else at that number can handle the transaction. A person-to-person call is made to a particular person only, and the caller is not charged for the call unless the person called is reached or the caller consents to speak to some other specifically identified individual. Charges start as soon as the caller consents to the call and begins speaking; therefore, the secretary should not start a conversation, but must make sure that the employer is ready to take the call immediately. A "1" is not needed in person-to-person calls because the operator intercepts.

Direct distance dialing. Almost all calls in the United States and abroad may be put through by means of direct distance dialing. A "1" must precede the area code. A list of the area codes one must use for direct dialing is found at the beginning of the telephone directory or in the expanded area code directory available from the telephone company. The direct dialing system works by dialing "1" and a three-digit area code, followed by the local telephone number. There are no two areas that have the same area code, nor are there two identical telephone numbers in an area. The numbers of adjacent geographical area codes are widely different numerically to help avoid confusion and error. It is a quick and accurate system. If a wrong number is reached, the secretary, before disconnecting, should ascertain the name of the city that was reached. He or she should then dial the operator, or in some cases the credit bureau, and promptly report that an incorrect destination was reached, so that the telephone bill will not reflect a charge for the wrong number. Also, if the transmission was poor or the call was cut off, the operator or the credit bureau should be called in order that the appropriate adjustment may be made.

The phone directory also explains how to use direct dialing for credit-card and collect calls and for overseas calls. A "1" must also precede the area code.

Time differences. It is vital to check the differences in time when planning to place a long-distance call. One must be aware not only that this country is divided into time zones, but also that certain regions change to daylight saving time during the summer months and that differences in time exist in all countries. For example, the United States (excluding Alaska and Hawaii) is divided into four standard-time zones: Eastern, Central, Mountain, and Pacific. Each zone is one hour earlier than the zone immediately to the east of it: when it is 12 noon Eastern Standard Time, it is 11 A.M. in the Central zone, 10 A.M. in the Mountain zone, and 9 A.M. Pacific time. Greenwich Mean Time, which is the mean solar time of the meridian at Greenwich, England, is used as the basis for standard time throughout most of the world. For specific time information, consult the tables in Chapter 25.

Appointment Calls

The telephone operator is asked to put through a person-to-person call at a specified hour. Contact is established at the time indicated and the caller is then notified that the connection has been made. The charge for such a call is the same as that for an ordinary person-to-person call. This service is not available for international calls.

Sequence Calls

The sequence-calls service is of value when a number of calls are to be made to out-of-town points. Much time is saved by furnishing the operator with a list, oral or written, of the calls to be made at the specified times. The secretary should supply the names of the individuals to be called, the cities and states where they are located, their telephone numbers, if known, and the hour at which the executive wishes to speak to each person on the list. However, it should be noted that this is an expensive procedure, as each call is charged at the "operator-assisted call" rate. If the secretary makes the calls by direct dialing, money is saved.

Conference Calls

Another instance of the various accommodations that the telephone company offers its subscribers is the conference service. It is of particular value to executives of organizations with branches and/or plants located over a wide area who find it necessary to confer speedily with those at the different branches. The telephone company provides two methods for setting up a telephone conference.

1. An arrangement can be made with the conference operator to connect several people in various cities simultaneously for a conference or discussion. No special equipment is required for this hookup.

2. An arrangement can be made with the conference operator whereby a conference call can be placed to a large group of employees. This type of call requires setting up a loudspeaker at the called point in a different city, so that the executive can talk by phone to the entire group at one time.

When placing such a call, the secretary should signal the operator; ask for the conference operator; describe the setup desired; and furnish the names of the people to be called, their telephone numbers, if known, the city and state where each is located, and the time of the conference.

Collect Calls

Calls can be charged to the phone of the person who is being called. The individual called may either accept the call and be charged for it or refuse the call and, of course, not be charged. Collect call rates are higher than direct-dialed station-to-station rates. A subscriber can also charge to his or her own phone long-distance calls placed from other phones. It behooves the efficient secretary to discuss with the employer when collect charges should be accepted. Determine from whom collect charges will be honored. If in doubt, ask the operator to wait while the matter is checked with the executive.

Overseas Calls

You can direct-dial many overseas points. Information on such calls can be obtained from the front pages of the directory, the International Dial brochures, or from the long-distance operator. For person-to-person overseas calls, the secretary must dial the long-distance operator and ask for an overseas operator. The name of the person to be called and the telephone number, if known, must be provided. The charges for this service are higher than those for domestic calls. There are reduced rates for evenings and for nights and weekends. (See section on "Telephoning a Telegram.")

Calls to Ships, Planes, Trains, and Automobiles

Telephone calls to mobile conveyances by way of radio telephone are similarly made by the operator. Such service is not available without the installation of special equipment by the telephone company in the car, plane, or ship, of course. Calls can then be placed directly from the office telephone to the destination desired. (See section on "Satellite Communications Network.")

Returning Long-Distance Calls

Frequently a long-distance call is received when the executive is not in the office to take it. In such a case, the long-distance operator will give the secretary the operator's number, the city calling, and the name and telephone number of the person calling. To return the call, the secretary must dial the operator, ask by number for the operator who placed the call, and identify the city from which the call originated. When the connection is made with the proper operator, the secretary should tell the employer the name and telephone number of the person who placed the call. Collect calls are excluded from this service.

Telephone Record Keeping

Many organizations require that a record be kept of all long-distance calls made, in order to verify the telephone bill, and have special printed forms for this purpose. The secretary may ask the telephone operator, when placing such calls, to provide the charges when the call is completed. However, the request for charges must be made in advance, not after the call is completed. If you log long-distance calls, record the following: date, time, and caller.

Special Telephone Equipment and Systems

A good secretary should be familiar with the various types of telephone equipment available, in order to meet the needs of the company and those of the executive. Tremendous strides have been made in the field of telephone research. Not only business but also the world in general benefits from the discoveries made by telephone technicians and telephone researchers.

Call director. A push-button telephone that provides the capacity of several ordinary push-button phones in one compact, attractive unit is known as the Call Director. It can handle up to 29 lines and is available in 18- to 30-button models, which can be adjusted as needs change. The Call Director can be combined with the speakerphone feature (see below), which makes it possible to telephone with the hands free when needed. A plug-in headset model is also available; this frees the hands so that the secretary can take notes, consult records, and so forth.

The telephone company has also added the conference feature to the Call Director. This permits an executive to set up an intercom conference by merely dialing a code or pushing a button.

Speakerphone set. The speakerphone consists of a microphone and a loudspeaker and permits the user to carry on a telephone conversation clearly from anywhere in an office without lifting the receiver from its rest. The microphone picks up the user's voice, and the loudspeaker, with an adjustable volume control, broadcasts it to the party at the other end of the line. By sitting around the microphone, all members of a group can engage in a telephone conversation at one time. Everybody can talk and offer a viewpoint, and everybody can hear and understand fully what is being discussed.

Direct inward dialing. A setup is available whereby an outside caller can dial the central office designation, followed by the extension needed, and thereby put the call directly to the office desired instead of to the switchboard operator.

Dataphone. The Dataphone is a telephone-computer setup which, after activation by human hands, enables office machines to talk to one another and transmit data at tremendous speeds in various machine-usable forms.

AT&T's Merlin. This system is equipped with a microprocessor and has its own internal software. Programming features are possible.

These include automatic dialing, privacy, and "do not disturb" mechanisms. Expansion is possible with other custom features and outside lines.

AT&T's Key 416. The key system links a group of key telephones. Each telephone permits the user to select an intercom or outside line. Paging is possible. The ultimate capacity is 16 stations, 4 central office lines, and 2 intercom paths. It is also possible to set up multiline conferences. Other systems include:

System			Lines	Stations
Com	Key	718	7	18
Com	Key	1434	14	34
Com	Key	2152	21	52

The Com Key system offers many standard and optional features and a choice of telephone sets in various colors.

Custom Calling services. These services are available on individual and auxiliary lines for both business and residence telephones. These features can be provided if a customer is served by the central office of ESS (Electronic Switching System). Custom Calling services will operate in connection with rotary or touch-tone service. There are four Custom Calling services.

Call waiting. This service is designed to let the called party know that someone is trying to call while the telephone is in use.

Call forwarding. This service transfers calls to another number when the called party is not at the office or at home.

Three-way calling. A third party may be cut into an existing conversation.

Speed calling. One or two digits can be dialed in order to reach local or long-distance numbers more quickly.

To obtain Custom Calling services, it is not necessary to install extra equipment nor to have an installer visit. These services are available with the regular telephone setup and may be attained by request at the central telephone office.

Dimension PBX. This electronic system uses stored program control, a time division switching network, and switched loop consoles. It is modular in design and has a solid-state system; therefore it saves space, speeds operation, and simplifies installation and maintenance. There are two types of systems that are available to customers:

Dimension 400 has an approximate capacity of 400 lines and 90 trunks.

Dimension 2000 has an approximate capacity of 2000 lines and 350 trunks.

However, the capacity of lines and trunks for both Dimension 400 and 2000 may change depending upon the line and trunk combinations and how they are used. Information on Dimension PBX or any other type PBX telephone system or service may be obtained by calling the local telephone company.

Dataspeed 40 service. This communication service transmits the written word. It is available for private-line and expanded switched networks. The Dataspeed 40 Selective Calling System is designed for use with private-line applications in both half duplex and full duplex. ("Full duplex" pertains to a simultaneous two-way and independent transmission in both directions. "Half duplex" service permits communication alternately in either direction or in one direction only.) Data is always prepared on a typewriter prior to transmission. All transmissions are fast, because the data proceeds at a maximum speed rather than the slower keyboard speed. The transmission accuracy is high, since the data is displayed on a monitor in its entirety before it is sent. This permits editing of data before transmission if necessary.

Horizon communications system. This is a microprocessor-controlled system that utilizes stored programs and multibutton electronic telephone (MET) sets. It has a capacity of 32 lines and 79 stations (excluding bridged, not MET, stations). A customer access unit (CAU) provides the ability to make feature changes or telephone-set rearrangements. There are further standard and optional features for both the stations and the system that are too numerous to mention. Local telephone companies can be called for further detailed information.

Picturephone meeting service. With this service a videophone, which is a telephone combined with a television receiver and transmitter, enables users to see, as well as speak to, one another. The service is offered in color in a limited area and in black and white between several large cities. It brings people together for an important meeting so that everyone can participate. It makes it possible to conduct monthly or quarterly administrative reviews, to introduce new products to the sales force, to screen applicants for employment, to resolve production or distribution conflicts, to handle emergencies, etc. Visual aids such as slides, charts, artwork, or graphs may be used to illustrate or clarify facts discussed. Hard copies of information can be transmitted and videotapes can be sent or received. This service has now advanced to video-conferencing, a new technology.

Portable conference telephone set. This permits individuals from an audience to speak directly to the speaker, to ask or answer questions, by means of a standard telephone receiver that may be carried anywhere; it connects to a standard telephone jack.

Computerized Branch Exchange (CBX). This system is used for large offices. This type of exchange can handle up to 800 stations. It is controlled by a microcomputer that automatically chooses the circuits to use and determines holding times.

Touch-tone telephones. These telephones have buttons. All numbers are used; the symbols # and * are for special services. The "tone" permits the transmission of data to computers, similar to voice communications, a new technology. They are much easier to use than rotary-dial telephones.

Touch-A-Matic. This automatic telephone dialer "remembers" up to 15 (or 31, depending on the type) numbers. It dials them at the touch of a button. Numbers may be added or changed at will.

Wide Area Telecommunications Service (WATS). This service allows subscribers to contract for station-to-station calls within a specified service area at a fixed monthly rate, in lieu of individual call billing. It includes a listing in the National Information Center Records (800-555-1212); by calling this number a subscriber can obtain the number of any other WATS-line subscriber.

Outward WATS provides outgoing direct-distance dialing of long-distance calls by means of a WATS line from the customer's premises to other telephones within a specified service area. Each WATS line has its own WATS number.

Inward WATS allows a subscriber to receive calls over a WATS line without charge to the originating party. The call is automatically charged to the called number without the announcement and acceptance necessary with a collect call.

Service areas number 1 through 7 indicate interstate service. Included within the range of WATS service is all of the United States including Alaska, Hawaii, Puerto Rico, and the U.S. Virgin Islands (St. Thomas, St. Croix, and St. John). The purchase of one service area, 2 through 7, includes the area or areas in the lower numbered service area or areas. Service area "0" is an intrastate service available only in some states. WATS service is available in either of two forms.

Full business day. The initial period allows 240 hours including up to 14,400 completed incoming station-to-station calls a month from any telephone within the specified service area.

Measured. The initial period allows 10 hours including up to 600 completed station-to-station calls a month from any telephone within the specified service area.

Card dialers. A plastic card is inserted in an automatic dialing telephone. The cards are coded with frequently called numbers. The number is dialed rapidly and accurately by the telephone mechanism. In a business that makes a great many calls to the same numbers, the amount of time saved by these cards can be considerable. The telephone that takes the cards may be used in a normal way.

Bellboy. This is a signaling device that may be kept in the pocket, purse, or briefcase. When the user is within a certain range of the office, the Bellboy will beep when the secretary dials its number. The user then goes to the nearest telephone and calls the office to receive the message.

Another name for Bellboy is "Beeper." Due to the advances in electronic communication, beepers may be activated up to 30 miles. Specially manufactured, "high-tech" beepers may range 30 miles plus. These are now common communication devices for top executives.

Telephone Answering Services

Many offices maintain contact with customers or others in the business world through an answering service that takes calls at night and on weekends and holidays. For a small office that closes entirely for vacations, an answering service is valuable.

The answering service may transfer the messages taken by calling at the beginning of the next business day. However, it is more common for the secretary to call in periodically and take the messages that have been received.

Trial and error may be necessary in finding a reliable answering service. If the service does not have enough lines or operators and callers are put on "hold" for unreasonable lengths of time, much good will can be lost. Then again, it is important to have a service that can be trusted to take messages accurately. The secretary planning to engage an answering service will do well to consult other secretaries and take their recommendations. Once the system is in operation, the secretary should check response time regularly.

When it comes time to take the messages from an answering service, the secretary should have pen and paper on hand and be scrupulously accurate in transcribing any messages given, and especially so if the answering device does not have playback equipment. A set of priorities may be set up in advance with the employer as to which messages call for immediate action and which may be delayed for a shorter or greater length of time.

A sophisticated service available through the telephone company has an apparatus by which the subscriber can dial a two-digit code and have incoming calls transferred to an answering service. This does not "tie up" the line, as the subscriber may still make outgoing calls. When the subscriber wishes to disengage the service, a second two-digit code will restore the incoming calls to the client's own telephone line. Telephone answering services also provide "wake-up" calls, courtesy calls, and reminder-of-appointment calls at an additional cost.

Telephone Answering Devices

A great variety of telephone answering devices, usually activating a cassette tape recorder, are available. The simplest of these give a recorded message, as for example a statement telling the caller when the person called will be available, telling hours when the business is open, or the like. An equally common type is the recorder in which the person called has prerecorded a message that invites the caller to leave a message. When a tone sounds, the caller can talk for varying lengths of time, depending upon the way in which the recorder is set to operate.

Messages recorded by such a device should be transcribed by the secretary as early as possible at the start of a business day. If it is not possible to understand clearly any portion of a message, a notation should be placed on the transcript to alert the employer that the secretary was not sure of the message given.

A remote-control feature on such devices as the Phone-mate allows the user to call the device on any telephone from anyplace in the world and hear whatever messages have been recorded. One phone call plays all messages, and a special feature allows the user to replay any given message without waiting for the entire tape to rewind and replay.

Record Keeping

8

Data Management

by Charlotte B. Holmquest
revised by Julie Eichenberger

An efficient filing system is one that reduces clutter, separates information into recognizable categories, and makes possible the rapid and accurate retrieval of documents. There are several standard methods, and each has its advantages and disadvantages. Nevertheless, it is not the system but the use of it that determines its effectiveness. Documents are filed so they can be found. This applies especially to information needed for making day-to-day management decisions. Given the system, the secretary should be able to pull a document from a file within five minutes of a request.

A large organization may employ a number of clerks who are responsible for maintaining company records kept in a central area. In a small office there may be only a few file cabinets. In either case, the secretary must be familiar with the systems commonly used, because every office depends on one or another of them.

In today's offices the processing of data in ever-increasing amounts has led to the proliferation of desk-top computers. Many have the capability to tie in with mainframe computers. Even though traditional filing systems continue to be used, the secretary in the electronic office must be prepared to access computer-generated documents quickly and efficiently.

TRADITIONAL FILING SYSTEMS

The basic filing systems in use in the modern office are alphabetic, combination subject, numeric, and phonetic. Alphabetic filing encompasses filing papers by name, subject, or geographic location in alphabetical order. Combination subject systems utilize both numbers and words or numbers and letters arranged in alphabetical order. Such names as alpha-numeric, subject-numeric, and duplex-numeric appear in this category. Non-alphabetic filing exercises the use of numbers for filing purposes; and such terms as numeric, decimal, terminal digit, triple digit, and middle digit are in this category. The phonetic filing system involves using letters and sounds in code number form.

Filing systems may be direct or indirect. In a *direct method of filing,* a person can locate a file immediately, without first having to refer to a cross-index file to find out where to look. In an *indirect filing system,* a person cannot immediately locate the file but must refer to a cross-index file to determine where to locate it. For example, if the basic filing system is a subject system and the secretary wishes to locate the file for a specific firm, he or she must either know the subject under which the firm is filed or refer to an alphabetical cross-index, looking up the firm name and finding out in which subject file the file is located.

Alphabetic Systems

Almost 90% of all filing that is done in the office is alphabetic. In this type of system the office correspondence and other papers are filed alphabetically according to name, geographic location, or subject.

Name

In a name file, all papers are filed alphabetically according to the last name of the person or the name of a company. It is a direct method of filing. It is very simple to expand a name file because any new name is filed alphabetically without disturbing the name before or after it.

Geographic Location

In the geographic system the papers are filed alphabetically according to the name of the state; then alphabetically according to the town or city within that state; then alphabetically according to the name of the correspondent within the town or city. Mail-order houses, public-utility companies, publishing houses, and organizations that serve a geographic district or have branch offices in different areas use this system of filing.

The geographic system of filing is an indirect system. It is not possible to locate the file for a specific firm without first referring to a cross-index that lists the names of the firms in alphabetical order and gives the location of each firm. In other words, if you do not know the location of the firm, you must refer to the cross index under the firm name and determine under what geographic location to find the file.

Subject

When a company deals with products, supplies, materials, advertising, and so forth, the subject system is used. It is an indirect system, because a cross-index file is used to save time in filing and finding material and in locating correspondence by firm name when the subject is doubtful. The folders in the subject file are arranged alphabetically by the name of the product. The material within the folders is arranged by date, with the latest date in the front of the folder.

Often a combination of subject file and name file is used. If there is not enough material to set up a separate subject file, the subject captions are set up in a name file.

Combination Subject Systems

Some companies that use the subject filing system have found it necessary to use major subject titles with separate sub-categories relating to that major topic so that locating specific information is quicker. A major subject outline containing the most important titles is set up in alphabetical order. Next, subcategory subject titles within each area are placed beneath the major subject titles. Then, numbers are used in combination with the subjects in the outline to make up the *combination subject filing system.*

When a company uses the combination subject filing system, it is extremely important that an up-to-date list be kept of all subjects and their code letters and numbers. This list should be circulated to all persons and departments needing access to the files. Likewise, a *relative index* should be made, listing all possible subjects and where information might be located pertaining to that subject. This list, too, should be updated frequently and distributed to those using the files.

Types of Combination Subject Files

Some of the combination subject filing systems used are:

Subject-Numeric. This system uses the major subject title with numbers assigned to the subcategories underneath it. For example, the subject heading "Automobile Accessories" would be treated in this manner:

AUTOMOBILE ACCESSORIES
1 Automobile Accessories: Tires
1-1 Standard Black
1-2 Whitewall

Duplex-Numeric. This system makes use of both numbers and letters of the alphabet. A digit is selected for the subject; this is followed by a dash and another digit for a division of the subject, plus a letter for further subdivision. For example, the subject heading "Automobile Accessories" might be given the number 8; the division "Automobile Accessories: Tires" would be numbered 8-1; a further subdivision, "Automobile Accessories: Tires, Standard Black," would be numbered 8-1a; "Automobile Accessories: Tires, Whitewall" would be numbered 8-1b. The outline would look like this:

8 AUTOMOBILE ACCESSORIES
8-1 Automobile Accessories: Tires
8-1a Standard Black
8-1b Whitewall

Alpha-Numeric. This system uses letters of the alphabet for the major subject titles along with letters and numbers for subtopics:

A ADMINISTRATION
A1 Long-Range Planning
A1-1 Guidelines and Schedules
A2 Competition
A2-1 Survey Reports
A3 Public Relations

G GOVERNMENT RELATIONS
G1 Air Pollution Control
G1-1 Vehicle Emissions
G1-1-1 Health Hazards

Numeric Systems

Numeric filing systems are nonalphabetic. All records are filed solely by numbers.

When the numeric system is used, an *accession register* must be kept to make retrieving a particular file a quick process. The accession register is a book or card file that contains each file number beginning with the first number as well as the correspondent's name on that file. The correspondents' names should be alphabetized so that one can get the file quickly if a correspondent's file number has been forgotten.

Types of Numeric Filing Systems

There are several types of numeric filing systems, some used only in highly specialized businesses.

Straight numeric. This system has records filed according to strict numeric sequence. Folder number 1 is given to the first client or account; folder number 2 is given to the second, and so forth, in strict numeric order.

Terminal digit. In this system, numbers on a file are read from right to left. Usually, the last, or terminal, two digits are the drawer number, the next two digits are the folder number, and any other numbers indicate the sequence within the folders. For example, an insurance policy numbered 567,123 would be stored in drawer 23, folder 71, and the 56 would refer to its sequence in the folder.

Triple digit. This system is similar to the terminal-digit system, except that the numbers are read in three digits instead of two. The terminal three digits of a number are called the "primary" numbers, and the remaining digits refer to the sequence of the papers in the folders bearing the primary numbers. For example, the insurance policy numbered 567,123 would be found in folder 123, and 567 would refer to its sequence in the folder.

Middle digit. The third and fourth digits from the right are separated from the last two digits on the right. For example, in the insurance policy number 567,123, the policy would be filed in folder 71, and 23 would refer to its sequence in the folder.

Decimal system. The decimal system is used only in highly specialized businesses. The system may be based on the Dewey decimal system, which is the system commonly used by public libraries, though many are switching to the Library of Congress Catalog card system.

Phonetic Systems

The phonetic filing system is a filing method based on the use of letters and sounds. Organizations that file records by individuals' surnames encounter the problem of filing names that sound alike but are spelled differently, such as Smith and Smyth or Schmidt and Schmitt. To eliminate this problem, the Remington Rand Office Systems Division of the Sperry Rand Corporation developed the Soundex Phonetic Filing System. Soundex is a combination of spelling, or sounds, and numbers. Basic sounds are represented by six fundamental letters, the consonants B, C, D, L, M, and R, which make up the entire Soundex alphabet. Each of these consonants is given a separate code number: B is 1, C is 2, D is 3, L is 4, M is 5, and R is 6. The remaining consonants in the alphabet have the same relative sounds as the six basic Soundex consonants and are grouped with the *basic* consonant. All vowels and the letters W, H, and Y have no number and are not coded. To use this system, look at the *first* letter of the *surname* and sort by *that letter* first. Then code the *remaining* letters in the surname by looking at the following chart.

Code	Key Letters and Equivalents
1	B F P V
2	C G J K Q S X Z
3	D T
4	L
5	M N
6	R

To file the surname "Snyder," the first letter, S, is recorded. The next letter to be coded is N, which is code 5. Y is disregarded, D is code 3, E is disregarded, and R is code 6. The surname "Snyder" is thus coded S536.

To file the surname "Day," code a D and three zeros to show that only vowels follow the first consonant, D. When no consonants or not enough consonants follow the first letter in the surname, use one, two, or three zeros to give the name a three-digit code. The code for "Day" is D000. The surname "Shaw" is S000, Levy is L100, and Kelly is K400.

PHYSICAL SETUP OF FILES

The file drawer contains primary guides that divide the file into alphabetic sections or numeric sections. These primary guides are placed at the beginning of each section. The tabs may be on the left-hand side or in the middle of the file drawer. Secondary guides are used to subdivide the section or to call attention to important names or numbers. Individual folders, arranged alphabetically, chronologically, or in numeric sequence, are placed directly behind the guides. Individual folders are used for correspondents who communicate frequently with the firm. When there are from five to eight pieces of correspondence from the same source, an individual folder is set up. The full name of the correspondent is on the tab. Tabs are usually alternated in position so that one does not come directly behind another. When material is arranged in an individual folder, the latest date is always in the front of the folder.

When material is placed in a miscellaneous folder, it should be arranged alphabetically with the latest date in front for each person or subject. Miscellaneous folders follow the individual folders at the end of each major division. They are used for correspondence that does not warrant individual folders. The tab on the miscellaneous folder may be of a different size or be marked with a distinctive color so that it can be easily located.

In preparing index tabs and labels for guides and folders, type the letter of the alphabet or the name. The first typing space below the fold of the file-drawer label should be used, and typing should start two spaces from the left of the label. Use initial capitals and indent the second and each succeeding line two spaces so that the first word on the top line will stand out. Use abbreviations if the name or subject is long. Use the largest type possible when typing file-drawer labels, or print these labels.

PREPARATION OF MATERIAL FOR FILING

Check all papers to see whether they are to be filed and have been released for filing. Sort the correspondence into personal, business, contracts, and the like. Remove all staples, paper clips, or other paper holders. Underline the name in colored pencil to indicate where the letter is to be filed. Indicate the guide number in the upper right-hand corner. Use a colored pencil to circle important words to help to locate a particular paper when it is needed. Make any cross-reference sheets that are required. A *cross-reference sheet* is made out when a letter or a record may be filed in one of two places. File the letter or record under the most important name and cross-refer the second name or subject. For example, a letter may be received from Jordan Marsh Company. It would be filed under Jordan (first unit) Marsh (second unit) Company (third unit), and a cross-reference made out for Marsh, Jordan Company. The cross-reference sheet would read:

Marsh, Jordan Company
SEE
Jordan Marsh Company

Below is a simple step-by-step checklist to use when getting ready to file material:

1. *Inspection*. Read or scan the material. Put a check mark in the upper left-hand corner to signal that this material should be filed.
2. *Indexing*. Determine which *name* or *subject* to use for filing the material. This is vital, as poor indexing means poor "finding" and a loss of time.
3. *Coding*. Coding is the physical act of marking the name, subject, etc., under which the material is to be filed. Put the code in the upper right-hand corner. Make cross-reference sheets at this point.
4. *Sorting*. Sort the material in a rough, superficial manner—all A's together, all B's together, etc., in alphabetical order. Put all 10's together, all 20's together, etc., for numeric filing. Then sort each stack according to "strict sorting," using the standard filing rules the firm uses.
5. *Filing*. Place correspondence in the folders, top to the left of the folder. Put material in the miscellaneous folder alphabetically, with the latest date on top. Place material in individual folders chronologically, latest date on top.

REMOVING FILES

When it is necessary to take material from the file, replace the record or correspondence with an "out" guide or card. On the "out" guide, record the date, the name of the record taken, who has it, and the date it is to be returned. The word "out" should be printed on the tab, and stock of a different color should be used so that the guide stands out. It is necessary to record the withdrawal of the material if it goes out of the office for a period of time or if the employer is going to use it away from the office. Confidential records should be used in the office and returned to the files immediately.

CARD FILE

A card file (usually with 3″ × 5″ cards) arranged alphabetically by name of person or subject is often imperative for finding needed manuscripts or correspondence. In many offices, two separate card files are maintained, one for subject and the second for the name of the writer of each piece of material. If there are a great many different sets of files in an office, each needs to be clearly identified to make the card file useful.

Each card should hold as much information as necessary for retrieval of needed material. It should contain subject, along with any pertinent subcategory; name of person and/or date (if pertinent); set of files in which the material is stored; and any notes that will aid the secretary or executive in learning exactly what will be found in the file being sought.

FILING EQUIPMENT

Files may be kept in standard four-drawer file cabinets or in open-shelf files.

File Cabinets

The standard office filing cabinet has four drawers that hold file folders enclosing material on the regulation $8\frac{1}{2}'' \times 11''$ typing paper. A law office or company with many legal papers will need a wider cabinet to accommodate legal cap.

The standard drawer will carry a load of from 60 to 70 pounds. For efficient filing, the file drawers should not be overcrowded. The secretary should take note at what intervals the files start to become overcrowded and take appropriate action.

The files should be arranged so that there is a minimum of walking required to and from the files. The file drawers may be labeled in either vertical (top to bottom) or horizontal (left to right) order. Space may be saved if the file cabinets are backed up against a wall. If there are many cabinets, it may be more efficient to arrange them in a cluster in the center of a room. Floor space is expensive; therefore, some consideration should be given to arranging cabinets economically. Adequate aisle space between cabinets must be allowed. At least 28 inches must be allowed for a file drawer when it is opened into the aisle. There should be gaps in long rows of cabinets to save time in getting from one row to another. This is particularly important for the file supervisor who has to make spot checks of the file drawers and to assist the file clerks.

Lateral or Open-Shelf Filing

For certain kinds of filing, the open-shelf method is more appropriate than the use of file drawers. This "lateral" or shelf filing may result in the saving of as much as 40 percent of the office floor space needed for files. The aisles between the shelves can be considerably narrower than those needed between cabinets with drawers, because the additional space for pulling out drawers is not needed. Also, files can be stacked higher than drawers—in many instances, to the ceiling.

Lateral filing is particularly useful for active files in which papers are inserted and withdrawn constantly and which are not to be retained for a long period of time. Proponents of lateral filing claim much time is saved by having the files immediately at hand and in sight.

COLOR CODING

Color coding can be a worthwhile expedient, permitting easier location of specific files or file sections. Before making a decision about color coding, the secretary should study the various methods available and determine which would be best for the particular type of material filed in the office for which the system is intended.

Color coding is usually employed to identify a filing series that has been categorized by the alphabetic system or any of the several numeric systems discussed earlier in this chapter. A specific color is assigned to each number or letter. One manufacturer of filing materials (Datafile) uses twelve colors twice, the second time with a white bar that sets it apart from the first. These 24 colors, with white for Y and gray for Z, serve for the 26 letters of the alphabet.

This represents one of the great variety of color coding systems that have been worked out. The pattern used depends on the complexity of the material to be filed. Datafile, using its twelve colors, also has folders with two color bands for identification of the first two letters of a word or name. By identifying two letters, the file is expanded from the 26 letters of the alphabet to about three or four hundred segments. The possible total is 26×26, or 676, but all combinations of letters do not occur at the beginning of words or names.

Color coding may be used with either open-shelf filing or with files in closed file cabinets.

With Open-Shelf Files

For some kinds of open-shelf filing, the plain manila folder and/or hanging file folders are used, with a much simpler color code. One company that keeps order files for exactly two years before discard uses a color-coded dot on the folders holding the records for alternate years. Thus the file at any particular time consists of folders marked in one color for one of the years represented, unmarked folders for another, and a second colored dot for the third. If, for example, the date is March 1986, the folders for April through December of 1984 (January through March having been discarded) have dots of one color, the folders for 1985 are plain, and the folders for January to date in 1986 have dots of a second color. Folders for 1987 will be plain, and the system will repeat.

In summary, color coding may be effected on shelf filing by folders of a solid color; by folders with color bands; by stick-on dots in an upper corner of a manila file folder; by tabs that protrude; or by tabs that slip on, clip on, or are pasted on the folders. The tabbed folders may be bought prepared or assembled by the secretary or file clerk.

In File Cabinets

Color coding of files within drawers can be equally effective. Durable plastic file folders may be purchased in a wide variety of colors, or a color tab may be affixed to manila folders or hanging dividers. One of the common ways to use these is to select a new color for each year within an alphabetic file.

INDEXING AND ALPHABETIZING

Indexing is the arrangement of the names on the folder tab or on cards. The folders and cards are arranged alphabetically for simplicity of filing and finding. The following indexing rules are standard rules for filing. The Association of Records Managers and Administrators, Inc. (ARMA) uses these guidelines with minor exceptions, which will be noted toward the end of this section.

Individual names. Names of individuals are indexed by the last name (the surname) first, then the first name, and then the middle initial or middle name, if any:

Name	Indexing Order
Alfred M. Amell	Amell, Alfred M.
Grace R. Gladd	Gladd, Grace R.
J. Thomas Williams	Williams, J. Thomas

Business names. The names of business establishments, institutions, and organizations are indexed as they are written, unless they embody the name of an individual. An exception to this rule is the names of schools. When the individual's name is part of a firm name, index by considering the last name (surname) first, then the first name and the middle initial or middle name, if any.

Name	Indexing Order
Atlantic Service Station	Atlantic Service Station
Earl A. Stone Book Publishers	Stone, Earl A. Book Publishers
General Department Store	General Department Store
James A. Carson Company	Carson, James A. Company
J. M. Morgan Sign Company	Morgan, J. M. Sign Company
Nathan Hale Junior High School	Nathan Hale Junior High School
Rose and Peter Beauty Supplies	Rose and Peter Beauty Supplies
Rose Peter Beauty Shoppe	Peter, Rose Beauty Shoppe
Rose's Beauty Salon	Rose's Beauty Salon
Stone and Book Publishing Company	Stone and Book Publishing Company
Stone Book Publishers	Stone Book Publishers
Thomas Milford Stiles Florist Shop	Stiles, Thomas Milford Florist Shop
Troy Sand and Gravel, Inc.	Troy Sand and Gravel, Inc.

Alphabetical order. Names are alphabetized by comparing each of their letters. If the first units are alike, compare the second units. If there is no second unit, the single name is filed first. The rule of "nothing before something" applies here. A surname followed by a first initial only goes before the same surname followed by a complete first name beginning with the same letter as the initial—again, "nothing before something."

	Indexing Order	
Name	*Unit 1*	*Unit 2*
Carson	Carson	
Carson Brothers	Carson	Brothers
J. Carson	Carson	J.
James Carson	Carson	James

Letters used as words. Consider any single letter as a word and not part of a cluster or part of an acronym.

	Indexing Order			
Name	*Unit 1*	*Unit 2*	*Unit 3*	*Unit 4*
N A P A Jobbers	N	A	P	A
N C R Accounting Company	N	C	R	Accounting
Pacific Car Company	Pacific	Car	Company	
R & B Auto Service	R	B	Auto	Service

Abbreviations. Abbreviations are indexed as though they are the words they are representing written out in full; hence, "Mme." is indexed as "Madame."

	Indexing Order		
Name	*Unit 1*	*Unit 2*	*Unit 3*
Mme. Sophie's Boutique	Madame	Sophie's	Boutique
Mr. Pete's Grocery	Mister	Pete's	Grocery
St. Alexis Hospital	Saint	Alexis	Hospital

Article "the." When *the* is part of the name, it is disregarded in filing. If it is the initial word, it is placed at the end of the name in parentheses.

If *the* occurs in the body of the name, it is placed in parentheses and disregarded.

Name	Indexing Order
The Cleveland Boat Company	Cleveland Boat Company (The)
Danny the Tailor	Danny (the) Tailor
Stanley of the Ritz	Stanley (of the) Ritz

Such words as *and, for, on, in, by,* and *of the* are disregarded in indexing and filing. However, they are placed in parentheses when writing names on folders and cards.

Hyphenated names. Hyphenated firm names are treated as separate names, because they represent separate individuals; when listed among other proper names, the second name is to be regarded as a given name for alphabetizing purposes.

Name	Indexing Order
Branch-Merrill Company	Branch Merrill Company
Richard T. Branch	Branch, Richard T.
Winifred I. Wilson	Wilson, Winifred I.
Wilson-Wyman, Inc.	Wilson Wyman, Inc.

Hyphenated individual names are treated as one name, because they represent one individual.

Name	Indexing Order
James A. Gladd-Monroe	GladdMonroe, James A.
Patricia Lloyd-Taylor	LloydTaylor, Patricia
Jane L. Marin-Jones	MarinJones, Jane L.

One- or two-word names. Names that may be spelled as one word or two words are usually considered as one word.

Name	Indexing Order Unit 1	Unit 2	Unit 3
Raybrook Cleaners	Raybrook	Cleaners	
Ray Brook Paint Company	RayBrook	Paint	Company
South East Electric Shop	SouthEast	Electric	Shop
Southeast Supply Company	Southeast	Supply	Company
Good Will Cleaners	GoodWill	Cleaners	
Goodwill Industries	Goodwill	Industries	

Individual surnames with prefixes. Prefixes such as D', d', De, de, Del, Des, Di, Du, Fitz, l', La, Le, M', Mac, Mc, O', Van, Von, and so on, are indexed as written and treated as one word.

	Indexing Order		
Name	*Unit 1*	*Unit 2*	*Unit 3*
D'Aoust, James	D'Aoust	James	
Darling, John E.	Darling	John	E.
De Lancett, Morris	De Lancett	Morris	
DeLancey, Lincoln	DeLancey	Lincoln	
MacDonald, George H.	MacDonald	George	H.
McCasland, Raymond A.	McCasland	Raymond	A.
Van Cour, Elsie A.	Van Cour	Elsie	A.
Von Ottenfeld, Oscar M.	Von Ottenfeld	Oscar	M.

Words ending in "s." When a name ends in "s'" or "'s," the "s" is considered part of the name.

	Indexing Order		
Name	*Unit 1*	*Unit 2*	*Unit 3*
Bob's Sport Shop	Bob's	Sport	Shop
Boy Scout Camp	Boy	Scout	Camp
Boys' Clothing Store	Boys'	Clothing	Store
Williams' Dry Cleaning	Williams'	Dry	Cleaning
William's Service Station	William's	Service	Station
Wilson, John M.	Wilson	John	M.

Titles. A personal or professional title or degree is usually not considered in indexing and filing. When the name is written, the title is placed in parentheses at the end of the name.

Name	*Indexed as*
Dr. Richard P. Bellaire	Bellaire, Richard P. (Dr.)
Ms. Helen Hayles	Hayles, Helen (Ms.)
Grace M. Janson, D.D.	Janson, Grace M. (D.D.)

A religious or foreign title is considered as the first indexing unit when it is followed by a given name only.

Indexed and filed as

Brother Francis
Madame Eugenie
Prince Charles
Princess Anne
Sister Mary Megan

Married women's names. The name of a married woman is indexed according to the name by which she prefers to be known. Some women retain their maiden names after marriage and this preference should be respected. A married name could be a woman's given first name, her maiden surname, and her husband's surname, or it could be her given first and middle names (or initial for the middle name) and her husband's surname. The title "Mrs." is disregarded in filing, but it is placed in parentheses after the name. If signatures on correspondence from a married woman indicate that she prefers "Ms.," then that is the title placed in parentheses after her name. The name of the husband may be given in parentheses below the woman's legal name.

Name	Indexing Order
Mrs. John F. Matson (Mary Nelson)	Matson, Mary Nelson (Mrs.) (Mrs. John F. Matson)
Mrs. Lucien (Louise S.) Platt	Platt, Louise S. (Mrs.) (Mrs. Lucien Platt)
Mrs. Robert (Mary Lee) Young	Young, Mary Lee (Mrs.) (Mrs. Robert Young)

Names with numbers. When a name contains a number, it is considered as if the number was written as a single unit and is spelled as it is pronounced.

	Indexing Order		
Name	Unit 1	Unit 2	Unit 3
A 1 Garage	A	One	Garage
The 400 Club	Fourhundred	Club (The)	
7th Ave. Building	Seventh	Avenue	Building

Geographic names. An easy rule to follow in arranging geographic names is to treat them as they are written. Each element in a compound name of a geographic location is indexed as a separate unit.

	Indexing Order			
Name	Unit 1	Unit 2	Unit 3	Unit 4
Mount Holly, New Jersey	Mount	Holly	New	Jersey
New Bedford, Massachusetts	New	Bedford	Massachusetts	
Newburgh, New York	Newburgh	New	York	

When the first element of a geographic name is not of English origin, that element is considered part of the first unit.

	Indexing Order	
Name	Unit 1	Unit 2
Des Moines, Iowa	DesMoines	Iowa
Las Vegas Hotel	LasVegas	Hotel
Los Angeles, California	LosAngeles	California
San Francisco, California	SanFrancisco	California

Government offices and departments. The name of a federal government office is indexed as follows:

1. United States Government (whether or not it is written as part of the name).

2. Principal word or words in the name of the department.

3. Principal word or words in the name of the bureau.

4. Principal word or words in the name of the division.

"Department of," "Bureau of," and "Division of" are disregarded but are usually placed in parentheses.

Name	Indexing Order

Bureau of the Census
  U.S. Department of Commerce
	United States Government
	  Commerce (Department of)
	  Census (Bureau of the)

Office of Indian Affairs
  U.S. Department of the Interior
	United States Government
	  Interior (Department of)
	  Indian Affairs (Office of)

U.S. Postal Service
  Bureau of Accounts
  Division of Cost Ascertainment
	United States Government
	  Postal Service
	  Accounts (Bureau of)
	  Cost Ascertainment (Division of)

Foreign government names. Names pertaining to foreign governments are indexed under names of countries and subdivided by title of the department and then by bureau, division, commission, or board.

Name	Indexing Order

Republic of India
  Department of Energy
	India (Republic of)
	  Energy Department

Other political divisions. Names pertaining to other political divisions are indexed under the name of the political division followed by its classification, such as *state, county,* or *city,* and then subdivided by the title of the department, bureau, division, commission, or board.

Name	Indexing Order

Bureau of Statistics
  State of Maine
	Maine, State (of)
	  Statistics (Bureau of)

Harris County
  Bureau of Personnel
	Harris, County (of)
	  Personnel (Bureau of)

Department of Safety
  City of Anaheim
	Anaheim, City (of)
	  Safety (Department of)

Banks. Banks are indexed under the names of the communities in which they are located, then by bank name. The state is the last indexing unit.

Name	Indexing Order

First National Bank
  Cleveland, Ohio
	Cleveland: First National Bank,
	  Ohio

Bank of New Jersey
  Newark
	Newark: Bank of New Jersey,
	  New Jersey

Wells Savings Bank
  Wells, Maine
	Wells Savings Bank,
	  Maine

If the name of the community is a part of the name of the bank, the name of the community is not repeated but is considered the first unit as it occurs.

Churches, schools, and other organizations. The names of churches, schools, and other organizations are indexed as follows. Cross-references may be used when necessary to file or find these names more efficiently.

Name	*Indexing Order*
American Legion	American Legion
University of California	California, University (of)
Lakewood Kiwanis Club	Kiwanis Club, Lakewood
First Lutheran Church	Lutheran Church, First
Martin Luther King High School	Martin Luther King High School
The Salvation Army	Salvation Army, The

Addresses. If two or more persons or firms have the same name but different addresses, alphabetize them according to city or town. In the event that the persons or firms also have the same city or town name, then alphabetize according to the state name. Should persons or firms having the same name be in the same community but have different addresses, alphabetize these names according to the name of the street. In the event that the same name has more than one address on the same street of that city or town, then index from the lowest to highest street number.

| 125 Main Street goes before 126 Main Street.

The Association of Records Managers and Administrators indexing and filing rules. The Association of Records Managers and Administrators, Inc., in its book of indexing rules, *Rules for Alphabetical Filing,* has established three classifications for indexing: individual names, business establishment names, and government/political designations. ARMA recommends separating index units with the diagonal (/). ARMA rules are essentially the same as the ones given above with the following differences:

1. The hyphenated company name is treated as one unit.
   | Brown-Jacobs/Company/

2. Compound geographical names are treated as separate units.
   | Las/Vegas/Construction/Company/
   | Del/Rio/Music/Store/

3. Company names that have compass points as part of the name are indexed as separate units.

Name	*Indexing Order*
North East Alignment	North/East/Alignment/
Southeastern Transfer	South/eastern/Transfer/

4. The "'s" is included as part of the indexing unit; that is, the apostrophe, "'", is disregarded.

Name	Indexing Order
Leon's Barbecue	Leon's/Barbecue/
Leons' Music Store	Leons'/Music/Store/

5. Company names that are numbers and written in figure form, such as *500 Club,* are arranged in strict numeric sequence and are *not* spelled out. They are filed at the *front* of the entire alphabetic file.

Name	Indexing Order
1 Hour Cleaners	1/Hour/Cleaners/
7th Street Auto Shop	7(th)/Street/Auto/Shop/
8 Ball Eatery	8/Ball/Eatery/
400 Executive Clothiers	400/Executive/Clothiers/
500 Club	500/Club/

RECORDS RETENTION SCHEDULE

The secretary should keep a copy of the company's records retention schedule and update it when revisions occur. This schedule is a listing of all types of records a firm has and how long these items are to be kept in the office or in the records center. The schedule lists which records must be microfilmed and how long they must be retained. Also, the schedule contains a timetable for disposing of records and a permanent records list.

The company's attorney and representatives of top management should set up the retention schedule following guidelines based on the many federal and state regulations that apply to the firm.

TRANSFERRING RECORDS

When records become inactive in the file, they should be transferred to storage files. Thus, the expensive filing equipment is used only for active material. The material that is removed from the active files and placed in the *inactive,* or *transfer,* files should be well arranged, so that no time is wasted in locating this material if it is needed. Many firms plan to transfer the material in the files annually. The entire file drawer is transferred to the inactive file. The secretary needs to make new guides and prepare new folders for the new files.

If the guides and folders are going to be kept in the office, the transferred material may be placed in inexpensive folders that have been labeled with the same captions as those in the active-file drawer.

All transfer files or boxes should be labeled to indicate their contents, dates, and so forth, so that they can easily be located when needed.

Many business papers, correspondence, and some records that will not be needed in the future may be destroyed to conserve space and save time in transferring files. Material should not be destroyed without consideration of the statute of limitations in the state and other laws that require business firms to retain certain types of records.

MICROGRAPHICS

Micrographics is the term used to designate reproduced information in miniature form on film. Storing information on microfilm has saved firms great amounts of money, space, and retrieval time. Records are photographed onto film in a microfilmer so that many small images in color or black and white will appear on a reel of 16-millimeter or 35-millimeter film. Records can be viewed in enlarged form on a reader.

Computer Output Microfilm (COM). COM is a method of microfilming in which data that are stored in a computer can be recorded directly onto microfilm. This process eliminates recording the data on paper printouts before microfilming can take place. COM speeds getting information to persons needing it on film rather than on paper.

Microfilm Storage

Microfilm may be stored in any of several ways.

Rolls. Roll film can be stored in cartons and cabinets. A plastic collar snapped over the film roll becomes a magazine that self-threads to readers.

Jackets. Jackets contain chambers that hold short lengths of film. A 4″ × 6″ jacket holds 70 images of letter-sized documents.

Microfiche. Microfiche, often called simply "fiche," contains rows of documents on sheet film about 4″ × 6″. Full-color or black-and-white images can appear on microfiche (98 full-color or more than 300 black-and-white images).

Aperture cards. Aperture cards are tab-card-sized cards that have chambers to hold one or more pieces of film and room on the card for identification.

Film folios. Film folios are a combination of aperture cards and jackets. They are cards the size of microfiche with chambers to hold film of microfiche size. The card also contains space for identification.

FILING ELECTRONIC DOCUMENTS

Because electronic documents (ED) can be manipulated in memory, storage and filing procedures differ greatly from standard filing practices.

Documents are stored on disks. A single floppy disk can hold many units of information, or *records*. Each record is composed of discrete areas called *fields*. For the purpose of filing, a field may be

alphabetic, containing only letters and blanks

numeric, containing only digits and certain characters, such as + or −

alphanumeric, containing any characters.

Within a field, numeric data are right justified; alphabetic and alphanumeric data are left justified. Examples of fields can be seen in Table 8.1.

File structure on a floppy disk is fairly simple. With a program such as DisplayWrite or Multimate, data control is increased by using the comment field, as illustrated in Table 8.2.

Methods of Organizing Computer Documents

There are three methods for organizing computer documents: sequential, direct, and indexed.

Sequential, or Serial, File

A sequential, or serial, file controls data on a medium such as magnetic tape. It is one-directional, and reading and writing are done while advancing the tape. Many files are intended to be used sequentially. Data to print onto a document are effectively handled as a serial file since printing itself is a serial process.

TABLE 8.1

Examples of Fields

Alphabetic	Numeric	Alphanumeric
ROGER	321	14 Oak St
CREDIT	9246	72,400
AMES CORP	100543	24 DOZ APPLES

TABLE 8.2

Display Directory

ID	NAME	EXT	DATE	COMMENT
a	TELEMEMO	TXT	04-01-88	Memo to H. Hadley
b	FILES	TXT	04-19-88	Personnel Change/IS Dept.
c	ANDREWS	TXT	04-24-88	Forsythe & Rhoades (Phillip)

Direct File

Any record stored on a direct file can be accessed immediately if its location or address is known. This is the method used by airline reservation agents. The flight number and date of flight are keyed in and the record is displayed on a terminal screen.

Indexed File

An indexed file offers the simplicity of sequential file processing and the capability for direct access. Using programs such as ISAM or VSAM, the indexes are searched for key values, which, in turn, provide the name of the record.

Database

A database is a set of logically related files organized for easy access and minimal overlap. In a database management system (DBMS), access usually is possible only through programming languages such as COBOL, FORTRAN, PL/I, or Pascal. With integrated software, a DBMS is capable of using files from outside sources. For example, data might be read into a word processing program. The secretary revises the text and then reads back into the DBMS for report generation.

A type of information network is called an online real-time information system, which provides two-way communication between individual terminals and a central processing unit (CPU). The database consists of large-volume, random-access files. The secretary in a sales office would use this system to good advantage. When an order is keyed in, the CPU responds with required data: cost, availability, quantity discount, shipping information, and so forth; creates an invoice, if the item is in stock; and updates inventory files. These programs are designed for specific applications; therefore, processing methods vary.

Utilities

Utilities are programs that manipulate files, disks, and subdocuments. Any electronic document can become an electronic subdocument (ESD), depending on how it is used. Pages, paragraphs, phrases, or text material common to many documents can be filed as an ESD and appended to future EDs. To create an ESD, request *block write* and give it a name, or request *phrase write* and give it a name. A phrase will be stored on the disk, but not in the text. Although a disk can be used hundreds of times, it is good practice to copy frequently used records onto a new disk to avoid the problems associated with worn or defective disks.

There are many occasions when the secretary will want to *sort* records and *merge* documents as part of file management. Most record processors will display a list of fields and an empty column for specifying the order of sort. Similarly, data from subfiles can be merged into a single document. Even though these features eliminate needless repetition, a quicker method is always welcome. Let us assume the secretary wants to compile a list of employees with dependents. Rather than scroll through records on the dependent field, it is less time-consuming to request all records *excluding* those with no dependents. Simply key in a dependent field value of 0, and that record will be excluded.

Directories

Directories provide information about existing documents. When the secretary reads a directory, it is presented either alphabetically by name, by creation date, by revision date, or in the order documents appear on the disk. Most record processors have a directory maintenance program, and most provide a single directory format.

Although some offices do keep records indefinitely, many documents are short-lived. A company report, for instance, may have several authors. After a first draft is assembled, the subdocuments can be disposed of. This procedure applies also to subsequent revisions. It is wise, however, to check with the author(s) before destroying any records. In any event, it is imperative that the secretary keep an up-to-date directory printout.

Subdirectories

The majority of computers in the modern office contain one floppy disk drive and one hard or fixed drive. Fixed drives cannot be removed and are capable of storing large amounts of data. Clearly, the greater the storage capability of a computer, the more precise the filing methods must be, not only to expedite retrieval but also to minimize the possibility of "losing" a file. There might be so many documents on a hard disk that to view all the file names and comments could, conceivably, take several hours. To avoid this, the secretary would set up *subdirectories* for greater control.

On most (if not all) computers, the "C" drive is the hard disk. Whenever subdirectories are established, all information is stored in C⟩. If, for example, you are the secretary to four people, and your program is DisplayWrite3, one of the subdirectories might read:

C   = "C" drive
cd   = a subdirectcry
DW3 = first level of subdirectory: the program
TDE = second level of subdirectory: TDE's files

The variations are endless: C⟩cd\DW3\1988\Budget\Variance. . . .

A word of caution, however. If too many subdirectories are set up, locating documents will become extremely difficult. A simple, broad-based system affords the two most desirable qualities of any filing system: easy access and rapid retrieval. It is always well to remember that documents are filed so they can be found.

9

Managing Funds, Bookkeeping, and Record Keeping

by Abba Spero
revised by Linda A. Bruce

A secretary will often be required to handle cash, either from the business operations or the employer's personal funds. This, in turn, may require the recording of these transactions. The figures recorded will be used in preparing income-tax returns and in determining the profitability of the firm's operations. It is important for the secretary to be able to handle various aspects of cash transactions and to be familiar with the basic procedures in record keeping. The purpose of this chapter is to provide information that will enable the secretary to carry out these duties proficiently.

Specifically, the chapter will deal with (1) managing all cash transactions, including receiving cash, writing checks, reconciling bank statements with records, and handling petty cash; (2) record keeping as it affects the determination of profits; and (3) record keeping for income-tax and payroll purposes.

MANAGING CASH TRANSACTIONS

Cash will come into the company from various sources, especially as fees collected for services or as the personal funds of the employer. Personal funds can be received for salaries, interest and dividends on investments, and rents from income-producing property. Usually this money will be in the form of checks; occasionally, cash itself is received.

It is important that all monies received be deposited into the appropriate bank account on the day they are received. This procedure is the best insurance against thefts and robberies. Checks should be examined to determine whether they are properly made out. Attention should be paid to the date; postdated checks cannot be deposited or cashed before the date written on the check. Checks that are not made out correctly should be set aside to be discussed with the employer. Whenever cash is received, the secretary should prepare a receipt in duplicate (blank forms are available at any stationery store), one copy to be given to the person making payment and the other to be retained as a record of the transaction.

If the secretary's duties include record keeping, entries should be made in the proper records. Arrangements for night deposits should be made if funds cannot be deposited before the bank closes.

HANDLING THE BANK ACCOUNT

Making Bank Deposits

When cash is to be deposited in a bank, a deposit slip is made out (see below). Although banks do accept deposit slips improperly prepared, the competent secretary is careful to do the job correctly. The company bank-deposit slips are usually imprinted with the company name and the bank account number. If these are not available,

CHECKING DEPOSIT	0008 1·0l5·781	NATIONAL CITY BANK

CHECKING DEPOSIT
SUBJECT TO RULES AND REGULATIONS GOVERNING CHECKING ACCOUNTS

NATIONAL CITY BANK
CLEVELAND, OHIO

DATE *Aug. 14, 19-*   ACCOUNT NO. 0 4 7 5 2 6 1

CREDIT THE ACCOUNT OF *Dorothy Jones*

OFFICE WHERE ACCOUNT IS CARRIED   Be Sure Each Item is Properly Endorsed.

Broadway — 65th

CASH — List Checks Single		
	22	50
	150	00
	43	75
TOTAL	276	25

⑆041000124⑆

then this information must be filled in on a blank slip. The account number is important since it is the number, rather than the name, that the bank uses for its records.

Currency is counted, and the total is entered on the slip. Coins, if in large quantities, should be rolled in wrappers provided by the bank. Each check included in the deposit is listed separately. Occasionally traveler's checks or money orders may be a part of the deposit. These are entered in the same manner as ordinary checks. After all checks have been listed, the amounts of all items on the slip are added and the total is placed in the space provided.

The bank will give a receipt for the deposit. The receipt should be retained until the bank statement is received and then used to check the statement and be sure that all deposits have been properly recorded.

Endorsing Checks

Checks are written orders by which the depositor, known as the "drawer," directs the bank, referred to as the "drawee," to pay money to the "payee" or to a third party designated by the payee. Checks are sometimes made payable to "bearer," a practice generally frowned upon because they are negotiated by simple delivery and can be cashed by persons who wrongfully receive them. Checks need not be made payable to real persons. Business checks are frequently made out to "Petty Cash" or to "Payroll." A check is made payable to Payroll, for example, when money is needed to make up pay envelopes.

If a check is made out to a definite payee, this person must write on the back of the check directions for its disposition and sign his or her name. This is known as an "endorsement." Endorsements are placed on the back of the check on the left-hand side. The endorser should sign exactly as the name is written on the face of the check. If the name is misspelled or differs in any manner from the way it appears on the bank records, the payee should sign twice, first as it is written on the face of the check and then correctly.

Forms of Endorsement

There are three principal forms of endorsement: blank, in full, and restrictive. (See Figure 9-1.)

Blank endorsement. In a blank endorsement, the endorser's signature is simply written across the back of the check. The effect of a blank endorsement is to make the check payable to the bearer. If it is lost or stolen, it can be cashed by the holder without further endorsement. Although they are commonly used, blank endorsements are not recommended. They should be made only at the time a check is being cashed or deposited at the bank.

Endorsement in full. In an endorsement in full, the endorser transfers the check to a designated party by writing the words "Pay to the order of" followed by the name of the person to whom payment is to be made and then signs the check. A check so endorsed can be cashed or negotiated only after the person named in the endorsement has signed it. It is not good in the hands of a person who wrongfully possesses it.

Restrictive endorsement. In a restrictive endorsement, the endorser limits further negotiation of the check by writing above his or her signature definite instructions on what may be done with it. Thus, a check might be made payable to one person only or it might be endorsed "For deposit only." Except when checks are being deposited in the bank, restrictive endorsements are almost never used. Business checks are usually endorsed for deposit with a rubber stamp; no written signature is needed.

Dishonored Checks

A bank accepts checks for deposit subject to their final payment. If the drawer has directed the bank to refuse payment or if there are insufficient funds on deposit, the bank will return the check and charge it to the drawer's account. Such a check is known as a "dishonored check," or an "NSF (insufficient funds) check." Informal arrangements for payment or redeposit of a dishonored check are usually made with the drawer. However, if the drawer is a stranger, it would be advisable for the holder of a dishonored check to take legal steps and file a formal notice of protest. In this way, the holder is assured of protecting full rights against the drawer.

Dishonored checks that have been returned by the bank should

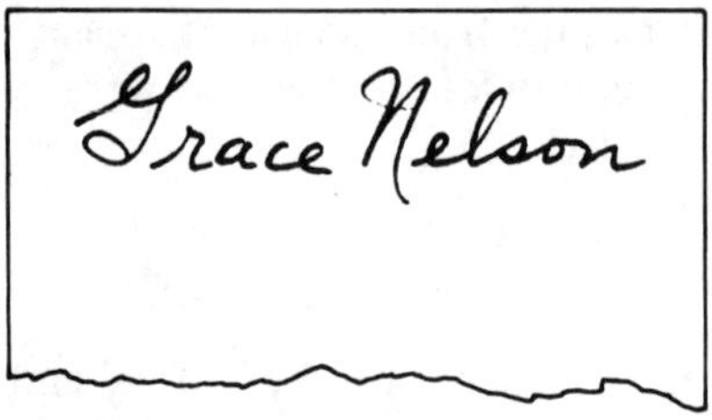
Grace Nelson

Blank Endorsement
Payable to bearer
without further endorsement

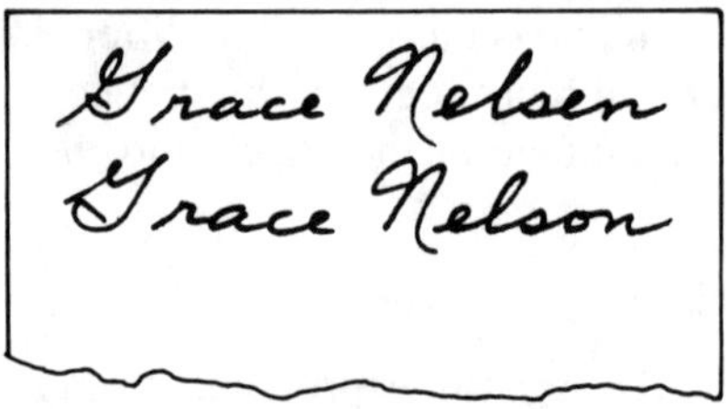
Grace Nelsen
Grace Nelson

Blank Endorsement
Name misspelled

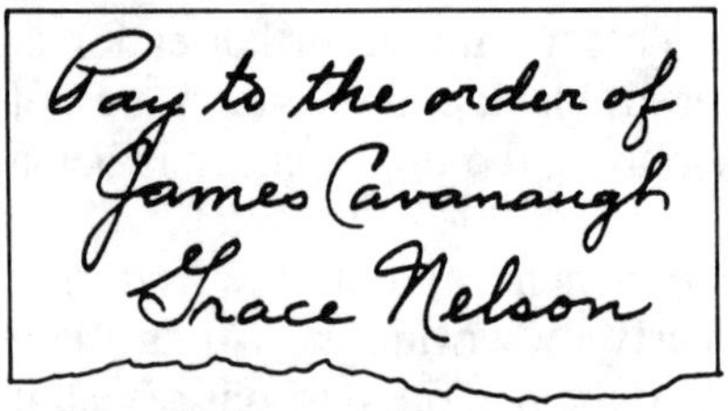
Pay to the order of
James Cavanaugh
Grace Nelson

Endorsement in Full
Payable as James Cavanaugh directs

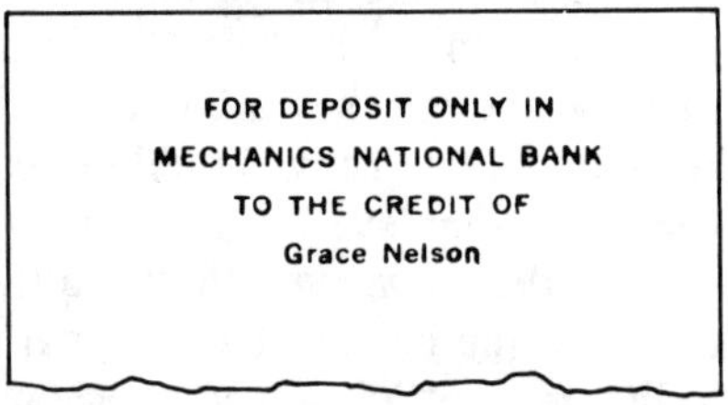
FOR DEPOSIT ONLY IN
MECHANICS NATIONAL BANK
TO THE CREDIT OF
Grace Nelson

Restrictive Endorsement
Further negotiation prohibited

Figure 9-1.

be deducted from the bank balance on the depositor's cash records and then be redeposited or filed for safekeeping until the drawer has made settlement. Any fees that may have been paid for the protest or collection can rightfully be collected from the drawer.

Bank Statements

At regular intervals, usually monthly, or sometimes upon request of the depositor, the bank renders a bank statement, showing what has taken place in the account since the last statement was prepared and the present balance according to the bank's records. The statement shows the balance carried forward from the previous statement, all deposits and all charges made to the account during the period, and the balance on the date the statement was rendered. Sent along with the statements are canceled checks, credit memos, and debit memos.

Today, many financial institutions provide checkbooks that make self-carbon copies of checks written. These copies remain in the check register and are used just as the traditional canceled and returned checks at the end of the statement period to balance the account.

Canceled checks are the depositor's checks that have been returned to the bank, charged against the account, and stamped "PAID." *Credit memos* are notices of amounts added to the account for such sums as interest allowed by the bank or proceeds of items left with the bank for collection—notes and bond coupons, for example. *Debit memos* are notices of deductions made from the account for service charges, interest on bank loans, and the like.

Bank Reconciliation

Seldom will the balance showing in the checkbook agree with the balance reported on the bank statement, even though no errors have been made in either place. Disagreement results from the following causes:

Deposits that were made near or after the date of the statement have not yet been posted on the bank records. They do, however, appear in the checkbook.

Credits that have been made to the account by the bank, as indicated on the credit memos, have not yet been entered in the checkbook.

Checks issued by the depositor and deducted in the checkbook are still outstanding; that is, they have not yet been presented to the bank for payment and therefore do not appear on the bank statement.

Charges that have been made against the account by the bank, as indicated on the debit memos, have not yet been entered in the checkbook.

Errors have been made either in the checkbook or on the bank's records, or in both places.

As soon as possible after receiving a statement, the depositor should locate the reasons for differences between the bank statement and the checkbook and find the correct balance in the account. This is done on a bank reconciliation statement, prepared by the following steps:

1. Compare deposits entered in the checkbook with those recorded on the bank statement. Check discrepancies against deposit slips to determine which record is correct. Make a note of deposits that do not appear on the bank statement and credits made by the bank that have not been added in the checkbook.
2. Take checks returned by the bank or self-carbon copies in the checkbook and arrange them in numerical order. Compare them with their stubs or other notations in the checkbook, taking

careful notice to see whether the amounts agree. Make a note of differences. Place a check mark or other symbol on stubs of the checks that have been returned. Prepare a list of the outstanding checks, noting the check numbers, the dates, and the names of the payees. Do not include certified checks on this list, since they have already been charged against the account. Make a note of any bank charges that have not been entered in the checkbook.

3. Arrange the information that has been assembled on a bank reconciliation statement. The form and preparation of this statement are explained and illustrated below.

If the checkbook and bank statement are both correct, the balances can be brought into agreement and the reconciliation is complete. If the accounts cannot be reconciled after adjustments have been made for omissions, there is probably an error in addition or subtraction in the checkbook. Check the check stubs, paying particular attention to the balances carried forward from one stub to another.

Bank Reconciliation Statements

Bank reconciliation statements are prepared in three ways:

Adjustments are made to the balance reported by the bank to bring it into agreement with the checkbook balance.

Adjustments are made in the checkbook balance to bring it into agreement with the balance according to the bank statement.

Adjustments are made to both balances to get the correct balance.

Since neither of the first two methods provides the correct balance, the third method is the preferred procedure and is the one explained here. The sources of the data are the bank statement and the checkbook or a cash ledger account if one was prepared.

Comparison of the deposits that were made during the month with those recorded on the bank statement reveals that the bank has not entered a deposit of $1,000 made on July 31; this amount is added to the balance reported by the bank. Comparison of the canceled checks returned by the bank with the checks drawn during the period shows that the following checks are still outstanding:

Check No.	Date	Payee	Amount
633	7/22	Bean & Co.	$2,180
634	7/28	Blue Cross	50
			$2,230

Reconciliation Statement (July 31)

Balance on bank statement			$7,328
Deposits made after date of statement			1,000
Add			$8,328

Checks Outstanding

Check No.	Date	Payee	Amount
633	7/22	Bean & Co.	$2,180
634	7/28	Blue Cross	50
			$2,230

Deduct checks outstanding	2,230
Corrected bank balance	6,098
Balance according to checkbook	6,100
Service charge not recorded	2
Corrected checkbook balance	$6,098

The total of the outstanding checks is deducted from the balance reported on the bank statement. Adding the unrecorded deposits and deducting the outstanding checks takes care of all omissions on the bank statement. The correct bank balance is determined to be $6,098.

The bank statement shows a service charge of $2.00 that has not been entered in the cash records; this amount is deducted from the checkbook balance. Now the corrected checkbook balance is also $6,098, and it has been proved that no errors have been made.

After the reconciliation has been completed, errors should be corrected and entries should be made in the depositor's cash records and checkbook for any omissions, such as the service charge discussed above, so that the records will reflect the correct balance. Adjustments in the checkbook can be made on the stub for the last check drawn. It is not necessary to correct all preceding balances. Any bank errors uncovered in the reconciliation should be reported to the bank immediately.

The bank reconciliation statement should be filed for future reference. It will prove useful when the next reconciliation is made. The canceled checks are receipts for payments that have been made. They should be kept on file as long as proof of payment might be necessary.

Investigating Outstanding Checks

Ordinarily checks should clear through the bank and be returned to the depositor (not the case with self-carbon checks) within a few weeks after issue. Checks that have been outstanding for unreasonably long periods of time should be investigated. Outstanding checks are not only annoying when bank accounts are being reconciled but also pose a question as to what may have happened to them. Perhaps the checks have been lost or mislaid by the payee. Communication with the payee is in order.

If the payee claims not to have received a check, a new one will have to be issued in its place. This should be done, however, only after a stop-payment notice has been filed on the old check. How to stop payment on a check is described later in this chapter.

HANDLING CASH PAYMENTS

The secretary who takes care of the company bills accepts responsibility for paying the correct amount at the right time. To ensure proper payment, the secretary should (1) check to make sure that bills submitted to the employer are correct and (2) take measures to ensure that bills are at hand for payment when they are due.

Before drawing checks for the employer's signature, the secretary should thoroughly check the accuracy of the statements received. Compare the charges listed on the statement with the sales slips that are attached or other supporting evidence and make sure that proper credits have been allowed for returns and for payments that have been made on the account. The mathematical accuracy of all calculations on the statement should be verified.

Prompt payment of all bills is desirable; on some bills, payment on or before a given date is essential. Particular attention must be paid to insurance premiums, because policies lapse if premiums are not paid before a certain date, and to those bills that are subject to some form of additional charge if payment is not made within a stated period. Also, bills that allow for cash discount if paid within a certain time should be earmarked for timely payment. For example, the expression "2/10; n/30" stands for a 2-percent discount if paid within ten days; if not taken, the total is due within thirty days. In terms of annual notes, this is the equivalent of almost a 35-percent interest charge if the discount is not taken. One method of ensuring payment at the right time is the use of a tickler file in which bills are filed by the dates on which they should be paid.

Occasionally payments must be made in a foreign currency (see Chapter 22). The easiest means of making remittances to foreign countries is a draft payable in the funds of the country to which payment is to be sent. Drafts can be purchased at any bank. Personal checks can be used in some instances; however, this poses the problem of exchange rates and presents the possibility of over- or underpayment. The exchange rates fluctuate.

Writing Checks

Care should be exercised in writing checks. It is good policy to fill in the check stub first, to prevent the possibility of drawing a check without recording it. The date, the check number, the name of the payee, and the reason for the payment should all be listed on the stub. The reason for payment should contain enough information to permit later entry in the cash records. The check is filled in with the number (if not preprinted), the date, the name of payee, the amount in both figures and words, and the signature. Checks should be written legibly. No blank spaces that might be used to alter the check should be left. The amount in figures is placed close to the dollar sign, and the amount in words is started close to the left-hand side. The amount in words should agree with the amount in figures. In case of disagreement, the bank may refuse to honor the check. If the check is honored, the amount written in words governs. If the amount of the check is less than one dollar, it is customary to cross out the word "Dollars" and write "Only . . . cents."

Titles such as "Dr." or "Rev." are not used; it is "Ben Kildare," not "Dr. Ben Kildare." "Mrs." is used only in connection with the husband's name; it is either "Mrs. Roy Roe" or "Ruth Roe." Checks issued to organizations should be made payable to the organization, not to some individual in the organization. Likewise, checks should be made payable to companies rather than to their agents. Checks for

Figure 9-2.

insurance premiums, for example, would be drawn in favor of the insurance company rather than the agent who handles the account.

It is not wise to sign blank checks. Should this be necessary when the employer will be absent from the office, the checkbook should be kept in a place where it will be safe from theft. Checks, like money, are a medium of exchange and should be guarded as carefully as money.

Erasures and alterations should never be made on checks. Banks are reluctant to accept checks if there is any suspicion that they have been tampered with. If mistakes are made in preparing a check, the word "VOID" should be written across the face of the check and on its stub. If the checks are prenumbered, spoiled checks should not be discarded; they should be kept with canceled checks so that there can be no question concerning the whereabouts of a missing check.

Certified Checks

Often checks for large amounts drawn by a person whose financial status is unknown to the payee must be certified by the bank before they are issued. To secure certification, the depositor takes a completed check to the bank. After the cashier has ascertained that the account has sufficient funds to cover it, the cashier stamps the check "CERTIFIED" and signs it. Immediately upon certification, the amount of the check is charged against the depositor's account. There can be no question concerning whether funds are available for payment when the check is presented. So far as the bank is concerned, it has already been paid. Thus in a bank reconciliation, a certified check is never outstanding, since it has been charged in advance.

Certified checks should never be destroyed. In the event that they are not sent to the payee, they should be redeposited in the bank.

Stopping Payment on a Check

The drawer of a check has the power to stop payment on it at any time prior to its presentation to the bank for payment. This is accomplished by filing a stop-payment notice at the bank on a form that the bank will provide. Oral notice is insufficient. So that the bank can identify the check when it is presented, it will ask for such information as the number of the check, its date, the name of the payee, and the amount. If a check is lost, a stop-payment notice should be filed immediately.

As soon as the stop-payment notice is filed with the bank, the check stub should be marked "Payment stopped." The amount of the check should then be added to the current balance. This can be done on the check stub open at the time; it is not necessary to go back and correct all preceding balances.

Petty-Cash Fund

Although it is good policy to make all payments by check, since a check provides a written record of the transaction and serves as a receipt, it is impractical to write checks for small amounts to cover items such as collect telegrams, postage due, carfare, supper money, and incidental purchases of office supplies. In some instances, too, cash is needed immediately. To meet these needs, it is customary to set up what is generally called a "petty-cash fund." Operation of the petty-cash fund is described in the following paragraphs.

Establishing the petty-cash fund. First, it is decided how much cash should be placed in the fund. This is determined by the expenditures that are anticipated. The amount should not be too high, yet it should not be so low that too-frequent reimbursements are required. When the amount has been set, a check is drawn payable to Petty Cash. The check is cashed and the funds are placed in a locked cash box or drawer, generally referred to as the petty-cash drawer. Responsibility for the fund should be placed in one person, and this person alone should have access to it.

Payments from the petty-cash fund. All payments from the petty-cash fund should be supported by documentary evidence in the form of a petty-cash voucher, showing the date of payment, the name of the payee, the reason for payment, and the amount paid out (see Figure 9-3). The petty-cash voucher is initialed by the person making payment and signed by the person who has received the cash. Printed forms for this purpose can be purchased at any stationery store.

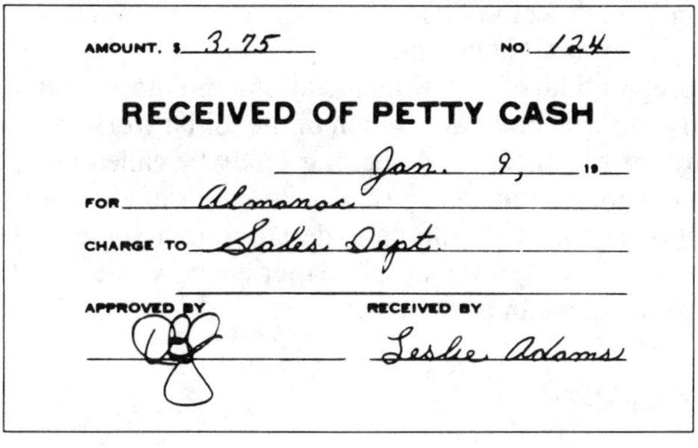

AMOUNT. $ 3.75 NO. 124

RECEIVED OF PETTY CASH

Jan. 9, 19

FOR Almanac

CHARGE TO Sales Dept.

APPROVED BY RECEIVED BY

Leslie Adams

Figure 9-3.

Paid vouchers are placed in the petty-cash drawer or in a special envelope kept for this purpose. In addition, some firms maintain a petty-cash record. This is simply a form on which paid vouchers can be summarized. Columns are provided for the voucher number, date, name of payee, explanation of payment, and a summary of the expenditures made. Seldom is there a real need for such a record; the petty-cash vouchers themselves usually provide an adequate record. However, in a company with a system of bookkeeping that accounts for every expenditure, regardless of how small, the inclusion of petty-cash payments in the accounting books as part of the daily record may be the best procedure.

Replenishing the petty-cash fund. Whenever the cash in the petty-cash fund gets low, the fund is replenished. A check is written payable to Petty Cash for the amount that has been spent from the fund. The check is cashed and the proceeds are placed in the petty-cash drawer. After replenishment, the cash in the fund should amount to the fund originally established. If replenishment of the fund is taking place too often, consideration should be given to increasing the size of the fund.

BOOKKEEPING

There is a need to properly record the income and expense transactions of any business operation. There are two major purposes for this recordkeeping. One objective is to determine the profitability of the business. By being able to calculate the profit or loss of the operation and then to be able to analyze in detail the individual items of income and expense, the company is in a position to act with greater knowledge in its decisions. The second objective is to gather the necessary information required by the governmental tax agencies such as the Internal Revenue Service. These tax reports not only require a calculation of net income (income less total expense) but also detailed substantiation of individual amounts.

The preparation of these financial statements is usually the responsibility of the accountant. Much of the initial work, however, may be done by the bookkeeper. A secretary may be called upon to handle these bookkeeping duties. At this point, a brief description of the duties will be given. It should be understood that some of these tasks can be handled with little or no experience, while others require complete training as an accountant.

Business Records

Careful records of all payments, expenses, and other transactions must be kept to determine the profitability (or losses) of a business. Some of the tasks involved in keeping complete business records follow.

Recording business transactions originally in journals. Most companies use what is referred to as a "double entry" system that has a "debit" and "credit" entry for each item.

Posting the journal to the ledger. There will be a general ledger and there may be subsidiary ledgers for specific accounts, such as accounts receivable and accounts payable.

Calculating a trial balance of all accounts in the ledger to determine if the accounts are in balance in terms of debits and credits.

Adjusting journal entries to bring all accounts up to date. For example, any bills owed at the end of the year are recorded even though they will not be paid until the next year.

Preparing the financial statements, primarily the Balance Sheet and the Income Statement. This usually involves the use of a worksheet.

The first two items and possibly the third are considered work normally done by the bookkeeper. The last two items are more often the job of the accountant. How a secretary fits into this process will, of course, depend upon the practice of the individual company.

Tax Records

Aside from the bookkeeping described above, there is a need to keep adequate tax records. Every business must pay a tax on its profits. A corporation pays its own income tax; income from a partnership or an individually owned business is added to the personal tax return of the individual owner. In each case there must be proof of the amounts recorded in the tax returns for income and expense.

A check canceled is often sufficient proof of the validity of a business expense. However, at other times, a company may be called upon to document specific items. A sales invoice, a bill, a receipt for cash payment—all of these can be useful in providing the necessary documentation. A filing system that allows the accountant to find the necessary papers easily should be maintained.

A filing system can be set up on the basis of (1) date, with bills and invoices filed according to month; (2) type of expense—for example, office supplies or utilities; or (3) type of document—for example, invoice, cash receipt, or bill. Combinations of these systems are often used. The main point is that the system be based on a common-sense approach that other people can follow. The secretary is in a central position to see to it that the filing is correctly handled.

Travel and Entertainment Expenses

There are specific expense items for which the IRS requires a detailed record. An example of this type of expense and the additional recordkeeping involved is the travel and entertainment deduction (T & E). Adequate records would include:

the amount of the expenditure

the dates of departure and return for each trip and the number of days spent on business

the business purpose of the expenditure

the place of travel or entertainment

the business relationship to the taxpayer of the person(s) being entertained.

Documentary evidence in the form of credit-card stubs and receipts of paid bills is required for (1) all expenditures for lodging while traveling away from home, and (2) any expenditure over the amount specified by the Internal Revenue Service. It is good practice to record all expenditures in an account book or diary and to attach receipts, paid bills, and other substantiating documents to the back of the page on which the expenditure is recorded. Employers will expect secretaries to handle this type of detailed record keeping. Usually the employer will turn over the raw information to the secretary and expect the secretary to put it together in a formal record. (See Figure 9-4.)

Automobile Expense Record

The taxpayer who uses a personal automobile in connection with business or employment is entitled to deduct automobile expenses (in whole if the auto is used exclusively for business, or in part if it is used for both business and pleasure) on the income-tax return. Expenses include not only all the operating costs but also a reasonable allowance for depreciation. To ensure receiving full benefit from allowable deductions, the taxpayer would be wise to keep careful account of expenses and mileage on an automobile-expense record. A simple form for this purpose, set up to accumulate expenses on an annual basis, is shown in Figure 9-5.

The secretary can keep the record by using information supplied by the employer or, better yet, by making entries from bills routinely filed. The calculation for depreciation can best be made by the accountant responsible for preparing the tax return.

If records are not kept on automobile expenses, an optional tax-deduction method is allowed by the IRS. A standard mileage rate for business use each year instead of a record of the actual operating and fixed expenses and separate deduction for depreciation may be used by an individual. Interest payments on loans and state and local taxes (other than the gasoline tax) attributable to the business use of the car are deductible in addition to the standard mileage rate.

TRAVEL EXPENSE REPORT

Name				Sales No		Dept No		Date		Approvals
Harriet Blasko						510-076		8/16		HBm

Business Purpose: Annual Convention of Purchasing Agents

Debit Acct   Credit Acct

Day	Date	Mil/Dr	Location	Hotel	Meals	Ent'm't	Tel/Tel	Air	Transportation Gas/Oil	Transportation Other	Park/Tolls	Other	TOTALS
Sun.													
Mon.													
Tue.													
Wed.													
Thu.	8/12		Kansas City	28.50	21.75	45.00	2.30	82.73		10.30		50.00	240.58
Fri.	8/13		"	--	19.80					10.50			30.30
Sat.			"										
			TOTALS										270.88

Miles @ 10¢

TOTAL	270.88
Less Airline Charges	82.73
Less Other Charges	
TOTAL	188.15
Cash Advance	
Due Me	188.15
Returned Herewith	

ITEMIZED ENTERTAINMENT RECORD

Date	Location	Business Purpose	Persons Ent'ed/Business Relationship	Amount
8/12	Jet Night Club	Inquiry on discounts for processing equipment	Elvin Hawes & Adele Vasquez, Acme Products	45.00

DETAIL OF OTHER EXPENDITURES

Date	Item	Total
8/12	cab; airport – hotel	10.30
8/13	" hotel – airport	10.50
8/12	Convention Registration fee	50.00

INSTRUCTIONS:

1. Receipts for lodging, the customer copy of airline tickets, receipts for supplies and each item over $25 should be attached to the report.
2. Meal charges may be included in the report if the employee is away from home "overnight."
3. Include tips for meals and taxis in meal and transportation charges. Tipping for other services should be listed under "Other" expenses and itemized in the space provided.
4. Under "Other" expenditures include items such as luggage tips, supplies, postage, valet, and laundry
5. Charges for transportation should be identified, such as bus, taxi, train, or rental car. Rental car receipts should be attached to the report
6. If the space provided for entertainment is inadequate, use a separate memorandum for the overflow
7. Expense reports are to be submitted weekly and should be sent to the office no later than the Friday following the week in which the expenditures occur.

Signed Harriet Blasko   Send Check To   Harriet Blasko, Purchasing Dept.

Figure 9-4.

    Always check current IRS booklets for detailed information and for rules on necessary record keeping.

Employer's Personal Tax Records

There are a number of different nonbusiness expenses that are deductible on the individual's personal income tax return. As with business expenses, it is important that there exist adequate evidence of the payment of these expenses. The secretary may be called upon

RECORD OF AUTOMOBILE UPKEEP FOR THE   Month of *January*   19**34**

DATE	MILEAGE	GASOLINE		OIL AND GREASE	STORAGE and PARKING	AUTO REPAIRS	CLEANING AND WASHING	ACCESS-ORIES	MISCEL-LANEOUS	
		No. Gals.	Amount							
1										
2	22,346	10	11	40						
3					2	00				
4							3	75		
5					2	75				
6				16	00		18	00		54	30
7		14	15	96						
29					3	15				
30		12	13	72						
31	24,180									
TOTAL	1,834			16	00	10	70	18	00	7	50		54	30

Figure 9-5.

by the employer to keep an additional set of records for these personal expenses. The expense deductions include: (1) contributions to charities, colleges, etc., (2) medical and dental expenses, (3) interest on mortgages, loans, etc., and (4) taxes. The most important proof is the canceled check indicating payment. In most situations this is usually sufficient. However, occasionally more evidence is required. Thus a file of the bills would be helpful in substantiating a tax deduction. The employer should turn over personal bank statements with the canceled checks, or at least the ones to be recorded, along with the bills received. The degree that the employer wants the secretary involved in personal financial matters will obviously affect the amount of record keeping that will be necessary.

PAYROLL

The secretary may be called in to handle the payroll of the company. This will involve (1) calculating the net amount to be paid out and (2) keeping payroll records required for computing the various kinds of payroll taxes and for the government reports. The following section describes these procedures in some detail.

The federal government requires that the employer withhold from each employee's salary a sufficient amount that will at year's end add up to the amount of income tax due. The employee when first hired must fill out a form indicating the number of exemptions claimed. The number of exemptions is then used in calculating, according to IRS guidelines, how much tax should be withheld for each salary level.

There also may be state and city income taxes that will require additional withholdings from the employee's payroll check. While the general procedures are basically the same, it is important that the secretary follow the specific requirements of each governmental agency.

Beside the various income taxes, the Federal Insurance Contributions Act (FICA) requires employees to pay a percentage of their salary as their contribution to the social security program. (There is a matching contribution that is paid by the employer.) The rate is fixed at a certain percentage of the annual salary up to a given amount. After this figure is reached, no more FICA tax is to be paid. Each year FICA tables are prepared for the various salary levels.

The following example uses the figure 7.51% FICA tax to be withheld from the first $22,900 of annual salary:

> Employee A, married with two children, may claim four exemptions. If A's weekly salary were $300, the payroll check would be calculated as follows:
>
> | | | |
> |---|---:|---:|
> | Gross Pay | | $300.00 |
> | Less: Federal Income Tax Withheld | $33.30 | |
> | FICA Tax Withheld (7.51% × $300) | 22.53 | |
> | Total Withheld | | − 55.83 |
> | Net Pay—Amount of Check | | 244.17 |

The illustration could have been more complex if state and city income taxes were included. Beside the taxes that are withheld, the company sometimes withholds medical insurance, union dues, contributions to charity or retirement programs, and other agreed-upon items.

The monies withheld from the employee's pay check have to be remitted periodically to the respective agencies. Thus, for example, the federal income tax withheld, plus the FICA tax withheld, and the employer's matching FICA tax contribution must be sent to the Internal Revenue Service (or a bank authorized to act as the depositor). How often this is to be done depends upon the dollar amount:

> Less than $500 a month—Every three months
> More than $500 but less than $3000 a month—Every month
> More than $3000 a month—Every two weeks

At the end of each three-month period, a payroll tax return form is required to be filed with the IRS. This requirement normally is not the responsibility of the secretary. However, keeping the detailed payroll records may be one of the duties. This will require a record of each pay period showing the dates, hours, and earnings of each employee and a record of each employee's earnings showing date of employment and discharge, social security number, rate or method of pay, and summary of wages and all deductions by quarter and calendar year.

There are additional reports required at the end of each year. These include the *Employer's Annual Federal Unemployment Tax Return* (Form 940) and a *Wage and Tax Statement* (Form W-2) for each employee. On the state and local governmental level, quarterly and annual income and unemployment tax returns may be required depending on state and local regulations.

It is important to point out that the ability to manage all of these tax and payroll reports is normally *not* the responsibility of the secretary. Usually the company has an accountant who handles these items. However, the accountant may delegate much of the work to the bookkeeper or the secretary and act only as a supervisor. Therefore, it is helpful to be familiar with payroll procedures and tax reports in case these areas become your responsibility.

Special Functions

10

Special Secretarial Functions

by Jeanette L. Bely
revised by Barry Persky

MAKING TRAVEL ARRANGEMENTS

Many firms today have extended and expanded their interests and scope into the international picture. This broadening of the horizons makes it more likely that the executive will travel to maintain contacts with the firm's branches and customers, to attend meetings and conventions, to lecture, or just to relax. With the need for increased travel, the means of transportation have become more convenient and many-faceted. To ensure a smooth and enjoyable trip for the employer, the secretary should be familiar with the various means of transportation that are available. It is the secretary's responsibility to make sure that the executive gets to the destination on time and in comfort and that the supplies and documents necessary for a successful trip are at the disposal of the traveler.

Before the secretary can make any arrangements for the trip, certain facts need to be compiled. The planner must know departure date and time, cities to be visited, length of time to be spent in each locality, the purpose of each visit, the time and day the traveler must arrive in each city to keep scheduled appointments, preferences as to means of travel, and how many people will be traveling. Supplied with this information, the secretary can take the next step in making travel arrangements—the compiling of an itinerary—and then proceed to complete all other tasks necessary.

Compiling an Itinerary

At first, as pieces and bits of information are gathered, it is a good practice to draw up a tentative itinerary or a work sheet on which notations of alternate flights, alternate train schedules, costs, and so forth can be presented for the executive's approval and selection. Such a work sheet might contain the following information: dates, destination, airport, railroad station, departure time, time of arrival, hotel accommodations, appointments (where and with whom), and reference materials.

The secretary should start the preliminary planning of the itinerary from the dates and times provided by the executive. Then a listing of whatever travel methods the employer prefers that are available at the times indicated should be added to the work sheet. If the means of transportation are left open, complete information on all airlines and railroads serving the city of destination, with arrival and departure times and the costs of each, should be obtained. Information about car rental agencies at the various destinations may be included. It is wise to indicate all possible choices available and permit the executive to make the decision as to which means of travel is preferred. The work sheet should be revised periodically with the approval of the executive until the decisions are complete and the itinerary is ready for final typing.

In planning an itinerary, the secretary must bear in mind that the traveler must eat regularly while traveling, must rest, must have enough time to get from a terminal to the place of an appointment, and so forth. Therefore, the following information should be included in the schedule:

eating locations (plane, train, hotel, restaurant, etc.)

allowance of time to go from the point of arrival to the appointment at the designated hour and without pressure

applicable time zones, noted in indicated time on the itinerary (EST, EDST, etc.)

all confirmations for hotel accommodations, attached to the itinerary

all confirmations for transportation, airline tickets, etc., attached to the itinerary.

Multiple copies of the final draft should be prepared by the secretary: one for the office files, one or two for the executive, one for the traveler's family, and, if customary, copies for key people in the organization. The typed form of the itinerary would appear as on the example on pages 294 and 295.

Data and Supplies for the Trip

If the executive's trip is entirely for business or is part business and part pleasure, the secretary's duties in making travel arrangements do not stop with the completion of the itinerary. The secretary should prepare an appointments schedule; pertinent files, including past correspondence and memory refresher notes; stationery and other supplies that might be needed; an expense record book; and any other supplies the traveler may need to be prepared for the calls, be able to communicate with the home office, and keep necessary records.

Appointments Calendar

The secretary should prepare an appointments calendar listing all the calls to be made while traveling. Such a schedule is usually made only for the executive and secretary, and it is not distributed to anyone else. It can be either combined with the itinerary or prepared as a separate schedule, depending on the executive's preference.

Charles Murray Itinerary February 19, 19__

Tuesday, February 19 (New York to Raleigh)

10:00 a.m.　Leave West Side Airline Terminal, New York, by limousine or van for Newark airport.

11:10 a.m.　Leave Newark airport on Eastern Airlines Flight #275 (lunch). (Ticket attached)

1:19 p.m.　Arrive Raleigh. Van to Hotel Hilton. (Reservation attached)

2:00 p.m.　Robert Lee, Office Manager at Raleigh branch, will pick you up at the Hilton. Conference scheduled at branch office. (File #1 in briefcase)

Wednesday, February 20 (Raleigh)

9:00 a.m.　Robert Lee will pick you up at the hotel for inspection of Raleigh plant. (File #2 in briefcase contains facts and statistics on plant operation)

8:00 p.m.　Company dinner at Hotel Hilton. (Speech in File #3 in briefcase)

Thursday, February 21 (Raleigh to Winston-Salem via Greensboro)

9:30 a.m.　Robert Lee will pick you up at the hotel and drive you to the airport.

9:56 a.m.　Leave Raleigh on Delta Airlines Flight #101. (Ticket attached)

10:18 a.m.　Arrive Greensboro airport. Limousine or van to Winston-Salem Hotel in Winston-Salem. (Reservation attached) Lunch at hotel.

3:00 p.m.　Appointment with John Spaaks, Office Manager at Winston-Salem branch, and Al Smith, Sales Director. Hotel Winston-Salem, Green Room. (File #4 in briefcase)

7:00 p.m.　Dinner at Bill Lawson's home. (Telephone 722-1234)

Friday, February 22 (Winston-Salem)

9:00 a.m.　Golf with Bill Lawson.

1:00 p.m.　Conference with staff at Winston-Salem offices. (File #5 in briefcase)

8:00 p.m.　Company dinner at Winston-Salem Hotel. (Speech in File #6 in briefcase)

<u>Saturday, February 23 (Winston-Salem to Greenville via Asheville)</u>

9:02 a.m.   Leave Winston-Salem on Southern Airlines Flight #501. (Ticket attached)

10:10 a.m.   Arrive Asheville. Limousine or van to Greenville Hotel in Greenville. (Reservation attached) Lunch at hotel.

2:00 p.m.   Conference with Greenville branch office manager Jim Turrell at Greenville Hotel, Mezzanine Lounge. (File #7 in briefcase)

7:00 p.m.   Company dinner at hotel. (Speech in File #8 in briefcase)

<u>Sunday, February 24 (Greenville to Columbia)</u>

3:00 p.m.   Leave Greenville/Spartanburg airport on Southern Airlines commuter flight #38. (Ticket attached)

4:00 p.m.   Arrive Columbia. George Lewis, Office Manager, will meet you at airport. Magnolia Hotel. (Reservation attached)

<u>Monday, February 25 (Columbia)</u>

9:00 a.m.   Conference at Columbia offices. George Lewis will pick you up at the hotel. (File #9 in briefcase contains statistics and progress reports from this branch)

7:00 p.m.   Dinner meeting of Columbia staff at Magnolia Hotel. (Speech in File #10 in briefcase)

<u>Tuesday, February 26 (Columbia to New York)</u>

10:00 a.m.   George Lewis will pick you up to take you to the airport.

11:07 a.m.   Leave Columbia on Eastern Airlines Flight #666 (lunch). (Ticket attached)

2:33 p.m.   Arrive Newark airport. Limousine to New York offices.

The appointments schedule should include the following:

the name of the city and state in which the call is to be made

the date and time of the appointment

the name and address of the firm to which the executive is going

the name of the individual with whom the appointment is made

the telephone number of the firm or individual (if known)

remarks or special reminders about each visit

a reference to the file number of the data the traveler is taking
along for each call.

Pertinent Files

The secretary should prepare a file for each firm to be visited. Then, the executive will not need to rely on memory alone for information regarding the firm and past associations with the firm or individuals in it. A memory refresher file may, indeed, help make the call productive.

A separate folder should be prepared for each call, and each folder should bear a reference number that is keyed to the schedule of appointments. The folders should be arranged in the order in which the executive will make the calls.

Each folder should contain:

copies of past correspondence with the firm or individual

letters or memos concerning the problem to be discussed

a list of the persons to see and their positions in the company

a list of the officers and executives of the organization

a list of the persons with whom the executive has had contact in
the past, other than those with whom appointments are scheduled, and the circumstances of these contacts

other bits of information, regardless of how insignificant they may
seem.

Stationery and Other Supplies

In addition to the files of correspondence and other data that the executive will take along, it is wise to provide the traveler with some stationery and supplies for communication with the office and with others while traveling. For this purpose the secretary should draw up a checklist of those supplies to be taken, assemble all the materials, and pack them in the briefcase. Supplies that the executive might require include company stationery, plain paper, onionskin or copy paper, carbon paper, envelopes of various sizes, memo paper or pads, a legal pad, an address book, legal-size folders, letter-size folders, business cards, dictation equipment (portable recorder), cassette tapes or belts for recorder, mailing folders or boxes for dictation tapes or belts, office account checks, expense forms, other office forms, pens and pencils, erasers, clips, scissors, rubber bands, transparent tape, paste, calendar, pins, a bottle opener, a ruler, first-aid items, aspirin, a timetable, and postage stamps. The materials that the executive selects from the checklist should be assembled by the secretary, checked by the executive, and made ready for packing at least a day before departure.

Expense Record Book

The expense record forms or expense book should be packed on top, so that expenses can be recorded as the executive goes along. This is a very important detail, because the expense record is needed for income-tax and accounting purposes. Generally the following information is needed if the executive is to be reimbursed in part or whole for the trip or to be able to deduct business-incurred travel expense from income tax: date of trip; description of how expense was incurred; types of expense (transportation, entertainment, breakfast, lunch, dinner, and so forth); and amount reimbursed by company. In some instances receipts must be obtained for travel expenses. Therefore a secretary should be familiar with the company and income-tax requirements in this area and should attach a reminder to the expense forms or expense book for the traveling executive to obtain these receipts as the occasions arise.

Arrangements for Domestic Trips

Large organizations generally have traffic departments that make all the arrangements pertinent to a trip. If the company has a traffic department, the executive's secretary submits to this department the data that has been obtained from the executive about the trip, and then the department takes over. It works out the itinerary with the traveler's approval, makes all the reservations for transportation and accommodations, and obtains the confirmations. This information is sent to the executive's office well in advance of the departure date.

Where there is no traffic department in an organization, the secretary may either call on the services of a reliable travel agency or take care of the arrangements personally.

The easiest way to obtain reservations for domestic and foreign travel is through the services of a reliable travel agency. Many executives rely on these services to plan their trips and to make their reservations. This method saves the secretary considerable time. Furthermore, travel agencies can usually obtain better and faster services than an individual who lacks their contacts and their specialized experience and knowledge.

If the secretary or the executive does not know the name of a good travel agency, he or she can contact other firms whose executives travel or get a list from The American Society of Travel Agents, Inc., at 501 Fifth Avenue, New York, NY 10017. However, not all of the good travel agents belong to this society. Others may be listed in the classified telephone directory.

The secretary must provide the travel agent with the executive's name, business and home telephone numbers, credit card number (if pertinent), detailed information on dates and times of arrival and departure desired for each city to be visited, and the type of transportation preferred. Although the agent will report periodically the progress made, it is the secretary's responsibility to keep in touch with the agent in order to see to it that tickets and reservations arrive at the office in plenty of time to check the dates, times, destinations, and so forth before they are turned over to the traveler.

These agencies do not charge for making airline or hotel reservations, since they receive a commission from the hotel or airline with which the reservation is placed. There is sometimes a charge, however, for rail reservations unless they are part of a prearranged package tour. Refunds for any unused tickets are obtained by the agency and should be reflected as deductions from the charges made on bills. The agency should be instructed that all bills are to be sent to the attention of the executive or the secretary, so that they can be checked before being forwarded to the accounting department.

Making Reservations for Transportation

Plane travel. The types of plane service available are first class and coach. Both types of accommodations are often available on the same plane. The differences between first class and coach are the size and comfort of the seats and the type of meals. First-class passengers enjoy wider seats and more leg room. They are served meals and complimentary alcoholic beverages. The coach section of the plane may be larger with smaller seats set closer together. The meals are less elaborate than in first class and alcoholic beverages must be purchased separately.

It has become the policy of many companies to request traveling personnel to use coach service on plane travel. The executive who prefers to travel first class must personally pay the difference between coach fare and first-class fare. The secretary should check company policy on this and then determine the executive's preference each time a trip is to be made. The executive may be willing to pay the difference if a very long flight is involved. If a first-class flight is to be made, the difference in cost must be entered in the correct place in the expense sheet.

Shuttle plane service may offer only a single class, especially when the flight is made in a smaller plane.

The secretary whose executive travels extensively should add an airline guidebook to the desk reference library for information on airlines servicing each city in the nation. The *Official Airlines Guide* may be obtained by writing to Official Airlines Guide, 2000 Clearwater Drive, Oak Brook, Illinois 60521. Each city in the United States and its possessions and each city in Canada that is serviced by an airline is listed in this book; the book indicates the airlines that service each city and gives information on car-rental and taxi service in each city.

Airline schedules may be kept on hand and the executive and the secretary may check the schedule before calling for reservations. The schedules need to be updated regularly, because flights may have been added or canceled or have changes of time.

To make a plane reservation, the secretary should call the reservation desk of the airline chosen by the executive and give the executive's name, the name and address of the firm, the credit card number, the executive's home telephone number, the desired flight number, the city of departure and the city of destination, and the time that the flight is scheduled to leave. If the flight is already filled or a considerable change in time has been posted, the secretary should ask for alternative suggestions. If none of the suggestions is acceptable to the executive, ask to be placed on the standby list and then try to make reservations on some other airline. As soon as a reservation is available and a definite confirmation is received, the secretary should immediately cancel all the other pending alternative arrangements. This will ensure the good will of persons the secretary may want to deal with in the future.

In placing airline reservations, the secretary should get the name of the airline clerk who makes the original reservations. If flight plans are extremely involved, with layovers in different cities and changes of time zones, the secretary may avoid repeating the information if the same clerk is available when checking or changing plans.

Payment for airline tickets is generally made by credit card or standard billing. The secretary should be absolutely certain that there is time for an airline ticket to arrive in the mail prior to a flight. If there is some doubt, the executive should pick up the ticket at the airport before boarding the plane. If the ticket comes in advance, the various parts must be checked carefully against the information on the itinerary as to the correctness of flight numbers, the time of departure, the departure airport, and the city of destination. If any discrepancies are noted, the secretary must immediately notify the reservation clerk.

Train travel. The choice of available train accommodations may depend upon the length of the trip and the price of the accommodations. The least expensive way of traveling is by coach. For long trips, the traveler may prefer a Pullman accommodation. For the most part, Pullman accommodations offered are roomettes and bedrooms. A roomette is a private room, usually for one person, with a bed folding into the wall, a sofa seat for daytime use, and toilet facilities in the same room. A bedroom is a private room with lower and upper berths, the lower berth serving as a sofa for daytime use, and toilet facilities in the same room. Bedrooms are more expensive than roomettes.

The secretary should be aware that not all trains provide all the above accommodations. Railroad connections to many destinations are increasingly limited.

Automobile travel. Sometimes a trip may be more easily and conveniently made by car, or the executive may rent a car to reach the desired destination after disembarking from plane or train. In that case, and if the executive is a member of the American Automobile Association (AAA), help can be obtained from its travel department in planning the route that should be followed on the trip. The AAA will prepare a "Triptik," which is a detailed, up-to-the-minute strip map of the entire trip, listing recommended hotels and AAA service stations along the route. This association also assists members in obtaining hotel and resort accommodations.

If the executive is not a member of the AAA, the secretary's task is more complicated. Road maps and city maps may be obtained from the Tourist Bureaus in the various states and cities, but they must be sent for well in advance. Nowadays there is sometimes a fee involved and the secretary will have to write a second letter after the amount of this is made known.

Most drivers have a preferred method of mapping out the route for a trip. If the secretary is asked to determine the best driving route to a destination, the executive's preferred method of recording this should be determined. Some drivers mark out a route directly on the map with a transparent felt-tipped pen. Others write out an itinerary to be followed.

If a car is to be rented, arrangements should be made as far in advance as possible. Rates vary according to the size of car to be rented, so the executive's preference should be determined before the reservations are made. If the car is to be left at a different city or airport from the one where it is rented, the secretary will need to make sure that the car-rental agency has a branch at the second location.

Bus travel. With the improvements in equipment and services offered by bus lines, the economy-minded traveler may choose to use this means of travel for all or intervening portions of a trip. Bus lines have passenger service agents who will assist in planning either long or short trips. Timetables should be obtained and the route laid out well before reservations are placed for a bus trip.

Refunds for Unused Tickets

On occasion the executive may need to change travel plans en route. In such a case the traveler is entitled to a refund on the unused portion of the ticket. The transportation line should be informed at once when the need for cancellation becomes apparent.

The secretary may send an unused flight ticket with a covering letter to the Refund Accounting Department of the airline involved. In the letter the secretary should mention the date of the flight that the executive was to have taken, the city of departure, the city of destination, the ticket number, the flight number, the credit card number, and the cost of the ticket. Refunds for train travel may be handled in a similar fashion.

Making Motel or Hotel Reservations

Reservations for motel or hotel accommodations should be made as soon as possible. Delay can cause the executive to arrive in a strange city without any place to stay. Therefore the secretary must be certain that reservations for all motel or hotel accommodations have been made and confirmed before the executive leaves on a trip.

If the motel or hotel at which the executive plans to stay is part of a chain, the easiest and quickest way for the secretary to make reservations is to call the chain's toll-free number for the central location through which all reservations for motels or hotels in the chain are handled.

In making reservations for overnight accommodations, the following sources contain information:

Hotel and Motel Red Book, published annually by the American Hotel Association Directory Corporation, 888 Seventh Avenue, New York, New York 10019. This book lists the hotels and motels by city and state; indicates the number of rooms, rates, and plans under which they operate (American, with meals; European, without meals); lists recreational facilities; gives telephone and toll-free telephone or TWX numbers for each hotel; and indicates whether the hotel or motel belongs to a chain. A special section lists number and types of meeting rooms

of various seating capacities, along with facilities available in
these rooms for PA systems, lecterns, showing of films, etc.

*Leahy's Hotel Guide and Travel Atlas of the United States,
Canada, Mexico, and Puerto Rico*, published by the American
Hotel Register Company, 2775 Shermer Road, Northbrook,
Illinois 60062.

Chamber of Commerce or Tourist Information Bureau in city of
destination.

Folders from the American Automobile Association, which list
motels, hotels, and inns for automobile travelers.

In making reservations for overnight accommodations, the following information must be supplied to the person taking reservations:
the name and address of the traveler, the type of accommodations
desired, the date of arrival, the approximate time of day of arrival,
and the probable departure date. The secretary should be sure to
obtain the checkout time, since this varies from one place to another,
and to request a confirmation of the reservation by mail. These
confirmations should be attached to the traveler's itinerary. Unless a
request for accommodations has been confirmed, there is no assurance
that a room will be held for the traveler. Some motels and hotels
confirm reservations only if a deposit is made in advance.

Generally if a reservation is not picked up by 6 P.M., the room is
not held. Therefore, if the traveler will arrive later than 6 P.M., it
would be wise to make a deposit to ensure that the room will be held
for the traveler. If such a deposit is not made and the traveler is held
up along the way, he or she should call the motel or hotel if possible
and ask that the reservation be held.

If the executive changes plans about itinerary or hotel after the
reservation is made, the secretary should contact the motel or hotel
to cancel the reservation.

Arrangements for Foreign Travel

Preparations for foreign travel should be made far in advance of the
departure date. There are many more details to be considered than in
domestic travel arrangements, and many phases of such an undertaking
involve much time. Before any arrangements for travel accommodations are started, the traveler should know

1. the names of the persons to be seen in what countries and for
   how long
2. the U.S. government requirements regarding travel to foreign
   countries

3. the requirements of the government of the country or countries to be visited

4. any conditions that are imposed on business travelers but not on tourists, and

5. something about the countries to be visited.

Using a travel agency. It is advisable that the arrangements for foreign travel be made by a reliable travel agency, unless the organization has a traffic department and foreign branches in the countries to be visited. Under any circumstances, the executive's secretary must know where to obtain information in preparation for the executive's trip abroad and the data that will be needed for such a trip. The travel agency chosen should be one that will work out a personal itinerary for the traveling executive, rather than an agency that specializes in package tours. A reliable agency will take care of all of the details pertaining to the trip and will perform the following services for its clientele:

Prepare a tentative itinerary, which the executive can approve or change.

Handle all the arrangements for traveling, for hotels, and perhaps for sightseeing for the entire trip.

Provide information as to exactly which documents will be needed (passport, visas, health and police certificates, etc.) and how to obtain them.

Obtain all the documents that they can (certain documents the executive must obtain personally).

Provide a small amount of currency in the denominations of the country or countries to be visited, in exchange for the equivalent in U.S. money.

Help to obtain a letter of credit or traveler's checks.

Arrange to have a rental car waiting for the executive at the destination point, if desired.

Handle both personal and baggage insurance, if desired.

If the executive is uncertain about accommodations and is unable to make arrangements before leaving, supply the name of a desirable hotel in the country of destination, as well as a letter of introduction to the manager of the hotel.

Preliminary preparations. For help in arranging a foreign business trip, the secretary can contact the Bureau of International Commerce in the Department of Commerce. This government department maintains a staff of specialists on individual countries and can contact foreign-trade experts who are stationed at each of the Department's field offices. This bureau will supply information on economic developments, regulations and trade statistics on any country, distribution methods, foreign costs and their effect on sales prices, types of distributors, and names of key commercial officers to contact both in the United States and in the countries to be visited. It will also set up the executive's overseas appointments and will notify all U.S. Foreign Service posts, such as the embassies, consulates, and consuls general, that the executive is coming to those countries and alert them as to the purpose of the visit. The bureau will request that these posts provide any assistance that is needed. Furthermore, the Washington Bureau of International Commerce maintains a trade complaint service, with which a traveler can communicate if any dispute with a foreign country should arise; this bureau safeguards and protects the industrial property rights to patents, trademarks, and copyrights abroad.

A very important secretarial duty in making preparations for the executive's trip abroad is writing letters to pave the way for a good reception in the countries to be visited. The secretary should write to the firms to be visited to make and confirm appointments, giving the time of arrival, the length of time the executive expects to stay, the address where reservations have been made, and any other pertinent information that will make it possible to aid the executive in the country of destination. The secretary should not overlook checking the holiday dates of the countries to be visited (see Chapter 26), so that an appointment will not be planned for a day when the offices will be closed. It should be borne in mind that many countries celebrate holidays that differ from those in the United States. (See Chapter 26 for additional hints on foreign travel.)

Visas. Some, but not all, countries require that visitors obtain permission to enter the country through a document referred to as a "visa." Therefore the secretary should call the consulates of the countries that the executive intends to visit and find out whether a visa is necessary. If it is, a passport must be presented by the traveler at the consulate and a visa form filled out. Since the length of time it takes to process a visa varies with the country to be visited, this must be done well in advance of the set departure date. The secretary should also find out from the consulate what the fee for the visa will be, since a charge for this document is generally made.

Customs regulations. In order to avoid difficulties upon the traveler's return to this country, the secretary should obtain information about the customs regulations for travelers abroad and present it to the executive. Such information can be procured from pamphlets issued by the U.S. Treasury Department, Bureau of Commerce, Washington, D.C., and from the travel agent who is arranging the trip.

The secretary should remind the executive that if a watch, a camera, or any other item of foreign manufacture that was purchased in the United States is being taken abroad, it will be necessary to carry proof of purchase such as a sales slip for each of the items. Such possessions should also be registered with the U.S. Customs officials before the executive leaves, in order to eliminate possible customs problems upon reentry.

During the trip, the executive will expect to be kept posted on events occurring at the home office. Therefore, it is important to determine which items are to be referred to other people in the organization and which are to be forwarded to the traveler. Some employers request that the secretary keep a log of daily events and send it on to them at specific times. If the secretary keeps abreast of the traveler's itinerary and uses airmail, the traveler can be kept informed about events in the home office. The secretary should keep a duplicate copy of all correspondence that is forwarded and number each packet sent, so that any loss can be detected.

If it is necessary to send a package to the executive in some foreign country, the secretary should first check with the post office about mailing regulations, restrictions, and requirements (see Chapter 7).

For urgent messages that need immediate attention, the secretary can rely on telephone, telegram, or cablegram services, which are described in Chapter 7.

The Traveling Secretary

At times it is necessary for the executive to take along a secretary on a business trip. Although today the executive has several means to facilitate business needs, such as portable recorders, public stenographers, and the like, an employer may prefer to take the secretary on the trip because much of the work to be done would take a great deal of explaining to one unfamiliar with it.

A secretary who travels with an employer should be prepared for and try to foresee all contingencies that may arise during the trip. The secretary should determine which supplies should be taken along and which will be easily available at the destination.

If the executive will want material typed, arrangements for a typewriter must be made. A portable typewriter may be taken along if one is available. If not, the secretary may write ahead to the hotel or motel and arrange for the rental of a typewriter. Then again, it may be possible for the traveling secretary to type up reports or speeches as needed in a branch office of the company. If arrangements for this courtesy can be made in advance, the way may be paved for a harmonious sharing of space and office equipment during the trip.

SOCIAL AMENITIES

Visiting Cards

Executives must use both business and personal cards. A secretary encloses an executive's business card when sending a gift to a business associate. However, if the individual becomes a personal friend—that is, someone whom the executive sees outside of business hours—the executive's personal card should be used. The secretary should also enclose the executive's personal card in greetings and presents that are sent to personal friends and to relatives.

Visiting cards that are collected from clients or other visitors should be stored in a reference file for easy access when they are needed.

Donations

An executive usually receives many requests for donations annually, and many individuals respond to these pleas. It is not the secretary's responsibility to screen such requests before submitting them to the employer. Every request for a donation must be submitted for the executive's attention and decision. However, it is the secretary's responsibility to keep a record, and (if possible) a receipt, for all donations made by the executive to educational, religious, and philanthropic organizations. These records are very important for income-tax purposes and for the donor's own information.

When a request for a donation or contribution comes into the office, it will aid the executive if the secretary notes on each request the amount given to that organization in the preceding year and the total amount of contributions made during the current year. If a pledge was made that is payable in installments, the due dates of the payments should be entered on the secretary's calendar or in the card tickler and brought to the executive's attention as they occur. At the end of the year a list should be compiled of all the organizations to which the executive has contributed, with the amounts of the donations given to each organization clearly shown.

Invitations

Invitations extended by the executive to two types of functions are of particular concern to the secretary. These functions are formal dinners that are given personally and official entertainments given by the executive in an official capacity.

Invitations for either of these functions are usually formal in style.

This means that they should be written in the third person. They may be engraved, partly engraved, or handwritten.

An executive who entertains frequently may wish to have a quantity of partially engraved invitations made up. When the time comes to put them to use, the name of the guest, the kind of gathering, and the time and date can be filled in by hand. A partially engraved invitation generally follows this form:

Mr. and Mrs. Harold Jones
request the pleasure of
(name written in)
company at
on
at   o'clock
35 Woodlawn Avenue

Answers to Invitations

Etiquette requires that an invitation be answered promptly in the same form in which it was issued; that is, if the invitation was issued in the third person, it should be answered in the third person. Formal answers are used in reply to formal invitations.

The full name of the person answering the invitation should appear. If the invitation is proffered in more than one name, all the names mentioned should be shown in the reply. The date and the hour that the function is to take place should be specified in an acceptance, but only the date need be mentioned in a regret. The year of the date is omitted. When referring to the invitation in a reply, it is courteous to refer to it as a "very kind invitation."

Answers to invitations to social business functions, such as luncheons, dinners, or receptions, should be on business letterhead paper. If it is necessary to explain the reason for declining such an invitation, a letter of explanation should follow the formal note of regret. Generally no reason need be given.

The secretary should keep a record of invitations received by the executive. The events should also be marked on the calendar or in the tickler file so that the employer can be reminded of them in advance. Also, if the employer should take the invitation home, the secretary will have a record of the host, time, place, and date of the affair, so that the invitation can be answered correctly when the decision on attendance is made.

If the invitation originates with the executive, the secretary should type a list of the guests to whom the invitations were sent. As the acceptances and regrets come in, a notation should be made next to the name of each guest, and the letters should be attached to the list. It is helpful to make a daily summary of the total number of acceptances, regrets, and nonresponses to the invitations sent out. This summary should be placed on the executive's desk at the end of each day.

When dinner or luncheon invitations have specified a definite return date for reply and no reply has been received from some of the guests on the list, it is perfectly permissible for the secretary to telephone the invited guests three or four days before the event. This is done in order to determine the number of guests who will be present.

Theater Tickets

A secretary is sometimes called upon to obtain theater tickets for the executive and guests. The executive may name several shows in order of preference. The usual procedure in buying tickets is to call the box office and charge tickets to the executive's credit-card account. Or, the secretary may go in person to a Ticketron location if there is one nearby.

It is often difficult to obtain tickets by either of these methods for hit shows unless they are bought far in advance. However, advance notice is not always possible. The secretary may establish an account in the executive's name with a reliable theater-ticket agency in order to have a better chance of obtaining tickets on short notice.

When the tickets arrive at the office, the secretary should enclose them in an envelope on which have been typed the date and day of the week of the performance, the curtain time, the name and address of the theater, and the name of the show.

If the tickets must be sent through the mail for any reason, the secretary should enclose with them a letter of transmittal in which reference has been made to the name of the show, the name and address of the theater, the date of the performance, and the seat numbers. Thus, if the tickets are lost, and particularly if the executive has planned to attend several different shows, the carbon copy of the letter contains all the information necessary for follow-up. The letter also provides all the pertinent information to the individual receiving the tickets and acts as a reminder of the date.

Gift and Card Lists

A secretary may also have the responsibility of reminding the executive of an approaching occasion such as a birthday, anniversary, or graduation. He or she may also be expected to send holiday remembrances. For this purpose, a record of these events and lists of the persons to whom the executive sends cards and presents must be kept. Separate lists should be maintained for friends, relatives, and business acquaintances to whom holiday greetings are sent by the executive, those to whom cards are sent by the executive jointly with husband or wife, those who receive company cards, those to whom holiday gifts are given, and those who receive gifts at other times of the year.

These lists and records should be kept up to date, with names added or deleted and addresses checked periodically. It will aid the executive in the selection of gifts if the secretary keeps a cumulative record of the gifts previously given the individual, their cost, and the occasions for which they were given. Since the secretary in many cases is asked to select and purchase the cards and gifts and to address and mail them, these lists should be submitted to the employer well in advance of the occasion, so that sufficient time will be allowed for shopping, preparation, and mailing.

Holiday gifts or greeting cards should be thought of at least six or eight weeks in advance, particularly if the gift is to be sent abroad. If greeting cards are to have the executive's name imprinted, they need to be ordered early.

At Time of Death

At the time of a death, a friend or acquaintance of the deceased usually expresses sympathy by sending a token remembrance to the bereaved family. The form of this expression of sympathy depends upon the religious affiliation, if any, of the deceased. These expressions may take any one or a combination of several of the following forms:

Flowers. It is customary to send flowers to the bereaved family, except one of the Jewish faith. From close friends or relatives, prepared dishes for meals that will save the family from food preparation is considered a proper and accepted expression of sympathy to the Jewish family in mourning.

Flowers may take the form of a floral piece—a spray, wreath, or basket. It is also appropriate to send a floral piece to memorial services when the deceased is cremated or buried immediately. A card should always accompany the floral piece. If a visiting card is used for this purpose, the engraved name should be crossed out in ink and a few words of sympathy added. The floral piece is usually ordered by the secretary from the florist by telephone, and the florist supplies an appropriate card on which the name of the person sending the flowers is written, along with any message the sender desires. When ordering the floral piece, the secretary must be prepared to tell the florist the name of the deceased, where the flowers are to be sent, the time and date of the services, and the kind and size of floral piece desired.

Letters of sympathy. Letters expressing sympathy to the bereaved family may be sent to people of any faith and may be sent in addition to flowers, fruit, or any of the other expressions noted here. The secretary should inquire about the customs in the business and social community of the executive.

Mass cards. Mass cards indicate that arrangements have been made to have a Mass or Masses said in memory of the deceased and for the repose of the soul. It is appropriate to send such cards to a Roman Catholic family. They may be sent by either a Roman Catholic or a non-Catholic. The cards may be obtained from a priest, church office, or sometimes a funeral parlor. It is customary to make an offering when such cards are obtained. Although a Roman Catholic could ask a priest to say Mass for a non-Catholic, Mass cards are not usually sent to a non-Catholic family.

Charitable contributions. Some families specify that, instead of flowers, they would prefer friends and business associates to send contributions to charities or organizations in which the deceased was interested. If this is done, the organization that receives these donations in the name of the deceased usually notifies the bereaved family that such contributions were received. The donor may also write to the family to inform them that a donation is being sent to the charitable or educational institution in the name of the deceased.

Death of a member of the executive's family. When a member of the executive's family dies, the secretary may be asked to keep a record of those who send expressions of sympathy and what was sent. A description of the floral piece that was received should be written on the back of each accompanying card. In addition, a separate alphabetic file of all Mass cards and letters should be kept. From these data, separate lists can be made of those who sent flowers alone, of those who sent both Mass cards and flowers, of those who wrote and also sent flowers or Mass cards, and of those who sent contributions to institutions, and appropriate acknowledgments sent.

Two opinions exist concerning the type of acknowledgment that is appropriate at this time. According to one, the cards acknowledging expressions of sympathy should be formal and engraved. According to the other, it is perfectly proper to have the acknowledgments typed. Acknowledgments may be written out in longhand if only a few need to be sent, but if the deceased was a prominent person and hundreds of remembrances were received, engraved cards should be sent only to those who are unknown to the bereaved, not to acquaintances. The type of remembrance sent—flowers, Mass cards, or contributions—should be mentioned in the acknowledgment.

The secretary should also keep a list of the names and addresses of those who performed outstanding services, such as doctors, nurses, a priest, minister, or rabbi, editorial writers, and the like, so that letters of appreciation can be sent to them for their kindness and understanding. Also, thank-you letters should be sent to those who sent memorial contributions to organizations.

All the lists should be submitted to the executive, who will select those to whom letters will be dictated, those to whom acknowledgments will be written in longhand, and those for whom the secretary is to draft and type acknowledgments.

Death of the executive. The details that the secretary takes care of in the event of the executive's death depend upon the wishes of the family. The secretary can offer assistance in a number of ways:

Help to compile material for newspaper obituaries. This would include dates and history of the executive's career and the names of organizations to which the executive belonged and offices held in each. The secretary can write or help to write the obituary or call the newspapers and give the information to the writer responsible for this. The funeral director supplies the funeral notice to the newspapers; the secretary can supply information for this.

Notify branch offices, foreign offices, or affiliates of the company of the death of the executive.

Notify the executive's lawyer and the secretaries of organizations to which the executive belonged.

Notify the insurance company or companies, the Social Security Administration, and any other institution or agency from which a monetary death benefit may derive.

Arrange for the personal effects of the executive to be removed from the office and taken home or disposed of as the family requests.

Keep a file of clippings from the newspapers bearing items about the deceased.

TALKING TO VISITORS

When visitors arrive they should find a courteous, professional secretary who is pleasant and attentive. The secretary should take the visitor's name, company, and reason for the visit and notify the executive that the person is waiting. It may help the executive if the secretary escorts the visitor to the office or conference room and announces or introduces the person to the executive. If the visitor is required to wait and wishes to talk, the secretary should engage in light conversation and avoid details about office matters.

Some executives suggest that visitors be offered coffee or tea while they wait. The secretary should ask if the visitor wishes refreshments and either serve it or direct the visitor to the area in the office where coffee and tea can be obtained.

Visitors without appointments should be told politely that the executive has a very busy schedule and cannot see people without an appointment. Then, the person's name, company, and phone number should be taken and arrangements for a future appointment made.

TALKING TO REPORTERS

If the executive is a government official or in the public eye, the secretary may find it necessary to deal with reporters and others from the media. Be courteous and professional; however, do not volunteer information. If the executive has a prepared statement, have it ready and distribute it without comment. If the executive asks the secretary to make a verbal statement, prepare the statement beforehand, type it, and read it as written. After the statement is read, it may be necessary to make a dismissal statement such as "This is the information that has been prepared for you. There is no further statement at this time. Thank you for your cooperation." If reporters persist, security may need to be called.

ORGANIZING MEETINGS AND CONFERENCES

The secretary may be called upon to assist with meetings and conferences—the preparation phase, tasks during the meeting, and the completion of tasks after the meeting.

Preparation Phase

During the preparation phase the secretary may be responsible for notifying the staff, directors, and persons outside the office headquarters, sometimes in other cities or countries, of the planned meeting or conference. Invitations may be mailed or telephoned. The secretary should make a list of those to be notified, check that all are informed, and check responses so that a final list of those who will be able to attend is prepared. If invitations are mailed, a reply card and a self-addressed envelope are enclosed.

The secretary may also work with the executive in preparing the agenda and materials for the participants; arranging for special services, sites, and speakers; arranging the physical site (the size of the room, the positioning of tables and chairs, etc.); and taking care of other miscellaneous details (providing water for the participants, locating coat racks, etc.)

The following page shows a typical agenda for a monthly staff meeting.

During the preparation phase special services such as multimedia equipment, tours of plants or offices, printing of agendas, mailing press coverage, security, and duplicating and organizing information folders will be attended to by the secretary. The secretary should also make sure that microphones, slide projectors, overhead projectors, video machines, and the like are available and functioning.

During the Meeting

During the meeting or conference, the secretary should be sure that everything ordered has arrived in working order and should organize material such as folders, pencils, and pads for the speakers and those who attend. The secretary may also arrange for greeting those who speak and attend, directing participants and speakers to conference rooms, and making introductions.

In addition, the secretary may be required to take the minutes, list participants, handle correspondence and telephone messages, deal with last-minute problems or changes, distribute press releases, arrange for luncheons, and summarize presentations.

After the Meeting

After the meeting or conference the secretary may be asked to prepare the minutes for distribution, collect extra agendas and materials, and list persons who will receive copies of the minutes, "thank-you" letters, and conference-related information.

Meeting/conference minutes should be prepared according to a specific format (see Chapter 6). The secretary will need copies of the agenda, notices of the meeting, lists of those who attended and spoke, and the file on current papers related to the meeting/conference.

Annual meetings and conferences require knowledge of the last meeting, the schedule, people involved, travel arrangements, contacts such as caterers, hotels, sites, and speakers. This job is easier if the office maintains a tickler file. One need only locate the conference folder from the last meeting or conference to begin the cycle of preparation.

Chapter 20, "Membership Secretary," provides additional information (and checklists) on handling conferences and meetings.

Agenda for Monthly Staff Meeting
January 15, 19__

SCHEDULE	EVENT	PLACE
9:30 A.M.	Call to Order Old Business Read Minutes of Last Meeting Committee Reports	Suite 1215
10 A.M.	New Business	Suite 1221

	1. Peter Doyle -
	   Demonstration of New
	   Computer System for
	   Accounting
	2. Helen Brown-
	   Dealing with Executive
	   Stress: New Techniques	

Noon	President's Report	Suite 1221
1-2 P.M.	Lunch	Suite 1232

DAILY AGENDA FOR A CONFERENCE
Monday, February 15

9 A.M.-Noon	Phillip White, Susan MacKay Our New Line of Sofware	Harrison Room
Noon-1 P.M.	Informal Discussion	Harrison Room
1-2:30 P.M.	Lunch Mary Alice Bender New Market Opportunities	Sky Terrace

Tuesday, February 16

9-11 A.M.	James Williams, Dawn Petersen Hardware - Old and New	Columbia Room
11:35 A.M.-1 P.M.	Plenary Margaret Snow and Anita Cuttitta Management Systems for Small Companies	Wintergreen Room
1:15-2:30 P.M.	Lunch Karen Trainer Business Run by Women	Sky Room

Time Management

by Murray Bromberg

In an attempt to improve employee performance, many large corporations routinely administer needs assessment questionnaires to staff members. In so doing, they seek to find out employee weaknesses and needs and determine in which areas training should be focused.

Research into the responses has shown that the entire range of office personnel, including secretaries, middle-management people, and top executives, often pinpoint similar concerns, such as how to handle stress, reduce paperwork, gain greater familiarity with state-of-the-art equipment, improve human relations, read faster, and comprehend better. However, almost without exception, the single topic that appears most often on most respondents' surveys is *time management*.

Some secretaries are able to deal with a tremendous workload within the normal working day without appearing frazzled or harassed. They rarely need to stay late to catch up on correspondence, get out a critical mailing, meet a deadline, or photocopy the agenda for the next day's important conference. As the popular saying goes, it's not that they work harder, but that they work smarter.

Admittedly, such performers are in the minority. Most secretaries in a busy environment complain that there just is not enough time during the normal work day to do everything required. When the pressure becomes intense ("I need that contract typed in a half hour," "Fish out everything we have on those mortgage applications before lunch," etc.), some secretaries almost panic and yearn for more time. But what they need is time management skills.

The good news about time management is that it is a skill that almost anyone can master. Application of the suggestions given in this chapter will restore a secretary's confidence, probably bring about renewed job satisfaction, and possibly even help the secretary advance in his or her career.

The remainder of this chapter discusses ten proven methods of time management for secretaries.

One: Analyzing the Way You Use Time Now

Before you start to draw up meaningful rules for streamlining your performance and managing your time, you should diagnose the problem. In short, try to determine how you spend your time now and decide whether or not you are using it to its best advantage. After you have analyzed how you spend your time now, you can determine how you can make better use of it in the future.

Just as a research-oriented employer might bring in a time-study expert to watch employees in action, you, the secretary, should keep a log of your daily expenditure of time. Over a period of two weeks, record your activities every half hour. Then study the log and focus on the recurring items that cause you to use your time inefficiently. Is it numerous trips to the mail room (and possible socializing en route)? Is it repeated jaunts to the executive's office for clarification of dictation, instructions, or other matters?

With the patterns apparent, you will be in a better position to draw up a trim schedule that will enable you to function in an orderly environment. After analyzing your movements, you may find that personally attending to every phase of every job that comes across your desk is a poor way to budget your time. Is it really necessary for you to collate multiple copies, to staple a newsletter, or to run envelopes through a postage meter? Are clerical assistants available for such tasks?

When executives enroll in time management seminars, they spend many hours learning how to delegate responsibility. Assuming that there is help available in the office, the secretary should also learn how to delegate. If you instruct and train people properly, you will very likely be able to assign them routine tasks, thus freeing yourself for those tasks that you and only you were hired to do.

Two: Living with a Schedule

The next step is the organization of a daily schedule. It may be more interesting to ad lib, and of course it is necessary to vary routines once in a while, but secretaries who do careful planning are on the road to becoming successful time managers.

Let's look at one secretary's schedule:

```
9:00 to 9:15 A.M.   - Play back telephone messages

9:15 to 9:40        - Go through the morning's mail

9:40 to 10:40       - Complete yesterday's correspondence

10:40 to 11:30      - Make business calls; set up appointments;
                      respond to inquiries

11:30 to 12:00      - Clip relevant articles from daily
                      newspapers

12:00 to 1:00 P.M.  - Lunch

1:00 to 2:00        - Take dictation

2:00 to 3:00        - Type the letters

3:00 to 4:00        - Take minutes at office meeting and
                      transcribe them

4:00 to 5:00        - Filing, mailing
```

Of course, the typical secretary is not a robot. There are coffee breaks, minor crises, photocopying, trips to the mailroom, etc. However, those secretaries who are guided by a schedule—somewhat rigid, somewhat flexible—will often find that they have those extra minutes each day to accomplish the tasks they need to complete.

An important hint: one sure way to negate the advantages to be gained from a daily schedule is to be intransigent and to tolerate no deviations from the schedule. In short, the secretary should be guided by the planned schedule but not shackled by it. Special needs will require modifying the schedule, but after that, the secretary can go back to its general outline.

Three: Working with a "To Do" List

Going hand in hand with the daily schedule is the "to do" list, a compilation of outstanding matters that require the secretary's attention. A typical "to do" list might include:

- Type letters to new sales reps
- Call service company for copying machine
- Order office supplies
- Revise file card tabs
- Prepare labels for mailing to prospective customers
- Place help wanted ad for office receptionist
- Have Mr. Berman's new business cards picked up at the printers
- Call DHL for pickup of letter to our Bangkok office
- Confirm Mr. Berman's reservation with Delta Airlines
- Order new name stamp for Mr. Berman

The "to do" list should be drawn up at the start of the week, reviewed daily, and updated as progress is made.

Some secretaries combine the "to do" list with a control sheet. Next to each important or multi-step item, they record steps taken toward its completion. In that way, they have a progress report as well as a visible reminder.

It is reasonable to assume that there will usually be about ten or more items on the "to do" list. The list is likely to have some tasks that will take five minutes to accomplish (e.g., a phone call) and some that are multi-step and challenging (e.g., reviewing the minutes of all unit meetings for the previous year and preparing an executive summary). In addition, some tasks require immediate attention; others are long-range in nature.

Start by grouping the tasks on the list: those that are routine and can be accomplished promptly in one column and other, more complex and time-consuming tasks in another column. The tasks in each column can then be prioritized so that the more important ones and/or the ones to which the executive gives greater weight are at the top. It is good practice to divide the larger tasks into smaller parts and do one part at a time.

Four: Hesitating to Take on Others' Responsibilities

A secretary naturally wants to please not only the executive but also coworkers. This can sometimes lead to problems if, for example, the secretary takes on responsibilities that are not his or hers and in so doing becomes overburdened with work that other staff members should be doing. Let's examine some practical examples.

Your fellow secretary, Miss Adams, makes personal calls throughout the day. As a result, she doesn't have enough time to complete an important assignment from the Vice President for whom she works. She asks for your assistance. While you are willing to help a colleague, when you repeatedly undertake such activities your own work suffers. The time-management strides that you have been making are seriously threatened. How do you get Miss Adams to stop taking advantage of your good nature? You might say, "Gloria, you have to respect the fact that my time is as important as yours. I'll pitch in whenever I have nothing pressing to do, but if you are a real friend, you won't ask me to bail you out regularly." (Notice, you are not lecturing her about her telephone activity, since that would chill your relationship permanently, but you are leading her to feel the guilt and to change her ways—if that is at all possible.)

Another example: The account executive for whom you work, Mr. Baker, asks you to shop for him, return purchases for credit, pick up theater tickets, etc. He tells you to take a two-hour lunch, leave the office an hour early, or punch in an hour late as compensation for taking care of his personal errands. One possible way to handle this is to say, "Mr. Baker, I love the job, and I think I'm making a genuine contribution toward our unit's effectiveness. If you want me to help you out on the special missions, I'm pleased to be of service, too, but I'm concerned about completing my basic daily tasks. Of course, the final decision is yours."

Five: Handling the Mail Efficiently

Some secretaries receive a daily bag of mail for all the staff and sort it before delivering it to the correct desks. The personal or executive secretary, however, usually opens the executive's mail and some secretaries, usually experienced ones in whom the executive has a great deal of confidence, have complete jurisdiction over the mail. They know which letters require immediate attention from their employers, which should be forwarded to other office personnel for action, which are considered to be the kind of junk mail that the executive does not wish to see, and which should be routinely filed.

Tackling the mail in a large office can be an onerous, time-consuming job that may wreak havoc with a well-planned schedule. Obviously, there is nothing to be gained by reading every word of every document. The secretary who is managing time efficiently determines the importance of each letter swiftly and steers it in the right direction.

Just as the executive's time management skills can be improved by handling each piece of mail once (and only once), so can the secretary's. If the mail is to be placed in the executive's in-basket, do so. If it goes to his/her associate, send it there promptly without keeping it on your desk, where it might be subjected to multiple handling. If it is a solicitation from an organization that your executive has told you to ignore, put it directly into the trash basket.

Six: Learning to Use the Phone Efficiently

The telephone can upset the most carefully thought-out schedule, but there are some general guidelines to follow in using it. Skillful secretaries make sure that their telephone conversations are brief, concise, and businesslike—albeit friendly. Some executives simply want to know the name of the caller, but others prefer that the secretary elicit the purpose of the call. Whatever the protocol in your particular office, be sure to follow it expeditiously. (Refer to Chapter 7 for additional advice on telephone communications.) Here are a few sample lines experienced secretaries use:

"Good morning, M & S furniture. May I help you?"
"For Miss Carter? Whom shall I say is calling?"
"Does Miss Carter know what the call is about?"
"Miss Carter is out of the office. May I take a message?"

As you can see, there are no wasted words in these brief exchanges, but they are polite.

If the secretary needs to make several outside calls, it is advisable to set aside a specific time of the day, group the calls, and place them. This saves interruptions during other daily tasks.

Needless to say, personal phone calls, incoming and outgoing, should be kept to a minimum. In a survey done at a large insurance company employing more than 50 secretaries, a time study expert found that 40% of secretarial telephone activity involved personal calls.

Seven: Avoiding Costly Interruptions

Concentrating on business without being distracted by a host of interruptions can spell success for a secretary's time-management program. When a steady stream of people swirl around a secretary's desk and engage him or her in conversation, all good resolutions and time-management plans are worthless. Some time-management consultants advise clients about the placement of office furniture to lessen interruptions. A person who can be seen from the hallway is often the one people interrupt. Consider moving your desk, if your particular office situation will permit it.

A secretary's behavior does not have to be austere just to demonstrate concern for proper time management. As in all things, moderation is called for. When there is no pressure to complete a task, a little sociability is in order, but when pressing business is being conducted, social exchanges must take a back seat.

Eight: Keeping Your Desk Neat and Clean

A secretary should have a clean and orderly desk for the obvious reason that it makes a good impression on staff and visitors. It's impossible to maintain one's self-esteem when seated behind a sloppy desk with mounds of paper, coffee cups, leftover food, etc. However, the more important reason for keeping a neat desk, especially for the purposes of this chapter, is that it is very difficult to locate material on a messy desk. Time spent searching for misplaced notes, files, or messages is time lost. Get into the habit of using clearly marked file folders for the temporary storage of materials—until you are ready to file them in the central system.

Nine: Being Sure the Filing System Is a Help, Not a Hindrance

Consider whether your filing system is an aid or a detriment. If it takes many minutes to locate a needed document, and questions such as "Is it filed under 'Correspondence' or 'Conference Notes'?" come up, you should consider setting up a new filing system.

Filing is discussed in detail in Chapter 8. In the context of time management, the best advice is simply to draw up a list of every category now being used in the filing system and review it with a supervisor or an experienced coworker. Eliminate what is no longer relevant; consolidate where you find redundancies; revise categories for greater clarity, etc. The small time investment in reviewing the filing system will pay huge dividends in time saved later.

Ten: Some Final Don'ts

There are a few additional hints that are helpful for secretaries trying to manage their time efficiently. First, don't allow yourself to be sidetracked. You should have goals for every job you engage in, and not until these objectives are met should you be ready to move on to a new project. (Of course, when a legitimate "crisis" arises, all current matters must be delayed to accommodate the emergency.)

Second, don't take on more work than you can handle. Be realistic about your work load, and do not take on extra assignments if you do not realistically have the time. It will only dilute your effectiveness in all areas.

Third, don't say "yes" to every request. If another secretary stops by and asks "May I see you for a few minutes?" it is not essential that you drop whatever you are doing. You may politely say that you are busy and cannot interrupt what you are doing but that you will see him or her later, perhaps at lunch.

A Final Word

Following the ten suggestions given in this chapter will help a secretary stretch his or her working day and improve overall performance. In closing, it should be noted that another aspect of office efficiency is the way a secretary manages the time of the executive for whom he or she works. Maintaining an executive's calendar intelligently, confirming or cancelling meetings or appointments, and using tickler files to ensure compliance with deadlines and other commitments are critical time-management assets discussed elsewhere in this book. Suffice it to say that if you are the type of secretary who is eager to enhance your time-management skills, you will also be the team player who enables the executive to make every minute count. Secretaries with such attitudes possess the hallmarks of the respected professional.

Business English

Sample Business Letters and Memos

by Lois M. Burns

- *Business Letters*
    Basic Principles
    Samples
- *Interoffice Memorandums*
    Use and Format
    Samples
- *Electronic Mail—Telegrams, Mailgrams, Telexes,*
  and Facsimiles
    Basic Principles of a Mailgram®
    Basic Principles of Telegrams
    Basic Principles of Telexes
    Basic Principles of Facsimiles

One essential skill that a secretary must possess is the ability to compose letters and memorandums. Being asked to write letters for your employer indicates confidence in your ability. It gives you the opportunity to show your creativity. Accept the assignment as a challenge.

There are certain basic principles you must adhere to when you write a letter or a memorandum. This chapter presents guidelines and discusses procedures for preparing several kinds of written communications that a secretary may be asked to compose. Included are sample letters that show how to use the principles and procedures for specific kinds of letters and sample memos that illustrate typical interoffice communication.

BUSINESS LETTERS

The most important principle to remember in writing a business letter is to plan—before you begin to write. Then, follow a logical sequence in writing the letter. The following guidelines and sample letters should be helpful.

General Guidelines for Organizing a Business Letter

1. Establish what type of letter you are writing (the purpose of the letter). Is it a request for information, an order, or an acknowledgment? } First paragraph

2. State items that need action, answer questions, and give information. In other words, give the details of the letter. } Middle paragraphs

3. Summarize briefly. End with a friendly greeting, if appropriate. } Last paragraph

Other Guidelines in Writing an Effective Business Letter

1. Reflect the employer's style of writing in presenting the message.
2. Write with clarity.
3. Write concisely.
4. Write the message in a personal tone.
5. Write with a positive approach.
6. Write with diplomacy and tact.
7. Endeavor to create good will and interest.

Guidelines for Answering a Letter

1. Read the letter to be answered carefully.
2. Jot down points of inquiry or other important points.
3. Place these items in priority order.
4. Decide the answers to all questions.
5. Verify all data.
6. Organize the letter and begin to write.

Guidelines for Initiating a Letter

1. Establish the purpose of the letter.
2. Collect all necessary material—information, enclosures, etc.
3. Organize material.
4. Compose the letter in a style suitable for the intended purpose.

Sample Acknowledgment Letter

1. Answer immediately.
2. State what you are acknowledging.
3. Give information requested.
4. If appropriate, end with a ''thank you'' or an expression of interest.

December 3, 19__

Mr. Joseph Peters
124 Main Street
New York, NY 11201-6734

Dear Mr. Peters:

    Your letter regarding the figures in our current window
display has been received. The dolls that aroused your curiosity
were made in Yugoslavia. They are not antique, but were made and
purchased within the past year.

    Thank you for your kind words about this display. Our
decorators spent many hours planning and setting up the scene, and
it is nice to know it is appreciated and enjoyed.

                    Sincerely,

                    Jane Jones

                    Ms. Jane Jones
                    Senior Decorator

ss

Sample Adjustment Letter

1. Describe original action or purchase.
2. State complaint.
3. Request adjustment.

May 23, 19--

Mr. Richard White
Sales Manager
Richard Office Equipment Corporation
888 Mill Road
Abilene, TX 79601-5739

Dear Mr. White:

On February 14 of this year, your company shipped a
paper shredder to our office. It is the Prestige
brand labeled Model 433. It was installed by your
local agency, Richard Electric Company.

At our request, Richard Electric Company service
representatives came to try to adjust this piece of
equipment twice in February and four times in March.
It is inoperative most of the time, and at this time
it is again not working. It seems fairly clear by
now that we have a defective machine. Richard Electric
Company says we must deal directly with you regarding
this matter.

Please have a representative contact us for arrangements to replace this paper shredder.

Sincerely yours,

Sharon Flemmings

Miss Sharon Flemmings
Office Manager

rm

Sample Appointment Letter

1. Be specific as to time, place, and date of appointment.
2. State purpose of appointment.
3. Specify any special information, file, etc., necessary for the appointment.
4. Ask for confirmation.

July 26, 19__

Mr. John Lettier
Auditing Department
Muskins and Sells, Inc.
876 Indiana Avenue
Washington, DC 20001-1438

Dear Mr. Lettier

Mr. Thomas will be returning from his vacation next week and will
be able to meet with you to discuss the audit report in the Board
Room, Thursday, August 9, at 10 a.m.

Please bring File No. 306 with you to the meeting, as there are a
few questions to be answered.

We would appreciate your confirming this appointment by Monday,
August 6.

Sincerely

Catherine Thompson

Mrs. Catherine Thompson
Administrative Assistant

ia

Sample Cancellation of Appointment Letter

1. Be specific about time and date of appointment being cancelled.
2. Give reason for cancellation, if appropriate.
3. Request rescheduled appointment.

```
                        OLYMPIA GREENE, M.D.
                         22 CENTRAL AVENUE
                      GLENDALE, NY 11385-7342
                          (718) 381-2345



                                    October 13, 19__



Dr. Matthew Bavetta
123 Myrtle Avenue
Glendale, NY 11385-7342

Dear Dr. Bavetta:

Dr. Greene would like to cancel her appointment for Saturday,
October 18, at 10:30 a.m.  She will be out of town attending a
seminar on that day.

Please reschedule Dr. Greene's appointment for the same time on
Saturday, October 25.

If this is inconvenient, please telephone our office.

                         Sincerely,

                         Marilyn Landry

                         Ms. Marilyn Landry
                         Medical Secretary
```

Sample Appreciation Letter

1. State ceremony or occasion for which thanks is being expressed or enjoyment is being acknowledged.
2. State briefly subsidiary reasons, if any, for writing letter.
3. If appropriate, express wishes for future success.

October 3, 19__

Miss Margaret Bauer
21 Applegate Drive
Hamden, CT 06514-3456

Dear Margaret

    The speech that you gave at the in-house workshop last week was stimulating as well as informative. The people I spoke with after your presentation also responded favorably.

    It has been ten years since we were in college, and it was good to see you again. It certainly brought back many memories for me.

    I look forward to your presentation next weekend and know that it will be as successful as the last one.

Sincerely yours

Judith Karp

Ms. Judith Karp
Office Administrator

es

Sample Collection Letter

1. State the problem—that is, the amount due, dates of letters or orders, and mention of specific merchandise where necessary. This should usually be done in the first paragraph, unless the first paragraph is an attention-arousing device.
2. Present the argument for payment (two paragraphs).
3. Motivate action in the closing paragraph.

July 24, 19__

Mr. Walter Whitcomb
Administrator
XYZ Company
123 Main Street
Philadelphia, PA 30001-3456

Dear Mr. Whitcomb

In our letters of June 17, July 2, and July 16, we tried unsuccessfully to obtain payment of your past-due account of $184.02 or to gain some explanation from you.

We are sorry that you have made no reply because we want to help our customers whenever possible. We filled your order promptly and in a manner that must have been satisfactory to you since you have made no reply to our offer of adjustment.

As you know, our credit terms call for payment within 30 days. You have not complied with these terms nor given us the facts by which we might arrive at a solution.

Won't you use the enclosed envelope to send us your check or an explanation of why your payment is so long overdue?

Yours truly

Jane Adams

Ms. Jane Adams
Credit Manager

ms

Enclosure

Sample Request for Payment Letter

1. State the problem.
2. Express concern about lack of payment.
3. Request a response.

OLYMPIA GREENE, M.D.
22 CENTRAL AVENUE
GLENDALE, NY 11385-7342
(718) 381-2345

October 13, 19__

Mr. Stanley Bailey
97-81 111 Street
Richmond Hill, NY 11418-2901

Dear Mr. Bailey

After reviewing our accounts, I find that your account is three
months overdue.

Enclosed is a copy of the statement.

Dr. Greene is a little concerned that the bill has not been paid.
Perhaps you would like to discuss it with her.

Please telephone Dr. Greene at your earliest convenience.

Sincerely

Marilyn Landry

Ms. Marilyn Landry
Medical Secretary

Enclosure

Sample Covering Letter

1. Inform recipient of what is being sent and whether it is enclosed or sent separately.
2. Tell when item was (or will be) sent.
3. Tell by what class of mail or method of shipment.
4. Give further information (if appropriate).

December 4, 19__

Professor John Hunter
Communications Department
Woods Collegiate School
22 Fifth Avenue
New York, NY 10001-1017

Dear Professor Hunter:

Your request to rent an 8-mm film, "Telephone Techniques," has been received. The film was sent this afternoon via Special Delivery.

We have other films on this subject and can furnish a list upon request.

Sincerely,

DUART FILMS, INC.

Joseph De Martino

Joseph DeMartino
Film Supervisor

bd

Sample Letter Acknowledging Applications for Credit

1. Welcome new customer.
2. Explain firm's policy.
3. Request that credit references be sent or that a credit form be filled out.
4. Provide an incentive to action.
5. Close with a sales statement about service, quality of merchandise, or your future mutual relationship.

SUPERIOR BUSINESS FORMS, INC.
222 Main Street
Hamden, CT 06514-5678
(203) 479-1234

December 3, 19__

Mr. James Weldon
Office Manager
New Business Systems, Inc.
333 Park Avenue
New York, NY 10001-3456

Dear Mr. Weldon:

We certainly appreciate the opportunity you have given us in your first order to do business with your firm. Your expression of confidence in us is most gratifying, and we will do everything in our power to live up to it.

Since you probably need this merchandise as soon as possible, we are shipping your order by express tomorrow. So that we can handle your future needs without delay, we would appreciate your sending us your financial statement. Or, if you prefer, just fill out and return the enclosed credit form.

This credit information will, of course, be kept absolutely confidential. We are looking forward to having you as a regular customer. May we have your credit information soon?

Cordially yours,

Harvey Froman

Harvey Froman
Purchasing Manager

lb

Enclosure

Sample Follow-Up or Reminder Letter

1. Make reference to previous letter or request.
2. State what is needed and why.
3. Emphasize deadline.

June 24, 19__

Professor Arlene Smith
Advertising Department
Institute of Technology
300 Jay Street
Brooklyn, NY 11201-2983

Dear Professor Smith

    At the June Directors' Meeting, the chairpersons were asked to submit their department budgets to the Vice President within two weeks.

    Three weeks have elapsed and your budget is needed in order that we be able to submit the overall budget report to the President. Our deadline is next week.

    Office Services will be able to assist you in typing the report.

                    Sincerely

                    Wanda Spear

                    Ms. Wanda Spear
                    Secretary to Vice President

ws

pc: Division Dean

Sample Notice of Meeting Letter

1. Specify day, date, time, place, and purpose of meeting.
2. Specify if it is a special meeting.
3. State agenda of meeting.
4. Inquire about additional items to be placed on agenda.
5. Request reply.

October 3, 19__

Mr. Clark Cason
Vice President
XYZ Company
228 Clark Street
Brooklyn, NY 11201-2983

Dear Mr. Cason:

An Advisory Committee meeting will be held in the Board Room,
Thursday, October 19, at noon. This is a special meeting, called
because of the upcoming change in the price of our product.

An agenda for the meeting is enclosed. If you have any additional
items to be placed on the agenda, please send them to Mr. Price by
October 13.

Please notify me by Monday, October 16, of whether or not you will
attend the meeting.

Sincerely,

Herbert Price

Herbert Price
Vice President

lmb

Enclosure

Sample Letter of Regret or Rejection

1. State circumstances.
2. Give background information telling why decision was made.
3. End with expression of good will, showing appreciation or interest.

July 1, 19__

Ms. Mary Popkins, Secretary
Delta Pi Epsilon
2 Stuyvesant Oval
New York, NY 10001-1234

Dear Miss Popkins

Our President, Mrs. Beatrice R. Stokes, has received your letter
asking her to speak to your membership on "The Office of the
Future," Saturday, August 4.

Unfortunately, Mrs. Stokes will be on a business trip at that
time. Thus, it will not be possible for her to accept your kind
invitation.

If your organization has a need for a speaker at some other time,
Mrs. Stokes hopes you will remember her then.

Sincerely

Judith McGee

Miss Judith McGee
Secretary to President

jm

Sample Reservation Letter

1. State who wants the reservation and the number of people in the party.
2. State number of rooms and type of accommodations (single, double, suite, deluxe suite) desired.
3. State planned length of stay and approximate rate desired.
4. State arrival time and departure time. If arriving late, ask about guaranteed arrival and deposit requirements.
5. Request confirmation.

February 2, 19__

Glenpointe Hotel
Attention Reservations Manager
Route 80 West
Teaneck, NJ 07728-0897

Dear Sir:

Please reserve a medium-priced living room and bedroom suite for Mr. and Mrs. Albert Clark, who will arrive late Monday evening, April 6. They will leave Thursday afternoon, April 9, on a 3 p.m. flight and will require transportation to the airport.

Please confirm the room reservation for late arrival and advise me of your deposit requirements.

Mr. Clark, Vice President of the ABZ Corporation, will be attending the NSW workshop that will be held in your hotel.

Sincerely,

Janice Theodore

Ms. Janice Theodore
Secretary to Vice President

jt

Sample Deferral Letter

1. Answer immediately.
2. State matter under discussion.
3. Explain why answers must be deferred.
4. Tell when answer may be expected.

October 3, 19__

Ms. Nancy Adams, Marketing Manager
Adams Associates, Inc.
234 Maple Avenue
Maplewood, NJ 07748-9876

Dear Ms. Adams,

Your letter to Ms. Jones asking her approval of your new sales
brochures has been received.

Ms. Jones is attending our annual international conference in
Denver.

I am sure she will give your letter her immediate attention when
she returns. You should hear from her within the next three
weeks.

Sincerely,

Renee Johnson

Ms. Renee Johnson
Executive Secretary

rj

Sample Letter of Inquiry or Request

1. Give background to explain why letter is being written.
2. Ask question or make request.
3. Tell when information or material is needed.
4. Close with expression of appreciation or good will.

December 15, 19__

Mr. Alfred Reed
Marketing Manager
Consumers Corporation
189 Tacoma Street
Seattle, WA 98765-4321

Dear Mr. Reed:

Our company is planning its annual sales meeting, to be held in
Seattle. Over 200 salespersons will attend.

We would appreciate having copies of your booklet "The Way to a
Consumer's Heart" to pass out to those attending our conference.

Could you please have them sent directly to the Seattle Hotel,
addressed to me, by January 15?

Your cooperation would be greatly appreciated.

Sincerely yours,

Thomas J. Jones

Thomas J. Jones
Consumer Affairs Specialist

jv

Sample Order Letter

1. Tell where order is to be sent.
2. List items wanted, giving all pertinent numbers, description of the products, price, and any other necessary information such as color and size.
3. Tell how payment is to be made (check is enclosed, bill is to be sent to a specified address, the order is to be put on a regular account, etc.).
4. Tell when order should be sent.

BUSINESS SYSTEMS, INC.
8 Jay Street
Brooklyn, NY 11201-2983
(718) 843-4567

October 3, 19__

Manhattan Stationers, Inc.
Attention Order Department
5 Lafayette Street
New York, NY 10001-2345

Gentlemen:

Please send the following items to the above address:

Quantity	Catalog No.	Item	Unit Price	Total
200	N238	No. 2 pencils Eberhard (blue)	.15	$30.00
25	N357	wooden rulers (blue)	.84	21.60
				$51.60
			sales tax	4.13
				$55.73

Our check for $55.73 is enclosed. We would appreciate having these items sent at once.

Yours truly,

Joan Bennett

Ms. Joan Bennett

Final Check after Writing the Letter

After you have planned and written the letter, ask yourself these questions:

1. Is my message clear?
2. Will the recipient interpret my message as I intended?
3. Have I presented facts clearly and correctly?
4. Have I kept the message concise?
5. Have I been diplomatic?
6. Have I used personal, positive, and natural tones throughout?
7. Have I created good will regardless of the situation?

INTEROFFICE MEMORANDUMS

Use and Format

The written communications passing between offices, departments, or branches of an organization are usually transmitted in a form known as an "interoffice memorandum." This form has the advantage of dispensing with the salutation, the complimentary close, and the signature of the dictator or originator.

The headings most frequently found on all interoffice memorandums are TO, FROM, DATE, and SUBJECT. In most firms, this heading, together with the firm name and, perhaps, address, are printed. Signed initials are frequently placed on the memo to show that it has been read and approved. The initials of the typist appear on the memorandum, just as in a letter. Enclosures and attachments should be indicated.

Some organizations have memorandum forms prepared in carbon packs. Other organizations prepare an original and use the copier for multiple copies. Several names may be typed after TO or they may be listed at the bottom of the memorandum. In this way, the recipients know which persons will be receiving the same message.

Interoffice correspondence should include most of the essential characteristics of a good letter. The tone should be considerate and courteous. The message should be clear, concise, and complete. (See also Chapter 6.)

COMMUNICATIONS ASSOCIATES

22 North Broad Street / Philadelphia, PA 19185-4752

INTEROFFICE COMMUNICATION

TO: All Information Processors

FROM: Catherine Quintana

DATE: December 2, 19__

SUBJECT: Interoffice Correspondence

Correspondence within a company is frequently formatted on inter-office forms, either half or full sheets, depending on the length of the message. The following points describe the features of a memorandum prepared on a printed form:

1. Space twice after the colon in the first line of the printed heading and set the left margin. The heading items will begin at this point. The body of the memo may begin at the same point, or it may be aligned with the letter "S" in the word SUBJECT. Set the right margin stop an equal distance from the right edge.

2. Omit full addresses, the salutation, the complimentary close, and the signature.

3. Omit personal titles from the memo heading. They are included on the interoffice envelope, however.

4. Triple-space between the last item in the heading and the body of the message. Single-space the paragraphs, but double-space between them. Double-space above and below a table or a numbered list when one is included in the message. Space twice after the number in an enumerated list; align the whole paragraph under the first line.

5. Include reference initials, enclosure or attachment notations, and copy notations.

6. Be sure the originator initials the memo opposite his or her name to show that it has been read and approved.

Special colored envelopes usually are used for memorandums. Type the addressee's name, title or name of department, and room number for the address.

ms

pc Naomi Greenfield

```
         OFFICE COMMUNICATIONS SYSTEMS, INC.

              INTEROFFICE MEMORANDUM


     TO:  John Doyle

   FROM:  William Jones

   DATE:  October 23, 19__

SUBJECT:  Employees' Sick Days


        Your memo about the increase in the number of days of
        sick leave that our employees are taking has been given
        my attention.

        A study of our sales reports and conversations with many
        of our employees revealed the cause of the problem.

        For many years it was our policy to close down our
        operations completely for the month of June.  All of our
        employees took their vacations at the same time, and most
        of our workers were very happy with this arrangement.
        Our decision to keep the plant in operation 12 months of
        the year was supposed to increase production.  It has not
        worked.

        Perhaps if we returned to the previous vacation time
        policy, our workers would be much happier and the number
        of days of sick leave would decrease to its previous
        level.

        lb
```

ABZ CORPORATION

INTEROFFICE MEMORANDUM

TO: Lori Nichols, Accounting Department

FROM: Arthur J. Brown, Administrator

DATE: October 3, 19__

SUBJECT: Salary Increases

We are sending memos to all our employees informing them of their salary increases effective next month.

Since the recommendations for salary increases start at your level, you should be prepared to answer any questions that members of your department may have. In those cases where my office decided on a salary increase other than that you recommended, I will be happy to discuss the increase with you and with the person who is to receive it.

The attached list of salary increases represents our best effort to be fair and remain within our budget.

ms

Attachment

ELECTRONIC MAIL— TELEGRAMS, MAILGRAMS, TELEXES, AND FACSIMILES

Basic Principles of a Mailgram®

The Mailgram® is a service offered jointly by the Postal Service and Western Union. The messages are transmitted by the wire facilities of Western Union to any address in the United States for delivery the next business day. After the local Western Union office receives the message, it is sent electronically to the destination post office for delivery to the addressee. Western Union has installed in certain post offices equipment that receives messages on a continuous roll of paper. A post office employee tears off the message, inserts it in a window envelope, and distributes it for delivery in the next business day's mail.

Sending Blank   western union **Mailgram**

MESSAGE NO.	OFFICE	NO. WDS.	DATE AND FILING TIME	CTB OPR	SENT TIME

Miss Mary Bayer
Name
12 East Gate Lane
Street & Number
Hamden,   CT   06514
City   State   ZIP

MESSAGE:

The closing on your house is delayed two weeks because of

construction crew's vacation time.

SIGNATURE *Ronald Dyece*

SENDER'S TEL. NO. (718) 381-1119   NAME AND ADDRESS: Ronald Dyece
Home Federal Bank, 234 Myrtle Avenue, Glendale, NY 11385

Basic Principles of Telegrams

The telegram has traditionally been used by businesses to send an urgent but brief message. Most firms simply telephone the message to the telegraph office. Many offices require that a typed copy (see sample) be placed in their files.

Telegrams are accepted for immediate transmission for delivery within two hours by telephone and five hours by messenger, subject to the open hours of the delivery office and special holiday conditions.

The typed telegram is spaced to fit the printed lines on the form.

Basic Principles of Telexes

Telex is a Western Union-operated network connected through the use of teletypewriters. The teletypewriter combines the immediacy of the telephone with the documentation provided by a letter. A message store-and-forward computer-switching system is used in conjunction with the Telex. A Telex subscriber may transmit a message to another subscriber. If the teletypewriter at the destination is busy, the message is stored and then forwarded as soon as the teletypewriter is available.

Basic Principle of Facsimiles

Facsimile is the transmission of a copy of a document by electronic means. It is also known as FAX. A special copying machine, called a facsimile unit or copier, sends the images of a document over telephone lines to a similar copying machine in another location. The transmitted document looks exactly like the original. Virtually any document can be telecopied within a matter of minutes. Facsimile, or FAX, is becoming widely used nationally and internationally, due to its low cost and extreme ease of use.

Grammar and Usage

by John I. McCollum

Contrary to the view held by a majority of people, grammar and rhetoric are not devices conjured by fiendish teachers to bedevil defenseless students. They are useful studies, the mastery of which is the mark of a sophisticated person. In general, it may be said that their value is both functional and esthetic. There is efficiency in a precisely worded statement, just as there may be pleasure in a well-turned phrase.

Of the various theories relative to the development of language, the social view seems most reasonable. The theory that languages have arisen, developed, and modified as a result of social necessity or convenience is the one from which most of the advice contained in the following pages springs. That is to say, the statements as to practice reflect usage widely adopted by informed writers and speakers. "Good" English is, in general, a somewhat debatable issue. What may at one time or in one place be good English may vary significantly from what is so considered at another time or in another place. The assumptions here are based on practices that may currently be considered acceptable by those who use the language clearly, efficiently, effectively, and artistically.

This section of the book contains basically useful advice for the development of an acceptable writing and speaking style. No attempt has been made to give a complete survey of the intricacies of grammar and rhetoric, and there is little or no theorizing. In many ways the material here is in the nature of a reminder of what should be brought to one's writing.

In matters of debate, and there are many, the practice is to adopt the more conservative position. To those who would argue that some of the best writers ignore, overlook, or transcend "mere rules," we offer the counterargument that in so doing such writers offer significant stylistic or artistic compensation and that they are generally capable of such compensation only after a long apprenticeship in which they acquired the tools with which to shape their greater achievement.

It may be argued, as well, that many decisions concerning propriety and style are essentially matters of taste. Indeed, such may be the case; one may, therefore, adopt a single rule: What is clearest, most precise, most useful, and most pleasing should prevail. One must learn to perceive and abhor vague, slovenly, impoverished, and inaccurate language.

The purpose of this section is to record useful statements of practice in the hope of leading secretaries easily and quickly through what is often considered a tangle of rule and rhetoric. What we generally call grammar is simply a description of the way words function and relate to one another in a sentence. This is to say that instead of prescribing a set of rules handed down by the gods of grammarians, rhetoricians, and linguists, we merely describe the way people have used their language in the past and thereby suggest possibilities for success through similar practice.

Effective communication is not easy, but we can reduce the difficulty somewhat by developing as great a familiarity with language as possible. The more we understand about how our sentences can be put together, how we can by punctuation marks pull together or separate a variety of ideas, how we can substitute one word for another to gain a more precise meaning or a more pleasing manner of expression, the easier and more successful our communication will be.

PARTS OF SPEECH

Sentences are composed by combining a series of words, each of which functions in a specific way within the particular context. That is to say, the word itself is called a *noun* or a *verb* or an *adjective* or an *adverb* because it functions as such in a sentence, not because it is arbitrarily a particular part of speech. In identifying parts of speech, always think of the *function* of the word (or word group) in a specific sentence. For example, the word *light* may function as a noun, a verb, an adverb, or an adjective.

> The *light* shines in the night. (Noun)
> *Light* the fire. (Verb)
> She struck him a *light* blow. (Adjective)

Functions of Words

Obviously, it is necessary to identify a word (or word group) not as a particular part of speech but as a *functioning* part of the sentence. In this sense words may be divided according to four general functions:

1. To name or identify—a word or word group (noun, pronoun, gerund, infinitive, noun phrase, or noun clause—all substantives) that names a person, place, thing, condition, quality, or action.

2. To assert—a word or word group (verb) that indicates action, state of being, or occurrence.
3. To modify—a word, phrase, or clause (adjective, adverb, or participle) that describes, limits, restricts, or qualifies the meaning of another word or word group.
4. To connect—a word (preposition) that may join a substantive to another word in the sentence; a word (conjunction) that may join words, phrases, or clauses.

Nouns

A noun is a word that names a person, place, thing, action, idea, quality, group, etc.

Classification

All nouns belong to one of two main classifications:

a. *Proper nouns* name specific persons, groups, organizations, places, things, or ideas.

> *John Smith, Hamlet, Pittsburgh, White House*

b. *Common nouns* name members of a group of persons, places, things, ideas, or conditions.

> *book, health, house, man, children, city, liberty*

Common nouns are variously classified according to what they name: *collective, concrete, abstract, mass.*

Agreement

a. For consistency, every verb must agree in number with its subject.

> FAULTY: In each room *is* ten *typists.*
> IMPROVED: In each room *are* ten *typists.*
> FAULTY: The *quality* of a company's products often *determine* the reputation of the company.
> IMPROVED: The *quality* of a company's products often *determines* the reputation of the company.

b. Nouns or pronouns placed between the subject and the verb do not affect the number of the subject.

> The *sound* of the violins *seems* very faint.

c. The number of the subject is not changed by the use of parenthetical expressions that begin with such terms as *as well as, no less than, including, together with,* etc.

> *Dr. Smith,* together with his wife and two sons, *is* to arrive on the evening flight.

d. Usually subjects joined by *and* take a plural verb.

> A *dictionary* and a *typewriter* are two tools of a secretary.
> *Mother, Father,* and *I were* at home when he called.

When the words joined by *and* refer to the same person or thing, the verb is singular:

> Your family *physician* and *friend is* the man to see.

e. When *each* or *every* precedes a singular subject, the verb is singular. When *each* follows the subject and the subject is plural, the verb is plural.

> *Each* member of the class *has* been urged to vote.
> *Every* person *is* to vote if he possibly can.
> They *each want* to go.

f. Singular subjects joined by *or, nor, either . . . or,* and *neither . . . nor* generally take a singular verb.

> *Neither* a doctor *nor* a nurse *was* available.
> *Either* the teacher *or* the principal *attends* the conference.

When one part of the subject is singular and one is plural, the verb usually agrees with the one closer to it.

> Neither Bill nor his *parents are* at home.
> He did not know where his pencil or his *books were.*
> Either the eggs or the *milk has* to be used.
> Either the milk or the *eggs have* to be used.

When the two parts of the subject are pronouns in different persons, usage is generally according to the following: If the sense is singular, the verb is singular and agrees with the closer pronoun.

> Either you or *I am* able to attend the conference.

If the sense is plural, the verb is plural.

> Neither you nor I *are* able to attend the conference.

g. Special care must be taken with sentences beginning with *there is* or *there are. There* is an expletive, not a substantive, and therefore cannot serve as a subject.

> There *are* to be at least ten *floats* in the parade. (*Floats,* not the expletive *there,* is the subject.)
> There *is* no *point* in questioning him further.

h. A collective noun (*class, committee, jury*) may be either singular or plural, depending upon the meaning of the noun in the particular context: If the items or people are considered as a group, the noun takes a singular verb; if they are considered as separate individuals in a group, the noun takes a plural verb. (Remember, too, that a collective noun can also be used in the plural form when more than one group is meant: *classes, committees, juries.* For some collective nouns the plural form is the same as the singular: *offspring*.)

> The *jury was* in session for two days. (A group)
> The *jury come* from several areas of the city. (Separate individuals)

A collective noun should not be used in both the singular and plural numbers within the same sentence.

> FAULTY: Since the school *board hires* the teachers, *they may* also *dismiss* them. (*Board* is singular with *hires*, then inconsistently plural with *they*.)
> IMPROVED: Since the school *board hires* the teachers, *it may* also *dismiss* them.

i. Some nouns that are plural in form but singular in meaning take singular verbs. *Esthetics, civics, economics, linguistics, mathematics, mumps, news*, and *semantics*, for example, are regularly singular. Verb agreement with words like *measles, physics*, and *politics* depends upon the specific use of the word.

> Your *politics* are going to get you into trouble with the company. (Your political opinions are going to . . . .)
> *Politics has* always interested him. ([The subject of] politics has always interested him.)

Checking your dictionary will help you with similar words you are not sure of.

j. The title of a single published work or work of art takes a singular verb.

> *Canterbury Tales* was written by Chaucer.

k. A word used as a word, even when it is plural in form, takes a singular verb.

> *They is* a pronoun.
> *Scissors comes* before *scissortail* in the dictionary.

Case

Differentiations between the nominative and objective cases of nouns are not observed in the English language. A few special rules, however, are generally applied to nouns in the possessive case.

a. The possessive case of nouns denoting inanimate objects is usually formed with an *of* phrase. (See also *Apostrophe* in the section on punctuation later in this chapter.)

> FAULTY: The room's ceiling
> IMPROVED: The ceiling *of* the room

Exceptions to this practice are found in certain familiar expressions that are idiomatically correct.

a year's labor	his heart's content
a moment's notice	for heaven's sake
a stone's throw	a mile's end

b. A noun preceding a gerund is usually in the possessive case.

> FAULTY: I don't understand William being gone so long.
>
> IMPROVED: I don't understand William's being gone so long. (It is not *William* that is not understood; it is *being gone,* which is adjectivally identified by the word *William's.*)

Distinction should be made between gerunds and participles. (See *Verbals,* under *Verbs,* in this chapter.)

> Everett doesn't like *Mary's working.* (Everett disapproves of the fact that Mary works. *Working* is a gerund here.)
>
> Everett doesn't like *Mary working.* (Everett doesn't like Mary when she is at work. *Working* is a participle here.)

Nouns Used as Adjectives

Although many nouns are used as adjectives effectively, especially when no suitable adjectives can be found, such forms should be avoided if they are awkward or ambiguous.

a. Nouns used acceptably as adjectives:

> *opera* tickets   *automobile* race

b. Nouns used awkwardly or ambiguously as adjectives:

> FAULTY: Many people now become seriously involved in a race argument. (Race is ambiguous; does the writer mean *racing* or *racial* issues?)
>
> IMPROVED: Many people now become seriously involved in arguments about *racial issues.*
>
> Many people now become seriously involved in arguments about *horse racing.*

Pronouns

A *pronoun* is a word that may be substituted for a noun. It performs all the functions of a noun but is not as specific. Because a pronoun is a substitute and depends on other words for its meaning, it must refer expressly or by clear implication to a noun or another pronoun previously mentioned (called the *antecedent*).

Classification

Pronouns are usually classified descriptively.

a. *Personal pronouns* designate the person speaking, the person spoken to, or the person or thing spoken of.

Declension of Personal Pronouns

Person	Case	Singular	Plural
1st person	nominative	I	we
	objective	me	us
	possessive	my, mine	our, ours
2nd person	nominative	you	you
	objective	you	you
	possessive	your, yours	your, yours
3rd person	nominative	he, she, it	they
	objective	him, her, it	them
	possessive	his, her, hers, its	their, theirs

(Note that the possessive forms *ours, yours, hers, its,* and *theirs* are each written without the apostrophe.)

b. *Demonstrative pronouns* point out or identify specific objects (*this, that, these, those, such*). The choice of pronoun depends on the relative proximity of the speaker to the object.

> this house, these houses (Near)
> that house, those houses (Farther away)

c. *Relative pronouns* connect a subordinate clause to the main clause. *Who, whom, whose* (and the compounds *whoever, whomever, whosoever,* and *whomsoever*) refer to persons; *which* and *whichever* refer to things or objects and to living creatures (but not to persons except groups of people regarded impersonally or categories of persons regarded as such); *that* and *what* may refer to either persons or objects.

> Homer, *who* is the first among the epic writers, has been called the father of heroic literature.
> The writer of *whom* I speak is Sylvia Warner.
> Is he the man *whose* hat is on my desk?
> *Whoever* is first receives the award.
> Grace will admit *whomever* she sees first.
> This is the book of *which* I spoke.
> The television set, *which* was repaired only last week, is broken again.
> You may have *whichever* book you want.
> He is a man *that* we all admire.
> Is this the face *that* launched a thousand ships?
> She is *what* I call a genius.
> This is about *what* I would expect of him.

d. *Interrogative pronouns* are used to introduce a question. The pronouns *who, whose, which,* and *what* (and the compounds *whoever* and *whatever*) can become *interrogative.*

> *Who* shall cast the first stone?
> *Whose* gloves are these?
> *Which* is yours?
> *What* do you want?
> *Whoever* told you that lie?
> *Whatever* does she mean?

e. *Indefinite pronouns* are ones whose antecedents are not explicit or precise persons, places, or things. Some of the most frequently used indefinite pronouns are listed below.

all	each one	neither	other
another	either	nobody	some
any	everyone	none	somebody
anyone	everybody	no one	someone
anything	everything	nothing	something
both	few	one	such
each	much		

f. *Reflexive pronouns* direct or reflect the action back to the subject. In form they represent a compound of one of the personal pronouns and *self* or *selves.*

> He taught *himself* to read.

g. *Intensive pronouns* appear in an appositive position and serve to emphasize or intensify a substantive. The forms are the same as the reflexive forms above.

> The students *themselves* made the decision.

h. *Reciprocal pronouns* indicate an interchange or mutual action. *Each other* and *one another* are the only two such pronouns in English.

> The two girls very seldom saw *each other.*
> As they passed, all the soldiers nodded to *one another.*

Case

The case of a pronoun is determined not by its antecedent but by the construction that it is a part of.

a. *Personal pronouns* have different forms for different cases. (See the table *Declension of Personal Pronouns,* above.)

(1) The subject of the verb is in the nominative case.

> *He* and *I* are going.
> Dave and *she* are going.

(2) The complements of all forms of the verb *to be* (except the infinitive) are in the nominative case.

> This is *she* speaking.
> The speaker was neither *he* nor *she*.
> It is *they* whom you seek.
> It is *we* who must remain to spread your message.

(3) The subject and the complement of the infinitive are in the objective case if the subject is also the object of a verb or preposition.

> He invited *them* and *us* to go to the party.
> We believed *him* to be wrong.
> He asked *you* and *me* to be ready at noon.
> The judges declared the winner to be *her*.

(4) The object of a preposition is in the objective case.

> Let's keep this secret *between you* and *me*.
> I bought birthday presents *for him* and *her*.
> Come to lunch *with* Judy and *me*.
> I typed the letters *for* Mr. Miller and *him*.

Note: In (1) through (4) above, when a pronoun follows *and*, it sometimes becomes a problem to choose the correct case (*I* or *me*, *he* or *him*, *she* or *her*, *we* or *us*, *they* or *them*). Very often the correct form can be determined if the sentence is tried out with the *pronoun in question used by itself*. Some of the sentences above would be tried out as follows:

> Come to lunch *with* [Judy and] *me*.
> I typed the letters *for* [Mr. Miller and] *him*.
> He invited *them* [and us] to go to the party.
> He invited [them and] *us* to go to the party.
> He asked [you and] *me* to be ready at noon.

(5) The proper case for a pronoun used in an elliptical clause introduced by *than* or *as* can be determined by the meaning of the complete form of the clause.

> He is more understanding than *I* [am understanding]. (*I* is the subject of the verb in the clause *I am understanding*.)
> I can write as well as *he* [can write]. (*He* is the subject of the verb in the clause *he can write*.)
> She speaks to Helen more often than [she speaks to] *me*. (*Me* is the object of the preposition *to*.)
> She speaks to Helen more often than *I* [speak to Helen]. (*I* is the subject of the verb *speak* in the clause *I speak to* Helen.)

(6) With gerunds the possessive case is most often used, although the choice of case sometimes depends on the emphasis intended.

> *Your* reading aloud disturbs me.
> Have you ever thought about *his* leaving the company? (The *leaving* is emphasized here.)
> Have you ever thought about *him* leaving the company? (The person named [*him*] is emphasized here.)

(See *Verbals*, under *Verbs*.)

(7) The possessive case of *it* has no apostrophe.

> The bird built *its* nest in the tree.

b. The case of a *relative pronoun* is determined by the construction of the clause in which it appears. Difficulties frequently arise in the use of *who* and *whom*. In formal English *who* and *whoever* serve as subjects of a verb; *whom* and *whomever* serve as objects.

Nominative Case	Objective Case	Possessive Case
who	whom	whose
whoever	whomever	whosever
that	that	of that
which	which	of which, whose
what	what	of what

> Jean, *who* lives next door, was married last week. (Subject of the verb *lives*)
> Ann, *whom* I have known all my life, was there. (Object of the verb *have known*)
> John, to *whom* we looked for help, was not at home. (Object of the preposition *to*)
> He spoke to *whoever* answered the telephone. (Subject of the verb *answered* in a noun clause that serves as the object of the preposition *to*)

Whose is often used as the possessive of *which*, in place of *of which*, to avoid an awkward or formal-sounding construction.

> I'd like to have a desk the drawers *of which* don't stick.
> I'd like to have a desk *whose* drawers don't stick.

c. Some *indefinite pronouns* can be made possessive in form through the addition of an apostrophe and an *s*.

> another's glove   anyone's house   everybody's responsibility

d. A *pronoun* used *in apposition* with a noun or another pronoun is in the same case as the noun or other pronoun.

> We—James and *I*—will never betray your confidence. (*I*, in apposition with *we*, the subject, is in the nominative case.)
> He asked three men—Bob, Joe, and *me*—to be ready. (*Me*, in apposition with *men*, the subject of the infinitive *to be*, is in the objective case.)
> The men—Bob, Joe, and *I*—met him at the river. (*I*, in apposition with *men*, the subject, is in the nominative case.)

Note: The correct form may be determined easily be dropping the noun with which the pronoun is in apposition and allowing the pronoun to function alone; *e.g.*, *I* met him at the river.

Reference

A pronoun should refer clearly to its antecedent if the meaning is to be precise. Each pronoun should refer to a definite person, place, or thing in order to avoid the following difficulties:

(1) Remote antecedent. The pronoun should be placed as close as possible to its antecedent.

> FAULTY: He wore a flower in his lapel, *which* he had received from an admirer. (What had he received from an admirer, his lapel or a flower?)
>
> IMPROVED: In his lapel he wore a flower, *which* he had received from an admirer.

(2) Ambiguous reference. There should be no question as to the specific antecedent for each pronoun; if the antecedent involves the possibility of choice, it is ambiguous and thus the reference is faulty.

> FAULTY: Last Tuesday James told Mr. Adams that *he* must find the money or face bankruptcy. (Who is to find the money or face bankruptcy?)
>
> IMPROVED: Last Tuesday James told Mr. Adams to find the money or face bankruptcy.
>
> *or:*
>
> IMPROVED: Last Tuesday James told Mr. Adams, "You must find the money or face bankruptcy."
>
> *or:*
>
> IMPROVED: Last Tuesday James told Mr. Adams, "I must find the money or face bankruptcy."

(3) Broad or weak reference. A pronoun should refer to a definite word, not to an entire clause, idea, action, modifier, or understood or unexpressed word.

> FAULTY: Bill was the star of the game, *which* led to his promotion to the first string.
>
> IMPROVED: Bill's starring in the game led to his promotion to the first string.
>
> FAULTY: Helen is learning to play the piano. *It* is a subject I know nothing about.
>
> IMPROVED: Helen is learning to play the piano. I know nothing about piano music.

(4) Indefinite reference with second- and third-person pronouns. Consistency of reference must be applied, or the passive voice may be used.

FAULTY: If you hope to pass, you must study; however, *anybody* can get help if *you* ask for it.

IMPROVED: If you hope to pass, you must study; however, *you* can get help if *you* ask for it.
or:

IMPROVED: If one hopes to pass, he must study; however, *anyone* can get help if *he* asks for it.

FAULTY: *They* have no income-tax law in the state of Florida.

IMPROVED: Florida has no state income-tax law.

Agreement

Although pronouns are effective instruments by which we can secure variety, emphasis, and economy, they may merely confuse if consistent grammatical patterns are not maintained.

a. The pronoun should agree with its antecedent in number, person, and gender.

If a new *secretary* wants to succeed, *he* or *she* must work hard. (Singular antecedent requires a singular pronoun.)

She is one of those people *who hate* early morning appointments. (*Who* refers to *people*; it is therefore plural and thus takes the plural form of the verb *hate*.)

b. The indefinite pronouns (*each, one, someone, somebody, any, anyone, everyone, everybody, none, nobody, either, neither*) are usually considered singular.

If *anyone* wishes to speak, *he* may do so now.
Neither of the men would answer when *he* was questioned.
Everyone present cast *his* vote.
Everybody must turn in *his* expense account by Thursday.

Verbs

A verb is a word that makes a statement about a subject. Its function is to convey a positive assertion, to make a statement of condition or probability, to give a command, to ask a question, or to make an exclamation.

Classification

a. A *transitive verb* is one that requires a direct object to complete its meaning (as the word *transitive* suggests, the action passes from one thing to another).

I *carried* the *book*.
Donne *wrote* intriguing *poetry*.
Alice *closed* the *book* with a sigh of relief.

b. An *intransitive verb* simply states something about the subject; there is no direct object to receive the action.

> The sun *rose* at six o'clock.
> The old dog *lay* sleeping in the sun.
> James *sat* for two hours waiting for the train.

c. A *linking verb*, or *copula*, is an intransitive verb that makes no complete statement itself but links the subject with a subjective complement (predicate noun or predicate adjective). *To be* is the most common linking verb; other principal ones are *taste, smell, become, feel, seem*, and *appear*.

> The coffee *tastes* good.
> I *am* the victor.
> His account *seems* improbable.
> She *felt* bad.

d. Many verbs serve an *auxiliary*, or *helping*, function; that is, they are used with another verb to form a verb phrase. They help indicate tense, mood, and voice. (See *Properties*, below.) Among the more common auxiliaries are *be, have, do, may, can, shall*, and *will*.

> I <u>*am*</u> going.
> She <u>*has*</u> been ill.
> I <u>*do*</u> want to go.

Properties

Verbs regularly show the following qualities, or properties: *person, number, mood, voice*, and *tense*.

a. Verbs (except *to be*) change in form to denote *person* and *number* only in the third person singular of the present tense.

To stop	*Singular*	*Plural*
1st person:	I stop	we stop
2nd person:	you stop	you stop
3rd person:	he, she, it stops	they stop

To be	*Singular*	*Plural*
1st person:	I am	we are
2nd person:	you are	you are
3rd person:	he, she, it is	they are

b. *Mood* (or *mode*) is the property of a verb that denotes the state of mind in which the action is conceived:

(1) The *indicative* mood makes a statement or asks a question.

> He *closed* the door.
> Who *is* the hero of the play?

(2) The *imperative* mood expresses a command or makes a request.

> *Take* time to compose a letter.
> *Listen* well; *respect* wisdom.
> *Stop!*
> Please *come* as early as you can.

(3) The *subjunctive* mood expresses a condition contrary to fact, a doubt, a regret or a wish, a concession, or a supposition.

> If I *were* you, I would study more regularly.
> I wish I *were* in command here.
> I move that the treasurer *be* instructed to pay our debts.
> Suppose she *were* too late to be considered.
> He acts as though he *were* the only person present.
> If this *be* treason, make the most of it.

In English, the subjunctive mood has largely been displaced by the indicative. The subjunctive occurs most frequently in the third person singular of the present tense (*I desire that he go at once,* instead of the indicative form, *I desire that he goes at once*) and in the verb *to be,* as indicated below:

Present Indicative		Present Subjunctive	
I am	we are	if I be	if we be
you are	you are	if you be	if you be
he is	they are	if he be	if they be

c. *Voice* is the property of the verb that indicates whether the subject of a sentence or of a clause is *acting* or *being acted upon.* When the subject performs the action, the verb is said to be in the *active voice.* When the subject is acted upon, it is said to be in the *passive voice*; the subject is literally passive and is a receiver rather than an actor. The passive is formed by the use of some form of the verb *to be* as an auxiliary to the past participle of another verb.

> The ball *struck* the player. (Active)
> The player *was struck* by the ball. (Passive)
> Mary *started* a rumor about two of her co-workers. (Active)
> A rumor *was started* about two of Mary's co-workers. (Passive)

Although the passive voice is sometimes weak, it has certain uses that are worth consideration by the careful writer.

(1) The passive voice may be used when the subject is not known or is not to be revealed.

> A bomb *was found* in the railway station.
> The invoice *was mailed* under separate cover.

(2) It may be used to emphasize the *action* in a sentence rather than the *actor.*

> Good health *is sought* by everyone.
> This lesson *will be learned* before we leave.

(3) It may be used to achieve variety in sentence structure.

Inexperienced writers often use the passive in an attempt to create an impression of authority and learning, but excessive use of the passive often results in vague and wordy constructions. When possible, use the active voice.

d. The word *tense* comes from the Latin word *tempus* (time) and refers to the forms of verbs denoting the time and the distinct nature of the action or existence (continuing or completed). In English six tenses are commonly used: present, past, future, present perfect, past perfect, and future perfect. (For more information on tenses, see *Principal Parts, Conjugation,* and *Sequence of Tenses,* below.)

Principal Parts

The *principal parts* of a verb are the *present stem,* which is the same as the infinitive (*jump*), the *past tense* (*jumped*), and the *past participle* (*jumped*). The past tense and past participle of most verbs in English are formed by adding *–ed* to the present stem; these verbs are called "regular" verbs. The principal parts of many other verbs in English are formed in an "irregular" manner—some through a vowel change (*sing, sang, sung*), others in some other "irregular" manner (*catch, caught, caught*). The principal parts are important because the six tenses are built from the three principal parts. From the present stem are formed the present and future tenses; from the past participle are formed the present perfect, past perfect, and future perfect tenses.

The word list in Chapter 14 includes the principal parts of all irregularly formed verbs. You may also consult this list to learn when the final consonant is doubled to form the past tense, past participle, and present participle of a verb (*hop, hopped, hopping*) and to learn when a final *e* is dropped before the *–ed* is added to form the past tense and past participle or before the *–ing* is added to form the present participle (*hope, hoped, hoping*).

Verbals

Because *participles, gerunds,* and *infinitives* are derived from verbs, they are called *verbals.* They are like verbs in that they have different tenses, may have subjects and objects, and may be modified by adverbs; but they cannot make a statement and therefore cannot be used in the place of verbs.

a. A *participle* may be used as an adjective.

A *working* man is generally busy. (Present participle used as an adjective to modify the noun *man*)

Polished silver always looks elegant. (Past participle used as an adjective to modify the noun *silver*)

Having completed his work, he retired for the night. (Perfect participle used as an adjective to modify the pronoun *he*)

b. A *gerund* ends in *–ing* and functions as a noun.

Your *working* is greatly appreciated. (Gerund used as the subject of the sentence)

He objected to my *speaking* without permission. (Gerund used as the object of the preposition *to*)

A noun or pronoun preceding a gerund is usually in the possessive case.

Most companies disapprove of an *employee's* being late.

However, a plural noun preceding a gerund is often not in the possessive case.

Most companies disapprove of *employees* being late.

When the noun preceding the gerund denotes an inanimate object or an abstract idea, the noun is usually not in the possessive case.

They blamed the plane crash on the *engine* falling in midair.

c. An *infinitive* is usually preceded by *to* and functions as a noun, an adjective, or an adverb.

To succeed was my greatest ambition. (Infinitive used as a noun, subject to the verb *was*)

The person *to choose* is the one now in office. (Infinitive used as an adjective to modify the noun *person*)

We came *to help*. (Infinitive used as an adverb to modify the verb *came*)

Conjugation

Following is the conjugation of the verb *to see* in its various forms (principal parts: *see, saw, seen*).

Indicative Mood

Present Tense	
1st person	
ACTIVE: I see	we see
PASSIVE: I am seen	we are seen
2nd person	
ACTIVE: you see	you see
PASSIVE: you are seen	you are seen
3rd person	
ACTIVE: he, she, it sees	they see
PASSIVE: he, she, it is seen	they are seen

Past Tense

1st person
ACTIVE: I saw   we saw
PASSIVE: I was seen   we were seen

2nd person
ACTIVE: you saw   you saw
PASSIVE: you were seen   you were seen

3rd person
ACTIVE: he saw   they saw
PASSIVE: he was seen   they were seen

Future Tense

1st person
ACTIVE: I shall see   we shall see
PASSIVE: I shall be seen   we shall be seen

2nd person
ACTIVE: you will see   you will see
PASSIVE: you will be seen   you will be seen

3rd person
ACTIVE: he will see   they will see
PASSIVE: he will be seen   they will be seen

Present Perfect Tense

1st person
ACTIVE: I have seen   we have seen
PASSIVE: I have been seen   we have been seen

2nd person
ACTIVE: you have seen   you have seen
PASSIVE: you have been seen   you have been seen

3rd person
ACTIVE: he has seen   they have seen
PASSIVE: he has been seen   they have been seen

Past Perfect Tense

1st person
ACTIVE: I had seen   we had seen
PASSIVE: I had been seen   we had been seen

2nd person
ACTIVE: you had seen   you had seen
PASSIVE: you had been seen   you had been seen

3rd person
ACTIVE: he had seen   they had seen
PASSIVE: he had been seen   they had been seen

Future Perfect Tense

1st person
ACTIVE: I shall have seen   we shall have seen
PASSIVE: I shall have been seen   we shall have been seen

2nd person
ACTIVE: you will have seen   you will have seen
PASSIVE: you will have been seen   you will have been seen

3rd person
ACTIVE: he will have seen   they will have seen
PASSIVE: he will have been seen   they will have been seen

Subjunctive Mood

Active Voice	*Passive Voice*
Present Tense	
SINGULAR: if I, you see (if he sees)	if I, you, he be seen
PLURAL: if we, you, they see	if we, you, they be seen
Past Tense	
SINGULAR: if I, you, he saw	if I, you, he were seen
PLURAL: if we, you, they saw	if we, you, they were seen
Present Perfect Tense	
SINGULAR: if I, you have seen	if I, you have been seen
(if he has seen)	(if he has been seen)
PLURAL: if we, you, they have seen	if we, you, they have been seen
Past Perfect Tense	
(Same as the Indicative Mood)	

Imperative Mood

Present Tense	
see	be seen

Infinitives

Present Tense	
to see	to be seen
Present Perfect Tense	
to have seen	to have been seen

Participles

Present Tense	
seeing	being seen

Past Tense	
seen	been seen

Present Perfect Tense	
having seen	having been seen

Gerunds

Present Tense	
seeing	being seen

Present Perfect Tense	
having seen	having been seen

In addition to the six simple tenses in English, there are two other forms that are frequently recognized:

a. *Progressive* verb forms show action in progress.

> I *am seeing.*
> I *was seeing.*
> I *am being seen.*

b. *Emphatic* verb forms employ *do* or *does* as an auxiliary. (These forms are used also for questions and negations.)

> I *do see;* he *does see.*
> *Does* he *see* it? *Did* he *see* it?
> He *does* not *see* it; he *did* not *see* it.

Sequence of Tenses

Tense reveals not only the time of the action (present, past, and future) but also the continuity of related action. Shifts in tense must conform to the logical order or sequence of action. In most instances a knowledge of the denotation of time in the six tenses and the application of common sense will aid in developing consistent practices.

a. The tense of a verb in a subordinate element should *agree* logically with the thought suggested by the governing verb in the main clause. Note that statements regarded as universally or permanently true are expressed in the present.

FAULTY: This book *is written* for an audience that *felt* that political favors *are* to be dispensed without particular regard for merit or justice.

IMPROVED: This book *was written* for an audience that *feels* that political favors *are* to be dispensed without particular regard for merit or justice.

b. A major difficulty arises from the use of verbals.

(1) The *present infinitive* is used to express action of the same time as, or future to, that of the governing verb.

> She wants *to read* each new book.
> He wanted *to improve* his efficiency.

(2) The *perfect infinitive* is used to express action previous to that of the governing verb.

> I *should* like *to have seen* his face when you told him.
> I consider it a privilege *to have worked* with him in the recent political campaign.

(3) The *present participle* is used to express action simultaneous with that of the governing verb.

> *Looking* up from her book, she was startled to see her supervisor enter the room.

(4) The *perfect participle* is used to express action prior to that of the governing verb.

> *Having found* his place, he sat down hurriedly.

Shall and Will, Should and Would

Although in informal usage the differences between *shall* and *will* and *should* and *would* are hardly discernible, careful writers still recognize the distinctions. In more conservative practice the use of *should* and *would* follows the same patterns as those established for *shall* and *will*.

a. In expressing expectation and in the simple future, *shall* is used in the first person and *will* in the second and third persons.

I shall	we shall
you will	you will
he, she, it will	they will

> I *shall* be in the office next Monday at 10 o'clock.
> They said that they *would* be on time.
> I *should* think that they *would* be more careful.

b. *Will* is used in the first person and *shall* in the second and third persons to express determination, command, or promise.

I *will* have my way in this matter.
I *would* do it if I could.
They *shall* not pass.

c. *Should* may be used in all persons to express obligation or condition.

I *should* follow your advice, but I'm too lazy.
If he *should* leave now, all work would stop.

d. *Would* may be used in all persons to express determination, habitual action, or a wish.

Only on one condition *would* we be willing to consider such a proposal.
I *would* read for an hour or two each night before going to sleep.
If he *would* leave now, all work would stop.

Adjectives and Adverbs

Modifiers are words or groups of words that describe or qualify other words. *To modify* means to describe, limit, or in any other way make the meaning more precise or exact. The two kinds of modifiers are *adjectives* and *adverbs*.

Adjectives

An *adjective* is a word that *modifies a noun or pronoun*.

blue bird   *the* chair
easy assignment   *his* grade
crushed flower   *several* people
a book   *seventh* day
an apple   *former* employer

Some adjectives form the comparative degree by adding *–er* and the superlative by adding *–est*; others form the comparative degree by the use of *more* (*less*) and *most* (*least*) for the superlative degrees. Still others have an irregular comparison.

Positive	Comparative	Superlative
cool	cooler	coolest
tired	more tired	most tired
bad	worse	worst
good	better	best

The comparative degree should be used to indicate the relationship between two persons or things.

I am the *taller* of the two children in our family.
This book is *better* than that one.
I am *more optimistic* than he.

The superlative degree should be used when three or more persons or things are compared.

This is the *warmest* day of the year.
I am the *tallest* of the three boys.
This is the *most pleasant* experience I can recall.

Adverbs

An *adverb* is a word that *modifies an adjective, a verb, or another adverb*. Frequently, adverbs can be distinguished from adjectives only by the context in which they appear.

Children like books. (No modifier)
Young children *usually* like *story* books. (*Young* and *story* are adjectives; *usually* is an adverb.)
Very young children *almost always* like *highly illustrated* books, books *that can be read quickly*. (*Young, illustrated,* and the clause *that can be read quickly* are adjectives; *very, almost, always, highly,* and *quickly* are adverbs.)

In the comparison of adverbs, some shorter adverbs form the comparative degree by adding *-er* (*fast, faster*) and the superlative by adding *-est* (*fastest*), but most adverbs form the comparative degree by using *more* (*less*) and the superlative by adding *most* (*least*). Others are irregularly formed.

Positive	Comparative	Superlative
calmly	more calmly	most calmly
badly	worse	worst
well	better	best

Adverbs have certain distinguishing characteristics:

a. They are frequently distinguished from corresponding adjectives by ending in *-ly*. Although many adverbs end in *-ly*, this ending is not a certain device for recognizing this part of speech; some adverbs do not and some adjectives (*early, cowardly*) do end in *-ly*. Several common words that do not end in *-ly* may be either adjectives or adverbs depending on their function in a given context: *fast, little, near, late, well*.

b. Some adverbs are distinguished from corresponding nouns by *-wise* or *-ways* used as a suffix: *sideways, lengthwise*.

c. Some adverbs are distinguished from the same word used as a preposition in that they have no noun as an object.

The sun came *up*. (Adverb)
Henry came *up* the hill. (Preposition)

d. Adverbs, like adjectives, may be preceded by words that intensify their meaning.

> The *very hastily* written paper was much better than the author had expected.
> He walked *right by* without speaking.

Prepositions

Simple Prepositions

A *simple preposition* shows the relationship of a noun or a pronoun (the object of the preposition) to some other word: stayed *at* school, lived *in* the house, the neighborhood *across* the way. The following list contains the words most commonly used as prepositions:

about	beside	in	since
above	besides	inside	through
across	between	into	throughout
after	beyond	like	till
against	but	near	to
along	by	of	toward
amid	concerning	off	until
among	despite	on	under
around	down	onto	underneath
at	during	outside	up
before	except	over	upon
behind	excepting	per	with
below	for	regarding	within
beneath	from	save	without

A preposition is usually followed by its object, which may be a noun, a pronoun, a noun phrase, or a noun clause. Occasionally, however, the object may appear earlier in the sentence:

> Which church are you going *to*?
> The company I am employed *by* is a reliable one.

> This is the sort of foolishness that we will not put up with.
> We will not put up with this sort of foolishness.

Although some writers object to the use of a preposition at the end of a sentence, others accept such usage unless the final preposition is weakening. The practice should always depend upon its effectiveness.

Compound Prepositions

A *compound preposition* serves the same purpose as a single one.

as for	for fear of	in view of
as to	for the sake of	on account of
aside from	in accordance with	owing to
because of	in addition to	pertaining to
by means of	in behalf of	regardless of
by way of	in case of	with reference to
contrary to	in favor of	with regard to
due to	in regard to	with respect to
exclusive of	in spite of	with the exception of

Conjunctions

Conjunctions are used to connect words or groups of words in sentences; they are identified generally according to their function as *coordinating* or *subordinating* elements. If the words or word groups are of equal value in the sentence, the conjunction is said to be *coordinating*; if the words or word groups are unequal, the conjunction is said to be *subordinating*.

Coordinating Conjunctions

Coordinating conjunctions link words, phrases, clauses, or sentences of equal rank—elements that are not grammatically dependent on one another.

a. *Pure*, or *simple*, conjunctions join two or more words, phrases, clauses, or sentences of equal rank—that is, having similar importance in the grammatical unit. The simple conjunctions are *and, but, for, or*, and *nor* (some writers include *yet* and *so*).

b. *Correlative* conjunctions are words used in pairs to emphasize the relationship between two ideas. The most commonly used correlatives are *either . . . or, both . . . and, neither . . . nor*, and *not only . . . but also*.

Subordinating Conjunctions

Subordinating conjunctions relate a noun clause or an adverb clause to its independent clause. (The adjective clause is usually related by a relative pronoun.) Some common subordinating conjunctions are *because, if, since, as, while, although, unless, before*, and *so that*.

Although English grammar is not difficult, many students never master it.
Peter cannot hope to buy a car *unless* he begins to save money.

Conjunctive Adverbs

Conjunctive adverbs are words or phrases that ordinarily are used parenthetically but also are often used to relate two independent clauses or two words, phrases, or sentences; the more common are *however, thus, in fact, for example, still,* and *then.*

> I worked for three hours on the bookkeeping; *then* I began to review the correspondence.
>
> English grammar is not difficult; *however*, many students never master it.

Interjections

An *interjection* is an exclamatory or parenthetical word that has little relation to the remainder of the sentence. Frequently it is a sentence in itself:

> *Ouch!*
> *Oh*, why didn't you come earlier?
> *Alas*, youth too soon is gone.

Commonly used interjections include the following:

ah	boo	hurrah	pshaw
aha	bravo	hush	so
ahoy	encore	indeed	tut
alas	gosh	lo	what
amen	hello	O	whoa
ay	hey	off	whoopee
bah	ho	oh	why
behold	huh	ouch	woe

Interjections should be used sparingly in serious writing because they are for the most part colloquial and conversational. When overused, they give the effect of a strained, melodramatic, or immature style.

CLAUSES AND PHRASES

The sentence, which is in itself a group or cluster of words in a meaningful pattern, is often made up of a number of subordinate groups or clusters of words that form *clauses* and *phrases* and that function as individual parts of speech.

A *clause* is a closely related group of words containing a subject and a verb. There are two general types of clauses:

Independent Clauses

An *independent* (principal or main) *clause* expresses a complete thought and may stand alone as a sentence. The underscored sections represent the independent clause.

> Today's newspaper is on my desk.
> The theater section, which begins on page 30, reviews the new play.

Dependent Clauses

A *dependent* (subordinate) *clause* cannot stand alone as a sentence, although it contains a subject and a verb. Such a clause depends for its meaning upon the principal clause of the sentence in which it occurs; it functions as a noun or a modifier, and it is usually introduced by a subordinating conjunction, an adverb, or a relative pronoun. Dependent clauses are used as adverbs (adverbial clause), as adjectives (adjective clause), or as nouns (noun clause) and are identified according to their function.

a. An *adverbial clause* modifies a verb, an adjective, or an adverb.

> *When the humidity is high,* we suffer from the heat. (The adverbial clause modifies the verb *suffer*.)
>
> We are sorry *that he is ill.* (The adverbial clause modifies the adjective *sorry*.)
>
> She does her work more quickly *than I do.* (The adverbial clause modifies the adverbs *more quickly*.)

b. An *adjective clause* modifies a noun or a pronoun.

> We saw a replica of the capsule *that John Glenn used in his orbital flight.* (The adjective clause modifies the noun *capsule*.)
>
> The employee *who applies himself* will succeed. (The adjective clause modifies the noun *employee*.)
>
> The woman *who applies herself* will succeed. (The adjective clause modifies the noun *woman*.)
>
> Give the book to anyone *who may want to use it.* (The adjective clause modifies the pronoun *anyone*.)

c. A *noun clause* serves as a subject, a complement, or an object.

> *What we need most* is more money. (The noun clause is the subject of the verb *is*.)
>
> That is *what he had in mind.* (The noun clause is a predicate nominative following the linking verb *is*.)
>
> Macbeth stated *that he was governed only by his vaulting ambition.* (The noun clause is the direct object of the verb *stated*.)
>
> Give *whoever needs one* a book. (The noun clause is the indirect object of the verb *give*.)
>
> I will speak to *whoever answers the telephone.* (The noun clause is the object of the preposition *to*.)

Phrases

A *phrase* is a group of related words having no subject and predicate. It is used as a noun or as a modifier (adjective or adverb) and is connected to the rest of the sentence by a preposition, a participle, a gerund, or an infinitive.

Her ambition was *to learn another language*. (The infinitive phrase is used as a noun, serving as a predicate nominative.)

Milton hoped *to write the great English epic*. (The infinitive phrase is used as a noun, serving as the direct object of the verb.)

To succeed was my greatest ambition. (The infinitive phrase is used as a noun, serving as the subject of the sentence.)

Her energies were directed to *writing a notable epic*. (The gerund phrase is used as a noun, serving as the object of the preposition *to*.)

Fishing with his friends was his favorite pastime. (The gerund phrase is used as a noun, serving as the subject of the sentence.)

He considered *peddling old clothes* undignified. (The gerund phrase is used as a noun, serving as the object of the verb.)

The Greeks sailed *to Troy*. (The prepositional phrase is used as an adverb.)

We went *to visit our brother at camp*. (The infinitive phrase is used as an adverb.)

The cover *of the book* was blue. (The prepositional phrase is used as an adjective.)

Her ambition *to climb the mountain* was never fulfilled. (The infinitive phrase is used as an adjective.)

The mysterious stranger, *wearing a black coat*, disappeared into the night. (The participial phrase is used as an adjective.)

The *absolute phrase* is somewhat unlike other kinds of phrases in that it usually consists of a noun followed and modified by a participle or participial phrase. Because it cannot stand alone as a sentence, it is a phrase; but it modifies no single word in the sentence, although it is closely related in thought to the rest of the sentence or to some part of it. The phrase is *absolute* in that it has no grammatical relationship to the main clause.

The dishes having been done, she curled up in the chair for a nap.

The king having died, the prince assumed the throne.

An *appositive phrase* is a group of words naming again a substantive previously mentioned.

Washington, *our first president*, was an astute politician.

Chicago, *an inland city*, has grown in importance as an ocean port since the opening of the St. Lawrence Seaway.

SENTENCES

Communication in English begins with the sentence. Depending on the circumstances, a sentence may be a fully developed statement or it may contain implied elements. In many instances, our spoken language can be reduced to writing; however, the written statement does not have accompanying aids like gesture and vocal intonation, nor does it permit immediate questioning or requests for repetition when it is unclear. A good sentence, and thus effective communication, requires clarity, unity, and propriety. In order to achieve these qualities, writing generally follows a set of rules and conventions.

With the proper inflection a single word could be considered a sentence—or at least a sentence by implication.

> Oh? (Is that so?)
> Oh! (That hurts!)
> Come! (You come here!)
> [Who is that?] John. (That is John.)

As questions, exclamations, commands, and responses, such units may function satisfactorily as sentences. In general, however, it is convenient to define a sentence as *a group of words conveying a single complete thought*. If the group of words contains more than one statement, such statements should be so closely related that they convey a single impression.

Parts of a Sentence

The typical English sentence contains a *subject* and a *predicate*. As previously suggested, either the subject or the predicate may be expressed or implied. In order to work meaningfully with such matters, one must understand the structure of the sentence; one must recognize the function of words as they stand in a particular relationship with one another. The following comments are basic to that understanding.

a. The *subject* (*S*) is the person, thing, or idea about which an assertion is made. The *predicate* (*P*) (in its most expanded form composed of a verb, its modifiers, and its object and modifiers) makes an assertion (of action, state of being, or condition) about the subject.

> I read a book.
> S   P
>
> The old man spoke softly.
> S   P

b. Both the subject and the predicate may be simple or compound.

> John and Mary read and sing well.
> S (compound)   P (compound)
>
> John stated his opinion and sat down.
> S (simple)   P (compound)
>
> John and Mary are present.
> s (compound)   P (simple)
>
> John's briefcase and hat were found beside the wreck.
> S (compound)   P (simple)

Note: A simple device by which the subject may be located is to ask *who* or *what* of the verb. Observe the sentences above:

> *Who* read and sing well? *John and Mary* are thus identified as the subject.
> *Who* stated his opinion and sat down? *John.*
> *Who* are present? *John and Mary.*
> *What* were found beside the wreck? *John's briefcase and hat.*

c.   Although a sentence needs only a subject and a verb to fulfill the requirement of the definition, many sentences contain other elements to complete their meanings. Among these are two general classifications: *objects* and *complements.*

   (1)   The *direct object (DO)* is a word or group of words that receives the action of a transitive verb.

   >   *DO*
   > Joan typed the *letter.*
   >   *DO*
   > I have read *War and Peace.*

   (2)   The *indirect object (IO)* identifies the person or thing receiving the action suggested by the verb and direct object. The indirect object usually precedes the direct object; the preposition *to* or *for* is implied.

   >   *IO   DO*
   > He gave *her* a *box* of candy.
   >   *IO*   *DO*
   > She told *him* a bedtime *story.*
   >   *IO*   *DO*
   > Bring *me* the *report.* (Subject *you* understood)

   (3)   The *object of a preposition (OP)* is the substantive that follows a preposition *(P)* and completes its meaning. The complete prepositional phrase functions either as an adjective or as an adverb.

   >   *P*   *OP*
   > She wore a dress *with* lace *trim.*
   >   *P*   *OP*
   > Your money is *in* the *bank.*
   >   *P*   *OP*
   > He spoke *to* the *manager.*
   >   *P*   *OP*
   > The boat was built *by* three old *men.*

   (4)   A *subjective complement (SC)* (also called a *predicate nominative* when a noun or pronoun, and a *predicate adjective* when an adjective) is a noun, pronoun, or adjective following a linking verb and completing the assertion made about the

subject or modifying the subject. (For more about linking verbs, see *Verbs* earlier in this chapter.)

> *SC* (or *predicate nominative*)
> Tom is the *hero* of the play.
> *SC* (or *predicate nominative*)
> This is *he* speaking.
> *SC* (or *predicate adjective*)
> This coffee smells *good.*

(5) The *objective complement* (*OC*) is a noun, pronoun, or adjective following the direct object and completing the assertion made about the object.

> *OC*
> The president appointed him *chairman.*
> *OC*
> He washed his face *clean.*

Types of Sentences

Sentences may be classified according to their purpose or according to their structure.

Purpose

According to their purpose, sentences are classified as declarative, imperative, interrogative, or exclamatory.

> I enjoy my work. (A declaration or a statement)
> Learn to write well. (An imperative request or command)
> Have you read the *Odyssey*? (An interrogation or question)
> Look out! (An exclamation)

Structure

Sentences may also be classified according to their *structure,* that is, according to the kind and number of clauses of which they are composed.

a. A *simple sentence* contains one independent clause.

> I work in an office.

b. A *compound sentence* contains two or more independent clauses.

> She works in the city, but John works on the farm.
> I like the theater; Bill, however, prefers the movies.

c. A *complex sentence* contains one independent and at least one dependent clause.

> Although she has traveled a great deal, she still finds charm in new places.

d.   A *compound-complex sentence* contains two or more independent clauses and one or more dependent clauses.

> My black dress, which I wore to the party last week, is at the cleaner's, and my blue dress is not suitable for the occasion.

Sentence Fragments

Usually, every sentence should be gramatically complete. Sometimes, however, a group of words stands alone as a sentence but is not grammatically complete and therefore not really a sentence in the strictest meaning. Such a group of words is called a *sentence fragment*.

a.   Although many skilled writers use fragments purposely to achieve particular effects, the inexperienced writer should be certain that he or she is able to write complete sentences when appropriate and that fragments are used knowingly and purposefully. The following sentences, while grammatically incomplete, are not considered real fragments, for the reader understands the writer's intent and the communication is complete.

> QUESTIONS AND ANSWERS: Why are you going? Because I want to.
>   Do you want to speak with me? No.
> EXCLAMATIONS: Too bad!   So sorry!

The sentence fragments that should be avoided are those that have no specific meaning for the reader and do not communicate the intent of the author.

> Increasingly large numbers of young people are seeking admission to colleges and universities, which are already overcrowded with students who have difficulty completing their work. Business and professions are demanding men and women with college degrees. *Because of a widespread idea that everyone should have a college education.*

The fragment is not clearly related to the sentences preceding it. Are large numbers of young people seeking admission to colleges and universities because of the widespread idea that everyone should have a college education, or do businesses and professions demand men and women with college degrees for that reason? The ambiguity cannot be resolved without grammatically associating the fragment with one of the complete sentences.

b.   Many fragments occur because the writer is careless in making dependent elements a part of the sentence to which they belong; correction can usually be made by *modifying the punctuation*.

FAULTY: He asked me to forgive him. *Although I don't know why.*
IMPROVED: He asked me to forgive him, although I don't know why.
FAULTY: I was unable to gain admittance to the supply room. *The door having been locked five minutes before my arrival.*
IMPROVED: I was unable to gain admittance to the supply room, the door having been locked five minutes before my arrival.

c. A sentence fragment is not to be confused with *elliptical construction* (also called *ellipsis*), an acceptable construction in which a word or more is omitted but whose meaning can be supplied from the rest of the sentence.

He is as tall as she [is tall].

Characteristics of an Effective Sentence

Effective sentences must be more than grammatically correct; they must be unified, coherent, and skillfully arranged through the coordination and subordination of ideas and structure. Poor sentences frequently result from a failure to organize ideas in such a way as to indicate clearly their relationship and relative importance to one another.

Coordination

The basic principle of coordination is parallelism, a means of achieving unity, emphasis, and coherence. Ideas of equal importance and elements with similar functions in a sentence should be made structurally parallel; that is, coordinate elements in a compound structure are most effectively stated when given similar word patterns. In such compound constructions, nouns will be parallel with nouns, verbs with verbs, phrases with phrases, dependent clauses with dependent clauses, independent clauses with independent clauses.

(1) Coordinating conjunctions (*and, but, for, or, nor*) are definite indicators of parallel structure; they should warn the writer to be careful in constructing the sentence and alert the reader to look for ideas or elements of equal importance in the statement.

FAULTY: I like *to read, to listen* to good music, and *watching* television. (The conjunction *and* joins improperly in this sentence two infinitive phrases—*to read, to listen*—and a gerund—*watching.*)
IMPROVED: I like *to read, to listen* to good music, and *to watch* television.
or:
IMPROVED: I like *reading, listening* to good music, and *watching* television.

> FAULTY: The duties of the president are *presiding* .at meetings, *appointment* of committees, and *to call* special meetings.
>
> IMPROVED: The duties of the president are *to preside* at meetings, *to appoint* committees, and *to call* special meetings.

(2) Comparisons should be stated in parallel structures.

> FAULTY: A ditchdigger is a less rewarding occupation than teaching. (A ditchdigger is not an occupation; teaching is.)
>
> IMPROVED: Ditchdigging is a less rewarding occupation than teaching.
>
> FAULTY: He protested that his job was more rewarding than a common laborer.
>
> IMPROVED: He protested that his job was more rewarding than a common laborer's [job].
>
> *or:*
>
> IMPROVED: He protested that his job was more rewarding than that of a common laborer.

(3) A frequent error in parallelism occurs in the improper use of correlative conjunctions (conjunctions occurring in pairs): *either . . . or, neither . . . nor, not only . . . but also, both . . . and.* Elements compared or contrasted through the use of such conjunctions are best stated in parallel form: The second conjunction should be followed by a construction parallel to that following the first; if a prepositional phrase follows one conjunction, a prepositional phrase should follow the other conjunction.

> FAULTY: She is not only *a tennis player* but *plays softball* as well.
>
> IMPROVED: She is not only *a tennis player* but also *a softball player.*
>
> FAULTY: He either was *a successful industrialist* or *an accomplished liar.*
>
> IMPROVED: He was either *a successful industrialist* or *an accomplished liar.*
>
> FAULTY: I talked both *to the student* and *his parents.*
>
> IMPROVED: I talked to both *the student* and *his parents.*

Subordination

The mature writer recognizes that not all details and thoughts are of equal importance. He or she learns to give certain details a primary or secondary position in the sentence in order to communicate accurately to the reader; in other words, the writer learns to apply the principle of *subordination.* The relationships of the writer's ideas are thus revealed with greater exactness. The main clause will convey the major idea, and the modifiers (words, phrases, dependent clauses) will convey additional and clarifying information. Effective subordination is a means of achieving not only clarity but also variety and coherence.

(1) Short, choppy sentences (often a mark of immature writing) may be eliminated.

FAULTY: He is a man. He is fifty years old. He works hard. He wants to give his family a good home.

IMPROVED: He is a fifty-year-old man who works hard to give his family a good home.

(2) Rambling sentences composed of short clauses joined by *ands* and *buts* may be improved.

FAULTY: The alarm rings and she sits up in bed and she rubs her eyes.

IMPROVED: When the alarm rings, she sits up in bed and rubs her eyes.

(3) Important ideas may be expressed emphatically in main clauses, and less important ideas through subsidiary constructions (modifying words; prepositional, infinitive, participial, and gerund phrases; appositives; dependent clauses).

FAULTY: I came to the office and found that I was behind in my work.

IMPROVED: When I came to the office, I found that I was behind in my work.

(4) Faulty subordination frequently results when conjunctions fail to express clearly the relationship between ideas. (*Like* is not a subordinating conjunction and is not used to join two clauses: *as* is ordinarily used to show time, not causal, relationships.)

FAULTY: I don't know *as* I want to go.

IMPROVED: I don't believe I want to go.

or:

IMPROVED: I don't want to go.

FAULTY: It looked *like* he would win the match.

IMPROVED: It looked *as if* he would win the match.

FAULTY: I liked the play *while* I didn't care for the movie.

IMPROVED: *Although* I liked the play, I didn't care for the movie.

FAULTY: I read in the paper *where* he had been elected.

IMPROVED: I read in the paper *that* he had been elected.

(5) *Because, where,* and *when* are subordinating elements and should not be used as the subject or the complement of a verb.

FAULTY: The reason he won is *because* he is fifty pounds heavier than his opponent.

IMPROVED: He won because he is fifty pounds heavier than his opponent.

FAULTY: Trusting him is *where* I made my mistake.

IMPROVED: My mistake was trusting him.

or:

IMPROVED: Trusting him was my mistake.

FAULTY: A quatrain is *when* you have a verse of four lines.

IMPROVED: A quatrain is a verse of four lines.

Consistent Construction

The careful writer avoids unnecessary or illogical shifts within the structure of an individual sentence or of closely related sentences. Although such a shift may not obscure the meaning, it may result in awkwardness, incongruity, and general loss of effectiveness and emphasis. In order to present ideas clearly and appropriately, the writer must be as consistent as possible in the use of voice, tense, mood, person, number, and style.

> FAULTY: When Meg returned to her home, a new car was found waiting for her. (Illogical shift from active to passive)
>
> IMPROVED: When Meg returned to her home, she found a new car waiting for her.
>
> FAULTY: When he hears that his friend is there, he hurried home. (Inconsistence in sequence of tenses)
>
> IMPROVED: When he heard that his friend was there, he hurried home.
>
> FAULTY: Everyone should be careful of their grammar. (Inconsistency of number)
>
> IMPROVED: Everyone should be careful of his grammar.
>
> FAULTY: If a man is to succeed, you must work hard. (Illogical shift in person)
>
> IMPROVED: If a man is to succeed, he must work hard.
>
> FAULTY: First prepare your notes carefully; then the report may be written. (Unnecessary shift in voice)
>
> IMPROVED: You should first prepare your notes carefully and then write your report.
>
> FAULTY: She asked me would I help her with her expense account. (Inappropriate shift from indirect to direct discourse)
>
> IMPROVED: She asked me to help her with her expense account.
>
> FAULTY: Although the party has made significant contributions to the community, the big wheels grab all the glory. (Inappropriate shift from formal to colloquial diction)
>
> IMPROVED: Although the party has made significant contributions to the comunity, the leaders do not recognize the contributions of others.

Correct Use of Modifiers

Modifiers, for clarity, must refer to specific words and should be placed as close as possible to the words they modify. A modifier is *misplaced* if it seems to modify a word that it logically should not or cannot; it is considered *dangling* if it has nothing to modify.

(1) Misplaced modifiers may be corrected by revising the sentence to place the modifier in such a position that its object of modification may be clearly discerned.

FAULTY: After driving blindly for hours, a local resident helped us find our way back to the main road.

IMPROVED: A local resident helped us find our way back to the main road after we had driven blindly for hours.

FAULTY: I only need a few more minutes.

IMPROVED: I need only a few more minutes.

(2) Dangling modifiers may be corrected by supplying the word that the phrase logically describes or by revising the dangling construction to make a complete clause.

FAULTY: Having taken our seats, the players began the game. (Dangling participial phrase)

IMPROVED: After we had taken our seats, the players began the game.

FAULTY: To appreciate good music, vigorous study must be undertaken. (Dangling infinitive phrase)

IMPROVED: To appreciate good music, one must study vigorously.

PUNCTUATION

Formal writing generally employs close punctuation because the sentences are often long and tend to contain more involved construction than informal writing. Punctuation serves two purposes: to make the structure of the sentence readily apparent and to establish minor relationships within the sentence. The marks of punctuation with conventional applications are listed in alphabetical order below.

Ampersand   &

The ampersand (&) is a symbol meaning "and." In general, it should not be used in formal writing. There are, however, a few situations in which its use is correct:

a. when it is part of the official name of a company

Johnson & Johnson
Little, Brown & Co.

b. in reports in which author–date references are given in parentheses (not in the body of the text)

(Smith & Robbins 1987)
Smith and Robbins (1987)

c. in tables, directories, advertising copy, and some informal writing to save space.

Apostrophe   '

The apostrophe is used to indicate possession, contraction, and plurality of certain words and symbols.

a. To show possession in singular nouns and indefinite pronouns, add an apostrophe and *s*.

Tom's book   anybody's guess

b. To show possession in plural nouns ending in *s*, add only an apostrophe.

the students' grades   the soldiers' allegiance

c. To show possession in plural and collective nouns that end in a letter other than *s*, add an apostrophe and *s*.

the people's choice   the children's wishes

d. To show possession with names of inanimate objects, it is more common to use an "of" phrase, but the apostrophe with *s* is also used. Sound, meaning, rhythm in the sentence, and the emphasis desired determine the choice.

the brightness of the sun   the sun's brightness
the power of the state   the state's power
the lesson of today   today's lesson

e. To indicate measurement (of time, amount, degree, etc.), add an apostrophe (and with the singular an *s*).

one day's work   a week's time
two weeks' notice   three dollars' worth

f. To show joint possession, add an apostrophe and *s* only to the last element.

Tom and Robert's office (Both share one office.)

NOTE: Individual or alternative possession may be indicated by adding an apostrophe and *s* to each element.

Tom's and Robert's offices (Each has a separate office.)
Hitler's or Mussolini's dictatorship

g. To form the possessive of compounds, add an apostrophe and *s* to the last element of the unit only.

my brother-in-law's request   anyone else's belief

h. To indicate omission of letters in contractions, insert an apostrophe at the point of elision.

Can't, isn't, won't, haven't

NOTE: *It's* is a contraction of *it is; its* is the possessive pronoun.

i. To indicate the omission of the first figures from dates, insert an apostrophe at the point of elision.

Class of '09   Spirit of '76

j. To form the plural of a word used as a word, without regard to its meaning, add an apostrophe and *s*.

There are too many *but's* in this sentence.

k. To indicate the plural of symbols and letters, add an apostrophe and *s.*

10's, two 5's, H's, &'s

NOTE: The possessive forms of personal and relative pronouns do not require the apostrophe: *his, hers, its, ours, theirs, whose.* The possessive forms of indefinite pronouns do require an apostrophe: *one's* book, *anyone's* opinion, *somebody's* mistake.

Brackets [ ]

a. Brackets are commonly used to enclose comments, insertions, corrections, etc., made by a person other than the author of the quoted material.

"He [Abraham Lincoln] became known as a great humanitarian."

b. Brackets are used to enclose material within parentheses to avoid the confusion of double parentheses.

The Voyages of the English Nation to America, before the Year 1600, from Hakluyt's Collection of Voyages **(1598–1600 [III, 121–128]). Edited by Edmund Goldsmid.**

Colon   :

a. The colon is a formal mark indicating introduction or anticipation. It ordinarily is used to precede a series or a statement that has already been introduced by a completed statement.

There is only one course of action: We must work more conscientiously.
The library has ordered the following books: *Don Quixote, The Pilgrim's Progress,* **and** *Alice in Wonderland.*
There are several schools and colleges in the university system: arts and sciences, business administration, education, music, and engineering.

b. The colon may be used to introduce an extended quotation.

In a long speech President Roosevelt said: "We have nothing to fear but . . . ."

c. The colon is conventionally used after a formal salutation in a letter.

Dear Sir:
Dear Mr. Adams:

d. The colon is used to separate chapter and verse numbers in Biblical citations and volume and page numbers in references containing Arabic numerals.

John 3:16   *I Corinthians 13:1–12*   *PMLA 72:19–25*

e. The colon is regularly used between numerals designating hours and minutes.

12:15 A.M.

Comma   ,

The comma is the most frequently used mark of punctuation; its misuse often produces confusion and misunderstanding.

a. A comma is used to separate two independent clauses joined in a compound sentence by a coordinating conjunction (*and, but, for, or, nor*).

He spoke clearly, but his father did not hear him.

NOTE: In less formal writing the comma is frequently omitted between short clauses joined by *and;* it is rarely omitted before *or* or *but.*

b. The comma is used to set off nonrestrictive modifiers. (A nonrestrictive modifier is one that is not essential to the meaning of the sentence but that supplies incidental information about a word already identified. A restrictive modifier restricts, limits, or defines; it cannot be left out without changing the meaning of the sentence.)

> NONRESTRICTIVE MODIFIER: **Grace's father,** *who is a grocer,* **ran for the city council. (The clause** *who is a grocer* **can be eliminated without robbing the sentence of meaning.)**
> RESTRICTIVE MODIFIER: **An employee** *who is always late* **may be fired. (The clause** *who is always late* **is necessary to the meaning of the sentence.)**

c. The comma is used to separate elements (words, phrases, clauses) in a series of three or more.

> **The vegetables included corn, beans, tomatoes, and asparagus.**
> **Tell me what you wore, where you went, and what you did.**

NOTE: Commas should not be used before the first or after the last element in the series unless needed for other reasons.

d. The comma is used to set off terms of direct address.

> **Professor Jones, please be seated.**

e. The comma is used after a long introductory phrase or clause. Such "signal" words as *when, although, as, if, while, since,* and *because* usually indicate that a comma will occur before the main clause.

> **After setting up our tent and getting the camp in order, we took a swim.**
> **Although I am no scholar, I enjoy historical research.**

f. The comma is used both before and after a dependent clause that appears in the body of a sentence.

> **His car, although he bought it only last year, looked ready for the junk heap.**

g. The comma is used to separate elements of a date, an address, or other statistical details.

> **Monday, September 1, 1952, was an important day.**
> **The address is 1172 Louis Plaza, Arlington, Kentucky.**
> **The quotation occurs on page 16, line 6, of the manual.**

h. The comma is used to set off direct quotations.

> **He said, "I am prepared."**

i. The comma is used between coordinate adjectives (usually coordination can be tested by substituting *and* for the comma).

> COORDINATE: **He sat in a poorly made, old-fashioned chair.**
> NOT COORDINATE: **He was a member of the large freshman class.**

j. Commas should not be used to separate the subject from the verb or the verb from the complement.

> FAULTY: **Careful study, may produce good grades.**
> IMPROVED: **Careful study may produce good grades.**

k. One of the most common errors in punctuation is the *comma splice,* the separation of two independent clauses by only a comma. Fused or run-together sentences result when two or more independent clauses are included in a single sentence without punctuation to separate them. Independent clauses should be separated by a comma and a coordinating conjunction or by a semicolon.

> FAULTY: **It was raining, he could not walk to work.**
> IMPROVED: **It was raining, and he could not walk to work.**
>> *or:*
> IMPROVED: **It was raining; he could not walk to work.**

(1) Frequently a comma splice can be best corrected by effective subordination.

> FAULTY: **It was raining, he could not walk to work.**
> IMPROVED: **Because it was raining, he could not walk to work.** (The first clause is now a subordinate clause.)
>> *or:*
> IMPROVED: **Because of the rain he could not walk to work.** (The first clause is now a prepositional phrase.)
>> *or:*
> IMPROVED: **The rain kept him from walking to work.** (The two clauses are combined to form one simple sentence.)

(2) If the two independent clauses are not closely related in meaning, each may be made into a sentence.

> FAULTY: **Swimming is good exercise, I like to swim in the summer.**
> IMPROVED: **Swimming is good exercise. I like to swim in the summer.**

l. Conjunctive adverbs (such as *moreover, therefore, thus, hence, then,* and *still*) should not be used to connect independent clauses unless a semicolon or a coordinating conjunction is also used.

> FAULTY: **The two boys meet each morning, then they spend the day together.**
> IMPROVED: **The two boys meet each morning; then they spend the day together.**
>> *or:*
> IMPROVED: **The two boys meet each morning, and then they spend the day together.**

m. When a conjunctive adverb of more than one syllable (*however, moreover, consequently, therefore,* etc.) is used to connect two independent clauses, a semicolon comes before the adverb and a comma after it.

The flood destroyed many houses; however, the church remained undamaged.

n. The comma is used to set off conjunctive adverbs or short transitional phrases.

We do not, moreover, need your advice.

o. The comma is often used before the conjunction *for* to avoid faulty interpretation.

We hurried, for the plane was about to leave.

p. The comma is used after the complimentary closing of a letter.

Very truly yours,   Sincerely,

q. The comma is used after the salutation of a personal letter.

Dear Sandra,

Dash   —

Dashes are frequently overused by inexperienced writers; they are more emphatic than commas and less emphatic than parentheses.

a. The dash is used to emphasize or to indicate hesitation or a sharp break or change in thought.

I must tell you—now what was I going to tell you?
He ought to be satisfied—if he is ever to be satisfied.

b. The dash is used to set off parenthetical material when commas might be confusing or inadequately emphatic.

Three books—a dictionary, a grammar book, and a novel—lay on the desk.

c. The dash is used before a statement or word that summarizes what has been said.

The mayor, the aldermen, the lesser officials, and the citizenry—all were gathered in front of the city hall.
Kindness, understanding, and honor—these are needed virtues.

Ellipsis   . . .

The ellipsis (. . .) is a mark used to indicate the omission of a part of quoted material or of words needed to complete a sentence. Three dots are used to indicate the omission; if the ellipsis occurs at the end of a sentence, a period is added.

The war, which had been in progress for ten years, was ended by mutual agreement.
The war . . . was ended by mutual agreement.
The war . . . was ended . . . .

Exclamation Point   !

The exclamation point is used to indicate an emphatic utterance.

For heaven's sake!   Ready, set, go!

Hyphen   -

Whenever possible, avoid breaking words from one line to the next. When hyphenation is necessary, (a) the hyphen should be placed at the end of a line, never at the beginning, and (b) only words of two or more syllables should be divided, with the division occurring only between syllables. The word list in Chapter 14 shows these syllable breaks.

a. The hyphen is used to divide at syllable breaks a word that must be carried over from one line to another. Words should be so divided that a single letter does not stand alone (*fault-y, a-bove*). Hyphenated words should be divided at the hyphen.

b. The hyphen is used to join compound numbers from twenty-one through ninety-nine.

c. The hyphen is used to join words that function as a single adjective before a substantive.

a broken-down nag
up-to-date methods

d. The hyphen is often used to join such prefixes as *self-, ex-,* and, when it is followed by a capital letter, *anti-.*

self-help   **anti-American**   **ex-governor**

e. The hyphen is used in compounds containing forms like *-elect* and *-in-law.*

President-elect Wilson   **sister-in-law**

f. The hyphen may be employed to eliminate confusion in the meaning of words to which prefixes are added.

re-creation (in contrast to *recreation*)
re-form (in contrast to *reform*)

g. The hyphen is now frequently used to join a single capital letter to a noun.

H-bomb, I-beam, U-boat

h. The hyphen is used to join a verb modifier except when the adverb ends in *-ly* or following such common adverbs as *very* and *most.*

a *fast-paced* horse
a *widely known* author

Be careful to recognize that some words ending in *-ly* are adjectives (*cowardly, friendly*) and that there may be times when the adjective and another word should be joined with a hyphen to form a modifier of a noun.

a *friendly-acting* animal
a *cowardly-looking* bullfighter

i. Although many modifiers are hyphenated when they come before the word they modify, they usually are not hyphenated when they are in the predicate position.

He is a *well-known* scientist. The scientist is *well known*.

Sometimes, however, the meaning of the modifier is such that the hyphen should be retained even in the predicate position.

That man is *big-hearted*.
His appearance was *awe-inspiring*.

j. Usage is divided on hyphenating noun phrases used as modifiers (*income tax* laws, *income-tax* laws; *life insurance* policies, *life-insurance* policies). Usually a hyphen is not needed when the significance of the compound modifier is so well established that no ambiguity can result (*public health* program).

k. Sometimes two words mean one thing hyphenated and quite another without the hyphen. Contrast the difference in meaning between:

a light green coat   **and**   *a light-green coat*

Be careful not to use hyphens in constructions like *a long telephone conversation,* where each word modifies the noun separately.

a new company policy
a large cardboard box

The hyphen should be used in two-word modifiers like the following:

a *four-year* term
a *first-class* cabin

Italics   *italic*

Italics are indicated in manuscript and typescript by underlining.

a. Italics are used to identify the titles of books, magazines, newspapers, and the names of ships and aircraft.

I have recently read Hemingway's novel *The Sun Also Rises.*
The *Queen Mary* was one of the world's finest ships.

b. Italics may be used to indicate emphasis.

I am *always* on time.

c. Italics are used to identify foreign words or phrases.

He is *persona non grata* in this country.
She lacks *joie de vivre.*

d. Italics (but frequently quotation marks) are used to identify words used as words (that is, without reference to their meanings).

The word *go* will be the signal.

e. Italics are used for Latin expressions used in bibliographical references.

op. cit.
ibid.

f. Italics are used for legal citations.

Smith v. Jones

g. Italics are used for the scientific (Latin) name of an organism.

***Homo sapiens* (human)**
***Pelecanus occidentalis* (brown pelican)**
***Paeonia officinalis* (common peony)**

h. Italics are used for algebraic symbols.

$a + b + c$

Parentheses   ( )

Parentheses are used to set off explanatory or supplementary material (definitions, additional information, illustration) not essential to the meaning of the sentence or to enclose numbers or letters in enumeration.

Many of our Presidents (Washington, Lincoln, Wilson, and Roosevelt, for example) rose above mere party politics.
(1), (a)

Period   .

The period is used to indicate the end of a sentence and to mark abbreviations.

Question Mark   ?

---

a. The question mark is used to mark the end of a question.

Do you really care?

b. A question mark is used to show doubt, uncertainty, or approximation.

Sir Thomas Wyatt, the English poet, lived from 1503? to 1542.

c. Question marks are used in a series of questions.

Several questions remained to be answered: How many were going? How many cars would be needed? What time would we return?

d. The question mark is not needed at the end of a courteous request that is phrased as a question.

Will you please return the completed form as soon as possible.

e. A question mark is not used after an indirect question.

He asked whether he would be allowed to go.

f. When quotation marks and a question mark are used together, the question mark is placed *before* the closing quotation marks if the quoted material is a question and *after* the closing quotation marks if the whole sentence is a question. (If both are questions, only one question mark is used, *before* the closing quotation marks.)

He said, "Are you here?"
Did he say, "I am here"?
Did he say, "Are you here?"

(See also *Quotation Marks,* below.)

Quotation Marks   " "

Quotation marks serve to indicate spoken dialogue and to acknowledge specifically reproduced material.

a. Quotation marks are used to enclose direct quotations.

The supervisor said, "Come to my desk, young man."

NOTE: Single quotation marks (' ') are used to enclose a quotation within a quotation.

The student asked, "Who popularized the statement 'This is the best of all possible worlds'?"

b. Quotation marks should be used to enclose titles of short poems, stories, and articles that are usually printed as a part of a larger work.

She read "Ode on a Grecian Urn" from an anthology.

c. Quotation marks may be used to enclose a word used as a word (rather than for its meaning). (See also item *d* under *Italics*.)

The word "school" brings back pleasant memories.
Do not overuse the word "and" in formal writing.

NOTE: When other marks of punctuation are used with quotation marks, the following practices should be observed:

(1) A question mark or an exclamation point is placed inside the final quotation mark if it is a part of the quotation, outside if it is a part of the sentence that includes the quoted material.

(2) Periods and commas are always placed inside the closing quotation marks.

(3) Semicolons and colons are always placed outside the closing quotation marks.

Semicolon   ;

---

a. A semicolon is used to separate two independent clauses not joined by a coordinating conjunction.

He annoyed me; I regretted having invited him.

b. A semicolon is used to separate two independent clauses that are joined by a coordinating conjunction when either or both of the clauses contain one or more commas.

The office manager, a woman I admired, was pleased with the results of the survey; but she was not happy to lose two of her best workers.

c. A semicolon is used to separate two independent clauses joined by a conjunctive adverb.

We placed our order with your sales representative two weeks ago; however, we have not yet received delivery.

d. A semicolon is used to separate two independent clauses when the second is introduced by such expressions as *namely, for example, that is,* and *in fact.*

She is a poor example of what we expect; that is, she just doesn't meet our requirements for a person in such a position.

e. The semicolon may be used to separate items in a series containing internal punctuation.

Our tour carried us to all parts of the country—from Seattle, Washington, to Miami, Florida; from El Paso, Texas, to Bangor, Maine.
Among our greatest Presidents we include George Washington, the father of our country; Abraham Lincoln, the great emancipator; and Theodore Roosevelt, the hero of San Juan.

Solidus (Slash or Virgule)   /

The solidus, or slash, should be used only in specific situations:

a. to represent the word "per"

9 ft/sec

b. to indicate periods of time or seasons that exend over two successive calendar years

fiscal year 1987/88
winter 1986/87

c. to indicate alternatives, as in *and/or*

my son and/or daughter

d. to mark the end of a line of poetry when more than one line is run into the text

She quoted William Blake's lines, "To see a world in a grain of sand/And a heaven in a wild flower."

CAPITALIZATION

The use of the capital letter generally is standardized, but some situations call for personal judgment based on the writer's taste and the level of writing in question. The following conventions are generally employed in formal writing.

1. Capitalize the first word of a sentence and of each line of poetry.

2. Capitalize the first word of a direct quotation. No capitalization is required at the resumption of a quotation interrupted by such expressions as *he said* and *he responded.*

> He said, "This is your last opportunity to change your mind."
> "This is your last chance," he said, "and I advise you to take it."

3. Capitalize proper nouns and adjectives derived from such nouns.

   a. Capitalize the names of specific persons and places, as well as their nicknames and titles.

   > Winston Churchill, Professor Smith, Major Adams, Grandma Moses, Boston, Bostonians

   b. Some words that were originally proper names but are no longer identified with those names are not capitalized. (Check the dictionary when in doubt.)

   > manila paper   india ink

   c. Titles used with a name, as on the envelope or inside address of a letter, are capitalized; but they are not capitalized when used alone.

   > John Jones, Director of Training
   > ABC Company
   > John Jones, the director of training of the ABC Company

d. Capitalize racial, religious, and political designations.

> Indian, Negro, Baptist, Republican

e. Capitalize names of languages.

> French, English, Latin, Aramaic

f. Capitalize days of the week, the months, and the holidays.

> Monday, July, Christmas, Labor Day, Easter

g. Capitalize names of organizations and membership designations.

> Phi Beta Kappa, Boy Scouts, Rotary Club, Rotarians, Socialists

h. Capitalize references to a divine being.

> Lord, Jehovah, Christ, Savior, Holy Ghost, God

i. Capitalize names of historical events and documents.

> Renaissance, Monroe Doctrine, French Revolution, Magna Carta

j. Capitalize names of specific institutions, ships, airplanes, academic courses, geographical features, and regions.

> First National Bank of Miami, *Queen Mary, Columbine,* History 101 (as distinguished from *my history class*), World War II (as distinguished from *a world war*), the South (as distinguished from *turn south on Main Street*)

k. Words denoting a definite geographical region or locality are proper names and therefore should be capitalized. However, compass points or words designating mere direction or position are not proper names and therefore should not be capitalized.

> the Far East
> Traveling south, we arrived . . .

4. Capitalize the first word and all important subsequent words (nouns, pronouns, adjectives, adverbs, verbs) in the titles of books, articles, musical compositions, motion pictures, and works of art.

> *The Sun Also Rises*   *A Place in the Sun*

5. Capitalize names of family relationship when used with the person's name or in place of the name, but not otherwise.

> I bought Mother a box of candy.
> I bought my mother a box of candy.

6. Capitalize the pronoun *I* and the interjection *O* (but not *oh,* except at the beginning of a sentence).

7. Capitalize the word *the* in the title of a company or organization only when it is actually part of the name.

> The Ohio Electric Company
> the Girl Scouts of America

8. Once an organization or group has been referred to by name in full in a letter or other piece of writing, a shortened version of the name, using one of the words in the name, should be capitalized.

> Acme Life Insurance Company . . . . the Company
> Federal Communications Commission . . . . . . the Commission
> Federal Bureau of Investigation . . . . the Bureau

(In expressions such as *our company policy, company* is not capitalized.)

9. Names of the seasons are ordinarily not capitalized.

10. Government organizations are capitalized when they are referred to by specific name.

> House of Representatives   Peace Corps
> Senate   Internal Revenue Service

11. Capitalize the material that follows a colon if it is in the form of a complete sentence. Do not capitalize it when it is not a sentence (unless the first word following the colon is capitalized for some other reason).

> We had two alternatives: We could either go to the movies or stay home and watch television.
> We had two alternatives: to go to the movies or to stay home and watch television.
> We had two alternatives: Aileen's plan or Marilyn's plan.

USE OF NUMBERS

Numbers often present a problem in formal writing. Should they be written out, or should numerals be used? The handling of numbers in reports is covered in Chapter 6, "Special Report Format," but some general guidelines are repeated here.

Use numerals (figures) for

- exact numbers above ten, except when the number begins a sentence
- ages (5 years old)
- exact amounts of money ($15.67)
- percentages (35%)
- measurements and dimensions (6 feet 4 inches)

- time of day when a.m. or p.m. is used (4 a.m.)
- plurals of numbers (6's)
- street names above ten (98 West 32 Street)
- dates (July 4, 1776)
- enumeration (1. dictation; 2. transcription; 3. proofreading)
- large even amounts (24 billion dollars)
- house or building numbers (19 Liliac Drive)
- federal, state, and interstate highways (U.S. 67)

Use words for

- numbers at the beginning of a sentence (Twenty-four boys were on the team.)
- numbers preceding figures (eleven 17-pound turkeys)
- exact numbers below ten (five boys and three girls)
- approximate numbers (about six hundred cars in the lot)
- approximate age (about fourteen or fifteen years old)
- sessions of Congress (Eighty-seventh Congress)
- centuries and decades (the twentieth century; the eighties)
- sums of money used as adjectives (fifty-dollar wallet)
- ordinals (the third person to enter; Third Avenue).

SPELLING RULES

Spelling rules represent generalizations that are applicable to large numbers of words; however, it should be noted that exceptions often occur. Proper understanding of prefixes, suffixes, syllabification, pronunciation, and definition will eliminate many spelling errors. Chapter 14 of this book is a guide to the correct spelling and syllabification of the 33,000 most frequently used words in English.

1. When the sound is long *e* (as in *believe*), *i* is placed before *e* except after *c*.

> achieve, chief, relief, yield, piece, receive, deceive, conceive, ceiling

> EXCEPTIONS: *neither, either, seize, weird, leisure*

When the *ie* combination is pronounced as separate syllables, the rule does not apply.

> society, deity, science

When the *ie* combination follows a *c* to produce the *sh* sound, *i* is placed before *e*.

> deficient, efficient, conscience, ancient

2. The final *e* preceded by a consonant is dropped before a suffix beginning with a vowel and retained before a suffix beginning with a consonant.

hope——hoping	pure——purely
desire——desirable	use——useful
allure——alluring	state——statement

After *c* or *g,* the *e* is retained before a suffix beginning with *a, o,* or *u* to preserve the soft *c* or *g.*

peaceable, courageous, changeable, serviceable

3. Monosyllables and words accented on the last syllable ending in a single consonant preceded by a single vowel *double* the consonant before a suffix beginning with a vowel.

prefer——preferred	hop——hopped
occur——occurrence	forbid——forbidden
red——redder	control——controlled

When the accent shifts to another syllable with the addition of the suffix, the stress in the new word determines the application of the rule.

| confer——conference | refer——reference |
| prefer——preference | |

4. Words ending in *y* usually change the *y* to *i* before all suffixes except *–ing*.

lonely——loneliness   try——tried   lady——ladies

The *y* is usually retained if preceded by a vowel.

valleys   plays

EXCEPTIONS: *lay——laid   pay——paid   say——said*

5. In the formation of plurals, most nouns add *s* or *es*. Some ending in *z* double this letter.

   a. Nouns ending in *s, z, x, sh,* or *ch* add *es*.

| church——churches | box——boxes |
| quiz——quizzes | loss——losses |

   b. Nouns ending in *y* preceded by a consonant or by *qu* change the *y* to *i* and add *es*.

| fly——flies | lily——lilies |
| sky——skies | soliloquy——soliloquies |

   c. Compound nouns usually form the plural by adding *s* or *es* to the principal word.

attorneys-at-law	brothers-in-law
consuls-general	master sergeants
commanders in chief	

    d. When the noun ends in *fe*, the *fe* is usually changed to *ve* and *s* is added.

> | knife——knives   wife——wives

    e. Nouns ending in *o* usually add *s* to form the plural.

> | radio——radios   cameo——cameos
>
> | EXCEPTIONS: *echo——echoes   hero——heroes*

6. When diacritical marks are a part of the foreign spelling, such marks are retained when the words are used in English sentences (fiancé, auto-da-fé, chargé d'affaires), but many words completely Anglicized no longer require diacritical marks.

> | cafe, canape, fete, habitue, naive, depot, denouement

7. Only one word ends in *sede* (*supersede*); three words end in *ceed* (*exceed, proceed, succeed*); all other words with this final sound end in *cede* (*precede, secede*).

USAGE

This section contains a list of words and phrases that are often used incorrectly or for some other reason cause a writer or speaker difficulty. In addition, the word list in Chapter 14 has many cross-references to help you decide which is the appropriate word to use when confusion might arise (for example, *adapt, adept, adopt*).

A, AN: *a* is used before words beginning with consonants or with initial vowels that have consonant sounds (*a* book, *a* one-way street, *a* historian, *a* uniform); *an* is used before words beginning with vowels or with a silent *h* (*an* apple, *an* hour). Before an abbreviation that consists of letters sounded separately, use the article that agrees with the *pronunciation* of the first letter of the abbreviation (an SOS, an FM radio, a UN committee).

ACCEPT, EXCEPT: *accept* means *to receive something offered*; *except*, as a verb, means *to exclude*; as a preposition, *except* means *with the exclusion of*.

ACCIDENTLY: used incorrectly for *accidentally*; the *–ly* suffix should be added to the adjective and not to the noun.

ACQUIRE: often pretentious for *get*.

AFFECT, EFFECT: *affect* is a verb meaning, in one sense, *to pretend* or *to assume* and, in another sense, *to influence* or *to move*; *effect*, as a verb, means *to bring about*; as a noun, *effect* means *result* or *consequence*.

AGGRAVATE: in formal English, *to make worse or more severe*; in colloquial English, *to annoy or irritate.*

ALL RIGHT, ALRIGHT: *all right* means *satisfactory, correct,* or *yes*; *alright* is a misspelling.

ALOT: used incorrectly for *a lot.*

ALREADY, ALL READY: frequently confused: *Already* means *before* or *before this time*; *all ready* means *completely ready.*

ALTOGETHER, ALL TOGETHER: frequently confused: *Altogether* means *completely, on the whole*; *all together* means *in a group.*

A.M., P.M., a.m., p.m.: should not be used as synonyms for *morning* and *afternoon*; the abbreviations should be used only with the figures designating the time.

AND ETC.: redundant: *Etc.* is an abbreviation of the Latin *et* (and) *cetera* (others); *and etc.* would mean *and and so forth.*

AND WHICH: correct only when the clause that follows it is coordinate with a previous clause introduced by *which.*

ANECDOTE, ANTIDOTE: an *anecdote* is a short, entertaining account of some event; an *antidote* is a remedy for poison.

ANGRY: *at* a thing and *with* a person.

ANYPLACE, EVERY PLACE, NO PLACE, SOMEPLACE: colloquialisms for *anywhere, everywhere, nowhere, somewhere.*

ANYWAY: sometimes misspelled as *anyways.*

ANYWHERES: a misspelling of *anywhere.*

AS: sometimes used as a weak synonym for *since* or *because*; used incorrectly as a conjunction in place of *for, that,* or *whether* in sentences like these: "I didn't buy the hat, *as* [use *for*] red is not my color." "I don't know *as* [use *that* or *whether*] I can go." See also LIKE.

AT: redundant in such sentences as "Where are we at?"

AWFUL, AWFULLY: overworked intensives for *very.*

AWHILE: an adverb improperly used as the object of the preposition *for*; the acceptable form is *for a while.* Use *awhile* without the preposition *for*: He has been gone *awhile.*

BAD, BADLY: linking verbs *appear, be, seem, sound, taste, smell, feel, look,* and *become* are followed by an adjective; hence *bad* is the proper form in such sentences as "This coffee tastes *bad.*" Remember, however, that a linking verb can also be used as a transitive verb, and the modifier may be an adverb, as in "He sounded the bell *loudly.*"

BADLY: colloquial for *very much, greatly.*

BECAUSE: a conjunction should not be used as a subject, object, or complement; thus, the construction beginning "The reason is because . . ." is incorrect.

BEFORE: redundant in such usage as "*Before, I used to* get sick if I saw blood."

BEING THAT, BEING AS HOW: misused for *as, since, because.*

BESIDE, BESIDES: only *beside* can be used as a preposition ("That is *beside* the point"), but both *beside* and *besides* can be used as an adverb ("*Besides*, there is no place to go." "*Beside*, there is no place to go").

BIANNUAL, BIENNIAL: *biannual* means *twice* (at any two times) *every year* (as distinguished from *semiannual*, which means *once regularly every six months*); *biennial* means *once every two years.*

CONTINUAL, CONTINUOUS: *continual* means *happening again and again*; *continuous* means *going on without interruption.*

CUTE: overused as a vague term of approval.

DEFINITELY: overused as an intensive modifier.

DEPRECIATE IN VALUE: redundant: *depreciate* means *lessen in value.*

DIFFERENT THAN: improperly used for *different from* except when the object is a clause: "This room is *different from* that one." "This room is *different than* I expected."

DUE TO: controversy among authorities exists about the use of *due to.* Some insist that *due to* should be used only as an adjective ("The leak was *due to* a break in the line"), never as a preposition ("*Due to* a break in the line, there was a leak"). They recommend that *owing to, because of,* or *as a result of* be substituted for *due to* in the second example.

EACH AND EVERY: needless repetition; use one word or the other.

EFFECT: see AFFECT.

ENTHUSE: colloquially used as a verb; not acceptable in formal writing as a substitute for *be enthusiastic about.*

EQUALLY AS: redundant; use *equally* ("Both men were *equally* guilty").

EXCEPT: improperly used for *unless.* See also ACCEPT.

EXCEPT FOR THE FACT THAT: wordy for *except that.*

FARTHER, FURTHER: now infrequently distinguished; in formal usage *farther* indicates distance and *further* indicates degree or extent.

FEWER, LESS: *fewer* refers to number; *less* refers to quantity or degree.

FIRST OFF: use instead *in the first place.*

FLAUNT, FLOUT: *flaunt* means *to display defiantly or impudently* ("The little girl *flaunted* her new dress in front of her friends''); *flout* means *to show scorn or contempt for* (''The employee who continually reports late to work *flouts* discipline'').

GOES ON TO SAY: wordy for *adds, continues.*

HARDLY: do not use a negative before *hardly* when you mean *with effort or difficulty* (''I *can hardly* read his handwriting''; not ''I *can't hardly . . .*'').

HAVE: see OF.

IDEA: often vague for *belief, scheme, theory, conjecture,* or *plan.*

INCREDIBLE, INCREDULOUS: *incredible,* said of a situation, means *unbelievable* (''That he went swimming in the ocean in freezing weather is *incredible*''); *incredulous,* said of a person, means *unbelieving* (''I was *incredulous* that he would do such a thing'').

INDULGE: often used improperly for *take part.*

INFER, IMPLY: often confused: *Infer* means *to draw a conclusion from facts or premises*; *imply* means *to hint or suggest.*

IN MY ESTIMATION, IN MY OPINION: often unnecessary or pretentious for *I think, I believe.*

IN REGARDS TO: a confusion of the British idiom *as regards* with the American idiom *in regard to.*

INSIDE OF: colloquial for *within* when used in a time sense (''I will see you *within* an hour'').

IS WHEN, IS WHERE: frequently used erroneously in definitions; the verb *to be* requires a noun or an adjective as a complement.

IT BEING, THERE BEING: awkward for introducing a clause that should be introduced by *since* (''There being little time left, we hurried to the airport'' should be changed to ''Since there was little time left, . . .'').

ITS, IT'S: *its* is the possessive form of the pronoun *it*; *it's* is a contraction of *it is.*

KIND OF: colloquial for *somewhat.*

LAY, LIE: often confused: *Lay* is a transitive verb meaning *to put* or *to place something* (''*Lay* the book on the table''); its principal parts are *lay, laid, laid. Lay* is also the past tense of the intransitive verb *lie,* meaning *to recline, to assume a position,* or *to remain in a position* (''I will *lie* here until morning''); the principal parts of the verb *lie* are *lie, lay, lain.*

LEARN: not to be confused with or used as a synonym for *teach.*

LEAVE, LET: *leave* should not be used as a synonym for *permit* or *let*; use *let me alone* to mean *do not bother me.*

LIABLE, LIKELY: *liable* means *subject to the possibility of*, but in a disagreeable way ("He is *liable* to be caught if he continues stealing"); *likely* means, simply, *subject to the possibility of* ("If the Pirates continue to win games, they are *likely* to win the pennant this year").

LIKE: should not be used as a substitute for *as* or *as if*; *like* is a preposition and governs a noun or pronoun ("He looks *like* me"); *as* and *as if* introduce clauses ("He looks *as if* he wants to speak to me").

–LOOKING: often a redundant suffix to an adjective.

LOT, LOT OF: vague, colloquial terms suggesting *many* or *much*.

MANNER: often unnecessarily used in phrases such as "in a clumsy manner"; a single adverb or a "with" phrase would suffice.

MARVELOUS: overused as a vague word of approval.

MINUS: colloquial for *lacking* or *without*.

MR., MRS.: in American usage the abbreviations are followed by a period and are now rarely written out except ironically.

MYSELF: often improperly used as a substitute for *I* or *me*.

NEVER-THE-LESS: should be written as one solid word (*nevertheless*).

NOT TOO: colloquial for *not very*.

NOWHERES: incorrect for *nowhere*.

OF: *could of, may of, might of, must of, should of*, and *would of* are often used incorrectly for *could have, may have, might have, must have, should have*, and *would have*.

OFF OF, OFF FROM: a doubling of prepositions that should be reduced to *off* (She stepped *off* the escalator). However, verb–adverb combinations ending with *off* may be followed by *of* or *from* ("The helicopter *took off from* the roof").

ONE AND THE SAME: needless repetition.

ONLY: should be placed in the sentence according to the meaning intended: contrast the following meanings: "*Only* men work in these rooms." "Men *only* work in these rooms." "Men work in *only* these rooms."

OUTSIDE OF: *of* is usually superfluous; *outside of* should not be used as a substitute for *aside from, except*, or *besides*.

PERSONS, PEOPLE: *persons* is used when the separateness of the individuals in a group is stressed ("Five *persons* applied for the job"); *people* is used when a large, indefinite, and anonymous mass is meant ("Jackson was a man of the *people*").

PLAN ON: the idiom is *plan to*.

PLENTY: should not be used adverbially as a substitute for *very*, as in *plenty good* or *plenty tired*.

PLUS: colloquial for *in addition to, having something added.*

PRACTICAL, PRACTICABLE: *practical* stresses effectiveness as tested by actual experience; *practicable* stresses capability of being put into effect ("Before the era of electronics, television did not seem *practicable*; today, however, it is only one of the *practical* applications of the science").

PRETTY: colloquial for *rather, somewhat,* or *very.* (Faulty: "He is a *pretty* good clerk." Improved: "He is a *rather* good clerk." "He is a *very* good clerk.")

PRINCIPAL, PRINCIPLE: often confused: *Principal* may be used as a modifier meaning *first in importance,* or as a noun naming a person or a thing of chief importance; *principle* is always a noun meaning *fundamental truth* or *motivating force.*

REASON WHY: *why* is redundant. See also BECAUSE.

SEEING THAT, SEEING AS HOW: an appropriate subordinating conjunction (*since, because,* etc.) should be substituted for these phrases.

SO: colloquial as a conjunction meaning *with the result that* between independent clauses. Colloquial as an intensive ("He's *so* handsome"); substitute *very.*

SOME TIME, SOMETIME, SOMETIMES: *some time* is used when a vague lapse of time is stressed (It has been *some time* since the objects were first sighted); *sometime,* used as an adverb, means at some unspecified time, usually in the future ("He will come back *sometime*"), and, used as an adjective, it means *having been formerly* or *occasional* ("the *sometime* president of the company"); *sometimes* means *on various occasions, usually unspecified* ("*Sometimes* I wish I were still working there").

–STYLE, –TYPE: redundant suffixes to adjectives.

SURE: an adjective used colloquially as an adverb, as in "He was *sure* thorough."

THEIR, THERE, THEY'RE: frequently confused in spelling: *Their* is the possessive form of *they; there* is an adverb meaning *in that place; they're* is a contraction of *they are.*

TOO: overused as a substitute for *very.*

TRY AND: colloquial for *try to.*

WHILE: frequently overused as a substitute for *although, but,* and *whereas.*

YOU: often improperly used indefinitely, in the sense of *a person, anyone, someone,* or *one.*

14

33,000-Word Spelling and Syllabification List

- *Basic Hints*
  Word Division
  Accent Marks
  Parts of Speech
  Inflected Forms
  Use of Identifying Definitions
  More than One Accepted Spelling
  Prefixes
- *Word Finder Table*
- *33,000-Word List*

This chapter provides a quick, accurate, up-to-date guide to the correct spelling and syllabification of more than 33,000 words, based on the widely accepted *Webster's New World Dictionary of the American Language, Second College Edition.* A special feature is the *Word Finder Table,* which will help you locate a word even though all you know about the word is how to pronounce it.

Many of the entries will settle questions as to whether a certain term is written as one word or with a hyphen or as two words. Answers to specific questions such as the following can be found easily: Do I want the word *anecdote* or *antidote*? When is *hanged* preferred as the past tense and past participle of *hang*? Is the word I want spelled *moot* or *mute*? When is *ringed* used correctly as a verb?

An almost infinite number of words can be formed through the addition of certain prefixes or suffixes to base words. Many of these derived words have been entered. Those that present any question of spelling have been included. For example:

a·gree′a·ble	di·ag′o·nal	di·dac′tic	gar′lic
a·gree′a·bly	di·ag′o·nal·ly	di·dac′ti·cal·ly	gar′lick·y

Obsolete, rare, and archaic forms have been omitted. Many technical terms, especially those in general use, and many colloquial words in common use have been included.

This list has been designed to be a complete and timesaving aid. A few general rules and an explanation of the symbols used in the list are given first. And, don't forget to use the Word Finder Table if you have trouble locating a word in the list.

BASIC HINTS

Each of the words in the alphabetical list in this chapter is referred to here as an *entry* or *entry word*. Symbols are used with the entry words to indicate word divisions, accents, parts of speech, and other useful information.

Word Division

All the entry words have been divided into syllables. Each syllable break is indicated by a centered dot, an accent mark, or, in certain cases, a hyphen. Wherever a hyphen is used in an entry word, that hyphen is part of the spelling of the word.

A word can be divided from one line to the next between any of its syllables except in the following cases:

a. Never separate from the rest of the word a first or last syllable of only one letter or, if you can avoid it, two letters.

b. Never divide a hyphenated word at any point other than the hyphen.

Accent Marks

Accent marks are included to help you find words more quickly. In some cases the accent mark will distinguish one word from another word spelled almost the same way.

| lo′cal / lo·cale′   kar′at / ka·ra′te

Two kinds of accent marks are used. The accent mark in heavy type shows that the syllable preceding it receives the main stress, or accent. The lighter one, wherever used, indicates that the preceding syllable receives less stress than the main one but somewhat more than an unmarked syllable.

| ag′gra·vate′ / dem′on·stra′tion / su′per·vise′

Parts of Speech

Part-of-speech labels (*n.* = noun, *v.* = verb, *adj.* = adjective, *adv.* = adverb) are included here only in special cases. Sometimes this label will give you information about current usage. In all cases the main purpose is to help you be sure you have the word you are looking for. Two of these special cases are explained here.

  a. Sometimes a word is accented and syllabified in one way as one part of speech and differently as another. These changes in accent and syllabification are indicated, and the word is identified with the appropriate part-of-speech label; for example: re·cord′ *v.* / rec′ord *n.*

  b. Sometimes two words are related in meaning and close in spelling and pronunciation. A part-of-speech label is all that is needed to identify each word:

ad·vice′ *n.*	proph′e·cy *n.*
ad·vise′ *v.*	·cies
·vised′ ·vis′ing	proph′e·sy′ *v.*
	·sied′ ·sy′ing

Inflected Forms

Inflected forms include the plurals of nouns, the parts of the verb, and the comparative and superlative forms of the adjective and adverb. All irregular inflected forms have been entered as part of the entry for the base word. To save space, these forms have been shortened in most cases to show only those syllables that are different from the base word:

please	li′a·bil′i·ty	pic′nic
pleased pleas′ing	·ties	·nicked ·nick·ing
fly	eas′y	date
flies	·i·er ·i·est	dat′ed dat′ing
flew flown fly′ing		

For verbs, when two forms are given, the first is the past tense and past participle and the second is the present participle. When three forms are given, the first is the past tense, the second is the past participle, and the third is the present participle. Noun, adjective, and adverb forms are easy to identify.

  Again to save space, inflected forms of some compound words and derived words have been omitted. These forms can easily be found with the entry for the base word:

po·lice′man	pre·pack′age	un′der·score′

Occasionally certain inflected forms are used for certain meanings. These are identified. For example:

staff	ring
staffs *or* staves	rang rung ring′ing
(*sticks; music*)	(*sound* . . .)
staffs	ring
(*people*)	ringed ring′ing
	(*circle* . . .)

This system of entering inflected forms as part of the entry for the base word accomplishes at least three things: (1) It helps you distinguish between words that might be confused if entered separately:

| hop | hope |
| hopped hop'ping | hoped hop'ing |

(2) It saves the time and trouble of searching for a word you might think is spelled one way but is, in fact, spelled differently:

swim
swam swum swim'ming

(3) It establishes, without further identification under a separate entry, the specific inflected form that you are looking for (see *fly*, above).

One last point: when an entry contains verb forms, this does not necessarily mean that the word is used only as a verb. On the contrary, many of the entries represent the spelling for more than one part of speech. If, for example, a word used as an adjective is already entered as a verb form, and the spelling and syllabification are exactly the same, this word is not entered again separately. You may accept the verb form as the correct spelling for the adjective (see *please*, above). If, too, a noun has the same spelling as a verb, no special notation is given (see *picnic*, above). Where confusion might exist, some kind of identification is given.

Use of Identifying Definitions

It is no doubt clear that this list is not meant to replace the dictionary. It is also clear that in attempting to learn the correct spelling for a specific word, you may run into the difficulty of confusing another word with it. Many instances of such confusion are present in the English language. To help you find the exact word you are seeking, this list contains many cross-references. Each cross-reference supplies you with a very short *identifying definition* and refers you to another word that may be the one you want.

Confusion may result for any of several reasons. Two of the most common are: (1) similar (but not exactly the same) pronunciation:

| mou'ton' | mut'ton |
| (*fur*; see mutton) | (*food*; see mouton) |

(2) exactly the same pronunciation but, usually, a different spelling (such words are called *homonyms*):

la'ma	leak
(*monk*; see llama)	(*escape*; see leek)
lla'ma	leek
(*animal*: see lama)	(*vegetable*: see leak)

Often the words involved are very close alphabetically. In such cases only the identifying terms are given, as in:

less'en	les'son
(*make less*)	(*instruction*)
less'er	les'sor
(*smaller*)	(*one who leases*)

An important thing to note here is that these *identifying definitions* are meant only as an aid to your locating or identifying the word you want. They are not meant to replace or by any means cover the entire dictionary definition.

More than One Accepted Spelling

Many words in the English language have more than one accepted spelling in use today. Because of space limitations, only the variant spellings of the more common words have been included. To help you identify them as variants of the same word, they have, in most cases, been entered together, as part of the same entry. Usually, the first spelling given is the one more frequently used. Sometimes, if they are far apart alphabetically, they are entered as separate entries. Whichever variant spelling you decide on, it is advisable to be consistent and use that same spelling throughout any one piece of writing.

Prefixes

Many derived words have been entered. Since all such words cannot possibly be included, the information given below about certain prefixes will be helpful.

The prefix . . . is usually added to the base word . . .

self	with a hyphen.
out	without a hyphen.
over	without a hyphen.
anti . . . .⎫	
pre. . . . .⎪	without a hyphen *except* when the prefix is followed by a capital
pro. . . . .⎬	letter.
semi. . . . .⎪	
un . . . .⎭	
non	without a hyphen *except* when the prefix is followed by a capital letter or a word that has a hyphen in it.
re . . . . . :	without a hyphen *except* to distinguish between a word in which the prefix means *again* or *anew* and a word having a special meaning (*re-lay* and *relay*).

WORD FINDER TABLE

Have you ever tried to look up a word in order to find its spelling when you don't have any idea how to find it—simply because you can't spell it? This *Word Finder Table,* which gives the most common spellings for sounds, will help you end this vicious circle.

Think of the word in terms of its pronounced syllables. *Be sure you are pronouncing the word correctly.*

If the sound is like the	*try also the spelling . . .*	*as in the words . . .*
a in fat	ai, au	pl*ai*d, dr*au*ght
a in lane	ai, au, ay, ea, ei, eigh, et, ey	r*ai*n, g*au*ge, r*ay*, br*ea*k, r*ei*n, w*eigh*, sach*et*, th*ey*
a in care	ai, ay, e, ea ei	*ai*r, pr*ay*er, th*e*re, w*ea*r, th*ei*r
a in father	au, e, ea	g*au*nt, s*e*rgeant, h*ea*rth
a in ago	e, i, o, u, *and combinations, as* ou	*a*gent, san*i*ty, c*o*mply, foc*u*s, vici*ou*s
b in big	bb	ru*bb*er
ch in chin	tch, ti, tu	ca*tch*, ques*ti*on, na*tu*re
d in do	dd, ed	pu*dd*le, call*ed*
e in get	a, ae, ai, ay, ea, ei, eo, ie, u	*a*ny, *ae*sthete, s*ai*d, s*ay*s, br*ea*d, h*ei*fer, l*eo*pard, fr*ie*nd, b*u*ry
e in equal	ae, ay, ea, ee, ei, eo, ey, i, ie, oe	alumn*ae*, qu*ay*, l*ea*n, fr*ee*, dec*ei*t, p*eo*ple, k*ey*, mach*i*ne, ch*ie*f, ph*oe*nix
e in here	ea, ee, ei, ie	*ea*r, ch*ee*r, w*ei*rd, b*ie*r
er in over	ar, ir, or, our, re, ur, ure, yr	li*ar*, elix*ir*, auth*or*, glam*our*, ac*re*, aug*ur*, meas*ure*, zeph*yr*
f in fine	ff, gh, lf, ph	cli*ff*, lau*gh*, ca*lf*, *ph*rase
g in go	gg, gh, gu, gue	e*gg*, *gh*oul, *gu*ard, prolo*gue*
h in hat	wh	*wh*o
i in it	a, e, ee, ia, ie, o, u, ui, y	us*a*ge, *E*nglish, b*ee*n, carr*ia*ge, s*ie*ve, w*o*men, b*u*sy, b*ui*lt, h*y*mn
i in kite	ai, ay, ei, ey, ie, igh, uy, y, ye	*ai*sle, *ay*e, sl*ei*ght, *ey*e, t*ie*, n*igh*, b*uy*, fl*y*, r*ye*
j in jam	d, dg, di, dj, g, gg	gra*d*uate, ju*dg*e, sol*di*er, a*dj*ective, ma*g*ic, exa*gg*erate
k in keep	c, cc, ch, ck, cqu, cu, lk, q, qu, que	*c*an, a*cc*ount, *ch*orus, ta*ck*, la*cqu*er, bis*cu*it, wa*lk*, *q*uick, liq*u*or, baro*que*
l in let	ll, sl	ca*ll*, i*sl*e
m in me	chm, gm, lm, mb, mm, mn	dra*chm*, paradi*gm*, ca*lm*, li*mb*, dru*mm*er, hy*mn*
n in no	gn, kn, mm, nn, pn	*gn*u, *kn*eel, *mn*emonic, di*nn*er, *pn*eumatic
ng in ring	n, ngue	pi*n*k, to*ngue*
o in go	au, eau, eo, ew, oa, oe, oh, oo, ou, ough, ow	m*au*ve, b*eau*, y*eo*man, s*ew*, b*oa*t, t*oe*, *oh*, br*oo*ch, s*ou*l, d*ough*, r*ow*
o in long	a, ah, au, aw, oa, ough	*a*ll, Ut*ah*, fr*au*d, th*aw*, br*oa*d, *ough*t
oo in tool	eu, ew, o, oe, ou, ough, u, ue, ui	man*eu*ver, dr*ew*, m*o*ve, sh*oe*, gr*ou*p, thr*ough*, r*u*le, bl*ue*, fr*ui*t

If the sound is like the	*try also the spelling . . .*	*as in the words . . .*
oo in look	o, ou, u	wolf, would, pull
oi in oil	oy	toy
ou in out	ough, ow	bough, crowd
p in put	pp	clipper
r in red	rh, rr, wr	rhyme, berry, wrong
s in sew	c, ce, ps, sc, sch, ss	cent, rice, psychology, scene, schism, miss
sh in ship	ce, ch, ci, s, sch, sci, se, si, ss, ssi, ti	ocean, machine, facial, sure, schwa, conscience, nauseous, tension, issue, fission, nation
t in top	ed, ght, pt, th, tt	walked, bought, ptomaine, thyme, better
u in cuff	o, oe, oo, ou	son, does, flood, double
u in use	eau, eu, eue, ew, ieu, iew, ue, ui, you, yu	beauty, feud, queue, few, adieu, view, cue, suit, youth, yule
ur in fur	ear, er, eur, ir, or, our, yr	learn, germ, hauteur, bird, word, scourge, myrtle
v in vat	f, lv, ph	of, salve, Stephen
w in will	o, u, wh	choir, quaint, wheat
y in you	i, j	onion, hallelujah
z in zero	s, sc, ss, x, zz	busy, discern, scissors, xylophone, buzzer
z in azure	ge, s, si, zi	garage, leisure, fusion, glazier

Sometimes, certain letter combinations (rather than single sounds) cause problems when you are trying to find a word. Here are some common ones:

If you've tried . . .	*then try . . .*	*If you've tried . . .*	*then try . . .*	*If you've tried . . .*	*then try . . .*
pre	per, pro, pri, pra, pru	cks, gz	x	fiz	phys
		us	ous	ture	teur
per	pre, pir, pur, par, por	tion	sion, cion, cean, cian	tious	seous, cious
				air	are
is	us, ace, ice	le	tle, el, al	ance	ence
ere	eir, ear, ier	kw	qu	ant	ent
wi	whi	cer	cre	able	ible
we	whe	ei	ie	sin	syn, cin,
zi	xy	si	psy, ci		cyn

A

aard'vark'
aard'wolf'
· wolves'
ab'a·cus'
· cus·es or ·ci'
ab'a·lo'ne
a·ban'don
a·base'
· based' bas'ing
a·bash'
a·bat'a·ble
a·bate'
· bat'ed bat'ing
ab'a·tis
ab'at·toir'
ab'ax'i·al
ab'ba·cy
· cies
ab'bé
ab'bess
ab'bey
ab'bot
ab·bre'vi·ate'
· at'ed ·at'ing
ab·bre'vi·a'tion
ab·bre'vi·a'tor
ab'di·cate'
· cat'ed ·cat'ing
ab'di·ca'tion
ab'di·ca'tor
ab'do·men
ab·dom'i·nal
ab·duct'
ab·duc'tion
ab·duc'tor
ab·er'rant
ab'er·ra'tion
a·bet'
· bet'ted ·bet'ting
a·bey'ance
ab·hor'
· horred' ·hor'ring
ab·hor'rence
ab·hor'rent
a·bide'
· bode' or ·bid'ed
· bid'ing
a·bil'i·ty
· ties
ab'ject
ab·jec'tion
ab'ju·ra'tion
ab·jure'
· jured' ·jur'ing
ab'la·tive
a·blaze'
a'ble
· bler ·blest
a'ble-bod'ied
ab·lu'tion
ab'ne·gate'
· gat'ed ·gat'ing
ab'ne·ga'tion

ab·nor'mal
ab'nor·mal'i·ty
· ties
ab·nor'mi·ty
· ties
a·board'
a·bode'
a·bol'ish
ab'o·li'tion
A'l-bomb
a·bom'i·na·ble
a·bom'i·nate'
· nat'ed ·nat'ing
a·bom'i·na'tion
a·bom'i·na'tor
ab'o·rig'i·nal
ab'o·rig'i·ne
· nes
a·bort'
a·bor'ti·cide
a·bor'ti·fa'cient
a·bor'tion
a·bor'tive
a·bound'
a·bout'-face'
-faced' -fac'ing
a·bove'bóard'
ab'ra·ca·dab'ra
ab·rade'
· rad'ed ·rad'ing
ab·ra'sion
ab·ra'sive
ab're·act'
ab're·ac'tion
a·breast'
a·bridge'
· bridged'
· bridg'ing
a·bridg'ment
or ·bridge'ment
a·broad'
ab'ro·gate'
· gat'ed ·gat'ing
ab'ro·ga'tion
ab'ro·ga'tor
a·brupt'
ab'scess
ab'scessed
ab·scis'sa
· sas or ·sae
ab·scond'
ab'sence
ab'sent adj.
ab·sent' v.
ab'sen·tee'ism
ab'sent-mind'ed
ab'sinthe or ·sinth
ab'so·lute'
ab'so·lu'tion
ab'so·lut'ism
ab·solve'
· solved' solv'ing
ab·solv'ent
ab·sorb'
· sorbed' sorb'ing
ab·sorb'a·ble
ab·sorb'en·cy
ab·sorb'ent

ab·sorp'tion
ab·stain'
ab·ste'mi·ous
ab·sten'tion
ab'sti·nence
ab'sti·nent
ab·stract'
ab·strac'tion
ab·struse'
ab·surd'
ab·surd'i·ty
· ties
a·bun'dance
a·bun'dant
a·buse'
· bused' bus'ing
a·bus'er
a·bu'sive
a·but'
· but'ted ·but'ting
a·but'ment
a·but'ter
a·bys'mal
a·bys'mal·ly
a·byss'
a·ca'cia
ac'a·de'mi·a
ac'a·dem'ic
ac'a·dem'i·cal
ac'a·dem'i·cal·ly
a·cade'mi'cian
ac'a·dem'i·cism
a·cad'e·my
· mies
ac'a·jou'
a·can'thus
· thus·es or ·thi
a' cap·pel'la
A'ca·pul'co
ac·cede'
· ced'ed ·ced'ing
(agree; see
exceed)
ac·cel'er·an'do
ac·cel'er·ant
ac·cel'er·ate'
· at'ed ·at'ing
ac·cel'er·a'tion
ac·cel'er·a'tor
ac·cel'er·om'e·ter
ac'cent
ac·cen'tu·al
ac·cen'tu·al·ly
ac·cen'tu·ate'
· at'ed ·at'ing
ac·cen'tu·a'tion
ac·cept'
(receive; see
except)
ac·cept'a·bil'i·ty
ac·cept'a·ble
ac·cept'a·bly
ac·cept'ance
ac'cep·ta'tion
ac·cept'ed
(approved; see
excepted)
ac·cep'tor

ac'cess
(approach; see
excess)
ac·ces'si·bil'i·ty
ac·ces'si·ble
ac·ces'sion
ac·ces'so·ry
or ·sa·ry
· ries
ac'ci·dent
ac'ci·den'tal
ac'ci·den'tal·ly
ac·claim'
ac'cla·ma'tion
ac'cli·mate'
· mat'ed ·mat'ing
ac·cli'ma·tize'
· tized' ·tiz'ing
ac·cliv'i·ty
ac·cli'vous
ac'co·lade'
ac·com'mo·date'
· dat'ed ·dat'ing
ac·com'mo·da'·
tion
ac·com'pa·ni·
ment
ac·com'pa·nist
ac·com'pa·ny
· nied ·ny·ing
ac·com'plice
ac·com'plish
ac·com'plished
ac·cord'
ac·cord'ance
ac·cord'ant·ly
ac·cord'ing
ac·cor'di·on
ac·cost'
ac·count'
ac·count'a·bil'·
i·ty
ac·count'a·ble
ac·count'a·bly
ac·count'ant
ac·count'ing
ac·cou'ter
ac·cou'ter·ments
ac·cred'it
ac·cred'it·a'tion
ac·cre'tion
ac·cru'al
ac·crue'
· crued' ·cru'ing
ac·cul'tu·rate'
· rat'ed ·rat'ing
ac·cul'tu·ra'tion
ac·cu'mu·la·ble
ac·cu'mu·late'
· lat'ed ·lat'ing
ac·cu'mu·la'tion
ac·cu'mu·la'tor
ac'cu·ra·cy
ac'cu·rate
ac'cu·rate·ly
ac·curs'ed or
ac·curst'

ac·cus'al
ac'cu·sa'tion
ac·cu'sa·tive
ac·cu'sa·to'ry
ac·cuse'
· cused' ·cus'ing
ac·cus'tom
ac·cus'tomed
a·cer'bi·ty
· ties
ac'e·tate'
ac'e·tone'
a·cet'y·lene'
ache
ached ach'ing
a·chiev'a·ble
a·chieve'
· chieved'
· chiev'ing
a·chieve'ment
ach'ro·mat'ic
a·chro'ma·tism
a·chro'ma·tize'
· tized' ·tiz'ing
A'chro·my'cin
ach'y
ach'i·er ach'i·est
ac'id-fast'
ac'id-form'ing
a·cid'ic
a·cid'i·fi'er
a·cid'i·fy'
· fied' ·fy'ing
a·cid'i·ty
ac'i·do'sis
a·cid'u·late'
· lat'ed ·lat'ing
a·cid'u·lous
ac·knowl'edge
· edged ·edg·ing
ac·knowl'edge·
a·ble
ac·knowl'edg·
ment or
· edge·ment
ac'me
ac'ne
ac'o·lyte'
ac'o·nite'
a'corn
a·cous'tic or
· ti·cal
a·cous'ti·cal·ly
ac·quaint'
ac·quaint'ance
ac'qui·esce'
· esced' ·esc'ing
ac'qui·es'cence
ac'qui·es'cent
ac·quir'a·ble
ac·quire'
· quired' ·quir'ing
ac·quire'ment
ac'qui·si'tion
ac·quis'i·tive
ac·quit'
· quit'ted
· quit'ting

ac·quit'tal
a'cre
a'cre·age
ac'rid
a·crid'i·ty
ac'ri·mo'ni·ous
ac'ri·mo'ny
ac'ro·bat'
ac'ro·bat'ic
ac'ro·bat'i·cal·ly
ac'ro·nym
ac'ro·pho'bi·a
a·crop'o·lis
a·cross'
a·cros'tic
a·cryl'ic
act'a·ble
act'a·bil'i·ty
act'ing
ac·tin'i·um
ac'ti·no·my'cin
ac'tion
ac'ti·vate'
· vat'ed ·vat'ing
ac'ti·va'tion
ac'ti·va'tor
ac'tive
ac'tiv·ism
ac'tiv·ist
ac·tiv'i·ty
· ties
ac'tiv·ize'
· ized' ·iz'ing
ac'tor
ac'tress
ac'tu·al
ac'tu·al'i·ty
· ties
ac'tu·al·ize'
· ized' ·iz'ing
ac'tu·al·ly
ac'tu·ar'i·al
ac'tu·ar'y
· ies
ac'tu·ate'
· at'ed ·at'ing
ac'tu·a'tion
ac'tu·a'tor
a·cu'i·ty
· ties
a·cu'men
ac'u·punc'ture
a·cute'
a·cute'ly
ad'age
a·da'gio
· gios
ad'a·mant
a·dapt'
(fit; see adept,
adopt)
a·dapt'a·bil'i·ty
a·dapt'a·ble
ad'ap·ta'tion or
a·dap'tion
a·dapt'er or
a·dap'tor

a·dap'tive
add'a·ble *or* ·i·ble
ad·den'dum
·da
ad'der
(*snake*)
add'er
(*one who adds*)
ad'dict
ad·dic'tion
ad·dic'tive
ad·di'tion
(*an adding; see
edition*)
ad·di'tion·al
ad·di'tion·al·ly
ad'di·tive
ad'dle
·dled ·dling
ad'dle·brained'
ad·dress'
ad'dress·ee'
ad·duce'
·duced' ·duc'ing
ad·duc'i·ble
ad·duc'tion
ade·e·noi'dal
ad'e·noids'
ad·ept'
(*skilled; see
adapt, adopt*)
ad'e·qua·cy
ad'e·quate
ad'e·quate·ly
ad·here'
·hered' ·her'ing
ad·her'ence
ad·her'ent
ad·he'sion
ad·he'sive
ad' hoc'
ad' hom'i·nem'
a·dieu'
ad in'fi·ni'tum
ad in'ter·im
ad'i·pose'
ad·ja'cen·cy
ad·ja'cent
ad'jec·tive
ad·join'
(*be next to*)
ad·journ'
(*suspend*)
ad·judge'
·judged'
judg'ing
ad·ju'di·cate'
·cat'ed ·cat'ing
ad·ju'di·ca'tion
ad·ju'di·ca'tor
ad'junct
ad'ju·ra'tion
ad·jure'
·jured' ·jur'ing
ad·just'
ad·just'a·ble
ad·just'er *or*

·jus'tor
ad·just'ment
ad'ju·tant
ad'-lib'
-libbed' -lib'bing
ad'man'
·men'
ad·min'is·ter
ad·min'is·tra·ble
ad·min'is·trate'
·trat'ed ·trat'ing
ad·min'is·tra'tion
ad·min'is·tra'tive
ad·min'is·tra'tor
ad'mi·ra·ble
ad'mi·ra·bly
ad'mi·ral
ad'mi·ral·ty
·ties
ad'mi·ra'tion
ad·mire'
·mired' ·mir'ing
ad·mir'er
ad·mis'si·bil'i·ty
ad·mis'si·ble
ad·mis'si·bly
ad·mis'sion
ad·mit'
·mit'ted ·mit'ting
ad·mit'tance
ad·mit'ted·ly
ad·mix'
ad·mix'ture
ad·mon'ish
ad·mo·ni'tion
ad·mon'i·to'ry
ad' nau'se·am
a·do'
a·do'be
ad·o·les'cence
ad·o·les'cent
a·dopt'
(*choose; see
adapt, adept*)
a·dop'tion
a·dop'tive
a·dor'a·ble
ad·o·ra'tion
a·dore'
·dored' ·dor'ing
a·dorn'
a·dorn'ment
ad·re'nal
ad·ren'al·in
a·drift'
a·droit'
ad·sorb'
ad·sor'bent
ad·sorp'tion
ad'u·late'
·lat'ed ·lat'ing
ad'u·la'tion
a·dul'ter·ant
a·dul'ter·ate'
·at'ed ·at'ing
a·dul'ter·a'tion
a·dul'ter·er
a·dul'ter·ess *n.*

a·dul'ter·ous *adj.*
a·dul'ter·y
a·dult'hood
ad·um'brate
·brat·ed ·brat·ing
ad' va·lo'rem
ad·vance'
·vanced'
·vanc'ing
ad·vance'ment
ad·van'tage
ad'van·ta'geous
ad·ven·ti'tious
ad·ven'ture
·tured ·tur·ing
ad·ven'tur·er
ad·ven'ture·some
ad·ven'tur·ous
ad'verb
ad·ver'bi·al
·ies
ad·ver·sar'y
ad·verse'
(*opposed; see
averse*)
ad·verse'ly
ad·ver'si·ty
·ties
ad·vert'
ad·vert'ent
ad·ver·tise' *or
·tize'*
·tised' *or* ·tized'
·tis'ing *or
·tiz'ing*
ad·ver·tise'ment
or ·tize'ment
ad·vice' *n.*
ad·vis'a·bil'i·ty
ad·vis'a·ble
ad·vis'a·bly
ad·vise' *v.*
·vised' ·vis'ing
ad·vis'ed·ly
ad·vise'ment
ad·vis'er *or
·vi'sor*
ad·vi'so·ry
ad'vo·ca·cy
ad'vo·cate'
·cat'ed ·cat'ing
Ae·ge'an
ae'gis
ae'on
aer'ate'
·at'ed ·at'ing
aer·a'tion
aer'a·tor
aer'i·al
aer'i·al·ist
aer'ie *or* ·y
aer'o·bal·lis'tics
aer'o·bat'ics
aer'obe
aer'o·dy·nam'i·
cal·ly
aer'o·dy·nam'ics
aer'o·me·chan'·ics

aer'o·med'i·cine
aer'o·nau'ti·cal
aer'o·nau'tics
aero'o·neu·ro'sis
aer'o·sol'
aer'o·space
aer'o·stat'ics
Ae'sop
aes'thete'
aes·thet'ic
aes·thet'i·cal·ly
aes·thet'i·cism
af'fa·bil'i·ty
af'fa·ble
af'fa·bly
af·fair'
af·fect'
(*to influence; see
effect*)
af'fec·ta'tion
af·fect'ed
af·fec'tion
af·fec'tion·ate
af·fec'tive
(*of feelings; see
effective*)
af·fi'ance
·anced ·anc·ing
af·fi·da'vit
af·fil'i·ate'
·at'ed ·at'ing
af·fil'i·a'tion
af·fin'i·ty
af·firm'
af·fir·ma'tion
af·firm'a·tive
af·firm'a·tive·ly
af·fix'
·fixed' *or* ·fixt'
·fix'ing
af·flict'
af·flic'tion
af'flu·ence
af'flu·ent
(*rich; see
effluent*)
af·ford'
af·fray'
af·front'
af'ghan
a·fi'cio·na'do
a·field'
a·fire'
a·flame'
a·float'
a·fore'men'tioned
a·fore'said'
a·fore'thought'
a·fore'time'
a·foul'
a·fraid'
A'-frame'
a·fresh'
Af'ri·can
af'ter
af'ter·birth'
af'ter·burn'er
af'ter·damp'

af'ter·ef·fect'
af'ter·glow'
af'ter·im'age
af'ter·life'
af'ter·math'
af'ter·noon'
af'ter·shock'
af'ter·taste'
af'ter·thought'
af'ter·ward
a·gain'
a·gainst'
a·gape'
ag'ate
ag'ate·ware'
age
aged, ag'ing *or*
age'ing
age'less
age'long'
a'gen·cy
·cies
a·gen'da
a'gent
age'-old'
ag·glom'er·ate'
·at'ed ·at'ing
ag·glom'er·a'tion
ag·glu'ti·nant
ag·glu'ti·nate'
·nat'ed ·nat'ing
ag·glu'ti·na'tion
ag·gran'dize'
·dized' ·diz'ing
ag·gran'dize·
ment
ag'gra·vate'
·vat'ed ·vat'ing
ag·gra·va'tion
ag'gre·gate'
·gat'ed ·gat'ing
ag·gre·ga'tion
ag·gres'sion
ag·gres'sive
ag·gres'sor
ag·grieve'
·grieved'
·griev'ing
a·ghast'
ag'ile
ag'ile·ly
a·gil'i·ty
ag'i·tate'
·tat'ed ·tat'ing
ag'i·ta'tion
ag'i·ta'tor
ag'it·prop'
a·gleam'
ag'let
a·glow'
ag·nos'tic
ag·nos'ti·cal·ly
ag·nos'ti·cism
a·gog'
ag'o·nize'
·nized' ·niz'ing
ag'o·ny
·nies

ag'o·ra·pho'bi·a
a·grar'i·an
a·gree'
greed' gree'ing
a·gree'a·bil'i·ty
a·gree'a·ble
a·gree'a·bly
ag'ri·busi'ness
ag'ri·cul'tur·al
ag'ri·cul'ture
ag'ri·cul'tur·ist
or ·tur·al·ist
a·gron'o·my
a·ground'
a'gue
a'gu·ish
a·head'
aid
(*help*)
aide
(*assistant*)
aide'-de-camp' *or*
aid'-de-camp'
aides'- *or* aids'-
ail
(*be ill; see ale*)
ai'le·ron'
ail'ing
ail'ment
aim'less
air
(*gases; see heir*)
air base
air'borne'
air brake
air'bra'sive
air'brush'
air coach
air'-con·di'tion
air'-con·di'tioned
air conditioner
air conditioning
air'-cool'
air'-cooled'
air'craft'
air'drome'
air'drop'
·dropped'
·drop'ping
air'-dry'
-dried' -dry'ing
air express
air'field'
air'foil'
air force
air'frame'
air gun
air hole
air'i·ly
air'i·ness
air'ing
air lane
air'lift'
air'line'
air'lin'er
air lock
air'mail'

air'man
·men
air'-mind'ed
air'mo'bile
air'plane'
air'port'
air pressure
air'proof'
air pump
air raid
air'scape'
air'ship'
air'sick'
air'space'
air'speed'
air'-sprayed'
air'stream'
air'strip'
air'tight'
air'waves'
air'wor'thy
air'y
air'i·er air'i·est
aisle
(*passage;* see isle)
a·kim'bo
Al'a·bam'a
al'a·bas'ter
a' la carte'
a·lac'ri·ty
à' la king'
a' la mode'
or à' la mode'
a·larm'ing
a·larm'ist
A·las'ka
al'ba·core'
al'ba·tross'
al·be'it
al'bi·nism
al·bi'no
·nos
al'bum
al·bu'men
(*egg white*)
al·bu'min
(*class of proteins*)
Al'bu·quer'que
al'che·mist
al'che·my
al'co·hol'
al'co·hol'ic
al'co·hol'i·cal·ly
al'co·hol'ism
al'cove
al'der·man
·men
ale
(*a drink;* see ail)
a'le·a·to'ry
ale'house'
a·lert'ly
A·leu'tian
ale'wife'
·wives'
al·fal'fa
al·fres'co
al'gae

al'gae·cide'
al'ge·bra
al'ge·bra'ic
al'ge·bra'i·cal·ly
al'i·as
al'i·bi'
·bis'
·bied' ·bi'ing
al'ien
al'ien·ate'
·at'ed ·at'ing
al'ien·a'tion
a·light'
·light'ed or ·lit'
·light'ing
a·lign' or a·line'
·ligned' or ·lined'
·lign'ing or
·lin'ing
a·lign'ment
or a·line'ment
a·like'
al'i·men'ta·ry
(*nourishing;* see
elementary)
al'i·mo'ny
al'i·quant
al'i·quot
a·live'
al'ka·li'
·lies' or ·lis'
al'ka·line
al'ka·lize'
·lized' ·liz'ing
al'ka·loid'
al'kyd
all'-A·mer'i·can
all'-a·round'
al·lay'
·layed' ·lay'ing
all'-clear'
al'le·ga'tion
al·lege'
·leged' ·leg'ing
al·leg'ed·ly
Al'le·ghe'ny
al·le'giance
al'le·gor'i·cal
al'le·go·rize'
·rized' ·riz'ing
al'le·go'ry
·ries
al'le·gret'to
al·le'gro
al'le·lu'ia
al'ler·gen
al'ler·gen'ic
al·ler'gic
al'ler·gist
al'ler·gy
·gies
al·le'vi·ate'
·at'ed ·at'ing
al·le'vi·a'tion
al'ley
·leys
(*narrow lane;*
see ally)

al'ley·way'
al·li'ance
al·lied'
al'li·ga'tor
all'-im·por'tant
all'-in·clu'sive
al·lit'er·ate'
·at'ed ·at'ing
al·lit'er·a'tion
al'lo·cate'
·cat'ed ·cat'ing
al'lo·ca'tion
al·lot'
·lot'ted ·lot'ing
al·lot'ment
al·lot'tee'
all'-out'
all'o'ver
al·low'
al·low'a·ble
al·low'ance
al·lowed'
(*permitted;* see
aloud)
al'loy
all'-pur'pose
all right
all'spice'
all'-star'
all'-time'
al·lude'
·lud'ed ·lud'ing
(*refer to;* see
elude)
al·lure'
·lured' ·lur'ing
al·lu'sion
(*mention;* see
elusion, illusion)
al·lu'sive
(*mentioning;* see
elusive, illusive)
al·lu'vi·al
al·lu'vi·um
·vi·ums or ·vi·a
al·ly' *v.* al'ly *n.*
·lied' ·ly'ing
·lies
(*join; partner;*
see alley)
al'ma ma'ter
al'ma·nac'
al·might'y
al'mond
al'mon·er
al'most
alms
a·loft'
a·lo'ha
a·long'shore'
a·long'side'
a·loof'
a·loud'
(*loudly;* see
allowed)
al·pac'a
al'pen·stock'
al'pha·bet'

al'pha·bet'i·cal
al'pha·bet'i·cal·ly
al'pha·bet·ize'
·ized' ·iz'ing
al·read'y
al'so-ran'
al'tar
(*table for
worship*)
al'ter
(*to change*)
al'ter·a'tion
al'ter·cate'
·cat'ed ·cat'ing
al'ter·ca'tion
al'ter·nate'
·nat'ed ·nat'ing
al'ter·na'tion
al·ter'na·tive
al'ter·na'tor
al·though'
al·tim'e·ter
al'ti·tude'
al'to
·tos
al·to·geth'er
al'tru·ism
al'tru·is'tic
a·lu'mi·num
a·lum'na *n.fem.*
·nae
a·lum'nus
n.masc.
·ni
al'ways
a·mal'ga·mate'
·mat'ed ·mat'ing
a·mal'ga·ma'tion
a·man'u·en'sis
·ses
am'a·ryl'lis
am'a·teur'
am'a·to'ry
a·maze'
·mazed'
·maz'ing
a·maze'ment
Am'a·zon'
am·bas'sa·dor
am·bas'sa·do'ri·al
am'ber
am'ber·gris'
am'bi·ance
am'bi·dex·ter'i·ty
am'bi·dex'trous
am'bi·ent
am'bi·gu'i·ty
am·big'u·ous
am·bi'tion
am·bi'tious
am·biv'a·lence
am'ble
·bled ·bling
am·bro'sia
am'bu·lance
am'bu·late'
·lat'ed ·lat'ing
am'bu·la·to'ry

am'bus·cade'
·cad'ed ·cad'ing
am'bush
a·me'ba
·bas or ·bae
a·mel'io·rate'
·rat'ed ·rat'ing
a·mel'io·ra'tion
a·mel'io·ra'tive
a·me'na·bil'i·ty
a·me'na·ble
a·mend'
(*revise;* see
emend)
a·mend'ment
a·men'i·ty
·ties
A·mer'i·can
A·mer'i·ca'na
A·mer'i·can·ism
A·mer'i·can·i·
za'tion
A·mer'i·can·ize'
·ized' ·iz'ing
Am'er·ind'
am'e·thyst
a'mi·a·bil'i·ty
a'mi·a·ble
a'mi·a·bly
am'i·ca·bil'i·ty
am'i·ca·ble
am'i·ca·bly
a·mid'
a·mid'ships
a·midst'
a·mi'no
Am'ish
a·miss'
am'i·ty
·ties
am'me'ter
am·mo'nia
am·mu·ni'tion
am·ne'sia
am·ne'si·ac' or
am·ne'sic
am'nes·ty
·ties, ·tied ·ty·ing
a·moe'ba
·bas or ·bae
a·mok'
a·mong'
a·mongst'
a·mon'til·la'do
a·mor'al
a'mor·al'i·ty
am'o·rous
a·mor'phous
am'or·ti·za'tion
am'or·tize'
·tized' ·tiz'ing
a·mount'
a·mour'
am'per·age
am'pere
am'per·sand'
am·phet'a·mine'
am·phib'i·an

am·phib'i·ous
am'phi·the'a·ter
am'pho·ra
·rae or ·ras
am'ple
am'pli·fi·ca'tion
am'pli·fi'er
am'pli·fy'
·fied' ·fy'ing
am'pli·tude'
am'ply
am'pul
am·pul'la
·las or ·lae
am'pu·tate'
·tat'ed ·tat'ing
am'pu·ta'tion
am'pu·tee'
a·muck'
am'u·let
a·muse'
·mused'
·mus'ing
a·muse'ment
a·nach'ro·nism
a·nach'ro·nis'tic
an'a·con'da
a·nae'mi·a
a·nae'mic
an'aes·the'sia
an'aes·thet'ic
an·aes'the·tize'
·tized' ·tiz'ing
an'a·gram'
a'nal
an'al·ge'si·a
an'al·ge'sic
an'a·log' computer
a·nal'o·gize'
·gized' ·giz'ing
a·nal'o·gous
a·nal'o·gy
·gies
a·nal'y·sis
·ses'
an'a·lyst
(*one who
analyzes;* see
annalist)
an'a·lyt'i·cal
or an'a·lyt'ic
an'a·lyt'i·cal·ly
an'a·lyze'
·lyzed' ·lyz'ing
an'a·pest'
an·ar'chic
or an·ar'chi·cal
an'ar·chism
an'ar·chist
an'ar·chis'tic
an'ar·chy
·chies
an·as'tig·mat'ic
a·nas'tro·phe
a·nath'e·ma
·mas
a·nath'e·ma·tize'
·tized' ·tiz'ing

an'a·tom'i·cal
or an'a·tom'ic
an'a·tom'i·cal·ly
a·nat'o·mist
a·nat'o·mize'
·mized' ·miz'ing
a·nat'o·my
·mies
an'ces'tor
an·ces'tral
an'ces'tress
an'ces'try
·tries
an'chor
an'chor·age
an'cho·rite'
an'cho'vy
·vies
an'cient
an'cil·lar'y
an·dan'te
and'i'ron
and/or
an'dro·gen
an'ec·dot'al
an'ec·do*e'
(story; see
antidote)
a·ne'mi·a
a·ne'mic
a·nem'o·graph'
an'e·mom'e·ter
a·nem'o·ne'
an'er·oid'
an'es·the'sia
an'es·the'si·
ol'o·gy
an'es·thet'ic
an·es'the·tist
an·es'the·tize'
·tized' ·tiz'ing
an'gel
(spirit; see angle)
an'gel·fish'
an·gel'ic
or an·gel'i·cal
an·gel'i·cal·ly
An'ge·lus
an'ger
an·gi'na
an'gle
·gled ·gling
(corner; scheme;
see angel)
an'gler
an'gle·worm'
An'gli·can
An'gli·cism
An'gli·cize'
·cized' ·ciz'ing
an'gling
An'glo-A·mer'i·
can
An'glo·ma'ni·a
An'glo·phile'
An'glo-Sax'on
An·go'ra
an'gos·tu'ra

an'gri·ly
an'gry
·gri·er ·gri·est
an'guish
an'gu·lar
an·gu·lar'i·ty
·ties
an'gu·la'tion
an·hy'drous
an'ile
a·nil'i·ty
an'i·mad·ver'
sion
an'i·mal
an'i·mal'cule
an'i·mal·ism
an'i·mal·is'tic
an'i·mal·ize'
·ized' ·iz'ing
an'i·mate'
·mat'ed ·mat'ing
an'i·ma'tor
or ·mat'er
an'i·ma'tion
an'i·mism
an'i·mos'i·ty
·ties
an'i·mus
an'i'on
an'ise
an'i·seed'
an'i·sette'
ankh
an'kle
an'kle·bone'
an'klet
an'nal·ist
(a writer of
annals; see
analyst)
an'nals
An·nap'o·lis
an·neal'
an'ne·lid
an·nex' v.
an'nex n.
an'nex·a'tion
an·ni'hi·late'
·lat'ed ·lat'ing
an·ni'hi·la'tion
an·ni'hi·la'tor
an'ni·ver'sa·ry
·ries
an'no·tate'
·tat'ed ·tat'ing
an'no·ta'tion
an·nounce'
·nounced'
·nounc'ing
an·nounce'ment
an·nounc'er
an·noy'
an·noy'ance
an·nu'al
an'nu·al·ly
an·nu'i·tant
an·nu'i·ty
·ties

an·nul'
·nulled'
·nul'ling
an·nu·lar
an·nul'ment
an'nu·lus
·li' or ·lus·es
an·nun'ci·ate'
·at'ed ·at'ing
(announce; see
enunciate)
an·nun'ci·a'tor
an'ode
an'o·dize'
·dized' ·diz'ing
an'o·dyne'
a·noint'
a·nom'a·lous
a·nom'a·ly
·lies
an'o·mie
an·o·nym'i·ty
a·non'y·mous
a·noph'e·les'
an·oth'er
an'swer
ant·ac'id
an·tag'o·nism
an·tag'o·nis'tic
an·tag'o·nize'
·nized' ·niz'ing
ant·al'ka·li'
·lies' or ·lis'
ant·arc'tic
Ant·arc'ti·ca
an'te
·ted or ·teed
·te·ing
an'te- prefix
(before; see
anti-)
ant'eat'er
an'te·bel'lum
an'te·cede'
·ced'ed ·ced'ing
an'te·ced'ence
an'te·ced'ent
an'te·cham'ber
an'te·date'
an'te·di·lu'vi·an
an'te·lope'
an'te me·ri'di·em
an·ten'na
·nae or ·nas
an'te·pe'nult
an'te·ri·or
an'te·room'
an'them
an'ther
an·thol'o·gist
an·thol'o·gy
·gies
an'thra·cite'
an'thrax
·thra·ces'
an'thro·poid'
an'thro·pol'o·gist
an'thro·pol'o·gy

an'thro·po·mor'·
phic
an'ti- prefix
(against; see
ante-)
an'ti·air'craft
an'ti·bac·te'ri·al
an'ti·bi·ot'ic
an'ti·bod'y
·ies
an'tic
·ticked ·tick·ing
an·tic'i·pant
an·tic'i·pate'
·pat'ed ·pat'ing
an·tic'i·pa'tion
an·tic'i·pa·to'ry
an'ti·cli·mac'tic
an'ti·cli'max
an'ti·de·pres'sant
an'ti·dote'
(remedy; see
anecdote)
an'ti·freeze'
an'ti·gen
an'ti·he'ro
an'ti·his'ta·mine'
an'ti·knock'
an'ti·la'bor
An·til'les
an'ti·ma·cas'sar
an'ti·mat'ter
an'ti·mo'ny
an'ti·nov'el
an'ti·par'ti·cle
an'ti·pas'to
an'ti·pa·thet'ic
an·tip'a·thy
·thies
an'ti·per'son·nel'
an'ti·phon
an·tiph'o·nal
an'ti·po'dal
an'ti·pode'
an·tip'o·des'
an'ti·quar'i·an
an·tiq'uar'y
·ies
an'ti·quate'
·quat'ed
·quat'ing
an·tique'
·tiqued'
·tiqu'ing
an·tiq'ui·ty
·ties
an'ti·Sem'ite
an'ti·Se·mit'ic
an'ti·Sem'i·tism
an'ti·sep'sis
an'ti·sep'tic
an'ti·so'cial
an·tith'e·sis
·ses'
an'ti·thet'i·cal
an'ti·thet'i·
cal·ly
an'ti·tox'in

an'ti·trust'
ant'ler
an'to·nym'
an'trum
·trums or ·tra
a'nus
·nus·es or ·ni
an'vil
anx·i'e·ty
·ties
anx'ious
an'y·bod'y
an'y·how'
an'y·one'
an'y·thing'
an'y·way'
an'y·where'
A'-OK' or
A'-O·kay'
a·or'ta
·tas or ·tae
a·pace'
a·part'heid
a·part'ment
ap'a·thet'ic
ap'a·thet'i·
cal·ly
ap'a·thy
·thies
ap'pe·ri·tif'
ap'er·ture
a'pex
a'pex·es or
ap'i·ces
a·pha'si·a
aph'o·rism
aph'ro·dis'i·ac'
a'pi·ar'y
·ies
a·piece'
a·plomb'
a·poc'a·lypse'
a·poc·a·lyp'tic
a·poc'ry·phal
ap'o·gee'
a·pol'o·get'ic
a·pol'o·get'i·
cal·ly
ap'o·lo'gi·a
a·pol'o·gize'
·gized' ·giz'ing
a·pol'o·gy
·gies
ap'o·plec'tic
ap'o·plex'y
a·pos'ta·sy
a·pos'tate
a'·pos·te'ri·o'ri
a·pos'tle
ap'os·tol'ic
a·pos'tro·phe
ap'os·troph'ic
a·pos'tro·phize'
·phized'
·phiz'ing
a·poth'e·car'y
·ies

ap'o·thegm'
(short saying)
ap'o·them'
(math. term)
a·poth'e·o'sis
·ses
Ap'pa·la'chi·an
ap·pall' or ·pal'
·palled' ·pal'ling
ap'pa·loo'sa
ap'pa·ra'tus
·tus or ·tus·es
ap·par'el
·eled or ·elled
·el·ing or ·el·ling
ap·par'ent
ap'pa·ri'tion
ap·peal'
ap·pear'ance
ap·peas'a·ble
ap·pease'
·peased'
·peas'ing
ap·pease'ment
ap·peas'er
ap·pel'lant
ap·pel'late
ap'pel·la'tion
ap·pend'
ap·pend'age
ap·pend'ant or
·ent
ap·pen·dec'to·my
·mies
ap·pen'di·ci'tis
ap·pen'dix
·dix·es or
·di·ces'
ap'per·cep'tion
ap·per·tain'
ap'pe·tite'
ap'pe·tiz'er
ap'pe·tiz'ing
ap·plaud'
ap·plause'
ap'ple·jack'
ap'ple·sauce'
ap·pli'ance
ap'pli·ca·bil'i·ty
ap'pli·ca·ble
ap'pli·cant
ap'pli·ca'tion
ap'pli·ca'tor
ap·plied'
ap'pli·qué'
·quéd' ·qué'ing
ap·ply'
·plied' ·ply'ing
ap·pog'gia·tu'ra
ap·point'
ap·point'ee'
ap·poin'tive
ap·point'ment
ap·por'tion
ap'po·site
ap'po·si'tion
ap·prais'a·ble
ap·prais'al

ap·praise'
·praised'
·prais'ing
(*estimate;* see
apprise)
ap·prais'er
ap·pre'ci·a·ble
ap·pre'ci·ate'
·at'ed ·at'ing
ap·pre'ci·a'tion
ap·pre'ci·a·tive
ap'pre·hend'
ap'pre·hen'sion
ap'pre·hen'sive
ap·pren'tice
·ticed ·tic·ing
ap·prise' or
·prize'
·prised' or
·prized'
·pris'ing or
·priz'ing
(*inform;* see
appraise)
ap·proach'
ap·proach'·
a·ble
ap'pro·ba'tion
ap·pro'pri·ate'
·at'ed ·at'ing
ap·pro'pri·ate·ly
ap·pro'pri·a'tion
ap·prov'a·ble
ap·prov'al
ap·prove'
·proved'
·prov'ing
ap·prox'i·mate'
·mat'ed ·mat'ing
ap·prox'i·mate·ly
ap·prox'i·ma'·
tion
ap·pur'te·nance
a'pri·cot'
A'pril
a' pri·o'ri
ap'ro·pos'
ap'ti·tude'
apt'ly
aq'ua·cade'
aq'ua·lung'
aq'ua·ma·rine'
aq'ua·naut'
aq'ua·plane'
a·quar'i·um
·i·ums or ·i·a
a·quat'ic
aq'ua·tint'
aq'ue·duct'
a'que·ous
aq'ui·line'
ar'a·besque'
A·ra'bi·an
Ar'a·bic
ar'a·ble
a·rach'nid
ar'bi·ter
ar'bi·tra·ble

ar·bit'ra·ment
ar'bi·trar'i·ly
ar'bi·trar'i·ness
ar'bi·trar'y
ar'bi·trate'
·trat'ed ·trat'ing
ar'bi·tra'tion
ar'bi·tra'tor
ar'bor
ar·bo're·al
ar'bo·re'tum
·tums or ·ta
ar'bor·vi'tae
arc
arced or arcked
arc'ing or arck'ing
(*curve;* see ark)
ar·cade'
ar'chae·o·log'i·cal
ar'chae·ol'o·gy
ar·cha'ic
arch·an'gel
arch'bish'op
arch'dea'con
arch'di'o·cese
arch'duch'y
·ies
arch'duke'
arched
arch'en'e·my
·mies
ar'che·o·log'i·cal
ar'che·ol'o·gy
arch'er·y
ar'che·type'
arch'fiend'
ar'chi·pel'a·go'
·goes' or ·gos'
ar'chi·tect'
ar'chi·tec·ton'ics
ar'chi·tec'tur·al
ar'chi·tec'tur·
al·ly
ar'chi·tec'ture
ar'chi·trave'
ar'chives
arch'priest'
arch'way'
arc'tic
ar'dent
ar'dor
ar'du·ous
ar'e·a·way'
a·re'na
aren't
Ar'gen·ti'na
ar'gon
ar'got
ar'gu·a·ble
ar'gu·a·bly
ar'gue
·gued ·gu·ing
ar'gu·ment
ar'gu·men·
ta'tion
ar'gu·men'ta·
tive
a'ri·a

a·rid'i·ty
ar'id·ness
a·rise'
·rose' ·ris'en
·ris'ing
ar'is·toc'ra·cy
·cies
a·ris'to·crat'
a·ris'to·crat'ic
a·ris'to·crat'i·
cal·ly
Ar'is·to·te'li·an
Ar'is·tot'le
a·rith'me·tic' *n.*
ar'ith·met'ic *adj.*
ar'ith·met'i·cal
ar'ith·met'i·
cal·ly
ar'ith·me·ti'cian
Ar'i·zo'na
ark
(*enclosure;*
see arc)
Ar'kan·sas'
ar·ma'da
ar'ma·dil'lo
·los
ar'ma·ment
ar'ma·ture
arm'chair'
armed
arm'ful
·fuls
arm'hole'
ar'mi·stice
arm'let
ar'mor
ar'mored
ar'mor-plat'ed
ar'mor·y
·ies
arm'pit'
arm'rest'
ar'my
·mies
ar'ni·ca
a·ro'ma
ar'o·mat'ic
ar'o·mat'i·cal·ly
a·round'
a·rous'al
a·rouse'
·roused'
·rous'ing
ar·peg'gio
·gios
ar·raign'
ar·range'
·ranged'
·rang'ing
ar·range'ment
ar·rang'er
ar'rant
ar·ray'
ar·ray'al
ar·rear'age
ar·rears'
ar·rest'

ar·riv'al
ar·rive'
·rived' ·riv'ing
ar'ro·gance
ar'ro·gant
ar'ro·gate'
·gat'ed ·gat'ing
ar'ro·ga'tion
ar'row·head'
ar'row·root'
ar·roy'o
·os
ar'se·nal
ar'se·nic
ar'son
ar'son·ist
ar'te·fact'
ar·te'ri·al
ar·te'ri·o·scle·
ro'sis
ar·te'ri·o·scle·
rot'ic
ar'ter·y
·ies
ar·te'sian
art'ful
art'ful·ly
ar·thrit'ic
ar·thri'tis
Ar·thu'ri·an
ar'ti·choke'
ar'ti·cle
ar·tic'u·late'
·lat'ed ·lat'ing
ar·tic'u·late·ly
ar·tic'u·la'tion
ar'ti·fact'
ar'ti·fice
ar·tif'i·cer
ar'ti·fi'cial
ar'ti·fi'cial·ly
ar'ti·fi'ci·al'i·ty
·ties
ar·til'ler·y
art'i·ness
ar'ti·san
art'ist
ar·tiste'
ar·tis'tic
ar·tis'ti·cal·ly
art'ist·ry
art'less
art'mo·bile'
art'sy-craft'sy
art'y
·i·er ·i·est
Ar'y·an
as·bes'tos
as·cend'
as·cend'a·ble
as·cend'an·cy
as·cend'ant
as·cen'sion
as·cent'
(*a rising;* see
assent)
as'cer·tain'
as·cet'ic

as·cet'i·cal·ly
as·cet'i·cism
a·scor'bic
as'cot
as·crib'a·ble
as·cribe'
·cribed'
·crib'ing
as·crip'tion
a·sep'tic
a·sep'ti·cal·ly
a·sex'u·al
a·shamed'
ash'can'
ash'en
ash'es
a·shore'
ash'y
·i·er ·i·est
A'sia
A'si·at'ic
as'i·nine'
as'i·nin'i·ty
·ties
a·skance'
a·skew'
a·sleep'
a·so'cial
as·par'a·gus
as'pect
as'pen
as·per'i·ty
as·perse'
·persed' ·pers'ing
as·per'sion
as'phalt
as·phyx'i·a
as·phyx'i·ant
as·phyx'i·ate'
·at'ed ·at'ing
as·phyx'i·a'tion
as·phyx'i·a'tor
as'pic
as'pir·ant
as'pi·rate'
·rat'ed ·rat'ing
as'pi·ra'tion
as'pi·ra'tor
as·pire'
·pired' ·pir'ing
as'pi·rin
as·sail'
as·sail'ant
as·sas'sin
as·sas'si·nate'
·nat'ed ·nat'ing
as·sas'si·na'tion
as·sault'
as·say'
(*analyze;* see
essay)
as·sem'blage
as·sem'ble
·bled ·bling
as·sem'bly
·blies
as·sem'bly·man
·men

as·sent'
(*consent;* see ascent)
as·sert'
as·ser'tion
as·ser'tive
as·sess'
as·ses'sor
as'set
as·sev'er·ate'
·at'ed ·at'ing
as·sev'er·a'tion
as'si·du'i·ty
as·sid'u·ous
as·sign'
as·sign'a·ble
as·sig·na'tion
as·sign'ee'
as·sign'ment
as·sim'i·la·ble
as·sim'i·late'
·lat'ed ·lat'ing
as·sim'i·la'tion
as·sim'i·la'tive
as·sim'i·la'tor
as·sist'
as·sist'ance
as·sist'ant
as·size'
as·so'ci·ate'
·at'ed ·at'ing
as·so'ci·a'tion
as·so'ci·a'tive
as'so·nant
as·sort'
as·sort'ed
as·sort'ment
as·suage'
·suaged'
·suag'ing
as·sua'sive
as·sum'a·ble
as·sume'
·sumed'
·sum'ing
as·sump'tion
as·sur'ance
as·sure'
·sured' ·sur'ing
as·sur'ed·ly
As·syr'i·a
as'ter·isk'
as'ter·oid'
asth'ma
asth·mat'ic
asth·mat'i·cal·ly
as'tig·mat'ic
as'tig·mat'i·cal·ly
a·stig'ma·tism
as·ton'ish
as·tound'
a·strad'dle
as'tra·khan
or ·chan
as'tral
a·stride'
as·trin'gen·cy
as·trin'gent

as'tro·dome'
as'tro·labe'
as·trol'o·ger
as'tro·log'i·cal
as·trol'o·gy
as'tro·naut'
as'tro·nau'ti·cal
as'tro·nau'tics
as·tron'o·mer
as'tro·nom'i·cal
  or ·nom'ic
as·tro·nom'i·cal·ly
as·tron'o·my
as'tro·phys'i·cal
as'tro·phys'i·cist
as'tro·phys'ics
as·tute'
a·sun'der
a·sy'lum
a'sym·met'ri·cal
  or ·met'ric
a·sym'me·try
as'ymp·tote'
at'a·vism
at'a·vis'tic
at'el·ier'
a'the·ism
a'the·ist
a'the·is'tic
ath'lete'
ath·let'ic
ath·let'i·cal·ly
at-home'
a·thwart'
a·tin'gle
At·lan'tic
at'las
at'mos·phere'
at'mos·pher'ic
at'mos·pher'i·
  cal·ly
at'oll
at'om
a·tom'ic
a·tom'ics
at'om·ize'
  ·ized' ·iz'ing
at'om·iz'er
a·ton'al
a'to·nal'i·ty
a·tone'
  ·toned' ·ton'ing
a·tone'ment
a'tri·um
  ·tri·a or ·tri·ums
a·tro'cious
a·troc'i·ty
  ·ties
at'ro·phy
  ·phied ·phy·ing
at·tach'
at'ta·ché'
at·tach'ment
at·tack'
at·tain'
at·tain'a·ble
at·tain'der
at·tain'ment

at·taint'
at'tar
at·tempt'
at·tend'
at·tend'ance
at·tend'ant
at·ten'tion
at·ten'tive
at·ten'u·ate'
  ·at'ed ·at'ing
at·ten'u·a'tion
at·ten'u·a'tor
at·test'
at'tes·ta'tion
at'tic
at·tire'
  ·tired' ·tir'ing
at'ti·tude'
at'ti·tu'di·nal
at·tor'ney
  ·neys
at·tract'
at·trac'tion
at·trac'tive
at·trib'ut·a·ble
at'tri·bute' n.
at·trib'ute v.
  ·ut·ed ·ut·ing
at'tri·bu'tion
at·trib'u·tive
at·tri'tion
at·tune'
  ·tuned' ·tun'ing
a·typ'i·cal
a·typ'i·cal·ly
au'burn
auc'tion
au·da'cious
au·dac'i·ty
  ·ties
au'di·bil'i·ty
au'di·ble
au'di·bly
au'di·ence
au'di·o
au'di·ol'o·gy
au'di·o-vis'u·al
au'di·phone'
au'dit
au·di'tion
au'di·tor
au·di·to'ri·um
au'di·to'ry
au'ger
  (tool; see augur)
aught
  (anything; see
  ought)
aug·ment'
aug'men·ta'tion
aug·ment'a·tive
au·gra'tin
au'gur
  (soothsayer;
  see auger)
Au'gust
au jus'

au na·tu·rel'
au'ra
  ·ras or ·rae
au'ral
  (of the ear; see
  oral)
au're·ole'
Au're·o·my'cin
au' re·voir'
au'ri·cle
  (earlike part;
  see oracle)
au·ric'u·lar
au·ro'ra bo're·
  a'lis
aus'cul·ta'tion
aus'pic·es'
aus·pi'cious
aus·tere'
aus·tere'ly
aus·ter'i·ty
  ·ties
Aus·tral'ia
au·then'tic
au·then'ti·cal·ly
au·then'ti·cate'
  ·cat'ed ·cat'ing
au·then'ti·ca'tion
au'then·tic'i·ty
au'thor
au·thor'i·tar'i·an
au·thor'i·ta'tive
au·thor'i·ty
  ·ties
au'thor·i·za'tion
au'thor·ize'
  ·ized' ·iz'ing
au'to
  ·tos
  ·toed ·to·ing
au'to·bi'o·
  graph'ic or
  graph'i·cal
au'to·bi·og'ra·
  phy
  ·phies
au·toc'ra·cy
  ·cies
au'to·crat'
au'to·crat'ic
au'to·crat'i·
  cal·ly
au'to·graph'
au'to·mat'
au'to·mate'
  ·mat'ed ·mat'ing
au'to·mat'ic
au'to·mat'i·cal·ly
au·tom'a·tion
au·tom'a·tism
au·tom'a·ton'
  ·tons' or ·ta
au'to·mo·bile'
au'to·mo'tive
au'to·nom'ic
au·ton'o·mous
au·ton'o·my
  ·mies

au'top·sy
  ·sies
au'to·sug·ges'·
  tion
au'tumn
au·tum'nal
aux·il'ia·ry
  ·ries
a·vail'a·bil'i·ty
a·vail'a·ble
a·vail'a·bly
av'a·lanche'
  ·lanched'
  ·lanch'ing
a·vant'-garde'
a·vant'-gard'ism
a·vant'-gard'ist
av'a·rice
av'a·ri'cious
a·venge'
  ·venged'
  ·veng'ing
a·veng'er
av'e·nue'
a·ver'
  ·verred'
  ·ver'ring
av'er·age
  ·aged ·ag·ing
a·verse'
  (unwilling; see
  adverse)
a·ver'sion
a·vert'
a'vi·ar'y
  ·ies
a'vi·a'tion
a'vi·a'tor
a'vi·a'trix
av'id·ly
av'o·ca'do
  ·dos
av'o·ca'tion
a·void'a·ble
a·void'a·bly
a·void'ance
av'oir·du·pois'
a·vow'al
a·vowed'
a·vun'cu·lar
a·wait'
a·wake'
  ·woke' or
  ·waked',
  ·waked',
  ·wak'ing
a·wak'en
a·wak'en·ing
a·ward'
a·ware'
a·weigh'
awe'some
awe'-struck'
aw'ful
aw'ful·ly
aw'ful·ness
a·while'
awk'ward

awn'ing
a·wry'
ax or axe
ax'es
axed ax'ing
ax'i·om
ax'i·o·mat'ic
ax'i·o·mat'i·
  cal·ly
ax'is
ax'es
ax'le
Ax'min·ster
a·zal'ea
az'i·muth
Az'tec
az'ure

B

bab'bitt
bab'ble
  ·bled ·bling
ba·boon'
ba·bush'ka
ba'by
  ·bies
  ·bied ·by·ing
ba'by-sit'
  ·sat' ·sit'ting
baby sitter
bac'ca·lau're·ate
bac'ca·rat'
bac'cha·nal
bac'cha·na'li·an
bac'chant
  ·chants or
  bac·chan'tes
bac·chan'te
bach'e·lor
ba·cil'lus
  ·li
back'ache'
back'bite'
  ·bit', ·bit'ten or
  ·bit', ·bit'ing
back'bend'
back'board'
back'bone'
back'break'ing
back'court'
back'date'
  ·dat'ed ·dat'ing
back'door'
back'drop'
back'field'
back'fire'
  ·fired' ·fir'ing
back'gam'mon
back'ground'
back'hand'
back'lash'
back'list'
back'log'
  ·logged'
  ·log'ging

back'rest'
back'side'
back'slide'
  ·slid', ·slid' or
  ·slid'den, ·slid'ing
back'space'
  ·spaced'
  ·spac'ing
back'spin'
back'stage'
back'stairs'
back'stop'
back'stretch'
back'stroke'
  ·stroked'
  ·strok'ing
back'track'
back'up' or
back'-up'
back'ward
back'wash'
back'wa'ter
back'woods'man
  ·men
ba'con
bac·te'ri·a
  (sing. bac·te'ri·um)
bac·te'ri·cide'
bac·te'ri·o·log'i·
  cal·ly
bac·te'ri·ol'o·gist
bac·te'ri·ol'o·gy
bad
  worse worst
badge
  badged badg'ing
badg'er
bad'i·nage'
  ·naged' ·nag'ing
bad'lands'
bad'min·ton
bad'-tem'pered
baf'fle
  ·fled ·fling
bag
  bagged bag'ging
bag'a·telle'
ba'gel
bag'ful'
  ·fuls'
bag'gage
bag'gy
  ·gi·er ·gi·est
bag'pipe'
ba·guette' or
  ·guet'
Ba·hai'
Ba·ha'mas
bail
  (money; see
  bale)
bai'liff
bai'li·wick
bails'man
  ·men
bait'ed
  (lured; see
  bated)

bake
  baked bak'ing
bak'er
bak'er·y
  ·ies
bal'a·lai'ka
bal'ance
  ·anced ·anc·ing
bal'ance·a·ble
bal·brig'gan
bal'co·ny
  ·nies
bal'der·dash'
bald'faced'
bald'head'ed
bald'ness
bale
  baled bal'ing
  (*bundle;* see
  bail)
bale'ful
balk'y
  ·i·er ·i·est
ball
  (*round object;*
  see bawl)
bal'lad
bal'lad·eer'
bal'last
ball bearing
bal'le·ri'na
bal'let
bal·lis'tic
bal·loon'ist
bal'lot
ball'park'
ball'play'er
ball'room'
balm'y
  ·i·er ·i·est
ba·lo'ney
bal'sa
bal'sam
Bal'tic
Bal'ti·more'
bal'us·ter
bal'us·trade'
bam·bi'no
  ·nos or ·ni
bam·boo'
bam·boo'zle
  ·zled ·zling
ban
  banned ban'ning
ba'nal
ba·nal'i·ty
  ·ties
ba·nan'a
band'age
  ·aged ·ag·ing
band'-aid' or
  band'aid'
ban·dan'na
band'box'
ban·deau'
  ·deaux'
ban'dit

band'mas'ter
ban'do·leer'
  or ·lier'
band saw
bands'man
  ·men
band'stand'
band'wag'on
ban'dy
  ·died ·dy·ing
ban'dy·leg'ged
bane'ful
ban'gle
bang'-up'
ban'ish
ban'is·ter
  or ban'nis·ter
ban'jo
  ·jos or ·joes
ban'jo·ist
bank'book'
bank note
bank'roll'
bank'rupt
bank'rupt·cy
  ·cies
ban'ner
banns or bans
  (*marriage notice*)
ban'quet
ban'tam
ban'tam·weight'
ban'ter
ban'zai'
bap'tism
bap·tis'mal
bap'tis·ter·y
  or ·tis·try
  ·ies or ·tries
bap'tize
  ·tized ·tiz·ing
bar
  barred bar'ring
bar·bar'i·an
bar·bar'ic
bar'ba·rism
bar·bar'i·ty
  ·ties
bar'ba·rous
bar'be·cue'
  ·cued ·cu'ing
barbed wire
bar'bel
  (*hairlike growth*)
bar'bell'
  (*bar with weights*)
bar'ber
bar'ber·shop'
bar'bi·tal'
bar·bi'tu·rate
bar'bule
bare
  bared bar'ing
  (*uncover;* see
  bear)
bare'back'
bare'faced'
bare'fac'ed·ly

bare'foot'
bare'foot'ed
bare'hand'ed
bare'head'ed
bare'leg'ged
bare'ly
bar'gain
barge
  barged barg'ing
bar'i·tone'
bar'keep'er
bark'en·tine'
bark'er
bar'ley·corn'
bar'maid'
bar'man
  ·men
bar mitz'vah or
  bar miz'vah
bar'na·cle
bar'na·cled
barn'storm'
barn'yard'
bar'o·graph'
ba·rom'e·ter
bar'o·met'ric
bar'on
  (*nobleman;* see
  barren)
bar'on·ess
bar'on·et
ba·ro'ni·al
ba·roque'
ba·rouche'
bar'racks
bar'ra·cu'da
bar·rage'
  ·raged' ·rag'ing
barred
bar'rel
  ·reled or ·relled
  ·rel·ing or
  ·rel·ling
bar'ren
  (*empty;* see
  baron)
bar·rette'
  (*hair clasp;*
  see beret)
bar'ri·cade'
  ·cad·ed ·cad·ing
bar'ri·er
bar'ring
bar'ris·ter
bar'room'
bar'row
bar'tend'er
bar'ter
Bart'lett pear
bas'al
bas'al·ly
ba·salt'
bas'cule
base
  bas'es
  based bas'ing
  (*foundation; vile;*
  see bass)

base'ball'
base'board'
base'born'
base'burn'er
base hit
base'less
base line
base'ly
base'man
  ·men
base'ment
base'ness
bas'es
  (*pl. of* base)
ba'ses
  (*pl. of* basis)
bash'ful
bash'ful·ly
bash'ful·ness
bas'ic
bas'i·cal·ly
bas'il
ba·sil'i·ca
ba'sin
ba'sis
  ·ses
bas'ket
bas'ket·ball'
bas'ket·work'
bas-re·lief'
bass
  (*singer;* see base)
bass
  (*fish*)
bass clef
bass drum
bas'set
bass horn
bas'si·net'
bas·soon'
bass viol
bass'wood'
bas'tard
baste
  bast'ed bast'ing
bas·tille'
bas'tion
bat
  bat'ted bat'ting
batch
bate
  bat'ed bat'ing
ba·teau'
  ·teaux'
bat'ed
  (*held in;* see
  baited)
bathe
  bathed bath'ing
bath'er
bath'house'
bath'i·nette'
ba'thos
bath'robe'
bath'room'
bath'tub'
bath'y·sphere'
ba·tik'

ba·tiste'
bat mitz'vah or
  bat miz'vah
ba·ton'
bat·tal'ion
bat'ten
bat'ter
bat'ter·y
  ·ies
bat'ting
bat'tle
  ·tled ·tling
bat'tle-ax' or -axe'
bat'tle·dore'
bat'tle·field'
bat'tle·ground'
bat'tle·ment
battle royal
battles royal
bat'tle-scarred'
bat'tle·ship'
bau'ble
baux'ite
bawd'y
  ·i·er ·i·est
bawl
  (*shout;* see ball)
bay'o·net'
  ·net'ed or ·net'ted
  ·net'ing or ·net'ting
bay'ou
ba·zaar'
  (*market;* see
  bizarre)
ba·zoo'ka
be
  was or were,
  been be'ing
beach
  (*shore;* see
  beech)
beach'comb'er
beach'head'
bea'con
bead'ing
bead'work
bead'y
  ·i·er ·i·est
bea'gle
beak'er
bean'bag'
bean'stalk'
bear
  (*animal;* see
  bare)
bear
  bore, borne or
  born,
bear'ing
  (*carry;* see bare)
bear'a·ble
bear'a·bly
beard'ed
bear'ish
bear'skin'
beast'li·ness
beast'ly
  ·li·er ·li·est

beat
  beat beat'en
  beat'ing
be'a·tif'ic
be·at'i·fi·ca'tion
be·at'i·fy'
  ·fied' ·fy'ing
be·at'i·tude'
beat'nik
beau
  beaus or beaux
  (*sweetheart;* see
  bow)
beau'te·ous
beau·ti'cian
beau'ti·fi·ca'tion
beau'ti·fi'er
beau'ti·ful
beau'ti·ful·ly
beau'ti·fy'
  ·fied' ·fy'ing
beau'ty
  ·ties
bea'ver
bea'ver·board'
be·calm'
be·cause'
beck'on
be·come'
  ·came' ·come'
  ·com'ing
bed
  bed'ded
  bed'ding
bed'bug'
bed'cham·ber
bed'clothes'
bed'cov'er
be·dev'il
  ·iled or ·illed
  ·il·ing or ·il·ling
bed'fast'
bed'fel'low
bed'lam
Bed'ou·in
bed'pan'
bed'post'
be·drag'gle
  ·gled ·gling
bed'rid'den
bed'rock'
bed'roll'
bed'room'
bed'side'
bed'sore'
bed'spread'
bed'spring'
bed'stead'
bed'time'
beech
  (*tree;* see beach)
beech'nut'
beef
  beeves or beefs
beef'eat'er
beef'steak'
beef'y
  ·i·er ·i·est

bee'hive'	be·la'bor	be·nev'o·lent	bet'tor or ·ter	big'ot·ry	bi·par'ti·san
bee'keep'er	be·lat'ed	ben'ga·line'	(one who bets)	·ries	bi·par'tite
bee'line'	be·lay'	be·night'ed	between'	bi'jou	bi'pro·pel'lant
beer	·layed' ·lay'ing	be·nign'	be·twixt'	·joux	bi·quar'ter·ly
(drink; see bier)	belch	be·nig'nan·cy	bev'a·tron'	bi·ki'ni	bi·ra'cial
beer'i·ness	be·lea'guer	be·nig'nant	bev'el	bi·la'bi·al	bird'bath'
beer'y	bel'fry	be·nig'ni·ty	·eled or ·elled	bi·lat'er·al	bird'call'
·i·er ·i·est	·fries	ben'i·son	·el·ing or ·el·ling	bilge	bird'ie
bees'wax'	be·lie'	be·numb'	bev'er·age	bi·lin'gual	bird'lime'
Bee'tho·ven	·lied' ·ly'ing	ben'zene	bev'y	bil'ious	bird'man'
bee'tle	be·lief'	(in chemistry)	·ies	bill'board'	·men'
bee'tle-browed'	be·liev'a·bil'i·ty	ben'zine	be·wail'	bil'let	bird'seed'
be·fall'	be·liev'a·ble	(cleaning fluid)	be·ware'	bil'let-doux'	bird's'-eye'
·fell' ·fall'en	be·liev'a·bly	be·queath'	·wared' ·war'ing	bil'lets-doux'	bi·ret'ta
·fall'ing	be·lieve'	·queathed'	be·wil'dered	bill'fold'	birth
be·fit'	·lieved' ·liev'ing	·queath'ing	be·witch'	bill'head'	(being born; see
·fit'ted ·fit'ting	be·liev'er	be·queath'al	be·yond'	bil'liards	berth)
be·fog'	be·lit'tle	be·quest'	bez'el	bill'ing	birth'day'
·fogged'	·tled ·tling	be·rate'	bi·an'nu·al	bil'lings·gate'	birth'mark'
·fog'ging	be·lit'tler	·rat'ed ·rat'ing	bi·an'nu·al·ly	bil'lion	birth'place'
be·fore'hand'	bel'la·don'na	be·reave'	bi'as	bil'lion·aire'	birth'rate'
be·friend'	bell'boy'	·reaved' or ·reft'	·ased or ·assed	bill of fare	birth'right'
be·fud'dle	(errand boy)	·reav'ing	·as·ing or ·as·sing	bill of lad'ing	birth'stone'
·dled ·dling	bell buoy	be·reave'ment	Bi'ble	bill of sale	bis'cuit
beg	(signal bell)	be·ret'	Bib'li·cal	bil'low	bi·sect'
begged beg'ging	belle	(flat cap; see	Bib'li·cal·ly	bil'low·i·ness	bi·sec'tion
be·get'	(pretty girl)	barrette)	bib'li·og'ra·phy	bil'low·y	bi·sec'tor
·got', ·got'ten or	belles-let'tres	ber'i·ber'i	·phies	·i·er ·i·est	bi·sex'u·al
·got', ·get'ting	bell'-bot'tom	Berke'ley	bib'li·o·phile'	bil'ly	bi·sex'u·al·ly
beg'gar	bel'li·cose'	Ber·mu'da	bib'u·lous	·lies	bish'op
be·gin'	bel'li·cos'i·ty	ber'ry	bi·cam'er·al	bi·man'u·al	bish'op·ric
·gan' ·gun'	bel·lig'er·ence	·ries	bi·car'bon·ate	bi·man'u·al·ly	bis'muth
·gin'ning	bel·lig'er·en·cy	·ried ·ry·ing	bi·cen·te'nar·y	bi·me·tal'lic	bi'son
(start; see beguine)	bel·lig'er·ent	(fruit; see bury)	·ies	bi·met'al·lism	bisque
be·gin'ner	bell'-like'	ber·serk'	bi·cen·ten'ni·al	bi·month'ly	bis'tro
be·gird'	bell'man	berth	bi'ceps	bin	bitch
·girt' or ·gird'ed,	·men	(bed; see birth)	·ceps or ·ceps·es	binned bin'ning	bite
·girt', ·gird'ing	bel'low	ber'yl	bick'er	bi'na·ry	bit, bit'ten or
be·gone'	bell'weth'er	be·ryl'li·um	bi·cus'pid	bind	bit, bit'ing
be·gon'ia	bel'ly	be·seech'	bi'cy·cle	bound bind'ing	bit'ter
be·grime'	·lies	·sought' or	·cled ·cling	bind'er	bit'tern
·grimed'	·lied ·ly·ing	·seeched'	bi'cy·clist	bind'er·y	bit'ter·sweet'
·grim'ing	bel'ly·band'	·seech'ing	bid	·ies	bi·tu'men
be·grudge'	be·long'	be·set'	bade or bid,	binge	bi·tu'mi·nous
·grudged'	be·loved'	·set' ·set'ting	bid'den or bid,	bin'go	bi·va'lent
·grudg'ing	be·low'	be·side'	bid'ding	bin'na·cle	bi'valve'
be·guile'	belt'ing	be·sides'	bid'da·ble	bin·oc'u·lars	biv'ou·ac'
·guiled' ·guil'ing	be·mire'	be·siege'	bi·det'	bi·no'mi·al	·acked' ·ack'ing
be·guine'	·mired' ·mir'ing	·sieged' ·sieg'ing	bi·en'ni·al	bi·no'mi·al·ly	bi·week'ly
(dance; see begin)	be·moan'	be·smirch'	bi·en'ni·al·ly	bi'o·as'tro·	·lies
be·half'	bend	be·sot'	bier	nau'tics	bi·year'ly
be·have'	bent bend'ing	·sot'ted ·sot'ting	(coffin stand; see	bi'o·chem'ist	bi·zarre'
·haved' ·hav'ing	be·neath'	Bes'se·mer	beer)	bi'o·chem'is·try	(odd; see bazaar)
be·hav'ior	ben'e·dict'	bes'tial	bi'fo'cals	bi'o·cide'	bi·zarre'ly
be·head'	Ben'e·dic'tine	bes·ti·al'i·ty	bi'fur·cate'	bi'o·e·col'o·gy	black'-a-moor'
be·he'moth	ben'e·dic'tion	·ties	·cat'ed ·cat'ing	bi·og'ra·pher	black'-and-blue'
be·hest'	ben'e·fac'tion	be·stow'	big	bi'o·graph'i·cal	black'ball'
be·hind'hand'	ben'e·fac'tor	best seller	big'ger big'gest	bi'o·graph'i·cal·ly	black'ber'ry
be·hold'	ben'e·fac'tress	bet	big'a·mist	bi·og'ra·phy	·ries
·held' ·hold'ing	ben'e·fice	bet or bet'ted	big'a·mous	·phies	black'bird'
be·hold'en	be·nef'i·cence	bet'ting	big'a·my	bi'o·log'i·cal	black'board'
be·hoove'	be·nef'i·cent	be'ta·tron'	·mies	bi'o·log'i·cal·ly	black'en
·hooved'	ben'e·fi'cial	be·tray'al	big'gish	bi·ol'o·gy	black'face'
·hoov'ing	ben'e·fi'ci·ar'y	be·troth'	big'heart'ed	bi·on'ics	black'guard'
beige	·ar'ies	be·troth'al	big'horn'	bi'o·phys'ics	black'head'
be·jew'el	ben'e·fit	be·trothed'	big·no'ni·a	bi'op'sy	black'heart'ed
·eled or ·elled	·fit·ed ·fit·ing	bet'ter	big'ot	·sies	black'jack'
·el·ing or ·el·ling	be·nev'o·lence	(compar. of good)	big'ot·ed	bi'o·sat'el·lite'	black'list'

black'mail'
black'out'
black'smith'
black'top'
·topped'
·top'ping
blad'der
blam'a·ble *or*
blame'a·ble
blame
blamed blam'ing
blame'wor'thy
blanc·mange'
blan'dish
blan'ket
blare
blared blar'ing
blar'ney
bla·sé'
blas·pheme'
·phemed'
·phem'ing
blas'phe·mous
blas'phe·my
·mies
blast'off' *or*
blast'-off'
bla'tan·cy
·cies
bla'tant
blaze
blazed blaz'ing
blaz'er
bla'zon
bleach'ers
bleak'ly
blear'i·ness
blear'y
·i·er ·i·est
blear'y-eyed'
bleed
bled bleed'ing
blem'ish
blend
blend'ed *or* blent
blend'ing
blend'er
bless
blessed *or* blest
bless'ing
bless'ed·ness
blight
blind'fold'
blintz
bliss'ful
bliss'ful·ly
blis'ter
blithe
blithe'some
blitz'krieg'
bliz'zard
bloat'ed
bloc
(*group*)
block
(*solid piece*)
block·ade'
·ad'ed ·ad'ing

block'bust'ing
block'head'
block'house'
blond *or* blonde
blood bank
blood count
blood'cur'dling
blood'hound'
blood'i·ness
blood'i·ly
blood'less
blood'let'ting
blood'mo·bile'
blood pressure
blood'shed'
blood'shot'
blood'stained'
blood'stream'
blood test
blood'thirst'y
blood vessel
blood'y
·i·er ·i·est
·ied ·y·ing
Bloody Mary
blos'som
blot
blot'ted blot'ting
blotch'y
·i·er ·i·est
blot'ter
blouse
bloused
blous'ing
blous'on
blow
blew blown
blow'ing
blow'gun'
blow'hole'
blow'out'
blow'pipe'
blow'torch'
blow'up'
blow'y
·i·er ·i·est
blowz'y
·i·er ·i·est
blub'ber
blu'cher
bludg'eon
blue
blued, blu'ing *or*
blue'ing
blue'ber'ry
·ries
blue'bird'
blue'-blood'ed
blue book
blue'-chip'
blue'-col'lar
blue'fish'
blue'grass'
blue jay
blue law
blue'-pen'cil
·ciled *or* ·cilled
·cil·ing *or* ·cil·ling

blue'print'
blue'stock'ing
bluff'er
blu'ing *or*
blue'ing
blu'ish *or*
blue'ish
blun'der
blun'der·buss'
blunt'ly
blur
blurred blur'ring
blur'ri·ness
blur'ry
·ri·er ·ri·est
blus'ter
blus'ter·y
bo'a
boar
(*hog;* see bore)
board'er
board foot
board feet
board'ing·house'
boarding school
board'walk'
boast'ful
boast'ful·ly
boat'house'
boat'ing
boat'load'
boat'man
·men
boat'swain
bob'bin
bob'ble
·bled ·bling
bob'o·link'
bob'sled'
·sled'ded
·sled'ding
bob'white'
bode
bod'ed bod'ing
bod'ice
bod'ied
bod'i·ly
bod'kin
bod'y
·ies
bod'y·guard'
bo'gey
·geys
bo'gey
·geyed ·gey·ing
(*golf term*)
bog'gy
·gi·er ·gi·est
(*like a bog*)
bo'gus
bo'gy
·gies
(*spirit*)
boil'ing
bois'ter·ous
bold'face'
bold'faced'
bo·le'ro
·ros

boll
(*pod;* see bowl)
boll weevil
boll'worm'
bo·lo'gna
bol'ster
bom·bard'
bom'bar·dier'
bom'bast
bom·bas'tic
bom·bas'ti·cal·ly
bomb'proof'
bomb'shell'
bomb'sight'
bo'na fi'de
bo·nan'za
bon'bon'
bond'age
bonds'man
·men
bone'-dry'
bon'fire'
bon'go
·gos
bon'i·ness
bon' mot'
bons' mots'
bon'net
bon'ny
·ni·er ·ni·est
bon·sai'
bo'nus
bon' vi·vant'
bons' vi·vants'
bon' voy·age'
bon'y
·i·er ·i·est
boo'by
·bies
boo·hoo'
·hoos'
·hooed' ·hoo'ing
book'bind'er
book'case'
book club
book'end'
book'ish
book'keep'er
book'keep'ing
book'let
book'mak'er
book'mark'
book'mo·bile'
book'plate'
book'rack'
book'sell'er
book'shelf'
·shelves'
book'stack'
book'stall'
book'stand'
book'store'
book'worm'
boom'er·ang'
boom'let
boon'docks'
boon'dog'gle
·gled ·gling

boor'ish
boost'er
boot'black'
boot'ee
(*baby's shoe;* see
booty)
boot'leg'
·legged'
·leg'ging
boot'leg'ger
boot'strap'
boo'ty
·ties
(*spoils;* see
bootee)
bo'rax
bor'der
bor'der·line'
bore
(*dull person;*
see boar)
bore
bored bor'ing
bore'dom
born
(*brought into
life*)
borne
(*participle of
bear*)
bor'ough
(*town;* see burro,
burrow)
bor'row
borsch *or* borsht
bos'om
boss'i·ness
boss'y
·i·er ·i·est
bo·tan'i·cal
bot'a·nist
bot'a·ny
botch
both'er·some
bot'tle
·tled ·tling
bot'tle·neck'
bot'tle·nose'
bot'tom
bot'u·lism
bou·clé' *or*
bou·cle'
bou'doir
bouf·fant'
bough
(*tree branch;*
see bow)
bought
bouil'la·baisse'
bouil'lon
(*broth;* see
bullion)
boul'der
boul'e·vard'
bounce
bounced
bounc'ing
bounc'er

bound'a·ry
·ries
bound'en
bound'less
boun'te·ous
boun'ti·ful
boun'ti·ful·ly
boun'ty
·ties
bou·quet'
bour'bon
bour·geois'
bour'geoi·sie'
bourse
bou·tique'
bou'ton·niere'
bo'vine
bow
(*curve;* see beau)
bow
(*of a ship;* see
bough)
bowd'ler·ize'
·ized' ·iz'ing
bow'el
bow'er
Bow'er·y
bow'ie knife
bow'knot'
bowl
(*dish;* see boll)
bow'leg'ged
bow'line
bowl'ing
bow'sprit'
bow'string'
bow tie
box'car'
box'er
box office
box'wood'
boy
(*child;* see buoy)
boy'cott
boy'friend'
boy'hood'
boy'ish
boy'sen·ber'ry
·ries
brace
braced brac'ing
brace'let
brack'et
brack'ish
brad'awl'
brag
bragged
brag'ging
brag'ga·do'ci·o'
brag'gart
Brah'ma
Brah'man·ism
braid
Braille
brain'child'
brain'i·ness
brain'pow'er
brain'storm'

brain'wash'
brain wave
brain'y
· i · er · i · est
braise
braised brais'ing
(cook; see braze)
brake
braked brak'ing
(stop; see break)
brake'man
· men
bram'ble
branch'ing
bran'dish
brand'-new'
bran'dy
· dies
· died · dy · ing
bras'sard
brass'ie n.
bras · siere'
brass'i · ness
brass'ware'
brass'-wind' adj.
brass winds
brass'y adj.
· i · er · i · est
braun'schwei'ger
bra · va'do
brave
braved brav'ing
brave'ly
brav'er · y
bra'vo
· vos
brawl
brawn'y
· i · er · i · est
braze
brazed braz'ing
(solder; see
braise)
bra'zen
bra'zen · ness
bra'zen · faced'
bra'zier
Bra · zil'
bra · zil'wood'
breach
(a gap; see
breech)
bread'bas'ket
bread'board'
bread'box'
breadth
(width; see
breath)
breadth'ways'
bread'win'ner
break
broke bro'ken
break'ing
(smash; see
brake)
break'a · ble
break'age
break'down'

break'fast
break'front'
break'neck'
break'out'
break'through'
break'up'
break'wa'ter
breast'bone'
breast'-feed'
-fed' -feed'ing
breast stroke
breast'work'
breath
(air; see breadth)
breath'a · lyz'er
breathe
breathed
breath'ing
breath'er
breath'less
breath'tak'ing
breech
(rear; see
breach)
breech'cloth'
breech'es
breech'-load'ing
breed
bred breed'ing
breez'i · ly
breez'i · ness
breeze'way'
breez'y
· i · er · i · est
breth'ren
bre'vi · ar'y
· ies
brev'i · ty
brew'er · y
· ies
brib'a · ble
bribe
bribed brib'ing
brib'er · y
· ies
bric'-a-brac'
brick'bat'
brick'lay'ing
brick'work'
brick'yard'
brid'al
(wedding; see
bridle)
bride'groom'
brides'maid'
bridge
bridged
bridg'ing
bridge'a · ble
bridge'head'
bridge'work'
bri'dle
(harness; see
bridal)
brief'case'
bri'er or bri'ar
bri · gade'
brig'a · dier'

brig'and
brig'an · tine'
bright'en
bril'liance
bril'liant
bril'lian · tine'
brim
brimmed
brim'ming
brim'ful'
brim'stone'
brin'dled
brine
brined brin'ing
bring
brought
bring'ing
brin'i · ness
brink'man · ship'
brin'y
· i · er · i · est
bri · oche'
bri · quette'
or · quet'
bris'ket
brisk'ly
bris'tle
· tled · tling
bris'tli · ness
bris'tly
· tli · er · tli · est
Bris'tol board
Brit'ain
(place)
Brit'i · cism
Brit'on
(person)
brit'tle
brit'tle · ly or
brit'tly
broach
(open; see
brooch)
broad'ax' or · axe'
broad'cast'
· cast' or · cast'ed
· cast'ing
broad'cloth'
broad'leaf'
broad'-leaved'
broad'loom'
broad'-mind'ed
broad'side'
broad'sword'
bro · cade'
· cad'ed · cad'ing
broc'co · li
bro · chette'
bro · chure'
bro'gan
brogue
broil'er
bro'ken-down'
bro'ken · heart'ed
bro'ker
bro'ker · age
bro'mide
bro · mid'ic

bro'mine
bro'mo selt'zer
bron'chi · al
bron · chi'tis
bron'chus
· chi
bron'co
· cos
bron'to · sau'rus
bronze
bronzed
bronz'ing
brooch
(pin; see broach)
brood'i · ness
broom'stick'
broth'el
broth'er-in-law'
broth'ers-in-law'
brougham
brought
brou'ha · ha'
brow'beat'
· beat' · beat'en
· beat'ing
brown'ie
brown'out'
brown'stone'
browse
browsed
brows'ing
bruise
bruised bruis'ing
bruis'er
bru · net' or
bru · nette'
brush'wood'
brush'work'
brusque
brusque'ly
brusque'ness
Brus'sels sprouts
bru'tal
bru · tal'i · ty
· ties
bru'tal · ize'
· ized' · iz'ing
brut'ish
bub'ble
· bled · bling
bub'ble-top'
bub'bly
bu · bon'ic
buc'ca · neer'
buck'board'
buck'et · ful'
· fuls'
bucket seat
buck'le
· led · ling
buck'-pass'er
buck'ram
buck'saw'
buck'shot'
buck'skin'
buck'tooth'
· teeth'

buck'toothed'
buck'wheat'
bu · col'ic
bud
bud'ded bud'ding
Bud'dha
Bud'dhism
budge
budged budg'ing
budg'et
budg'et · ar'y
buf'fa · lo'
· loes' or · los'
buff'er
buf'fet
buf · foon'er · y
bug'bear'
bug'gy
· gies
· gi · er · gi · est
bu'gle
· gled · gling
build
built build'ing
build'up' or
build'-up'
built'-in'
built'-up'
bul'bar
bul'bous
bulge
bulged bulg'ing
bulg'i · ness
bulk'i · ness
bulk'y
· i · er · i · est
bull'dog'
bull'doze'
· dozed' · doz'ing
bull'doz'er
bul'let
bul'le · tin
bul'let-proof'
bull'fight'er
bull'frog'
bull'head'ed
bull'horn'
bul'lion
(gold; see
bouillon)
bull'ish
bull'ock
bull'pen'
bull's'-eye'
bull'whip'
bul'ly
· lies
· lied · ly · ing
bul'rush'
bul'wark
bum'ble · bee'
bum'bling
bump'er
bump'kin
bump'tious
bump'y
· i · er · i · est
bun'combe

bun'dle
· dled · dling
bun'ga · low'
bung'hole'
bun'gle
· gled · gling
bun'ion
bunk'er
bun'ting
Bun'sen burner
buoy
(marker; see boy)
buoy'an · cy
buoy'ant
bur'ble
· bled · bling
bur'den · some
bu'reau
· reaus or · reaux
bu · reau'cra · cy
· cies
bu'reau · crat'
bu'reau · crat'ic
bu'reau · crat'i-
cal · ly
bu · rette' or · ret'
bur'geon
bur'glar
bur'gla · rize'
· rized' · riz'ing
bur'gla · ry
· ries
Bur'gun · dy
bur'i · al
bur'lap
bur · lesque'
· lesqued'
· lesqu'ing
bur'ley
(tobacco)
bur'li · ness
bur'ly
· li · er · li · est
(muscular)
burn
burned or burnt
burn'ing
burn'a · ble
bur'nish
bur · noose'
burn'out'
bur'ro
· ros
(donkey; see
burrow, borough)
bur'row
(hole; see burro,
borough)
bur'sa
· sae or · sas
bur'sar
bur · si'tis
burst
burst burst'ing
bur'y
· ied · y · ing
(cover; see
berry)

bus
bus'es *or* bus'ses
bused *or* bussed
bus'ing *or* bus'sing
(*motor coach;* see
buss)
bus'boy'
bus'by
·bies
bush'el·bas'ket
bush'ing
bush'man
·men
bush'rang'er
bush'whack'er
bush'y
·i·er ·i·est
bus'i·ly
busi'ness
busi'ness·like'
busi'ness·man'
·men
busi'ness·wom'an
·wom'en
bus'kin
bus'man
·men
buss
(*kiss;* see bus)
bus'tle
·tled ·tling
bus'y
·i·er ·i·est
·ied ·y·ing
bus'y·bod'y
·ies
bus'y·ness
butch'er·y
but'ler
butte
but'ter·fat'
but'ter·fin'gers
but'ter·fly'
·flies
but'ter·milk'
but'ter·nut'
but'ter·scotch'
but'ter·y
but'tocks
but'ton-down'
but'ton·hole'
·holed' ·hol'ing
but'tress
bux'om
buy
bought buy'ing
buz'zard
buz'zer
by'gone'
by'law'
by'line'
by'pass'
by'path'
by'play'
by'prod'uct *or*
by'-prod'uct
by'road'
by'stand'er

by'way'
by'word'

C

ca·bal'
·balled' ·bal'ling
cab'a·lism
ca·bal·le'ro
·ros
ca·ba'na
cab'a·ret'
cab'bage
cab'driv'er
cab'in
cab'i·net
cab'i·net·mak'er
cab'i·net·work'
ca'ble
·bled ·bling
ca'ble·gram'
ca·boose'
cab'ri·o·let'
cab'stand'
ca·ca'o
cac'ci·a·to're
cache
cached cach'ing
ca·chet'
cach'in·nate'
·nat'ed ·nat'ing
cach'in·na'tion
cack'le
·led ·ling
ca·cog'ra·phy
ca·coph'o·nous
ca·coph'o·ny
cac'tus
·tus·es *or* ·ti
ca·dav'er
ca·dav'er·ous
cad'die *or* ·dy
·dies
·died ·dy·ing
(*in golf*)
cad'dish
cad'dy
·dies
(*tea box*)
ca'dence
ca·den'za
ca·det'
cad'mi·um
ca'dre
ca·du'ce·us
·ce·i
Cae·sar'e·an
cae·su'ra
·ras *or* ·rae
ca·fé' *or* ca·fe'
caf'e·te'ri·a
caf'fe·ine *or* ·in
cage
caged cag'ing
ca'gey *or* ca'gy
·gi·er ·gi·est

ca'gi·ly
ca'gi·ness
cais'son
cai'tiff
ca·jole'
·joled' ·jol'ing
ca·jole'ment
ca·jol'er·y
cake
caked cak'ing
cal'a·bash'
ca·lam'i·tous
ca·lam'i·ty
·ties
cal·car'e·ous
cal'ci·fi·ca'tion
cal'ci·fy'
·fied' ·fy'ing
cal'ci·mine'
·mined' ·min'ing
cal'ci·um
cal'cu·la·ble
cal'cu·late'
·lat'ed ·lat'ing
cal'cu·la·ble
cal'cu·la'tor
cal'cu·lus
·li *or* ·lus·es
cal'dron
cal'en·dar
(*table of dates*)
cal'en·der
(*roller;* see
colander)
cal'ends
ca·les'cent
calf
calves
calf'skin'
cal'i·ber *or* ·bre
cal'i·brate'
·brat'ed ·brat'ing
cal'i·bra'tion
cal'i·co'
·coes' *or* ·cos'
Cal'i·for'ni·a
cal'i·pers
ca'liph
cal'is·then'ics
calk
call'board'
cal·lig'ra·phy
cal'lous *adj.*
cal'low
call'-up'
cal'lus *n.*
·lus·es
calm'ly
ca·lor'ic
cal'o·rie *or* ·ry
·ries
cal'o·rim'e·ter
cal'u·met'
ca·lum'ni·ate'
·at'ed ·at'ing
ca·lum'ni·ous
cal'um·ny
·nies

Cal'va·ry
(*Biblical place;*
see cavalry)
calve
calved calv'ing
Cal'vin·ism
ca·lyp'so
ca'lyx
ca'lyx·es *or*
ca'ly·ces'
ca·ma·ra'de·rie
cam'ber
cam'bric
Cam'bridge
cam'el
ca·mel'li·a
Cam'em·bert'
cam'e·o'
·os'
cam'er·a
cam'er·a·man'
·men'
cam'er·a-shy'
cam'i·sole'
cam'o·mile'
cam'ou·flage'
·flaged' ·flag'ing
cam·paign'
cam·pa·ni'le
·les *or* ·li
camp'er
camp'fire'
camp'ground'
cam'phor
cam'phor·ate'
·at'ed ·at'ing
camp'o·ree'
camp'site'
camp'stool'
cam'pus
cam'shaft'
can
canned can'ning
Ca'naan
Can'a·da
Ca·na'di·an
ca·naille'
ca·nal'
ca·nal'boat'
ca·nal'ize
·ized ·iz'ing
ca'na·pé
(*food;* see
canopy)
ca·nard'
ca·nar'y
·ies
ca·nas'ta
can'can'
can'cel
·celed *or* ·celled
·cel·ing *or*
·cel·ling
can'cel·la'tion
can'cer
can'cer·ous
can·de·la'bra
·bras

can·de·la'brum
·bra *or* ·brums
can·des'cence
can·des'cent
can'did
(*frank;* see
candied)
can'di·da·cy
·cies
can'di·date'
can'died
(*sugared;* see
candid)
can'dle·light'
candle power
can'dle·stick'
can'dle·wick'
can'dor
can'dy
·dies
·died ·dy·ing
can'dy-striped'
cane
caned can'ing
ca'nine
can'is·ter
can'ker
can'na·bis
can'ner·y
·ies
can'ni·bal
can'ni·bal·ize'
·ized' ·iz'ing
can'ni·ly
can'ni·ness
can'non
(*gun;* see canon,
canyon)
can'non·ade'
·ad'ed ·ad'ing
can'not
can'ny
·ni·er ·ni·est
ca·noe'
·noed' ·noe'ing
can'on
(*law;* see cannon,
canyon)
ca·non'i·cal
can'on·ize'
·ized' ·iz'ing
can'o·py
·pies
(*hood;* see
canapé)
can·ta'bi·le'
can'ta·loupe'
or ·loup'
can·tan'ker·ous
can·ta'ta
can·teen'
can'ter
(*gallop;* see
cantor)
can'ti·cle
can'ti·le'ver
can'to
·tos

can'ton
can·ton'ment
can'tor
(*singer;* see
canter)
can'vas
(*cloth*)
can'vass
(*to solicit*)
can'yon *or* ca'ñon
(*valley;* see
cannon, canon)
caou·tchouc'
cap
capped cap'ping
ca·pa·bil'i·ty
·ties
ca'pa·ble
ca'pa·bly
ca·pa'cious
ca·pac'i·tance
ca·pac'i·tor
ca·pac'i·ty
·ties
ca'per
cap'ful'
·fuls'
cap'il·lar'y
·ies
cap'i·tal
(*city; chief;* see
capitol)
cap'i·tal·ism
cap'i·tal·is'tic
cap'i·tal·is'ti-
cal·ly
cap'i·tal·i·za'tion
cap'i·tal·ize'
·ized' ·iz'ing
cap'i·tal·ly
cap'i·ta'tion
cap'i·tol
(*building;* see
capital)
ca·pit'u·late'
·lat'ed ·lat'ing
ca·pit'u·la'tion
ca'pon
ca·price'
ca·pri'cious
cap'ri·ole'
·oled' ·ol'ing
cap'size
·sized ·siz'ing
cap'stan
cap'stone'
cap'su·lar
cap'sule
·suled ·sul·ing
cap'sul·ize'
·ized' ·iz'ing
cap'tain
cap'tain·cy
·cies
cap'tion
cap'tious
cap'ti·vate'
·vat'ed ·vat'ing

cap'tive
cap·tiv'i·ty
·ties
cap'tor
cap'ture
·tured ·tur·ing
car'a·cul
ca·rafe'
car'a·mel
car'a·mel·ize'
·ized' ·iz'ing
car'a·pace'
car'at
(weight; see
caret, carrot)
car'a·van'
car·a·van'sa·ry
·ries
car'a·way'
car'bide
car'bine
car·bo·hy'drate
car·bol'ic
car'bon
car·bo·na'ceous
car'bon·ate'
·at'ed ·at'ing
car'bon·a'tion
car'bon-date'
-dat'ed -dat'ing
car·bon·if'er·ous
car'bon·ize'
·ized' ·iz'ing
car'bo·run'dum
car'bun·cle
car·bu·re'tion
car'bu·re'tor
car'cass
car·cin'o·gen
car·ci·no'ma
car'da·mom
card'board'
card'-car'ry·ing
car'di·ac'
car'di·gan
car'di·nal
car'di·o·gram'
car'di·o·graph'
card'sharp'
care
cared car'ing
ca·reen'
ca·reer'
care'free'
care'ful
care'ful·ly
care'less
ca·ress'
ca·res'sive·ly
car'et
(insert mark; see
carat, carrot)
care'tak'er
care'worn'
car'fare'
car'go
·goes or ·gos
car'hop'

Car'ib·be'an
car'i·bou'
car·i·ca·ture
·tured ·tur·ing
car·i·ca·tur·ist
car'ies
(decay; see
carries)
car'il·lon'
car'load'
car'man
·men
car'mine
car'nage
car'nal
car'nal·ly
car·na'tion
car·nel'ian
car'ni·val
car·niv'o·rous
car'ol
·oled or ·olled
·ol·ing or ·ol·ling
car'ol·er or ·ol·ler
Car'o·li'nas
Car'o·lin'i·an
car'om
car'o·tene' or ·tin
ca·rot'id
ca·rous'al
ca·rouse'
·roused'
·rous'ing
car'ou·sel'
car'pen·ter
car'pen·try
car'pet
car'pet·bag'ger
car'pet·ing
carp'ing
car'port'
car'riage
car'ri·er
car'ries
(form of carry;
see caries)
car'ri·on
car'rot
(vegetable; see
carat, caret)
car'rou·sel'
car'ry
·ried ·ry·ing
car'ry·all'
car'ry-out'
car'ry-o'ver
car'sick'
cart'age
carte' blanche'
cartes' blanches'
car·tel'
car'ti·lage
car'ti·lag'i·nous
car'to·gram'
car·tog'ra·phy
car'ton
car·toon'

car·toon'ist
car'tridge
carve
carved carv'ing
car'wash'
car'y·at'id
·ids or -i·des'
ca·sa'ba
or cas·sa'ba
cas'bah
cas·cade'
·cad'ed ·cad'ing
cas·car'a
case
cased cas'ing
case'book'
case'hard'ened
ca'se·in
case'load'
case'mate'
case'ment
case'work'er
cash'-and-car'ry
cash'book'
cash'ew
cash·ier'
cash'mere
cas'ing
ca·si'no
·nos
(gambling room)
cas'ket
cas·sa'va
cas'se·role'
cas·sette'
cas·si'no
(card game)
cas'sock
cas'so·war'y
·war'ies
cast
cast cast'ing
cas'ta·nets'
cast'a·way'
caste
(social class)
cas'tel·lat'ed
cast'er
cas'ti·gate'
·gat'ed ·gat'ing
cast'-i'ron
cas'tle
cast'off'
cas'tor
cas'trate
·trat·ed ·trat-ing
cas·tra'tion
cas'u·al
cas'u·al·ly
cas'u·al·ty
·ties
cas'u·ist
cas'u·is'tic
cas'u·ist·ry
cat'a·clysm
cat'a·comb'
cat'a·falque'
cat'a·lep'sy

cat'a·lep'tic
cat·a·lo'
·loes' or ·los'
cat'a·log' or
·logue'
·loged' or
·logued'
·log'ing or
·logu'ing
cat·a·log'er or
·logu'er
ca·tal'y·sis
·ses'
cat'a·lyst
cat·a·ma·ran'
cat'a·pult'
cat'a·ract'
ca·tarrh'
ca·tarrh'al
ca·tas'tro·phe
cat·a·stroph'ic
cat·a·stroph'i-
cal·ly
cat·a·to'ni·a
cat'call'
catch
caught catch'ing
catch'all'
catch'er
catch'ing
catch'pen'ny
·nies
catch'up
catch'word'
catch'y
·i·er ·i·est
cat'e·chism
cat'e·chize'
·chized' ·chiz'ing
cat'e·chu'men
cat·e·gor'i·cal
cat'e·go·rize'
·rized' ·riz'ing
cat'e·go'ry
·ries
ca'ter
cat'er-cor'nered
ca'ter·er
ca'ter·pil'lar
cat'er·waul'
cat'gut'
ca·thar'sis
ca·thar'tic
ca·the'dral
cath'e·ter
cath'e·ter·ize'
·ized' ·iz'ing
cath'ode
cath'o·lic
Ca·thol'i·cism
cath·o·lic'i·ty
ca·thol'i·cize'
·cized' ·ciz'ing
cat'i·on
cat'nap'
·napped'
·nap'ping
cat'nip

cat'-o'-nine'-tails'
cat's'-eye'
Cats'kill'
cat's'-paw'
cat'sup
cat'tail'
cat'ti·ly
cat'ti·ness
cat'tle
cat'tle·man
·men
cat'ty
·ti·er ·ti·est
cat'ty-cor'nered
cat'walk'
Cau·ca'sian
Cau'ca·soid'
cau'cus
cau'dal
cau'date
caul'dron
cau'li·flow'er
caulk
caus'a·ble
caus'al
caus'al·ly
cau·sal'i·ty
·ties
cau·sa'tion
caus'a·tive
cause
caused caus'ing
cau'se·rie'
cause'way'
caus'tic
cau'ter·i·za'tion
cau'ter·ize'
·ized' ·iz'ing
cau'ter·y
·ies
cau'tion
cau'tion·ar'y
cau'tious
cav'al·cade'
cav·a·lier'
cav'al·ry
·ries
(troops; see
Calvary)
cav'al·ry·man
·men
cave
caved cav'ing
ca've·at' emp'tor
cave'-in'
cav'ern
cav'ern·ous
cav'i·ar'
cav'il
·iled or ·illed
·il·ing or ·il·ling
cav'i·ty
·ties
ca·vort'
cay·enne'
cease
ceased ceas'ing
cease'-fire'

cease'less
ce'dar
cede
ced'ed ced'ing
ce·dil'la
ceil'ing
ceil·om'e·ter
cel'e·brant
cel'e·brate'
·brat'ed ·brat'ing
cel·e·bra'tion
cel'e·bra'tor
ce·leb'ri·ty
·ties
ce·ler'i·ty
cel'e·ry
ce·les'ta
ce·les'tial
cel'i·ba·cy
cel'i·bate
cel'lar
cel'lar·et'
cel'lar·way'
cel'list
or 'cel'list
cell'-like'
cel'lo
or 'cel'lo
·los or ·li
cel'lo·phane'
cel'lu·lar
cel'lu·loid'
cel'lu·lose'
Cel'o·tex'
Cel'si·us
ce·ment'
cem'e·ter'y
·ies
cen'o·bite'
Ce'no·zo'ic
cen'ser
(incense box)
cen'sor
(prohibiter)
cen'sored
cen·so'ri·al
cen·so'ri·ous
cen'sor·ship'
cen'sur·a·ble
cen'sure
·sured ·sur·ing
(blame)
cen'sus
cen'taur
cen·ta'vo
cen'te·nar'i·an
cen'te·nar'y
cen'ter
cen'ter·board'
cen'tered
cen'ter·piece'
cen·tes'i·mal
cen·tes'i·mal·ly
cen'ti·grade'
cen'ti·gram'
cen'ti·li·ter

cen'time	chain'man	change'ling	char'ter	cheer'ful·ly	child'bear'ing
cen'ti·me'ter	·men	change'o'ver	char·treuse'	cheer'i·ly	child'bed'
cen'ti·pede'	chain'-re·act'	change'-up'	char'wom'an	cheer'i·ness	child'birth'
cen'tral	chain'-smoke'	chan'nel	char'y	cheer'lead'er	child'hood'
cen'tral·i·za'tion	chair'lift'	·neled or ·nelled	·i·er ·i·est	cheer'less	child'ish
cen'tral·ize'	chair'man	·nel·ing or ·nel·ling	chase	cheer'y	child'like'
·ized' ·iz'ing	·men	chan'nel·ize'	chased chas'ing	·i·er ·i·est	chil'i
cen·trif'u·gal	chair'wom'an	·ized' ·iz'ing	chasm	cheese'burg'er	·ies
cen'tri·fuge'	·wom'en	chan·teuse'	chas·sé'	cheese'cake'	chill'i·ness
cen·trip'e·tal	chaise longue	chan'tey or ·ty	·séd' ·sé'ing	cheese'cloth'	chill'y
cen'trist	chaise or chaises	·teys or ·ties	chas'sis	chees'i·ness	·i·er ·i·est
cen'tu·ple	longues	Cha'nu·kah	·sis	chees'y	chime
cen·tu'ri·on	chaise lounge	cha'os	chaste'ly	·i·er ·i·est	chimed chim'ing
cen'tu·ry	chaise lounges	cha·ot'ic	chas'ten	chee'tah	chi·me'ra
·ries	chal·ced'o·ny	cha·ot'i·cal·ly	chas·tise'	chem'i·cal	chi·mer'i·cal
ce·phal'ic	cha·let'	chap	·tised' ·tis'ing	che·mise'	chim'ney
ce·ram'ic	chal'ice	chapped	chas·tise'ment	chem'ist	·neys
ce·ram'ist or	chalk'board'	chap'ping	chas'ti·ty	chem'is·try	chim·pan·zee'
ce·ram'i·cist	chalk'i·ness	chap'ar·ral'	chas'u·ble	·tries	chin
ce're·al	chalk'y	cha·peau'	chat	chem'ur·gy	chinned
(grain; see serial)	·i·er ·i·est	·peaus' or	chat'ted	che·nille'	chin'ning
cer'e·bel'lum	chal'lenge	·peaux'	chat'ting	cher'ish	chi'na·ware'
·lums or ·la	·lenged ·leng·ing	chap'el	châ·teau'	Cher'o·kee'	chin·chil'la
cer'e·bral	chal'leng·er	chap'er·on'	·teaux' or ·teaus'	che·root'	Chi·nese'
cer·e'bral·ly	chal'lis	or ·one'	chat'e·laine'	cher'ry	chi'no
cer'e·brate'	cham'ber	·oned' ·on'ing	cha·toy'ant	·ries	chin'qua·pin
·brat'ed ·brat'ing	cham'ber·lain	chap'fall'en	chat'tel	cher'ub	chintz
cer'e·bro·spi'nal	cham'ber·maid'	chap'lain	chat'ty	·ubs or ·u·bim	chip
cer'e·brum	cham'bray	chap'let	·ti·er ·ti·est	che·ru'bic	chipped
·brums or ·bra	cha·me'le·on	chap'ter	Chau'cer	che·ru'bi·cal·ly	chip'ping
cer'e·ment	cham'fer	char	chauf'fer	cher'vil	chip'munk'
cer'e·mo'ni·al	cham'ois	charred	(stove)	chess'board'	chi·rog'ra·phy
cer·e·mo'ni·al·ly	·ois	char'ring	chauf'feur	chess'man'	chi·rop'o·dist
cer'e·mo'ni·ous	cham'o·mile'	char'ac·ter	(driver)	ches'ter·field'	chi·rop'o·dy
cer'e·mo'ny	cham·pagne'	char'ac·ter·is'tic	chau·tau'qua	chest'nut	chi'ro·prac'tic
·nies	(wine)	char'ac·ter·is'ti·	chau'vin·ism	chev'i·ot	chi'ro·prac'tor
ce·rise'	cham·paign'	cal·ly	chau'vin·ist	chev'ron	chir'rup
cer'tain	(open field)	char'ac·ter·i·	chau'vin·is'tic	chew'y	chis'el
cer'tain·ly	cham'pi·on	za'tion	chau'vin·is'ti·	·i·er ·i·est	·eled or ·elled
cer'tain·ty	chance	char'ac·ter·ize'	cal·ly	Chi·an'ti	·el·ing or ·el·ling
·ties	chanced	·ized' ·iz'ing	cheap	chi·a'ro·scu'ro	chis'el·er or
cer'ti·fi'a·ble	chanc'ing	cha·rade'	(low in cost;	·ros	chis'el·ler
cer'ti·fi·a·bly	chan'cel	char'coal'	see cheep)	chic	chit'-chat'
cer·tif'i·cate	chan'cel·ler·y	chare	cheap'en	chic'quer	chit'chat'
cer'ti·fi·ca'tion	·ies	chared char'ing	cheat'er	chic'quest	chit'ter·lings
cer'ti·fy'	chan'cel·lor	charge	check'book'	chi·can'er·y	chiv'al·rous
·fied' ·fy'ing	chance'-med'ley	charged	check'er·board'	chi'chi or chi'-chi	chiv'al·ry
cer'ti·o·ra'ri	chan'cer·y	charg'ing	check'ered	chick'en-heart'ed	chlor'dane
cer'ti·tude'	·ies	charge'a·ble	check'list' or	chicken pox	chlo'ric
ce·ru'le·an	chan'cre	charge plate or	check list	chic'le	chlo'ride
ce·ru'men	chan'croid	charge'-a-plate'	check'mate'	chic'o·ry	chlo'ri·nate'
cer'vi·cal	chanc'y	charg'er	·mat'ed ·mat'ing	chide	·nat'ed ·nat'ing
cer'vix	·i·er ·i·est	char'i·ly	check'off'	chid'ed or chid,	chlo'ri·na'tion
·vi·ces' or ·vix·es	chan·de·lier'	char'i·ness	check'out' or	chid'ed or chid	chlo'rine
ces·sa'tion	chan·delle'	char'i·ot	check'-out'	or chid'den,	chlo'ro·form'
ces'sion	chan'dler·y	char'i·ot·eer'	check'point'	chid'ing	chlo'ro·phyll'
(a giving up; see	·ies	cha·ris'ma	check'rein'	chief'ly	or ·phyl'
session)	Cha·nel'	char·is·mat'ic	check'room'	chief'tain	chlo'rous
cess'pool'	change	char'i·ta·ble	check'up'	chif·fon'	chlor·tet'ra·cy'·
chafe	changed	char'i·ty	Ched'dar	chif'fo·nier'	cline
chafed chaf'ing	chang'ing	·ties	cheek'bone'	chig'ger	chock'a·block'
(rub)	change'a·bil'i·ty	cha·riv'a·ri'	cheek'i·ly	chi'gnon	chock'-full'
chaff	change'a·ble	char'la·tan	cheek'i·ness	chig'oe	choc'o·late
(husks of grain)	change'a·bly	charm'ing	cheek'y	·oes	choice
chaf'finch	change'ful	char'nel	·i·er ·i·est	Chi·hua'hua	choic'er choic'est
cha·grin'	change'ful·ly	char'ry	cheep	chil'blain'	choir
·grined'	change'less	·ri·er ·ri·est	(sound; see cheap)	child	(singers; see
·grin'ing			cheer'ful	chil'dren	quire)

choke
 choked chok'ing
chok'er
chol'er·a
chol'er·ic
cho·les'ter·ol'
choose
 chose cho'sen
 choos'ing
chop
 chopped
 chop'ping
chop'house'
chop'pi·ness
chop'py
 ·pi·er ·pi·est
chop'sticks'
chop su'ey
cho'ral
 (of a chorus)
cho·rale' or ·ral'
 (hymn tune)
chord
 (music; see cord)
chore
cho·re'a
chor·e·og'ra·pher
chor·e·o·graph'ic
chor·e·o·graph'·
 i·cal·ly
chor·e·og'ra·phy
chor'is·ter
chor'tle
 ·tled ·tling
cho'rus
cho'sen
chow'der
chow mein
chrism
chris'ten
Chris'ten·dom
Chris'tian
Chris'ti·an'i·ty
Chris'tian·ize'
 ·ized' ·iz'ing
chris'tie or ·ty
Christ'like'
Christ'mas
Christ'mas·tide'
chro·mat'ic
chro'ma·tin
chrome
chro'mic
chro'mi·um
chro'mo·some'
chron'ic
chron'i·cle
 ·cled ·cling
chron'o·log'i·cal
chro·nol'o·gy
chro·nom'e·ter
chro·nom'e·try
chrys'a·lis
chrys·an'the·
 mum
chrys'o·lite'
chrys'o·prase'
chub'bi·ness

chub'by
 ·bi·er ·bi·est
chuck'-full'
chuck'hole'
chuck'le
 ·led ·ling
chug
 chugged chug'ging
chuk'ka boot
chuk'ker or ·kar
chum'mi·ness
chum'my
 ·mi·er ·mi·est
chunk'i·ness
chunk'y
 ·i·er ·i·est
church'go'er
church'man
church'wom'an
church'yard'
churl'ish
churn
chute
chut'ney
chyle
chyme
ci·bo'ri·um
 ·ri·a
ci·ca'da
 ·das or ·dae
cic'a·trix
 ci·cat'ri·ces
cic'e·ly
Cic'er·o'
ci'der
ci·gar'
cig·a·rette'
 or ·ret'
cig'a·ril'lo
 ·los
cil'i·a
 (sing. cil'i·um)
cil'i·ar'y
cin·cho'na
Cin'cin·nat'i
cinc'ture
 ·tured ·tur·ing
cin'der
cin'e·ma
cin'e·mat'o·
 graph'
cin'e·rar'i·um
 ·rar'i·a
cin'er·a'tor
cin'na·bar'
cin'na·mon
cinque'foil'
ci'pher
cir'ca
cir'cle
 ·cled ·cling
cir'clet
cir'cuit
cir·cu'i·tous
cir'cuit·ry
cir'cu·lar
cir'cu·lar·i·
 za'tion

cir'cu·lar·ize'
 ·ized' ·iz'ing
cir'cu·late'
 ·lat'ed ·lat'ing
cir'cu·la'tion
cir'cu·la·to·ry
cir'cum·cise'
 ·cised' ·cis'ing
cir·cum·ci'sion
cir·cum'fer·ence
cir'cum·flex'
cir'cum·lo·
 cu'tion
cir'cum·nav'i·
 gate'
 ·gat'ed ·gat'ing
cir'cum·po'lar
cir'cum·scribe'
 ·scribed' ·scrib'ing
cir'cum·
 scrip'tion
cir'cum·spect'
cir'cum·spec'tion
cir'cum·stance'
cir'cum·stan'tial
cir'cum·stan'ti·
 ate'
 ·at'ed ·at'ing
cir'cum·vent'
cir'cum·ven'tion
cir'cus
cir·rho'sis
cir·ro·cu'mu·lus
cir·ro·stra'tus
cir'rus
 ·ri
cis·al'pine
cis·at·lan'tic
cis'tern
cit'a·del
ci·ta'tion
cite
 cit'ed cit'ing
 (mention; see
 sight)
cit'i·fied'
cit'i·zen
cit'i·zen·ry
cit'i·zen·ship'
cit'rate
cit'ric
cit'ron
cit'ron·el'la
cit'rous adj.
cit'rus n.
cit'y
 ·ies
cit'y·scape'
cit'y-state'
civ'et
civ'ic
civ'il
ci·vil'ian
ci·vil'i·ty
 ·ties
civ'i·li·za'tion
civ'i·lize'
 ·lized' ·liz'ing

civ'il·ly
civ'vies
claim'ant
clair·voy'ance
clair·voy'ant
clam
clammed
clam'ming
clam'bake'
clam'ber
clam'mi·ness
clam'my
 ·mi·er ·mi·est
clam'or
clam'or·ous
clan·des'tine
clan·des'tine·ly
clan'gor
clan'gor·ous
clan'nish
clans'man
clap
clapped
clap'ping
clap'board
clap'per
clap'trap'
claque
clar'et
clar·i·fi·ca'tion
clar'i·fi'er
clar'i·fy'
 ·fied ·fy'ing
clar'i·net'
clar'i·net'ist or
 clar'i·net'tist
clar'i·on
clar'i·ty
clas'sic
clas'si·cal
clas'si·cal·ly
clas'si·cism
clas'si·cist
clas'si·fi'a·ble
clas'si·fi·ca'tion
clas'si·fi'er
clas'si·fy'
 ·fied' ·fy'ing
class'mate'
class'room'
clat'ter
clause
claus'tro·
 pho'bi·a
clav'i·chord'
clav'i·cle
cla·vier'
clay'ey
clay'i·er
clay'i·est
clean'a·ble
clean'-cut'
clean'er
clean'hand'ed
clean'li·ly
clean'li·ness
clean'ly
 ·li·er ·li·est

clean'ness
cleanse
cleansed
cleans'ing
cleans'er
clean'shav'en
clean'up'
clear'ance
clear'-cut'
clear'eyed'
clear'head'ed
clear'ing·house'
clear'sight'ed
cleats
cleav'age
cleave
 cleaved or cleft
 or clove, cleaved
 or cleft or
 clo'ven,
 cleav'ing
 (to split)
cleave
 cleaved cleav'ing
 (to cling)
cleav'er
clem'en·cy
clem'ent
clere'sto'ry
 ·ries
cler'gy
 ·gies
cler'gy·man
 ·men
cler'ic
cler'i·cal
cler'i·cal·ly
cler'i·cal·ism
clev'er
clew
cli·ché'
click
cli'ent
cli·en·tele'
cliff'-dwell'ing
cliff'hang'er or
 cliff'-hang'er
cli·mac'ter·ic
cli·mac'tic
 (of a climax)
cli·mac'ti·cal·ly
cli'mate
cli·mat'ic
 (of climate)
cli·mat'i·cal·ly
cli'ma·tol'o·gy
cli'max
climb'er
clinch'er
cling
 clung cling'ing
clin'ic
clin'i·cal
cli·ni'cian
clink'er
cli·nom'e·ter
clip
 clipped clip'ping

clip'board'
clip'per
clique
cli'to·ris
clo·a'ca
 ·cae
cloak'room'
clob'ber
cloche
clock'wise'
clock'work'
clod'dish
clod'hop'per
clog
 clogged
 clog'ging
cloi'son·né'
clois'ter
close
 closed clos'ing
close
 clos'er clos'est
closed'-end'
close'fist'ed
close'fit'ting
close'grained'
close'-hauled'
close'ly
close'mouthed'
clos'et
close'-up'
clo'sure
clot
 clot'ted clot'ting
cloth n.
clothe v.
 clothed or clad
cloth'ing
clothes'line'
clothes'pin'
clothes'press'
cloth'ier
cloth'ing
clo'ture
cloud'burst'
cloud'i·ness
cloud'y
 ·i·er ·i·est
clo'ver·leaf'
 ·leafs'
cloy'ing·ly
clown'ish
club
 clubbed
 club'bing
club'foot'
club'house'
clue
 clued clu'ing
clum'si·ly
clum'si·ness
clum'sy
 ·si·er ·si·est
clus'ter
clut'ter
coach'man
co·ad'ju·tor
co·ag'u·la·ble

co·ag'u·lant
co·ag'u·late'
· lat'ed · lat'ing
co·ag'u·la'tion
co·ag'u·la'tor
co'a·lesce'
· lesced' · lesc'ing
co'a·les'cence
co'a·les'cent
co'a·li'tion
coarse
(common; see
course)
coarse'grained'
coars'en
coarse'ness
coast'al
coast'er
coast guard
coast'land'
coast'line'
coat'ing
coat'tail'
co·au'thor
co·ax'i·al
coax'ing·ly
co'balt
cob'ble
· bled · bling
cob'bler
cob'ble·stone'
co'bra
cob'web'
co·caine'
or ·cain'
coc'cus
coc'ci
coc'cyx
coc·cy'ges
cock'a·lo'rum
cock'boat'
cock'crow'
cock'er·el
cock'eyed'
cock'i·ly
cock'i·ness
cock'ney
· neys
cock'pit'
cock'roach'
cocks'comb'
cock'sure'
cock'tail'
co'coa
co'co·nut'
or co'coa·nut'
co·coon'
cod'dle
· dled · dling
code
cod'ed cod'ing
co'de·fend'ant
co'deine'
co'dex
· di·ces'
cod'fish'
codg'er

cod'i·cil
cod'i·fi·ca'tion
cod'i·fy'
· fied' · fy'ing
co'ed·u·ca'tion
co·ef·fi'cient
co·erce'
· erced' · erc'ing
co·er'cion
co·er'cive
co·e'val
co'ex·ist'ence
cof'fee·house'
cof'fee·pot'
cof'fer
cof'fer·dam'
cof'fin
co'gen·cy
co'gent
cog'i·tate'
· tat'ed · tat'ing
cog'i·ta'tion
co'gnac
cog'nate
cog·ni'tion
cog'ni·tive
cog'ni·zance
cog'ni·zant
cog·no'men
· no'mens or
· nom'i·na
cog'wheel'
co·hab'it
co·hab'i·ta'tion
co'heir'
co·here'
· hered' · her'ing
co·her'ence
co·her'ent
co·he'sion
co·he'sive·ness
co'hort
coif·fure'
coign
(position; see
coin, quoin)
coin
(metal money;
see coign, quoin)
coin'age
co'in·cide'
· cid'ed · cid'ing
co·in'ci·dence
co·in'ci·dent
co·in'ci·den'tal
co·in'ci·den'tal·ly
co·i'tion
co'i·tus
col'an·der
(draining pan;
see calender)
cold'blood'ed
cold'heart'ed
co·le·op'ter·ous
cole'slaw'
col'ic
col'ick·y
col'i·se'um

co·li'tis
col·lab'o·rate'
· rat'ed · rat'ing
col·lab'o·ra'tion
col·lab'o·ra'tor
col·lapse'
col·lapse'
· lapsed' · laps'ing
col·laps'i·bil'i·ty
col·laps'i·ble
col'lar
col'lar·bone'
col·late'
· lat'ed · lat'ing
col·lat'er·al
col·lat'er·al·ly
col·la'tion
col·la'tor
col'league
col·lect'a·ble
or ·i·ble
col·lec'tion
col·lec'tive·ly
col·lec'tiv·ism
col·lec'tiv·is'tic
col·lec·tiv'i·ty
col·lec'tiv·ize'
· ized' · iz'ing
col·lec'tor
col'leen
col'lege
col·le'gi·al'i·ty
col·le'gi·an
col·le'giate
col·lide'
· lid'ed · lid'ing
col'lie
col'li·gate'
· gat'ed · gat'ing
col'li·mate'
· mat'ed · mat'ing
co·lin'e·ar
col·li'sion
col'lo·ca'tion
col·lo'di·on
col'loid
col·lo'qui·al
col·lo'qui·al·ism
col·lo'qui·um
· qui·a
col'lo·quy
· quies
col'lo·type'
col·lude'
· lud'ed · lud'ing
col·lu'sion
col·lu'sive
co·lo'cate'
· cat'ed · cat'ing
co'·lo·ca'tion
co·logne'
co'lon
colo'nel
(officer; see
kernel)
co·lo'ni·al
col'o·nist

col'o·ni·za'tion
col'o·nize'
· nized' · niz'ing
col'on·nade'
col'o·ny
· nies
col'o·phon'
col'or
Col'o·rad'o
col'o·rant
col·or·a'tion
col'or·bear'er
col'or·blind'
col'or·cast'
· cast' or cast'ed
· cast'ing
col'ored
col'or·fast'
col'or·ful
col'or·less
co·los'sal
Col'os·se'um
co·los'sus
· los'si or
· los'sus·es
colt'ish
Co·lum'bi·a
col'umn
co·lum'nar
col'um·nist
co'ma
(stupor; see
comma)
com'a·tose'
com·bat'
· bat'ed or
· bat'ted
· bat'ing or
· bat'ting
· mat'ed · mat'ing
com'bat·ant
com·bat'ive
comb'er
com·bin'a·ble
com·bi·na'tion
com·bine'
· bined' · bin'ing
comb'ings
com·bus'ti·
bil'i·ty
com·bus'ti·ble
com·bus'ti·bly
com·bus'tion
com·bus'tor
come
came come
com'ing
come'back'
co·me'di·an
co·me'dic
co·me'di·enne'
come'down'
com'e·dy
· dies
come'li·ness
come'ly
· li·er · li·est
co·mes'ti·ble

col'o·ni·za'tion
com'et
come'up'pance
com'fit
com'fort
com'fort·a·ble
com'fort·a·bly
com'fort·er
com'ic
com'i·cal
com'i·cal·ly
com'i·ty
· ties
com'ma
(punctuation
mark; see coma)
com·mand'
com'man·dant'
com'man·deer'
com·mand'er
com·mand'ment
com·man'do
· dos or ·does
com·mem'o·rate'
· rat'ed · rat'ing
com·mem'o·
ra'tion
com·mem'o·
ra'tive
com·mence'
· menced'
· menc'ing
com·mence'·
ment
com·mend'
com·mend'a·ble
com·mend'a·bly
com'men·da'tion
com·mend'a·
to'ry
com·men'su·
ra·ble
com·men'su·
ra·bly
com·men'su·rate
com'ment
com'men·tar'y
· ies
com'men·tate'
· tat'ed · tat'ing
com'men·ta'tor
com'merce
com·mer'cial
com·mer'cial·ism
com·mer'cial·i·
za'tion
com·mer'cial·ize'
· ized' · iz'ing
com·min'gle
· gled · gling
com·mis'er·ate'
· at'ed · at'ing
com·mis'er·
a'tion
com'mis·sar'
com'mis·sar'i·at
com'mis·sar'y
· ies
com·mis'sion

com·mis'sion·er
com·mit'
· mit'ted · mit'ting
com·mit'ment
com·mit'ta·ble
com·mit'tal
com·mit'tee
com·mit'tee·man
com·mode'
com·mo'di·ous
com·mod'i·ty
· ties
com'mo·dore'
com'mon·al·ty
· ties
com'mon·er
com'mon·ness
com'mon·place'
com'mon·weal'
com'mon·wealth'
com·mo'tion
com'mu·nal
com'mu·nal·ly
com'mu·nal·ism
com·mune' v.
· muned'
· mun'ing
com'mune n.
com·mu'ni·ca·ble
com·mu'ni·cant
com·mu'ni·cate'
· cat'ed · cat'ing
com·mu'ni·
ca'tion
com·mu'ni·
ca'tive
com·mu'ni·ca'tor
com·mun'ion
com·mu'ni·qué'
com'mu·nism
com'mu·nist
com'mu·nis'tic
com'mu·nis'ti·
cal·ly
com·mu'ni·ty
· ties
com'mu·nize'
· nized' · niz'ing
com·mut'a·ble
com'mu·tate'
· tat'ed · tat'ing
com'mu·ta'tion
com'mu·ta'tive
com'mu·ta'tor
com·mute'
· mut'ed
· mut'ing
com·mut'er
com·pact'
com·pan'ion
com·pan'ion·
a·ble
com'pa·ny
· nies
com'pa·ra·ble
com'pa·ra·bly
com·par'a·tive
com·par'a·tive·ly

com·pare'
·pared' ·par'ing
com·par'i·son
com·part'ment
com·part'men'·
tal·ize'
·ized' -iz'ing
com'pass
com·pas'sion
com·pas'sion·ate
com·pat'i·bil'i·ty
com·pat'i·ble
com·pat'i·bly
com·pa'tri·ot
com'peer
com·pel'
·pelled' ·pel'ling
com·pen'di·ous
com·pen'di·um
·ums or ·a
com·pen'sa·ble
com'pen·sate
·sat'ed ·sat'ing
com'pen·sa'tion
com'pen·sa'tive
com'pen·sa'tor
com'pen·sa·to'ry
com·pete'
·pet'ed ·pet'ing
com'pe·tence
com'pe·ten·cy
com'pe·tent
com·pe·ti'tion
com·pet'i·tive
com·pet'i·tor
com·pi·la'tion
com·pile'
·piled' ·pil'ing
com·pil'er
com·pla'cence
com·pla'cen·cy
com·pla'cent
(*smug;* see
complaisant)
com·plain'
com·plain'ant
com·plaint'
com·plai'sance
com·plai'sant
(*obliging;* see
complacent)
com'ple·ment
(*completing part;*
see compliment)
com'ple·
men'ta·ry
com·plete'
·plet'ed ·plet'ing
com·ple'tion
com·plex'
com·plex'ion
com·plex'i·ty
·ties
com·pli'ance
com·pli'ant
com'pli·cate'
·cat'ed ·cat'ing
com'pli·ca'tion

com·plic'i·ty
com·pli'er
com'pli·ment
(*praise;* see
complement)
com'pli·men'·
ta·ry
com'pli·men·
tar'i·ly
com·ply'
·plied' ·ply'ing
com·po'nent
com·port'ment
com·pose'
·posed' ·pos'ing
com·pos'er
com·pos'ite
com'po·si'tion
com·pos'i·tor
com'pos men'tis
com'post
com·po'sure
com'pote
com·pound' *v.*
com'pound *n.*
com'pre·hend'
com'pre·hen'si·
ble
com'pre·hen'sion
com'pre·hen'sive
com·press'
com·pressed'
com·pres'si·ble
com·pres'sion
com·pres'sor
com·prise'
·prised' ·pris'ing
com'pro·mise'
·mised' ·mis'ing
comp·tom'e·ter
comp·trol'ler
com·pul'sion
com·pul'sive
com·pul'so·ri·ly
com·pul'so·ri·ness
com·pul'so·ry
com·punc'tion
com·punc'tious
com·put'a·bil'i·ty
com·put'a·ble
com'pu·ta'tion
com·pute'
·put'ed ·put'ing
com·put'er
com·put'er·ize'
·ized' ·iz'ing
com·put'er·i·
za'tion
com'rade
con·cat·e·na'tion
con·cave'
con·cav'i·ty
·ties
con·ca'vo-con·
cave'
con·ca'vo-con·
vex'
con·ceal'

con·cede'
·ced'ed ·ced'ing
con·ceit'
con·ceit'ed
con·ceiv'a·
bil'i·ty
con·ceiv'a·ble
con·ceiv'a·bly
con·ceive'
·ceived' ·ceiv'ing
con'cen·trate'
·trat'ed ·trat'ing
con'cen·tra'tion
con·cen'tric
con·cen'tri·cal·ly
con'cept
con·cep'tion
con·cep'tu·al
con·cep'tu·al·ize'
·ized' ·iz'ing
con·cep'tu·al·i·
za'tion
con·cep'tu·al·ly
con·cern'
con·cerned'
con·cern'ing
con'cert
con·cert'ed
con·cer·ti'na
con'cert·mas'ter
con·cer'to
·tos or ·ti
con·ces'sion
con·ces'sion·aire'
conch
conchs or
conch'es
con·chol'o·gy
con'ci·erge'
con·cil'i·ar
con·cil'i·ate'
·at'ed ·at'ing
con·cil'i·a·to'ry
con·cise'
con·cise'ly
con·cise'ness
con'clave
con·clude'
·clud'ed
·clud'ing
con·clu'sion
con·clu'sive
con·coct'
con·coc'tion
con·com'i·tance
con·com'i·tant
con'cord
con·cord'ance
con·cor'dat
con'course
con·crete'
con·cre'tion
con'cu·bine'
con·cu'pis·cence
con·cu'pis·cent
con·cur'
·curred'
·cur'ring

con·cur'rence
con·cur'rent
con·cus'sion
con·demn'
con·dem'na·ble
con'dem·na'tion
con·dem'na·to'ry
con·demn'er
con·den'sa·ble
or ·si·ble
con'den·sa'tion
con·dense'
·densed'
·dens'ing
con·dens'er
con'de·scend'
con'de·scend'ing
con'de·scen'sion
con·dign'
con'di·ment
con·di'tion
con·di'tion·al
con·di'tion·al·ly
con·do'la·to·ry
con·dole'
·doled' ·dol'ing
con·do'lence
con'dom
con'do·min'i·um
·i·ums or ·i·a
con'do·na'tion
con·done'
·doned' ·don'ing
con'dor
con·duce'
·duced' ·duc'ing
con·du'cive
con'duct'
con·duct'ance
con·duct'i·ble
con·duc'tion
con'duc·tiv'i·ty
con·duc'tor
con'duit
co'ney
·neys or ·nies
con·fab'u·late'
·lat'ed ·lat'ing
con·fec'tion
con·fec'tion·ar'y
adj.
con·fec'tion·er
con·fec'tion·er'y
n.
·ies
con·fed'er·a·cy
·cies
con·fed'er·ate'
·at'ed ·at'ing
con·fed'er·a'tion
con·fer'
·ferred' ·fer'ring
con·fer·ee'
con'fer·ence
con·fer·en'tial
con·fer'ment
con·fer'ral
con·fess'

con·fes'sed·ly
con·fes'sion
con·fes'sion·al
con·fes'sor
con·fet'ti
con·fi'dant' *n.*
con·fide'
·fid'ed ·fid'ing
con'fi·dence
con'fi·dent *adj.*
con'fi·den'tial
con'fi·den'tial·ly
con·fig'u·ra'tion
con·fin'a·ble *or*
con·fine'a·ble
con·fine'
·fined' ·fin'ing
con·fine'ment
con·firm'
con·fir·mand'
con·fir·ma'tion
con·firm'a·to'ry
con·firmed'
con'fis·cate'
·cat'ed ·cat'ing
con·fis·ca'tion
con'fla·gra'tion
con·flict'
con·flic'tion
con'flu·ence
con'form'
con·form'a·ble
con·form'a·bly
con·form'ance
con'for·ma'tion
con·form'ist
con·form'i·ty
con·found'ed
con·front'
con'fron·ta'tion
Con·fu'cius
con·fuse'
·fused' ·fus'ing
con·fu'sion
con·fu·ta'tion
con·fute'
·fut'ed ·fut'ing
con·geal'
con·gen'ial
con·gen'ial·ly
con·ge'ni·al'i·ty
con·gen'i·tal
con·gen'i·tal·ly
con·gest'
con·ges'tion
con·glom'er·ate'
·at'ed ·at'ing
con·glom'er·a'tion
con·grat'u·late'
·lat'ed ·lat'ing
con·grat'u·
la'tion
con·grat'u·
la·to'ry
con'gre·gant
con'gre·gate'
·gat'ed ·gat'ing
con'gre·ga'tion

con·gres'sion·al
con'gress·man
con'gru·ence
con'gru·ent
con·gru'i·ty
con'gru·ous
con'ic
con'i·cal
con'i·cal·ly
co'ni·fer
co·nif'er·ous
con·jec'tur·al
con·jec'ture
·tured ·tur·ing
con·join'
con·joint'ly
con'ju·gal
con'ju·gal·ly
con'ju·gate'
·gat'ed ·gat'ing
con'ju·ga'tion
con·junc'tive
con·junc'tive
con·junc·ti·vi'tis
con·junc'ture
con'jure
·jured ·jur·ing
con'jur·er *or* ·or
con·nect'
Con·nect'i·cut
con·nec'tion
con·nec'tive
con·nec'tor
or ·nect'er
conn'ing tower
con·niv'ance
con·nive'
·nived' ·niv'ing
con'nois·seur'
con·no·ta'tion
con'no·ta'tive
con·note'
·not'ed ·not'ing
con·nu'bi·al
con'quer
con'quer·or
con'quest
con·quis'ta·dor
·dors *or* ·dores
con·san'guin·e·
ous
con'science
con'sci·en'tious
con'scious
con'script'
con'se·crate'
·crat'ed ·crat'ing
con'se·cra'tion
con·sec'u·tive
con·sen'sus
con·sent'
con'se·quence
con'se·quen'tial
con'se·quent'ly
con·ser'van·cy
con·ser·va'tion
con·ser'va·tism
con·ser'va·tive
con·ser'va·to'ry
·ries

con·serve'
·served'
·serv'ing
con·sid'er
con·sid'er·a·ble
con·sid'er·a·bly
con·sid'er·ate
con·sid'er·a'tion
con·sid'ered
con·sign'
con·sign'a·ble
con·sign·ee'
con·sign'ment
con·sign'or
or ·er
con·sist'
con·sis'ten·cy
·cies
con·sis'tent
con·sis'to·ry
·ries
con·sol'a·ble
con·so·la'tion
con·sol'a·to'ry
con·sole'
·soled' ·sol'ing
con'sole
con·sol'i·date'
·dat'ed ·dat'ing
con·sol'i·da'tion
con·sol'i·da'tor
con·som·mé'
con'so·nance
con'so·nant
con'so·nan'tal
con'sort
con·sor'ti·um
·ti·a
con·spec'tus
con·spic'u·ous
con·spir'a·cy
·cies
con·spir'a·tor
con·spire'
·spired' ·spir'ing
con'sta·ble
con·stab'u·lar'y
·ies
con'stan·cy
con'stant
con'stel·la'tion
con'ster·na'tion
con'sti·pate'
·pat'ed ·pat'ing
con'sti·pa'tion
con·stit'u·en·cy
·cies
con·stit'u·ent
con'sti·tute'
·tut'ed ·tut'ing
con'sti·tu'tion
con'sti·tu'tion·al
al'i·ty
con'sti·tu'tion·
al·ly
con·strain'
con·straint'

con·strict'
con·stric'tion
con·stric'tor
con·stru'a·ble
con·struct'
con·struc'tion
con·struc'tive
con·struc'tor or
con·struct'er
con·strue'
·strued' ·stru'ing
con'sul
con'sul·ar
con'sul·ate
con·sult'
con·sult'ant
con'sul·ta'tion
con·sul'ta·tive
con·sum'a·ble
con·sume'
·sumed'
·sum'ing
con·sum'er
con'sum·mate'
·mat'ed ·mat'ing
con·sum'mate·ly
con'sum·ma'tion
con'sum·ma'tor
con·sump'tion
con·sump'tive
con'tact
con·ta'gion
con·ta'gious
con·tain'er
con·tain'er·ize'
·ized' ·iz'ing
con·tain'ment
con·tam'i·nant
con·tam'i·nate'
·nat'ed ·nat'ing
con·tam'i·na'tion
con·tam'i·na'tor
con·temn'
con'tem·plate'
·plat'ed
·plat'ing
con'tem·pla'tion
con'tem·pla'tive
con'tem·pla'tor
con·tem'po·
ra'ne·ous
con·tem'po·rar'y
con·tempt'
con·tempt'i·bil'·
i·ty
con·tempt'i·ble
con·tempt'i·bly
con·temp'tu·ous
con·tend'
con·tent'
con'tent
con·tent'ed·ly
con·ten'tion
con·ten'tious
con·tent'ment
con·test'
con·test'a·ble
con·test'ant

con'text
con·tex'tu·al
con'ti·gu'i·ty
con·tig'u·ous
con'ti·nence
con'ti·nent
con'ti·nen'tal
con·tin'gen·cy
·cies
con·tin'gent
con·tin'u·a·ble
con·tin'u·al
con·tin'u·ance
con·tin'u·a'tion
con·tin'ue
·ued ·u·ing
con'ti·nu'i·ty
·ties
con·tin'u·ous
con·tin'u·um
·u·a or ·u·ums
con·tort'
con·tor'tion
con'tour
con'tra·band'
con'tra·bass'
con'tra·cep'tion
con'tra·cep'tive
con'tract
con·tract'i·bil'i·ty
con·tract'i·ble
con·trac'tile
con·trac'tion
con'trac·tor
con·trac'tu·al
con·trac'tu·al·ly
con'tra·dict'
con'tra·dic'tion
con'tra·dic'to·ry
con'tra·dis·
tinc'tion
con'trail'
con·tral'to
·tos or ·ti
con'tra·pun'tal
con'trar·i·ly
con'trar·i·ness
con'trar·i·wise'
con'trar·y
con·trast'
con'tra·vene'
·vened' ·ven'ing
con'tra·ven'tion
con·trib'ute
·ut·ed ·ut·ing
con'tri·bu'tion
con·trib'u·tor
con·trib'u·to'ry
con·trite'
con·tri'tion
con·triv'a·ble
con·triv'ance
con·trive'
·trived' ·triv'ing
con·trol'
·trolled'
·trol'ling
con·trol'la·bil'i·ty

con·trol'la·ble
con·trol'ler
con'tro·ver'sial
con'tro·ver'sy
·sies
con'tro·vert'
con'tro·vert'i·ble
con·tu·ma'cious
con'tu·ma·cy
con·tu·me'li·ous
con'tu·me·ly
con·tuse'
·tused' ·tus'ing
con·tu'sion
co·nun'drum
con'ur·ba'tion
con'va·lesce'
·lesced' ·lesc'ing
con'va·les'cence
con'va·les'cent
con·vec'tion
con·vec'tive
con·vec'tor
con·vene'
·vened' ·ven'ing
con·ven'ience
con·ven'ient
con'vent
con·ven'ti·cle
con·ven'tion
con·ven'tion·al
con·ven'tion·
al'i·ty
con·ven'tion·
al·ize'
·ized' ·iz'ing
con·ven'tion·eer'
con·verge'
·verged'
·verg'ing
con·ver'gence
con·vers'a·ble
con·ver'sant
con'ver·sa'tion
con'ver·sa'tion·al
con·verse'
·versed' ·vers'ing
con'verse
con·ver'sion
con·vert'
con·vert'er
or ·ver'tor
con·vert'i·ble
con·vex'
con·vex'i·ty
con·vex'o-con·
cave'
con·vex'o-con·
vex'
con·vey'
con·vey'ance
con·vey'or or ·er
con·vict'
con·vic'tion
con·vince'
·vinced'
·vinc'ing

con·vin'ci·ble
con·viv'i·al
con·viv'i·al'i·ty
con'vo·ca'tion
con·voke'
·voked' ·vok'ing
con'vo·lut'ed
con'vo·lu'tion
con'voy
con·vulse'
·vulsed'
·vuls'ing
con·vul'sion
con·vul'sive
cook'book'
cook'out'
cook'ie or ·y
·ies
cool'ant
cool'head'ed
coo'lie
(Oriental laborer;
see coolly,
coulee)
cool'ly
(in a cool manner;
see coolie, coulee)
co'-op
co·op'er·ate'
or co-op'·
·at'ed ·at'ing
co·op'er·a'tion
or co-op'·
co·op'er·a·tive
or co-op'·
co-opt'
co·or'di·nate'
or co-or'·
·nat'ed ·nat'ing
co·or'di·na'tor
or co-or'·
co·part'ner
cope
coped cop'ing
cop'i·er
co'pi·lot
co'pi·ous
cop'-out'
cop'per
cop'per·plate'
co'pra
cop'u·late'
·lat'ed ·lat'ing
cop'u·la'tion
cop'y
·ies
·ied ·y·ing
cop'y·cat'
cop'y·hold'er
cop'y·read'er
cop'y·right'
cop'y·writ'er
co·quet'
·quet'ted
·quet'ting
co'quet·ry
co·quette'

co·quet'tish
co·quille'
cor'al
cor'bel
cord
(string; see
chord)
cord'age
cor'date
cor'dial
cor'di·al'i·ty
·ties
cor'dil·le'ra
cord'ite
cor'don
cor'do·van
cor'du·roy'
cord'wood'
core
cored cor'ing
co're·spond'ent
(in law; see
correspondent)
Cor'fam
co'ri·an'der
Co·rin'thi·an
cork'screw'
cor'mo·rant
corn borer
corn bread
corn'cob'
cor'ne·a
cor'nered
cor'ner·stone'
cor'ner·wise'
cor·net'
cor·net'ist
or ·net'tist
corn'field'
corn'flow'er
corn'husk'ing
cor'nice
corn'meal'
corn'stalk'
corn'starch'
cor'nu·co'pi·a
corn'y
·i·er ·i·est
co·rol'la
cor'ol·lar'y
·ies
co·ro'na
·nas or ·nae
cor'o·nar'y
cor'o·na'tion
cor'o·ner
cor'o·net'
cor'po·ral
cor'po·rate
cor'po·ra'tion
cor'po·ra·tive
cor·po're·al
corps
corps
(group of people)
corpse
(dead body)
corps'man

cor'pu·lence
cor'pu·lent
cor'pus
  cor'po·ra
cor'pus·cle
cor·ral'
  ·ralled' ·ral'ling
cor·rect'
cor·rect'a·ble
cor·rec'tion
cor·rec'tive
cor·rec'tor
cor're·late'
  ·lat'ed ·lat'ing
cor're·la'tion
cor·rel'a·tive
cor're·spond'
cor're·
  spond'ence
cor're·
  spond'ent
  (*writer;* see
  corespondent)
cor'ri·dor
cor'ri·gi·ble
cor'ri·gi·bly
cor·rob'o·rate'
  ·rat'ed ·rat'ing
cor·rob'o·ra'tion
cor·rob'o·ra'tive
cor·rob'o·ra'tor
cor·rode'
  ·rod'ed ·rod'ing
cor·rod'i·ble
cor·ro'sion
cor·ro'sive
cor'ru·gate'
  ·gat'ed ·gat'ing
cor'ru·ga'tion
cor·rupt'
cor·rupt'i·bil'i·ty
cor·rupt'i·ble
cor·rupt'i·bly
cor·rup'tion
cor·rup'tive
cor·sage'
cor'sair
corse'let
cor'set
cor'se·tiere'
cor·tege' or ·tège'
cor'tex
  ·ti·ces'
cor'ti·cal
cor'ti·cal·ly
cor'ti·sone'
co·run'dum
cor'us·cate'
  ·cat'ed ·cat'ing
cor·vette'
co·se'cant
co'sign'
co'sign'er
co·sig'na·to'ry
  ·ries
co'sine
cos·met'ic
cos'me·ti'cian

cos'me·tol'o·gy
cos'mic
cos'mi·cal·ly
cos·mog'o·ny
cos·mog'ra·phy
cos'mo·line'
cos·mol'o·gy
cos'mo·naut'
cos·mop'o·lis
cos·mo·pol'i·tan
cos'mos
cos'mo·tron'
co'spon'sor
cost
  cost cost'ing
cost'li·ness
cost'ly
  ·li·er ·li·est
cost'-plus'
cos'tume
  ·tumed ·tum·ing
cos·tum'er
co·tan'gent
co'te·rie
co·til'lion
cot'tage
cot'ton
cou'gar
cough
cou'lee
  (*gulch;* see
  coolie, coolly)
cou·lomb'
coun'cil
  (*legislature;* see
  counsel)
coun'cil·man
coun'ci·lor
  or ·cil·lor
  (*council member;*
  see counselor)
coun'sel
  ·seled or ·selled
  ·sel·ing or
  ·sel·ling
  (*advice; advise;*
  see council)
coun'se·lor
  or ·sel·lor
  (*adviser;* see
  councilor)
count'down'
coun'te·nance
count'er
  (*one that counts*)
coun'ter
  (*opposite*)
coun'ter·act'
coun'ter·ac'tion
coun'ter·at·tack'
coun'ter·bal'·
  ance
coun'ter·claim'
coun'ter·clock'·
  wise
coun'ter·feit
coun'ter·foil'

coun'ter·ir'ri·
  tant
coun'ter·man'
coun'ter·mand'
coun'ter·march'
coun'ter·meas'·
  ure
coun'ter·move'
coun'ter·of·fen'·
  sive
coun'ter·pane'
coun'ter·part'
coun'ter·plot'
coun'ter·point'
coun'ter·poise'
coun'ter·sign'
coun'ter·sink'
  ·sunk' ·sink'ing
coun'ter·spy'
coun'ter·weight'
count'ess
count'less
coun'tri·fied'
coun'try
  ·tries
coun'try·man
coun'try·side'
coun'ty
  ·ties
coup de grâce'
coup d'é·tat'
coupe
cou'ple
  ·pled ·pling
cou'pler
cou'plet
cou'pon
cour'age
cou·ra'geous
cou'ri·er
course
coursed
cours'ing
  (*way; run;* see
  coarse)
cour'te·ous
cour'te·san
cour'te·sy
  ·sies
  (*polite act;*
  see curtsy)
court'house'
cour'ti·er
court'li·ness
court'ly
  ·li·er ·li·est
court'-mar'tial
courts'-mar'tial
  ·tialed or
  ·tialled
  ·tial·ing or
  ·tial·ling
court'room'
court'yard'
cous'in
cou·ture'
cou·tu·rier'
cou·tu·rière'

cov'e·nant
Cov'en·try
cov'er·age
cov'er·alls'
cov'ered
cov'er·ing
cov'er·let
cov'ert
cov'er-up'
cov'et·ous
cov'ey
cow'ard
cow'ard·ice
cow'ard·li·ness
cow'ard·ly
cow'boy'
cow'catch'er
cow'er
cow'herd'
cow'hide'
  ·hid'ed ·hid'ing
cowled
cow'lick
cowl'ing
co'-work'er
cow'pox'
cow'rie or ·ry
  ·ries
cow'shed'
cox'comb'
cox'swain
coy'ly
coy·o'te
co'zi·ly
co'zi·ness
co'zy
  ·zies
  ·zi·er ·zi·est
crab
  crabbed crab'bing
crab'bed
crab'bi·ness
crab'by
  ·bi·er ·bi·est
crack'brained'
crack'down'
cracked
crack'er
crack'ing
crack'le
  ·led ·ling
crack'lings
crack'up'
cra'dle
  ·dled ·dling
cra'dle·song'
craft'i·ly
craft'i·ness
crafts'man
craft'y
  ·i·er ·i·est
crag'gi·ness
crag'gy
  ·gi·er ·gi·est
cram
crammed
  cram'ming
cramped

cram'pon
cran'ber'ry
  ·ries
crane
craned cran'ing
cra'ni·al
cra'ni·ol'o·gy
cra'ni·um
  ·ni·ums or ·ni·a
crank'case'
crank'i·ness
crank'shaft'
crank'y
  ·i·er ·i·est
cran'ny
  ·nies
crap'u·lence
crash'-land'
crass'ly
crass'ness
cra'ter
cra·vat'
crave
craved crav'ing
cra'ven
crawl'er
cray'fish'
cray'on
craze
crazed craz'ing
cra'zi·ly
cra'zi·ness
cra'zy
  ·zi·er ·zi·est
creak
  (*squeak;* see
  creek)
creak'i·ness
creak'y
  ·i·er ·i·est
cream'er·y
  ·ies
cream'i·ness
cream'y
  ·i·er ·i·est
crease
creased
creas'ing
cre·ate'
  ·at'ed ·at'ing
cre·a'tion
cre·a'tive
cre'a·tiv'i·ty
cre·a'tor
crea'ture
cre'dence
cre·den'tial
cre·den'za
cred'i·bil'i·ty
cred'i·ble
cred'i·bly
cred'it·a·bil'i·ty
cred'it·a·ble
cred'it·a·bly
cred'i·tor
cre'do
  ·dos
cre·du'li·ty

cred'u·lous
creek
  (*stream;* see
  creak)
creep
  crept creep'ing
creep'i·ness
creep'y
  ·i·er ·i·est
cre'mate
  ·mat·ed ·mat·ing
cre·ma'tion
cre'ma·to'ry
  ·ries
cre'o·sote'
crepe or crêpe
cre·scen'do
  ·dos
cres'cent
crest'fall'en
cre'tin
cre'tonne
cre·vasse'
crev'ice
crew'el·work'
crib'bage
crick'et
cri'er
crim'i·nal
crim'i·nol'o·gy
crim'son
cringe
cringed
cring'ing
crin'kle
  ·kled ·kling
crin'o·line
crip'ple
  ·pled ·pling
crip'pler
cri'sis
  ·ses
crisp'er
crisp'i·ness
crisp'y
  ·i·er ·i·est
criss'cross'
cri·ter'i·on
  ·i·a or ·i·ons
crit'ic
crit'i·cal
crit'i·cal·ly
crit'i·cism
crit'i·cize'
  ·cized' ·ciz'ing
cri·tique'
croak
cro·chet'
  ·cheted'
  ·chet'ing
crock'er·y
croc'o·dile'
cro'cus
crois·sant'
crom'lech
cro'ny
  ·nies
crook'ed·ness

croon'er
crop
cropped
crop'ping
crop'-dust'ing
cro·quet'
·queted'
·quet'ing
(game)
cro·quette'
(food)
cro'sier
cross'bar'
cross'beam'
cross'bow'
cross'breed'
·bred' ·breed'ing
cross'-check'
cross'-coun'try
cross'cur'rent
cross'cut'
cross'-ex·am'i·
na'tion
cross'-ex·am'ine
cross'-eyed'
cross'-fer'ti·lize'
cross'-grained'
cross'hatch'
cross'-in'dex
cross'ing
cross'-leg'ged
cross'o'ver
cross'piece'
cross'-pur'pose
cross'-re·fer'
cross'-ref'er·ence
cross'road'
cross'ruff'
cross section
cross'-stitch'
cross'tie'
cross'-town'
cross'walk'
cross'wise'
cross'word'
crotch'et·i·ness
crotch'et·y
crou'pi·er'
crou'ton
crow'bar'
crowd'ed
crow's'-foot'
-feet'
crow's'-nest'
cru'cial
cru'cial·ly
cru'ci·ble
cru'ci·fix'
cru'ci·fix'ion
cru'ci·form'
cru'ci·fy'
·fied' ·fy'ing
crude'ly
cru'di·ty
·ties
cru'el·ly
cru'el·ty
·ties

cru'et
cruise
cruised cruis'ing
cruis'er
crul'ler
crum'ble
·bled ·bling
crum'bly
·bli·er ·bli·est
crum'by
·bi·er ·bi·est
crum'pet
crum'ple
·pled ·pling
crunch'i·ness
crunch'y
·i·er ·i·est
crup'per
cru·sade'
crush'a·ble
crus·ta'cean
crust'ed
crust'i·ness
crust'y
·i·er ·i·est
crux
crux'es or cru'ces
cry
cries
cried cry'ing
cry'o·gen'ics
crypt
cryp'tic
cryp'ti·cal·ly
cryp'to·gram'
cryp'to·gram'mic
cryp'to·graph'ic
cryp'to·graph'i·
cal·ly
cryp·tog'ra·phy
crys'tal
crys'tal·line
crys'tal·liz'a·ble
crys'tal·li·za'tion
crys'tal·lize'
·lized' ·liz'ing
crys'tal·log'ra·phy
cub'by·hole'
cube
cubed cub'ing
cu'bic
cu'bi·cal
(cube-shaped)
cu'bi·cal·ly
cu'bi·cle
(compartment)
cu'bit
cuck'old
cuck'oo'
cu'cum·ber
cud'dle
·dled ·dling
cud'dly
·dli·er ·dli·est
cudg'el
·eled or ·elled
·el·ing or
·el·ling

cue
cued cu'ing
or cue'ing
(signal; see
queue)
cui·rass'
cui·sine'
cul'-de-sac'
cu'li·nar'y
cull
cul'mi·nate'
·nat'ed ·nat'ing
cul'mi·na'tion
cu·lottes'
cul'pa·bil'i·ty
cul'pa·ble
cul'pa·bly
cul'prit
cult'ist
cul'ti·va·ble
cul'ti·vate'
·vat'ed ·vat'ing
cul'ti·va'tion
cul'ti·va'tor
cul'tur·al
cul'ture
·tured ·tur·ing
cul'vert
cum'ber·some
cum'mer·bund'
cu'mu·late'
·lat'ed ·lat'ing
cu'mu·la'tive
cu'mu·lous adj.
·li
cu·ne'i·form'
cun'ning·ly
cup'board
cup'ful'
·fuls'
cu·pid'i·ty
cu'po·la
cur'a·ble
cu·ra·çao'
cu'rate
cur'a·tive
cu·ra'tor
curb'stone'
curd'le
·dled ·dling
cure
cured cur'ing
cure'-all'
cur'few
cu'rie
cu·ri·o'
·os'
cu·ri·os'i·ty
·ties
cu'ri·ous
curl'i·cue'
curl'i·ness
curl'y
·i·er ·i·est
cur·mudg'eon
cur'rant
(fruit)

cur'ren·cy
·cies
cur'rent
(a flowing)
cur·ric'u·lar
cur·ric'u·lum
·u·la or ·u·lums
cur'ry
·ried ·ry·ing
cur'ry·comb'
curse
cursed or curst
curs'ing
cur'sive
cur'so·ri·ly
cur'so·ri·ness
cur'so·ry
cur·tail'
cur'tain
curt'ness
curt'sy
·sies
·sied ·sy·ing
(knee bend;
see courtesy)
cur'va·ture
curve
curved curv'ing
cur'vi·lin'e·ar
curv'y
·i·er ·i·est
cush'ion
cus'pid
cus'pi·dor'
cus'tard
cus·to'di·al
cus·to'di·an
cus'to·dy
cus'tom
cus'tom·ar'i·ly
cus'tom·ar'y
cus'tom-built'
cus'tom·er
cus'tom·house'
cus'tom-made'
cut
cut cut'ting
cu·ta'ne·ous
cut'a·way'
cut'back'
cut'i·cle
cut'lass or ·las
cut'ler·y
cut'let
cut'off'
cut'out'
cut'-rate'
cut'ter
cut'throat'
cy'a·nide'
cy'ber·cul'ture
cy'ber·na'tion
cy'ber·net'ics
cy'cla·mate'
cy'cle
cy'cled cy'cling
cy'clic
cy'cli·cal

cy'clist
cy'cli·zine'
cy'clom'e·ter
cy'clone
cy'clo·pe'di·a
cy'clo·ra'ma
cy'clo·tron'
cyg'net
cyl'in·der
cy·lin'dri·cal
cym'bal
(brass plate;
see symbol)
cyn'ic
cyn'i·cal
cyn'i·cal·ly
cyn'i·cism
cy'no·sure'
cy'press
cyst'ic
cyst'oid
cy·tol'o·gy
cy'to·plasm
czar
Czech'o·slo·
va'ki·a

D

dab'ble
·bled ·bling
dachs'hund
Da'cron
dac'tyl
dad'dy
·dies
da'do
·does
daf'fo·dil'
dag'ger
da·guerre'o·type'
dahl'ia
dai'ly
·lies
dain'ti·ly
dain'ti·ness
dain'ty
·ties
·ti·er ·ti·est
dair'y
·ies
dair'y·maid'
dair'y·man'
da'is
dai'sy
·sies
dal'li·ance
dal'ly
·lied ·ly·ing
Dal·ma'tian
dam
dammed
dam'ming
(barrier; see
damn)

dam'age
·aged ·ag·ing
dam'age·a·ble
dam'a·scene'
dam'ask
damn
damned
damn'ing
(condemn; see
dam)
dam'na·ble
dam'na·bly
dam·na'tion
dam'na·to'ry
damp'-dry'
-dried' -dry'ing
damp'en
damp'er
dam'sel
dance
danced danc'ing
danc'er
dan'de·li'on
dan'dle
·dled ·dling
dan'druff
dan'ger
dan'ger·ous
dan'gle
·gled ·gling
Dan'ish
dan·seuse'
dap'ple
·pled ·pling
dare
dared dar'ing
dare'dev'il
Dar·jee'ling
dark'en
dark'room'
dar'ling
Dar·win'i·an
dash'board'
das'tard·li·ness
das'tard·ly
da'ta
(sing. da'tum)
date
dat'ed dat'ing
daugh'ter
daugh'ter-in-law'
daugh'ters-
in-law'
daunt'less
dav'en·port'
dav'it
daw'dle
·dled ·dling
day'bed'
day'book'
day'break'
day'dream'
day letter
day'light'
day'long'
day room
day'time'
day'-to-day'

day'work'
daze
 dazed daz'ing
daz'zle
 ·zled ·zling
D'-day'
dea'con
dea'con·ess
de·ac'ti·vate'
dead'en
dead'-end'
dead'head
dead'line'
dead'li·ness
dead'lock'
dead'ly
 ·li·er ·li·est
dead'wood'
deaf'en·ing·ly
deaf'-mute'
deal
 dealt deal'ing
deal'er·ship'
dean'er·y
 ·ies
dear'ly
dearth
death'bed'
death'blow'
death'less
death'ly
death'trap'
death'watch'
de·ba'cle
de·bar'
 ·barred' ·bar'ring
de·bark'
de'bar·ka'tion
de·base'
 ·based' ·bas'ing
de·bat'a·ble
de·bate'
 ·bat'ed ·bat'ing
de·bauch'
deb·au·chee'
de·bauch'er·y
 ·ies
de·ben'ture
de·bil'i·tate'
 ·tat'ed ·tat'ing
de·bil'i·ta'tion
de·bil'i·ty
 ·ties
deb'it
deb'o·nair'
 or ·naire'
deb'o·nair'ly
de·brief'
de·bris'
debt'or
de·bunk'
de·but'
deb'u·tante'
dec'ade
dec'a·dence
dec'a·dent
dec'a·gon'
dec'a·gram'

dec'a·he'dron
 ·drons or ·dra
de·cal'ci·fy'
 ·fied' ·fy'ing
de·cal'co·ma'ni·a
dec'a·li'ter
Dec'a·logue'
 or ·log'
dec'a·me'ter
de·camp'
de·cant'
de·cant'er
de·cap'i·tate'
 ·tat'ed ·tat'ing
de·cap'i·ta'tion
de·cath'lon
de·cay'
de·ce'dent
de·ceit'ful
de·ceiv'a·ble
de·ceive'
 ·ceived'
 ·ceiv'ing
de·cel'er·ate'
 ·at'ed ·at'ing
de·cel'er·a'tion
de·cel'er·a'tor
de·cel'er·on'
De·cem'ber
de'cen·cy
 ·cies
de·cen'ni·al
de'cent
 (proper; see
 descent, dissent)
de·cen'tral·i·
 za'tion
de·cen'tral·ize'
 ·ized' ·iz'ing
de·cep'tion
de·cep'tive·ly
dec'i·bel
de·cide'
 ·cid'ed ·cid'ing
de·cid'ed·ly
de·cid'u·ous
dec'i·mal
dec'i·mal·ize'
 ·ized' ·iz'ing
dec'i·mal·ly
dec'i·mate'
 ·mat'ed ·mat'ing
de·ci'pher
de·ci'sion
de·ci'sive
deck'le
de·claim'
dec'la·ma'tion
de·clam'a·to'ry
de·clar'a·ble
dec'la·ra'tion
de·clar'a·tive
de·clare'
 ·clared'
 ·clar'ing

de·clas'si·fy'
 ·fied' ·fy'ing
de·clen'sion
dec'li·na'tion
de·cline'
 ·clined' ·clin'ing
de·cliv'i·ty
 ·ties
de·code'
de·cod'er
dé·col'le·tage'
dé·col'le·té'
de'com·pos'a·ble
de'com·pose'
de'com·po·si'tion
de'com·pres'sion
de'con·gest'ant
de·con·tam'i·nate'
de'con·trol'
 ·trolled'
 ·trol'ling
dé·cor' or de·cor'
dec'or·ate'
 ·at'ed ·at'ing
dec'o·ra'tion
dec'o·ra·tive
dec'o·ra'tor
dec'o·rous
de·co'rum
de'cou·page'
de·coy'
de·crease'
 ·creased'
 ·creas'ing
de·cree'
 ·creed' ·cree'ing
de·crep'it
de·crep'i·tude'
de'cre·scen'do
de·cres'cent
de·cri'al
de·cry'
 ·cried' ·cry'ing
de·crypt'
de·cum'bent
ded'i·cate'
 ·cat'ed ·cat'ing
ded'i·ca'tion
ded'i·ca·to'ry
de·duce'
 ·duced' ·duc'ing
de·duc'i·ble
de·duct'
de·duct'i·ble
de·duc'tion
de·duc'tive
de-em'pha·sis
de-em'pha·size'
deep'-chest'ed
deep'-dyed'
deep'freeze'
 ·froze' or
 ·freezed'
 ·fro'zen or
 ·freezed'
 ·freez'ing
deep'-fry'
 -fried' -fry'ing

deep'-laid'
deep'-root'ed
deep'-seat'ed
deep'-set'
deer'skin'
de-es'ca·late'
de-es'ca·la'tion
de·face'
de fac'to
de·fal'cate
 ·cat·ed ·cat·ing
def'a·ma'tion
de·fam'a·to'ry
de·fame'
 ·famed'
 ·fam'ing
de·fault'
de·fea'sance
de·feat'
de·feat'ist
def'e·cate'
 ·cat'ed ·cat'ing
def'e·ca'tion
de·fect'
de·fec'tion
de·fec'tive
de·fec'tor
de·fend'
de·fend'ant
de·fense'
de·fen'si·ble
de·fen'sive
de·fer'
 ·ferred' ·fer'ring
def'er·ence
def'er·en'tial
de·fer'ment
de·fi'ance
de·fi'ant
de·fi'cien·cy
 ·cies
de·fi'cient
def'i·cit
de·fi'er
de·file'
 ·filed' ·fil'ing
de·fin'a·ble
de·fine'
 ·fined' ·fin'ing
def'i·nite
def'i·ni'tion
de·fin'i·tive
de·flate'
 ·flat'ed ·flat'ing
de·fla'tion
de·fla'tion·ar'y
de·fla'tor
de·flect'
de·flec'tion
de·flec'tor
de·flow'er
de·fo'li·ate'
 ·at'ed ·at'ing
de'for·ma'tion
de·formed'
de·form'i·ty
 ·ties
de·fraud'

de·fray'
de·fray'al
de·frost'
de·funct'
de·fuse'
de·fy'
 ·fied' ·fy'ing
dé·ga·gé'
de·gen'er·a·cy
de·gen'er·ate'
 ·at'ed ·at'ing
de·gen'er·a'tion
de·gen'er·a·tive
de·grad'a·ble
deg'ra·da'tion
de·grade'
 ·grad'ed
 ·grad'ing
de·gree'
de'hu·mid'i·fy'
de·hy'drate
 ·drat·ed ·drat·ing
de'hy·dra'tion
de·hy'dra·tor
de·ic'er
de'i·fi·ca'tion
de'i·fy'
 ·fied' ·fy'ing
deign
de'ism
de'i·ty
 ·ties
de·ject'ed
de·jec'tion
Del'a·ware'
de·lay'
de·lec'ta·ble
del'e·gate'
 ·gat'ed ·gat'ing
del'e·ga'tion
de·lete'
 ·let'ed ·let'ing
del·e·te'ri·ous
de·le'tion
delft'ware'
de·lib'er·ate'
de·lib'er·ate·ly
de·lib'er·a'tion
del'i·ca·cy
 ·cies
del'i·cate
del'i·cate·ly
del'i·ca·tes'sen
de·li'cious
de·light'ful
de·light'ful·ly
de·lin'e·ate'
 ·at'ed ·at'ing
de·lin'e·a'tion
de·lin'e·a'tor
de·lin'quen·cy
de·lin'quent
de·lir'i·ous
de·lir'i·um
de·liv'er·a·ble
de·liv'er·ance
de·liv'er·y
 ·ies

de·lude'
 ·lud'ed ·lud'ing
del'uge
 ·uged ·ug·ing
de·lu'sion
de·lu'sive
de·luxe'
delve
 delved delv'ing
de·mag'net·ize'
dem'a·gog'ic
dem'a·gog'i·cal·ly
dem'a·gogue'
 or ·gog'
dem'a·gog'y
de·mand'ing
de·mar'cate
 ·cat·ed ·cat·ing
de'mar·ca'tion
de·mean'or
de·men'tia
de·mer'it
de·mesne'
dem'i·john'
de·mil'i·ta·rize'
de·mise'
dem'i·tasse'
de·mo'bi·lize'
de·moc'ra·cy
 ·cies
dem'o·crat'ic
dem'o·crat'i·cal·ly
de·moc'ra·ti·
 za'tion
de·moc'ra·tize'
 ·tized' ·tiz'ing
de·mog'ra·phy
de·mol'ish
dem'o·li'tion
de'mon
de·mon'e·tize'
 ·tized' ·tiz'ing
de·mo'ni·ac'
de·mon'ic
de·mon'i·cal·ly
de·mon'stra·ble
dem'on·strate'
 ·strat'ed
 ·strat'ing
dem'on·stra'tion
de·mon'stra·tive
de·mon'stra·tor
de·mor'al·ize'
de·mote'
 ·mot'ed ·mot'ing
de·mo'tion
de·mount'
de·mul'cent
de·mur'
 ·murred'
 ·mur'ring
 (to object)
de·mure'
 (coy)
de·mur'rage
de·mur'rer
de·na'tion·al·ize'
de·nat'u·ral·ize'

de·na'ture
·tured ·tur·ing
de·ni'a·ble
de·ni'al
de·nier'
de·ni'er
den'im
den'i·zen
de·nom'i·nate'
·nat'ed ·nat'ing
de·nom'i·na'tion
de·nom'i·na'tor
de'no·ta'tion
de·note'
·not'ed ·not'ing
de·noue'ment
de·nounce'
·nounced'
·nounc'ing
dense
dens'er dens'est
dense'ly
den'si·ty
·ties
den'tal
den'tal·ly
den'ti·frice'
den'tin
den'tist
den'tist·ry
den'ture
de·nude'
·nud'ed ·nud'ing
de·nun'ci·a'tion
de·ny'
·nied' ·ny'ing
de·o'dor·ant
de·o'dor·ize'
·ized' ·iz'ing
de·o'dor·iz'er
de·part'ed
de·part'ment
de·part'men'tal
de·part'men'tal·ize'
·ized' ·iz'ing
de·par'ture
de·pend'a·bil'i·ty
de·pend'a·ble
de·pend'a·bly
de·pend'ence
de·pend'en·cy
·cies
de·pend'ent
de·per'son·al·ize'
de·pict'
de·pic'tion
de·pil'a·to'ry
·ries
de·plane'
de·plete'
·plet'ed ·plet'ing
de·ple'tion
de·plor'a·ble
de·plore'
·plored'
·plor'ing
de·ploy'

de·pon'ent
de·pop'u·late'
de·port'a·ble
de'por·ta'tion
de·port'ment
de·pose'
de·pos'it
de·pos'i·tar'y
·ies
dep'o·si'tion
de·pos'i·tor
de·pos'i·to'ry
·ries
de'pot
dep'ra·va'tion
(a corrupting;
see deprivation)
de·prave'
·praved'
·prav'ing
de·prav'i·ty
·ties
dep're·cate'
·cat'ed ·cat'ing
dep're·ca'tion
dep're·ca·to'ry
de·pre'ci·a·ble
de·pre'ci·ate'
·at'ed ·at'ing
de·pre'ci·a'tion
de·pre·da'tion
de·pres'sant
de·pressed'
de·press'ing
de·pres'sion
de·pres'sive·ly
dep'ri·va'tion
(a taking away;
see depravation)
de·prive'
·prived' ·priv'ing
depth
dep'u·ta'tion
dep'u·tize'
·tized' ·tiz'ing
dep'u·ty
·ties
de·rail'
de·range'
·ranged'
·rang'ing
der'e·lict'
der'e·lic'tion
de·ride'
·rid'ed ·rid'ing
de ri·gueur'
de·ri'sion
de·ri'sive
de·riv'a·ble
der'i·va'tion
de·riv'a·tive
de·rive'
·rived' ·riv'ing
der'ma·tol'o·gist
der'o·ga'tion
de·rog'a·to'ri·ly
de·rog'a·to'ry
der'rick

der'ri·ère'
der'ring·do'
der'rin·ger
de·sal'i·na'tion
de·salt'
des'cant
de·scend'
de·scend'ant
de·scend'i·ble
de·scent'
(going down; see
decent, dissent)
de·scrib'a·ble
de·scribe'
·scribed'
·scrib'ing
de·scrip'tion
de·scrip'tive
de·scry'
·scried'
·scry'ing
des'e·crate'
·crat'ed ·crat'ing
des'e·cra'tion
de·seg're·gate'
·gat'ed ·gat'ing
de·seg're·ga'tion
de·sen'si·tize'
de·sen'si·tiz'er
de·sert'
(abandon; see
dessert)
des'ert
(dry area)
de·ser'tion
de·serts'
(reward, etc.)
de·serve'
·served'
·serv'ing
de·serv'ed·ly
des'ic·cant
des'ic·cate'
·cat'ed ·cat'ing
des'ic·ca'tion
de·sign'
des'ig·nate'
·nat'ed ·nat'ing
des'ig·na'tion
des'ig·na'tor
de·signed'
de·sign'er
de·sir'a·bil'i·ty
de·sir'a·ble
de·sir'a·bly
de·sire'
·sired' ·sir'ing
de·sir'ous
de·sist'
des'o·late'
·lat'ed ·lat'ing
des'o·la'tion
de·spair'
des'per·a'do
·does or ·dos
des'per·ate
(hopeless; see
disparate)

des'per·a'tion
des'pi·ca·ble
de·spise'
·spised'
·spis'ing
de·spite'
de·spoil'
de·spo'li·a'tion
de·spond'en·cy
de·spond'ent
des'pot
des·pot'ic
des·pot'i·cal·ly
des'pot·ism
des·sert'
(food; see desert)
des·sert'spoon'
des'ti·na'tion
des'tine
·tined ·tin·ing
des'tin·y
·ies
des'ti·tute'
des'ti·tu'tion
de·stroy'er
de·struct'
de·struct'i·bil'i·ty
de·struct'i·ble
de·struc'tion
de·struc'tive
de·struc'tor
des'ue·tude'
des'ul·to'ry
de·tach'
de·tach'a·ble
de·tach'ment
de·tail'
de·tain'
de·tect'
de·tect'a·ble
or ·i·ble
de·tec'tion
de·tec'tive
de·tec'tor
dé·tente'
de·ten'tion
de·ter'
·terred'
·ter'ring
de·ter'gent
de·te'ri·o·rate'
·rat'ed ·rat'ing
de·te'ri·o·ra'tion
de·ter'ment
de·ter'mi·na·ble
de·ter'mi·na·bly
de·ter'mi·nant
de·ter'mi·nate
de·ter'mi·na'tion
de·ter'mine
·mined ·min·ing
de·ter'min·ism
de·ter'rence
de·ter'rent
de·test'
de·test'a·ble
de·test'a·bly
de·tes·ta'tion

de·throne'
·throned'
·thron'ing
det'o·nate'
·nat'ed ·nat'ing
det'o·na'tion
det'o·na'tor
de'tour
de·tract'
de·trac'tor
det'ri·ment
det'ri·men'tal
de·tri'tus
deuce
de·val'u·a'tion
de·val'ue
dev'as·tate'
·tat'ed ·tat'ing
dev'as·ta'tion
de·vel'op·ment
de·vel'op·men'tal
de'vi·ant
de'vi·ate'
·at'ed ·at'ing
de'vi·a'tion
de·vice'
dev'il·ish
dev'il·ment
dev'il·try
·tries
de'vi·ous
de·vis'a·ble
(that can be devised;
see divisible)
de·vise'
·vised' ·vis'ing
de·vi'tal·ize'
de·void'
de·volve'
·volved'
·volv'ing
de·vote'
·vot'ed ·vot'ing
de·vo·tee'
de·vo'tion
de·vour'
de·vout'
dew'drop'
dew'lap'
dew'y
·i·er ·i·est
dex·ter'i·ty
dex'ter·ous
or dex'trous
dex'trose
di'a·be'tes
di'a·bet'ic
di'a·bol'ic
di'a·bol'i·cal
di'a·bol'i·cal·ly
di'a·crit'i·cal
di'a·dem'
di'ag·nos'a·ble
di'ag·nose'
·nosed' ·nos'ing
di'ag·no'sis
·no'ses
di'ag·nos'tic

di'ag·nos'ti·cal·ly
di'ag·nos·ti'cian
di·ag'o·nal
di·ag'o·nal·ly
di'a·gram'
·gramed' or
·grammed'
·gram'ing or
·gram'ming
di'a·gram·mat'ic
di'al
·aled or ·alled
·al·ing or ·al·ling
di'a·lect'
di'a·lec'tal
di'a·lec'tic
di'a·lec·ti'cian
di·al'o·gist
di'a·logue' or
·log'
di·am'e·ter
di'a·met'ri·cal
di'a·met'ri·cal·ly
di'a·mond
di'a·pa'son
di'a·per
di·aph'a·nous
di'a·phragm'
di'a·rist
di·ar'rhe·a
or ·rhoe'a
di'a·ry
·ries
di'a·stase'
di'a·ther'my
di'a·ton'ic
di'a·tribe'
dib'ble
·bled ·bling
dice
diced dic'ing
(sing. die or dice)
di·chot'o·mize'
·mized' ·miz'ing
di·chot'o·my
dick'er
dick'ey
·eys
Dic'ta·phone'
dic'tate
·tat·ed ·tat·ing
dic·ta'tion
dic'ta·tor
dic'ta·to'ri·al
dic'tion·ar'y
·ies
Dic'to·graph'
dic'tum
·tums or ·ta
di·dac'tic
di·dac'ti·cal·ly
die
dice
(cube)
die
dies
died die'ing
(mold; stamp)

die	dil'i·gence	dire'ful	dis·com'fit	dis·gorge'	dis·par'age
died dy'ing	dil'i·gent	dirge	dis·com'fi·ture	dis·grace'	·aged ·ag·ing
(*stop living;*	dil'ly·dal'ly	dir'i·gi·ble	dis·com'fort	·graced'	dis'pa·rate
see dye)	·lied ·ly·ing	dirn'dl	dis·com·pose'	·grac'ing	(*not alike;* see
die'-hard' *or*	dil'u·ent	dirt'i·ness	dis·com·po'sure	dis·grace'ful	desperate)
die'hard'	di·lute'	dirt'y	dis·con·cert'	dis·grun'tle	dis·par'i·ty
diel'drin	·lut'ed ·lut'ing	·i·er ·i·est	dis·con·nect'	·tled ·tling	dis·pas'sion·ate
di·e·lec'tric	di·lu'tion	dis·a·bil'i·ty	dis·con'so·late	dis·guise'	dis·patch'
di·er'e·sis	di·lu'vi·al	·ties	dis·con·tent'	·guised'	dis·patch'er
·ses'	dim	dis·a'ble	dis·con·tin'u·ance	·guis'ing	dis·pel'
die'sel	dim'mer	·bled ·bling	dis·con·tin'ue	dis·gust'	·pelled' ·pel'ling
die'sink'er	dim'mest	dis'a·buse'	dis·con·ti·nu'i·ty	dis·ha·bille'	dis·pen'sa·bil'i·ty
di'e·sis	dimmed	·bused' ·bus'ing	dis·con·tin'u·ous	dis·har'mo·ny	dis·pen'sa·ble
·ses'	dim'ming	dis'ad·van'tage	dis'co·phile'	dish'cloth'	dis·pen'sa·ry
di'e·tar'y	di·men'sion	dis·ad'van·ta'·	dis'cord	dis·heart'en	·ries
di'e·tet'ic	di·min'ish	geous	dis·cord'ant	di·shev'el	dis'pen·sa'tion
di'e·tet'i·cal·ly	di·min'u·en·do	dis'af·fect'ed	dis'co·thèque'	·eled *or* ·elled	dis·pense'
di'e·ti'tian	dim'i·nu'tion	dis'a·gree'	dis'count	·el·ing *or*	·pensed'
or ·cian	di·min'u·tive	dis'a·gree'a·ble	dis·cour'age	·el·ling	·pens'ing
dif'fer·ence	dim'i·ty	dis'a·gree'a·bly	·aged ·ag·ing	dis·hon'est	dis·pen'ser
dif'fer·ent	dim'out'	dis'a·gree'ment	dis·cour'age·ment	dis·hon'es·ty	dis·per'sal
dif'fer·en'tial	dim'ple	dis'al·low'	dis'course	dis·hon'or	dis·perse'
dif'fer·en'ti·ate'	·pled ·pling	dis'ap·pear'ance	dis·cour'te·ous	dis·hon'or·a·ble	·persed' ·pers'ing
·at'ed ·at'ing	din	dis'ap·point'ment	dis·cour'te·sy	dish'pan'	dis·pers'i·ble
dif'fer·en'ti·a'tion	dinned din'ning	dis'ap·pro·ba'tion	dis·cov'er	dish towel	dis·per'sion
dif'fi·cult	dine	dis'ap·prov'al	dis·cov'er·er	dish'wash'er	dis·pir'it·ed
dif'fi·cul'ty	dined din'ing	dis'ap·prove'	dis·cov'er·y	dish'wa'ter	dis·place'
·ties	din'er	dis·ar'ma·ment	·ies	dis'il·lu'sioned	dis·place'ment
dif'fi·dence	(*person eating;*	dis·arm'ing	dis·cred'it	dis'in·cli·na'tion	dis·play'
dif'fi·dent	see dinner)	dis·ar·range'	dis·creet'	dis'in·cline'	dis·please'
dif·fract'	din·ette'	dis·ar·ray'	(*prudent;* see	dis'in·fect'	dis·pleas'ure
dif·frac'tion	din'ghy	dis'as·sem'ble	discrete)	dis'in·fect'ant	dis·port'
dif·fuse'	·ghies	dis'as·so'ci·ate'	dis·crep'an·cy	dis'in·gen'u·ous	dis·pos'a·ble
·fused' ·fus'ing	(*boat*)	dis·as'ter	·cies	dis'in·her'it	dis·pos'al
dif·fus'i·ble	din'gi·ness	dis·as'trous	dis·crete'	dis·in'te·grate'	dis·pose'
dif·fu'sion	din'gy	dis'a·vow'	(*separate;* see	·grat'ed	·posed' ·pos'ing
dif·fu'sive	·gi·er ·gi·est	dis'a·vow'al	discreet)	·grat'ing	dis·po·si'tion
dig	(*not bright*)	dis·band'	dis·cre'tion	dis·in'te·gra'tion	dis·pos·sess'
dug dig'ging	din'ner	dis·bar'	dis·cre'tion·ar'y	dis·in'ter'	dis·proof'
dig'a·my	(*meal;* see diner)	dis·be·lief'	dis·crim'i·nate'	dis'in·ter'est·ed	dis·pro·por'tion
di'gest	din'ner·ware'	dis·be·lieve'	·nat'ed ·nat'ing	dis·join'	dis·pro·por'tion·
di·gest'i·ble	di'no·saur'	dis·be·liev'er	dis·crim'i·na'tion	dis·joint'	ate
di·ges'tive	di·oc'e·san	dis·burse'	dis·crim'i·na·	dis·junc'tion	dis·prove'
dig'ger	di'o·cese	·bursed'	to'ry	disk	dis·pu'ta·ble
dig'it	di'o·ra'ma	·burs'ing	dis·cur'sive	dis·like'	dis'pu·tant
dig'it·al	di·ox'ide	dis·burse'ment	dis'cus	dis'lo·cate'	dis'pu·ta'tion
dig'i·tal'is	dip	disc	·cus·es *or* dis'ci	dis'lo·ca'tion	dis·pu·ta'tious
dig'i·ti·grade'	dipped dip'ping	dis·card'	dis·cuss'	dis·lodge'	dis·pute'
dig'ni·fy	diph·the'ri·a	dis·cern'	dis·cus'sion	dis·loy'al	·put'ed ·put'ing
·fied' ·fy'ing	diph'thong	dis·cern'i·ble	dis·dain'ful	dis·loy'al·ty	dis·qual'i·fi·ca'·
dig'ni·tar'y	di·plo'ma	dis·cern'ing	dis·ease'	dis'mal	tion
·ies	di·plo'ma·cy	dis·cern'ment	·eased' ·eas'ing	dis'mal·ly	dis·qual'i·fy'
dig'ni·ty	·cies	dis·charge'	dis·em·bark'	dis·man'tle	dis·qui'et
·ties	dip'lo·mat'	dis·ci'ple	dis·em·bod'y	dis·may'	dis·qui'e·tude
di·gress'	(*government*	dis'ci·plin·a·ble	dis·em·bow'el	dis·mem'ber	dis'qui·si'tion
di·gres'sion	*representative*)	dis'ci·pli·nar'i·an	·eled *or* ·elled	dis·miss'	dis·re·gard'
di·lan'tin	dip'lo·mate'	dis'ci·pli·nar'y	·el·ing *or*	dis·miss'al	dis·re·pair'
di·lap'i·date'	(*doctor*)	dis'ci·pline	·el·ling	dis·mount'	dis·rep'u·ta·ble
·dat'ed ·dat'ing	dip'lo·mat'i·cal·ly	·plined ·plin·ing	dis·en·chant'	dis'o·be'di·ence	dis·rep'u·ta·bly
di·lat'a·ble	dip'so·ma'ni·a	disc jockey	dis·en·cum'ber	dis'o·be'di·ent	dis·re·pute'
di·late'	di·rect'	dis·claim'	dis·en·gage'	dis'o·bey'	dis·re·spect'ful
·lat'ed ·lat'ing	di·rec'tion	dis·claim'er	dis·en·tan'gle	dis·or'der	dis·robe'
di·la'tion	di·rec'tive	dis·close'	dis·es·tab'lish	dis·or'der·ly	dis·rupt'
dil'a·to'ry	di·rec'tor	dis·clo'sure	dis·fa'vor	dis·or'gan·i·za'·	dis·rup'tion
di·lem'ma	di·rec'tor·ate	dis·cog'ra·phy	dis·fig'ure	tion	dis·rup'tive
dil'et·tante'	di·rec'to'ri·al	dis'coid	dis·fig'ure·ment	dis·or'gan·ize'	dis·sat'is·fac'tion
·tantes' *or* ·tan'ti	di·rec'to·ry	dis·col'or	dis·fran'chise	dis·o'ri·ent'	dis·sat'is·fy'
dil'et·tant'ish	·ries	dis·col'or·a'tion	·chised ·chis·ing	dis·own'	·fied' ·fy'ing

dis·sect'
dis·sec'tion
dis·sec'tor
dis·sem'blance
dis·sem'ble
·bled ·bling
dis·sem'i·nate'
·nat'ed ·nat'ing
dis·sem'i·na'tion
dis·sen'sion
dis·sent'
(disagree; see
decent, descent)
dis·sen'tient
dis·sen'tious
dis'ser·ta'tion
dis·serv'ice
dis·sev'er
dis'si·dence
dis'si·dent
dis·sim'i·lar
dis·sim'i·lar'i·ty
dis·sim'i·la'tion
dis·sim'u·late'
dis'si·pate'
·pat'ed ·pat'ing
dis'si·pa'tion
dis·so'ci·ate'
·at'ed ·at'ing
dis·so'ci·a'tion
dis·sol'u·ble
dis·so·lute'
dis'so·lu'tion
dis·solv'a·ble
dis·solve'
·solved'
·solv'ing
dis·sol'vent
dis'so·nance
dis'so·nant
dis·suade'
·suad'ed
·suad'ing
dis·sua'sion
dis·sym'me·try
dis'taff
dis'tance
dis'tant
dis·taste'ful
dis·tem'per
dis·tend'
dis·ten'si·ble
dis·ten'tion or
dis·ten'sion
dis'tich
dis·till' or ·til'
·tilled' ·till'ing
dis'til·late
dis'til·la'tion
dis·till'er
dis·till'er·y
·ies
dis·tinct'
dis·tinc'tion
dis·tinc'tive
dis·tin·gué'
dis·tin'guish
dis·tin'guish·a·ble

dis·tin'guish·a·bly
dis·tort'
dis·tor'tion
dis·tract'
dis·tract'i·ble
dis·trac'tion
dis·trait'
dis·traught'
dis·tress'
dis·trib'ut·a·ble
dis·trib'ute
·ut·ed ·ut·ing
dis'tri·bu'tion
dis·trib'u·tive
dis·trib'u·tor
dis'trict
dis·trust'ful
dis·turb'
dis·turb'ance
dis·un'ion
dis'u·nite'
dis·u'ni·ty
dis·use'
ditch
dith'er
dit'to
·tos
dit'ty
·ties
di'u·ret'ic
di·ur'nal
di'va
di·van'
dive
dived or dove
dived div'ing
di·verge'
·verged'
·verg'ing
di·ver'gence
di·ver'gent
di'vers
(sundry)
di·verse'
(different)
di·ver'si·fi·ca'·
tion
di·ver'si·form'
di·ver'si·fy'
·fied' ·fy'ing
di·ver'sion
di·ver'sion·ar'y
di·ver'si·ty
di·vert'
di·ver'tisse·ment
di·vest'
di·vest'i·ture
di·vid'a·ble
di·vide'
·vid'ed ·vid'ing
div'i·dend'
div'i·na'tion
di·vine'
·vined' ·vin'ing
di·vin'i·ty
·ties
di·vis'i·bil'i·ty

di·vis'i·ble
(that can be divided;
see devisable)
di·vi'sion
di·vi'sor
di·vorce'
·vorced' ·vorc'ing
di·vor'cé' masc.
di·vor'cée' or
·cee' fem.
div'ot
di·vulge'
·vulged'
·vulg'ing
di·vul'gence
diz'zi·ly
diz'zi·ness
diz'zy
·zi·er ·zi·est
·zied ·zy·ing
do'a·ble
dob'bin
do'cent
doc'ile
doc'ile·ly
do·cil'i·ty
dock'age
dock'et
dock'yard'
doc'tor
doc'tor·al
doc'tor·ate
doc'tri·naire'
doc'tri·nal
doc'trine
doc'u·ment
doc'u·men'tal
doc'u·men'ta·ry
·ries
doc'u·men·ta'tion
dod'der·ing
dodge
dodged
dodg'ing
dodg'y
·i·er ·i·est
do'er
does
doe'skin'
does'n't
dog'catch'er
dog'ear'
dog'ged·ly
dog'ger·el
dog'gy or ·gie
·gies
(dog)
do'gie or ·gy
·gies
(calf)
dog'ma
·mas or ·ma·ta
dog·mat'ic
dog·mat'i·cal·ly
dog'ma·tism
dog'ma·tize'
·tized' ·tiz'ing
dog'nap'

do'-good'er
dog'trot'
dog'watch'
dog'wood'
doi'ly
·lies
do'-it-your·self'
doll'ce
doll'drums
dole
doled dol'ing
dole'ful
dol'lar
dol'lop
dol'man
·mans
(robe)
dol'men
(tomb)
do'lor·ous
dol'phin
dolt'ish
do·main'
do·mes'tic
do·mes'ti·cate'
·cat'ed ·cat'ing
do'mes·tic'i·ty
·ties
dom'i·cile'
dom'i·nance
dom'i·nant
dom'i·nate'
·nat'ed ·nat'ing
dom'i·na'tion
dom'i·neer'ing
do·min'i·cal
do·min'ion
dom'i·no'
·noes' or ·nos'
don
donned don'ning
do'nate
·nat·ed ·nat·ing
do·na'tion
do·nee'
Don Ju'an
don'key
·keys
don'ny·brook'
do'nor
do'-noth'ing
Don Qui·xo'te
don't
doo'dle
·dled ·dling
doo'hick'ey
dooms'day'
door'bell'
do'-or-die'
door'jamb'
door'keep'er
door'knob'
door'man'
door'mat'
door'nail'
door'plate'
door'sill'
door'step'

door'stop'
door'-to-door'
door'way'
dope
doped dop'ing
dor'man·cy
dor'mant
dor'mer
dor'mi·to·ry
·ries
dor'mouse'
·mice'
dor'sal
do'ry
·ries
dos'-à-dos'
dos'age
dos'si·er'
dot
dot'ted dot'ting
dot'age
dot'ard
dote
dot'ed dot'ing
dou'ble
·bled ·bling
dou'ble-bar'reled
dou'ble-breast'ed
dou'ble-check'
dou'ble-cross'
dou'ble-date'
dou'ble-deal'ing
dou'ble-deck'er
dou'ble-edged'
dou'ble-
en·ten'dre
dou'ble-faced'
dou'ble-head'er
dou'ble-joint'ed
dou'ble-knit'
dou'ble-park'
dou'ble-quick'
dou'ble-space'
dou'blet
dou'ble-tongued'
dou'bly
doubt
doubt'ful
doubt'ful·ly
doubt'less
douche
douched
douch'ing
dough
dough'i·ness
dough'nut'
dough'y
·i·er ·i·est
doup'pi·o'ni or
dou'pi·o'ni
douse
doused dous'ing
dove'cote'
dove'tail'
dow'a·ger
dow'di·ness
dow'dy
·di·er ·di·est

dow'el
dow'er
down'beat'
down'cast'
down'fall'
down'grade'
down'heart'ed
down'hill'
down'i·ness
down'pour'
down'range'
down'right'
down'spout'
down'stage'
down'stairs'
down'state'
down'stream'
down'swing'
down'time'
down'-to-earth'
down'town'
down'trod'den
down'turn'
down'ward
down'wash'
down'wind'
down'y
·i·er ·i·est
dow'ry
·ries
dox·ol'o·gy
doze
dozed doz'ing
doz'en
drab
drab'ber
drab'best
draft·ee'
draft'i·ness
drafts'man
draft'y
·i·er ·i·est
drag
dragged
drag'ging
drag'gle
·gled ·gling
drag'gy
·gi·er ·gi·est
drag'net'
drag'o·man
·mans or ·men
drag'on
drag'on·fly'
·flies'
dra·goon'
drain'age
drain'pipe'
dra'ma
dra·mat'ic
dra·mat'i·cal·ly
dram'a·tist
dram'a·ti·za'tion
dram'a·tize'
·tized' ·tiz'ing
dram'a·tur'gy
drape
draped drap'ing

dra'per·y
· ies
dras'tic
dras'ti·cal·ly
draughts'man
· men
draw
drew drawn
draw'ing
draw'back'
draw'bridge'
draw·ee'
draw'er
draw'knife'
· knives'
drawl
drawn'work'
draw'string'
dray'age
dray'man
dread'ful
dread'ful·ly
dread'nought'
dream'i·ly
dream'i·ness
dream'y
· i·er · i·est
drear'i·ly
drear'i·ness
drear'y
· i·er · i·est
dredge
dredged
dredg'ing
drenched
dress
dressed or drest
dress'ing
dress'er
dress'i·ly
dress'i·ness
dress'ing-down'
dress'mak·er
dress'y
· i·er · i·est
drib'ble
· bled · bling
drib'let
dri'er or dry'er
drift'wood'
drill'mas·ter
drill press
drink
drank drunk
drink'ing
drink'a·ble
drip
dripped or dript
drip'ping
drip'-dry'
drive
drove driv'en
driv'ing
drive'-in'
driv'el
· eled or ·elled
· el·ing or
· el·ling

driv'er
drive'way'
driz'zle
· zled · zling
driz'zly
droll'er·y
· ies
drol'ly
drom'e·dar'y
· ies
drone
droned dron'ing
droop'i·ly
droop'i·ness
droop'y
· i·er · i·est
drop
dropped
drop'ping
drop'cloth'
drop'-forge'
· -forged'
· -forg'ing
drop'let
drop'out'
drop'per
dross
drought
or drouth
dro'ver
drown
drowse
drowsed
drows'ing
drow'si·ly
drow'si·ness
drow'sy
· si·er · si·est
drub
drubbed
drub'bing
drudge
drudged
drudg'ing
drudg'er·y
drug
drugged
drug'ging
drug'gist
drug'store'
drum
drummed
drum'ming
drum'beat'
drum'head'
drum'mer
drum'stick'
drunk'ard
drunk'en·ness
drunk·o'me·ter
drupe'let
dry
dri'er dri'est
dried dry'ing
dry'as·dust'
dry'-clean'
dry cleaner
dry cleaning

dry'er
dry'-eyed'
dry ice
dry'ly or dri'ly
dry'ness
du'al
(of two; see duel)
du'al·ism
du'al·is'tic
du'al·ly
du'al-pur'pose
dub
dubbed dub'bing
du·bi'e·ty
du'bi·ous
du'cal
duc'at
duch'ess
duch'y
· ies
duck'ling
duck'pins'
duc'tile
duct'less
dudg'eon
due bill
du'el
· eled or ·elled
· el·ing or
· el·ling
(fight; see dual)
du·et'
duf'fel or ·fle
dug'out'
dul'cet
dul'ci·mer
dull'ard
dull'ness
dul'ly
(in a dull manner)
du'ly
(as due)
dumb'bell'
dumb'found' or
dum'found'
dumb'ly
dumb'wait·er
dum'dum'
dum'my
· mies
dump'i·ness
dump'ling
dump'y
· i·er · i·est
dun
dunned
dun'ning
dun'der·head'
dun'ga·ree'
dun'geon
dung'hill'
dun'nage
du'o
du'os or du'i
du·o·dec'i·mal
du'o-de'nal
du'o·logue'
du·op'o·ly

du'o·tone'
du'o·type'
dupe
duped dup'ing
du'ple
du'plex
du'pli·cate'
· cat'ed · cat'ing
du'pli·ca'tion
du'pli·ca'tor
du·plic'i·ty
· ties
du·ra·bil'i·ty
du'ra·ble
du'ra·bly
dur'ance
du·ra'tion
du·ress'
dur'ing
du'rum
dusk'i·ness
dusk'y
· i·er · i·est
dust'i·ness
dust'pan'
dust'y
· i·er · i·est
du'te·ous
du'ti·a·ble
du'ti·ful
du'ti·ful·ly
du'ty
· ties
du'ty-free'
dwarf
dwarfs or
dwarves
dwell
dwelt or dwelled
dwell'ing
dwin'dle
· dled · dling
dy'ad
dyb'buk
dye
dyed dye'ing
(color; see die)
dyed'-in-the-wool'
dy'er
dye'stuff'
dy·nam'ic
dy·nam'i·cal·ly
dy'na·mism
dy'na·mite'
· mit'ed · mit'ing
dy'na·mo'
· mos'
dy·na·mom'e·ter
dy'na·mo'tor
dy'nas·ty
· ties
dyne
dy·nel'
dys'en·ter'y
dys·func'tion
dys·pep'si·a
dys·pep'tic
dys'tro·phy

E

ea'ger
ea'gle
ea'gle-eyed'
ear'ache'
ear'drum'
ear'ly
· li·er · li·est
ear'mark'
ear'muffs'
ear'nest
earn'ings
ear'phone'
ear'plug'
ear'ring'
ear'shot'
earth'en·ware'
earth'i·ness
earth'ly
earth'quake'
earth'shak·ing
earth'ward
earth'y
· i·er · i·est
ear'wax'
ease
eased eas'ing
ea'sel
ease'ment
eas'i·ly
eas'i·ness
east'er·ly
east'ern
east'ward
eas'y
· i·er · i·est
eas'y-go'ing
eat
ate eat'en
eat'ing
eat'a·ble
eaves'drop'
ebb tide
eb'on·y
e·bul'lient
e'bul·li'tion
ec·cen'tric
ec·cen'tri·cal·ly
ec'cen·tric'i·ty
· ties
ec·cle'si·as'ti·cal
ech'e·lon'
ech'o
· oes
e·cho'ic
é·clair'
é·clat'
ec·lec'tic
ec·lec'ti·cism
e·clipse'
· clipsed'
· clips'ing
e·clip'tic
ec'o·log'i·cal

ec'o·log'i·cal·ly
e·col'o·gist
e·col'o·gy
e'co·nom'ic
e'co·nom'i·cal
e'co·nom'i·cal·ly
e·con'o·mist
e·con'o·mize'
· mized' · miz'ing
e·con'o·my
· mies
e'co·sys'tem
e'co·tone'
ec'ru
ec'sta·sy
· sies
ec·stat'ic
ec·stat'i·cal·ly
ec'u·men'i·cal
ec'ze·ma
ed'dy
· dies
e'del·weiss'
e·de'ma
· mas or ·ma·ta
edge
edged edg'ing
edge'ways'
edge'wise'
edg'i·ly
edg'i·ness
edg'y
· i·er · i·est
ed'i·bil'i·ty
ed'i·ble
e'dict
ed'i·fi·ca'tion
ed'i·fice
ed'i·fy'
· fied' · fy'ing
e·di'tion
(form of book;
see addition)
ed'i·tor
ed'i·to'ri·al
ed'i·to'ri·al·ize'
· ized' · iz'ing
ed'i·to'ri·al·ly
ed·u·ca·bil'i·ty
ed'u·ca·ble
ed'u·cate'
· cat'ed · cat'ing
ed·u·ca'tion
ed'u·ca'tive
ed'u·ca'tor
e·duce'
· duced' · duc'ing
e·duc'i·ble
ee'rie or ·ry
· ri·er · ri·est
ee'ri·ly
ee'ri·ness
ef·face'
· faced' · fac'ing
ef·face'a·ble
ef·fect'
(result; see
affect)

ef·fec'tive
(having effect;
see affective)
ef·fec'tu·al
ef·fec'tu·ate
·at'ed ·at'ing
ef·fem'i·na·cy
ef·fem'i·nate
ef'fer·ent
ef'fer·vesce'
·vesced'
·vesc'ing
ef'fer·ves'cence
ef'fer·ves'cent
ef·fete'
ef·fi·ca'cious
ef'fi·ca·cy
ef·fi'cien·cy
ef·fi'cient
ef'fi·gy
·gies
ef'flo·resce'
·resced'
·resc'ing
ef'flo·res'cence
ef'flu·ence
ef'flu·ent
(flowing; see
affluent)
ef·flu'vi·um
·vi·a or ·vi·ums
ef'fort
ef·fron'ter·y
·ies
ef·ful'gence
ef·fu'sion
ef·fu'sive
e·gal'i·tar'i·an
egg'nog'
egg'shell'
e'go
e'go·cen'tric
e'go·cen'tri·cal·ly
e'go·ism
e'go·ist
e'go·ma'ni·a
e'go·tism
e'go·tist
e'go·tis'tic
e'go·tis'ti·cal·ly
e·gre'gious
e'gress
e'gret
ei'der·down'
ei·det'ic
eight'een'
eighth
eight'i·eth
eight'y
·ies
ei'ther
ei'ther-or'
e·jac'u·late'
·lat'ed ·lat'ing
e·jac'u·la'tion
e·jac'u·la'tor
e·ject'
e·jec'tion

e·jec'tor
eke
eked ek'ing
e·kis'tics
e·kis'ti·cal
e·lab'o·rate'
·rat'ed ·rat'ing
e·lab'o·rate·ly
e·lab'o·ra'tion
e·lapse'
·lapsed'
·laps'ing
e·las'tic
e·las'tic'i·ty
e·las'ti·cize'
·cized' ·ciz'ing
e·late'
·lat'ed ·lat'ing
e·la'tion
el'bow·room'
eld'er·ly
eld'est
e·lec'tion
e·lec'tion·eer'
e·lec'tive
e·lec'tor
e·lec'tor·al
e·lec'tor·ate
e·lec'tric
e·lec'tri·cal
e·lec'tri·cal·ly
e·lec·tri'cian
e·lec·tric'i·ty
e·lec'tri·fi·ca'tion
e·lec'tri·fy'
·fied' ·fy·ing
e·lec'tro·cute'
·cut'ed ·cut'ing
e·lec'tro·cu'tion
e·lec'trode
e·lec'trol'y·sis
e·lec'tro·lyte'
e·lec'tro·lyt'ic
e·lec'tro·lyze'
·lyzed' ·lyz'ing
e·lec'tro·mag'net
e·lec'trom'e·ter
e·lec'tro·mo'tive
e·lec'tron
e·lec'tron'ic
e·lec·tron'i·cal·ly
e·lec'tro·plate'
e·lec'tro·scope'
e·lec'tro·stat'ics
e·lec'tro·ther'a·py
e·lec'tro·type'
e·lec'tro·typ'y
el'ee·mos'y·nar'y
el'e·gance
el'e·gant
el'e·gi'ac
el'e·gize'
·gized' ·giz'ing
el'e·gy
·gies
el'e·ment
el'e·men'tal
el'e·men'ta·ri·ness

el'e·men'ta·ry
(basic; see
alimentary)
el'e·phant
el'e·phan·ti'a·sis
el'e·phan'tine
El'eu·sin'i·an
el'e·vate'
·vat'ed ·vat'ing
el'e·va'tion
el'e·va'tor
e·lev'enth
elf
elves
elf'in
e·lic'it
(draw forth;
see illicit)
e·lide'
·lid'ed ·lid'ing
el'i·gi·bil'i·ty
el'i·gi·ble
el'i·gi·bly
e·lim'i·nate'
·nat'ed ·nat'ing
e·lim'i·na'tion
e·li'sion
e·lite' or é·lite'
e·lix'ir
E·liz'a·be'than
el·lipse'
el·lip'sis
·ses
el·lip'ti·cal
el·lip'ti·cal·ly
el'o·cu'tion
e·lon'gate'
·gat'ed ·gat'ing
e·lon·ga'tion
e·lope'
·loped' ·lop'ing
e·lope'ment
el'o·quence
el'o·quent
else'where'
e·lu'ci·date'
·dat'ed ·dat'ing
e·lu'ci·da'tion
e·lude'
·lud'ed ·lud'ing
(escape; see
allude)
e·lu'sion
(an escape; see
allusion, illusion)
e·lu'sive
(hard to grasp;
see allusive,
illusive)
e·ma'ci·ate'
·at'ed ·at'ing
e·ma·ci·a'tion
em'a·nate'
·nat'ed ·nat'ing
em'a·na'tion
e·man'ci·pate'
·pat'ed ·pat'ing
e·man'ci·pa'tion

e·man'ci·pa'tor
e·mas'cu·late'
·lat'ed ·lat'ing
e·mas'cu·la'tion
e·mas'cu·la'tor
em·balm'
em·bank'ment
em·bar'go
·goes
em·bark'
em'bar·ka'tion
em·bar'rass
em·bar'rass·ment
em'bas·sy
·sies
em·bat'tle
·tled ·tling
em·bed'
em·bel'lish
em'ber
em·bez'zle
·zled ·zling
em·bez'zler
em·bla'zon
em'blem
em'blem·at'ic
em·bod'i·ment
em·bod'y
·ied ·y·ing
em·bold'en
em'bo·lism
em'bo·lus
·li
em·boss'
em'bou·chure'
em·brace'
·braced'
·brac'ing
em·brace'a·ble
em·bra'sure
em·broi'der
em·broi'der·y
·ies
em·broil'
em'bry·o'
·os'
em'bry·ol'o·gy
em'bry·on'ic
em·cee'
·ceed' ·cee'ing
e·mend'
(to correct;
see amend)
e'men·da'tion
em'er·ald
e·merge'
·merged'
·merg'ing
(appear; see
immerge)
e·mer'gence
e·mer'gen·cy
·cies
e·mer'i·tus
em'er·y
e·met'ic
em'i·grant

em'i·grate'
·grat'ed
·grat'ing
em'i·gra'tion
em'i·nence
em'i·nent
(prominent; see
imminent)
em'is·sar'y
·ies
e·mis'sion
e·mit'
·mit'ted
·mit'ting
e·mol'li·ent
e·mol'u·ment
e·mo'tion·al
e·mo'tion·al·ize'
·ized' ·iz'ing
em·path'ic
em'pa·thize'
·thized' ·thiz'ing
em'pa·thy
em'pen·nage'
em'per·or
em'pha·sis
·ses'
em'pha·size'
·sized' ·siz'ing
em·phat'ic
em'phy·se'ma
em'pire
em·pir'i·cal
em·pir'i·cism
em·place'ment
em·ploy'
em·ploy'a·ble
em·ploy'ee
em·ploy'er
em·ploy'ment
em·po'ri·um
·ri·ums or ·ri·a
em·pow'er
em'press
emp'ti·ly
emp'ti·ness
emp'ty
·ti·er ·ti·est
·ties
·tied ·ty·ing
emp'ty-hand'ed
emp'ty-head'ed
em'u·late'
·lat'ed ·lat'ing
em'u·la'tion
em'u·lous
e·mul'si·fi·ca'tion
e·mul'si·fi'er
e·mul'si·fy'
·fied' ·fy'ing
e·mul'sion
en·a'ble
·bled ·bling
en·act'ment
en·am'el
·eled or ·elled
·el·ing or
·el·ling

en·am'el·ware'
en·am'ored
en·camp'ment
en·case'
·cased' ·cas'ing
en·caus'tic
en·ceph'a·li'tis
en·chant'ment
en'chi·la'da
en·cir'cle
en'clave
en·close'
·closed'
·clos'ing
en·clo'sure
en·code'
en·co'mi·ast'
en·co'mi·um
·ums or ·a
en·com'pass
en'core
en·coun'ter
en·cour'age
·aged ·ag'ing
en·cour'age·ment
en·croach'
en·cum'ber
en·cum'brance
en·cyc'li·cal
en·cy'clo·pe'di·a
or ·pae'di·a
en·dan'ger
en·dear'
en·dear'ment
en·deav'or
en·dem'ic
end'ing
en'dive
end'less
end'most'
en'do·crine'
en·dog'a·my
en'do·me'tri·um
en·dorse'
·dorsed'
·dors'ing
en·dorse'ment
en·dors'er
en·dow'
en·dow'ment
end'pa'per
en·dur'a·ble
en·dur'a·bly
en·dur'ance
en·dure'
·dured' ·dur'ing
end'ways'
en'e·ma
en'e·my
·mies
en'er·get'ic
en'er·get'i·cal·ly
en'er·gize'
·gized' ·giz'ing
en'er·giz'er
en'er·gy
·gies

en'er·vate'	en·roll·ee'	en'try	ep'i·thet'	e·rad'i·cate'	es'ca·role'
·vat'ed ·vat'ing	en·roll'ment or	·tries	e·pit'o·me	·cat'ed ·cat'ing	es·carp'ment
en·fee'ble	·rol·l'ment	en·twine'	e·pit'o·mize'	e·rad'i·ca'tion	es·cha·rot'ic
·bled ·bling	en route'	e·nu'mer·ate'	·mized' ·miz'ing	e·rad'i·ca'tor	es·cha·tol'o·gy
en'fi·lade'	en·sconce'	·at'ed ·at'ing	ep'och	e·ras'a·ble	es·cheat'
·lad'ed ·lad'ing	·sconced'	e·nu'mer·a'tion	(period; see epic)	e·rase'	es·chew'
en·fold'	·sconc'ing	e·nu'mer·a'tor	ep'och·al	·rased' ·ras'ing	es·chew'al
en·force'	en·sem'ble	e·nun'ci·ate'	ep'o·nym'	e·ras'er	es'cort
·forced'	en·shrine'	·at'ed ·at'ing	ep·ox'y	e·ra'sure	es'cri·toire'
·forc'ing	·shrined'	(pronounce; see	ep'si·lon'	e·rect'	es'crow
en·force'a·ble	·shrin'ing	annunciate)	eq'ua·bil'i·ty	e·rec'tile	es'cu·lent
en·fran'chise	en'sign	e·nun'ci·a'tion	eq'ua·ble	e·rec'tion	es·cutch'eon
en·gage'	en·slave'	e·nun'ci·a'tor	eq'ua·bly	e·rec'tor	Es'ki·mo'
·gaged' ·gag'ing	en·snare'	en·vel'op v.	e'qual	erg	·mos' or ·mo'
en·gage'ment	en·snarl'	en'vel·ope' n.	·qualed or	er'go	e·soph'a·gus
en·gen'der	en·sue'	en·ven'om	·qualled	er·gos'ter·ol'	·a·gi'
en'gine	·sued' ·su'ing	en'vi·a·ble	·qual·ing or	er'got	es'o·ter'ic
en'gi·neer'	en·sure'	en'vi·a·bly	·qual·ling	er'mine	es'o·ter'i·cal·ly
Eng'lish	en·tail'	en'vi·ous	e·qual'i·tar'i·an	e·rode'	es'pa·drille'
en·gorge'	en·tan'gle	en·vi'ron·ment	e·qual'i·ty	·rod'ed ·rod'ing	es·pal'ier
·gorged' ·gorg'ing	en·tente'	en·vi'ron·men'tal	·ties	e·rog'e·nous	es·pe'cial
en·grave'	en'ter·prise'	en·vi'rons	e'qual·i·za'tion	e·ro'sion	es·pe'cial·ly
·graved'	en'ter·pris'ing	en·vis'age	e'qual·ize'	e·ro'sive	Es'pe·ran'to
·grav'ing	en'ter·tain'	·aged ·ag·ing	·ized' ·iz'ing	e·rot'ic	es'pi·o·nage'
en·grav'er	en·thrall' or	en·vi'sion	e'qual·ly	e·rot'i·ca	es'pla·nade'
en·gross'	en·thral'	en'voy	e'qua·nim'i·ty	e·rot'i·cal·ly	es·pous'al
en·gulf'	·thralled'	en'vy	e·quate'	e·rot'i·cism	es·pouse'
en·hance'	·thrall'ing	·vies	·quat'ed	er'o·tism	·poused' ·pous'ing
·hanced'	en·throne'	·vied ·vy·ing	·quat'ing	e·ro'to·gen'ic	es·pres'so
·hanc'ing	en·thuse'	en'zyme	e·qua'tion	err	·sos
e·nig'ma	·thused'	e'o·lith'ic	e·qua'tor	er'ran·cy	es·prit' de corps'
e'nig·mat'ic	·thus'ing	e'on	e·qua·to'ri·al	·cies	es·py'
e'nig·mat'i·cal·ly	en·thu'si·asm	ep'au·let' or	eq'uer·ry	er'rand	·pied' ·py'ing
en·join'	en·thu'si·as'tic	·lette'	·ries	er'rant	es'quire
en·joy'a·ble	en·thu'si·as'ti·	e·pergne'	e·ques'tri·an	er·ra'ta	es·say'
en·joy'a·bly	cal·ly	e·phem'er·al	e·ques'tri·enne'	(sing. er·ra'tum)	(try; see assay)
en·joy'ment	en·tice'	ep'ic	e'qui·an'gu·lar	er·rat'ic	es'say·ist
en·kin'dle	·ticed' ·tic'ing	(poem; see	e'qui·dis'tant	er·rat'i·cal·ly	es'sence
·dled ·dling	en·tice'ment	epoch)	e'qui·lat'er·al	er·ro'ne·ous	es·sen'tial
en·lace'	en·tire'	ep'i·cen'ter	e·quil'i·brant	er'ror	es·sen'ti·al'i·ty
en·large'	en·tire'ly	ep'i·cure'	e·quil'i·brate'	er'satz	es·sen'tial·ly
·larged'	en·tire'ty	ep'i·cu·re'an	·brat'ed ·brat'ing	erst'while'	es·tab'lish
·larg'ing	·ties	ep'i·dem'ic	e'qui·lib'ri·um	e·ruct'	es·tab'lish·ment
en·large'ment	en·ti'tle	ep'i·der'mis	·ri·ums or ·ri·a	e·ruc'tate	es·tate'
en·larg'er	·tled ·tling	ep'i·glot'tis	e'quine	·tat·ed ·tat·ing	es·teem'
en·light'en	en'ti·ty	ep'i·gram'	e'qui·noc'tial	e·ruc'ta'tion	es'thete
en·light'en·ment	·ties	ep'i·gram·mat'ic	e'qui·nox'	er'u·dite'	es·thet'ic
en·list'	en·tomb'	ep'i·gram·mat'i·	e·quip'	er'u·di'tion	es·thet'i·cal·ly
en·list'ment	en'to·mol'o·gy	cal·ly	·quipped'	e·rupt'	es·thet'i·cism
en·liv'en	(insect study; see	ep'i·graph'	·quip'ping	e·rupt'i·ble	es'ti·ma·ble
en masse'	etymology)	ep'i·graph'ic	eq'ui·page	e·rup'tion	es'ti·mate'
en·mesh'	en·tou·rage'	ep'i·graph'i·cal·ly	e·quip'ment	e·rup'tive	·mat'ed ·mat'ing
en'mi·ty	en·tr'acte'	ep'i·lep'sy	e'qui·poise'	e·ryth'ro·my'cin	es'ti·ma'tion
·ties	en'trails	ep'i·lep'tic	eq'ui·pol'lent	es'ca·drille'	es'ti·ma'tor
en·no'ble	en·train'	ep'i·logue' or	eq'ui·ta·ble	es'ca·lade'	es'ti·val
·bled ·bling	en'trance	·log'	eq'ui·ta·bly	·lad'ed ·lad'ing	es'ti·vate'
en'nui	en·trance'	E·piph'a·ny	eq'ui·ty	es'ca·late'	·vat'ed ·vat'ing
e·nor'mi·ty	·tranced'	e·pis'co·pal	·ties	·lat'ed ·lat'ing	es·trange'
·ties	·tranc'ing	E·pis'co·pa'li·an	e·quiv'a·lence	es·ca·la'tion	·tranged'
e·nor'mous	en'trant	ep'i·sode'	e·quiv'a·lent	es·ca·la'tor	·trang'ing
e·nough'	en·trap'	ep'i·sod'ic	e·quiv'o·cal	es·cal'lop or ·op	es·trange'ment
en·plane'	en·treat'	ep'i·sod'i·cal·ly	e·quiv'o·cal·ly	es'ca·pade'	es'tro·gen
en·rage'	en·treat'y	e·pis'tle	e·quiv'o·cate'	es·cape'	es'trous adj.
en·rap'ture	·ies	e·pis'to·lar'y	·cat'ed ·cat'ing	·caped' ·cap'ing	es'trus n.
·tured ·tur·ing	en'tree or ·trée	ep'i·taph	e·quiv'o·ca'tion	es·cap·ee'	es·tu·ar'i·al
en·rich'	en·trench'ment	ep'i·the'li·al	e·quiv'o·ca'tor	es·cape'ment	es'tu·ar'y
en·roll' or ·rol'	en'tre·pre·neur'	ep'i·the'li·um	e'ra	es·cap'ism	·ies
·rolled' ·roll'ing	en·trust'	·li·ums or ·li·a	e·rad'i·ca·ble	es·cap'ist	et·cet'er·a

et·cet'er·as
etch'ing
e·ter'nal
e·ter'nal·ly
e·ter'ni·ty
· ·ties
e'ther
e·the're·al
e·the're·al·ize'
· ·ized' ·iz'ing
e'ther·ize'
· ·ized' ·iz'ing
eth'i·cal
eth'i·cal·ly
eth'ics
eth'nic
eth'ni·cal·ly
eth'no·cen'tri·
· ·cal·ly
eth'no·cen'trism
eth·nog'ra·phy
eth'no·log'i·cal
eth·nol'o·gy
e'thos
eth'yl
e'ti·ol'o·gy
et'i·quette
é'tude
et'y·mo·log'i·cal
et'y·mol'o·gy
· ·gies
(word study; see
entomology)
et'y·mon'
eu'ca·lyp'tus
· ·tus·es or ·ti
Eu'cha·rist
eu'chre
eu·gen'i·cal·ly
eu·gen'ics
eu'lo·gize'
· ·gized' ·giz'ing
eu'lo·gy
· ·gies
eu'nuch
eu'phe·mism
eu'phe·mis'tic
eu'phe·mis'ti·
· ·cal·ly
eu'phe·mize'
· ·mized' ·miz'ing
eu·phon'ic
eu·pho'ni·ous
eu·pho'ni·um
eu'pho·ny
· ·nies
eu·pho'ri·a
eu·phor'ic
eu'phu·ism
eu'phu·is'tic
Eur·a'sian
Eur'a·tom'
eu·re'ka
Eu'ro·crat'
Eu'ro·dol'lars
Eu'ro·pe'an
eu·ryth'mics
eu·ryth'my

Eu·sta'chi·an
eu'tha·na'si·a
e·vac'u·ate'
· ·at'ed ·at'ing
e·vac'u·a'tion
e·vac'u·ee'
e·vade'
· ·vad'ed ·vad'ing
e·val'u·ate'
· ·at'ed ·at'ing
e·val'u·a'tion
ev'a·nesce'
· ·nesced' ·nesc'ing
ev'a·nes'cence
ev'a·nes'cent
e'van·gel'i·cal
e'van·gel'i·cal·ly
e·van'gel·ism
e·van'gel·ist
e·van'gel·is'tic
e·van'gel·ize'
· ·ized' ·iz'ing
e·vap'o·rate'
· ·rat'ed ·rat'ing
e·vap'o·ra'tion
e·va'sion
e·va'sive
e'ven·hand'ed
eve'ning
e'ven·ness
e·vent'
e'ven-tem'pered
e·vent'ful
e·ven'tu·al
e·ven'tu·al'i·ty
· ·ties
e·ven'tu·al·ly
e·ven'tu·ate'
· ·at'ed ·at'ing
ev'er·glade'
ev'er·green'
ev'er·last'ing
ev'er·more'
e·vert'
ev'er·y·bod'y
ev'er·y·day'
ev'er·y·one
ev'er·y·thing'
ev'er·y·where'
e·vict'
e·vic'tion
ev'i·dence
· ·denced ·denc·ing
ev'i·dent
ev'i·den'tial
e'vil-do'er
e'vil·ly
e'vil-mind'ed
e·vince'
· ·vinced'
· ·vinc'ing
e·vin'ci·ble
e·vis'cer·ate'
· ·at'ed ·at'ing
e·vis'cer·a'tion
ev'o·ca'tion
e·voke'
· ·voked' ·vok'ing

ev'o·lu'tion
ev'o·lu'tion·ar'y
ev'o·lu'tion·ist
e·volve'
· ·volved' ·volv'ing
ewe
(sheep; see yew)
ew'er
ex·ac'er·bate'
· ·bat'ed ·bat'ing
ex·ac'er·ba'tion
ex·act'
ex·act'ing
ex·ac'tion
ex·ac'ti·tude'
ex·act'ly
ex·ag'ger·ate'
· ·at'ed ·at'ing
ex·ag'ger·a'tion
ex·ag'ger·a'tor
ex·alt'
ex·al·ta'tion
ex·am'i·na'tion
ex·am'ine
· ·ined ·in·ing
ex·am'in·er
ex·am'ple
ex·as'per·ate'
· ·at'ed ·at'ing
ex·as'per·a'tion
ex'ca·the'dra
ex'ca·vate'
· ·vat'ed ·vat'ing
ex'ca·va'tion
ex'ca·va'tor
ex·ceed'
(surpass; see
accede)
ex·ceed'ing·ly
ex·cel'
· ·celled' ·cel'ling
ex'cel·lence
ex'cel·len·cy
· ·cies
ex'cel·lent
ex·cel'si·or'
ex·cept'
(omit; see accept)
ex·cept'ed
(left out; see
accepted)
ex·cep'tion
ex·cep'tion·a·ble
ex·cep'tion·al
ex·cep'tion·al·ly
ex·cerpt'
ex·cess'
(surplus; see
access)
ex·ces'sive
ex·ces'sive·ly
ex·change'
· ·changed'
· ·chang'ing
ex·change'·
a·bil'i·ty
ex·change'a·ble
ex·cheq'uer

ex·cis'a·ble
ex'cise
ex·cise'
· ·cised' ·cis'ing
ex·ci'sion
ex·cit'a·bil'i·ty
ex·cit'a·ble
ex·cit'a·bly
ex·ci·ta'tion
ex·cite'
· ·cit'ed ·cit'ing
ex·cite'ment
ex·claim'
ex·cla·ma'tion
ex·clam'a·to'ry
ex'clave
ex·clud'a·ble
ex·clude'
· ·clud'ed
· ·clud'ing
ex·clu'sion
ex·clu'sive
ex·clu·siv'i·ty
ex'com·mu'ni·
cate'
· ·cat'ed ·cat'ing
ex·co'ri·ate'
· ·at'ed ·at'ing
ex·co'ri·a'tion
ex'cre·ment
ex·cres'cence
ex·crete'
· ·cret'ed
· ·cret'ing
ex·cre'tion
ex'cre·to'ry
ex·cru'ci·ate'
· ·at'ed ·at'ing
ex'cul·pate'
· ·pat'ed ·pat'ing
ex'cul·pa'tion
ex·cur'sion
ex·cus'a·ble
ex·cus'a·bly
ex·cuse'
· ·cused' ·cus'ing
ex'e·cra·ble
ex'e·crate'
· ·crat'ed
· ·crat'ing
ex'e·cra'tion
ex'e·cute'
· ·cut'ed ·cut'ing
ex'e·cu'tion
ex'e·cu'tion·er
ex·ec'u·tive
ex·ec'u·tor
ex'e·ge'sis
ex·em'plar
ex·em'pla'ri·ly
ex·em'pla·ri·ness
ex·em'pla·ry
ex·em'pli·fi·
ca'tion
ex·em'pli·fy'
· ·fied' ·fy'ing
ex·empt'
ex·emp'tion

ex'er·cis'a·ble
ex'er·cise'
· ·cised' ·cis'ing
(use; see exorcise)
ex·ert'
ex·er'tion
ex'e·unt
ex·ha·la'tion
ex·hale'
· ·haled' ·hal'ing
ex·haust'
ex·haust'i·ble
ex·haus'tion
ex·haus'tive
ex·hib'it
ex·hi·bi'tion
ex·hi·bi'tion·ism
ex·hib'i·tor
ex·hil'a·rant
ex·hil'a·rate'
· ·rat'ed ·rat'ing
ex·hil'a·ra'tion
ex·hort'
ex·hor·ta'tion
ex·hu·ma'tion
ex·hume'
· ·humed'
· ·hum'ing
ex'i·gen·cy
· ·cies
ex'i·gent
ex'ile
ex·ist'
ex·ist'ence
ex·ist'ent
ex·is·ten'tial
ex·is·ten'tial·ism
ex'it
ex'o·dus
ex' of·fi'ci·o'
ex·og'a·my
ex·on'er·ate'
· ·at'ed ·at'ing
ex·on'er·a'tion
ex'o·ra·ble
ex·or'bi·tance
ex·or'bi·tant
ex'or·cise' or
· ·cize'
· ·cised' or ·cized'
· ·cis'ing or ·ciz'ing
(expel; see
exercise)
ex'or·cism
ex'o·ter'ic
ex·ot'ic
ex·ot'i·ca
ex·ot'i·cal·ly
ex·pand'
ex·panse'
ex·pan'si·ble
ex·pan'sion
ex·pan'sive
ex·pa'ti·ate'
· ·at'ed ·at'ing
ex·pa'ti·a'tion
ex·pa'tri·ate'
· ·at'ed ·at'ing

ex·pa'tri·a'tion
ex·pect'
ex·pect'an·cy
ex·pect'ant
ex·pec·ta'tion
ex·pec'to·rant
ex·pec'to·rate'
· ·rat'ed ·rat'ing
ex·pec'to·ra'tion
ex·pe'di·ence
ex·pe'di·en·cy
· ·cies
ex·pe'di·ent
ex'pe·dite'
· ·dit'ed ·dit'ing
ex'pe·dit'er
ex·pe·di'tion
ex·pe·di'tion·ar'y
ex·pe·di'tious
ex·pel'
· ·pelled' ·pel'ling
ex·pel'la·ble
ex·pel·lee'
ex·pend'
ex·pend·a·bil'i·ty
ex·pend'a·ble
ex·pend'i·ture
ex·pense'
ex·pen'sive
ex·pen'sive·ly
ex·pe'ri·ence
· ·enced ·enc·ing
ex·pe·ri·en'tial
ex·per'i·ment
ex·per'i·men'tal
ex·per'i·men·
ta'tion
ex'pert
ex·pert·ise'
ex'pi·a·ble
ex'pi·ate'
· ·at'ed ·at'ing
ex'pi·a'tion
ex'pi·a'tor
ex'pi·ra'tion
ex·pir'a·to'ry
ex·pire'
· ·pired' ·pir'ing
ex·plain'a·ble
ex'pla·na'tion
ex·plan'a·to'ry
ex'ple·tive
ex'pli·ca·ble
ex'pli·cate'
· ·cat'ed ·cat'ing
ex'pli·ca'tion
ex·plic'it
ex·plod'a·ble
ex·plode'
· ·plod'ed
· ·plod'ing
ex'ploit
ex'ploi·ta'tion
ex'plo·ra'tion
ex·plor'a·to'ry
ex·plore'
· ·plored'
· ·plor'ing

ex·plor'er
ex·plo'sion
ex·plo'sive
ex·po'nent
ex·po·nen'tial
ex·port'
ex'por·ta'tion
ex·pose'
 ·posed' ·pos'ing
ex'po·sé'
ex·po·si'tion
ex·pos'i·tor
ex·pos'i·to·ry
ex post fac'to
ex·pos'tu·late'
 ·lat'ed ·lat'ing
ex·pos'tu·la'tion
ex·pos'tu·la'tor
ex·po'sure
ex·pound'
ex·press'
ex·press'age
ex·press'i·ble
ex·pres'sion
ex·pres'sion·ism
ex·pres'sion·
 is'tic
ex·pres'sive
ex·press'man
ex·press'way
ex·pro'pri·ate'
 ·at'ed ·at'ing
ex·pro'pri·a'tion
ex·pul'sion
ex·punge'
 ·punged'
 ·pung'ing
ex'pur·gate'
 ·gat'ed ·gat'ing
ex'pur·ga'tion
ex'qui·site
ex'tant
 (existing; see extent)
ex·tem'po·ra'ne·ous
ex·tem'po·re
ex·tem'po·rize'
 ·rized' ·riz'ing
ex·tend'
ex·ten'si·ble
ex·ten'sion
ex·ten'sive
ex·tent'
 (scope; see extant)
ex·ten'u·ate'
 ·at'ed ·at'ing
ex·ten'u·a'tion
ex·te'ri·or
ex·ter'mi·nate'
 ·nat'ed ·nat'ing
ex·ter'mi·na'tion
ex·ter'mi·na'tor
ex·ter'nal
ex·ter'nal·ize'
 ·ized' ·iz'ing
ex·tinct'
ex·tinc'tion

ex·tin'guish
ex'tir·pate'
 ·pat'ed ·pat'ing
ex'tir·pa'tion
ex·tol' or ·toll'
 ·tolled' ·tol'ling
ex·tort'
ex·tor'tion
ex·tor'tion·ate
ex·tor'tion·er
ex·tor'tion·ist
ex'tra
ex·tract'
ex·tract'a·ble
 or ·i·ble
ex·trac'tion
ex·trac'tor
ex'tra·cur·ric'u·lar
ex'tra·dit'a·ble
ex'tra·dite'
 ·dit'ed ·dit'ing
ex'tra·di'tion
ex'tra·le'gal
ex'tra·mar'i·tal
ex'tra·mu'ral
ex·tra'ne·ous
ex·traor'di·nar'i·ly
ex·traor'di·nar'y
ex·trap'o·late'
 ·lat'ed ·lat'ing
ex'tra·sen'so·ry
ex'tra·ter·ri·to'ri·al
ex·trav'a·gance
ex·trav'a·gant
ex·trav'a·gan'za
ex'tra·ve·hic'u·lar
ex·treme'
ex·treme'ly
ex·trem'ism
ex·trem'ist
ex·trem'i·ty
 ·ties
ex'tri·cate'
 ·cat'ed ·cat'ing
ex'tri·ca'tion
ex·trin'sic
ex·trin'si·cal·ly
ex'tro·ver'sion
ex'tro·vert'
ex·trude'
 ·trud'ed
 ·trud'ing
ex·tru'sion
ex·u'ber·ance
ex·u'ber·ant
ex'u·da'tion
ex·ude'
 ·ud'ed ·ud'ing
ex·ult'
ex·ult'ant
ex'ul·ta'tion
ex'urb'
ex·ur'ban·ite'
ex·ur'bi·a

eye
eyed eye'ing
 or ey'ing
eye'ball'
eye'brow'
eye'-catch'er
eye'cup'
eye'ful'
eye'glass'
eye'hole'
eye'lash'
eye'let
 (hole; see islet)
eye'lid'
eye liner
eye'-o'pen·er
eye'piece'
eye shadow
eye'shot'
eye'sight'
eye'sore'
eye'strain'
eye'tooth'
eye'wash'
eye'wink'
eye'wit'ness

F

fa'ble
 ·bled ·bling
fab'ric
fab'ri·cate'
 ·cat'ed ·cat'ing
fab'ri·ca'tion
fab'ri·ca'tor
Fab'ri·koid'
fab'u·lous
fa·cade' or ·cade'
face
 faced fac'ing
face'plate'
face'-sav'ing
fac'et
fa·ce'tious
fa'cial
fac'ile
fa·cil'i·tate'
 ·tat'ed ·tat'ing
fa·cil'i·ta'tion
fa·cil'i·ty
 ·ties
fac·sim'i·le
 ·led ·le·ing
fac'tion
fac'tious
fac·ti'tious
 (artificial; see fictitious)
fac'tor
fac·to'ri·al
fac'to·ry
 ·ries
fac·to'tum
fac'tu·al
fac'tu·al·ly

fac'ul·ty
 ·ties
fad'dish
fad'dism
fade
 fad'ed fad'ing
fade'-in'
fade'-out'
fag
 fagged
 fag'ging
fag'ot·ing
Fahr'en·heit'
fail'-safe'
fail'ure
faint
 (weak; see feint)
faint'heart'ed
fair'ground'
fair'-haired'
fair'ly
fair'-mind·ed
fair'-spo'ken
fair'-trade'
fair'way'
fair'-weath'er
fair'y
 ·ies
fair'y·land'
faith'ful
faith'ful·ly
faith'less
fake
 faked fak'ing
fak'er
 (fraud)
fa·kir'
 (Moslem beggar)
fal'cate
fal'con
fal'con·ry
fall
 fell fall'en
fall'ing
fal·la'cious
fal'la·cy
 ·cies
fal·li·bil'i·ty
fal'li·ble
fal'li·bly
fall'ing-out'
fall'off'
fall'out'
fal'low
false
 fals'er fals'est
false'heart'ed
false'hood'
fal·set'to
fal'si·fi·ca'tion
fal'si·fi'er
fal'si·fy'
 ·fied' ·fy'ing
fal'si·ty
 ·ties
fal'ter
fa·mil'ial
fa·mil'iar

fa·mil'i·ar'i·ty
 ·ties
fa·mil'iar·i·
 za'tion
fa·mil'iar·ize'
 ·ized' ·iz'ing
fam'i·ly
 ·lies
fam'ine
fam'ish
fa'mous
fan
 fanned fan'ning
fa·nat'ic
fa·nat'i·cal·ly
fa·nat'i·cism
fan'ci·ful
fan'cy
 ·cies
 ·ci·er ·ci·est
 ·cied ·cy·ing
fan'cy-free'
fan'cy·work'
fan'fare'
fan'light'
fan'tail'
fan·ta'si·a
fan'ta·size'
 ·sized' ·siz'ing
fan·tas'tic
fan·tas'ti·cal·ly
fan'ta·sy
 ·sies
 ·sied ·sy·ing
far
far'ther
far'thest
far'ad
far'a·day'
far'a·way'
farce
 farced farc'ing
far'ci·cal
far'ci·cal·ly
fare
 fared far'ing
fare'well'
far'fetched'
far'-flung'
fa·ri'na
far·i·na'ceous
farm'hand'
farm'house'
farm'stead'
farm'yard'
far'o
far'-off'
far'-out'
far'-reach'ing
far'row
far'see'ing
far'sight'ed
far'ther
far'thing
fas'ces
fas'ci·cle
fas'ci·nate'
 ·nat'ed ·nat'ing

fas'ci·na'tion
fas'ci·na'tor
fas'cism
fas'cist
fash'ion
fash'ion·a·ble
fash'ion·a·bly
fast'back'
fas'ten
fas'ten·er
fas'ten·ing
fas·tid'i·ous
fat
 fat'ter fat'test
 fat'ted fat'ting
fa'tal
fa'tal·ism
fa'tal·ist
fa'tal·is'tic
fa·tal'i·ty
 ·ties
fa'tal·ly
fate'ful
fa'ther·hood'
fa'ther-in-law'
fa'thers-
 in-law'
fa'ther·land'
fa'ther·less
fa'ther·li·ness
fa'ther·ly
fath'om
fath'om·a·ble
fath'om·less
fat'i·ga·ble
fa·tigue'
 ·tigued'
 ·tigu'ing
fat'-sol'u·ble
fat'ten
fat'ti·ness
fat'ty
 ·ti·er ·ti·est
fa·tu'i·ty
 ·ties
fat'u·ous
fat'-wit'ted
fau'cet
fault'find'ing
fault'i·ness
fault'less
fault'y
 ·i·er ·i·est
faun
 (deity; see fawn)
fau'na
 ·nas or ·nae
faux' pas'
faux' pas'
fa'vor·a·ble
fa'vor·a·bly
fa'vored
fa'vor·ite
fa'vor·it·ism
fawn
 (deer; act ser-
 vilely; see faun)

faze
fazed faz'ing
(disturb; see
phase)
fe'al·ty
fear'ful
fear'ful·ly
fear'less
fear'some
fea·si·bil'i·ty
fea'si·ble
fea'si·bly
feast
feat
(deed; see feet)
feath'er·bed'
feath'er·
bed'ding
feath'er·
brain'
feath'ered
feath'er·edge'
feath'er·i·ness
feath'er·stitch'
feath'er·weight'
feath'er·y
fea'ture
·tured ·tur·ing
fea'ture-length'
feb'ri·fuge'
fe'brile
Feb'ru·ar'y
fe'cal
fe'ces
feck'less
fe'cund
fe'cun·date'
·dat'ed ·dat'ing
fe·cun'di·ty
fed'er·al
fed'er·al·ism
fed'er·al·i·
za'tion
fed'er·al·ize'
·ized' ·iz'ing
fed'er·ate'
·at'ed ·at'ing
fed'er·a'tion
fe·do'ra
fee'ble
·bler ·blest
fee'ble·mind'ed
feed
fed feed'ing
feed'back'
feel
felt feel'ing
feel'-split'ting
feet
(pl. of foot;
see feat)
feign
feint
(pretense; see
faint)
fe·lic'i·tate'
·tat'ed ·tat'ing
fe·lic'i·ta'tion

fe·lic'i·tous
fe·lic'i·ty
·ties
fe'line
fel'low·ship'
fel'on
fe·lo'ni·ous
fel'o·ny
·nies
fe·luc'ca
fe'male
fem'i·nine
fem'i·nin'i·ty
fem'i·nism
fem'i·nize'
·nized' ·niz'ing
femme fa·tale'
femmes fa·tales'
fence
fenced fenc'ing
fend'er
fen'es·tra'tion
fen'nel
fer'ment
fer'men·ta'tion
fern
fe·ro'cious
fe·roc'i·ty
fer'ret
fer'ri·age
Fer'ris wheel
fer'rule
(metal ring;
see ferule)
fer'ry
·ries
·ried ·ry·ing
fer'ry·boat'
fer'tile
fer·til'i·ty
fer'til·iz'a·ble
fer·til·i·za'tion
fer'til·ize'
·ized' ·iz'ing
fer'til·iz'er
fer'ule
(stick; see
ferrule)
fer'vent
fer'vid
fer'vor
fes'cue
fes'tal
fes'ter
fes'ti·val
fes'tive
fes·tiv'i·ty
·ties
fes·toon'
fe'tal
fetch'ing
fete or fête
fet'ed or fêt'ed
fet'ing or fêt'ing
fet'i·cide'
fet'id
fet'ish
fet'ish·ism

fet'lock'
fet'ter
fet'tle
fet'tuc·ci'ne
fe'tus
·tus·es
feu'dal
feu'dal·ism
feu'dal·is'tic
fe'ver·ish
fez
fez'zes
fi'an·cé' masc.
fi'an·cée' fem.
fi·as'co
·coes or ·cos
fi'at
fib
fibbed fib'bing
fib'ber
fi'ber or ·bre
fi'ber·board'
Fi'ber·glas'
fi'bril·la'tion
fi'broid
fi'brous
fib'u·la
·lae or ·las
fick'le
fic'tion·al·ize'
·ized' ·iz'ing
fic·ti'tious
(imaginary; see
factitious)
fid'dle
·dled ·dling
fi·del'i·ty
·ties
fidg'et
fidg'et·i·ness
fidg'et·y
fi·du'ci·ar'y
·ies
field'er
field'-strip'
field'-test'
field'work'
fiend'ish
fierce
fierc'er
fierc'est
fierce'ly
fi'er·i·ness
fi'er·y
·i·er ·i·est
fi·es'ta
fif'teen'
fif'ti·eth
fif'ty
·ties
fight
fought
fight'ing
fig'ment
fig'u·ra'tion
fig'u·ra·tive
fig'ure
·ured ·ur·ing

fig'ure·head'
fig'u·rine'
fil'a·ment
fi'lar
fil'bert
file
filed fil'ing
fi·let' mi·gnon'
fil'i·al
fil'i·a'tion
fil'i·bus'ter
fil'i·gree'
·greed'
·gree'ing
fill'ings
Fil'i·pi'no
·nos
fil'let
fill'-in'
fill'ing
fil'lip
fil'ly
·lies
film'strip'
film'y
·i·er ·i·est
fil'ter
(strainer; see
philter)
fil'ter·a·ble
filth'i·ly
filth'i·ness
filth'y
·i·er ·i·est
fil'trate
·trat·ed ·trat·ing
fin'a·ble
fi·na'gle
·gled ·gling
fi·na'le
fi'nal·ist
fi·nal'i·ty
fi'nal·ize'
·ized' ·iz'ing
fi'nal·ly
fi·nance'
·nanced'
·nanc'ing
fi·nan'cial
fi·nan'cial·ly
fin'an·cier'
find
found find'ing
find'er
fine
fin'er fin'est
fined fin'ing
fine'-cut'
fine'-drawn'
fine'-grained'
fine'ly
fine'ness
fin'er·y
·ies
fine'spun'
fi·nesse'
·nessed'
·ness'ing

fine'-toothed'
fin'ger·board'
fin'gered
fin'ger·nail'
fin'ger·print'
finger tip
fin'i·al
fin'i·cal
fin'ick·i·ness
fin'ick·y
fi'nis
fin'ish
fin'ished
fi'nite
fin'nan had'die
fiord
fir
(tree; see fur)
fire
fired fir'ing
fire'arm'
fire'ball'
fire'boat'
fire'bomb'
fire'box'
fire'brand'
fire'break'
fire'brick'
fire'bug'
fire'clay'
fire'crack'er
fire'-cure'
fire'damp'
fire'dog'
fire'-eat'er
fire escape
fire'fly'
·flies'
fire'man
fire'place'
fire'plug'
fire'pow'er
fire'proof'
fire'side'
fire'trap'
fire'wa'ter
fire'wood'
fire'works'
fir'kin
fir'ma·ment
firm'ly
first'born'
first'-class'
first'hand'
first'ly
first'-rate'
firth
fis'cal
fis'cal·ly
fish'bowl'
fish'er·man
fish'er·y
·ies
fish'hook'
fish'i·ness
fish'mon'ger
fish'plate'
fish'pond'

fish'tail'
fish'wife'
fish'y
·i·er ·i·est
fis'sion
fis'sion·a·ble
fis'sure
·sured ·sur·ing
fis'ti·cuffs'
fis'tu·lous
fit
fit'ted fit'ting
fit'ter fit'test
fit'ful
fit'ful·ly
fit'ness
five'fold'
fix'ate
·at·ed ·at·ing
fix·a'tion
fix'a·tive
fixed
fix'ed·ly
fix'ture
fiz'zle
·zled ·zling
fjord
flab'ber·gast'
flab'bi·ness
flab'by
·bi·er ·bi·est
flac'cid
flac·cid'i·ty
fla·con'
flag
flagged
flag'ging
flag'el·lant
flag'el·late'
·lat'ed ·lat'ing
flag'el·la'tion
fla·gel'lum
·la or ·lums
flag'eo·let'
flag'on
flag'pole'
fla'gran·cy
fla'grant
flag'ship'
flag'stone'
flag'-wav'ing
flail
flair
(knack; see flare)
flake
flaked flak'ing
flak'i·ness
flak'y
·i·er ·i·est
flam·bé'
flam'beau
·beaux or ·beaus
flam·boy'ance
flam·boy'ant
flame
flamed flam'ing
fla·men'co
·cos

flame'out'
flame'proof'
fla·min'go
 ·gos *or* ·goes
flam'ma·bil'i·ty
flam'ma·ble
flange
 flanged
 flang'ing
flank
flan'nel
flan'nel·ette'
flan'nel-mouthed'
flap
 flapped
 flap'ping
flap'jack'
flap'per
flare
 flared flar'ing
 (*blaze;* see flair)
flare'-up'
flash'back'
flash'bulb'
flash'card'
flash'cube'
flash'i·ly
flash'i·ness
flash'light'
flash'y
 ·i·er ·i·est
flat
 flat'ter flat'test
 flat'ted flat'ting
flat'boat'
flat'car'
flat'fish'
flat'-foot'ed
flat'i'ron
flat'ten
flat'ter
flat'ter·y
flat'u·lent
flat'ware'
flat'work'
flaunt
flau'tist
fla'vor·ful
fla'vor·ing
fla'vor·less
flaw'less
flax'en
flax'seed'
flea'-bit'ten
fledg'ling
flee
 fled flee'ing
fleece
 fleeced fleec'ing
fleec'i·ness
fleec'y
 ·i·er ·i·est
fleet'ing
flesh'-col'ored
flesh'i·ness
flesh'pots'
flesh'y
 ·i·er ·i·est

fleur'-de-lis'
fleurs'-de-lis'
flex'i·bil'i·ty
flex'i·ble
flex'i·bly
flick'er
flied
 (*only in baseball*)
fli'er *or* fly'er
flight'i·ness
flight'less
flight'y
 ·i·er ·i·est
flim'si·ly
flim'si·ness
flim'sy
 ·si·er ·si·est
flinch'ing·ly
fling
 flung fling'ing
flint'lock'
flint'y
 ·i·er ·i·est
flip
 flipped flip'ping
flip'pan·cy
 ·cies
flip'pant
flip'per
flir·ta'tion
flir·ta'tious
flit
 flit'ted flit'ting
float'er
float'ing
floc'cu·late'
 ·lat'ed ·lat'ing
floc'cu·lent
floe
 (*ice;* see flow)
flog
 flogged
 flog'ging
flood'gate'
flood'light'
 ·light'ed *or* ·lit'
 ·light'ing
floor'ing
floor'walk'er
flop
 flopped
 flop'ping
flo'ra
 ·ras *or* ·rae
flo'ral
flo·res'cence
 (*blooming;* see
 fluorescence)
flo·res'cent
flo'ret
flo'ri·cul'ture
flor'id
Flor'i·da
flo·rid'i·ty
flor'in
flo'rist
floss'y
 ·i·er ·i·est

flo·ta'tion
flo·til'la
flot'sam
flounce
 flounced
 flounc'ing
floun'der
flour'ish
flout
flow
 (*glide;* see floe)
flow'ered
flow'er·i·ness
flow'er·pot'
flow'er·y
 ·i·er ·i·est
flu
 (*influenza*)
fluc'tu·ate'
 ·at'ed ·at'ing
flue
 (*pipe*)
flu'en·cy
flu'ent
fluff'i·ness
fluff'y
 ·fi·er ·fi·est
flu'id
flu·id'i·ty
flun'ky
 ·kies
flu'o·resce'
 ·resced'
 ·resc'ing
flu'o·res'cence
 (*light;* see
 florescence)
flu'o·res'cent
fluor'i·date'
 ·dat'ed ·dat'ing
fluor'i·da'tion
fluor'i·nate'
 ·nat'ed ·nat'ing
fluor'o·scope'
flu'o·ros'co·py
flur'ry
 ·ries
 ·ried ·ry·ing
flus'ter
flute
 flut'ed flut'ing
flut'ist
flut'ter
flu'vi·al
fly
 flies
 flew flown
fly'ing
fly'a·ble
fly'a·way'
fly'-by-night'
fly'catch'er
fly'leaf'
 ·leaves'
fly'pa'per
fly'speck'
fly'trap'
fly'weight'

fly'wheel'
foam'i·ness
foam'y
 ·i·er ·i·est
fo'cal
fo'cal·ize'
 ·ized' ·iz'ing
fo'cus
 ·cus·es *or* ·ci
 ·cused *or* ·cussed
 ·cus·ing *or*
 ·cus·sing
fod'der
fog
 fogged fog'ging
fog'bound'
fog'gi·ly
fog'gi·ness
fog'gy
 ·gi·er ·gi·est
fog'horn'
fo'gy *or* fo'gey
 ·gies *or* ·geys
foi'ble
foist
fold'a·way'
fold'er
fo'li·age
fo'li·ate'
 ·at'ed ·at'ing
fo'li·a'tion
fo'li·o'
 ·os', ·oed' ·o'ing
folk'lore'
folk'way'
fol'li·cle
fol'low·er
fol'low-through'
fol'low-up'
fol'ly
 ·lies
fo·ment'
fo'men·ta'tion
fon'dant
fon'dle
 ·dled ·dling
fond'ness
fon·due'
food'stuff'
fool'har'di·ness
fool'har'dy
fool'ish·ness
fool'proof'
fools'cap'
foot
 feet
foot'age
foot'ball'
foot'bridge'
foot'-can'dle
foot'fall'
foot'hold'
foot'ing
foot'lights'
foot'lock'er
foot'loose'
foot'note'
foot'path'

foot'-pound'
foot'print'
foot'race'
foot'rest'
foot'sore'
foot'step'
foot'stool'
foot'-ton'
foot'wear'
foot'work'
fop'pish
for'age
for'ay
for·bear'
 ·bore' ·borne'
 ·bear'ing
 (*abstain;* see
 forebear)
for·bear'ance
for·bid'
 ·bade' *or* ·bad'
 ·bid'den
 ·bid'ding
force
 forced forc'ing
force'ful
for'ceps
 ·ceps
for'ci·ble
for'ci·bly
fore'arm'
fore'bear'
 (*ancestor;* see
 forbear)
fore·bode'
 ·bod'ed ·bod'ing
fore'cast'
 ·cast' *or* ·cast'ed
 ·cast'ing
fore'cas'tle
fore·close'
fore·clo'sure
fore·doom'
fore'fa'ther
fore'fin'ger
fore'foot'
fore·go'
 ·went' ·gone'
 ·go'ing
 (*precede;* see
 forgo)
fore·go'ing
fore'ground'
fore'hand'
fore·hand'ed
fore'head
for'eign
for'eign-born'
for'eign·er
fore'knowl'edge
fore'leg'
fore'lock'
fore'man
fore'most'
fore'named'
fore'noon'
fo·ren'sic
fo·ren'si·cal·ly

fore'or·dain'
fore'paw'
fore'play'
fore'quar'ter
fore'run'ner
fore'sail'
fore·see'
 ·saw' ·seen'
 ·see'ing
fore·see'a·ble
fore·se'er
fore·shad'ow
fore·short'en
fore·show'
 ·showed',
 ·shown' *or*
 ·showed',
 ·show'ing
fore'sight'
fore'skin'
for'est
fore·stall'
for'est·a'tion
for'est·er
for'est·ry
fore'taste'
fore·tell'
 ·told' ·tell'ing
fore'thought'
for·ev'er
fore·warn'
fore'word'
 (*preface;* see
 forward)
for'feit
for'fei·ture
forge
 forged forg'ing
forg'er
for'ger·y
 ·ies
for·get'
 ·got', ·got'ten
 or ·got',
 ·get'ting
for·get'ful
for·get'-me-not'
for·get'ta·ble
for·giv'a·ble
for·give'
 ·gave' ·giv'en
 ·giv'ing
for·give'ness
for·go' *or* fore·
 ·went' ·gone'
 ·go'ing
 (*do without;*
 see forego)
forked
fork'lift'
for·lorn'
for'mal
form·al'de·hyde'
for·mal'i·ty
 ·ties
for'mal·i·za'tion
for'mal·ize'
 ·ized' ·iz'ing

for'mal·ly
for'mat
for·ma'tion
form'a·tive
for'mer
For·mi'ca
for'mi·da·ble
for'mi·da·bly
form'less
for'mu·la
 ·las or ·lae'
for'mu·late'
 ·lat'ed ·lat'ing
for'mu·la'tion
for'ni·cate'
 ·cat'ed ·cat'ing
for'ni·ca'tion
for'ni·ca'tor
for·sake'
 ·sook' ·sak'en
 ·sak'ing
for·swear'
 ·swore' ·sworn'
 ·swear'ing
for·syth'i·a
fort
(fortified place)
forte
(special skill)
forth'com'ing
forth'right'
forth'with'
for'ti·eth
for'ti·fi·ca'tion
for'ti·fi'er
for'ti·fy'
 ·fied' ·fy'ing
for'ti·tude'
for'tress
for·tu'i·tous
for·tu'i·ty
 ·ties
for'tu·nate
for'tune
for'tune·tell'er
for'ty
 ·ties
fo'rum
 ·rums or ·ra
for'ward
(to the front;
see foreword)
fos'sil
fos'ter
foul
(filthy; see fowl)
fou·lard'
foul'mouthed'
foun·da'tion
foun'der v.
found'er n.
found'ling
found'ry
 ·ries
foun'tain
foun'tain·head'
four'-flush'er
four'fold'

four'-foot'ed
Four'-H' club or
4'-H' club
four'-in-hand'
four'-post'er
four'score'
four'some
four'square'
four'-star'
four'teen'
fourth
fourth'-class'
four'-way'
fowl
(bird; see foul)
fox'hole'
fox'hound'
fox'i·ly
fox'i·ness
fox'y
 ·i·er ·i·est
foy'er
fra'cus
frac'tion
frac'tious
frac'ture
 ·tured ·tur·ing
frag'ile
fra·gil'i·ty
frag'ment
frag·men'tal·ly
frag'men·tar'y
fra'grance
fra'grant
frail'ty
 ·ties
frame
framed
fram'ing
frame'-up'
frame'work'
franc
(coin; see frank)
fran'chise
 ·chised ·chis·ing
fran'gi·bil'i·ty
fran'gi·ble
frank
(free; see franc)
frank'furt·er
frank'in·cense'
fran'tic
fran'ti·cal·ly
frap·pé'
fra·ter'nal
fra·ter'nal·ly
fra·ter'ni·ty
 ·ties
frat'er·ni·za'tion
frat'er·nize'
 ·nized' ·niz'ing
frat'ri·cide'
fraud'u·lence
fraud'u·lent
fraught
freak'ish
freck'le
 ·led ·ling

free
fre'er fre'est
freed free'ing
free'bie or ·by
 ·bies
free'born'
freed'man
free'dom
free'-for-all'
free'-form'
free'hand'
free'-lance'
free'load'er
free'man
Free'ma'son
free'-spo'ken
free'-stand'ing
free'stone'
free'think'er
free'way'
free'wheel'ing
freez'a·ble
freeze
froze froz'en
freez'ing
(become ice; see
frieze)
freeze'-dry'
 -dried' -dry'ing
freez'er
freight'age
freight'er
French cuff
French doors
French fry
 French fries
French toast
fre·net'ic
fre·net'i·cal·ly
fren'zy
 ·zies
 ·zied ·zy·ing
fre'quen·cy
 ·cies
fre'quent
fres'co
 ·coes or ·cos
fresh'en
fresh'et
fresh'man
fresh'wa'ter
fret
fret'ted
fret'ting
fret'ful
fret'ful·ly
fret'work'
Freud'i·an
fri'a·bil'i·ty
fri'a·ble
fri'ar
fric'as·see'
 ·seed' ·see'ing
fric'tion
Fri'day
friend'li·ness
friend'ly
 ·li·er ·li·est

friend'ship
frieze
(in architecture;
see freeze)
frig'ate
fright'ened
fright'ful
frig'id
fri·gid'i·ty
frill'y
 ·i·er ·i·est
fringe
fringed
fring'ing
frip'per·y
 ·ies
Fris'bee
fri·sé'
frisk'i·ness
frisk'y
 ·i·er ·i·est
frit'ter
fri·vol'i·ty
 ·ties
friv'o·lous
friz'zi·ness
frog'man'
frol'ic
 ·icked ·ick·ing
frol'ick·er
frol'ic·some
front'age
fron'tal
fron·tier'
fron·tiers'man
fron'tis·piece'
front'let
frost'bite'
 ·bit' ·bit'ten
 ·bit'ing
frost'i·ly
frost'i·ness
frost'ing
frost'y
 ·i·er ·i·est
froth'i·ly
froth'i·ness
froth'y
 ·i·er ·i·est
fro'ward
frown
frow'zi·ness
frow'zy
 ·zi·er ·zi·est
fro'zen
fruc'ti·fy'
 ·fied' ·fy'ing
fru'gal
fru·gal'i·ty
fru'gal·ly
fruit'cake'
fruit'ful
fruit'i·ness
fru·i'tion
fruit'less
fruit'wood'
fruit'y
 ·i·er ·i·est

frump'ish
frus'trate
 ·trat·ed ·trat·ing
frus·tra'tion
frus'tum
 ·tums or ·ta
fry
fried fry'ing
fry'er or fri'er
f'-stop'
fuch'sia
fudge
fudged
fudg'ing
fu'el
 ·eled or ·elled
 ·el·ing or ·el·ling
fuel cell
fu'gi·tive
fugue
ful'crum
 ·crums or ·cra
ful·fill' or ·fil'
 ·filled' ·fill'ing
ful·fill'ment
 or ·fil'ment
full'back'
full'-blood'ed
full'-blown'
full'-bod'ied
full'-dress'
full'er's earth
full'-faced'
full'-fash'ioned
full'-fledged'
full'-length'
full'-scale'
full'-time'
full'y
ful'mi·nate'
 ·nat'ed ·nat'ing
ful'some
fum'ble
 ·bled ·bling
fume
fumed fum'ing
fu'mi·gant
fu'mi·gate'
 ·gat'ed ·gat'ing
fu'mi·ga'tion
fu'mi·ga'tor
func'tion·al
func'tion·al·ly
func'tion·ar'y
 ·ar'ies
fun'da·men'tal
fun'da·men'tal·
ism
fun'da·men'tal·ly
fund'-rais'er
fu'ner·al
fu·ne're·al
fun'gi·cid'al
fun'gi·cide'
fun'gous adj.
fun'gus n.
 ·gi or ·gus·es
fu·nic'u·lar

fun'nel
 ·neled or ·nelled
 ·nel·ing or
 ·nel·ling
fun'ni·ness
fun'ny
 ·ni·er ·ni·est
fur
furred fur'ring
(hair; see fir)
fur'be·low'
fur'bish
fu'ri·ous
fur'long
fur'lough
fur'nace
fur'nish·ings
fur'ni·ture
fu'ror
fur'ri·er
fur'ri·ness
fur'row
fur'ry
 ·ri·er ·ri·est
fur'ther
fur'ther·ance
fur'ther·more'
fur'ther·most'
fur'thest
fur'tive
fu'ry
 ·ries
fuse
fused fus'ing
fu'se·lage'
fu'si·bil'i·ty
fu'si·ble
fu'sil·lade'
 ·lad'ed ·lad'ing
fu'sion
fuss'i·ness
fuss'y
 ·i·er ·i·est
fus'tian
fust'y
 ·i·er ·i·est
fu'tile
fu'tile·ly
fu·til'i·ty
fu'ture
fu·tu'ri·ty

G

gab'ar·dine'
ga'ble
gad'a·bout'
gadg'et
gag
gagged
gag'ging

gage
(*pledge;* see
gauge)
gag'gle
gag'man'
gai'e·ty
gai'ly
gain'er
gain'ful
gain'ful·ly
gain'li·ness
gain'ly
·li·er ·li·est
gain'say'
·said' ·say'ing
gait
(*way of walking;*
see gate)
gai'ter
ga'la
Gal'a·had'
gal'ax·y
·ies
gal'lant
gal'lant·ry
·ries
gal'le·on
gal'ler·y
·ies
·ied ·y·ing
gal'ley
·leys
gall'ing
gal'li·vant'
gal'lon
gal'lop
gal'lows
·lows·es *or* ·lows
gall'stone'
ga·lore'
ga·losh'
or ·loshe'
ga·lumph'
gal·van'ic
gal'va·nism
gal'va·ni·za'tion
gal'va·nize'
·nized' ·niz'ing
gal'va·nom'e·ter
gam'bit
gam'ble
·bled ·bling
(*risk;* see
gambol)
gam'bler
gam'bol
·boled *or* ·bolled
·bol·ing *or*
·bol·ling
(*frolic;* see
gamble)
gam'brel
game'cock'
game'keep'er
games'man·ship'
gam'in
gam'i·ness
gam'ma

gam'ut
gam'y
·i·er ·i·est
gan'der
Gan'dhi·ism
ga'nef *or* ·nof
gang'land'
gan'gling
gan'gli·on
·gli·a *or* ·gli·ons
gang'plank'
gan'grene
gan'gre·nous
gang'ster
gang'way'
gant'let
gan'try
·tries
gap
gapped
gap'ping
gape
gaped gap'ing
ga·rage'
·raged' ·rag'ing
gar'bage
gar'ble
·bled ·bling
gar·çon'
·çons'
gar'den·er
gar·de'ni·a
Gar·gan'tu·an *or*
gar·gan'tu·an
gar'gle
·gled ·gling
gar'goyle
gar'ish
gar'land
gar'lic
gar'lick·y
gar'ment
gar'ner
gar'net
gar'nish
gar'nish·ee'
·eed' ·ee'ing
gar'nish·ment
gar'ret
gar'ri·son
gar·rote'
·rot'ed *or*
·rot'ted
·rot'ing *or*
·rot'ting
gar·ru'li·ty
gar'ru·lous
gar'ter
gas
gassed
gas'sing
gas'e·ous
gas'ket
gas'light'
gas'o·line' *or*
·lene'
gas'sy
·si·er ·si·est

gas'tric
gas'tro·nome'
gas·tro·nom'i·cal
gas·tron'o·my
gate
(*door;* see gait)
gate'way'
gath'er·ing
gauche
(*lacking grace;*
see gouache)
gau'che·rie'
gaud'i·ly
gaud'i·ness
gaud'y
·i·er ·i·est
gauge
gauged
gaug'ing
(*measure;* see
gage)
gauge'a·ble
gaunt
gaunt'let
gauze
gauz'y
·i·er ·i·est
gav'el
gawk'i·ness
gawk'y
·i·er ·i·est
gay'ly
gaze
gazed gaz'ing
ga·ze'bo
·bos *or* ·boes
ga·zelle'
ga·zette'
gaz'et·teer'
gear'box'
gear'shift'
gear'wheel'
Gei'ger
gei'sha
·sha *or* ·shas
gel
gelled gel'ling
gel'a·tin *or* ·tine
ge·lat'i·nize'
·nized' ·niz'ing
ge·lat'i·nous
geld
geld'ed *or* gelt
geld'ing
gel'id
ge·lid'i·ty
gem'i·nate'
·nat'ed ·nat'ing
Gem'i·ni'
gen'darme
gen'der
ge·ne·a·log'i·cal
ge·ne·al'o·gy
·gies
gen'er·al
gen'er·al'i·ty
·ties
gen'er·al·i·za'tion

gen'er·al·ize'
·ized' ·iz'ing
gen'er·al·ly
gen'er·ate'
·at'ed ·at'ing
gen'er·a'tion
gen'er·a'tor
ge·ner'ic
ge·ner'i·cal·ly
gen'er·os'i·ty
·ties
gen'er·ous
gen'e·sis
·ses'
ge·net'ic
ge·net'i·cal·ly
ge'nial
ge·ni·al'i·ty
ge'nial·ly
ge'nie
gen'i·tal
gen'ius
gen'o·cide'
gen'o·type'
gen're
gen·teel'
gen·teel'ly
gen'tile
gen·til'i·ty
gen'tle
·tler ·tlest
gen'tle·man
gen'tle·man·ly
gen'tle·wom'an
gent'ly
gen'try
gen'u·flect'
gen'u·ine
gen'u·ine·ly
ge'nus
gen'er·a
ge'o·cen'tric
ge·og'ra·pher
ge'o·graph'i·cal
ge·og'ra·phy
·phies
ge'o·log'ic
ge'o·log'i·cal·ly
ge·ol'o·gist
ge·ol'o·gy
·gies
ge'o·met'ric
ge'o·met'ri·cal·ly
ge·om'e·try
·tries
ge'o·phys'i·cal
ge'o·phys'i·cist
ge'o·phys'ics
ge'o·po·lit'i·cal
ge'o·pol'i·tics
Geor'gia
ge'o·stat'ics
ge·ot'ro·pism
ge·ra'ni·um
ger'bil *or* ·bille
ger'i·at'rics
ger·mane'
ger'mi·cid'al

ger'mi·cide'
ger'mi·nate'
·nat'ed ·nat'ing
ger'mi·na'tion
ger'on·tol'o·gy
ger'ry·man'der
ger'und
Ge·stalt'
ges'tate
·tat·ed ·tat·ing
ges·ta'tion
ges·tic'u·late'
·lat'ed ·lat'ing
ges·tic'u·la'tion
ges·tic'u·la'tor
ges'ture
·tured ·tur·ing
get
got, got *or*
got'ten,
get'ting
get'a·way'
get'-to·geth'er
gew'gaw
gey'ser
ghast'li·ness
ghast'ly
·li·er ·li·est
gher'kin
ghet'to
·tos *or* ·toes
ghet'to·ize'
·ized' ·iz'ing
ghil'lie
ghost'li·ness
ghost'ly
·li·er ·li·est
ghost'write'
ghost'writ'er
ghoul'ish
gi'ant
gib'ber·ish
gib'bet
gib'bon
gib·bos'i·ty
·ties
gib'bous
gibe
gibed gib'ing
(*taunt;* see jibe)
gib'let
gid'di·ly
gid'di·ness
gid'dy
·di·er ·di·est
gift'ed
gift'-wrap'
-wrapped'
-wrap'ping
gig
gigged gig'ging
gig'gle
·gled ·gling
gig'o·lo'
·los'

gild
gild'ed *or* gilt
gild'ing
(*coat with gold;*
see guild)
gilt
(*gold;* see guilt)
gilt'-edged'
gim'bals
gim'crack'
gim'let
gim'mick
gin'ger
gin'ger·bread'
ging'ham
gi·raffe'
gird
gird'ed *or* girt
gird'ing
gird'er
gir'dle
·dled ·dling
girl'ish
gist
give
gave giv'en
giv'ing
give'a·way'
giz'zard
gla·cé'
·céed' ·cé'ing
gla'cial
gla'ci·ate'
·at'ed ·at'ing
gla'cier
glad
glad'der
glad'dest
glad'den
glad'i·a'tor
glad'i·o'lus *or* ·la
·lus·es *or* ·li, ·las
glad'some
glair
(*glaze;* see glare)
glam'or·ize'
·ized' ·iz'ing
glam'or·ous
glam'our *or* ·or
glance
glanced
glanc'ing
glan'du·lar
glare
glared glar'ing
(*strong light;*
see glair)
glar'i·ness
glar'y
·i·er ·i·est
glass'ful'
·fuls'
glass·ine'
glass'i·ness
glass'ware'
glass'y
·i·er ·i·est
glau·co'ma

glaze
 glazed glaz'ing
gla'zier
glean'ings
glee'ful
glee'ful·ly
glib
 glib'ber
 glib'best
glib'ly
glide
 glid'ed glid'ing
glid'er
glim'mer
glimpse
 glimpsed
 glimps'ing
glis·sade'
 ·sad'ed ·sad'ing
glis'ten
glit'ter
glit'ter·y
gloam'ing
gloat
glob'al
globe'-trot'ter
glob'u·lar
glob'ule
glock'en·spiel'
gloom'i·ly
gloom'i·ness
gloom'y
 ·i·er ·i·est
glo'ri·fi·ca'tion
glo'ri·fy'
 ·fied' ·fy'ing
glo'ri·ous
glo'ry
 ·ries
 ·ried ·ry·ing
glos'sa·ry
 ·ries
gloss'i·ness
gloss'y
 ·i·er ·i·est
 ·ies
glot'tal
glove
 gloved glov'ing
glow'er
glow'ing·ly
glow'worm'
glu'cose
glue
 glued glu'ing
glue'y
 glu'i·er
 glu'i·est
glum'ly
glut
 glut'ted
 glut'ting
glu'ten
glu'ten·ous
 (having gluten)
glu'ti·nous
 (gluey)
glut'ton

glut'ton·ous
 (greedy)
glut'ton·y
glyc'er·in or ·ine
gnarled
gnash
gnat
gnaw
 gnawed
 gnaw'ing
gneiss
gnoc'chi
gnome
gno'mic
gno'mon
gnos'tic
gnu
go
 went gone
 go'ing
goad
go'-a·head'
goal'keep'er
goat·ee'
gob'ble
 bled bling
gob'ble·dy·gook'
go'-be·tween'
gob'let
gob'lin
god'child'
god'daugh·ter
god'dess
god'fa·ther
God'-giv'en
god'li·ness
god'ly
 ·li·er ·li·est
god'moth·er
god'par·ent
god'send'
god'son'
God'speed'
go'-get'ter
gog'gle
 ·gled ·gling
go'-go'
goi'ter or ·tre
gold'en
gold'-filled'
gold'fish'
gold leaf
gold'smith'
golf'er
gon'do·la
gon'do·lier'
gon'or·rhe'a
 or ·rhoe'a
good
 bet'ter best
good'bye' or
 good'-bye'
 ·byes' or -byes'
good'-for-
 noth'ing
good'-heart'ed
good'-hu'mored
good'-look'ing

good'ly
 ·li·er ·li·est
good'-na'tured
good night
good'-sized'
good'-tem'pered
good'y
 ·ies
goo'ey
goo'i·er goo'i·est
goo'gol
goose
 geese
goose'neck'
goose'-step'
go'pher
gore
 gored gor'ing
gorge
 gorged gorg'ing
gor'geous
go·ril'la
 (ape; see guerrilla)
gor'i·ness
gor'mand·ize'
 ·ized' ·iz'ing
gor'y
 ·i·er ·i·est
gos'hawk'
gos'ling
gos'pel
gos'sa·mer
gos'sip
got'ten
gouache
 (painting; see
 gauche)
gouge
 gouged
 goug'ing
gou'lash
gourd
gour'mand
gour'met
gout
gov'ern·ess
gov'ern·ment
gov'ern·men'tal
gov'er·nor
grab
 grabbed
 grab'bing
grace'ful
grace'ful·ly
grace'less
gra'cious
gra'date
 ·dat·ed ·dat·ing
gra·da'tion
grade
 grad'ed grad'ing
grad'u·al
grad'u·ate'
 ·at'ed ·at'ing
grad'u·a'tion
graf·fi'ti
 (sing. graf·fi'to)
graft'er

gra'ham
grain'i·ness
grain'y
 ·i·er ·i·est
gram'mar
gram·mar'i·an
gram·mat'i·cal
gran'a·ry
 ·ries
grand'aunt'
grand'child'
grand'daugh'ter
gran'deur
grand'fa'ther
gran·dil'o·quent
gran'di·ose'
grand'moth'er
grand'neph'ew
grand'niece'
grand'par'ent
grand'son'
grand'stand'
grand'un'cle
gran'ite
gran'ite·ware'
grant·ee'
grant'in-aid'
 grants'-in-aid'
grant'or
gran'u·lar
gran'u·late'
 ·lat'ed ·lat'ing
gran'ule
grape'fruit'
grape'vine'
graph'ic
graph'i·cal·ly
graph'ite
graph·ol'o·gy
grap'nel
grap'ple
 ·pled ·pling
grap'pler
grasp'ing
grass'hop'per
grass'y
 ·i·er ·i·est
grate
 grat'ed grat'ing
grate'ful
grate'ful·ly
grat'i·fi·ca'tion
grat'i·fy'
 ·fied' ·fy'ing
gra'tis
grat'i·tude
gra·tu'i·tous
gra·tu'i·ty
 ·ties
grave
 graved, grav'en
 or graved,
 grav'ing
 (carve out)
grave
 graved grav'ing
 (clean the hull)
grave'clothes'

grav'el
 ·eled or ·elled
 ·el·ing or ·el·ling
grav'el·ly
grave'ly
grave'side'
grave'stone'
grave'yard'
grav'i·tate'
 ·tat'ed ·tat'ing
grav·i·ta'tion
grav'i·ty
 ·ties
gra'vy
 ·vies
gray
gray'-head'ed
graze
 grazed graz'ing
grease
 greased
 greas'ing
grease'paint'
greas'i·ness
greas'y
 ·i·er ·i·est
great'-aunt'
great'coat'
great'-grand'child'
great'-grand'par'·
 ent
great'ly
great'-neph'ew
great'ness
great'-niece'
great'-un'cle
greed'i·ly
greed'i·ness
greed'y
 ·i·er ·i·est
Greek'-let'ter
green'back'
green'er·y
green'-eyed'
green'gage'
green'horn'
green'house'
green'room'
green'sward'
greet'ing
gre·gar'i·ous
grem'lin
gre·nade'
gren'a·dier'
gren'a·dine'
grey'hound' or
 gray'
grid'dle
 ·dled ·dling
grid'dle·cake'
grid'i'ron
grief'-strick'en
griev'ance
grieve
 grieved
 griev'ing
griev'ous
grif'fin

grill
 (broiler grid)
grille
 (open grating)
grill'room'
grim
 grim'mer
 grim'mest
gri·mace'
 ·maced'
 ·mac'ing
grime
 grimed grim'ing
grim'i·ly
grim'i·ness
grim'y
 ·i·er ·i·est
grin
 grinned
 grin'ning
grind
 ground
 grind'ing
grind'stone'
grip
 gripped or gript
 grip'ping
 (hold)
gripe
 griped grip'ing
 (distress)
grippe
 (influenza)
gris'li·ness
gris'ly
 ·li·er ·li·est
 (horrid)
gris'tle
gris'tly
 (of gristle)
grist'mill'
grit
 grit'ted
 grit'ting
grit'ti·ness
grit'ty
 ·ti·er ·ti·est
griz'zly bear
groan'ing
gro'cer·y
 ·ies
grog'gi·ly
grog'gi·ness
grog'gy
 ·gi·er ·gi·est
groin
grom'met
groom
groove
 grooved
groov'ing
groov'y
 ·i·er ·i·est
grope
 groped grop'ing
gros'grain'
gross'ly
gross'ness

gro·tesque'
gro·tesque'ly
grot'to
· toes *or* ·tos
grouch'i·ly
grouch'i·ness
grouch'y
· i·er ·i·est
ground'less
grounds'keep'er
ground'speed'
ground'work'
group
grout
grove
grov'el
· eled *or* ·elled
· el·ing *or* ·el·ling
grow
grew grown
grow'ing
growl'er
grown'-up'
growth
grub
grubbed
grub'bing
grub'bi·ness
grub'by
· bi·er ·bi·est
grub'stake'
grudge
grudged
grudg'ing
gru'el
gru'el·ing *or*
gru'el·ling
grue'some
grue'some·ly
gruff'ly
grum'ble
· bled ·bling
grum'bler
grum'bly
grump'i·ness
grump'y
· i·er ·i·est
grun'ion
grunt
Gru·yère'
G'-string'
G'-suit'
guar'an·tee'
· teed' ·tee'ing
guar'an·tor'
guar'an·ty
· ties
· tied ·ty·ing
guard'ed
guard'house'
guard'i·an
guard'rail'
guard'room'
guards'man
gua'va
gu'ber·na·to'ri·al
Guern'sey
· seys

guer·ril'la *or* gue·
(*soldier;* see
gorilla)
guess'work'
guest
guid'a·ble
guid'ance
guide
guid'ed
guid'ing
guide'book'
guide'line'
guide'post'
guild
(*union;* see gild)
guilds'man
guile'ful
guile'less
guil'lo·tine'
· tined' ·tin'ing
guilt
(*blame;* see gilt)
guilt'i·ly
guilt'i·ness
guilt'y
· i·er ·i·est
guin'ea pig
guise
gui·tar'
gui·tar'ist
gulch
gul'let
gul'li·bil'i·ty
gul'li·ble
gul'li·bly
gul'ly
· lies
gum'drop'
gum'mi·ness
gum'my
· mi·er ·mi·est
gun
gunned
gun'ning
gun'cot'ton
gun'fire'
gung'-ho'
gun'lock'
gun'man
gun'ner·y
gun'ny·sack'
gun'play'
gun'point'
gun'pow'der
gun'run'ning
gun'shot'
gun'shy'
gun'smith'
gun'stock'
gup'py
· pies
gur'gle
· gled ·gling
gu'ru
gush'er
gush'i·ness
gush'y
· i·er ·i·est

gus'set
gus'ta·to'ry
gus'to
gust'y
· i·er ·i·est
gut
gut'ted
gut'ting
gut'ta-per'cha
gut'ter·snipe'
gut'tur·al
guy
guz'zle
· zled ·zling
guz'zler
gym·na'si·um
· si·ums *or* ·si·a
gym'nast
gym·nas'tics
gym'no·sperm'
gyn'e·col'o·gist
gyn'e·col'o·gy
gyp
gypped gyp'ping
gyp'sum
Gyp'sy
· sies
gy'rate
· rat·ed ·rat·ing
gy·ra'tion
gy'ro·com'pass
gy'ro·scope'
gy'ro·scop'ic
gy'ro·sta'bi·liz'er

H

ha'be·as cor'pus
hab'er·dash'er·y
· ies
ha·bil'i·tate'
· tat'ed ·tat'ing
hab'it
hab'it·a·ble
hab'i·tat'
hab'i·ta'tion
hab'it-form'ing
ha·bit'u·al
ha·bit'u·ate'
· at'ed ·at'ing
hab'i·tude'
ha·bit'u·é
ha'ci·en'da
hack'ney
· neys
hack'neyed
hack'saw'
had'dock
hag'gard
hag'gle
· gled ·gling
hai'ku
· ku
hail
(*ice;* see hale)
hail'stone'

hail'storm'
hair'breadth'
hair'cut'
hair'do'
hair'dress'er
hair'i·ness
hair'line'
hair'piece'
hair'-rais'ing
hair'split'ting
hair'spring'
hair'y
· i·er ·i·est
hal'cy·on
hale
haled hal'ing
(*healthy; force;*
see hail)
half
halves
half'back'
half'-baked'
half'-breed'
half'-caste'
half'-cocked'
half'heart'ed
half'-hour'
half'-mast'
half'-moon'
half'tone'
half'track'
half'-truth'
half'way'
half'-wit'ted
hal'i·but
hal'i·to'sis
hal'le·lu'jah
or ·iah
hall'mark'
hal'lowed
Hal'low·een'
hal·lu'ci·nate'
· nat'ed ·nat'ing
hal·lu'ci·na'tion
hal·lu'ci·na·to'ry
hal·lu'ci·no·gen
hall'way'
hal'lo
· los *or* ·loes
hal'ter
halt'ing·ly
ha·lutz'
ha'lutz·im'
halve
halved halv'ing
hal'yard
ham'burg'er
ham'let
ham'mer
ham'mer·head'
ham'mock
ham'per
ham'ster
ham'string'
hand'bag'
hand'ball'
hand'bar'row
hand'bill'

hand'book'
hand'breadth'
hand'clasp'
hand'cuff'
hand'ful'
· fuls'
hand'gun'
hand'i·cap'
· capped
· cap'ping
hand'i·craft'
hand'i·ly
hand'i·ness
hand'i·work'
hand'ker·chief
· chiefs
han'dle
· dled ·dling
han'dle·bar'
hand'ler
hand'made'
hand'-me-down'
hand'out'
hand'picked'
hand'rail'
hand'saw'
hand'sel
· seled *or* ·selled
· sel·ing *or* ·sel·ling
hand'set'
hand'shake'
hands'-off'
hand'some
hand'spring'
hand'stand'
hand'-to-hand'
hand'-to-mouth'
hand'work'
hand'writ'ing
hand'y
· i·er ·i·est
han'dy·man'
hang
hung hang'ing
(*suspend*)
hang
hanged hang'ing
(*put to death*)
hang'ar
(*aircraft shed*)
hang'dog'
hang'er
(*garment holder*)
hang'er-on'
hang'ers-on'
hang'man
hang'nail'
hang'o'ver
hang'-up'
hank'er
han'ky-pan'ky
han'som (cab)
Ha'nu·ka'
hap'haz'ard
hap'less
hap'pen
hap'pen·stance'
hap'pi·ly

hap'pi·ness
hap'py
· pi·er ·pi·est
hap'py-go-luck'y
ha'ra-ki'ri
ha·rangue'
· rangued'
· rangu'ing
ha·rangu'er
har·ass'
har'bin·ger
har'bor
hard'back'
hard'-bit'ten
hard'-boiled'
hard'-bound'
hard'-core'
hard'-cov'er
hard'en
hard'fist'ed
hard'goods'
hard'head'ed
hard'heart'ed
har'di·hood'
har'di·ly
har'di·ness
hard'ly
hard'pan'
hard'-shell'
hard'ship'
hard'tack'
hard'top'
hard'ware'
hard'wood'
har'dy
· di·er ·di·est
hare'brained'
hare'lip'
ha'rem
har'le·quin
harm'ful
harm'less
har·mon'ic
har·mon'i·ca
har·mo'ni·ous
har'mo·nize'
· nized' ·niz'ing
har'mo·ny
har'ness
harp'ist
har·poon'
harp'si·chord'
har'py
· pies
har'ri·er
har'row
har'row·ing
har'ry
· ried ·ry·ing
harsh'ness
har'te·beest'
har'um-scar'um
har'vest·er
has'-been'
ha'sen·pfef'fer
hash'ish *or* ·eesh
has'sle
· sled ·sling

has'sock
haste
has'ten
hast'i·ly
hast'i·ness
hast'y
  ·i·er ·i·est
hat'band'
hatch'er·y
  ·ies
hatch'et
hatch'ing
hatch'way'
hate
  hat'ed hat'ing
hate'a·ble
hate'ful
hat'rack'
ha'tred
hat'ter
haugh'ti·ly
haugh'ti·ness
haugh'ty
  ·ti·er ·ti·est
haul'age
haunch
haunt'ed
haunt'ing
hau·teur'
have
  had hav'ing
have'lock
ha'ven
have'-not'
hav'er·sack'
hav'oc
Ha·wai'i
Ha·wai'ian
hawk
hawk'-eyed'
hawk'ish
haw'ser
hay fever
hay'field'
hay'loft'
hay'ride'
haz'ard
haz'ard·ous
haze
  hazed haz'ing
ha'zel·nut'
ha'zi·ly
ha'zi·ness
ha'zy
  ·zi·er ·zi·est
H'-bomb'
head'ache'
head'board'
head'cheese'
head'dress'
head'first'
head'gear'
head'hunt·er
head'i·ly
head'i·ness
head'land
head'less
head'light'

head'line'
head'long'
head'man
head'mas'ter
head'mis'tress
head'-on'
head'phone'
head'piece'
head'quar'ters
head'rest'
head'room'
head'set'
head'stand'
head start
head'stock'
head'strong'
head'wait·er
head'wa'ters
head'way'
head wind
head'y
  ·i·er ·i·est
heal
  (cure; see heel)
health'ful
health'i·ly
health'i·ness
health'y
  ·i·er ·i·est
heap
hear
  heard hear'ing
hark'en
hear'say'
hearse
heart'ache'
heart'beat'
heart'break'
heart'bro'ken
heart'burn'
heart'en
heart'felt'
hearth'stone'
heart'i·ly
heart'i·ness
heart'less
heart'-rend'ing
heart'sick'
heart'strings'
heart'-to-heart'
heart'warm'ing
heart'y
  ·i·er ·i·est
heat'ed·ly
heat'er
heath
hea'then
heath'er
heat'stroke'
heave
  heaved or hove
heav'ing
heav'en·ly
heav'en·ward
heav'i·ly
heav'i·ness
heav'y
  ·i·er ·i·est

heav'y-du'ty
heav'y-hand'ed
heav'y-heart'ed
heav'y·set'
heav'y·weight'
He·bra'ic
He'brew
heck'le
  ·led ·ling
hec'tic
hec'ti·cal·ly
hec'to·graph'
hedge
  hedged
  hedg'ing
hedge'hop'
he'don·ism
he'do·nis'tic
heed'ful
heed'less
heel
  (foot part;
  see heal)
heft'y
  ·i·er ·i·est
heif'er
height
height'en
hei'nous
heir
  (inheritor; see
  air)
heir'ess
heir'loom'
hel'i·cal
hel'i·cop'ter
he'li·o·graph'
he'li·o·trope'
he'i·port'
he'li·um
he'lix
  ·lix·es or ·li·ces'
hell'ion
hel·lo'
  ·los'
  ·loed' ·lo'ing
hel'met
helms'man
help'ful
help'ful·ly
help'less
hel'ter-skel'ter
hem
  hemmed
  hem'ming
he'ma·tol'o·gy
hem'i·sphere'
hem'i·spher'i·cal
hem'line'
he'mo·glo'bin
he'mo·phil'i·a
hem'or·rhage
  ·rhaged
  ·rhag·ing
hem'or·rhoid'
hem'stitch'
hence'forth'
hench'man

hen'na
  ·naed ·na·ing
hen'ner·y
  ·ies
hen'pecked'
hen'ry
  ·rys or ·ries
he·pat'ic
hep'a·ti'tis
hep'ta·gon'
her'ald
he·ral'dic
her'ald·ry
her·ba'ceous
her'bi·cide'
her'bi·vore'
her·biv'o·rous
herds'man
here'a·bout'
here·af'ter
here'by'
he·red'i·tar'y
he·red'i·ty
  ·ties
here·in'
here'in·af'ter
here's
her'e·sy
  ·sies
her'e·tic
he·ret'i·cal
here'to·fore'
here·with'
her'it·a·ble
her'it·age
her·maph'ro·dite'
her·met'i·cal·ly
her'mit
her'ni·a
  ·as or ·ae'
her'ni·ate'
  ·at'ed ·at'ing
he'ro
  ·roes
he·ro'ic
he·ro'i·cal·ly
her'o·in
  (narcotic)
her'o·ine
  (female hero)
her'o·ism
her'pes
her'ring·bone'
her·self'
hes'i·tan·cy
  ·cies
hes'i·tant
hes'i·tate'
  ·tat'ed ·tat'ing
hes'i·ta'tion
het'er·o·dox'
het'er·o·dox'y
  ·ies
het'er·o·dyne'
  ·dyned' ·dyn'ing
het'er·o·ge·ne'i·ty
  ·ties
het'er·o·ge'ne·ous

het'er·o·nym'
het'er·o·sex'u·al
heu·ris'tic
heu·ris'ti·cal·ly
hew
  hewed, hewed or
  hewn, hew'ing
  (chop; see hue)
hex'a·gon'
hex·ag'o·nal
hex'a·he'dron
  ·drons or ·dra
hey'day'
H'-hour'
hi·a'tus
  ·tus·es or ·tus
hi·ba'chi
hi'ber·nate'
  ·nat'ed ·nat'ing
hi'ber·na'tion
hi'ber·na'tor
hi·bis'cus
hic'cup or ·cough
  ·cuped or ·cupped
  ·cup·ing or
  ·cup·ping
hick'o·ry
  ·ries
hide
  hid, hid'den or
  hid, hid'ing
hide'a·way'
hide'bound'
hid'e·ous
hide'-out'
hie
  hied, hie'ing
  or hy'ing
hi'er·ar'chi·cal
hi'er·ar'chy
  ·chies
hi'er·o·glyph'ic
hi'-fi'
high'ball'
high'born'
high'boy'
high'bred'
high'brow'
high'chair'
high'-class'
high'er-up'
high'fa·lu'tin
high'-flown'
high'-grade'
high'hand'ed
high'-keyed'
high'land·er
high'-lev'el
high'light'
high'ly
high'-mind'ed
high'-pitched'
high'-pow'ered
high'-pres'sure
high'-priced'
high'-rise'
high'-sound'ing
high'-spir'it·ed

high'-strung'
high'-ten'sion
high'-test'
high'-toned'
high'way'
hi'jack'
hike
  hiked hik'ing
hi·lar'i·ous
hi·lar'i·ty
hill'i·ness
hill'ock
hill'side'
hill'y
  ·i·er ·i·est
him·self'
hind
  hind'er,
  hind'most' or
  hind'er·most'
hin'der
hin'drance
hind'sight'
hinge
  hinged hing'ing
hin'ter·land'
hip'bone'
hip'pie
hip'po·drome'
hip'po·pot'a·mus
  ·mus·es or ·mi
hir'a·ble or hire'·
hire
  hired hir'ing
hire'ling
hiss'ing
his'ta·mine'
his·tol'o·gy
his·to'ri·an
his·tor'i·cal
his·tor'i·cal·ly
his'to·ry
  ·ries
his'tri·on'ic
hit
  hit hit'ting
hit'-and-run'
hitch'hike'
hith'er·to'
hit'-or-miss'
hives
hoard
  (reserve; see
  horde)
hoar'frost'
hoar'i·ness
hoarse
hoar'y
  ·i·er ·i·est
hob'ble
  ·bled ·bling
hob'by
  ·bies
hob'by·horse'
hob'gob'lin
hob'nail'
hob'nob'
  ·nobbed' ·nob'bing

ho'bo
· bos *or* · boes
hock'ey
ho'cus·po'cus
hodge'podge'
hoe
  hoed hoe'ing
hoe'down'
hog'gish
hogs'head'
hog'tie'
  ·tied', ·ty'ing
  or ·tie'ing
hog'wash'
hoi' pol·loi'
hoist
hold
  held hold'ing
hold'out'
hold'o·ver
hold'up'
hole
  holed hol'ing
hole'y
  (*with holes;* see
  holy, wholly)
hol'i·day
ho'li·ly
ho'li·ness
hol'lan·daise'
hol'low
hol'lo·ware'
hol'ly
  ·lies
hol'ly·hock'
hol'o·caust'
ho·log'ra·phy
Hol'stein
hol'ster
ho'ly
  ·li·er ·li·est
  ·lies
  (*sacred;* see
  holey, wholly)
hom'age
hom'burg
home
  homed hom'ing
home'bod'y
home'bred'
home'-brew'
home'com'ing
home'-grown'
home'land'
home'less
home'li·ness
home'ly
  ·li·er ·li·est
  (*plain;* see
  homey)
home'made'
home'mak'er
home'own'er
home'sick'
home'spun'
home'stead'
home'stretch'
home'ward

home'work'
home'y
hom'i·er
hom'i·est
  (*cozy;* see
  homely)
home'y·ness
hom'i·ci'dal
hom'i·cide'
hom'i·let'ics
hom'i·ly
  ·lies
hom'i·ny
ho'mo·ge·ne'i·ty
ho'mo·ge'ne·ous
ho·mog'e·nize'
  ·nized' ·niz'ing
hom'o·graph'
ho·mol'o·gous
hom'o·nym
hom'o·phone'
Ho'mo sa'pi·ens'
ho'mo·sex'u·al
ho'mo·sex'u·
  al'i·ty
hone
  honed hon'ing
hon'est
hon'es·ty
hon'ey
  ·eys, ·eyed *or*
  ·ied, ·ey·ing
hon'ey·bee'
hon'ey·comb'
hon'ey·dew'
hon'ey·moon'
hon'ey·suck'le
hon'or·a·ble
hon·o·ra'ri·um
  ·ri·ums *or* ·ri·a
hon'or·ar'y
hon'or·if'ic
hood'ed
hood'lum
hood'wink'
hoof
hoof'beat'
hook'ah *or* ·a
hook'up'
hook'y
hoo'li·gan
hoop'la
hoot'en·an'ny
  ·nies
hop
  hopped hop'ping
hope
  hoped hop'ing
hope'ful
hope'ful·ly
hope'less
hop'per
horde
hord'ed hord'ing
  (*crowd;* see
  hoard)
hore'hound'
ho·ri'zon

hor'i·zon'tal
hor·mo'nal
hor'mone
hor'net
horn'i·ness
horn'pipe'
horn'y
  ·i·er ·i·est
ho·rol'o·gy
hor'o·scope'
hor·ren'dous
hor'ri·ble
hor'ri·bly
hor'rid
hor'ri·fy'
  ·fied' ·fy'ing
hor'ror
hors' d'oeu'vre
  ·vres
horse'back'
horse'fly'
  ·flies'
horse'hair'
horse'hide'
horse'laugh'
horse'man
horse'play'
horse'pow'er
horse'rad'ish
horse'shoe'
  ·shoed' ·shoe'ing
horse'tail'
horse'whip'
horse'wom'an
hors'i·ness
hors'y
  ·i·er ·i·est
hor'ta·to'ry
hor'ti·cul'ture
hor'ti·cul'tur·ist
ho·san'na
hose
  hosed hos'ing
ho'sier·y
hos'pice
hos'pi·ta·ble
hos'pi·ta·bly
hos'pi·tal
hos·pi·tal'i·ty
  ·ties
hos'pi·tal·i·za'tion
hos'pi·tal·ize'
  ·ized' ·iz'ing
hos'tage
hos'tel
  (*inn;* see hostile)
hos'tel·ry
  ·ries
host'ess
hos'tile
  (*unfriendly;* see
  hostel)
hos·til'i·ty
  ·ties
hos'tler
hot
  hot'ter hot'test

hot'bed'
hot'-blood'ed
hot'box'
ho·tel'
ho·tel·ier'
hot'foot'
  ·foots'
hot'head'ed
hot'house'
hot'tem'pered
hound'ed
hour'glass'
hour'ly
house
  housed hous'ing
house'boat'
house'break'
  ·broke' ·bro'ken
  ·break'ing
house'clean'ing
house'dress'.
house'coat'
house'fly'
  ·flies'
house'ful'
house'hold'
house'keep'er
house'lights'
house'maid'
house'man'
house'moth·er
house organ
house party
house'-rais'ing
house'warm'ing
house'wife'
  ·wives'
house'work'
hous'ing
hov'el
  ·eled *or* ·elled
  ·el·ing *or* ·el·ling
hov'er
how'dah
how·ev'er
how'itz·er
howl'ing
how'so·ev'er
how'-to'
hoy'den
hua·ra'ches
hub'bub'
hub'cap'
huck'le·ber'ry
  ·ries
huck'ster
hud'dle
  ·dled ·dling
hue
  (*color;* see hew)
huff'i·ly
huff'i·ness
huff'y
  ·i·er ·i·est
hug
  hugged hug'ging
huge'ness
hulk'ing

hul'la·ba·loo'
hum
  hummed
  hum'ming
hu'man
hu·mane'
hu'man·ism
hu'man·is'tic
hu·man·is'ti·cal·ly
hu·man'i·tar'i·an
hu·man'i·ty
  ·ties
hu'man·ize'
  ·ized' ·iz'ing
hu'man·kind'
hu'man·ly
hu'man·ness
hu'man·oid'
hum'ble
  ·bler ·blest
  ·bled ·bling
hum'bly
hum'bug'
hum'drum'
hu·mec'tant
hu'mer·us
  ·mer·i'
  (*bone;* see
  humorous)
hu'mid
hu·mid'i·fi·ca'tion
hu·mid'i·fi'er
hu·mid'i·fy'
  ·fied' ·fy'ing
hu·mid'i·ty
hu'mi·dor'
hu·mil'i·ate'
  ·at'ed ·at'ing
hu·mil'i·a'tion
hu·mil'i·ty
hum'ming·bird'
hum'mock
hu'mor
hu'mor·esque'
hu'mor·ist
hu'mor·ous
  (*funny;* see
  humerus)
hump'back'
hu'mus
hunch'back'
hun'dred·fold'
hun'dredth
hun'dred·weight'
hun'ger
hun'gri·ly
hun'gri·ness
hun'gry
  ·gri·er ·gri·est
hunt'er
hunt'ress
hunts'man
hur'dle
  ·dled ·dling
  (*barrier;* see
  hurtle)
hur'dy-gur'dy
hurl'er

hurl'y-burl'y
hur·rah'
hur'ri·cane'
hur'ried·ly
hur'ry
  ·ried ·ry·ing
hurt
  hurt hurt'ing
hurt'ful
hur'tle
  ·tled ·tling
  (*rush;* see hurdle)
hus'band
hus'band·ry
hush'-hush'
husk'i·ly
husk'i·ness
hus'ky
  ·kies
  (*dog*)
husk'y
  ·i·er ·i·est, ·ies
  (*hoarse; robust*)
hus'sy
  ·sies
hus'tle
  ·tled ·tling
hus'tler
hya'cinth'
hy'brid
hy'brid·ize'
  ·ized' ·iz'ing
hy·dran'ge·a
hy'drant
hy'drate
  ·drat·ed ·drat·ing
hy'dra·tor
hy·drau'lic
hy'dro·chlo'ric
hy'dro·dy·nam'ics
hy'dro·e·lec'tric
hy'dro·foil'
hy'dro·gen
hy'dro·gen·ate'
  ·at'ed ·at'ing
hy'dro·gen·a'tion
hy'dro·ki·net'ics
hy·drol'o·gy
hy·drol'y·sis
hy'dro·lyt'ic
hy'dro·me·
  chan'ics
hy·drom'e·ter
hy'dro·naut'
hy'dro·pho'bi·a
hy'dro·plane'
hy'dro·pon'ics
hy'dro-ski'
hy'dro·stat'ics
hy'dro·ther'a·py
hy'drous
hy·e'na
hy'giene
hy·gi·en'ic
hy·gi·en'i·cal·ly
hy'gi·en·ist
hy·grom'e·ter
hy'gro·scope'

hy'men
hy·me·ne'al
hymn
hym'nal
hym·nol'o·gy
hy'per·a·cid'i·ty
hy'per·ac'tive
hy·per'bo·la
  (curve)
hy·per'bo·le
  (exaggeration)
hy·per·bol'ic
hy'per·crit'i·cal
  (too critical; see
   hypocritical)
hy'per·sen'si·tive
hy'per·son'ic
hy'per·ten'sion
hy'per·ven'ti·
   la'tion
hy'phen
hy'phen·ate'
  ·at'ed ·at'ing
hy'phen·a'tion
hyp·no'sis
  ·ses
hyp·not'ic
hyp·not'i·cal·ly
hyp'no·tism
hyp'no·tiz'a·ble
hyp'no·tize'
  ·tized' ·tiz'ing
hy·po·chon'dri·a
hy·po·chon'dri·ac'
hy·po·chon·
   dri'a·cal
hy·po·chon·
   dri'a·sis
hy·poc'ri·sy
  ·sies
hyp'o·crite
hyp'o·crit'i·cal
  (deceitful; see
   hypercritical)
hy'po·der'mic
hy·pot'e·nuse'
hy·poth'e·cate'
  ·cat'ed ·cat'ing
hy·poth'e·sis
  ·ses'
hy·poth'e·size'
  ·sized' ·siz'ing
hy'po·thet'i·cal
hy'po·thet'i·cal·ly
hys'ter·ec'to·my
  ·mies
hys·te'ri·a
hys·ter'ic
hys·ter'i·cal
hys·ter'i·cal·ly

I

i·am'bic
ice
  iced ic'ing

ice'berg'
ice'bound'
ice'box'
ice'break'er
ice'cap'
ice cream
ice field
ice'house'
ice'man'
ice milk
ich'thy·ol'o·gy
i'ci·cle
i'ci·ly
i'ci·ness
ic'ing
i'con
i·con'ic
i·con'o·clast'
i'cy
i'ci·er i'ci·est
I'da·ho'
i·de'a
i·de'al
i·de'al·ism
i·de'al·ist
i·de·al·is'tic
i·de'al·i·za'tion
i·de'al·ize'
  ·ized' ·iz'ing
i·de'al·ly
i'de·ate'
  ·at'ed ·at'ing
i'de·a'tion
i·den'ti·cal
i·den'ti·cal·ly
i·den'ti·fi'a·ble
i·den'ti·fi·ca'tion
i·den'ti·fi'er
i·den'ti·fy'
  ·fied' ·fy'ing
i·den'ti·ty
  ·ties
id'e·o·gram'
id'e·o·graph'ic
i'de·o·log'i·cal
i'de·o·log'i·cal·ly
i'de·ol'o·gist
i'de·ol'o·gize'
  ·gized' ·giz'ing
i'de·ol'o·gy
  ·gies
id'i·o·cy
id'i·om
id'i·o·mat'ic
id'i·o·mat'i·cal·ly
id'i·o·syn'cra·sy
  ·sies
id'i·o·syn·crat'ic
id'i·ot
id'i·ot'ic
id'i·ot'i·cal·ly
i'dle
i'dler i'dlest
i'dled i'dling
  (not active; see
   idol, idyll)
i'dle·ness

i'dler
i'dly
i'dol
  (image worshiped;
   see idle, idyll)
i·dol'a·ter
i·dol'a·trous
i·dol'a·try
i'dol·ize'
  ·ized' ·iz'ing
i'dyll or i'dyl
  (pastoral poem;
   see idle, idol)
i·dyl'lic
ig'loo
  ·loos
ig'ne·ous
ig·nit'a·ble
  or ·i·ble
ig·nite'
  ·nit'ed ·nit'ing
ig·ni'tion
ig·no'ble
ig'no·min'i·ous
ig'no·min'y
  ·ies
ig·no·ra'mus
ig'no·rance
ig'no·rant
ig·nore'
  ·nored' ·nor'ing
i·gua'na
ill'e·um
  (intestine)
il'i·um
  (bone)
ill
  worse worst
ill'-ad·vised'
ill'-be'ing
ill'-bod'ing
ill'-bred'
ill'-con·sid'ered
ill'-dis·posed'
il·le'gal
il'le·gal'i·ty
  ·ties
il·le'gal·ly
il'leg·i·bil'i·ty
il·leg'i·ble
il·leg'i·bly
il'le·git'i·ma·cy
  ·cies
il'le·git'i·mate
il'le·git'i·mate·ly
ill'-fat'ed
ill'-fa'vored
ill'-found'ed
ill'-got'ten
ill'-hu'mored
il·lib'er·al
il·lic'it
  (unlawful; see
   elicit)
il·lim'it·a·ble
il·lim'it·a·bly
Il'li·nois'
il·lit'er·a·cy

il·lit'er·ate
il·lit'er·ate·ly
ill'-man'nered
ill'-na'tured
ill'ness
il·log'i·cal
il·log'i·cal·ly
ill'-sort'ed
ill'-spent'
ill'-starred'
ill'-suit'ed
ill'-tem'pered
ill'-timed'
ill'-treat'
il·lu'mi·nate'
  ·nat'ed ·nat'ing
il·lu'mi·na'tion
il·lu'mi·na'tor
ill'-us'age
ill'-use'
il·lu'sion
  (false idea; see
   allusion, elusion)
il·lu'sive
  (deceptive; see
   allusive, elusive)
il·lu'so·ri·ly
il·lu'so·ri·ness
il·lu'so·ry
il'lus·trate'
  ·trat'ed ·trat'ing
il·lus·tra'tion
il·lus'tra·tive
il·lus'tra·tor
il·lus'tri·ous
im'age
  ·aged ·ag·ing
im'age·ry
  ·ries
i·mag'i·na·ble
i·mag'i·na·bly
i·mag'i·nar'i·ness
i·mag'i·nar'y
i·mag'i·na'tion
i·mag'i·na·tive
i·mag'ine
  ·ined ·in·ing
im'ag·ism
im·bal'ance
im'be·cile
im'be·cil'ic
im'be·cil'i·ty
  ·ties
im·bibe'
  ·bibed' ·bib'ing
im·bib'er
im'bri·cate'
  ·cat'ed ·cat'ing
im'bri·ca'tion
im·bro'glio
  ·glios
im·brue'
  ·brued' ·bru'ing
im·bue'
  ·bued' ·bu'ing
im'i·ta·ble
im'i·tate'
  ·tat'ed ·tat'ing

im'i·ta'tion
im'i·ta'tive
im'i·ta'tor
im·mac'u·late
im'ma·nent
  (inherent; see
   imminent)
im'ma·te'ri·al
im'ma·ture'
im'ma·tu'ri·ty
im·meas'ur·a·ble
im·me'di·a·cy
im·me'di·ate
im·me'di·ate·ly
im·me·mo'ri·al
im·mense'
im·mense'ly
im·men'si·ty
im·merge'
  ·merged'
  ·merg'ing
  (plunge; see
   emerge)
im·mer'gence
im·merse'
  ·mersed'
  ·mers'ing
im·mers'i·ble
im·mer'sion
im'mi·grant
im'mi·grate'
  ·grat'ed ·grat'ing
im'mi·gra'tion
im'mi·nence
im'mi·nent
  (impending; see
   eminent,
   immanent)
im·mis'ci·ble
im·mit'i·ga·ble
im·mo'bile
im·mo·bil'i·ty
im·mo'bi·li·
   za'tion
im·mo'bi·lize'
  ·lized' ·liz'ing
im·mod'er·ate
im·mod'er·a'tion
im·mod'est
im·mod'es·ty
im'mo·late'
  ·lat'ed ·lat'ing
im'mo·la'tion
im·mor'al
im'mo·ral'i·ty
  ·ties
im·mor'tal
im'mor·tal'i·ty
im·mor'tal·i·
   za'tion
im·mor'tal·ize'
  ·ized' ·iz'ing
im·mov'a·bil'i·ty
im·mov'a·ble
im·mune'
im·mu'ni·ty
  ·ties
im'mu·ni·za'tion

im'mu·nize'
  ·nized' ·niz'ing
im'mu·nol'o·gy
im·mure'
  ·mured' ·mur'ing
im·mu'ta·bil'i·ty
im·mu'ta·ble
im·mu'ta·bly
im·pact'ed
im·pac'tion
im·pair'
im·pale'
  ·paled' ·pal'ing
im'pal·pa·bil'i·ty
im·pal'pa·ble
im·pan'el
  ·eled or ·elled
  ·el·ing or ·el·ling
im·part'
im·part'a·ble
im·par'tial
im'par·ti·al'i·ty
im·part'i·ble
im·pas'sa·bil'i·ty
im·pass'a·ble
  (not passable;
   see impassible)
im'passe
im·pas'si·bil'i·ty
im·pas'si·ble
  (unfeeling; see
   impassable)
im·pas'sioned
im·pas'sive
im'pas·siv'i·ty
im·pa'tience
im·pa'tient
im·peach'
im·peach'a·ble
im·pec'ca·bil'i·ty
im·pec'ca·ble
im·pec'ca·bly
im'pe·cu'ni·
   os'i·ty
im'pe·cu'ni·ous
im·ped'ance
im·pede'
  ·ped'ed ·ped'ing
im·ped'i·ment
im·ped'i·men'ta
im·pel'
  ·pelled' ·pel'ling
im·pel'lent
im·pel'ler
im·pend'
im·pend'ing
im·pen'e·tra·
   bil'i·ty
im·pen'e·tra·ble
im·pen'i·tence
im·pen'i·tent
im·per'a·tive
im'per·cep'ti·ble
im'per·cep'ti·bly
im·per'fect
im·per·fec'tion
im·per'fo·rate
im·pe'ri·al

im·pe'ri·al·ism
im·pe'ri·al·is'tic
im·pe'ri·al·ly
im·per'il
im·pe'ri·ous
im·per'ish·a·ble
im·per'ma·nent
im·per'me·a·ble
im'per·mis'si·ble
im·per'son·al
im·per'son·al'i·ty
im·per'son·al·ize'
im·per'son·ate'
·at'ed ·at'ing
im·per'son·a'tion
im·per'son·a'tor
im·per'ti·nence
im·per'ti·nent
im'per·turb'a·
bil'i·ty
im·per·turb'a·ble
im·per'vi·ous
im·pe·ti'go
im·pet'u·os'i·ty
im·pet'u·ous
im'pe·tus
im·pi'e·ty
·ties
im·pinge'
·pinged' ·ping'ing
im·pinge'ment
im'pi·ous
imp'ish
im·pla'ca·ble
im·plant'
im·plan·ta'tion
im·plau'si·ble
im'ple·ment
im'ple·men'tal
im'ple·men·ta'tion
im'pli·cate'
·cat'ed ·cat'ing
im'pli·ca'tion
im'pli·ca'tive
im·plic'it
im·plode'
·plod'ed ·plod'ing
im·plore'
·plored' ·plor'ing
im·plo'sion
im·ply'
·plied' ·ply'ing
im'po·lite'
im·pol'i·tic
im·pon'der·a·ble
im·port'
im·port'a·ble
im·por'tance
im·por'tant
im'por·ta'tion
im·port'er
im·por'tu·nate
im'por·tune'
·tuned' ·tun'ing
im'por·tu'ni·ty
·ties
im·pose'
·posed' ·pos'ing

im'po·si'tion
im·pos'si·bil'i·ty
·ties
im·pos'si·ble
im'post
im·pos'tor
(*deceiver*)
im·pos'ture
(*deception*)
im'po·tence
im'po·tent
im·pound'
im·pov'er·ish
im·prac'ti·ca·
bil'i·ty
im·prac'ti·ca·ble
im·prac'ti·cal
im'pre·cate'
·cat'ed ·cat'ing
im'pre·ca'tion
im'pre·cise'
im·preg'na·bil'i·ty
im·preg'na·ble
im·preg'nate
·nat·ed ·nat·ing
im'preg·na'tion
im'pre·sa'ri·o
·ri·os
im'pre·scrip'ti·ble
im·press'
im·press'i·ble
im·pres'sion
im·pres'sion·a·ble
im·pres'sion·a·bly
im·pres'sion·ism
im·pres'sive
im·pres'sive·ly
im·pri'ma·tur
im·print'
im·pris'on
im·prob'a·ble
im·promp'tu
im·prop'er
im·pro·pri'e·ty
·ties
im·prov'a·ble
im·prove'
·proved' ·prov'ing
im·prove'ment
im·prov'i·dent
im·prov'i·sa'tion
im'pro·vise'
·vised' ·vis'ing
im·pru'dence
im·pru'dent
im'pu·dence
im'pu·dent
im·pugn'
im·pugn'a·ble
im'pulse
im·pul'sion
im·pul'sive
im·pul'sive·ly
im·pu'ni·ty
im·pure'
im·pu'ri·ty
·ties
im·put'a·bil'i·ty

im·put'a·ble
im'pu·ta'tion
im·put'a·tive
im·pute'
·put'ed ·put'ing
in'a·bil'i·ty
in·ac'ces'si·ble
in·ac'cu·ra·cy
·cies
in·ac'cu·rate
in·ac'tion
in·ac'ti·vate'
·vat'ed ·vat'ing
in·ac·ti·va'tion
in·ac'tive
in·ac·tiv'i·ty
in·ad'e·qua·cy
·cies
in·ad'e·quate
in·ad·mis'si·ble
in·ad·vert'ence
in·ad·vert'ent
in'ad·vis'a·bil'i·ty
in'ad·vis'a·ble
in·al'ien·a·ble
in·al'ter·a·ble
in·ane'
in·an'i·mate
in·an'i·ty
·ties
in'ap·pli·ca·ble
in·ap·pre'ci·a·ble
in·ap·proach'a·ble
in·ap·pro'pri·ate
in·ar·tic'u·late
in·ar·tis'tic
in·as·much' as
in·at·ten'tion
in·at·ten'tive
in·au'di·ble
in·au'gu·ral
in·au'gu·rate'
·rat'ed ·rat'ing
in·aus·pi'cious
in'board'
in'born'
in'breed'
·bred' ·breed'ing
in·cal'cu·la·ble
in·cal'cu·la·bly
in·can·des'cence
in·can·des'cent
in·can·ta'tion
in·ca·pa·bil'i·ty
in·ca'pa·ble
in'ca·pac'i·tate'
·tat'ed ·tat'ing
in'ca·pac'i·ta'tion
in'ca·pac'i·ty
in·car'cer·ate'
·at'ed ·at'ing
in·car·cer·a'tion
in·car'nate
·nat·ed ·nat·ing
in·car·na'tion
in·cau'tious
in·cen'di·ar'y
·ies

in'cense
in·cense'
·censed' ·cens'ing
in·cen'tive
in·cep'tion
in·cep'tive
in·cer'ti·tude'
in·ces'sant
in'cest
in·ces'tu·ous
in·cho'ate
in'ci·dence
in'ci·dent
in'ci·den'tal
in'ci·den'tal·ly
in·cin'er·ate'
·at'ed ·at'ing
in·cin·er·a'tion
in·cin'er·a'tor
in·cip'i·ence
in·cip'i·ent
in·cise'
·cised' ·cis'ing
in·ci'sion
in·ci'sive
in·ci'sor
in·cite'
·cit'ed ·cit'ing
in·cit'er
in'ci·vil'i·ty
·ties
in·clem'en·cy
in·clem'ent
in·clin'a·ble
in'cli·na'tion
in·cline'
·clined' ·clin'ing
in·cli·nom'e·ter
in·clude'
·clud'ed
·clud'ing
in·clu'sion
in·clu'sive
in'co·er'ci·ble
in'cog·ni'to
·tos
in·cog'ni·zance
in·cog'ni·zant
in'co·her'ence
in'co·her'ent
in'com·bus'ti·ble
in'come
in'com'ing
in'com·men'su-
ra·ble
in'com·men'su-
rate
in'com·mode'
·mod'ed ·mod'ing
in'com·mo'di·ous
in'com·mu'ni-
ca·ble
in'com·mu'ni-
ca'do
in·com'pa·ra·ble
in'com·pat'i-
bil'i·ty
·ties

in'com·pat'i·ble
in·com'pe·tence
in·com'pe·tent
in'com·plete'
in'com·pre-
hen'si·ble
in'com·press'i·ble
in'com·put'a·ble
in'con·ceiv'a·ble
in·con·clu'sive
in·con'dite
in'con·form'i·ty
in·con'gru·ent
in·con·gru'i·ty
in·con'gru·ous
in·con·se-
quen'tial
in'con·sid'er·a·ble
in'con·sid'er·ate
in'con·sid'er-
ate·ly
in'con·sid'er-
a'tion
in'con·sis'ten·cy
·cies
in'con·sis'tent
in·con·sol'a·ble
in'con·spic'u·ous
in·con'stan·cy
in·con'stant
in'con·sum'a·ble
in·con·test'a·ble
in·con'ti·nent
in·con·trol'la·ble
in'con·tro·vert'i-
ble
in'con·ven'ience
in'con·ven'ient
in'con·vert'i·ble
in·cor'po·rate'
·rat'ed ·rat'ing
in·cor'po·ra'tion
in·cor'po·ra'tor
in'cor·po're·al
in'cor·rect'
in·cor'ri·gi·bil'i·ty
in·cor'ri·gi·ble
in·cor'ri·gi·bly
in'cor·rupt'
in'cor·rupt'i·ble
in·creas'a·ble
in·crease'
·creased'
·creas'ing
in·creas'ing·ly
in·cred'i·bil'i·ty
in·cred'i·ble
in·cred'i·bly
in·cre·du'li·ty
in·cred'u·lous
in'cre·ment
in'cre·men'tal
in·crim'i·nate'
·nat'ed ·nat'ing
in·crim'i·na'tion
in·crim'i·na·to'ry

in·crust'
in'crus·ta'tion
in'cu·bate'
·bat'ed ·bat'ing
in'cu·ba'tion
in'cu·ba'tor
in·cul'cate
·cat·ed ·cat·ing
in·cul·ca'tion
in·culp'a·ble
in·cul·pa'tion
in·cum'ben·cy
·cies
in·cum'bent
in·cu·nab'u·la
in·cur'
·curred'
·cur'ring
in·cur'a·bil'i·ty
in·cur'a·ble
in·cur'a·bly
in·cu'ri·ous
in·cur'sion
in·debt'ed
in·de'cen·cy
·cies
in·de'cent
in·de·ci'pher-
a·ble
in·de·ci'sion
in·de·ci'sive
in·de·clin'a·ble
in·dec'o·rous
in·de·co'rum
in·deed'
in·de·fat'i·ga·ble
in·de·fat'i·ga·bly
in·de·fea'si·ble
in·de·fect'i·ble
in·de·fen'si·ble
in·de·fin'a·ble
in·def'i·nite
in·del'i·ble
in·del'i·bly
in·del'i·ca·cy
·cies
in·del'i·cate
in·dem'ni·fi·
ca'tion
in·dem'ni·fy'
·fied' ·fy'ing
in·dem'ni·ty
·ties
in·dent'
in·den·ta'tion
in·den'tion
in·den'ture
·tured ·tur·ing
in·de·pend'ence
in·de·pend'ent
in'·depth'
in·de·scrib'a·ble
in·de·scrib'a·bly
in·de·struct'i·ble
in·de·ter'mi·na-
ble
in·de·ter'mi·na·cy
in·de·ter'mi·nate

in·de·ter·mi·
na'tion
in'dex
·dex·es *or* ·di·ces'
In'di·an'a
in'di·cate'
·cat·ed ·cat'ing
in'di·ca'tion
in·dic'a·tive
in'di·ca'tor
in·dict'
(*accuse formally;*
see indite)
in·dict'a·ble
in·dict'ment
in·dif'fer·ence
in·dif'fer·ent
in'di·gence
in·dig'e·nous
in'di·gent
in·di·gest'i·ble
in·di·ges'tion
in·dig'nant
in·dig·na'tion
in·dig'ni·ty
·ties
in'di·go'
in·di·rect'
in·di·rec'tion
in·dis·cern'i·ble
in'dis·creet'
(*lacking prudence*)
in'dis·crete'
(*not separated*)
in'dis·cre'tion
(*indiscreet act*)
in'dis·crim'i·nate
in'dis·pen'sa·ble
in'dis·pose'
in'dis·po·si'tion
in'dis·pu'ta·ble
in'dis·sol'u·ble
in'dis·tinct'
in'dis·tinc'tive
in'dis·tin'guish·
a·ble
in·dite'
·dit'ed ·dit'ing
(*write;* see indict)
in'di·vid'u·al
in'di·vid'u·al·ism
in'di·vid'u·al·
is'tic
in'di·vid'u·al'i·ty
in'di·vid'u·al·ize'
·ized' ·iz'ing
in'di·vid'u·al·ly
in'di·vid'u·ate'
·at'ed ·at'ing
in'di·vis'i·bil'i·ty
in'di·vis'i·ble
in·doc'tri·nate'
·nat'ed ·nat'ing
in·doc'tri·na'tion
in·doc'tri·na'tor
in'do·lence
in'do·lent
in·dom'i·ta·ble

in·dom'i·ta·bly
in'door'
in'doors'
in·dorse'
·dorsed'
·dors'ing
in·du'bi·ta·ble
in·du'bi·ta·bly
in·duce'
·duced' ·duc'ing
in·duce'ment
in·duct'
in·duct'ance
in·duct'ee'
in·duc'tile
in·duc'tion
in·duc'tive
in·duc'tor
in·dulge'
·dulged'
·dulg'ing
in·dul'gence
in·dul'gent
in'du·rate'
·rat'ed ·rat'ing
in'du·ra'tion
in·dus'tri·al
in·dus'tri·al·ism
in·dus'tri·al·ist
in·dus'tri·al·i·
za'tion
in·dus'tri·al·ize'
·ized' ·iz'ing
in·dus'tri·ous
in'dus·try
·tries
in·e'bri·ate'
·at'ed ·at'ing
in·e'bri·a'tion
in·e'bri·e·ty
in·ed'i·ble
in·ed'u·ca·ble
in·ef'fa·ble
in·ef'fa·bly
in'ef·face'a·ble
in'ef·fec'tive
in'ef·fec'tu·al
in'ef·fi·ca'cious
in·ef'fi·ca·cy
in'ef·fi'cien·cy
in'ef·fi'cient
in'e·las'tic
in'e·las·tic'i·ty
in·el'e·gance
in·el'e·gant
in·el'i·gi·bil'i·ty
in·el'i·gi·ble
in'e·luc'ta·ble
in'e·lud'i·ble
in·ept'
in·ept'i·tude'
in'e·qual'i·ty
·ties
in·eq'ui·ta·ble
in·eq'ui·ty
·ties
(*unfairness;*
see iniquity)

in'e·rad'i·ca·ble
in·er'ra·ble
in·er'rant
in·ert'
in·er'tia
in'es·cap'a·ble
in'es·cap'a·bly
in'es·sen'tial
in·es'ti·ma·ble
in·ev'i·ta·bil'i·ty
in·ev'i·ta·ble
in·ev'i·ta·bly
in·ex·act'
in'ex·cus'a·ble
in'ex·haust'i·ble
in·ex'o·ra·ble
in'ex·pe'di·ent
in'ex·pen'sive
in'ex·pe'ri·ence
in·ex'pert
in·ex'pi·a·ble
in·ex'pli·ca·ble
in·ex'pli·ca·bly
in'ex·press'i·ble
in'ex·press'i·bly
in'ex·pres'sive
in'ex·ten'si·ble
in'ex·tin'guish·a·
ble
in·ex'tri·ca·ble
in·ex'tri·ca·bly
in·fal'li·bil'i·ty
in·fal'li·ble
in·fal'li·bly
in'fa·mous
in'fa·my
·mies
in'fan·cy
·cies
in'fant
in·fan'ti·cide'
in'fan·tile'
in'fan·ti·lism
in'fan·try
·tries
in'fan·try·man
in·fat'u·ate'
·at'ed ·at'ing
in·fat'u·a'tion
in·fect'
in·fec'tion
in·fec'tious
in·fec'tive
in·fec'tor
in'fe·lic'i·tous
in'fe·lic'i·ty
·ties
in·fer'
·ferred'
·fer'ring
in·fer'a·ble
in'fer·ence
in'fer·en'tial
in·fe'ri·or
in·fe'ri·or'i·ty
in·fer'nal
in·fer'no
·nos

in·fer'tile
in·fest'
in'fi·del
in'fi·del'i·ty
·ties
in'field'
in·fil'trate
·trat·ed ·trat·ing
in'fil·tra'tion
in'fil·tra'tor
in'fi·nite
in'fi·nite·ly
in·fin·i·tes'i·mal
in·fin'i·tive
in·fin'i·ty
·ties
in·firm'
in·fir'ma·ry
·ries
in·fir'mi·ty
·ties
in·flame'
·flamed'
·flam'ing
in·flam'ma·ble
in·flam·ma'tion
in·flam'ma·to'ry
in·flate'
·flat'ed
·flat'ing
in·fla'tion
in·fla'tion·ar'y
in·flect'
in·flec'tion
in·flex'i·ble
in·flex'i·bly
in·flict'
in·flic'tion
in'-flight'
in'flow'
in'flu·ence
·enced ·enc·ing
in·flu·en'tial
in·flu·en'za
in'flux'
in·form'
in·for'mal
in'for·mal'i·ty
in·form'ant
in'for·ma'tion
in·form'a·tive
in·form'er
in·frac'tion
in·fran'gi·ble
in'fra·red'
in·fre'quent
in·fringe'
in·fringe'ment
in·fu'ri·ate'
·at'ed ·at'ing
in·fuse'
·fused' ·fus'ing
in·fu'sion
in·gen'ious
(*clever;* see
ingenuous)
in·gé·nue'
in·ge·nu'i·ty

in·gen'u·ous
(*frank;* see
ingenious)
in·gest'
in·ges'tion
in·glo'ri·ous
in'got
in·grained'
in'grate
in·gra'ti·ate'
·at'ed ·at'ing
in·grat'i·tude'
in·gre'di·ent
in'gress
in'-group'
in'grown'
in·hab'it
in·hab'it·a·ble
in·hab'it·ant
in·hal'ant
in'ha·la'tion
in·hale'
·haled' ·hal'ing
in·hal'er
in·har·mon'ic
in·har·mo'ni·ous
in·here'
·hered' ·her'ing
in·her'ence
in·her'ent
in·her'it
in·her'it·a·ble
in·her'it·ance
in·her'i·tor
in·hib'it
in·hi·bi'tion
in·hib'i·tive
in·hib'i·tor
in·hos'pi·ta·ble
in'hos·pi·tal'i·ty
in'-house'
in·hu'man
in·hu·mane'
in'hu·man'i·ty
·ties
in·im'i·cal
in·im'i·ta·ble
in·iq'ui·tous
in·iq'ui·ty
·ties
(*wickedness;*
see inequity)
in·i'tial
·tialed *or* ·tialled
·tial·ing *or* ·tial·ling
in·i'tial·ly
in·i'ti·ate'
·at'ed ·at'ing
in·i'ti·a'tion
in·i'ti·a'tor
in·ject'
in·jec'tion
in·jec'tor
in·ju·di'cious
in·junc'tion
in'jure
·jured ·jur·ing

in·ju'ri·ous
in'ju·ry
·ries
in·jus'tice
ink'blot'
ink'ling
ink'y
·i·er ·i·est
in'laid'
in'land'
in'-law'
in'lay'
·laid' ·lay'ing
·lays'
in'let
in'mate'
in me·mo'ri·am
in'most'
in'nards
in·nate'
in'ner·most'
in'ner·spring'
in·ner'vate
·vat·ed ·vat·ing
in'ning
inn'keep'er
in'no·cence
in'no·cent
in·noc'u·ous
in'no·vate'
·vat'ed ·vat'ing
in'no·va'tion
in'no·va'tive
in'no·va'tor
in·nu·en'do
·does *or* ·dos
in·nu'mer·a·ble
in·oc'u·late'
·lat·ed ·lat'ing
in·oc'u·la'tion
in'of·fen'sive
in·op'er·a·ble
in·op'er·a·tive
in·op'por·tune'
in·or'di·nate
in·or·gan'ic
in'pa'tient
in'put'
in'quest
in·qui'e·tude'
in·quire'
·quired'
·quir'ing
in'quir·y
·ies
in·qui·si'tion
in·quis'i·tive
in·quis'i·tor
in'road'
in·sane'
in·san'i·tar'y
in·san'i·ty
in·sa'ti·a·ble
in·scribe'
·scribed'
·scrib'ing
in·scrip'tion
in·scru'ta·bil'i·ty

in·scru'ta·ble	in'sti·ga'tion	in·tel'li·gence	in'ter·lin'e·ar	in'ter·sper'sion	in'un·date'
in'seam'	in'sti·ga'tor	in·tel'li·gent	in'ter·lin'ing	in'ter·state'	·dat'ed ·dat'ing
in'sect	in·still' or ·stil'	in·tel'li·gent'si·a	in'ter·lock'	in'ter·stel'lar	in'un·da'tion
in·sec'ti·cide'	·stilled' ·still'ing	in·tel'li·gi·bil'i·ty	in'ter·lo·cu'tion	in·ter'stice	in·ure'
in·se·cure'	in'stinct	in·tel'li·gi·ble	in'ter·loc'u·tor	·stic·es	·ured' ·ur'ing
in·se·cu'ri·ty	in·stinc'tive	in·tel'li·gi·bly	in'ter·loc'u·to'ry	in'ter·twine'	in·vade'
in·sem'i·nate'	in'sti·tute'	In'tel·sat'	in'ter·lope'	in'ter·ur'ban	·vad'ed ·vad'ing
·nat'ed ·nat'ing	·tut'ed ·tut'ing	in·tem'per·ance	·loped' ·lop'ing	in'ter·val	in·vad'er
in·sem'i·na'tion	in'sti·tu'tion	in·tem'per·ate	in'ter·lop'er	in'ter·vene'	in'va·lid
in·sen'sate	in'sti·tu'tion·al·	in·tend'	in'ter·lude'	·vened' ·ven'ing	in·val'id
in·sen·si·bil'i·ty	ize'	in·tend'ant	in'ter·mar'riage	in'ter·ven'tion	in·val'i·date'
in·sen'si·ble	·ized' ·iz'ing	in·tense'	in'ter·mar'ry	in'ter·view'	·dat'ed ·dat'ing
in·sen'si·tive	in·struct'	in·tense'ly	in'ter·me'di·ar'y	in'ter·view'er	in·val'i·da'tion
in·sen·si·tiv'i·ty	in·struc'tion	in·ten'si·fi·ca'tion	·ar'ies	in'ter·weave'	in·val'u·a·ble
in·sep'a·ra·ble	in·struc'tive	·fied' ·fy'ing	in'ter·me'di·ate	·wove' ·wov'en	in·val'u·a·bly
in·sert'	in·struc'tor	in·ten'si·fy'	in·ter'ment	·weav'ing	in·var'i·a·ble
in·ser'tion	in'stru·ment	in·ten'si·ty	in'ter·mez'zo	in·tes'tate	in·var'i·a·bly
in'·ser'vice	in'stru·men'tal	in·ten'sive	·zos or ·zi	in·tes'tin·al	in·va'sion
in'side'	in'stru·men·	in·tent'	in·ter'mi·na·ble	in·tes'tine	in·vec'tive
in·sid'i·ous	tal'i·ty	in·ten'tion	in'ter·min'gle	in'ti·ma·cy	in·veigh'
in'sight'	in'stru·men·	in·ten'tion·al	in'ter·mis'sion	·cies	in·vei'gle
in·sig'ni·a	ta'tion	in·ten'tion·al·ly	in'ter·mit'tent	in'ti·mate	·gled ·gling
in·sig·nif'i·cance	in·sub·or'di·nate	in·ter'	in'tern	in'ti·ma'tion	in·vent'
in·sig·nif'i·cant	in·sub·or'di·	·terred' ·ter'ring	(doctor)	in·tim'i·date'	in·ven'tion
in'sin·cere'	na'tion	in'ter·act'	in·tern'	·dat'ed ·dat'ing	in·ven'tive
in'sin·cere'ly	in·sub·stan'tial	in'ter·ac'tion	(detain)	in·tim'i·da'tion	in·ven'tor
in'sin·cer'i·ty	in·suf'fer·a·ble	in'ter·breed'	in·ter'nal	in·tol'er·a·ble	in'ven·to'ry
in·sin'u·ate'	in·suf·fi'cien·cy	·bred' ·breed'ing	in·ter'nal·ize'	in·tol'er·ance	·ries, ·ried ·ry·ing
·at'ed ·at'ing	·cies	in'ter·cede'	·ized' ·iz'ing	in·tol'er·ant	in·verse'
in·sin'u·a'tion	in·suf·fi'cient	·ced'ed ·ced'ing	in·ter'nal·ly	in'to·na'tion	in·ver'sion
in·sip'id	in'su·lar	in'ter·cept'	in'ter·na'tion·al	in·tone'	in·vert'
in·si·pid'i·ty	in'su·late'	in'ter·cep'tion	in'ter·ne'cine	in·tox'i·cant	in·ver'te·brate
in·sist'	·lat'ed ·lat'ing	in'ter·cep'tor	in·tern·ee'	in·tox'i·cate'	in·vert'i·ble
in·sist'ence	in·su·la'tion	in'ter·ces'sion	in'ter·nist	·cat'ed ·cat'ing	in·vest'
in·sist'ent	in'su·la·tor	in'ter·change'	in·tern'ment	in·tox'i·ca'tion	in·ves'ti·gate'
in·so·bri'e·ty	in'su·lin	in'ter·change'a·	in'tern·ship'	in·trac'ta·ble	·gat'ed ·gat'ing
in'so·far'	in·sult'	ble	in'ter·of'fice	in'tra·mu'ral	in·ves'ti·ga'tion
in'sole'	in·su'per·a·ble	in'ter·com'	in'ter·pen'e·	in'tra·mus'cu·lar	in·ves'ti·ga'tor
in'so·lence	in·sup·port'a·ble	in'ter·com·mu'ni·	trate'	in·tran'si·gent	in·ves'ti·ture
in'so·lent	in·sup·press'i·ble	cate'	in'ter·per'son·al	in·tran'si·tive	in·vest'ment
in·sol'u·ble	in·sur'a·bil'i·ty	in'ter·con·nect'	in'ter·phone'	in'tra·state'	in·vet'er·ate
in·sol'vent	in·sur'a·ble	in'ter·course'	in'ter·plan'e·	in'tra·u'ter·ine	in·vi'a·ble
in·som'ni·a	in·sur'ance	in'ter·de·nom'i·	tar'y	in'tra·ve'nous	in·vid'i·ous
in·sou'ci·ance	in·sure'	na'tion·al	in'ter·play'	in·trep'id	in·vig'or·ate'
in·sou'ci·ant	·sured' ·sur'ing	in'ter·de·part'·	in·ter'po·late'	in'tre·pid'i·ty	·at'ed ·at'ing
in·spect'	in·sur'er	men'tal	·lat'ed ·lat'ing	in'tri·ca·cy	in·vin'ci·bil'i·ty
in·spec'tion	in·sur'gence	in'ter·de·pend'·	in·ter'po·la'tion	·cies	in·vin'ci·ble
in·spec'tor	in·sur'gent	ence	in'ter·pose'	in'tri·cate	in·vin'ci·bly
in'spi·ra'tion	in'sur·mount'a·	in'ter·dict'	in·ter'pret	in·trigue'	in·vi'o·la·ble
in·spire'	ble	in'ter·dis'ci·	in·ter'pre·ta'tion	·trigued'	in·vi'o·late
·spired' ·spir'ing	in'sur·rec'tion	pli·nar'y	in·ter'pret·er	·trigu'ing	in·vis'i·ble
in·spir'it	in·tact'	in'ter·est	in'ter·ra'cial	in·trin'sic	in'vi·ta'tion
in·sta·bil'i·ty	in·tagl'io	in'ter·est·ed	in'ter·re·late'	in'tro·duce'	in·vite'
in·stall' or ·stal'	·ios	in'ter·faith'	in'ter·re·la'tion	·duced' ·duc'ing	·vit'ed ·vit'ing
·stalled' ·stall'ing	in'take'	in'ter·fere'	in·ter'ro·gate'	in'tro·duc'tion	in·vo·ca'tion
in·stal·la'tion	in·tan'gi·ble	·fered' ·fer'ing	·gat'ed ·gat'ing	in'tro·duc'to·ry	in'voice
in·stall'ment	in'te·ger	in'ter·fer'ence	in·ter'ro·ga'tion	in'tro·spec'tion	in·voke'
or ·stal'ment	in'te·gral	in'ter·fer'on	in·ter'ro·ga'tor	in'tro·spec'tive	·voked' ·vok'ing
in'stance	in'te·grate'	in'ter·im	in'ter·rog'a·tive	in'tro·ver'sion	in·vol'un·tar'i·ly
in'stant	·grat'ed ·grat'ing	in·te'ri·or	in·ter'ro·ga·to'ry	in'tro·vert'	in·vol'un·tar'y
in'stan·ta'ne·ous	in'te·gra'tion	in'ter·ject'	in'ter·rupt'	in·trude'	in'vo·lute'
in·stan'ter	in·teg'ri·ty	in'ter·jec'tion	in'ter·rup'tion	·trud'ed	in·volve'
in·state'	in·teg'u·ment	in'ter·lace'	in'ter·scho·las'tic	·trud'ing	·volved'
·stat'ed ·stat'ing	in'tel·lect'	in'ter·leaf'	in'ter·sect'	in·trud'er	·volv'ing
in·stead'	in'tel·lec'tu·al	·leaves'	in'ter·sec'tion	in·tru'sion	in·vul'ner·a·ble
in'step'	in'tel·lec'tu·al·ize'	in'ter·leave'	in'ter·sperse'	in·tru'sive	in'ward
in'sti·gate'	·ized' ·iz'ing	·leaved'	·spersed'	in·tu·i'tion	i'o·dine'
·gat'ed ·gat'ing	in'tel·lec'tu·al·ly	·leav'ing	·spers'ing	in·tu'i·tive	

i'on
i'on·i·za'tion
i'on·ize'
·ized' ·iz'ing
i·on'o·sphere'
i·o'ta
I'o·wa
ip'e·cac'
ip'so fac'to
i·ras'ci·bil'i·ty
i·ras'ci·ble
i·rate'
ire'ful·ly
ir'i·des'cence
ir'i·des'cent
irk'some
i'ron·bound'
i'ron·clad'
i·ron'i·cal
i·ron'i·cal·ly
i'ron·stone'
i'ron·work'
i'ro·ny
·nies
ir·ra'di·ate'
ir·ra'di·a'tion
ir·ra'tion·al
ir·ra'tion·al'i·ty
ir·ra'tion·al·ly
ir·re·claim'a·ble
ir·rec'on·cil'a·ble
ir·re·cov'er·a·ble
ir·re·deem'a·ble
ir·re·duc'i·ble
ir·ref'u·ta·ble
ir·reg'u·lar
ir·reg'u·lar'i·ty
·ties
ir·rel'e·vant
ir're·li'gious
ir're·me'di·a·ble
ir're·mis'si·ble
ir're·mov'a·ble
ir're·rep'a·ra·ble
ir're·place'a·ble
ir're·press'i·ble
ir're·proach'a·ble
ir're·sist'i·ble
ir·res'o·lute'
ir're·spec'tive
ir're·spon'si·ble
ir're·triev'a·ble
ir·rev'er·ence
ir·rev'er·ent
ir're·vers'i·ble
ir·rev'o·ca·ble
ir'ri·ga·ble
ir'ri·gate'
·gat'ed ·gat'ing
ir'ri·ga'tion
ir'ri·ta·bil'i·ty
ir'ri·ta·ble
ir'ri·ta·bly
ir'ri·tant
ir'ri·tate'
·tat'ed ·tat'ing
ir'ri·ta'tion
ir·rupt'

ir·rup'tion
i'sin·glass'
is'land
isle
(island; see aisle)
is'let
(small island;
see eyelet)
is'n't
i'so·bar'
i'so·late'
·lat'ed ·lat'ing
i'so·la'tion
i'so·la'tion·ist
i'so·mer
i'so·met'ric
i'so·met'ri·cal·ly
i·sos'ce·les'
i'so·therm'
i'so·tope'
i'so·trop'ic
Is'ra·el
Is·rae'li
is'su·ance
is'sue
·sued ·su·ing
isth'mus
·mus·es or ·mi
i·tal'ic
i·tal'i·cize'
·cized' ·ciz'ing
itch'i·ness
itch'y
·i·er ·i·est
i'tem·ize'
·ized' ·iz'ing
it'er·ate'
·at'ed ·at'ing
it'er·a'tion
i·tin'er·ant
i·tin'er·ar'y
·ies
i·tin'er·ate'
·at'ed ·at'ing
its
(of it)
it's
(it is)
it·self'
I've
i'vied
i'vo·ry
·ries
i'vy
i'vies

J

jab
jabbed jab'bing
jab'ber
ja·bot'
ja'cinth
jack'al
jack'a·napes'
jack'ass'

jack'boot'
jack'et
jack'ham'mer
jack'-in-the-box'
-box'es
jack'knife'
·knives'
·knifed' ·knif'ing
jack'-of-all'-
trades'
jacks'-
jack'-o'-lan'tern
·terns
jack'pot'
jack'screw'
jack'straw'
Jac·quard'
jade
jad'ed jad'ing
jag'ged
jag'uar
jai' a·lai'
jail'bird'
jail'er or ·or
jal'ou·sie'
(door; see
jealousy)
jam
jammed
jam'ming
jam'ba·lay'a
jam'bo·ree'
jan'gle
·gled ·gling
jan'i·tor
Jan'u·ar'y
·ar'ies
ja·pan'
·panned'
·pan'ning
jar
jarred jar'ring
jar'di·niere'
jar'gon
jas'mine
jas'per
ja'to or JA'TO
jaun'dice
·diced ·dic·ing
jaun'ti·ly
jaun'ti·ness
jaun'ty
·ti·er ·ti·est
jav'e·lin
jaw'bone'
jaw'break'er
Jay'cee'
jay'walk'er
jazz'i·ness
jazz'y
·i·er ·i·est
jeal'ous
jeal'ous·y
·ies
(envy; see
jalousie)
jeans
jeer'ing·ly

je·june'
jell'i·fy'
·fied' ·fy'ing
jel'ly
·lies, ·lied ·ly·ing
jel'ly·fish'
jel'ly·roll'
jen'ny
·nies
jeop'ard·ize'
·ized' ·iz'ing
jeop'ard·y
je·quir'i·ty
·ties
jer'e·mi'ad
jerk'i·ly
jer'kin
jerk'i·ness
jerk'wa'ter
jerk'y
·i·er ·i·est
(moving fitfully)
jer'ky
(dried beef)
Jer'sey
·seys
(dairy cattle)
jer'sey
·seys
(cloth; shirt)
jest'er
jet
jet'ted jet'ting
jet'-black'
jet'lin'er
jet'port'
jet'-pro·pelled'
jet'sam
jet stream
jet'ti·son
jet'ty
·ties, ·tied ·ty·ing
jew'el
·eled or ·elled
·el·ing or ·el·ling
jew'el·er or
·el·ler
jew'el·ry
Jew'ish
Jew'ry
·ries
jew's'-harp' or
jews'-harp'
Jez'e·bel
jib
jibbed jib'bing
jibe
jibed jib'ing
(nautical; agree;
see gibe)
jig'ger
jig'gle
·gled ·gling
jig'saw'
Jim'-Crow'
jim'my
·mies
·mied ·my·ing

jin'gle
·gled ·gling
jin'go
·goes
jin'go·ism
jin'go·is'ti·cal·ly
jin·ni'
jinn
jin·rik'i·sha
jinx
jit'ney
·neys
jit'ter·y
job
jobbed job'bing
job'ber
jock'ey
·eys
jock'strap'
jo·cose'
jo·cos'i·ty
·ties
joc'u·lar
joc'u·lar'i·ty
joc'und
jo·cun'di·ty
jodh'purs
jog
jogged jog'ging
jog'ger
jog'gle
·gled ·gling
john'ny·cake'
join'er
joint'ly
join'ture
joist
joke
joked jok'ing
jol'li·ness
jol'li·ty
jol'ly
·li·er ·li·est
jon'quil
jos'tle
·tled ·tling
jot
jot'ted jot'ting
jounce
jounced
jounc'ing
jour'nal
jour'nal·ese'
jour'nal·ism
jour'nal·is'tic
jour'ney
·neys
·neyed ·ney·ing
jour'ney·man
joust
jo'vi·al
jo'vi·al'i·ty
jo'vi·al·ly
jowl
joy'ful
joy'less
joy'ous

ju'bi·lant
ju'bi·la'tion
ju'bi·lee'
Ju·da'i·ca
Ju'da·ism
judge
judged judg'ing
judg'ment or
judge'-
ju'di·ca·to'ry
·ries
ju·di'cial
ju·di'ci·ar'y
·ies
ju·di'cious
ju'do
jug
jugged jug'ging
jug'ger·naut'
jug'gle
·gled ·gling
jug'u·lar
juice
juiced juic'ing
juic'er
juic'i·ly
juic'i·ness
juic'y
·i·er ·i·est
ju·jit'su or
ju·jut'su
ju'jube
juke'box'
ju'lep
ju'li·enne'
Ju·ly'
·lies'
jum'ble
·bled ·bling
jum'bo
jump'er
jump'i·ness
jump'y
·i·er ·i·est
junc'tion
junc'ture
June
jun'gle
jun'ior
jun·ior'i·ty
ju'ni·per
jun'ket
junk'man'
jun'ta
jun'to
·tos
ju·rid'i·cal
ju·rid'i·cal·ly
ju·ris·dic'tion
ju·ris·pru'dence
ju'rist
ju·ris'tic
ju'ror
ju'ry
·ries
ju'ry·man
jus'tice
jus'ti·fi'a·ble

jus'ti·fi'a·bly
jus'ti·fi·ca'tion
jus'ti·fy'
· fied' ·fy'ing
just'ly ·
jut
jut'ted jut'ting
jute
ju'ven·ile
jux·ta·pose'
· posed' ·pos'ing
jux'ta·po·si'tion

K

Ka·bu'ki
kaf'fee·klatsch'
kai'ser
ka·lei'do·scope'
ka·lei'do·scop'ic
kal'so·mine'
ka'mi·ka'ze
kan'ga·roo'
Kan'sas
ka'o·lin
ka'pok
ka·put'
kar'a·kul
kar'at
ka·ra'te
ka'sha
ka'ty·did'
katz'en·jam'mer
kay'ak
ka·zoo'
ke·bab'
kedge ·
kedged kedg'ing
keel'haul'
keel'son
keen'ness
keep
kept keep'ing
keep'sake'
keg'ler
ke'loid
kempt
ken'nel
·neled or ·nelled
·nel·ing or
·nel·ling
Ken·tuck'y
ker'a·tin
ker'chief
ker'miss or ·mess
ker'nel
(grain; see
colonel)
ker'o·sene' or
·sine'
ker'sey
·seys
ketch'up
ke'tone
ket'tle
ket'tle·drum'

key
keys
keyed key'ing
(lock; see quay)
key'board'
key club
key'hole'
key'note'
key punch
key'stone'
key'way'
kha'ki
kib'ble
kib·butz'
kib'but·zim'
kib'itz·er
kick'off'
kid'nap'
·napped' or
·naped'
·nap'ping or
·nap'ing
kid'nap'per or
kid'nap'er
kid'ney
·neys
kill'er
kill'-joy'
kiln
kil'o·gram'
kil'o·hertz'
·hertz'
kil'o·li'ter
ki·lo'me·ter
kil'o·volt'
kil'o·watt'
kil'o·watt'-hour'
kil'ter
ki·mo'no
·nos
kin'der·gar'ten
kin'der·gart'ner
kind'heart'ed
kin'dle
·dled ·dling
kind'li·ness
kind'ly
·li·er ·li·est
kin'dred
kin·e·mat'ics
kin'e·scope'
ki·ne'sics
kin'es·thet'ic
ki·net'ic
kin'folk'
king'bolt'
king'dom
king'fish'
king'li·ness
king'ly
·li·er ·li·est
king'pin'
king post
king'-size'
kink'i·ness
kink'y
·i·er ·i·est
kin'ship'

kins'man
ki'osk
kis'met
kitch'en
kitch'en·ette'
kitch'en·ware'
kit'ten
kit'ty
·ties
kit'ty-cor'nered
klax'on
Klee'nex
klep'to·ma'ni·ac
klieg light
knack
knack'wurst'
knap'sack'
knave
(rogue; see nave)
knav'er·y
knav'ish
knead
(press; see need)
knee
kneed knee'ing
knee'cap'
knee'-deep'
knee'-high'
knee'hole'
kneel
knelt or kneeled
kneel'ing
knee'pad'
knell
knick'er·bock'ers
knick'knack'
knife
knives
knifed knif'ing
knife'-edge'
knight
(rank; see night)
knight'hood'
knit
knit'ted or knit
knit'ting
knit'ter
knob'by
·bi·er ·bi·est
knock'a·bout'
knock'down'
knock'-kneed'
knock'out'
knoll
knot
knot'ted
knot'ting
knot'hole'
knot'ty
·ti·er ·ti·est
know
knew known
know'ing
know'a·ble
know'-how'
know'-it-all'
knowl'edge
knowl'edge·a·ble

knowl'edge·a·bly
knuck'le
·led ·ling
knurled
ko·a'la
ko'di·ak' bear
kohl'ra'bi
·bies
Ko·ran'
ko'sher
kow'tow'
ku'chen
ku'dos
küm'mel
kum'quat
kwa'shi·or'kor

L

la'bel
· beled or ·belled
· bel·ing or
· bel·ling
la'bi·al
la'bile
la'bor
lab'o·ra·to'ry
· ries
la'bor·er
la·bo'ri·ous
la'bor-sav'ing
lab'y·rinth'
lab'y·rin'thine
lace
laced lac'ing
lac'er·ate'
· at'ed ·at'ing
lac'er·a'tion
lace'work'
lach'ry·mose'
lac'i·ness
lack·a·dai'si·cal
lack'ey
· eys
lack'lus'ter
la·con'ic
la·con'i·cal·ly
lac'quer
la·crosse'
lac'tate
· tat·ed ·tat·ing
lac·ta'tion
lac'te·al
lac'tic
lac'tose
la·cu'na
· nas or ·nae
lac'y
· i·er ·i·est
lad'der
lad'en
lad'ing
la'dle
· dled ·dling
la'dy
· dies

la'dy·bug'
la'dy·fin'ger
la'dy·like'
la'dy·ship'
lag
lagged lag'ging
la'ger
lag'gard
la·gniappe'
la·goon'
lair
(den; see layer)
lais'sez faire'
la'i·ty
la'ma
(monk; see llama)
la'ma·ser'y
· ies
lam·baste'
· bast'ed ·bast'ing
lam'bent
lamb'kin
lam'bre·quin
lamb'skin'
lame
(crippled)
la·mé';
(fabric)
la·ment'
lam'en·ta·ble
lam'en·ta'tion
lam'i·nate'
· nat'ed ·nat'ing
lam'i·na'tion
lamp'black'
lam·poon'
lamp'post'
lance
lanced lanc'ing
lan'dau
land'fill'
land'hold'er
land'ing
land'la'dy
land'locked'
land'lord'
land'lub'ber
land'mark'
land'own'er
land'scape'
· scaped'
· scap'ing
land'slide'
lands'man
lan'guage
lan'guid
lan'guish
lan'guor
lan'guor·ous
lank'li·ness
lank'ness
lank'y
· i·er ·i·est
lan'o·lin
lan'tern
lan'yard
lap
lapped lap'ping

la·pel'
lap'i·dar'y
· ies
lap'in
lap'is laz'u·li'
lapse
lapsed laps'ing
lar'ce·nous
lar'ce·ny
lard'er
large
larg'er larg'est
large'ly
large'-scale'
lar'gess or ·gesse
lar'i·at
lar'va
· vae or ·vas
la·ryn'ge·al
lar'yn·gi'tis
lar'ynx
lar'ynx·es or
la·ryn'ges
la·sa'gna
las·civ'i·ous
lase
lased las'ing
(emit laser light;
see laze)
la'ser
lash'ing
las'si·tude'
las'so
· sos or ·soes
last'-ditch'
Las'tex
last'ing
latch'key'
latch'string'
late
lat'er or lat'ter
lat'est or last
la·teen'
late'ly
la'ten·cy
la'tent
lat'er·al
la'tex
lat'i·ces' or
la'tex·es
lath
(wood strip)
lathe
lathed lath'ing
(machine)
lath'er
lath'ing
lat'i·tude'
lat'ke
· kes
la·trine'
lat'ter-day'
lat'tice
· ticed ·tic·ing
lat'tice·work'
laud'a·ble
laud'a·bly
laud'a·to'ry

laugh'a·ble
laugh'ing·stock'
laugh'ter
laun'der
laun'dress
laun'dro·mat'
laun'dry
·dries
laun'dry·man
lau're·ate
lau'rel
la'va
la·va'bo
·boes
lav'a·liere'
lav'a·to'ry
·ries
lav'en·der
lav'ish
law'-a·bid'ing
law'break'er
law'ful
law'ful·ly
law'giv'er
law'less
law'mak'er
lawn mower
law'suit'
law'yer
lax'a·tive
lax'i·ty
lay
laid lay'ing
(put; see lie)
lay'er
(stratum; see
lair)
lay·ette'
lay'man
lay'off'
lay'out'
lay'o·ver
laze
lazed laz'ing
(loaf; see lase)
la'zi·ly
la'zi·ness
la'zy
·zi·er ·zi·est
leach
(filter; see leech)
lead
led lead'ing
lead'en
lead'er·ship'
lead'-in'
lead'off'
leaf
leaves
leaf'let
leaf'y
·i·er ·i·est
league
leagued
leagu'ing
leagu'er
leak
(escape; see leek)

leak'age
leak'y
·i·er ·i·est
lean
leaned or leant
lean'ing
lean
(thin; see lien)
lean'ness
lean'-to'
-tos'
leap
leaped or leapt
leap'ing
leap'frog'
·frogged'
·frog'ging
learn
learned or learnt
learn'ing
learn'ed adj.
leas'a·ble
lease
leased leas'ing
lease'-back'
lease'hold'er
least
leath'er
leath'er·ette'
leath'er·i·ness
leath'er·y
leave
left leav'ing
(let stay)
leave
leaved leav'ing
(bear leaves)
leav'en·ing
leave'-tak'ing
lech'er·ous
lec'i·thin
lec'tern
lec'ture
·tured ·tur·ing
ledge
ledg'er
leech
(worm; see
leach)
leek
(vegetable; see
leak)
leer'y
·i·er ·i·est
lee'ward
lee'way'
left'-hand'ed
left'ist
left'o·ver
left'-wing'er
leg
legged leg'ging
leg'a·cy
·cies
le'gal·ese'
le·gal'i·ty
·ties
le'gal·i·za'tion

le'gal·ize'
·ized' ·iz'ing
le'gal·ly
leg'a·tee'
le·ga'tion
le·ga'to
leg'end
leg'end·ar'y
leg'er·de·main'
leg'gi·ness
leg'gy
·gi·er ·gi·est
leg'i·bil'i·ty
leg'i·ble
leg'i·bly
le'gion
le'gion·naire'
leg'is·late'
·lat'ed ·lat'ing
leg'is·la'tion
leg'is·la'tive
leg'is·la'tor
leg'is·la'ture
le·git'i·ma·cy
le·git'i·mate
le·git'i·mize'
·mized' ·miz'ing
leg'man'
leg'room'
leg'ume
lei
lei'sure
lei'sure·ly
lem'on·ade'
lend
lent lend'ing
length'en
length'i·ness
length'wise'
length'y
·i·er ·i·est
le'ni·en·cy
le'ni·ent
len'i·tive
len'i·ty
lens
len'til
(pea; see lintel)
leop'ard
le'o·tard'
lep'er
lep're·chaun'
lep'ro·sy
lep'rous
les'bi·an
le'sion
les·see'
less'en
(make less)
less'er
(smaller)
les'son
(instruction)
les'sor
(one who leases)
let
let let'ting
let'down'

le'thal
le·thar'gic
le·thar'gi·cal·ly
leth'ar·gize'
·gized' ·giz'ing
leth'ar·gy
let'tered
let'ter·head'
let'ter-per'fect
let'ter·press'
let'tuce
let'up'
leu·ke'mi·a
lev'ee
·eed ·ee·ing
(embankment;
see levy)
lev'el
·eled or ·elled
·el·ing or ·el·ling
lev'el·head'ed
lev'el·ly
lev'er·age
lev'i·a·ble
lev'i·er
le'vis
lev'i·tate'
·tat'ed ·tat'ing
lev'i·ta'tion
lev'i·ty
lev'y
·ies, ·ied ·y·ing
(tax; see levee)
lewd'ness
lex'i·cog'ra·pher
lex'i·con
li'a·bil'i·ty
·ties
li'a·ble
(likely; see libel)
li'ai·son'
li'ar
(one who tells
lies; see lyre)
li·ba'tion
li'bel
·beled or ·belled
·bel·ing or
·bel·ling
(defame; see
liable)
li'bel·ous or
·bel·lous
lib'er·al
lib'er·al'i·ty
lib'er·al·ize'
·ized' ·iz'ing
lib'er·ate'
·at'ed ·at'ing
lib'er·a'tion
lib'er·a'tor
lib'er·tar'i·an
lib'er·tine'
lib'er·ty
·ties
li·bid'i·nous
li·bi'do
li·brar'i·an

li'brar'y
·ies
li·bret'tist
li·bret'to
·tos or ·ti
Lib'ri·um
li'cense
·censed ·cens·ing
li·cen'tious
li'chen
lic'it
lic'o·rice
lie
lay lain ly'ing
(to rest; see lay)
lie
lied ly'ing
(tell falsehood;
see lye)
li'en
(claim; see lean)
lieu
lieu·ten'an·cy
lieu·ten'ant
life
lives
life belt
life'blood'
life'boat'
life buoy
life'-giv'ing
life'guard'
life'less
life'like'
life'line'
life'long'
life'sav'er
life'-size'
life'time'
life'work'
lift'off'
lig'a·ment
lig'a·ture
·tured ·tur·ing
light
light'ed or lit
light'ing
light'en
·ened ·en·ing
(make light or less
heavy; see lightning)
light'face'
light'-fin'gered
light'-foot'ed
light'-hand'ed
light'head'ed
light'heart'ed
light'house'
light'ly
light'-mind'ed
light'ning
(flash of light;
see lighten)
light'weight'
light'-year'
lig'ne·ous
lig'nite
lik'a·ble or like'-

like
liked lik'ing
like'li·hood'
like'ly
like'-mind'ed
lik'en
like'ness
like'wise'
li'lac
Lil·li·pu'tian
lil'y
·ies
lil'y-liv'ered
lil'y-white'
limb
(branch; see limn)
lim'ber
lim'bo
lime
limed lim'ing
lime'light'
lim'er·ick
lime'stone'
lim'it·a·ble
lim'i·ta'tion
lim'it·ed
limn
(draw; see limb)
lim'ou·sine'
lim'pid
limp'ness
lin'age or line'-
(number of lines;
see lineage)
linch'pin'
Lin'coln
lin'den
line
lined lin'ing
lin'e·age
(ancestry; see
linage)
lin'e·al
lin'e·a·ment
(feature; see
liniment)
lin'e·ar
line'man
lin'en
lin'er
lines'man
line'up'
lin'ger
lin'ge·rie'
lin'go
·goes
lin'gual
lin'guist
lin·guis'tics
lin'i·ment
(medication;
see lineament)
lin'ing
link'age
links
(golf course;
see lynx)
li·no'le·um

lin'o·type'
lin'seed'
lin'sey-wool'sey
lin'tel
  (*beam; see* lentil)
li'on·ess
li'on·heart'ed
lip'-read'
  -read' -read'ing
lip'stick'
lip'-sync'
liq'ue·fac'tion
liq'ue·fi'a·ble
liq'ue·fi'er
liq'ue·fy'
  ·fied' ·fy'ing
li·ques'cent
li·queur'
liq'uid
liq'ui·date'
  ·dat'ed ·dat'ing
liq·ui·da'tion
liq'ui·da'tor
liq'uor
lisle
lisp'ing·ly
lis'some *or* ·som
lis'ten
list'less
lit'a·ny
  ·nies
li'tchi nut
li'ter
lit'er·a·cy
lit'er·al
  (*exact; see*
  littoral)
lit'er·al·ly
lit'er·ar'y
lit'er·ate
lit'er·a·ture
lithe'ly
lith'o·graph'
li·thog'ra·pher
li·thog'ra·phy
lith'o·sphere'
lit'i·ga·ble
lit'i·gant
lit'i·gate'
  ·gat'ed ·gat'ing
lit'i·ga'tion
lit'mus
li'to·tes
lit'ter
lit'ter·bug'
lit'tle
  lit'tler *or* less *or*
  less'er, lit'tlest
  or least
lit'to·ral
  (*shore; see*
  literal)
li·tur'gi·cal
lit'ur·gy
  ·gies
liv'a·ble *or* live'·
live
  lived liv'ing

live'li·hood'
live'li·ness
live'long'
live'ly
  ·li·er ·li·est
liv'en
liv'er·wurst'
liv'er·y
  ·ies
live'stock'
liv'id
liz'ard
lla'ma
  (*animal; see*
  lama)
load
  (*burden; see* lode)
load'stone'
loaf
loaves
loaf'er
loam'y
  ·i·er ·i·est
loan
  (*something lent;*
  see lone)
loath
  (*unwilling*)
loathe
  loathed loath'ing
  (*detest*)
loath'some
lob
  lobbed lob'bing
lob'by
  ·bies
  ·bied ·by·ing
lob'by·ist
lobe
lob'ster
lo'cal
lo·cale'
lo'cal·ism
lo·cal'i·ty
  ·ties
lo'cal·ize'
  ·ized' ·iz'ing
lo'cal·ly
lo'cate
  ·cat·ed ·cat·ing
lo·ca'tion
lock'er
lock'et
lock'out'
lock'smith'
lo'co·mo'tion
lo'co·mo'tive
lo'co·weed'
lo'cus
  ·ci
lo'cust
lo·cu'tion
lode
  (*ore; see* load)
lode'stone'
lodge
  lodged lodg'ing
  (*house; see* loge)

lodg'er
lodg'ment
loft'i·ly
loft'i·ness
loft'y
  ·i·er ·i·est
log
  logged log'ging
log'a·rithm
loge
  (*theater box;*
  see lodge)
log'ger·head'
log'gi·a
  ·gi·as
log'ic
log'i·cal
log'i·cal·ly
lo·gi'cian
lo·gis'tics
log'o·gram'
log'o·griph'
log'or·rhe'a
lo'gy
  ·gi·er ·gi·est
loin'cloth'
loi'ter
loll'li·pop' *or* ·ly·
lone
  (*solitary;*
  see loan)
lone'li·ness
lone'ly
  ·li·er ·li·est
lone'some
long'-dis'tance'
long'-drawn'
lon·gev'i·ty
long'hand'
lon'gi·tude'
lon'gi·tu'di·nal
long'-lived'
long'-play'ing
long'-range'
long'-run'
long'shore'man
long'stand'ing
long'-suf'fer·ing
long'-term'
long'-wind'ed
look'er-on'
  look'ers-on'
look'out'
loop'hole'
loose
  loosed loos'ing
  (*free; see*
  lose, loss)
loose'-joint'ed
loose'-leaf'
loose'ly
loos'en
loose'-tongued'
lop
  lopped lop'ping
lope
  loped lop'ing
lop'sid'ed

lo·qua'cious
lo·quac'i·ty
lor·do'sis
lor·gnette'
lor'ry
  ·ries
lose
  lost los'ing
  (*mislay;* see
  loose, loss)
los'er
loss
  (*thing lost;* see
  loose, lose)
Lo·thar'i·o'
lo'tion
lot'ter·y
  ·ies
loud'mouthed'
loud'speak'er
Lou·i'si·an'a
lounge
lounged
loung'ing
louse
lice
lout'ish
lou'ver
lov'a·ble *or*
love'·
love
  loved lov'ing
love'li·ness
love'lorn'
love'ly
  ·li·er ·li·est
lov'ing·kind'ness
low'boy'
low'bred'
low'brow'
low'-cost'
low'-down'
low'er
low'er·class'man
low'-grade'
low'-key'
low'-lev'el
low'li·ness
low'ly
  ·li·er ·li·est
low'-mind'ed
low'-necked'
low'-pitched'
low'-spir'it·ed
lox
loy'al
loy'al·ly
loy'al·ty
  ·ties
loz'enge
lu·au'
lu'bri·cant
lu'bri·cate'
  ·cat'ed ·cat'ing
lu'bri·ca'tion
lu'bri·ca'tor
lu'cid
lu·cid'i·ty

luck'i·ly
luck'i·ness
luck'y
  ·i·er ·i·est
lu'cra·tive
lu'cre
lu·cu·bra'tion
lu'di·crous
lug'gage
lu·gu'bri·ous
luke'warm'
lull'a·by'
  ·bies'
lum'bar
  (*of the loins*)
lum'ber
  (*timber*)
lum'ber·jack'
lum'ber·yard'
lu'men
  ·mi·na *or* ·mens
lu'mi·nar'y
  ·ies
lu'mi·nes'cent
lu'mi·nous
lump'i·ness
lump'y
  ·i·er ·i·est
lu'na·cy
lu'nar
lu'na·tic
lunch'eon
lunge
  lunged lung'ing
lu'pine
lure
  lured lur'ing
lu'rid
lurk'ing
lus'cious
lush'ness
lus'ter
lust'i·ness
lus'trous
lust'y
  ·i·er ·i·est
lux·u'ri·ance
lux·u'ri·ant
lux·u'ri·ate'
  ·at'ed ·at'ing
lux·u'ri·ous
lux'u·ry
  ·ries
ly·ce'um
lye
  (*alkaline sub-*
  stance; see lie)
ly'ing-in'
lym·phat'ic
lynch'ing
lynx
  (*animal; see* links)
ly'on·naise'
lyre
  (*harp;* see liar)
lyr'ic
lyr'i·cal
lyr'i·cist

M

ma·ca'bre
mac·ad'am
mac·ad'am·ize'
  ·ized' ·iz'ing
mac'a·ro'ni
mac'a·roon'
mac'er·ate'
  ·at'ed ·at'ing
ma·che'te
Mach'i·a·vel'li·an
mach'i·nate'
  ·nat'ed ·nat'ing
mach'i·na'tion
ma·chine'
  ·chined'
  ·chin'ing
ma·chin'er·y
ma·chin'ist
mack'er·el
mack'i·naw'
mack'in·tosh'
  (*coat;* see
  McIntosh)
mac'ra·me'
mac'ro·bi·ot'ics
mac'ro·cosm
ma'cron
mac'u·la
  ·lae
mad
  mad'der
  mad'dest
mad'am
mad'ame
  mes·dames'
mad'cap'
mad'den·ing
Ma·deir'a
ma'de·moi·selle'
made'-to-or'der
made'-up'
mad'house'
mad'man'
ma'dras
mad'ri·gal
mad'wo'man
mael'strom
ma'es·tro
  ·tros *or* ·tri
Ma'fi·a *or* Maf'·
mag'a·zine'
ma·gen'ta
mag'got
mag'ic
mag'i·cal·ly
ma·gi'cian
mag·is·te'ri·al
mag'is·trate'
mag'na·nim'i·ty
mag·nam'i·mous
mag'nate
  (*influential*
  person)

mag·ne'sia
mag'net
(iron attracter)
mag·net'ic
mag·net'i·cal·ly
mag'net·ism
mag'net·ize'
·ized' ·iz'ing
mag·ne'to
·tos
mag'ni·fi·ca'tion
mag·nif'i·cence
mag·nif'i·cent
mag'ni·fi'er
mag'ni·fy'
fied' ·fy'ing
mag·nil'o·quent
mag'ni·tude'
mag·no'li·a
mag'num
mag'pie
ma'ha·ra'jah or
·ra'ja
ma'ha·ra'ni or
·ra'nee
ma·hat'ma
mah'-jongg'
ma·hog'a·ny
maid'en
maid'ser'vant
mail'box'
mail'man'
maim
Maine
main'land'
main'line'
main'ly
main'spring'
main'stream'
main·tain'
main'te·nance
maî'tre d'hô·tel'
maize
(corn; see maze)
ma·jes'tic
ma·jes'ti·cal·ly
maj'es·ty
·ties
ma·jol'i·ca
ma'jor
ma'jor-do'mo
·mos
ma·jor'i·ty
·ties
ma·jus'cule
make
made mak'ing
make'-be·lieve'
make'shift'
make'up'
mal·a·dapt'ed
mal'ad·just'ed
mal'ad·min'is·ter
mal'a·droit'
mal'a·dy
·dies
ma·laise'
mal'a·prop·ism

mal'ap·ro·pos'
ma·lar'i·a
mal'con·tent'
mal de mer'
mal'e·dic'tion
mal'e·fac'tion
mal'e·fac'tor
ma·lef'i·cent
male'ness
ma·lev'o·lence
ma·lev'o·lent
mal·fea'sance
mal'for·ma'tion
mal·formed'
mal·func'tion
mal'ice
ma·li'cious
ma·lign'
ma·lig'nan·cy
ma·lig'nant
ma·lig'ni·ty
·ties
ma·lin'ger
ma·lin'ger·er
mall
(promenade; see
maul)
mal'lard
mal'le·a·bil'i·ty
mal'le·a·ble
mal'let
malm'sey
mal'nu·tri'tion
mal·oc·clu'sion
mal·o'dor·ous
mal·prac'tice
malt'ose
mal·treat'
mam'mal
mam·ma'li·an
mam'ma·ry
mam'mon
mam'moth
man
men, manned
man'ning
man'a·cle
·cled ·cling
man'age
·aged ·ag·ing
man'age·a·ble
man'age·ment
man'ag·er
man'a·ge'ri·al
ma·ña'na
man'-child'
men'-chil'dren
man·da'mus
man'da·rin
man'date
·dat·ed ·dat·ing
man'da·to'ry
man'di·ble
man'do·lin'
man'drel or ·dril
(metal spindle)
man'drill
(baboon)

man'-eat'er
ma·nège'
(horsemanship;
see ménage)
ma·neu'ver
ma·neu'ver·a·ble
man'ful·ly
man'ga·nese'
mange
man'ger
man'gi·ness
man'gle
·gled ·gling
man'go
·goes or ·gos
man'grove
man'gy
·gi·er ·gi·est
man'han'dle
Man·hat'tan
man'hole'
man'hood'
man'-hour'
man'hunt'
ma'ni·a
ma'ni·ac'
ma·ni'a·cal
man'ic
man'i·cot'ti
man'i·cure'
·cured' ·cur'ing
man'i·cur'ist
man'i·fest'
man'i·fes·ta'tion
man'i·fes'to
·toes
man'i·fold'
man'i·kin
Ma·ni'la
ma·nip'u·late'
·lat'ed ·lat'ing
ma·nip'u·la'tion
ma·nip'u·la'tive
ma·nip'u·la'tor
man'kind'
man'li·ness
man'ly
·li·er ·li·est
man'-made'
man'na
man'ne·quin
man'ner
(way; see manor)
man'ner·ism
man'ner·ly
man'nish
man'-of-war'
men'-of-war'
ma·nom'e·ter
man'or
(residence;
see manner)
man'pow'er
man'sard
man'ser'vant
men'ser'vants
man'sion
man'-sized'

man'slaugh'ter
man'teau
·teaus
man'tel
(fireplace fac-
ing; see mantle)
man'tel·et
man'tel·piece'
man·til'la
man'tis
·tis·es or ·tes
man'tle
·tled ·tling
(cloak; see
mantel)
man'tu·a
man'u·al
man'u·fac'to·ry
·ries
man'u·fac'ture
·tured ·tur·ing
man'u·fac'tur·er
ma·nure'
·nured' ·nur'ing
man'u·script'
man'y
more most
man'y-sid'ed
map
mapped
map'ping
ma'ple
mar
marred mar'ring
mar'a·bou'
ma·ra'ca
mar'a·schi'no
ma·ras'mus
mar'a·thon'
ma·raud'
mar'ble
·bled ·bling
mar'ble·ize'
·ized' ·iz'ing
mar'ca·site'
mar·cel'
·celled' ·cel'ling
March
mar'chion·ess
Mar'di gras'
mare's'-nest'
mare's'-tail'
mar'ga·rine
mar'gin
mar'gin·al
mar'gin·al·ly
mar'i·gold'
ma'ri·jua'na or
·hua'na
ma·rim'ba
ma·ri'na
mar'i·nade'
·nad'ed ·nad'ing
mar'i·nate'
·nat'ed ·nat'ing
ma·rine'
mar'i·ner
mar'i·o·nette'

mar'i·tal
(of marriage;
see martial)
mar'i·time'
mar'jo·ram.
mark'down'
marked
mark'ed·ly
mar'ket·a·bil'i·ty
mar'ket·a·ble
mar'ket·place'
marks'man
mark'up'
mar'lin
(fish)
mar'line
(cord)
mar'line·spike'
mar'ma·lade'
mar'mo·set'
mar'mot
ma·roon'
mar·quee'
mar'quess
mar'que·try
mar'quis
mar·quise'
mar'qui·sette'
mar'riage
mar'riage·a·ble
mar'row
mar'row·bone'
mar'ry
·ried ·ry·ing
Mar·sa'la
mar'shal
·shaled or
·shalled
·shal·ing or
·shal·ling
marsh'mal'low
mar·su'pi·al
mar·su'pi·um
·pi·a
mar'ten
(animal; see
martin)
mar'tial
(military; see
marital)
Mar'tian
mar'tin
(bird; see marten)
mar'ti·net'
mar'tin·gale'
mar·ti'ni
·nis
mar'tyr
mar'tyr·dom
mar'tyr·ize'
·ized' ·iz'ing
mar'vel
·veled or ·velled
·vel·ing or
·vel·ling
mar'vel·ous
Marx'ism
Mar'y·land

mar'zi·pan'
mas·ca'ra
·raed ·ra·ing
mas'con'
mas'cot
mas'cu·line
mas'cu·lin'i·ty
ma'ser
mash'ie
mask
(cover; see
masque)
masked
mas'och·ism
mas'och·is'tic
mas'och·is'ti·
cal·ly
ma'son
Ma'son·ite'
ma'son·ry
masque
(masked ball; see
mask)
mas'quer·ade'
·ad'ed ·ad'ing
Mas'sa·chu'setts
mas'sa·cre
·cred ·cring
mas·sage'
·saged' ·sag'ing
mas·seur'
mas·seuse'
mas'sive
mas'ter·ful
mas'ter·ly
mas'ter·mind'
mas'ter·piece'
mas'ter·y
·ies
mast'head'
mas'tic
mas'ti·cate'
·cat'ed ·cat'ing
mas'ti·ca'tion
mas'tiff
mas'to·don'
mas'toid
mas'tur·bate'
·bat'ed ·bat'ing
mas'tur·ba'tion
mat
mat'ted
mat'ting
mat'a·dor'
match'box'
match'less
match'lock'
match'mak'er
mate
mat'ed mat'ing
ma'te·las·sé'
ma·te'ri·al
(of matter;
see materiel)
ma·te'ri·al·ism
ma·te'ri·al·is'tic
ma·te'ri·al·ize'
·ized' ·iz'ing

ma·te'ri·al·ly
ma·te'ri·el'
or ·té·ri·el'
(equipment;
see material)
ma·ter'nal
ma·ter'ni·ty
math'e·mat'i·cal
math'e·ma·ti'cian
math'e·mat'ics
mat'i·nee'
or ·i·née'
ma'tri·arch'
ma'tri·ar'chal
ma'tri·ar'chy
·chies
ma'tri·cide'
ma·tric'u·lant
ma·tric'u·late'
·lat'ed ·lat'ing
ma·tric'u·la'tion
mat'ri·mo'ni·al
mat'ri·mo'ny
ma'trix
·tri·ces' or ·trix·es
ma'tron
ma'tron·li·ness
ma'tron·ly
mat'ter
mat'ter-of-fact'
mat'tock
mat'tress
mat'u·rate'
·rat'ed ·rat'ing
mat'u·ra'tion
ma·ture'
·tured' ·tur'ing
ma·ture'ly
ma·tu'ri·ty
mat'zo
·zot or ·zoth
or ·zos
maud'lin
maul
(mallet; injures;
see mall)
maun'der
mau'so·le'um
·le'ums or ·le'a
mauve
mav'er·ick
mawk'ish
max·il'la
max'il·lar'y
max'im
max'i·mal
max'i·mize'
·mized' ·miz'ing
max'i·mum
·mums or ·ma
May
may'be
May'day'
may'hem
may'on·naise'
may'or
may'or·al·ty
·ties

May'pole'
maze
(labyrinth; see
maize)
maz'el tov'
Mc'In·tosh'
(apple; see
mackintosh)
mead'ow
mea'ger
meal'time'
meal'y
·i·er ·i·est
meal'y-mouthed'
mean v.
meant mean'ing
mean adj., n.
(middle; low;
see mien)
me·an'der
mean'ing·ful
mean'ing·less
mean'ness
mean'time'
mean'while'
mea'sles
mea'sly
·sli·er ·sli·est
meas'ur·a·bil'i·ty
meas'ur·a·ble
meas'ur·a·bly
meas'ure
·ured ·ur·ing
meas'ure·less
meas'ure·ment
meas'ur·er
meat
(flesh; see
meet, mete)
meat'i·ness
me·a'tus
meat'y
·i·er ·i·est
me·chan'ic
me·chan'i·cal
mech'a·ni'cian
me·chan'ics
mech'a·nism
mech'a·ni·za'tion
mech'a·nize'
·nized' ·niz'ing
med'al
(award;
see meddle)
med'al·ist
me·dal'lion
med'dle
·dled ·dling
(interfere;
see medal)
med'dler
med'dle·some
me'di·a
(sing. medium)
me'di·al
me'di·an
me'di·ate'
·at'ed ·at'ing

me'di·a'tion
me'di·a'tor
Med'i·caid'
med'i·cal
Med'i·care'
med'i·cate'
·cat'ed ·cat'ing
med'i·ca'tion
me·dic'i·nal
med'i·cine
me'di·e'val
or ·ae'val
med'i·o'cre
me'di·oc'ri·ty
·ties
med'i·tate'
·tat'ed ·tat'ing
med'i·ta'tion
med'i·ta'tor
Med'i·ter·ra'ne·an
me'di·um
·di·ums or ·di·a
med'ley
·leys
meer'schaum
meet
met meet'ing
(come upon; see
meat, mete)
meg'a·death'
meg'a·hertz'
meg'a·lo·ma'ni·a
meg'a·lop'o·lis
meg'a·phone'
meg'a·ton'
mel'an·cho'li·a
mel'an·chol'ic
mel'an·chol'y
me·lange'
mel'a·nin
me'lee or mê'lée
mel'io·rate'
·rat'ed ·rat'ing
me'lio·ra'tion
mel·lif'lu·ous
mel'low
me·lo'de·on
me·lod'ic
me·lo'di·ous
mel'o·dra'ma
mel'o·dra·mat'ic
mel'o·dy
·dies
mel'on
melt'a·ble
mel'ton
mem'ber·ship'
mem'brane
mem'bra·nous
me·men'to
·tos or ·toes
mem'oir
mem'o·ra·bil'i·a
mem'o·ra·ble
mem'o·ra·bly
mem'o·ran'dum
·dums or ·da
me·mo'ri·al

me·mo'ri·al·ize'
·ized' ·iz'ing
mem'o·ri·za'tion
mem'o·rize'
·rized' ·riz'ing
mem'o·ry
·ries
men'ace
·aced ·ac·ing
mé·nage' or me·
(household; see
manège)
me·nag'er·ie
men·da'cious
men·dac'i·ty
Men·de'li·an
men'di·cant
me'ni·al
men'in·gi'tis
me·nis'cus
·cus·es or ·ci
Men'non·ite'
men'o·pause'
men'ses
men'stru·al
men'stru·ate'
·at'ed
·at'ing
men'stru·a'tion
men'sur·a·ble
men'su·ra'tion
mens'wear'
men'tal
men·tal'i·ty
men'thol
men'tho·lat'ed
men'tion
men'tor
men'u
·us
me·phit'ic
me·pro'ba·mate'
mer'can·tile
mer'can·til·ism
mer'ce·nar'y
·nar'ies
mer'cer·ize'
·ized' ·iz'ing
mer'chan·dise'
·dized' ·diz'ing
mer'chan·dis'er
mer'chant
mer'ci·ful
mer'ci·ful·ly
mer'ci·less
mer·cu'ri·al
Mer·cu'ro·
chrome'
mer'cu·ry
mer'cy
·cies
mere
mer'est
mere'ly
mer·en'gue
(dance; see
meringue)
mer'e·tri'cious

merge
merged merg'ing
merg'er
me·rid'i·an
me·ringue'
(pie topping;
see merengue)
me·ri'no
·nos
mer'it
mer'i·to'ri·ous
mer'maid'
mer'ri·ly
mer'ri·ment
mer'ri·ness
mer'ry
·ri·er ·ri·est
mer'ry-an'drew
mer'ry-go-round'
mer'ry·mak'ing
Mer·thi'o·late'
me'sa
mé·sal'li·ance
mes·cal'
mes'ca·line'
mes'dames'
mes'de·moi·selles'
me·shu'ga
mesh'work'
mes'mer·ism
mes'mer·ize'
·ized' ·iz'ing
mes'on
mes'sage
mes'sen·ger
mes·si'ah
mes'sieurs
mess'i·ly
mess'i·ness
mess'y
·i·er ·i·est
met'a·bol'ic
me·tab'o·lism
me·tab'o·lize'
·lized' ·liz'ing
met'al
·aled or ·alled
·al·ing or ·al·ling
(mineral; see
mettle)
me·tal'lic
met'al·lur'gi·cal
met'al·lur'gist
met'al·lur'gy
met'al·work'
met'a·mor'phic
met'a·mor'phism
met'a·mor'phose
·phosed phos·ing
met'a·mor'pho·sis
·ses
met'a·phor'
met'a·phor'i·cal
met'a·phor'i·
cal·ly
met'a·phys'i·cal
met'a·phys'ics
met'a·tar'sal

me·tath'e·sis
·ses'
mete
met'ed met'ing
(allot; see meat,
meet)
me'te·or
me'te·or'ic
me'te·or·ite'
me'te·or·oid'
me'te·or·o·
log'i·cal
me'te·or·ol'o·gist
me'te·or·ol'o·gy
me'ter
meth'a·done'
meth'ane
meth'a·nol'
meth'e·drine'
meth'od
me·thod'i·cal
me·thod'i·cal·ly
Meth'od·ist
meth'od·ize'
·ized' ·iz'ing
meth'od·ol'o·gy
me·tic'u·lous
mé·tier'
me·ton'y·my
met'ric
met'ri·cal
me'tro·nome'
me·trop'o·lis
met'ro·pol'i·tan
met'tle
(spirit; see metal)
mez'za·nine'
mez'zo-so·pra'no
·nos or ·ni
mez'zo·tint'
mi·as'ma
·mas or ·ma·ta
mi'ca
Mich'i·gan
mi'cro·bar'
mi'crobe
mi·cro'bic
mi'cro·cop'y
mi'cro·cosm
mi'cro·dot'
mi'cro·fiche'
mi'cro·film'
mi'cro·groove'
mi·crom'e·ter
mi'cro·or'gan
ism
mi'cro·phone'
mi'cro·print'
mi'cro·read'er
mi'cro·scope'
mi'cro·scop'ic
mi'cro·scop'i·
cal'ly
mi'cro·wave'
mid'air'
mid'cult'
mid'day'
mid'dle

mid'dle-aged'
mid'dle·brow'
mid'dle-class'
mid'dle·man'
mid'dle-of-the-
road'
mid'dle-sized'
mid'dle·weight'
mid'dling
mid'dy
·dies
midg'et
mid'i'ron
mid'land
mid'night'
mid'point'
mid'riff
mid'ship·man
midst
mid'stream'
mid'sum'mer
mid'term'
mid'-Vic·to'ri·an
mid'way'
mid'week'
Mid'west'
Mid'west'ern·er
mid'wife'
·wives'
mid'win'ter
mid'year'
mien
(manner; see
mean)
miffed
might
(power; see mite)
might'i·ly
might'i·ness
might'y
·i·er ·i·est
mi'gnon
mi'graine
mi'grant
mi'grate
·grat·ed ·grat·ing
mi·gra'tion
mi'gra·to'ry
mi·ka'do
·dos
mi·la'dy
mil'dew'
mild'ly
mile'age
mile'post'
mile'stone'
mi·lieu'
mil'i·tan·cy
mil'i·tant
mil'i·tar'i·ly
mil'i·ta·rism
mil'i·ta·ris'tic
mil'i·ta·ri·za'tion
mil'i·ta·rize'
·rized' ·riz'ing
mil'i·tar'y
mil'i·tate'
·tat'ed ·tat'ing

mi·li'tia
milk'i·ness
milk'maid'
milk'man'
milk'shake'
milk'shed'
milk'sop'
milk toast
(food; see
milquetoast)
milk'weed'
milk'y
·i·er ·i·est
mill'age
mill'dam'
milled
mil·len'ni·um
·ni·ums or ·ni·a
mill'er
mill'let
mil'liard
mill'li·bar'
mil'li·gram'
mill'li·li'ter
mil'li·me'ter
mill'line'
mill'li·ner
mil'li·ner'y
mill'ing
mil'lion
mil'lion·aire'
mill'lionth
mil'li·pede'
mill'pond'
mill'race'
mill'stone'
mill'stream'
mill wheel
mill'work'
mill'wright'
milque'toast'
(timid person;
see milk toast)
Mil·wau'kee
mime
mimed mim'ing
mim'e·o·graph'
mim'er
mi·met'ic
mim'ic
·icked ·ick·ing
mim'ick·er
mim'ic·ry
mi·mo'sa
min'a·ret'
min'a·to'ry
mince
minced minc'ing
mince'meat'
mind'ful
mind'less
mind reader
mine
mined min'ing
mine'lay'er
min'er
(mine worker;
see minor)

min'er·al
min'er·al·i·za'tion
min'er·al·ize'
·ized' ·iz'ing
min'er·al'o·gist
min'er·al'o·gy
mi'ne·stro'ne
min'gle
·gled ·gling
min'i·a·ture
min'i·a·tur'i·
za'tion
min'i·a·tur·ize'
·ized' ·iz'ing
min'i·bus'
min'i·fi·ca'tion
min'i·fy'
·fied' ·fy'ing
min'im
min'i·mal
min'i·mal·ly
min'i·mize'
·mized' ·miz'ing
min'i·mum
·mums or ·ma
min'ion
(deputy; see
minyan)
min'i·skirt'
min'is·ter
(diplomat; clergy-
man; see minster)
min'is·te'ri·al
min'is·trant
min'is·tra'tion
min'is·try
·tries
min'i·track'
min'i·ver
Min'ne·ap'o·lis
min'ne·sing'er
Min'ne·so'ta
min'now
mi'nor
(lesser; see
miner)
mi·nor'i·ty
·ties
min'ster
(church; see
minister)
min'strel
mint'age
min'u·end'
min'u·et'
mi'nus
mi·nus'cule
min'ute n.
mi·nute'ly
min'ute·man'
mi·nu'ti·ae'
(sing. mi·nu'ti·a)
minx
min·yan'
min'ya·nim'
(group; see
minion)

mir'a·cle
mi·rac'u·lous
mi·rage'
mire
mired mir'ing
mir'ror
mirth'ful
mirth'less
mir'y
·i·er ·i·est
mis'ad·ven'ture
mis'ad·vise'
mis'al·li'ance
mis·al'ly'
mis'an·thrope'
mis'an·throp'ic
mis·an'thro·py
mis'ap·pli·ca'tion
mis'ap·ply'
mis'ap·pre·hend'
mis'ap·pre·
hen'sion
mis'be·got'ten
mis'be·have'
mis'be·hav'ior
mis'be·lief'
mis'be·lieve'
mis·cal'cu·late'
mis'cal·cu·la'tion
mis·car'riage
mis·car'ry
mis·cast'
mis'ce·ge·na'tion
mis'cel·la'ne·a
mis'cel·la'ne·ous
mis'cel·la'ny
·nies
mis·chance'
mis'chief
mis'chief-mak'er
mis'chie·vous
mis·ci·bil'i·ty
mis'ci·ble
mis'con·ceive'
mis'con·cep'tion
mis·con'duct
mis'con·
struc'tion
mis'con·strue'
mis·count'
mis'cre·ant
mis·cue'
mis·date'
mis·deal'
·dealt' ·deal'ing
mis·deed'
mis'de·mean'or
mis'di·rect'
mi'ser
mis'er·a·ble
mis'er·a·bly
mi'ser·ly
mis'er·y
·ies
mis·es'ti·mate'
mis·fea'sance
mis·file'

mis·fire'
mis'fit'
mis·for'tune
mis·giv'ing
mis·gov'ern
mis·guid'ance
mis·guide'
mis·han'dle
mis'hap
mish'mash'
mis·in·form'
mis'in·for·ma'tion
mis·in·ter'pret
mis·judge'
mis·judg'ment
or ·judge'ment
mis·lay'
·laid' ·lay'ing
mis·lead'
·led' ·lead'ing
mis·man'age
mis·man'age·
ment
mis·match'
mis·mate'
mis·no'mer
mi·sog'a·mist
mi·sog'a·my
mi·sog'y·nist
mi·sog'y·ny
mis·place'
mis·print'
mis·pri'sion
mis'pro·nounce'
mis'pro·nun'ci·
a'tion
mis'quo·ta'tion
mis·quote'
mis·read'
·read' ·read'ing
mis'rep·re·sent'
mis'rep·re·sen·
ta'tion
mis·rule'
Miss
Miss'es
mis'sal
(book; see
missile, missive)
mis·shape'
mis·shap'en
mis'sile
(weapon; see
missal, missive)
mis'sion
mis'sion·ar'y
Mis'sis·sip'pi
mis'sive
(letter; see
missal, missile)
, Mis·sour'i
mis·speak'
·spoke' ·spo'ken
·speak'ing
mis·spell'
·spelled' or
·spelt'
·spell'ing

mis·spend'
·spent'
·spend'ing
mis·state'
mis·state'ment
mis·step'
mis·take'
·took' ·tak'en
·tak'ing
mist'i·ly
mist'i·ness
mis'tle·toe'
mis'tral
mis·treat'ment
mis'tress
mis·tri'al
mis·trust'
mist'y
·i·er ·i·est
mis'un·der·stand'
·stood' ·stand'ing
mis·us'age
mis·use'
mis·val'ue
mis·write'
·wrote' ·writ'ten
·writ'ing
mite
(arachnid; tiny
thing; see might)
mi'ter
mit'i·ga·ble
mit'i·gate'
·gat'ed ·gat'ing
mit'i·ga'tion
mit'i·ga'tor
mi'tral
mitt
mit'ten
mix
mixed or mixt
mix'ing
mix'er
mix'ture
mix'-up'
miz'zen·mast
mne·mon'ic
moan'ing
moat
(ditch; see mote)
mob
mobbed
mob'bing
mo'bile
mo·bil'i·ty
mo'bi·liz'a·ble
mo'bi·li·za'tion
mo'bi·lize'
·lized' ·liz'ing
mob·oc'ra·cy
·cies
moc'ca·sin
mo'cha
mock'er·y
·ies
mock'-he·ro'ic
mock'ing·bird'
mock'-up'

mod'a·cryl'ic
mod'al
  (of a mode)
mod'el
  ·eled or ·elled
  el·ing or ·el·ling
  (copy)
mod'er·ate'
  ·at'ed ·at'ing
mod'er·ate·ly
mod'er·a'tion
mod'er·a'tor
mod'ern
mod'ern·ism
mod'ern·is'tic
mo·der'ni·ty
mod'ern·i·za'tion
mod'ern·ize'
  ·ized' ·iz'ing
mod'ern·ness
mod'est
mod'es·ty
mod'i·cum
mod'i·fi·ca'tion
mod'i·fi'er
mod'i·fy'
  ·fied' ·fy'ing
mod'ish
mo·diste'
mod'u·lar
mod'u·late'
  ·lat'ed ·lat·ing
mod'u·la'tion
mod'u·la'tor
mod'ule
mo'gul
mo'hair
moi'e·ty
  ·ties
moire
moi·ré'
mois'ten
moist'ness
mois'ture
mois'tur·ize'
  ·ized' ·iz'ing
mo'lar
mo·las'ses
mold'board'
mold'er
mold'i·ness
mold'ing
mold'y
  ·i·er ·i·est
mole
mo·lec'u·lar
mol'e·cule'
mole'hill'
mole'skin'
mo·lest'
mo·les·ta'tion
mol'li·fy'
  ·fied' ·fy'ing
mol'lusk
mol'ly·cod'dle
  ·dled ·dling
molt
mol'ten

mo·lyb'de·num
mo'ment
mo'men·tar'i·ly
mo'men·tar'y
mo·men'tous
mo·men'tum
  ·tums or ·ta
mom'ism
mo·nan'drous
mon'arch
mo·nar'chal
mon'arch·ism
mon'arch·y
  ·ies
mon'as·ter'y
mo·nas'tic
mo·nas'ti·cism
mon·au'ral
Mon'day
mon'e·tar'y
mon'e·tize'
  ·tized' ·tiz'ing
mon'ey
  ·eys or ·ies
mon'ey·bag'
mon'ey-chang'er
mon'eyed
mon'ey-grub'ber
mon'ey·lend'er
mon'ey·mak'er
mon'ger
Mon'gol·ism
Mon'gol·oid'
mon'goose
  ·goos·es
mon'grel
mo·ni'tion
mon'i·tor
mon'i·to'ry
  ·ries
monk
mon'key
  ·keys
monk's cloth
mon'o·chro·
  mat'ic
mon'o·chrome'
mon'o·cle
mon'o·coque'
mo·noc'u·lar
mon'o·dra'ma
mo·nog'a·mist
mo·nog'a·mous
mo·nog'a·my
mon'o·gram'
  ·grammed'
  ·gram'ming
mon'o·graph'
mo·nog'y·ny
mon'o·lith'
mon'o·logue'
  or ·log'
mon'o·logu'ist or
  mo·nol'o·gist
mon'o·ma'ni·a
mon'o·met'al·lism
mon'o·nu'cle·o'sis

mon'o·plane'
mo·nop'o·list
mo·nop'o·list'tic
mo·nop'o·li·
  za'tion
mo·nop'o·lize'
  ·lized' ·liz'ing
mo·nop'o·ly
  ·lies
mon'o·rail'
mon'o·syl·lab'ic
mon'o·syl'la·ble
mon'o·the'ism
mon'o·the·is'tic
mon'o·tone'
mo·not'o·nous
mo·not'o·ny
mon'o·type'
mon·ox'ide
Mon'sei·gneur'
Mes'sei·gneurs'
mon·sieur'
mes'sieurs
Mon·si'gnor
mon·soon'
mon'ster
mon·stros'i·ty
  ·ties
mon'strous
mon·tage'
  ·taged' ·tag'ing
Mon·tan'a
month'ly
  ·lies
mon'u·ment
mon'u·men'tal
mood'i·ly
mood'i·ness
mood'y
  ·i·er ·i·est
moon'beam'
moon'-faced'
moon'light'
moon'light'ing
moon'lit'
moon'port'
moon'rise'
moon'set'
moon'shine'
moon'shot'
moon'stone'
moon'struck'
moor'age
moor'ing
moose
  moose
  (deer; see
  mouse, mousse)
moot
  (debatable;
  see mute)
mop
  mopped
  mop'ping
mope
  moped mop'ing
mop'pet
mop'-up'

mo·raine'
mor'al
mo·rale'
mor'al·ist
mor'al·is'tic
mor'al·is'ti·cal·ly
mo·ral'i·ty
mor'al·ize'
  ·ized' ·iz'ing
mor'al·ly
mo·rass'
mor'a·to'ri·um
  ·ri·ums or ·ri·a
mor'bid
mor·bid'i·ty
mor'dant
  (corrosive)
mor'dent
  (musical term)
more·o'ver
mo'res
mor'ga·nat'ic
morgue
mor'i·bund'
mor'i·bun'di·ty
Mor'mon
morn'ing
  (part of day;
  see mourning)
mo·roc'co
mo'ron
mo·ron'ic
mo·rose'
mor'phine
mor·phol'o·gy
mor'sel
mor'tal
mor·tal'i·ty
mor'tal·ly
mor'tar
mor'tar·board'
mort'gage
  ·gaged ·gag·ing
mort'ga·gee'
mort'ga·gor
mor·ti'cian
mor'ti·fi·ca'tion
mor'ti·fy'
  ·fied' ·fy'ing
mor'tise
  ·tised ·tis·ing
mor'tu·ar'y
  ·ies
mo·sa'ic
  ·icked ·ick·ing
mosque
mos·qui'to
  ·toes or ·tos
moss'back'
moss'i·ness
moss'y
  ·i·er ·i·est
most'ly
mote
  (speck; see moat)
mo·tel'
moth'ball'
moth'-eat'en

moth'er·hood'
moth'er-in-law'
  moth'ers-in-law'
moth'er·land'
moth'er·li·ness
moth'er·ly
moth'er-of-pearl'
moth'proof'
mo·tif'
mo'tile
mo·til'i·ty
mo'tion·less
mo'ti·vate'
  ·vat'ed ·vat'ing
mo'ti·va'tion
mo'ti·va'tor
mo'tive
mot'ley
mo'tor·bike'
mo'tor·boat'
mo'tor·bus'
mo'tor·cade'
mo'tor·cy'cle
mo'tor·drome'
mo'tor·ist
mo'tor·ize'
  ·ized' ·iz'ing
mo'tor·man
mot'tle
  ·tled ·tling
mot'to
  ·toes or ·tos
mou·lage'
mound
moun'tain
moun'tain·eer'
moun'tain·ous
moun'te·bank'
mourn'ful
mourn'ing
  (grieving;
  see morning)
mouse
  mice
  moused mous'ing
  (rodent; see
  moose, mousse)
mous'er
mouse'trap'
mous'i·ness
mousse
  (food; see
  moose, mousse)
mousse·line'
  de soie'
mous'y
  ·i·er ·i·est
mouth'ful'
  ·fuls'
mouth'part'
mouth'piece'
mouth'-to-mouth'
mouth'wash'
mouth'wa'ter·ing
mou'ton'
  (fur; see mutton)
mov'a·ble
  or move'·

mov'a·bly
move
  moved mov'ing
move'ment
mov'ie
mov'ie·go'er
mov'i·o'la
mow
  mowed, mowed
  or mown,
  mow'ing
moz'za·rel'la
Mr.
Messrs.
Mrs.
Mmes.
mu'ci·lage
mu'ci·lag'i·nous
muck'rake'
mu'cous adj.
mu'cus n.
mud'der
mud'di·ness
mud'dle
  ·dled ·dling
mud'dler
mud'dy
  ·di·er ·di·est
mud'sling'ing
Muen'ster
mu·ez'zin
muf'fin
muf'fle
  ·fled ·fling
muf'fler
muf'ti
mug
  mugged
  mug'ging
mug'gi·ness
mug'gy
  ·gi·er ·gi·est
mug'wump'
muk'luk'
mu·lat'to
  ·toes
mul'ber'ry
  ·ries
mulch
mulct
mul'ish
mul'li·ga·taw'ny
mul'lion
mul'ti·col'ored
mul'ti·far'i·ous
mul'ti·form'
mul'ti·lat'er·al
mul'ti·ple
mul'ti·plex'
mul'ti·pli'a·ble
mul'ti·pli·cand'
mul'ti·pli·ca'tion
mul'ti·plic'i·ty
mul'ti·pli'er
mul'ti·ply'
  ·plied' ·ply'ing
mul'ti·tude'
mul'ti·tu'di·nous

mul·ti·ver'si·ty
mum'ble
 ·bled ·bling
mum'bler
mum'mer·y
mum'mi·fy'
 ·fied' ·fy'ing
mum'my
 ·mies
munch
mun·dane'
mu·nic'i·pal
mu·nic'i·pal'i·ty
 ·ties
mu·nic'i·pal·ize'
 ·ized' ·iz'ing
mu·nif'i·cence
mu·nif'i·cent
mu·ni'tion
mu'ral
mur'der·er
mur'der·ous
murk'i·ly
murk'i·ness
murk'y
 ·i·er ·i·est
mur'mur
mur'mur·er
mus'ca·dine
mus'ca·tel'
mus'cle
 ·cled ·cling
 (body part;
 see mussel)
mus'cle-bound'
mus'cu·lar
mus'cu·la'ture
muse
 mused mus'ing
mu·sette'
mu·se'um
mush'i·ness
mush'room
mush'y
 ·i·er ·i·est
mu'sic
mu'si·cal adj.
mu'si·cale' n.
mu·si'cian
mu'si·col'o·gist
mu'si·col'o·gy
mus'kel·lunge'
mus'ket
musk'i·ness
musk'mel'on
musk'rat'
musk'y
 ·i·er ·i·est
mus'lin
mus'sel
 (shellfish;
 see muscle)
mus·tache'
 or mous·
mus'tang
mus'tard
mus'ter
mus'ti·ness

mus'ty
 ·ti·er ·ti·est
mu·ta·bil'i·ty
mu'ta·ble
mu'tant
mu'tate
 ·tat·ed ·tat·ing
mu·ta'tion
mute
 mut'ed mut'ing
 (silent; see moot)
mu'ti·late'
 ·lat'ed ·lat'ing
mu'ti·la'tion
mu'ti·neer'
mu'ti·nous
mu'ti·ny
 ·nies
 ·nied ·ny·ing
mut'ter
mut'ton
 (food; see
 mouton)
mu'tu·al
mu'tu·al'i·ty
mu'tu·al·ly
muu'muu
Mu'zak
muz'zle
 ·zled ·zling
my'e·li'tis
my'e·lo·gram'
my'lar
my'na or ·nah
my·o'pi·a
my·op'ic
myr'i·ad
myr'i·a·pod'
myr'mi·don'
myrrh
myr'tle
my·self'
mys·te'ri·ous
mys'ter·y
 ·ies
mys'tic
mys'ti·cal
mys'ti·cal·ly
mys'ti·cism
mys'ti·fi·ca'tion
mys'ti·fy'
 ·fied' ·fy'ing
mys·tique'
myth'i·cal
myth'o·log'i·cal
my·thol'o·gize'
 ·gized' ·giz'ing
my·thol'o·gy
 ·gies
myth'os

N

nab
 nabbed nab'bing
na·celle'

na'cre
na'cre·ous
na'dir
nag
 nagged nag'ging
nail'head'
nain'sook
na·ive' or ·īve'
na·ive·té' or ·īve·
na'ked·ness
nam'by-pam'by
 ·bies
name
 named nam'ing
name'a·ble
 or nam'·
name'-drop'per
name'less
name'ly
name'plate'
name'sake'
nan·keen' or ·kin'
nap
 napped nap'ping
na'palm
na'per·y
naph'tha
naph'tha·lene'
nap'kin
na·po'le·on
nap'per
nar·cis'sism
nar'cis·sist
nar'cis·sis'tic
nar·cis'sus
nar'co·lep'sy
nar·co'sis
nar·cot'ic
nar'co·tism
nar'rate
 ·rat·ed ·rat·ing
nar·ra'tion
nar'ra·tive
nar'ra·tor
nar'row-mind'ed
nar'whal
na'sal
na·sal'i·ty
na'sal·ize'
 ·ized' ·iz'ing
nas'cent
nas'ti·ly
nas'ti·ness
na·stur'tium
nas'ty
 ·ti·er ·ti·est
na'tal
na'tant
na'ta·to'ri·um
 ·ri·ums or ·ri·a
na'ta·to'ry
na'tion
na'tion·al
na'tion·al·ism
na'tion·al·is'ti·
 cal·ly
na'tion·al'i·ty
 ·ties

na'tion·al·i·za'tion
na'tion·al·ize'
 ·ized' ·iz'ing
na'tion·al·ly
na'tion·wide'
na'tive
na'tive-born'
na·tiv'i·ty
 ·ties
nat'ti·ly
nat'ty
 ·ti·er ·ti·est
nat'u·ral
nat'u·ral·ism
nat'u·ral·ist
nat'u·ral·is'tic
nat'u·ral·i·za'tion
nat'u·ral·ize'
 ·ized' ·iz'ing
nat'u·ral·ly
na'ture
naug'a·hyde'
naught
naugh'ti·ly
naugh'ti·ness
naugh'ty
 ·ti·er ·ti·est
nau'se·a
nau'se·ate'
 ·at'ed ·at'ing
nau'seous
nau'ti·cal
nau'ti·lus
 ·lus·es or ·li'
na'val
 (of a navy)
nave
 (part of a church;
 see knave)
na'vel
 (umbilicus)
nav'i·cert
nav'i·ga·ble
nav'i·ga'tion
nav'i·ga'tor
na'vy
 ·vies
nay
 (no; see nee,
 neigh)
Ne·an'der·thal'
near'by'
near'ly
near'sight'ed
neat'ly
neat'ness
neb'bish
Ne·bras'ka
neb'u·la
 ·lae' or ·las
neb'u·lar
neb·u·los'i·ty
neb'u·lous
nec'es·sar'i·ly
nec'es·sar'y
 ·ies

ne·ces'si·tate'
 ·tat'ed ·tat'ing
ne·ces'si·tous
ne·ces'si·ty
 ·ties
neck'er·chief
neck'lace
neck'line'
neck'piece'
neck'tie'
neck'wear'
ne·crol'o·gy
 ·gies
nec'ro·man'cy
nec'tar
nec'tar·ine'
nee or née
 (born; see nay,
 neigh)
need
 (require; see
 knead)
need'ful
need'i·ness
nee'dle
 ·dled ·dling
nee'dle-like'
nee'dle·point'
nee'dler
need'less
nee'dle·work'
need'n't
need'y
 ·i·er ·i·est
ne'er'-do-well'
ne·far'i·ous
ne·gate'
 ·gat'ed ·gat'ing
ne·ga'tion
neg'a·tive
neg'a·tiv·ism
neg·lect'
neg·lect'ful
neg'li·gee'
 ·gat'ed ·gat'ing
neg'li·gence
neg'li·gent
neg'li·gi·ble
neg'li·gi·bly
ne·go'ti·a·bil'i·ty
ne·go'ti·a·ble
ne·go'ti·ate'
 ·at'ed ·at'ing
ne·go'ti·a'tion
ne·go'ti·a'tor
Ne'gro
 ·groes
Ne'groid
neigh
 (whinny; see
 nay, nee)
neigh'bor
neigh'bor·hood'
neigh'bor·li·ness
neigh'bor·ly
nei'ther
 (not either;
 see nether)
nem'a·tode'

nem'e·sis
 ·ses'
ne'o·clas'sic
ne'o·lith'ic
ne·ol'o·gism
ne'o·my'cin
ne'on
ne'o·phyte'
ne'o·plasm
ne'o·prene'
ne·pen'the
neph'ew
ne·phri'tis
nep'o·tism
Nep'tune
nerve
 nerved nerv'ing
nerve'-rack'ing
 or -wrack'·
nerv'ous
nerv'y
 ·i·er ·i·est
nes'ci·ent
nes'tle
 ·tled ·tling
nest'ling
 (young bird)
net
 net'ted net'ting
neth'er
 (lower; see
 neither)
net'tle
 ·tled ·tling
net'work'
Neuf·châ·tel'
neu'ral
neu·ral'gia
neu'ras·the'ni·a
neu·ri'tis
neu'ro·log'i·cal
neu·rol'o·gist
neu·rol'o·gy
neu·ro'sis
 ·ses
neu·rot'ic
neu'ter
neu'tral
neu·tral'i·ty
neu'tral·i·za'tion
neu'tral·ize'
 ·ized' ·iz'ing
neu'tral·iz'er
neu·tri'no
neu'tron
Ne·vad'a
nev'er·more'
nev'er·the·less'
ne'vus
 ·vi
new'born'
new'com'er
new'el
new'fan'gled
new'-fash'ioned
New'found·land'
New Hamp'shire
New Jer'sey

new'ly·wed'
New Mex'i·co
news'boy'
news'cast'
news'deal·er
news'let·ter
news'man'
news'pa·per
new'speak'
news'print'
news'reel'
news'stand'
news'wor'thy
New York
next'-door'
nex'us
·us·es *or* nex'us
ni'a·cin
Ni·ag'a·ra
nib'ble
·bled ·bling
nib'lick
nice
nic'er nic'est
nice'ly
ni'ce·ty
·ties
niche
(*recess*)
nick
(*notch*)
nick'el
·eled *or* ·elled
·el·ing *or* ·el·ling
nick'el·o'de·on
nick'name'
nic'o·tine'
nic'o·tin·ism
nic'ti·tate'
·tat'ed ·tat'ing
niece
nig'gard·ly
nig'gling
night
(*darkness;* see
knight)
night'cap'
night'club'
night'dress'
night'fall'
night'gown'
night'in·gale'
night'long'
night'ly
night'mare'
night'mar·ish
night'shirt'
night'time'
ni'hil·ism
ni'hil·is'tic
nim'ble
·bler ·blest
nim'bly
nim'bus
·bi *or* ·bus·es
nin'com·poop'
nine'fold'
nine'pins'

nine'teen'
nine'ti·eth
nine'ty
·ties
nin'ny
·nies
ni'non
ninth
nip
nipped nip'ping
nip'per
nip'pi·ness
nip'ple
nip'py
·pi·er ·pi·est
nip'-up'
nir·va'na
ni'sei
·sei *or* ·seis
nit'-pick'ing
ni'tro·gen
ni·tro·glyc'er·in
or ·er·ine
nit'ty-grit'ty
no·bil'i·ty
no'ble
·bler ·blest
no'ble·man
no'bly
no'bod'y
·ies
noc·tur'nal
noc·tur'nal·ly
noc'turne
noc'u·ous
nod
nod'ded nod'ding
nod'al
node
nod'u·lar
nod'ule
no·el' *or* ·ël'
nog'gin
no'-hit'ter
noise
noised nois'ing
noise'less
noise'mak·er
nois'i·ly
nois'i·ness
noi'some
nois'y
·i·er ·i·est
no'mad
no·mad'ic
nom' de plume'
noms' de plume'
no'men·cla'ture
nom'i·nal
nom'i·nal·ly
nom'i·nate'
·nat'ed ·nat'ing
nom'i·na'tion
nom'i·na·tive
nom'i·na'tor
nom'i·nee'
non·a·ge·nar'i·an
non'-book'

nonce
nose cone
nose'-dive'
-dived' -div'ing
nose'gay'
nose'piece'
no'-show'
nos·tal'gia
nos·tal'gic
nos'tril
nos'trum
no'ta·ble
no'ta·bly
no'ta·ri·za'tion
no'ta·rize'
·rized' ·riz'ing
no'ta·ry public
no'ta·ries public
or no'ta·ry publics
no·ta'tion
notched
note
not'ed not'ing
note'book'
note'wor'thy
noth'ing·ness
no'tice
·ticed ·tic·ing
no'tice·a·ble
no'tice·a·bly
no·ti·fi'a·ble
no·ti·fi·ca'tion
no'ti·fy'
·fied' ·fy'ing
no'tion
no'to·ri'e·ty
no·to'ri·ous
no'-trump'
not'with·stand'ing
nou'gat
nought
nour'ish·ment
nou'veau riche'
nou'veaux riches'
no'va
·vas *or* ·vae
nov'el
nov'el·ette'
nov'el·ist
no·vel'la
nov'el·ty
·ties
No·vem'ber
nov'ice
no·vi'ti·ate
now'a·days'
no'where'
no'wise'
nox'ious
noz'zle
nu'ance
nub'bi·ness
nub'by
·bi·er ·bi·est
nu'bile
nu'cle·ar
nu'cle·ate'
·at'ed ·at'ing

nose'bleed'
non'cha·lance'
non'cha·lant'
non·com'bat·ant
non'com·mit'tal
non·com'pos
men'tis
non'con·form'ist
non'co·op'er·a'·
tion
non'de·script'
non·en'ti·ty
·ties
non'es·sen'tial
none'such'
none'the·less'
non·ex·ist'ent
non·fea'sance
non'he·ro
non·nu'cle·ar
no-non'sense
non'pa·reil'
non·par'ti·san
non·plus'
·plused' *or*
·plussed'
·plus'ing *or*
·plus'sing
non·prof'it
non·sched'uled
non·sec'tar'i·an
non'sense
non·sen'si·cal
non·sen'si·cal·ly
non' se'qui·tur
non'-sked'
non'skid'
non'stop'
non'sup·port'
non·un'ion
non·vi'o·lence
noo'dle
noon'day'
no one
noon'time'
noose
noosed noos'ing
no'-par'
nor'mal
nor'mal·cy
nor·mal'i·ty
nor'mal·ize'
·ized' ·iz'ing
nor'mal·ly
north'bound'
North Car'o·li'na
North Da·ko'ta
north'east'
north'east'er·ly
north'east'ern
north'er·ly
north'ern
north'ward
north'west'
north'west'er·ly
north'west'ern
nose
nosed nos'ing

nu·cle·on'ics
nu'cle·us
·cle·i' *or*
·cle·us·es
nude
nudge
nudged nudg'ing
nud'ist
nu'di·ty
nu'ga·to'ry
nug'get
nui'sance
nul'li·fi·ca'tion
nul'li·fy'
·fied' ·fy'ing
num'ber
num'ber·less
numb'ly
numb'ness
nu'mer·a·ble
nu'mer·al
nu'mer·ate'
·at'ed ·at'ing
nu'mer·a'tion
nu'mer·a'tor
nu·mer'i·cal
nu'mer·ol'o·gy
nu'mer·ous
nu'mis·mat'ic
nu·mis'ma·tist
num'skull'
nun'ner·y
·ies
nup'tial
nurse
nursed nurs'ing
nurse'maid'
nurs'er·y
·ies
nur'ture
·tured ·tur·ing
nut'crack'er
nut'gall'
nut'meat'
nut'meg'
nut'pick'
nu'tri·a
nu'tri·ent
nu'tri·ment
nu·tri'tion
nu·tri'tious
nu'tri·tive
nut'shell'
nuz'zle
·zled ·zling
ny'lon
nymph
nym'pho·
ma'ni·ac'

O

oaf'ish
oa'kum
oar
(*pole;* see ore)

oar'lock'
oars'man
o·a'sis
·ses
oath
oat'meal'
ob'bli·ga'to
·tos *or* ·ti
ob'du·ra·cy
ob'du·rate
o·be'di·ence
o·be'di·ent
o·bei'sance
o·bei'sant
ob'e·lisk'
o·bese'
o·be'si·ty
o·bey'
ob'fus·cate'
·cat'ed ·cat'ing
ob'i·ter dic'tum
ob'i·ter dic'ta
o·bit'u·ar'y
·ies
ob'ject
ob·jec'tion
ob·jec'tion·a·ble
ob·jec'tion·a·bly
ob·jec'tive
ob·jec'tive·ly
ob'jec·tiv'i·ty
ob·jec'tor
ob'jet d'art'
ob'jets d'art'
ob'jur·gate'
·gat'ed ·gat'ing
ob'jur·ga'tion
ob·la'tion
ob'li·gate'
·gat'ed ·gat'ing
ob'li·ga'tion
ob·lig'a·to'ry
o·blige'
o·bliged'
o·blig'ing
ob·lique'
ob·lique'ly
ob·liq'ui·ty
ob·lit'er·ate'
·at'ed ·at'ing
ob·lit'er·a'tion
ob·lit'er·a'tor
ob·liv'i·on
ob·liv'i·ous
ob'long
ob'lo·quy
·quies
ob·nox'ious
o'boe
o'bo·ist
ob·scene'
ob·scen'i·ty
·ties
ob·scure'
·scured' ·scur'ing
ob·scure'ly
ob·scu'ri·ty
·ties

ob'se·quies
ob·se'qui·ous
ob·serv'a·ble
ob·serv'ance
ob·serv'ant
ob·ser·va'tion
ob·serv'a·to·ry
 ·ries
ob·serve'
 served' ·serv'ing
ob·serv'er
ob·sess'
ob·ses'sion
ob·ses'sive
ob·sid'i·an
ob'so·lesce'
 ·lesced' ·lesc'ing
ob'so·les'cence
ob'so·les'cent
ob'so·lete'
ob'sta·cle
ob·stet'ric
ob·stet'ri·cal
ob'ste·tri'cian
ob'sti·na·cy
 ·cies
ob'sti·nate
ob'sti·nate·ly
ob·strep'er·ous
ob·struct'
ob·struc'tion
ob·struc'tion·ist
ob·struc'tive
ob·tain'
ob·trude'
 ·trud'ed
 ·trud'ing
ob·tru'sion
ob·tru'sive
ob·tru'sive·ly
ob·tuse'
ob·vert'
ob'vi·ate'
 ·at'ed ·at'ing
ob'vi·ous
ob'vi·ous·ly
oc'a·ri'na
oc·ca'sion
oc·ca'sion·al
oc·ca'sion·al·ly
Oc'ci·dent
Oc'ci·den'tal
oc·cip'i·tal
oc·clude'
 ·clud'ed
 ·clud'ing
oc·clu'sion
oc·cult'
oc'cul·ta'tion
oc·cult'ism
oc'cu·pan·cy
 ·cies
oc'cu·pant
oc'cu·pa'tion
oc'cu·pa'tion·al·ly
oc'cu·py'
 ·pied' ·py'ing

oc·cur'
 ·curred'
 ·cur'ring
oc·cur'rence
o'cean
o'cean·go'ing
o'ce·an'ic
o'ce·a·nog'ra·phy
o'ce·an·ol'o·gy
o'ce·lot'
o'cher or o'chre
o'·clock'
oc'ta·gon'
oc·tag'o·nal
oc'ta·he'dron
oc'tane
oc·tan'gu·lar
oc'tave
oc·ta'vo
 ·vos
oc·tet' or ·tette'
Oc·to'ber
oc'to·ge·nar'i·an
oc'to·pus
 ·pus·es or ·pi'
 or oc·top'o·des'
oc'tu·ple
oc'u·lar
oc'u·list
odd'i·ty
 ·ties
odd'ly
odds'-on'
o'di·ous
o'di·um
o·dom'e·ter
o'dor
o'dor·if'er·ous
o'dor·ous
Od'ys·sey
of'fal
off'beat'
off'-col'or
of·fend'
of·fense'
of·fen'sive
of'fer
of'fer·ing
of'fer·to'ry
 ·ries
off'hand'
off'hand'ed·ly
of'fice
of'fice·hold'er
of'fi·cer
of·fi'cial·ese'
of·fi'cial
of·fi'ci·ate'
 ·at'ed ·at'ing
of·fi'ci·a'tor
of·fi'cious
off'ing
off'-key'
off'-lim'its
off'-line'
off'print'
off'set'

off'shoot'
off'shore'
off'side'
off'spring'
 ·spring' or
 ·springs'
off'stage'
off'-white'
of'ten
of'ten·times'
o'gle
o'gled o'gling
o'gre
o'gre·ish or
 o'grish
O·hi'o
ohm'me'ter
oil'cloth'
oil'i·ness
oil'pa'per
oil'skin'
oil'stone'
oil'y
oint'ment
OK or O.K.
 OK's or O.K.'s
 OK'd or O.K.'d
 OK'ing or O.K.'ing
O'kla·ho'ma
old'-fash'ioned
old'ish
old'-line'
old'ster
old'-tim'er
old'-world'
o'le·o'
o'le·o·mar'ga·
 rine or ·rin
ol·fac'tion
ol·fac'to·ry
 ·ries
ol'i·garch'
ol'i·garch'y
 ·ies
ol'i·gop'o·ly
 ·lies
ol'ive
O·lym'pic
o·me'ga
om'e·let or
 ·lette
o'men
om'i·nous
o·mis'si·ble
o·mis'sion
o·mit'
o·mit'ted
o·mit'ting
om'ni·bus'
om'ni·far'i·ous
om·nip'o·tence
om·nip'o·tent
om'ni·pres'ence
om'ni·pres'ent
om'ni·range'
om·nis'cience
om·nis'cient

om·niv'o·rous
once'-o'ver
on'com'ing
one'ness
on'er·ous
one'self'
one'-sid'ed
one'-time'
one'-track'
one'-up'
 -upped'
 -up'ping
one'-up'man·ship'
one'-way'
on'go'ing
on'ion·skin'
on'-line'
on'look'er
on'ly
on'o·mat'o·poe'ia
on'rush'
on'set'
on'shore'
on'side'
on'slaught'
o'nus
on'ward
on'yx
oo'long
ooze
oozed ooz'ing
oo'zi·ness
oo'zy
 ·zi·er ·zi·est
o·pac'i·ty
o'pal
o'pal·es'cent
o·paque'
o'pen-and-shut'
o'pen-end'
o'pen'e·trist
o'pen-end'ed
o'pen·er
o'pen-eyed'
o'pen·hand'ed
o'pen·heart'ed
o'pen-hearth'
o'pen·ly
o'pen-mind'ed
o'pen-mouthed'
o'pen·ness
o'pen·work'
op'er·a
op'er·a·ble
op'er·ate'
 ·at'ed ·at'ing
op'er·at'ic
op'er·a'tion
op'er·a'tion·al
op'er·a'tion·al·ly
op'er·a·tive
op'er·a'tor
op'er·et'ta
oph'thal·mol'o·
 gist
oph'thal·mol'o·gy
oph·thal'mo·
 scope'
o'pi·ate

o·pin'ion
o·pin'ion·at'ed
o·pin'ion·a'tive
o'pi·um
o·pos'sum
op·po'nent
op'por·tune'
op'por·tun'ism
op'por·tun'ist
op'por·tu'ni·ty
 ·ties
op·pos'a·ble
op·pose'
 ·posed' ·pos'ing
op·pos'er
op'po·site
op'po·si'tion
op·press'
op·pres'sion
op·pres'sive
op·pres'sive·ly
op·pres'sor
op·pro'bri·ous
op·pro'bri·um
op'tic
op'ti·cal
op·ti'cian
op'ti·mal
op'ti·mism
op'ti·mist
op'ti·mis'tic
op'ti·mis'ti·cal·ly
op'ti·mize'
 ·mized' ·miz'ing
op'ti·mum
 ·mums or ·ma
op'tion
op'tion·al
op'tion·al·ly
op·tom'e·trist
op·tom'e·try
op'u·lence
op'u·lent
o'pus
op'er·a or
o'pus·es
or'a·cle
 (wise person;
 see auricle)
o·rac'u·lar
o'ral
 (of the mouth;
 see aural)
o'ral·ly
or'ange
or'ange·ade'
or'ange·wood'
o·rang'u·tan'
o·ra'tion
or'a·tor
or'a·tor'i·cal
or'a·tor'i·o'
 ·os'
or'a·to'ry
 ·ries
or·bic'u·lar
or'bit
or'chard

or'ches·tra
or·ches'tral
or'ches·trate'
 ·trat'ed ·trat'ing
or'ches·tra'tion
or'chid
or·dain'
or·deal'
or'der
or'der·li·ness
or'der·ly
 ·lies
or'di·nal
or'di·nance
 (law; see
 ordnance)
or'di·nar'i·ly
or'di·nar'y
 ·ies
or'di·nate
or'di·na'tion
ord'nance
 (artillery; see
 ordinance)
or'dure
ore
 (mineral; see oar)
o·reg'a·no
Or'e·gon
or'gan
or'gan·dy or ·die
or·gan'ic
or·gan'i·cal·ly
or'gan·ism
or'gan·ist
or'gan·iz'a·ble
or'gan·i·za'tion
or'gan·ize'
 ·ized' ·iz'ing
or'gan·iz'er
or·gan'za
or'gasm
or·gas'mic
or'gi·as'tic
or'gy
 ·gies
O'ri·ent n.
o'ri·ent' v.
O'ri·en'tal
o'ri·en·tate'
 ·tat'ed ·tat'ing
o'ri·en·ta'tion
or'i·fice
or'i·ga'mi
or'i·gin
o·rig'i·nal
o·rig'i·nal'i·ty
o·rig'i·nal·ly
o·rig'i·nate'
 ·nat'ed ·nat'ing
o·rig'i·na'tion
o·rig'i·na'tor
o'ri·ole'
or'lon
or'na·ment
or'na·men'tal
or'na·men·ta'tion
or·nate'

or·nate'ly
or'ni·thol'o·gy
o'ro·tund'
or'phan·age
or'thi·con'
or'tho·don'tics
or'tho·don'tist
or'tho·dox'
or'tho·dox'y
·ies
or·thog'ra·phy
or'tho·pe'dics
or'tho·pe'dist
os'cil·late'
·lat'ed ·lat'ing
(fluctuate; see
osculate)
os'cil·la'tion
os'cil·la'tor
os·cil'lo·scope'
os'cu·late'
·lat'ed ·lat'ing
(kiss; see
oscillate)
os·mo'sis
os'prey
·preys
os'si·fy'
·fied ·fy'ing
os·ten'si·ble
os·ten'si·bly
os·ten'sive
os·ten'sive·ly
os'ten·ta'tion
os'ten·ta'tious
os'te·o·path'
os'te·op'a·thy
os'tra·cism
os'tra·cize'
·cized ·ciz'ing
os'trich
oth'er-di·rect'ed
oth'er·wise'
o'ti·ose'
ot'ter
ot'to·man
·mans
ought
(be obliged; see
aught)
our·self'
our·selves'
oust'er
out'-and-out'
out'bid'
·bid' ·bid'ding
out'board'
out'bound'
out'break'
out'build'ing
out'burst'
out'cast'
out'class'
out'come'
out'crop'
out'cry'
·cries'
out'dat'ed

out'dis'tance
·tanced ·tanc·ing
out'do'
·did' ·done'
·do'ing
out'door'
out'doors'
out'er·most'
out'er space
out'er·wear'
out'face'
out'field'er
out'fit'
out'fit'ter
out'flank'
out'flow'
out'go'
·went' ·gone'
·go'ing
out'go'
·goes'
out'go'ing
out'-group'
out'grow'
·grew' ·grown'
·grow'ing
out'growth'
out'guess'
out'house'
out'ing
out'land'er
out·land'ish
out·last'
out'law'
out'law·ry
·ries
out'lay'
·laid' ·lay'ing
out'let'
out'li'er
out'line'
out'live'
out'look'
out'ly·ing
out'man'
out'ma·neu'ver
out'mod'ed
out'most'
out'num'ber
out'-of-date'
out'-of-doors'
out'-of-pock'et
out'-of-the-way'
out'-of-town'er
out'pa'tient
out'post'
out'pour'ing
out'put'
out'rage'
out·ra'geous
out'rank'
out'reach'
out'ride'
·rode' ·rid'den
·rid'ing
out'rid'er
out'rig'ger
out'right'

out'run'
·ran' ·run'
·run'ning
out'sell'
·sold' ·sell'ing
out'set'
out'shine'
·shone' ·shin'ing
out'side'
out'sid'er
out'sit'
·sat' ·sit'ting
out'size'
out'skirts'
out'smart'
out'speak'
·spoke' ·spo'ken
·speak'ing
out'spo'ken·ness
out'spread'
·spread'
·spread'ing
out'stand'ing
out'stare'
out'sta'tion
out'stay'
out'stretch'
out'strip'
out'talk'
out'think'
·thought'
·think'ing
out'vote'
out'ward
out'wear'
·wore' ·worn'
·wear'ing
out'weigh'
out'wit'
·wit'ted
·wit'ting
out'work'
o'val
o'val·ly
o·var'i·an
o'va·ry
·ries
o·va'tion
ov'en
o'ver·age
o'ver·all'
o'ver·alls'
o'ver·awe'
·awed' ·aw'ing
o'ver·bal'ance
o'ver·bear'
·bore' ·borne'
·bear'ing
o'ver·bid'
·bid' ·bid'ding
o'ver·bite'
o'ver·blouse'
o'ver·board'
o'ver·cap'i·tal·
ize'
o'ver·cast'
o'ver·charge'
o'ver·coat'

o'ver·come'
·came' ·come'
·com'ing
o'ver·com'pen·
sate'
o'ver·con'fi·dent
o'ver·crowd'ed
o'ver·do'
·did' ·done'
·do'ing
o'ver·dose'
o'ver·draft'
o'ver·draw'
·drew' ·drawn'
·draw'ing
o'ver·dress'
o'ver·drive'
o'ver·due'
o'ver·flight'
o'ver·flow'
o'ver·fly'
·flew' ·flown'
·fly'ing
o'ver·gar'ment
o'ver·glaze'
o'ver·grow'
·grew' ·grown'
·grow'ing
o'ver·hand'
o'ver·hang'
·hung'
·hang'ing
o'ver·haul'
o'ver·head'
o'ver·hear'
·heard'
·hear'ing
o'ver·heat'
o'ver·in·dul'·
gence
o'ver·is'sue
o'ver·joy'
o'ver·lad'en
o'ver·lap'
o'ver·lay'
·laid' ·lay'ing
o'ver·leap'
o'ver·lie'
·lay' ·lain'
·ly'ing
o'ver·load'
o'ver·look'
o'ver·ly
o'ver·nice'
o'ver·night'
o'ver·pass'
o'ver·pay'
·paid' ·pay'ing
o'ver·pop'u·late'
o'ver·pow'er
o'ver·pro·duce'
o'ver·pro·tect'
o'ver·rate'
o'ver·reach'
o'ver·ride'
·rode' ·rid'den
·rid'ing
o'ver·rule'

o'ver·run'
·ran' ·run'
·run'ning
o'ver·seas'
o'ver·see'
·saw' ·seen'
·see'ing
o'ver·se'er
o'ver·sell'
·sold' ·sell'ing
o'ver·sexed'
o'ver·shad'ow
o'ver·shoe'
o'ver·shoot'
·shot' ·shoot'ing
o'ver·sight'
o'ver·sim'pli·fy'
o'ver·size'
o'ver·skirt'
o'ver·slaugh'
o'ver·sleep'
·slept' ·sleep'ing
o'ver·spend'
·spent' ·spend'ing
o'ver·spread'
o'ver·state'
o'ver·stay'
o'ver·step'
o'ver·stock'
o'ver·strung'
o'ver·stuff'
o'ver·sub·scribe'
o'ver·sup·ply'
o·vert'
o'ver·take'
·took' ·tak'en
·tak'ing
o'ver·tax'
o'ver-the-count'er
o'ver·throw'
·threw' ·thrown'
·throw'ing
o'ver·time'
o'ver·tone'
o'ver·ture
o'ver·use'
o'ver·view'
o'ver·ween'ing
o'ver·weight'
o'ver·whelm'
o'ver·wind'
·wound' ·wind'ing
o'ver·work'
o'ver·write'
·wrote' ·writ'ten
·writ'ing
o'ver·wrought'
o·vip'a·rous
o'void
o'vu·late'
·lat'ed ·lat'ing
o'vu·la'tion
o'vule
o'vum
o'va
owe
owed ow'ing
owl'ish

own'er·ship'
ox
ox'en
ox'blood'
ox'bow'
ox'ford
ox'i·da'tion
ox'i·dize'
·dized' diz'ing
ox'tail'
ox'y·gen
ox'y·gen·ate'
·at'ed ·at'ing
ox'y·gen·a'tion
ox'y·mo'ron
·mo'ra
ox'y·tet'ra·cy'·
cline
oys'ter
o'zone

P

pab'lum
pace
paced pac'ing
pace'mak'er
pach'y·derm'
pach'y·san'dra
pac'i·fi'a·ble
pa·cif'ic
pac'i·fi·ca'tion
pac'i·fi'er
pac'i·fism
pac'i·fy'
·fied' fy'ing
pack'age
·aged ·ag·ing
pack'et
pack'ing
pack'sad'dle
pack'thread'
pact
pad
pad'ded
pad'ding
pad'dle
dled ·dling
pad'dock
pad'dy
·dies
(rice; see patty)
pad'lock'
pa'dre
·dres
pae'an
(song; see peon)
pa'gan
page
paged pag'ing
pag'eant
pag'eant·ry
·ries
page'boy'
pag'i·nate'
·nat'ed ·nat'ing

pag'i·na'tion
pa·go'da
pail
  (bucket; see
  pale)
pail'ful'
  ·fuls'
pain
  (hurt; see pane)
pain'ful
pain'less
pains'tak'ing
paint'brush'
paint'er
pair
  (two; see pare,
  pear)
pais'ley
pa·ja'mas
pal'ace
pal'an·quin'
pal'at·a·ble
pal'at·a·bly
pal'a·tal
pal'ate
  (roof of mouth;
  see palette, pallet)
pa·la'tial
pal'a·tine'
pa·lav'er
pale
  paled pal'ing
  (white; see pail)
pale'face'
pale'ly
pa'le·o·lith'ic
pa'le·on·tol'o·gy
pal'ette
  (paint board; see
  palate, pallet)
pal'in·drome'
pal'ing
pal'i·sade'
pall
  palled pall'ing
pal·la'di·um
pall'bear'er
pal'let
  (tool; bed; see
  palate, palette)
pal'li·ate'
  ·at'ed ·at'ing
pal'li·a'tive
pal'lid
pall'-mall'
  (game; see
  pell-mell)
pal'lor
palm
pal·met'to
  ·tos or ·toes
palm'is·try
pal'o·mi'no
  ·nos
pal'pa·ble
pal'pa·bly
pal'pate
  ·pat·ed ·pat·ing

pal'pi·tate'
  ·tat'ed ·tat'ing
pal'pi·ta'tion
pal'sy
  ·sied ·sy·ing
pal'tri·ness
pal'try
  ·tri·er ·tri·est
  (trifling;
  see poultry)
pam'pas
pam'per
pam'phlet
pam'phlet·eer'
pan
  panned pan'ning
pan'a·ce'a
pa·nache'
Pan'-A·mer'i·can
pan·a·tel'a
pan'cake'
pan'chro·mat'ic
pan'cre·as
pan'cre·at'ic
pan·dem'ic
pan'de·mo'ni·um
pan'der
pan·dow'dy
  ·dies
pane
  (window; see
  pain)
pan'e·gyr'ic
pan'e·gyr'i·cal
pan'el
  ·eled or ·elled
  ·el·ing or ·el·ling
pan'el·ist
pan'-fry'
  -fried' -fry'ing
pan'han'dle
pan'ic
  ·icked ·ick·ing
pan'ic·al·ly
pan'ick·y
pan'ic-strick'en
panne
pan'nier
pan'o·ply
  ·plies
pan'o·ra'ma
pan'o·ram'ic
pan'o·ram'i·cal·ly
pan'ta·loons'
pant'dress'
pan'the·ism
pan'the·is'tic
pan'the·on'
pan'ther
pant'ies
pan'to·graph
pan'to·mime'
  ·mimed'
  ·mim'ing
pan'to·mim'ic
pan'to·mim'ist
pan'try
  ·tries

pant'suit' or
  pants suit
pan'ty hose
pa'pa·cy
  ·cies
pa'pal
pa'paw
pa·pa'ya
pa'per·back'
pa'per·bound'
pa'per·hang'er
pa'per·weight'
pa'per·y
pa'pier-mâ·ché'
pa·poose'
pa·pri'ka
pap'ule
pa·py'rus
  ·ri or ·rus·es
par
  parred par'ring
par'a·ble
pa·rab'o·la
par'a·bol'ic
par'a·bol'i·cal·ly
par'a·chute'
  ·chut'ed
  ·chut'ing
par'a·chut'ist
pa·rade'
  ·rad'ed ·rad'ing
par'a·digm
par'a·dise'
par'a·dox'
par'a·dox'i·cal
par'a·dox'i·cal·ly
par'af·fin
par'a·gon'
par'a·graph'
par'a·keet'
par'al·lax'
par'al·lel'
  ·leled' or ·lelled'
  ·lel'ing or
  ·lel'ling
par'al·lel·ism
par'al·lel'o·gram'
pa·ral'y·sis
par'a·lyt'ic
par'a·lyze'
  ·lyzed' ·lyz'ing
par'a·me'ci·um
  ·ci·a
par'a·med'ic
par'a·med'i·cal
pa·ram'e·ter
  (math. term; see
  perimeter)
par'a·mount'
par'a·mour'
par'a·noi'a
par'a·noi'ac
par'a·noid'
par'a·pet
par'a·pher·na'li·a
par'a·phrase'
  ·phrased'
  ·phras'ing

par'a·ple'gi·a
par'a·ple'gic
par'a·prax'is
  ·es
par'a·psy·chol'o·gy
par'a·res'cue
par'a-sail'
par'a·site'
par'a·sit'ic
par'a·sol'
par'a·troops'
par'boil'
par'buck'le
par'cel
  ·celed or ·celled
  ·cel·ing or
  ·cel·ling
parch'ment
par'don·a·ble
par'don·a·bly
pare
  pared par'ing
  (trim; see pair,
  pear)
par'e·gor'ic
par'ent
par'ent·age
pa·ren'tal
pa·ren'the·sis
  ·ses'
pa·ren'the·size'
  ·sized' ·siz'ing
par'en·thet'i·cal
par'ent·hood'
pa·re'sis
par'e·ve
par ex'cel·lence'
par·fait'
par·he'li·on
  ·li·a
pa·ri'ah
pa·ri'e·tal
par'i·mu'tu·el
par'ish
pa·rish'ion·er
par'i·ty
  ·ties
par'ka
park'way'
parl'ance
par'lay
  (bet)
par'ley
  (confer)
par'lia·ment
par'lia·men·
  tar'i·an
par'lia·men'ta·ry
par'lor
pa·ro'chi·al
par'o·dist
par'o·dy
  ·dies
  ·died ·dy·ing
pa·role'
  ·roled' ·rol'ing
pa·rol'ee'

pa·rot'id
par'ox·ysm
par'ox·ys'mal
par·quet'
  ·queted'
  ·quet'ing
par'quet·ry
par'ra·keet'
par'ri·cid'al
par'ri·cide'
par'rot
par'ry
  ·ries
  ·ried ·ry·ing
par'sec'
par'si·mo'ni·ous
par'si·mo'ny
pars'ley
pars'nip
par'son
par'son·age
par·take'
  ·took' ·tak'en
  ·tak'ing
par·terre'
par'the·no·gen'e·sis
par'tial
par'ti·al'i·ty
par'tial·ly
par'ti·ble
par·tic'i·pant
par·tic'i·pate'
  ·pat'ed ·pat'ing
par·tic'i·pa'tion
par·tic'i·pa'tor
par'ti·cip'i·al
par'ti·ci·ple
par'ti·cle
par'ti-col'ored
par·tic'u·lar
par·tic'u·lar'i·ty
  ·ties
par·tic'u·lar·ize'
  ·ized' ·iz'ing
par·tic'u·lar·ly
par'ti·san
par·ti'tion
par'ti·tive
part'ner
part'ner·ship'
par'tridge
part'-time'
par·tu'ri·ent
par·tu·ri'tion
par'ty
  ·ties
par've·nu'
  ·nus'
pas'chal
pass'a·ble
pass'a·bly
pas'sage
pas'sage·way'
pass'book'
pas·sé'
passed
  (pp. of pass;
  see past)

pas'sen·ger
passe'-par·tout'
pass'er-by'
  pass'ers-by'
pas'sion
pas'sion·ate
pas'sion·ate·ly
pas'sive
pas'sive·ly
pas·siv'i·ty
pass'key'
Pass'o'ver
pass'port'
pass'-through'
pass'word'
past
  (gone by; over;
  see passed)
paste
  past'ed past'ing
paste'board'
pas·tel'
pas'teur·i·za'tion
pas'teur·ize'
  ·ized' ·iz'ing
pas·tille'
pas'time'
past'i·ness
pas'tor
pas'to·ral
pas'tor·ate
pas·tra'mi
pas'try
  ·tries
pas'ture
  ·tured ·tur·ing
past'y
  ·i·er ·i·est
pat
  pat'ted pat'ting
patch'work'
patch'y
  ·i·er ·i·est
pâ·té' de foie'
  gras'
pa·tel'la
  ·las or ·lae
pat'ent
pat'ent·ee'
pa·ter'nal
pa·ter'nal·is'tic
pa·ter'ni·ty
pa·thet'ic
pa·thet'i·cal·ly
path'find'er
path'o·gen'ic
path'o·log'i·cal
pa·thol'o·gy
  ·gies
pa'thos
pa'tience
pa'tient
pat'i·na
pa'ti·o'
  ·os'
pa·tis'se·rie
pat'ois
  ·ois

pa'tri·arch'
pa'tri·ar'chal
pa'tri·ar'chy
 ·chies
pa·tri'cian
pat'ri·cide'
pat'ri·mo'ny
 ·nies
pa'tri·ot
pa'tri·ot'ic
pa·tri·ot'i·cal·ly
pa'tri·ot·ism
pa·trol'
 ·trolled'
 ·trol'ling
pa·trol'man
pa'tron
pa'tron·age
pa'tron·ize'
 ·ized' ·iz'ing
pat'ro·nym'ic
pat'ter
pat'tern·mak'er
pat'ty
 ·ties
 (cake; see paddy)
pau'ci·ty
paunch'i·ness
paunch'y
pau'per
pause
 paused paus'ing
pave
 paved pav'ing
pave'ment
pa·vil'ion
pawn'bro'ker
pawn'shop'
pay
 paid pay'ing
pay'a·ble
pay'check'
pay'day'
pay·ee'
pay'load'
pay'mas'ter
pay'ment
pay'off'
pay'roll'
peace
 (harmony;
 see piece)
peace'a·ble
peace'a·bly
peace'ful
peace'ful·ly
peace'mak'er
peace pipe
peace'time'
peach
pea'cock'
peak
 (highest point;
 see peek, pique)
peaked
 (pointed)
peak'ed
 (thin and drawn)

peal
 (sound; see peel)
pea'nut
pear
 (fruit; see pair,
 pare)
pearl
 (gem; see purl)
pearl'y
 ·i·er ·i·est
pearl'-shaped'
peas'ant
peas'ant·ry
peat moss
peau' de soie'
peb'ble
 ·bled ·bling
peb'bly
 ·bli·er ·bli·est
pe·can'
pec'ca·dil'lo
 ·loes or ·los
pec'cant
peck
pec'tin
pec'to·ral
pec'u·late'
 ·lat'ed ·lat'ing
pec'u·la'tion
pec'u·la'tor
pe·cul'iar
pe·cu'li·ar'i·ty
 ·ties
pe·cu'ni·ar'i·ly
pe·cu'ni·ar'y
ped'a·gog'ic
ped'a·gogue'
 or ·gog'
ped'a·go'gy
ped'al
 ·aled or ·alled
 ·al·ing or
 ·al·ling
 (foot lever; see
 peddle)
ped'ant
pe·dan'tic
pe·dan'ti·cal·ly
ped'ant·ry
 ·ries
ped'dle
 ·dled ·dling
 (sell; see pedal)
ped'dler
ped'es·tal
pe·des'tri·an
pe'di·a·tri'cian
pe'di·at'rics
ped'i·cure'
ped'i·gree'
ped'i·greed'
ped'i·ment
pe·dom'e·ter
peek
 (look; see
 peak, pique)
peel
 (skin; see peal)

peep'hole'
peer
 (equal; look;
 see pier)
peer group
peer'less
peeve
 peeved peev'ing
pee'vish
peg
 pegged peg'ging
peg'board'
peign·oir'
pe'jo·ra'tion
pe·jo'ra·tive
Pe'king·ese'
pe'koe
pel'i·can
pel·la'gra
pel'let
pell'-mell'
 (without order;
 see pall-mall)
pel·lu'cid
pel'vic
pel'vis
pem'mi·can
pen
 penned or pent
 pen'ning
 (enclose)
pen
 penned pen'ning
 (write with pen)
pe'nal
pe'nal·i·za'tion
pe'nal·ize'
 ·ized' ·iz'ing
pen'al·ty
 ·ties
pen'ance
pen'chant
pen'cil
 ·ciled or ·cilled
 ·cil·ing or
 ·cil·ling
pend'ant or
 ·ent n.
pend'ent or
 ·ant adj.
pend'ing
pen'du·lous
pen'du·lum
pen'e·tra·bil'i·ty
pen'e·tra·ble
pen'e·tra·bly
pen'e·trate'
 ·trat'ed ·trat'ing
pen'e·tra'tion
pen'e·trom'e·ter
pen'guin
pen'hold'er
pen'i·cil'lin
pen·in'su·la
pen·in'su·lar
pe'nis
 ·nis·es or ·nes
pen'i·tence

pen'i·tent
pen'i·ten'tial
pen'i·ten'tia·ry
 ·ries
pen'knife'
 ·knives'
pen'light' or ·lite'
pen'man·ship'
pen name
pen'nant
pen'non
Penn'syl·va'ni·a
pen'ny
 ·nies
pen'ny ante
pen'ny·weight'
pen'ny-wise'
pen'ny·worth'
pe'no·log'i·cal
pe·nol'o·gist
pe·nol'o·gy
pen'sion
pen'sion·ar'y
 ·ies
pen'sive
pen'sive·ly
pen'stock'
pen'ta·gon'
pen·tag'o·nal
pen'ta·he'dral
pen'ta·he'dron
 ·drons or ·dra
pen·tam'e·ter
Pen'ta·teuch'
pen·tath'lon
Pen'te·cost'
pent'house'
pen·tom'ic
pent'-up'
pe·nu'che or ·chi
pe'nult
pe·nul'ti·mate
pe·num'bra
 ·brae or ·bras
pe·nu'ri·ous
pen'u·ry
pe'on
 (laborer; see
 paean)
pe'on·age
pe'o·ny
 ·nies
peo'ple
 ·pled ·pling
pep'lum
 ·lums or ·la
pep'per-and-salt'
pep'per·corn'
pep'per·i·ness
pep'per·mint'
pep'per·o'ni
 ·nis or ·ni
pep'per·y
 ·i·er ·i·est
pep'pi·ly
pep'pi·ness
pep'py
 ·pi·er ·pi·est

pep'sin
pep'tic
per·am'bu·late'
 ·lat'ed ·lat'ing
per·am'bu·la'tion
per·am'bu·la'tor
per an'num
per·cale'
per cap'i·ta
per·ceiv'a·ble
per·ceiv'a·bly
per·ceive'
 ·ceived' ·ceiv'ing
per·cent' or
 per cent
per·cent'age
per·cen'tile
per'cept
per·cep'ti·ble
per·cep'ti·bly
per·cep'tion
per·cep'tive
per·cep'tive·ly
per·cep'tu·al
per·chance'
Per'che·ron'
per·cip'i·ent
per'co·late'
 ·lat'ed ·lat'ing
per'co·la'tion
per'co·la'tor
per·cus'sion
per·cus'sive
per di'em
per·di'tion
per·du' or ·due'
per·dur'a·ble
per'e·gri·nate'
 ·nat'ed ·nat'ing
per'e·gri·na'tion
per·emp'to·ri·ly
per·emp'to·ri·ness
per·emp'to·ry
per·en'ni·al
per'fect
per·fect'i·bil'i·ty
per·fect'i·ble
per·fec'tion
per·fec'tion·ism
per·fec'to
 ·tos
per·fid'i·ous
per'fi·dy
 ·dies
per'fo·rate'
 ·rat'ed ·rat'ing
per'fo·ra'tion
per'fo·ra'tor
per·force'
per·form'
per·form'ance
per·fume'
 ·fumed' ·fum'ing
per'fume n.
per·fum'er
per·func'to·ri·ly
per·func'to·ry
per'go·la

per·haps'
per'i·gee'
per'i·he'li·on
 ·li·ons or ·li·a
per'il
 ·iled or ·illed
 ·il·ing or ·il·ling
per'il·ous
per'i·lune'
pe·rim'e·ter
 (boundary; see
 parameter)
pe'ri·od
pe'ri·od'ic
pe'ri·od'i·cal
pe'ri·od'i·cal·ly
pe'ri·o·dic'i·ty
per'i·pa·tet'ic
pe·riph'er·al
pe·riph'er·y
 ·ies
pe·riph'ra·sis
per'i·phras'tic
pe·rique'
per'i·scope'
per'i·scop'ic
per'ish
per'ish·a·bil'i·ty
per'ish·a·ble
per'i·stal'sis
per'i·style'
per'i·to·ni'tis
per'jure
 ·jured ·jur·ing
per'jur·er
per'ju·ry
 ·ries
perk'i·ness
perk'y
 ·i·er ·i·est
per'ma·frost'
perm'al·loy
per'ma·nence
per'ma·nent
per'me·a·bil'i·ty
per'me·a·ble
per'me·ate'
 ·at'ed ·at'ing
per'me·a'tion
per·mis'si·bil'i·ty
per·mis'si·ble
per·mis'si·bly
per·mis'sion
per·mis'sive
per·mis'sive·ly
per·mit'
 ·mit'ted
 ·mit'ting
per·mut'a·ble
per'mu·ta'tion
per·ni'cious
per·nod'
per'o·rate'
 ·rat'ed ·rat'ing
per'o·ra'tion
per·ox'ide
 ·id·ed ·id·ing
per'pen·dic'u·lar

per'pe·trate'
·trat'ed ·trat'ing
per'pe·tra'tion
per'pe·tra'tor
per·pet'u·al
per·pet'u·al·ly
per·pet'u·ate'
·at'ed ·at'ing
per·pet'u·a'tion
per·pet'u·a'tor
per'pe·tu'i·ty
·ties
per·plex'
per·plexed'
per·plex'ed·ly
per·plex'i·ty
·ties
per'qui·site
(privilege; see
prerequisite)
per se
per'se·cute'
·cut'ed ·cut'ing
(harass; see
prosecute)
per'se·cu'tion
per'se·cu'tor
per'se·ver'ance
per'se·vere'
·vered' ·ver'ing
per'si·flage'
per·sim'mon
per·sist'
per·sist'ence
per·sist'ent
per'son
per'son·a·ble
per'son·age
per'son·al
(private; see
personnel)
per'son·al'i·ty
·ties
per'son·al·ize'
·ized' ·iz'ing
per'son·al·ly
per'son·ate'
·at'ed ·at'ing
per'son·a'tion
per'son·a'tor
per·son'i·fi·
ca'tion
per·son'i·fy'
·fied' ·fy'ing
per'son·nel'
(employees; see
personal)
per·spec'tive
(view; see
prospective)
per'spi·ca'cious
per'spi·cac'i·ty
per'spi·cu'i·ty
per·spic'u·ous
per'spi·ra'tion
per·spir'a·to·ry
per·spire'
·spired' ·spir'ing

per·suad'a·ble
per·suade'
·suad'ed
·suad'ing
per·sua'si·bil'i·ty
per·sua'sion
per·sua'sive
per·tain'
per'ti·na'cious
per'ti·nac'i·ty
per'ti·nence
per'ti·nent
pert'ly
per·turb'
per'tur·ba'tion
pe·rus'al
pe·ruse'
·rused' ·rus'ing
per·vade'
·vad'ed ·vad'ing
per·va'sion
per·va'sive
per·verse'
per·verse'ly
per·ver'sion
per·ver'si·ty
per·vert'
per'vi·ous
Pe'sach
pe'so
·sos
pes'si·mism
pes'si·mist
pes'si·mis'tic
pes'si·mis'ti·
cal·ly
pes'ter
pest'hole'
pes'ti·cide'
pes'ti·lence
pes'ti·lent
pes'ti·len'tial
pes'tle
·tled ·tling
pet
pet'ted pet'ting
pet'al
pet'al·like'
pet'cock'
pe·tite'
pe'tit four'
pe'tits fours'
or pe'tit fours'
pe·ti'tion
pet'it jury
pe·tit' mal'
pet'it point
pe'tri dish
pet'ri·fac'tion
pet'ri·fy'
·fied' ·fy'ing
pet'ro·la'tum
pe·tro'le·um
pet'ti·coat'
pet'ti·fog'
·fogged'
·fog'ging
pet'ti·fog'ger

pet'ti·ly
pet'ti·ness
pet'ti·pants'
pet'tish
pet'ty
·ti·er ·ti·est
pet'u·lance
pet'u·lant
pew'ter
pha'e·ton
pha'lanx
·lanx·es or
pha·lan'ges
phal'lic
phal'lus
·li or ·lus·es
phan'tasm
phan'tom
phar'i·sa'ic
phar'i·see'
phar'ma·ceu'ti·cal
phar'ma·cist
phar'ma·col'o·gy
phar'ma·co·pe'ia
phar'ma·cy
·cies
phar'ynx
·ynx·es or
pha·ryn'ges
phase
phased phas'ing
(stage; see faze)
phase'-out'
pheas'ant
phe'no·bar'bi·tal'
phe·nom'e·nal
phe·nom'e·nal·ly
phe·nom'e·non'
·na or ·nons'
phi'al
Phil'a·del'phi·a
phi·lan'der·er
phil'an·throp'ic
phi·lan'thro·pist
phi·lan'thro·py
·pies
phil'a·tel'ic
phi·lat'e·list
phi·lat'e·ly
phil'har·mon'ic
Phil'ip·pine'
Phil'is·tine'
phil'o·den'dron
phil'o·log'i·cal
phi·lol'o·gist
phi·lol'o·gy
phi·los'o·pher
phil'o·soph'ic
phil'o·soph'i·
cal·ly
phi·los'o·phize'
·phized' ·phiz'ing
phi·los'o·phy
·phies
phil'ter
(potion; see
filter)
phle·bi'tis

phlegm
phleg·mat'ic
phlox
pho'bi·a
pho'bic
phoe'be
Phoe'nix
phone
phoned phon'ing
pho'neme
pho·net'ic
pho·net'i·cal·ly
pho·ne·ti'cian
phon'ics
pho'ni·ness
pho'no·graph'
pho·nol'o·gy
pho'ny
·ni·er ·ni·est
·nies
phos'phate
phos'pho·
res'cence
phos'pho·res'cent
pho'to·chron'o·
graph
pho'to·cop'i·er
pho'to·cop'y
·ies
·ied ·y·ing
pho'to·e·lec'tric
pho'to·en·grave'
·graved'
·grav'ing
pho'to·flash'
pho'to·flood'
pho'to·gen'ic
pho'to·graph'
pho·tog'ra·pher
pho'to·graph'ic
pho'to·graph'i·
cal·ly
pho·tog'ra·phy
pho'to·gra·vure'
pho'to·lith'o·
graph
pho'to·li·thog'ra·
phy
pho'to·map'
pho·tom'e·ter
pho'to·met'ric
pho·tom'e·try
pho'to·mon·tage'
pho'to·mu'ral
pho'to-off'set'
pho'to·sen'si·tive
pho'to·stat'
·stat'ed or
·stat'ted
·stat'ing or
·stat'ting
pho'to·stat'ic
pho'to·syn'the·sis
phras'al
phras'al·ly
phrase
phrased
phras'ing

phra'se·ol'o·gy
·gies
phre·net'ic
phre·nol'o·gy
phy·lac'ter·y
·ies
phy'lum
·la
phys'ic
·icked ·ick·ing
phys'i·cal
phys'i·cal·ly
phy·si'cian
phys'i·cist
phys'ics
phys'i·og'no·my
phys'i·og'ra·phy
phys'i·o·log'i·cal
phys'i·ol'o·gy
phys'i·o·ther'a·
pist
phys'i·o·ther'a·py
phy·sique'
pi
pied
pie'ing or pi'ing
(jumble; see pie)
pi
(Greek letter;
see pie)
pi'a·nis'si·mo'
pi·an'ist
pi·an'o
·os
pi·a·no'la
pi·az'za
pi'ca
pic'a·dor'
pic'a·resque'
pic'a·yune'
Pic'ca·dil'ly
pic'ca·lil'li
pic'co·lo'
·los'
pick'ax' or ·axe'
pick'er·el
pick'et
pick'le
·led ·ling
pick'pock'et
pick'up'
pic'nic
·nicked
·nick·ing
pic'nick·er
pi'cot
·coted ·cot·ing
pic'to·graph'
pic·to'ri·al
pic·to'ri·al·ly
pic'ture
·tured ·tur·ing
pic'tur·esque'
pid'dle
·dled ·dling
pidg'in English
pie
(food; see pi)

pie'bald'
piece
pieced piec'ing
(part; see peace)
pièce de ré·sis·
tance'
piece'-dyed'
piece'meal'
piece'work'
pied'mont
pier
(structure; see
peer)
pierce
pierced
pierc'ing
pier glass
pi'e·tism
pi'e·ty
·ties
pi'geon
pi'geon·hole'
·holed' ·hol'ing
pi'geon-toed'
pig'gish
pig'gy·back'
pig'head'ed
pig iron
pig'let
pig'ment
pig'men·ta'tion
pi·gno'li·a
pig'pen'
pig'skin'
pig'sty'
·sties'
pig'tail'
pi·laf' or ·laff'
pi·las'ter
pile
piled pil'ing
pi'le·ous
pile'up'
pil'fer
pil'fer·age
pil'grim
pil'grim·age
pil'lage
·laged ·lag·ing
pil'lar
pill'box'
pil'lion
pil'lo·ry
·ries
·ried ·ry·ing
pil'low
pil'low·case'
pi'lose
pi'lot
pi'lot·house'
Pil'sener or
Pil'sner
pi·men'to or
·mien'·
·tos
pim'ple
pim'ply
pin'a·fore'

pi·ña'ta
pin'ball'
pince'-nez'
pin'cers
pinch'beck'
pinch'-hit'
·hit' ·hit'ting
pin'cush'ion
pine
pined pin'ing
pine'ap'ple
pin'feath'er
ping'-pong'
pin'head'
pin'hole'
pin'ion
pink'eye'
pin'na·cle
·cled ·cling
(acme)
pi'noch'le or
·noc'·
(game)
pin'point'
pin stripe
pin'to
·tos
pint'-size'
pin'up'
pin'wale'
pin'wheel'
pin'worm'
pi'o·neer'
pi'ous
pipe
piped pip'ing
pipe'ful'
·fuls'
pipe'line'
pip'er
pipe'stem'
pi·pette' or ·pet'
·pet'ted ·pet'ting
pip'pin
pi'quan·cy
pi'quant
pique
piqued piqu'ing
(offend; see
peak, peek)
pi·qué' or ·que'
(fabric)
pi'ra·cy
pi·ra'nha
pi'rate
·rat·ed ·rat·ing
pir'ou·ette'
·et'ted ·et'ting
pis'ca·to'ri·al
pis'ci·cul'ture
pis·ta'chi·o'
·os'
pis'til
(part of plant)
pis'tol
·toled or ·tolled
·tol·ing or ·tol·ling
(firearm)

pis'tol-whip'
pis'ton
pit
pit'ted pit'ting
pitch'-black'
pitch'blende'
pitch'-dark'
pitch'er·ful'
·fuls'
pitch'fork'
pitch pipe
pit'e·ous
pit'fall'
pith'i·ness
pith'y
·i·er ·i·est
pit'i·a·ble
pit'i·ful
pit'i·less
pit'tance
Pitts'burgh
pi·tu'i·tar'y
pit'y
·ies, ·ied ·y·ing
piv'ot
piv'ot·al
pix'ie or ·y
·ies
piz'za
piz'ze·ri'a
piz'zi·ca'to
plac'a·bil'i·ty
plac'a·ble
plac'a·bly
plac'ard
pla'cate
·cat·ed ·cat·ing
place
placed plac'ing
pla·ce'bo
·bos or ·boes
place'ment
pla·cen'ta
·tas or ·tae
plac'er
plac'id
pla·cid'i·ty
plack'et
pla'gia·rism
pla'gia·rize'
·rized' ·riz'ing
pla'gia·ry
·ries
plague
plagued
plagu'ing
plagu'er
plaid
plain
(clear; simple;
see plane)
plain'ness
plains'man
plain'song'
plain'-spo·ken
plain'tiff
plain'tive
plain'tive·ly

plait
(pleat; braid;
see plate)
plan
planned
plan'ning
plane
planed plan'ing
(level; see plain)
plan'et
plan'e·tar'i·um
·i·ums or ·i·a
plan'e·tar'y
plan'e·tes'i·mal
plan'et·oid'
plank'ing
plank'ton
plan'ner
plan'tain
plan'tar
(of the sole)
plan·ta'tion
plant'er
(one that plants)
plan'ti·grade'
plaque
plas'ma
plas'ter
plas'ter·board'
plas'ter·er
plas'tic
plas'ti·cal·ly
plas'ti·cine
plas·tic'i·ty
plas'ti·cize'
·cized' ·ciz'ing
plat
plat'ted
plat'ting
(map)
plate
plat'ed plat'ing
(dish; see plait)
pla·teau'
·teaus' or
·teaux'
plate'ful'
·fuls'
plat'en
plat'form'
plat'i·num
plat'i·tude'
plat'i·tu'di·nous
pla·ton'ic
pla·ton'i·cal·ly
pla·toon'
plat'ter
plau'dit
plau'si·bil'i·ty
plau'si·ble
plau'si·bly
play'back'
play'bill'
play'boy'
play'-by-play'
play'ful·ly
play'go'er
play'ground'

play'house'
play'mate'
play'-off'
play'pen'
play'room'
play'thing'
play'wright'
pla'za
plea
plead
plead'ed or plead
plead'ing
pleas'ant
pleas'ant·ry
·ries
please
pleased
pleas'ing
pleas'ur·a·ble
pleas'ur·a·bly
pleas'ure
pleat
ple·be'ian
pleb'i·scite'
plec'trum
·trums or ·tra
pledge
pledged
pledg'ing
pledg'ee'
ple'na·ry
plen'i·po·ten'ti·
ar'y
·ies
plen'i·tude'
plen'te·ous
plen'ti·ful
plen'ti·ful·ly
plen'ty
ple'num
·nums or ·na
ple'o·nasm
pleth'o·ra
pleu'ral
(of the pleura;
see plural)
pleu'ri·sy
Plex'i·glas'
pli'a·bil'i·ty
pli'a·ble
pli'an·cy
pli'ant
pli'ers
plight
plis·sé' or ·se'
plod
plod'ded
plod'ding
plop
plopped
plop'ping
plot
plot'ted
plot'ting
plow'share'
pluck'i·ness
pluck'y
·i·er ·i·est

plug
plugged
plug'ging
plum
(fruit)
plum'age
plumb
(lead weight)
plumb'er
plumb'ing
plume
plumed
plum'ing
plum'met
plu'mose
plump'ness
plun'der
plunge
plunged
plung'ing
plung'er
plu·per'fect
plu'ral
(more than one;
see pleural)
plu'ral·ism
plu'ral·is'tic
plu·ral'i·ty
·ties
plu'ral·ize'
·ized' ·iz'ing
plush'i·ness
plush'y
·i·er ·i·est
plu·toc'ra·cy
·cies
plu'to·crat'
plu'to·crat'ic
plu·to'ni·um
plu'vi·al
ply
plies
plied ply'ing
ply'wood'
pneu·mat'ic
pneu·mo'ni·a
poached
poach'er
pock'et·book'
(purse)
pocket book
(small book)
pock'et·ful'
·fuls'
pock'et·knife'
·knives'
pock'et-size'
pock'mark'
po·di'a·trist
po·di'a·try
po'di·um
·di·a or ·di·ums
po'em
po·et'ic
po·et'i·cal·ly
po'et·ry
po·go'ni·a
po'go stick

po·grom'
poign'an·cy
poign'ant
poin·set'ti·a
point'-blank'
point'ed·ly
point'er
point'less
poise
poised pois'ing
poi'son·ous
poke
poked pok'ing
pok'er
pok'i·ness
pok'y
·i·er ·i·est
po'lar
po·lar'i·ty
po·lar·i·za'tion
po'lar·ize'
·ized' ·iz'ing
pole
poled pol'ing
(rod; see poll)
pole'ax' or ·axe'
po·lem'ic
po·lem'i·cist
pole'star'
pole'-vault' v.
po·lice'
·liced' ·lic'ing
po·lice'man
po·lice'wom'an
pol'i·clin'ic
(outpatient clinic;
see polyclinic)
pol'i·cy
·cies
pol'i·cy·hold'er
po'li·o·my'e·li'tis
pol'ish
po·lite'ly
po·lite'ness
pol'i·tic
·ticked ·tick·ing
po·lit'i·cal
po·lit'i·cal·ly
(in a political
manner)
pol'i·ti'cian
pol'i·tic·ly
(shrewdly)
po·lit'i·co'
·cos'
pol'i·tics
pol'i·ty
·ties
pol'ka
pol'ka dot
poll
(vote; see pole)
poll'ee'
poll'en
pol'li·nate'
·nat'ed ·nat'ing
pol'li·na'tion
pol'li·wog'

poll'ster
poll tax
pol·lu'tant
pol·lute'
  ·lut'ed ·lut'ing
pol·lu'tion
pol'ter·geist'
pol·troon'
pol'y·an'drous
pol'y·an'dry
pol'y·clin'ic
  (hospital; see
  policlinic)
pol'y·es'ter
pol'y·eth'yl·ene'
po·lyg'a·mous
po·lyg'a·my
pol'y·glot'
pol'y·gon'
pol'y·graph'
po·lyg'y·ny
pol'y·mer
pol'y·sty'rene
pol'y·syl·lab'ic
pol'y·syl'la·ble
pol'y·tech'nic
pol'y·the·ism
pol'y·un·sat'u·
  rat'ed
pom'ace
  (pulp; see
  pumice)
po·ma'ceous
po·made'
pome'gran'ate
pom'mel
  ·meled or
  ·melled
  ·mel·ing or
  ·mel·ling
pom'pa·dour'
pom'pa·no'
Pom·pei'i
pom'pon'
pom·pos'i·ty
pom'pous
pon'cho
  ·chos
pon'der
pon'der·a·ble
pon'der·ous
pon·gee'
pon'iard
pon'tiff
pon·tif'i·cal
pon·tif'i·cate'
  ·cat'ed ·cat'ing
pon·toon'
po'ny
  ·nies
po'ny·tail'
poo'dle
pooh'-pooh'
pool'room'
poor'house'
pop
  popped pop'ping
pop'corn'

pop'eyed'
pop'lar
  (tree; see
  popular)
pop'lin
pop'o·ver
pop'per
pop'pet
pop'py
  ·pies
pop'u·lace
  (the masses;
  see populous)
pop'u·lar
  (liked by many;
  see poplar)
pop'u·lar'i·ty
pop'u·lar·i·
  za'tion
pop'u·lar·ize'
  ·ized' ·iz'ing
pop'u·late'
  ·lat'ed ·lat'ing
pop'u·la'tion
pop'u·lous
  (full of people;
  see populace)
por'ce·lain
por'cu·pine'
pore
  pored por'ing
  (ponder; tiny
  opening; see
  pour)
pork'er
por·no·graph'ic
por·nog'ra·phy
po·ros'i·ty
po'rous
por'phy·ry
  ·ries
por'poise
por'ridge
por'rin·ger
port'a·bil'i·ty
port'a·ble
por'tage
  ·taged ·tag·ing
por'tal
port·cul'lis
por·tend'
por'tent
por·ten'tous
por'ter
por'ter·house'
port·fo'li·o'
  ·os'
port'hole'
por'ti·co'
  ·coes' or ·cos'
por·tiere'
por'tion
port'li·ness
port'ly
  ·li·er ·li·est
port·man'teau
  ·teaus or ·teaux
por'trait

por'trai·ture
por·tray'
por·tray'al
Por'tu·guese'
por'tu·lac'a
pose
  posed pos'ing
posh
po·si'tion
pos'i·tive
pos'i·tive·ly
pos'i·tiv·ism
pos'se
pos·sess'
pos·sessed'
pos·ses'sion
pos·ses'sive
pos·ses'sor
pos·si·bil'i·ty
  ·ties
pos'si·ble
pos'si·bly
post'age
post'al
post'box'
post card
post·date'
post'er
pos·te'ri·or
pos·ter'i·ty
post'grad'u·ate
post'haste'
post'hu·mous
post'hyp·not'ic
pos·til'ion
post'man
post'mark'
post'mas'ter
post'mis'tress
post'-mor'tem
post·na'tal
post'paid'
post·pone'
  ·poned' ·pon'ing
post·pone'ment
post'script'
pos'tu·late'
  ·lat'ed ·lat'ing
pos'tu·la'tion
pos'tu·la'tor
pos'tur·al
pos'ture
  ·tured ·tur·ing
post'war'
pot
  pot'ted pot'ting
po'ta·ble
po·ta'tion
po·ta'to
  ·toes
pot'bel'lied
pot'bel'ly
  ·lies
pot'boil'er
po'ten·cy
po'tent
po'ten·tate'

po·ten'tial
po·ten'ti·al'i·ty
  ·ties
po·ten'tial·ly
po'tent·ly
poth'er
pot'hold'er
pot'hole'
pot'hook'
po'tion
pot'latch'
pot'luck'
pot'pour·ri'
pot'sherd'
pot'shot'
pot'tage
pot'ter·y
  ·ies
pouch'i·ness
poul'tice
poul'try
  (fowls; see
  paltry)
pounce
pounced
poun'cing
pound'-fool'ish
pour
  (flow; see pore)
pout
pov'er·ty
pow'der·y
  ·i·er ·i·est
pow'er·ful
pow'er·ful·ly
pow'er·house'
pow'er·less
pow'wow'
pox
prac'ti·ca·bil'i·ty
prac'ti·ca·ble
prac'ti·ca·bly
prac'ti·cal
prac'ti·cal'i·ty
  ·ties
prac'ti·cal·ly
prac'tice
  ·ticed ·tic·ing
prac'tic·er
prac'ti·cum
prac·ti'tion·er
prag·mat'ic
prag·mat'i·cal·ly
prag'ma·tism
prag'ma·tist
prai'rie
praise
praised
prais'ing
praise'wor'thy
pra'line
prance
pranced
pranc'ing
prank'ish
prate
prat'ed
prat'ing

prat'tle
  ·tled ·tling
pray
  (implore; see
  prey)
pray'er
  (one who prays)
prayer
  (an entreaty)
preach'er
pre'am'ble
pre'ar·range'
  ·ranged'
  ·rang'ing
pre'ar·range'ment
preb'end
pre·can'cel
pre·car'i·ous
pre·cau'tion
pre·cau'tion·ar'y
pre·cede'
  ·ced'ed ·ced'ing
  (come before;
  see proceed)
prec'e·dence
  (priority)
prec'e·dent
  (example)
pre'-cen'sor
pre'cept
pre·cep'tor
pre·ces'sion
  (a going before;
  see procession)
pre·ces'sion·al
pre'cinct
pre·ci·os'i·ty
pre'cious
prec'i·pice
pre·cip'i·tate'
  ·tat'ed ·tat'ing
pre·cip'i·ta'tion
pre·cip'i·tous
pré·cis'
  ·cis'
  (abstract)
pre·cise'
  (definite)
pre·cise'ly
pre·ci'sion
pre·clude'
  ·clud'ed
  ·clud'ing
pre·clu'sion
pre·co'cious
pre·cog·ni'tion
pre·con·ceive'
pre·con·cep'tion
pre·con'scious
pre·cur'sor
pre·cur'so·ry
pre·da'cious
pre·date'
pred'a·tor
pred'a·to'ry
pre·de·cease'
pred'e·ces'sor
pre·des'ti·na'tion

pre·des'tine
  ·tined ·tin·ing
pre'de·ter'mine
pred'i·ca·bil'i·ty
pred'i·ca·ble
pre·dic'a·ment
pred'i·cate'
  ·cat'ed ·cat'ing
pred'i·ca'tion
pre·dict'
pre·dict'a·ble
pre·dic'tion
pre·dic'tive
pre·dic'tor
pre·di·gest'
pre'di·lec'tion
pre·dis·pose'
pre·dis·po·si'tion
pre·dom'i·nant
pre·dom'i·nate'
pre·em'i·nence
pre·em'i·nent
pre·empt'
pre·emp'tion
pre·emp'tive
pre·emp'tor
pre·es·tab'lish
pre·ex·ist'
pre·ex·ist'ence
pre'fab'
pre·fab'ri·cate'
pref'ace
  ·aced ·ac·ing
pref'a·to'ry
pre'fect
pre'fec·ture
pre·fer'
  ·ferred' ·fer'ring
pref'er·a·ble
pref'er·a·bly
pref'er·ence
pref'er·en'tial
pre·fer'ment
pre'fig·u·ra'tion
pre·fig'ur·a·tive
pre·fig'ure
pre'fix
pre'flight'
preg'na·ble
preg'nan·cy
  ·cies
preg'nant
pre·hen'sile
pre'his·tor'ic
pre·judge'
pre·judg'ment or
  ·judge'-
prej'u·dice
  ·diced ·dic·ing
prej'u·di'cial
prel'a·cy
prel'ate
pre·lim'i·nar'y
  ·ies
prel'ude
pre·mar'i·tal
pre'ma·ture'
pre'ma·ture'ly

pre·med'i·cal
pre·med'i·tate'
pre·mier'
(chief)
pre·mière'
·mièred'
·mièr'ing
(first showing)
prem'ise
·ised ·is·ing
pre'mi·um
pre'mo·ni'tion
pre·mon'i·to'ry
pre·na'tal
pre·oc'cu·pan·cy
pre·oc'cu·pa'tion
pre·oc'cu·py'
·pied' ·py'ing
pre'or·dain'
pre·pack'age
pre·paid'
prep'a·ra'tion
pre·par'a·tive
pre·par'a·to'ry
pre·pare'
·pared' ·par'ing
pre·par'ed·ness
pre·pay'
·paid' ·pay'ing
pre·pay'ment
pre·pon'der·ance
pre·pon'der·ant
pre·pon'der·ate'
·at'ed ·at'ing
prep'o·si'tion
pre'pos·sess'
pre'pos·sess'ing
pre·pos'ter·ous
pre're·cord'
pre·req'ui·site
(requirement; see
perquisite)
pre·rog'a·tive
pre·sage'
·saged' ·sag'ing
pres'by·ter
Pres'by·te'ri·an
pre'school'
pre'sci·ence
pre'sci·ent
pre·scribe'
·scribed'
·scrib'ing
(order; see
proscribe)
pre·scrip'tion
pre·scrip'tive
pres'ence
pres'ent
pre·sent'a·ble
pre'sen·ta'tion
pres'ent-day'
pre·sen'ti·ment
(premonition)
pre·sent'ment
(presentation)
pre·serv'a·ble
pres'er·va'tion

pre·serv'a·tive
pre·serve'
·served'
·serv'ing
pre·set'
pre'-shrunk'
pre·side'
·sid'ed ·sid'ing
pres'i·den·cy
·cies
pres'i·dent
pres'i·dent-e·lect'
pres'i·den'tial
pre·sid'i·um
·i·a or ·i·ums
pre·sig'ni·fy'
press box
press'ing
press'man
pres'sure
·sured ·sur·ing
pres'sur·ize'
·ized' ·iz'ing
press'work'
pres'ti·dig'i·ta'tor
pres·tige'
pres·ti'gious
pre'stressed'
pre·sum'a·ble
pre·sume'
·sumed'
·sum'ing
pre·sump'tion
pre·sump'tive
pre·sump'tu·ous
pre'sup·pose'
pre'sup·po·si'tion
pre·tend'
pre·tend'er
pre·tense'
pre·ten'sion
pre·ten'tious
pre'ter·nat'u·ral
pre'text
pret'ti·fy'
·fied' ·fy'ing
pret'ti·ly
pret'ti·ness
pret'ty
·ti·er ·ti·est
·tied ·ty·ing
pret'zel
pre·vail'
pre·vail'ing
prev'a·lence
prev'a·lent
pre·var'i·cate'
·cat'ed ·cat'ing
pre·var'i·ca'tion
pre·var'i·ca'tor
pre·ven'ient
pre·vent'
pre·vent'a·ble or
·i·ble
pre·ven'tion
pre·ven'tive or
·vent'a·tive

pre'view
pre'vi·ous
pre·vi'sion
pre'war'
prey
(victim; see
pray)
pri'a·pism
price
priced pric'ing
price'less
prick'le
·led ·ling
prick'li·ness
prick'ly
·li·er ·li·est
pride
prid'ed prid'ing
pri'er
(one who pries;
see prior)
priest
priest'ess
priest'hood
priest'ly
·li·er ·li·est
prig'gish
prim
prim'mer
prim'mest
pri'ma·cy
pri'ma don'na
pri'ma fa'ci·e'
pri'mal
pri·ma'ri·ly
pri'ma·ry
·ries
pri'mate
prime
primed prim'ing
prim'er
pri·me'val
prim'i·tive
prim'i·tive·ly
prim'i·tiv·ism
pri'mo·gen'i·tor
pri'mo·gen'i·ture
pri·mor'di·al
primp
prim'rose'
prince'ling
prince'ly
·li·er ·li·est
prin'cess
prin'ci·pal
(chief; see
principle)
prin'ci·pal'i·ty
·ties
prin'ci·pal·ly
prin'ci·ple
(basic rule; see
principal)
prin'ci·pled
print'a·ble
print'out'
pri'or
(previous; see
prier)

pri'or·ess
pri·or'i·ty
·ties
pri'o·ry
·ries
prism
pris·mat'ic
pris'on
pris'on·er
pris'tine
pri'va·cy
pri'vate
pri'va·teer'
pri·va'tion
priv'et
priv'i·lege
·leged ·leg·ing
priv'y
·ies
prize
prized priz'ing
prize'fight'
prob'a·bil'i·ty
prob'a·ble
prob'a·bly
pro'bate
·bat·ed ·bat·ing
pro·ba'tion
pro·ba'tion·ar'y
pro·ba'tion·er
pro'ba·tive
probe
probed prob'ing
prob'i·ty
prob'lem
prob'lem·at'ic
pro·bos'cis
·cis·es or ·ci·des'
pro·ce'dur·al
pro·ce'dure
pro·ceed'
(go on; see
precede)
pro'ceeds
proc'ess
pro·ces'sion
(parade; see
precession)
pro·ces'sion·al
proc'es·sor or
proc'ess·er
pro·claim'
proc'la·ma'tion
pro·cliv'i·ty
·ties
pro·cras'ti·nate'
·nat'ed ·nat'ing
pro·cras'ti·na'tion
pro·cras'ti·na'tor
pro'cre·ant
pro'cre·ate'
·at'ed ·at'ing
pro'cre·a'tor
proc·tol'o·gy
proc'tor
proc'to·scope'
pro·cum'bent
pro·cur'a·ble

proc'u·ra·tor
pro·cure'
·cured' ·cur'ing
pro·cure'ment
prod
prod'ded
prod'ding
prod'i·gal
prod'i·gal'i·ty
pro·di'gious
prod'i·gy
·gies
(genius; see
protégé)
pro·duce'
·duced'
·duc'ing
pro·duc'er
pro·duc'i·ble
prod'uct
pro·duc'tion
pro·duc'tive
pro·duc'tive·ly
pro'duc·tiv'i·ty
prof'a·na'tion
pro·fane'
·faned' ·fan'ing
pro·fane'ly
pro·fan'i·ty
·ties
pro·fess'
pro·fessed'
pro·fess'ed·ly
pro·fes'sion
pro·fes'sion·al·ly
pro·fes'sor
pro·fes'so·ri·al
pro·fes'so·ri·ate
prof'fer
pro·fi'cien·cy
pro·fi'cient
pro'file
·filed ·fil·ing
prof'it
(gain; see
prophet)
prof'it·a·ble
prof'it·a·bly
prof'i·teer'
prof'li·ga·cy
prof'li·gate
pro·found'
pro·fun'di·ty
·ties
pro·fuse'
pro·fuse'ly
pro·fu'sion
pro·gen'i·tor
prog'e·ny
·nies
prog'na·thous
prog·no'sis
·ses
prog·nos'tic
prog·nos'ti·cate'
·cat'ed ·cat'ing
prog·nos'ti·
ca'tion

prog·nos'ti·ca'tor
pro'gram
·grammed
or ·gramed
·gram·ming
or ·gram·ing
pro'gram·mat'ic
pro'gram·mer
or ·gram·er
prog'ress
pro·gres'sion
pro·gres'sive
pro·gres'siv·ism
pro·hib'it
pro·hi·bi'tion
pro·hib'i·tive
pro·hib'i·to'ry
proj'ect
pro·jec'tile
pro·jec'tion
pro·jec'tive
pro·jec'tor
pro·lep'sis
·ses
pro'le·tar'i·an
pro'le·tar'i·at
pro·lif'er·ate'
·at'ed ·at'ing
pro·lif'ic
pro·lix'
pro·lix'i·ty
pro·loc'u·tor
pro'logue
pro·long'
pro·lon'gate
·gat·ed ·gat·ing
pro'lon·ga'tion
prom'e·nade'
·nad'ed
·nad'ing
prom'i·nence
prom'i·nent
prom'is·cu'i·ty
·ties
pro·mis'cu·ous
prom'ise
·ised ·is·ing
prom'is·so'ry
pro·mon'to·ry
·ries
pro·mot'a·ble
pro·mote'
·mot'ed ·mot'ing
pro·mot'er
pro·mo'tion
prompt'er
prompt'i·tude'
prompt'ly
prom'ul·gate'
·gat'ed ·gat'ing
prom'ul·ga'tion
prom'ul·ga'tor
prone
pronged
pro'noun'
pro·nounce'
·nounced'
·nounc'ing

pro·nounce'a·ble
pro·nounce'ment
pro·nun'ci·a'tion
proof'read'
·read' ·read'ing
prop'a·gan'da
prop'a·gan'dize
·dized ·diz·ing
prop'a·gate'
·gat'ed ·gat'ing
prop'a·ga'tion
prop'a·ga'tor
pro'pane
pro·pel'
·pelled' ·pel'ling
pro·pel'lant or
·lent
pro·pel'ler
pro·pen'si·ty
·ties
prop'er·ly
prop'er·tied
prop'er·ty
·ties
proph'e·cy n.
·cies
proph'e·sy' v.
·sied' ·sy'ing
proph'et
(predictor; see
profit)
pro·phet'ic
pro·phet'i·cal·ly
pro'phy·lac'tic
pro'phy·lax'is
·lax'es
pro·pin'qui·ty
pro·pi'ti·ate'
·at'ed ·at'ing
pro·pi'ti·a'tion
pro·pi'ti·a·to'ry
pro·pi'tious
pro·po'nent
pro·por'tion
pro·por'tion·al
pro·por'tion·al·ly
pro·por'tion·ate
pro·por'tion·ate·
ly
pro·pos'al
pro·pose'
·posed' ·pos'ing
prop'o·si'tion
pro·pound'
pro·pri'e·tar'y
·ies
pro·pri'e·tor
pro·pri'e·tress
pro·pri'e·ty
·ties
pro·pul'sion
pro·pul'sive
pro ra'ta
pro·rat'a·ble
pro'rate'
·rat'ed ·rat'ing
pro'ro·ga'tion

pro·sa'ic
pro·sa'i·cal·ly
pro·sce'ni·um
·ni·ums or ·ni·a
pro·sciut'to
pro·scribe'
·scribed'
·scrib'ing
(forbid; see
prescribe)
pro·scrip'tion
prose
pros'e·cut'a·ble
pros'e·cute'
·cut'ed ·cut'ing
(legal term;
see persecute)
pros'e·cu'tion
pros'e·cu'tor
pros'e·lyte'
·lyt'ed ·lyt'ing
pros'e·lyt·ism
pros'e·lyt·ize'
·ized' ·iz'ing
pros'o·dy
·dies
pros'pect
pro·spec'tive
(expected; see
perspective)
pros'pec·tor
pro·spec'tus
pros'per
pros·per'i·ty
pros'per·ous
pros'tate
(gland; see
prostrate)
pros'the·sis
·the·ses
pros·thet'ic
pros'ti·tute'
·tut'ed ·tut'ing
pros'ti·tu'tion
pros'trate
·trat·ed ·trat·ing
(prone; see
prostate)
pros·tra'tion
pros'y
·i·er ·i·est
pro·tag'o·nist
pro·tect'
pro·tec'tion
pro·tec'tive
pro·tec'tor
pro·tec'tor·ate
pro'té·gé'
(one helped by
another; see
prodigy)
pro'tein
pro tem'po·re'
pro·test'
Prot'es·tant
prot'es·ta'tion
pro·test'er or
·tes'tor

pro·thon'o·tar'y
·ies
pro'to·col'
pro'ton
pro'to·plasm
pro'to·typ'al
pro'to·type'
pro'to·zo'an
pro·tract'
pro·tract'ed·ly
pro·tract'i·ble
pro·trac'tile
pro·trac'tion
pro·trac'tor
pro·trude'
·trud'ed
·trud'ing
pro·tru'sile
pro·tru'sion
pro·tru'sive
pro·tu'ber·ance
pro·tu'ber·ant
proud'ly
prov'a·bil'i·ty
prov'a·ble
prov'a·bly
prove
proved, proved
or prov'en,
prov'ing
prov'en·der
prov'erb
pro·ver'bi·al
pro·ver'bi·al·ly
pro·vide'
·vid·ed ·vid'ing
prov'i·dence
prov'i·dent
prov'i·den'tial
pro·vid'er
prov'ince
pro·vin'cial
pro·vin'cial·ism
pro·vin'cial·ly
pro·vi'sion
pro·vi'sion·al
pro·vi'sion·al·ly
pro·vi'so
·sos or ·soes
pro·vi'so·ry
prov'o·ca'tion
pro·voc'a·tive
pro·voc'a·tive·ly
pro·voke'
·voked' ·vok'ing
pro'vo·lo'ne
pro'vost
prow'ess
prowl'er
prox'i·mal
prox'i·mate
prox·im'i·ty
prox'i·mo'
prox'y
·ies
pru'dence
pru'dent
pru·den'tial

pru'dent·ly
prud'er·y
prud'ish
prune
pruned prun'ing
pru'ri·ence
pru'ri·ent
pry
pries, pried pry'ing
psalm'book'
psal'mo·dy
psal'ter·y
·ies
pse·phol'o·gy
pseu'do
pseu'do·nym'
pseu'do·nym'i·ty
pseu·don'y·mous
psit'ta·co'sis
pso·ri'a·sis
psy'che
psy'che·de'li·a
psy'che·del'ic
psy'che·del'i·cal·
ly
psy·chi·at'ric
psy'chi·at'ri·cal·
ly
psy·chi'a·trist
psy·chi'a·try
psy'chic
psy'chi·cal·ly
psy·cho·a·
nal'y·sis
psy'cho·an'a·lyst
psy'cho·an'a·
lyt'ic
psy'cho·an'a·
lyt'i·cal·ly
psy'cho·an'a·lyze'
·lyzed' ·lyz'ing
psy'cho·dra'ma
psy'cho·dy·nam'·
ics
psy'cho·gen'ic
psy'cho·log'i·cal
psy·chol'o·gist
psy·chol'o·gize'
·gized' ·giz'ing
psy·chol'o·gy
psy·chom'e·try
psy'cho·neu·ro'sis
·ses
psy'cho·neu·rot'ic
psy'cho·path'ic
psy'cho·path·ol'·
o·gy
psy'cho·sex'u·al
psy·cho'sis
·ses
psy'cho·so·mat'ic
psy'cho·ther'a·py
psy·chot'ic
pter'o·dac'tyl
pto'maine
pu'ber·ty
pu·bes'cence
pu'bic

pub'lic
pub'li·ca'tion
pub'li·cist
pub·lic'i·ty
pub'li·cize'
·cized' ·ciz'ing
pub'lic·ly
pub'lish
pub'lish·er
puck'er
pud'ding
pud'dle
·dled ·dling
pudg'i·ness
pudg'y
·i·er ·i·est
pueb'lo
·los
pu'er·ile
Puer'to Ri'co
puff'i·ness
puff'y
·i·er ·i·est
pu'gil·ism
pug·na'cious
pug·nac'i·ty
pul'chri·tude'
pul'chri·tu'di·
nous
pull
pul'let
pul'ley
·leys
pull'out'
pull'o'ver
pul'mo·nar'y
pul'mo'tor
pul'pit
pulp'wood'
pulp'y
·i·er ·i·est
pul'sate
·sat·ed ·sat·ing
pul·sa'tion
pulse
pulsed puls'ing
pul'ver·iz'a·ble
pul'ver·i·za'tion
pul'ver·ize'
·ized' ·iz'ing
pum'ice
(rock; see pomace)
pum'mel
·meled or
·melled
·mel·ing or
·mel·ling
pump'er·nick'el
pump'kin
pun
punned
pun'ning
punch card
pun'cheon
punc·til'i·o'
·os'
punc·til'i·ous
punc'tu·al
punc'tu·al'i·ty

punc'tu·al·ly
punc'tu·ate'
·at'ed ·at'ing
punc'tu·a'tion
punc'tu·a'tor
punc'tur·a·ble
punc'ture
·tured ·tur·ing
pun'dit
pun'gen·cy
pun'gent
pu'ni·ness
pun'ish
pun'ish·a·ble
pun'ish·ment
pu'ni·tive
pun'ster
pu'ny
·ni·er ·ni·est
pu'pil
pup'pet
pup'pet·eer'
pup'py
·pies
pur'chas·a·ble
pur'chase
·chased
·chas·ing
pure'bred'
pu·rée'
·réed' ·ré'ing
pure'ly
pur·ga'tion
pur'ga·tive
pur'ga·to'ry
purge
purged purg'ing
pu'ri·fi·ca'tion
pu'ri·fi'er
pu'ri·fy'
·fied' ·fy'ing
pur'ism
pu'ri·tan
pu'ri·tan'i·cal
pu'ri·ty
purl
(stitch; see pearl)
pur·loin'
pu'ro·my'cin
pur'ple
pur'plish
pur·port'
pur'pose
·posed ·pos·ing
pur'pose·ful
pur'pose·ful·ly
pur'pose·less
pur'pose·ly
purr
purs'er
pur·su'ance
pur·sue'
·sued' ·su'ing
pur·suit'
pu'ru·lence
pu'ru·lent
pur·vey'
pur·vey'ance

pur·vey'or
pur'view
push'cart'
push'o·ver
push'-up'
pu'sil·lan'i·mous
pus'sy
 ·si·er ·si·est
 (with pus)
puss'y
 ·ies
 (cat)
pus'tu·lant
pus'tule
put
 put put'ting
 (place; see putt)
pu'ta·tive
pu'tre·fac'tion
pu'tre·fy'
 ·fied' ·fy'ing
pu·tres'cence
pu·tres'cent
pu'trid
putt
 (golf term; see
 put)
put·tee'
putt'er
 (golf club)
put'ter
 (busy oneself)
put'ty
 ·tied ·ty·ing
puz'zle
 ·zled ·zling
puz'zler
pyg'my
 ·mies
py'lon
py'or·rhe'a
pyr'a·mid
py·ram'i·dal
pyre
py·ret'ic
Py'rex
py·rog'ra·phy
py'ro·ma'ni·a
py'ro·ma'ni·ac'
py'ro·tech'nics
py·rox'y·lin
Py·thag'o·ras
py'thon

Q

quack'er·y
 ·ies
quad'ran'gle
quad·ran'gu·lar
quad'rant
quad'rate
 ·rat·ed ·rat·ing
quad·rat'ic
quad·ren'ni·al
quad'ri·lat'er·al

qua·drille'
quad·ril'lion
quad'ri·ple'gi·a
quad'ru·ped'
quad·ru'ple
 ·pled ·pling
quad·ru'plet
quad·ru'pli·cate'
 ·cat'ed ·cat'ing
quaff
quag'mire'
quail
quaint'ly
quake
 quaked
 quak'ing
qual'i·fi·ca'tion
qual'i·fi'er
qual'i·fy'
 ·fied' ·fy'ing
qual'i·ta'tive
qual'i·ty
 ·ties
qualm
quan'da·ry
 ·ries
quan'ti·ta'tive
quan'ti·ty
 ·ties
quan'tum
 ·ta
quar'an·tin'a·ble
quar'an·tine'
 ·tined' ·tin'ing
quar'rel
 ·reled or ·relled
 ·rel·ing or
 ·rel·ling
quar'rel·some
quar'ry
 ·ries
 ·ried ·ry·ing
quart
quar'ter
quar'ter·back'
quar'ter-deck'
quar'ter·ly
 ·lies
quar'ter·mas'ter
quar'ter·saw'
 ·sawed', ·sawed'
 or ·sawn',
 ·saw'ing
quar·tet' or ·tette'
quar'tile
quar'to
 ·tos
quartz
qua'sar
quash
qua'si
qua'ter·na'ry
 ·ries
quat'rain
qua'ver
quay
 (wharf; see key)
quea'si·ness

quea'sy
 ·si·er ·si·est
queen'li·ness
queen'ly
 ·li·er ·li·est
queen'-size'
queer
quell
quench'a·ble
quer'u·lous
que'ry
 ·ries
 ·ried ·ry·ing
quest
ques'tion
ques'tion·a·ble
ques'tion·naire'
queue
queued
queu'ing
 (line; see cue)
quib'ble
 ·bled ·bling
quick'en
quick'-freeze'
 -froze' -froz'en
 -freez'ing
quick'sand'
quick'sil'ver
quick'-tem'pered
quick'-wit'ted
quid'nunc'
qui·es'cence
qui·es'cent
qui'et
 (still; see quite)
qui'e·tude'
qui·e'tus
quill
quilt'ing
quince
qui·nel'la
quin·quen'ni·al
quin·tes'sence
quin·tet'
 or ·tette'
quin·til'lion
quin·tu'ple
 ·pled ·pling
quin·tu'plet
quin·tu'pli·cate'
 ·cat'ed ·cat'ing
quip
 quipped
 quip'ping
quire
 (of paper; see
 choir)
quirk
quis'ling
quit
 quit or quit'ted
 quit'ting
quit'claim'
quite
 (fully; see quiet)
quit'tance
quit'ter

quiv'er
quix·ot'ic
quiz
 quiz'zes
 quizzed
 quiz'zing
quiz'zi·cal
quoin
 (wedge; corner;
 see coign, coin)
quoit
quon'dam
Quon'set hut
quo'rum
quo'ta
quot'a·ble
quo·ta'tion
quote
 quot'ed quot'ing
quo'tient

R

rab'bet
 (cut; see rabbit)
rab'bi
 ·bis or ·bies
rab·bin'i·cal
rab'bit
 (hare; see rabbet)
rab'ble
 ·bled ·bling
rab'id
ra'bies
rac·coon'
race
 raced rac'ing
race'horse'
rac'er
race track
race'way'
ra'cial
ra'cial·ly
rac'i·ly
rac'i·ness
rac'ism
rack'et
rack'et·eer'
rack'-rent'
rac·on·teur'
rac'y
 ·i·er ·i·est
ra'dar
ra'di·al
ra'di·ance
ra'di·ant
ra'di·ate'
 ·at'ed ·at'ing
ra'di·a'tion
ra'di·a'tor
rad'i·cal
rad'i·cal·ism
rad'i·cal·ly
ra'di·o'
 ·os', ·oed' ·o'ing
ra'di·o·ac'tive

ra'di·o·gram'
ra'di·o·graph'
ra'di·og'ra·phy
ra'di·o·i'so·tope'
ra'di·ol'o·gist
ra'di·ol'o·gy
ra'di·o·phone'
ra'di·o·pho'no·
 graph'
ra'di·o·pho'to
 ·tos
ra'di·os'co·py
ra'di·o·sonde'
ra'di·o·tel'e·
 phone'
ra'di·o·ther'a·py
ra'di·o·ther'my
rad'ish
ra'di·um
ra'di·us
 ·di·i' or ·di·us·es
ra'dix
 ra'di·ces' or
 ra'dix·es
ra'don
raf'fi·a
raf'fle
 ·fled ·fling
raft'er
rag'a·muf'fin
rage
 raged rag'ing
rag'ged
rag'lan
ra·gout'
rag'pick'er
rag'time'
rag'weed'
raid'er
rail'ing
rail'ler·y
 ·ies
rail'road'
rail'-split'ter
rail'way'
rai'ment
rain
 (water; see
 reign, rein)
rain'bow'
rain check
rain'coat'
rain'drop'
rain'fall'
rain'i·ness
rain'proof'
rain'storm'
rain'y
 ·i·er ·i·est
raise
 raised rais'ing
 (lift; see raze)
rai'sin
rai'son d'être'
ra'jah or ·ja
rake
 raked rak'ing
rak'ish

ral'li·er
ral'ly
 ·lies
 ·lied ·ly·ing
ram
 rammed
 ram'ming
ram'ble
 ·bled ·bling
ram'bler
ram·bunc'tious
ram'e·kin or ·quin
ram'i·fi·ca'tion
ram'i·fy'
 ·fied' ·fy'ing
ram'jet'
ramp
ram·page'
 ·paged' ·pag'ing
ram·pa'geous
ramp'ant
ram'part
ram'rod'
ram'shack'le
ranch'er
ran'cid
ran'cor
ran'cor·ous
ran'dom
ran'dom·ize'
 ·ized' ·iz'ing
range
 ranged
 rang'ing
rang'i·ness
rang'y
 ·i·er ·i·est
ran'kle
 ·kled ·kling
ran'sack
ran'som
rap
 rapped rap'ping
 (strike; see wrap)
ra·pa'cious
ra·pac'i·ty
rape
 raped rap'ing
rap'id-fire'
ra·pid'i·ty
rap'id·ly
ra'pi·er
rap'ine
rap'ist
rap·port'
rap·proche'ment
rap·scal'lion
rap·to'ri·a
rap'ture
rap'tur·ous
rare
 rar'er rar'est
rare'bit
rar'e·fy'
 ·fied' ·fy'ing
rare'ly
rar'i·ty
 ·ties

ras'cal
ras·cal'i·ty
ras'cal·ly
rash'er
rash'ness
rasp'ber'ry
 ·ries
rasp'i·ness
rasp'ing
rasp'y
 ·i·er ·i·est
rat
rat'ted rat'ting
rat'a·ble or rate'·
ratch'et
rate
 rat'ed rat'ing
rath'er
raths'kel'ler
rat'i·fi·ca'tion
rat'i·fi'er
rat'i·fy'
 ·fied' ·fy'ing
ra'tio
 ·tios
ra·ti·o'ci·nate'
 ·nat'ed ·nat'ing
ra'tion·al
ra'tion·ale'
ra'tion·al·ism
ra'tion·al'i·ty
ra'tion·al·i·za'tion
ra'tion·al·ize'
 ·ized' ·iz'ing
ra'tion·al·ly
rat'line or ·lin
rat'tail'
rat·tan' or ra·tan'
rat'tle
 ·tled ·tling
rat'tle·brained'
rat'tler
rat'tle·snake'
rat'tle·trap'
rat'tly
rau'cous
rav'age
 ·aged ·ag·ing
rave
 raved rav'ing
rav'el
 ·eled or ·elled
 ·el·ing or ·el·ling
ra'ven
rav'e·nous
ra·vine'
ra'vi·o'li
rav'ish
raw'boned'
raw'hide'
ray'on
raze
 razed raz'ing
 (demolish; see
 raise)
ra'zor
ra'zor·back'
reach

re·act'
 (respond)
re'-act'
 (act again)
re·ac'tion
re·ac'tion·ar'y
 ·ies
re·ac'ti·vate'
 ·vat'ed ·vat'ing
re·ac'tive·ly
re·ac'tor
read
 read read'ing
read'a·bil'i·ty
read'a·ble
read'i·ly
read'i·ness
re'ad·just'
read'out'
read'y
 ·i·er ·i·est
 ·ied ·y·ing
read'y-made'
re'al
 (actual; see reel)
re'al·ism
re'al·ist
re'al·is'tic
re'al·is'ti·cal·ly
re·al'i·ty
 ·ties
 (real thing; see
 realty)
re'al·iz'a·ble
re'al·i·za'tion
re'al·ize'
 ·ized' ·iz'ing
re'al-life'
re'al·ly
realm
Re'al·tor
re'al·ty
 (real estate; see
 reality)
ream'er
re·an'i·mate'
 ·mat'ed ·mat'ing
reap'er
re'ap·por'tion
rear guard
re·ar'ma·ment
re'ar·range'
re'ar·range'ment
rear'ward
rea'son·a·ble
rea'son·a·bly
re'as·sur'ance
re'as·sure'
 ·sured' ·sur'ing
re'bate
 ·bat·ed ·bat·ing
reb'el n.
re·bel' v.
 ·belled' ·bel'ling
re·bel'lion
re·bel'lious
re·birth'

re·bound'
re·buff'
 (blunt refusal)
re'-buff'
 (buff again)
re·buke'
 ·buked'
 ·buk'ing
re'bus
re·but'
 ·but'ted
 ·but'ting
re·but'tal
re·cal'ci·trant
re·call'
re·cant'
re·cap'
 ·capped'
 ·cap'ping
re·ca·pit'u·late'
 ·lat'ed ·lat'ing
re·ca·pit'u·la'tion
re·cap'pa·ble
re·cap'ture
re·cede'
 ·ced'ed ·ced'ing
re·ceipt'
re·ceiv'a·ble
re·ceive'
 ·ceived'
 ·ceiv'ing
re·ceiv'er·ship'
re·cen'sion
re'cent
re·cep'ta·cle
re·cep'tion
re·cep'tive
re·cep'tor
re'cess
re·ces'sion
re·ces'sive
re·charge'a·ble
re·cher'ché
re·cid'i·vism '
rec'i·pe
re·cip'i·ent
re·cip'ro·cal
re·cip'ro·cal·ly
re·cip'ro·cate'
 ·cat'ed ·cat'ing
re·cip'ro·ca'tion
re·cip'ro·ca'tor
rec'i·proc'i·ty
re·ci'sion
re·cit'al
rec'i·ta'tion
rec'i·ta·tive'
re·cite'
 ·cit'ed ·cit'ing
reck'less
reck'on·ing
re·claim'
 (restore for use)
re'-claim'
 (claim back)
rec'la·ma'tion
re·cline'
 ·clined' ·clin'ing

rec'luse
re·clu'sion
rec'og·ni'tion
rec'og·niz'a·ble
re·cog'ni·zance
rec'og·nize'
 ·nized' ·niz'ing
re·coil'
 (draw back)
re'-coil'
 (coil again)
re·coil'less
rec'ol·lect'
 (remember)
re'-col·lect'
 (collect again)
rec'ol·lec'tion
re·com·mend'
re·com·men·
 da'tion
re·com·mit'
rec'om·pense'
 ·pensed'
 ·pens'ing
rec'on·cil'a·ble
rec'on·cile'
 ·ciled' ·cil'ing
rec'on·cil'i·a'tion
rec'on·dite'
re'con·di'tion
re·con·nais·sance
re·con·struct'
rec'on·noi'ter
re·con·sid'er
re·con·ver'sion
re·con·vert'
re·cord' v.
rec'ord n.
re·cord'er
re·count'
 (narrate)
re'-count'
 (count again)
re·coup'
re'course
re·cov'er
 (get back)
re'-cov'er
 (cover again)
re·cov'er·y
 ·ies
rec're·ant
rec're·ate'
 ·at'ed ·at'ing
 (refresh)
re'-cre·ate'
 ·at'ed ·at'ing
 (create anew)
re'cre·a'tion
re'-cre·a'tion
re·crim'i·nate'
 ·nat'ed ·nat'ing
re·crim'i·na'tion
re·cruit'
rec'tal
rec'tan'gle
rec·tan'gu·lar
rec'ti·fi'a·ble

rec'ti·fi·ca'tion
rec'ti·fi'er
rec'ti·fy'
 ·fied' ·fy'ing
rec'ti·lin'e·ar
rec'ti·tude'
rec'tor
rec'to·ry
 ·ries
rec'tum
 ·tums or ·ta
re·cum'ben·cy
re·cum'bent
re·cu'per·ate'
 ·at'ed ·at'ing
re·cu'per·a'tion
re·cur'
 ·curred'
 ·cur'ring
re·cur'rence
re·cur'rent
re·cu'sant
re·cy'cle
re·dact'
re·dac'tion
re·dac'tor
red'bait'
red'-blood'ed
red'den
re·deem'a·ble
re·demp'tion
re'de·ploy'
re'de·vel'op·ment
red'-hand'ed
red'head'
red'-hot'
re·di·rect'
re·dis'trict
red'-let'ter
re·do'
 ·did' ·done'
 ·do'ing
red'o·lence
red'o·lent
re·dou'ble
re·doubt'
re·doubt'a·ble
re·dound'
red'out'
re·dress'
 (remedy)
re'-dress'
 (dress again)
re·duce'
 ·duced' ·duc'ing
re·duc'i·ble
re·duc'tion
re·dun'dan·cy
 ·cies
re·dun'dant
re·du'pli·cate'
re·du'pli·ca'tion
re·ech'o
reed'i·ness
re·ed'it
re·ed'u·cate'
reed'y
 ·i·er ·i·est

reek
 (emit a smell; see
 wreak)
reel
 (whirl; dance;
 spool; see real)
re'e·lect'
re'e·lec'tion
re'em·bark'
re'em·bod'y
re'em·brace'
re'e·merge'
re·em'pha·sis
re·em'pha·size'
re'em·ploy'
re'en·act'
re'en·dow'
re'en·gage'
re'en·list'
re·en'ter
re·en'try
re'e·quip'
re'es·tab'lish
re'e·val'u·ate'
re'ex·am'ine
re'ex·change'
re'ex·hib'it
re'ex·pe'ri·ence
re'ex·plain'
re'ex·port'
re·fec'tion
re·fer'
 ·ferred'
 ·fer'ring
ref'er·a·ble or
 ·i·ble
ref'er·ee'
 ·eed' ·ee'ing
ref'er·ence
ref'er·en'dum
 ·dums or ·da
ref'er·ent
re·fer'ral
re·fill'a·ble
re·fine'
 ·fined' ·fin'ing
re·fine'ment
re·fin'er·y
 ·ies
re·fit'
re·fla'tion
re·flect'
re·flec'tion
re·flec'tive
re·flec'tor
re'flex
re·flex'ive
re'for·est·a'tion
re·form'
 (make better)
re'-form'
 (form again)
re·for'ma·tion
re·form'a·to'ry
 ·ries
re·fract'
re·frac'tion
re·frac'to·ry

re·frain'
re·fran'gi·ble
re·fresh'
re·fresh'ment
re·frig'er·ant
re·frig'er·ate'
· at'ed ·at'ing
re·frig'er·a'tion
re·frig'er·a'tor
ref'uge
ref'u·gee'
re·ful'gent
re·fund'
re·fur'bish
re·fus'al
re·fuse' v.
· fused' fus'ing
ref'use n.
re·fut'a·ble
ref'u·ta'tion
re·fute'
· fut'ed ·fut'ing
re·gain'
re'gal adj.
re·gale' v.
· galed' gal'ing
re·ga'li·a
re·gal'i·ty
· ties
re·gard'ing
re·gard'less
re·gat'ta
re'gen·cy
· cies
re·gen'er·ate'
· at'ed ·at'ing
re·gen'er·a'tion
re·gen'er·a'tive
re·gen'er·a'tor
re'gent
reg'i·cide'
re·gime' or ré·
reg'i·men
reg'i·ment
reg'i·men'tal
reg'i·men·ta'tion
re'gion·al
reg'is·ter
reg'is·trant
reg'is·trar'
reg'is·tra'tion
reg'is·try
· tries
re'gress
re·gres'sion
re·gres'sive
re·gret'
· gret'ted
· gret'ting
re·gret'ful
re·gret'ful·ly
re·gret'ta·ble
re·gret'ta·bly
reg'u·lar
reg'u·lar'i·ty
· ties
reg'u·late'
· lat'ed ·lat'ing

reg'u·la'tion
reg'u·la'tor
re·gur'gi·tate'
· tat'ed ·tat'ing
re·gur'gi·ta'tion
re'ha·bil'i·tate'
· tat'ed ·tat'ing
re'ha·bil'i·ta'tion
re·hears'al
re·hearse'
· hearsed'
· hears'ing
reign
(*rule;* see rain, rein)
re'im·burs'a·ble
re'im·burse'
· bursed'
· burs'ing
rein
(*control;* see rain, reign)
re'in·car'nate
· nat·ed ·nat·ing
re'in·car·na'tion
re'in·cur'
rein'deer
re'in·force'
· forced'
· forc'ing
re'in·force'ment
re'in·state'
· stat'ed
· stat'ing
re·it'er·ate'
· at'ed ·at'ing
re·ject'
re·jec'tion
re·joice'
· joiced' joic'ing
re·join'der
re·ju've·nate'
· nat'ed ·nat'ing
re·lapse'
· lapsed'
· laps'ing
re·lat'a·ble
re·late'
· lat'ed ·lat'ing
re·la'tion·ship'
rel'a·tive
rel'a·tive·ly
rel'a·tiv'i·ty
re·lax'
re·lax'ant
re·lax·a'tion
re'lay
· layed ·lay·ing
(*send by relay*)
re'-lay'
· laid' -lay'ing
(*lay again*)
re·lease'
· leased'
· leas'ing
(*set free*)
re'-lease'
(*lease again*)

rel'e·gate'
· gat'ed ·gat'ing
rel'e·ga'tion
re·lent'less
rel'e·vance
rel'e·vant
re·li'a·bil'i·ty
re·li'a·ble
re·li'a·bly
re·li'ance
re·li'ant
rel'ic
re·lief'
re·liev'a·ble
re·lieve'
· lieved' liev'ing
re·liev'er
re·li'gion
re·li'gious
re·lin'quish
rel'i·quar'y
· ies
rel'ish
re·luc'tance
re·luc'tant
re·ly'
· lied' ·ly'ing
re·main'der
re·make'
· made' ·mak'ing
re·mand'
re·mark'a·ble
re·mark'a·bly
re·me'di·a·ble
re·me'di·al
rem'e·dy
· dies
· died ·dy·ing
re·mem'ber
re·mem'brance
re·mind'er
rem'i·nisce'
· nisced'
· nisc'ing
rem'i·nis'cence
rem'i·nis'cent
rem'i·nis'cer
re·miss'
re·mis'si·ble
re·mis'sion
re·mit'
· mit'ted
· mit'ting
re·mit'ta·ble
re·mit'tance
re·mit'tent
rem'nant
re·mod'el
re·mon'strance
re·mon'strate
· strat·ed
· strat·ing
re'mon·stra'tion
re·mon'stra·tor
re·morse'ful
re·morse'less
re·mote'
re·mote'ly

re·mov'a·ble
re·mov'al
re·move'
· moved'
· mov'ing
re·mu'ner·ate'
· at'ed ·at'ing
re·mu'ner·a'tion
re·mu'ner·a'tive
re·mu'ner·a'tor
ren'ais·sance'
re·nas'cent
rend
rent rend'ing
ren'der
ren'dez·vous'
· vous
· voused'
· vous'ing
ren·di'tion
ren'e·gade'
re·nege'
· neged' ·neg'ing
re·new'al
ren'net
re·nounce'
· nounced'
· nounc'ing
ren'o·vate'
· vat'ed ·vat'ing
ren'o·va'tion
re·nown'
re·nowned'
rent'al
rent'-free'
re·nun'ci·a'tion
re·or'der
re·or'gan·i·za'tion
re·or'gan·ize'
· ized' ·iz'ing
re·pair'man
rep'a·ra·ble
rep'a·ra'tion
rep'ar·tee'
re·past'
re·pa'tri·ate'
· at'ed ·at'ing
re·pa'tri·a'tion
re·pay'
· paid' ·pay'ing
(*pay back*)
re'-pay'
· paid' -pay'ing
(*pay again*)
re·peal'
re·peat'
re·pel'
· pelled' ·pel'ling
re·pel'lent
re·pent'
re·pent'ance
re·pent'ant
re·per·cus'sion
rep'er·toire'
rep'er·to·ry
· ries
rep'e·ti'tion
(*a repeating*)

re'-pe·ti'tion
(*petition again*)
rep'e·ti'tious
re·pet'i·tive
re·phrase'
re·place'
re·place'a·ble
re·place'ment
re·plen'ish
re·plete'
re·ple'tion
re·plev'in
rep'li·ca
re·ply'
· plies'
· plied' ·ply'ing
re·port'ed·ly
re·port'er
re·pose'
· posed' ·pos'ing
(*rest*)
re'-pose'
(*pose again*)
re·pos'i·to·ry
· ries
re'pos·sess'
re'pos·ses'sion
rep're·hend'
rep're·hen'si·ble
rep're·hen'sion
rep're·sent'
(*stand for*)
re'-pre·sent'
(*present again*)
rep're·sen·ta'tion
rep're·sent'a·tive
re·press'
(*restrain*)
re'-press'
(*press again*)
re·pressed'
re·press'i·ble
re·pres'sion
re·prieve'
· prieved'
· priev'ing
rep'ri·mand'
re·print'
re·pris'al
re·proach'
re·proach'ful
rep'ro·bate'
· bat'ed ·bat'ing
re·proc'essed
re'pro·duce'
re'pro·duc'i·ble
re'pro·duc'tion
re'pro·duc'tive
re·proof'
re·prove'
· proved'
· prov'ing
(*rebuke*)
re'-prove'
(*prove again*)
rep'tile
rep·til'i·an
re·pub'lic

re'-pe·ti'tion
re·pub'li·can
re·pu'di·ate'
· at'ed ·at'ing
re·pu'di·a'tion
re·pug'nance
re·pug'nant
re·pulse'
· pulsed'
· puls'ing
re·pul'sion
re·pul'sive
rep'u·ta·bil'i·ty
rep'u·ta·ble
rep'u·ta·bly
rep'u·ta'tion
re·pute'
· put'ed ·put'ing
re·quest'
Re'qui·em
re·quire'
· quired'
· quir'ing
re·quire'ment
req'ui·site
req'ui·si'tion
re·quit'al
re·quite'
· quit'ed
· quit'ing
rere'dos
re·route'
re·run'
· ran' ·run'
· run'ning
re·sal'a·ble
re'sale'
re·scind'
re·scind'a·ble
re·scis'sion
res'cu·a·ble
res'cue
· cued ·cu·ing
res'cu·er
re·search'
re·sem'blance
re·sem'ble
· bled ·bling
re·sent'
(*feel a hurt*)
re'-sent'
(*sent again*)
re·sent'ful
re·sent'ment
res'er·va'tion
re·serve'
· served'
· serv'ing
(*set aside*)
re'-serve'
(*serve again*)
re·serv'ed·ly
re·serv'ist
res'er·voir'
re·set'
· set' ·set'ting
re·ship'ment
re·side'
· sid'ed ·sid'ing

res'i·dence
res'i·den·cy
·cies
res'i·dent
res'i·den'tial
re·sid'u·al
re·sid'u·ar'y
res'i·due'
re·sign'
(give up)
re'-sign'
(sign again)
res'ig·na'tion
re·sil'i·ence
re·sil'i·ent
res'in
res'in·ous
re·sist'
re·sist'ance
re·sist'ant
re·sist'er
(one who resists)
re·sist'i·ble
re·sis'tor
(electrical device)
re'sole'
soled' sol'ing
res'o·lute'
res'o·lu'tion
re·solv'a·ble
re·solve'
solved'
solv'ing
(break into parts)
re'-solve'
(solve again)
re·sol'vent
res'o·nance
res'o·nant
res'o·na'tor
re·sort'
(go for help)
re'-sort'
(sort again)
re·sound'
(echo)
re'-sound'
(sound again)
re'source
re·source'ful
re·spect'a·bil'i·ty
re·spect'a·ble
re·spect'ful
re·spect'ful·ly
re·spec'tive
re·spec'tive·ly
res'pi·ra'tion
res'pi·ra'tor
res'pi·ra·to'ry
re·spire'
spired'
spir'ing
res'pite
pit·ed pit·ing
re·splend'ence
re·splend'ent
re·spond'
re·spond'ent

re·sponse'
re·spon'si·bil'i·ty
·ties
re·spon'si·ble
re·spon'si·bly
re·spon'sive
re·state'
stat'ed stat'ing
res'tau·rant
res'tau·ra·teur'
rest'ful
res'ti·tu'tion
res'tive
rest'less
res'to·ra'tion
re·stor'a·tive
re·store'
stored' stor'ing
re·strain'
(hold back)
re'-strain'
(strain again)
re·straint'
re·strict'
re·stric'tion
re·stric'tive
rest'room'
re·struc'ture
re·sult'
re·sult'ant
re·sum'a·ble
re·sume' *v.*
·sumed'
·sum'ing
ré'su·mé' *n.*
re·sump'tion
re·sur'face
re·sur'gence
re·sur'gent
res'ur·rect'
res'ur·rec'tion
re·sus'ci·tate'
·tat'ed ·tat'ing
re·sus'ci·ta'tion
re·sus'ci·ta'tor
re'tail
re·tain'
re·tain'er
re·take'
·took' ·tak'en
·tak'ing
re·tal'i·ate'
·at'ed ·at'ing
re·tal'i·a'tion
re·tal'i·a·to'ry
re·tard'
re·tard'ant
re·tar'date
re'tar·da'tion
retch
(strain to vomit; see wretch)
re·ten'tion
re·ten'tive
re'ten·tiv'i·ty
re·think'
ret'i·cence
ret'i·cent

re·tic'u·lar
re·tic'u·late'
·lat'ed ·lat'ing
ret'i·cule'
ret'i·na
·nas *or* ·nae'
ret'i·nue'
re·tire'
·tired' ·tir'ing
re·tire'ment
re·tool'
re·tort'
re·touch'
re·trace'
(go back over)
re'-trace'
(trace again)
re·trace'a·ble
re·tract'
re·tract'a·ble
re·trac'tile
re·trac'tion
re·trac'tor
re'tread' *v.*
·tread'ed
·tread'ing
re'tread' *n.*
re·treat'
(go back)
re'-treat'
(treat again)
re·trench'
ret'ri·bu'tion
re·triev'a·ble
re·triev'al
re·trieve'
·trieved'
·triev'ing
re·triev'er
ret'ro·ac'tive
ret'ro·ces'sion
ret'ro·fire'
ret'ro·fit'
ret'ro·grade'
·grad'ed
·grad'ing
ret'ro·gress'
ret'ro·gres'sion
ret'ro·rock'et *or*
ret'ro-rock'et
ret'ro·spect'
ret'ro·spec'tion
re·turn'
re·turn'ee'
re·un'ion
re·u'nite'
re·us'a·ble
re·use'
rev
revved rev'ving
re·vamp'
re·veal'
re'veil·le
rev'el
·eled *or* ·elled
·el·ing *or* ·el·ling
rev'e·la'tion

rev'el·ry
re·venge'
·venged'
·veng'ing
re·venge'ful
·veng'er
rev'e·nue'
re·ver'ber·ant
re·ver'ber·ate'
·at'ed ·at'ing
re·ver'ber·a'tion
re·ver'ber·a'tor
re·ver'ber·a·to'ry
re·vere'
·vered' ·ver'ing
rev'er·ence
rev'er·end
rev'er·ent
rev'er·en'tial
rev'er·ie
re·ver'sal
re·vers'
·vers'
(part of garment)
re·verse'
·versed'
·vers'ing
(turned backward)
re·vers'i·ble
re·vers'i·bly
re·ver'sion
re·ver'sion·ar'y
re·vert'
re·view'
re·view'al
re·view'er
re·vile'
·viled' ·vil'ing
re·vise'
·vised' ·vis'ing
re·vi'sion
re·vi'so·ry
re·vi'tal·ize'
re·viv'a·ble
re·viv'al
re·vive'
·vived' ·viv'ing
re·viv'i·fy'
rev'o·ca·ble
rev'o·ca·bly
rev'o·ca'tion
re·voke'
·voked' ·vok'ing
re·volt'
re·volt'ing
rev'o·lu'tion
rev'o·lu'tion·ar'y
·ies
rev'o·lu'tion·ize'
·ized' ·iz'ing
re·volv'a·ble
re·volve'
·volved'
·volv'ing
re·volv'er
re·vue' *or* ·view'
re·vul'sion
re·ward'

re·wind'
·wound'
·wind'ing
re·write'
·wrote' ·writ'ten
·writ'ing
rhap·sod'ic
rhap·sod'i·cal·ly
rhap'so·dize'
·dized' ·diz'ing
rhap'so·dy
·dies
rhe'o·stat'
rhe'sus
rhet'o·ric
rhe·tor'i·cal
rhe·tor'i·cal·ly
rhet'o·ri'cian
rheu·mat'ic
rheu'ma·tism
rheu'ma·toid'
rheum'y
·i·er ·i·est
Rh factor
rhine'stone'
rhi·ni'tis
rhi·noc'er·os
rhi'zome
Rhode Island
rho'do·den'dron
rhom'boid
rhom'bus
·bus·es *or* ·bi
rhu'barb
rhyme
rhymed
rhym'ing
(verse; see rime)
rhythm
rhyth'mic
rhyth'mi·cal·ly
rib
ribbed
rib'bing
rib'ald
rib'ald·ry
rib'bon
ri'bo·fla'vin
rice
riced ric'ing
rich'ness
rick'et·i·ness
rick'ets
rick·ett'si·a
·si·ae' *or* ·si·as
rick'et·y
rick'ey
rick'rack'
rick'shaw *or* ·sha
ric'o·chet'
·cheted' *or*
·chet'ted
·chet'ing *or*
·chet'ting
ri·cot'ta
rid
rid *or* rid'ded
rid'ding

rid'a·ble *or* ride'·
rid'dance
rid'dle
·dled ·dling
ride
rode rid'den
rid'ing
rid'er·less
ridge
ridged ridg'ing
ridge'pole'
rid'i·cule'
ri·dic'u·lous
rife
rif'fle
·fled ·fling
(shoal; shuffle)
riff'raff'
ri'fle
·fled ·fling
(gun; plunder)
ri'fle·man
rig
rigged rig'ging
ri'ga·to'ni
rig'ger
(one who rigs; see rigor)
right
(correct; see rite)
right'-an'gled
right'eous
right'ful·ly
right'-hand'ed
right'ist
rig'id
ri·gid'i·ty
rig'ma·role'
rig'or
(stiffness; see rigger)
rig'or mor'tis
rig'or·ous
rile
riled ril'ing
rim
rimmed
rim'ming
rime
rimed rim'ing
(hoarfrost; rhyme; see rhyme)
ring
rang rung
ring'ing
(sound; see wring)
ring
ringed ring'ing
(circle; see wring)
ring'er
ring'lead'er
ring'let
ring'mas'ter
ring'side'
rink

rinse
 rinsed rins'ing
ri'ot·ous
rip
 ripped rip'ping
ri·par'i·an
rip'en
ripe'ness
ri·poste' or
 ·post'
rip'per
rip'ple
 ·pled ·pling
rip'saw'
rip'tide'
rise
 rose ris'en
 ris'ing
ris'er
ris·i·bil'i·ty
 ·ties
ris'i·ble
risk'i·ly
risk'i·ness
risk'y
 ·i·er ·i·est
ris·qué'
ris'sole
rite
 (ceremonial act;
 see right, write)
rit'u·al
rit'u·al·is'tic
rit'u·al·ly
ri'val
 ·valed or ·valled
 ·val·ing or
 ·val·ling
ri'val·ry
 ·ries
rive
 rived, rived or
 riv'en, riv'ing
riv'er·side'
riv'et
riv'et·er
riv'u·let
roach
road'a·bil'i·ty
road'bed'
road'block'
road'show'
road'side'
road'ster
road'way'
road'work'
roam'er
roan
roar'ing
roast'er
rob
 robbed rob'bing
rob'ber
rob'ber·y
 ·ies
robe
 robed rob'ing
rob'in

ro'bot
ro·bust'
rock'-and-roll'
rock'-bound'
rock'er
rock'et
rock'e·teer'
rock'et·ry
rock'i·ness
 rock·oon'
rock'y
 ·i·er ·i·est
ro·co'co
ro'dent
ro'de·o'
 ·os'
roe
 (fish eggs; see
 row)
roent'gen
rogue
 rogued rogu'ing
ro'guer·y
 ·ies
ro'guish
roil
 (stir up; see royal)
roist'er·er
roist'er·ous
role or rôle
 (actor's part)
roll
 (revolve)
roll'a·way'
roll'back'
roll call
roll'er
roll'ick·ing
roll'-top'
ro·maine'
ro·mance'
 ·manced'
 ·manc'ing
ro·man'tic
ro·man'ti·cal·ly
ro·man'ti·cism
ro·man'ti·cize'
 ·cized' ·ciz'ing
ron'deau
 ·deaux
 (poem)
ron'do
 ·dos
 (music)
rood
 (cross; see rude)
roof'er
rook
rook'er·y
 ·ies
rook'ie
room'er
 (lodger; see
 rumor)
room·ette'
room'ful'
 ·fuls'
room'i·ness

room'mate'
room'y
 ·i·er ·i·est
roos'ter
root beer
root'er
root'less
root'let
rope
 roped rop'ing
rope'walk'
Roque'fort
ro'sa·ry
 ·ries
ro·sé'
ro'se·ate
rose'bud'
rose'bush'
rose'-col'ored
ro·se'o·la
ro·sette'
rose'wood'
Rosh' Ha·sha'na
ros'i·ly
ros'in
ros'i·ness
ros'ter
ros·trum
 ·trums or ·tra
ros'y
 ·i·er ·i·est
rot
 rot'ted
 rot'ting
ro'ta·ry
 ·ries
ro'tat·a·ble
ro'tate
 ·tat·ed ·tat·ing
ro·ta'tion
ro'ta·tor
rote
 (routine; see
 wrote)
ro·tis'ser·ie
ro'to·gra·vure'
ro'tor
rot'ten
ro·tund'
ro·tun'da
ro·tun'di·ty
rou·é'
rouge
 rouged roug'ing
rough
 (not smooth;
 see ruff)
rough'age
rough'cast'
 ·cast' ·cast'ing
rough'-dry'
 -dried' -dry'ing
rough'en
rough'-hew'
 -hewed', -hewed'
 or -hewn',
 -hew'ing
rough'ly

rough'shod'
rou·lade'
rou·leau'
 ·leaux' or ·leaus'
rou·lette'
round'a·bout'
roun·de·lay'
round'house'
round'up'
round'worm'
rouse
 roused rous'ing
roust'a·bout'
rout
 (noisy mob; dig
 up; defeat)
route
 rout'ed rout'ing
 (course)
rou·tine'
rove
 roved rov'ing
row n., v.
 (line; use oars;
 brawl; see roe)
row'boat'
row'di·ness
row'dy
 ·dies
 ·di·er ·di·est
row'dy·ism
row'el
 ·eled or ·elled
 ·el·ing or ·el·ling
roy'al
 (regal; see roil)
roy'al·ist
roy'al·ly
roy'al·ty
 ·ties
rub
 rubbed
 rub'bing
rub'ber·ize'
 ·ized' ·iz'ing
rub'ber·y
rub'bish
rub'ble
 (stone; see ruble)
rub'down'
ru·bel'la
ru'bi·cund'
ru'ble
 (money; see
 rubble)
ru'bric
ru'by
 ·bies
ruche
ruch'ing
ruck'sack'
rud'der
rud'di·ness
rud'dy
 ·di·er ·di·est
rude
 (crude; see rood)
rude'ly

ru'di·ment
ru'di·men'ta·ry
rue
 rued ru'ing
rue'ful
ruff
 (collar; see rough)
ruf'fi·an
ruf'fle
 ·fled ·fling
rug'ged
ru'in·a'tion
ru'in·ous
rule
 ruled rul'ing
rul'er
rum'ble
 ·bled ·bling
ru'mi·nant
ru'mi·nate'
 ·nat'ed ·nat'ing
ru'mi·na'tor
rum'mage
 ·maged
 ·mag·ing
ru'mor
 (hearsay; see
 roomer)
rum'ple
 ·pled ·pling
run
 ran run
 run'ning
run'a·bout'
run'a·way'
run'-down'
rung
 (crossbar; pp. of
 ring; see wrung)
run'-in'
run'ner-up'
run'ners-up'
run'ni·ness
run'ny
 ·ni·er ·ni·est
run'off'
run'-on'
run'way'
rup'ture
 ·tured ·tur·ing
ru'ral
ru'ral·ly
ruse
rush
rus'set
rus'tic
rus'ti·cal·ly
rus'ti·cate'
 ·cat'ed ·cat'ing
rust'i·ness
rus'tle
 ·tled ·tling
rus'tler
rust'proof'
rust'y
 ·i·er ·i·est
rut
 rut'ted rut'ting

ru'ta·ba'ga
ruth'less
rye
 (grain; see wry)

S

Sab'bath
sab·bat'i·cal
sa'ber or ·bre
sa'ble
sa'bot
sab'o·tage'
 ·taged' ·tag'ing
sab'o·teur'
sac
 (pouch; see sack)
sac'cha·rin n.
sac'cha·rine adj.
sac'er·do'tal
sa·chet'
sack
 (bag; see sac)
sack'cloth'
sack'ful'
 ·fuls'
sack'ing
sac'ra·ment
sac'ra·men'tal
sa'cred
sac'ri·fice'
 ·ficed' ·fic'ing
sac'ri·fi'cial
sac'ri·lege
sac'ri·le'gious
sac'ris·tan
sac'ris·ty
 ·ties
sac'ro·il'i·ac'
sac'ro·sanct'
sa'crum
 ·cra or ·crums
sad
 sad'der sad'dest
sad'den
sad'dle
 ·dled ·dling
sad'dle·bag'
sad'dle·cloth'
sad'dler
sad'i'ron
sad'ism
sad'ist
sa·dis'tic
sa·dis'ti·cal·ly
sa·fa'ri
 ·ris
safe
 saf'er saf'est
safe'-con'duct
safe'-de·pos'it
safe'guard'
safe'keep'ing
safe'ty
 ·ties
saf'fron

sag
 sagged sag'ging
sa'ga
sa·ga'cious
sa·gac'i·ty
sage
 sag'er sag'est
sage'brush'
sag'gy
 ·gi·er ·gi·est
sa'go
 ·gos
sail'boat'
sail'cloth'
sail'er
 (*boat*)
sail'fish'
sail'or
 (*person; hat*)
saint'li·ness
saint'ly
 ·li·er ·li·est
sa'ke
 (*rice wine*)
sake
 (*purpose*)
sa·laam'
sal'a·ble *or*
sale' ·
sa·la'cious
sal'ad
sal'a·man'der
sa·la'mi
sal'a·ried
sal'a·ry
 ·ries
sal'e·ra'tus
sales'clerk'
sales'man
sales'man·ship'
sales'peo'ple
sales'per'son
sales'wom'an
sa'lient
sa'line
sa·lin'i·ty
sa·li'va
sal'i·var'y
sal'i·vate'
 ·vat'ed ·vat'ing
sal'low
sal'ly
 ·lies, ·lied ·ly·ing
sal'ma·gun'di
salm'on
sal'mo·nel'la
 ·lae *or* ·la *or* ·las
sa·lon'
sa·loon'
sa·loon'keep'er
sal'si·fy'
salt'box'
salt'cel'lar
salt'i·ly
salt·ine'
salt'i·ness
salt'pe'ter
salt'shak'er

salt'wa'ter
salt'works'
 ·works'
salt'y
 ·i·er ·i·est
sa·lu'bri·ous
sal'u·tar'y
sal'u·ta'tion
sa·lu'ta·to'ri·an
sa·lu'ta·to'ry
 ·ries
sa·lute'
 ·lut'ed ·lut'ing
sal'vage
 ·vaged ·vag·ing
sal'vage·a·ble
sal·va'tion
salve
 salved salv'ing
sal'ver
sal'vo
 ·vos *or* ·voes
Sa·mar'i·tan
same'ness
sam'i·sen'
sam'o·var'
sam'pan
sam'ple
 ·pled ·pling
sam'pler
sam'u·rai'
 ·rai
san'a·tive
sanc'ti·fi·ca'tion
sanc'ti·fy'
 ·fied' ·fy'ing
sanc'ti·mo'ni·ous
sanc'ti·mo'ny
sanc'tion
sanc'ti·ty
sanc'tu·ar'y
 ·ies
sanc'tum
 ·tums *or* ·ta
san'dal
san'daled *or*
 ·dalled
san'dal·wood'
sand'bag'
sand bar
sand'blast'
sand'box'
san'dhi
sand'hog'
sand'i·ness
sand'lot'
sand'man'
sand'pa'per
sand'stone'
sand'storm'
sand'wich
sand'y
 ·i·er ·i·est
sane'ly
San'for·ize'
 ·ized' ·iz'ing
sang'-froid'
san'gui·nar'y

san'guine
san'i·tar'i·um
 ·i·ums *or* ·i·a
san'i·tar'y
san'i·ta'tion
san'i·tize'
 ·tized' ·tiz'ing
san'i·ty
San'skrit
sap
 sapped sap'ping
sa'pi·ent
sap'ling
sa·pon'i·fy'
 ·fied' ·fy'ing
sap'phire
sap'py
 ·pi·er ·pi·est
sap'suck'er
sa·ran'
sar'casm
sar·cas'tic
sar·cas'ti·cal·ly
sar·co'ma
 ·mas *or* ·ma·ta
sar·coph'a·gus
 ·a·gi
sar·dine'
sar·don'ic
sar·don'i·cal·ly
sar'do·nyx
sa'ri
 ·ris
sa·rong'
sar'sa·pa·ril'la
sar·to'ri·al
sas'sa·fras'
sa·tan'ic
sa·tan'i·cal·ly
satch'el
sate
 sat'ed sat'ing
sa·teen'
sat'el·lite'
sa'tia·ble
sa'ti·ate'
 ·at'ed ·at'ing
sa·ti'a·tion
sa·ti'e·ty
sat'in
sat'in·wood'
sat'in·y
sat'ire
sa·tir'i·cal
sat'i·rist
sat'i·rize'
 ·rized' ·riz'ing
sat'is·fac'tion
sat'is·fac'to·ri·ly
sat'is·fac'to·ry
sat'is·fy'
 ·fied' ·fy'ing
sa·to'ri
sa'trap
sat'su·ma
sat'u·ra·ble
sat'u·rate'
 ·rat'ed ·rat'ing

sat'u·ra'tion
Sat'ur·day
sat'ur·nine'
sat'yr
sat'y·ri'a·sis
sauce'pan'
sau'cer
sau'ci·ness
sau'cy
 ·ci·er ·ci·est
sau'er·bra'ten
sau'er·kraut'
sau'na
saun'ter
sau'sage
sau·té'
 ·téed' ·té'ing
sau·terne'
sav'a·ble *or*
 save' ·
sav'age
sav'age·ly
sav'age·ry
sa·van'na
sa·vant'
save
 saved sav'ing
sav'ior
sa'voir-faire'
sa'vor
sa'vor·i·ness
sa'vor·y
 ·i·er ·i·est
sa·voy'
saw
 sawed saw'ing
saw'dust'
saw'horse'
saw'mill'
saw'-toothed'
saw'yer
sax'o·phone'
sax'o·phon'ist
say
 said say'ing
says
say'-so'
scab
 scabbed scab'bing
scab'bard
scab'bi·ness
scab'by
 ·bi·er ·bi·est
scab'rous
scaf'fold
scagl·io'la
scal'a·ble
scal'a·wag'
scald
scale
 scaled scal'ing
scale'less
sca·lene'
scal'i·ness
scal'lion
scal'lop
scal'op·pi'ne
scal'pel

scalp'er
scal'y
 ·i·er ·i·est
scam'per
scan
 scanned
 scan'ning
scan'dal
scan'dal·ize'
 ·ized' ·iz'ing
scan'dal·mon'ger
scan'dal·ous
scan'na·ble
scan'ner
scan'sion
scant'i·ly
scant'i·ness
scant'ling
scant'ness
scant'y
 ·i·er ·i·est
scape'goat'
scape'grace'
scap'u·la
 ·lae' *or* ·las
scap'u·lar
scar
 scarred
 scar'ring
scar'ab
scar'a·mouch'
scarce'ly
scar'ci·ty
 ·ties
scare
 scared scar'ing
scare'crow'
scarf
 scarfs *or* scarves
 (*long cloth*)
scarf
 scarfs
 (*joint; cut*)
scar'i·fi·ca'tion
scar'i·fy'
 ·fied' ·fy'ing
scar'i·ness
scar'let
scarp
scar'y
 ·i·er ·i·est
scat
 scat'ted
 scat'ting
scathe
 scathed
 scath'ing
scat'ter
scat'ter·brain'
scav'enge
 ·enged ·eng·ing
scav'eng·er
sce·nar'i·o'
 ·os'
sce·nar'ist
scene
sce'ner·y
 ·ies

sce'nic
scent
 (*odor; see sent*)
scep'ter
sched'ule
 ·uled ·ul·ing
sche'ma
 ·ma·ta
sche·mat'ic
sche·mat'i·cal·ly
scheme
 schemed
 schem'ing
scher'zo
 ·zos *or* ·zi
schism
schis·mat'ic
schiz'oid
schiz'o·phre'ni·a
schiz'o·phren'ic
schnau'zer
schol'ar·ly
schol'ar·ship'
scho·las'tic
scho·las'ti·cal·ly
scho·las'ti·cism
school'boy'
school'girl'
school'house'
school'mate'
school'room'
school'teach'er
school'work'
schoon'er
schwa
sci·at'i·ca
sci'ence
sci'en·tif'ic
sci'en·tif'i·cal·ly
sci'en·tist
scim'i·tar
scin·til'la
scin'til·late'
 ·lat'ed ·lat'ing
scin'til·la'tor
sci'on
scis'sors
scle·ro'sis
scoff
scold'ing
sconce
scone
scoop'ful'
 ·fuls'
scoot'er
scope
scorch'ing
score
 scored scor'ing
score'less
scorn'ful
scor'pi·on
scot'-free'
scoun'drel
scour
scourge
 scourged
 scourg'ing

scout'mas'ter
scowl
scrab'ble
· bled · bling
scrag'gly
· gli · er · gli · est
scram'ble
· bled · bling
scrap
scrapped
scrap'ping
scrap'book'
scrape
scraped
scrap'ing
scrap'er
scrap'heap'
scrap'ple
scrap'py
· pi · er · pi · est
scratch'i · ness
scratch'y
· i · er · i · est
scrawl
scraw'ny
· ni · er · ni · est
scream'ing
screech'y
screen'play'
screw'driv'er
scrib'ble
· bled · bling
scrib'bler
scribe
scribed scrib'ing
scrim'mage
· maged · mag · ing
scrimp'i · ness
scrimp'y
· i · er · i · est
scrip
(certificate)
script
(manuscript)
scrip'tur · al
scrof'u · la
scroll'work'
scro'tum
· ta or · tums
scrounge
scrounged
scroung'ing
scrub
scrubbed
scrub'bing
scrub'by
· bi · er · bi · est
scruff
scrunch
scru'ple
· pled · pling
scru'pu · lous
scru'ta · ble
scru'ti · nize'
· nized' · niz'ing
scru'ti · ny

scu'ba
scuff
scuf'fle
· fled · fling
scull
(oar; boat; see skull)
scul'ler · y
· ies
sculpt
sculp'tor
sculp'tur · al
sculp'ture
· tured · tur · ing
scum'my
· mi · er · mi · est
scup'per · nong'
scur · ril'i · ty
· ties
scur'ril · ous
scur'ry
· ried · ry · ing
scur'vy
· vi · er · vi · est
scut'tle
· tled · tling
scythe
scythed
scyth'ing
sea'board'
sea'borne'
sea'coast'
sea'far'er
sea'far'ing
sea'food'
sea'go'ing
seal'ant
sea level
seal'skin'
seam
sea'man
seam'less
seam'stress
seam'y
· i · er · i · est
sé'ance
sea'plane'
sea'port'
sear
(burn; see seer)
search'light'
sea'scape'
sea'shell'
sea'shore'
sea'sick'ness
sea'side'
sea'son
sea'son · a · ble
sea'son · al
seat belt
sea'ward'
sea'way'
sea'weed'
sea'wor'thy
se · ba'ceous
se'cant
se · cede'
· ced'ed · ced'ing

se · ces'sion
se · clude'
· clud'ed
· clud'ing
se · clu'sion
se · clu'sive
sec'ond
sec'ond · ar'i · ly
sec'ond · ar'y
sec'ond-class'
sec'ond-guess'
sec'ond-hand'
sec'ond-rate'
se'cre · cy
se'cret
sec're · tar'i · al
sec're · tar'i · at
sec're · tar'y
· ies
se · crete'
· cret'ed · cret'ing
se · cre'tion
se'cre · tive
se · cre'to · ry
sect
sec · tar'i · an
sec'tion · al
sec'tion · al · ize'
· ized' · iz'ing
sec'tor
sec'u · lar
sec'u · lar · ize'
· ized' · iz'ing
se · cur'a · ble
se · cure'
· cured' · cur'ing
se · cure'ly
se · cu'ri · ty
· ties
se · dan'
se · date'
· dat'ed · dat'ing
se · date'ly
se · da'tion
sed'a · tive
sed'en · tar'y
sed'i · ment
sed'i · men'ta · ry
sed'i · men · ta'tion
se · di'tion
se · di'tious
se · duce'
· duced' · duc'ing
se · duc'i · ble
se · duc'tion
se · duc'tive
se · du'li · ty
sed'u · lous
see
saw seen see'ing
seed'bed'
seed'i · ness
seed'ling
seed'y
· i · er · i · est
seek
sought seek'ing
seem'ing · ly

seem'li · ness
seem'ly
· li · er · li · est
seep'age
seer
(prophet; see sear)
seer'suck'er
see'saw'
seethe
seethed
seeth'ing
seg'ment
seg · men'tal
seg'men · ta'tion
seg're · gate'
· gat'ed · gat'ing
seg · re · ga'tion
seg're · ga'tion · ist
sei'del
seis'mic
seis'mi · cal · ly
seis'mo · graph'
seis · mog'ra · pher
seis · mol'o · gist
seis · mol'o · gy
seize
seized seiz'ing
sei'zure
sel'dom
se · lect'
se · lect'ee'
se · lec'tion
se · lec'tive
se · lec'tiv'i · ty
se · lec'tor
self
selves
self'-act'ing
self'-ad · dressed'
self'-ap · point'ed
self'-as · sur'ance
self'-as · sured'
self'-cen'tered
self'-con'fi · dence
self'-con'scious
self'-con · tained'
self'-con · trol'
self'-de · fense'
self'-dis · ci · pline
self'-driv'en
self'-ed'u · cat'ed
self'-em · ployed'
self'-es · teem'
self'-ev'i · dent
self'-ex · plan'a · to'ry
self'-ex · pres'sion
self'-gov'ern · ing
self'-im'age
self'-im · por'tant
self'-im · posed'
self'-im · prove'ment
self'-in · duced'
self'-in · dul'gence
self'-in · flict'ed
self'-in'ter · est

self'ish
selfless
self'-load'ing
self'-love'
self'-made'
self'-pit'y
self'-por'trait
self'-pos · sessed'
self'-pres'er · va'· tion
self'-reg'u · lat'ing
self'-re · li'ance
self'-re · proach'
self'-re · spect'
self'-re · straint'
self'-right'eous
self'-ris'ing
self'-sac'ri · fice'
self'same'
self'-sat'is · fied'
self'-seal'ing
self'-serv'ice
self'-start'er
self'-styled'
self'-suf · fi'cient
self'-sup · port'
self'-taught'
self'-tor'ture
self'-willed'
self'-wind'ing
sell
sold sell'ing
sell'-off'
sell'out'
sel'vage or
· vedge
se · man'tic
sem'a · phore'
· phored
· phor'ing
sem'blance
se'men
sem'i · na
se · mes'ter
sem'i · an'nu · al
sem'i · au'to · mat'ic
sem'i · cir'cle
sem'i · co'lon
sem'i · con · duc'tor
sem'i · con'scious
sem'i · de · tached'
sem'i · fi'nal
sem'i · for'mal
sem'i · month'ly
sem'i · nal
sem'i · nar'
sem'i · nar'y
· ies
sem'i · of · fi'cial
sem'i · pre'cious
sem'i · pri'vate
sem'i · pro · fes'· sion · al
sem'i · rig'id
sem'i · skilled'
sem'i · sol'id
Sem'ite

Se · mit'ic
sem'i · trail'er
sem'i · trop'i · cal
sem'i · week'ly
sem'i · year'ly
sem'o · li'na
sen'ate
sen'a · tor
sen'a · to'ri · al
send
sent send'ing
send'-off'
se · nes'cent
se'nile
se · nil'i · ty
sen'ior
sen · ior'i · ty
sen · sa'tion
sen · sa'tion · al · ly
sense
sensed sens'ing
sense'less
sen'si · bil'i · ty
· ties
sen'si · ble
sen'si · bly
sen'si · tive
sen'si · tiv'i · ty
sen'si · ti · za'tion
sen'si · tize'
· tized' · tiz'ing
sen'so · ry
sen'su · al
sen'su · al'i · ty
sen'su · ous
sent
(transmitted;
see scent)
sen'tence
· tenced · tenc · ing
sen · ten'tious
sen'tient
sen'ti · ment
sen'ti · men'tal
sen'ti · men · tal'i · ty
sen'ti · men'tal · ize'
· ized' · iz'ing
sen'ti · nel
· neled or · nelled
· nel · ing or
· nel · ling
sen'try
· tries
sep'a · ra · ble
sep'a · rate'
· rat'ed · rat'ing
sep'a · ra'tion
sep'a · ra · tism
sep'a · ra'tor
se'pi · a
Sep · tem'ber
sep · tet' or
· tette'
sep'tic
sep'tu · a · ge ·· nar'i · an

sep·tu'ple
·pled ·pling
sep'ul·cher
se·pul'chral
se'quel
se'quence
se·quen'tial
se·ques'ter
se'quin
se·quoi'a
se·ra'pe
ser'e·nade'
·nad'ed ·nad'ing
ser'en·dip'i·ty
se·rene'
se·ren'i·ty
serf
(slave; see surf)
serge
(fabric; see surge)
ser'geant
se'ri·al
(in a series;
see cereal)
se'ri·al·ize'
·ized' ·iz'ing
se'ries
·ries
ser'if
se'ri·o·com'ic
se'ri·ous
se'ri·ous-mind'ed
ser'mon
se'rous
ser'pent
ser'pen·tine'
ser·rate'
·rat'ed ·rat'ing
se'rum
·rums or ·ra
ser'vant
serve
served serv'ing
serv'ice
·iced ·ic·ing
serv'ice·a·bil'i·ty
serv'ice·a·ble
serv'ice·a·bly
serv'ice·man'
ser'vi·ette'
ser'vile
ser·vil'i·ty
ser'vi·tor
ser'vi·tude'
ses'a·me'
ses'qui·cen·ten'·
ni·al
ses'sion
(meeting; see
cession)
set
set set'ting
set'back'
set'-in'
set'off'
set'screw'
set·tee'
set'ter

set'tle
·tled ·tling
set'tle·ment
set'tler
set'-to'
·tos'
sev'en·teen'
sev'enth
sev'en·ti·eth
sev'en·ty
·ties
sev'er
sev'er·al
sev'er·al·ly
sev'er·ance
se·vere'
se·vere'ly
se·ver'i·ty
·ties
sew
sewed, sewn or
sewed, sew'ing
(stitch; see sow)
sew'age
sew'er
sew'er·age
sex'a·ge·nar'i·an
sex'i·ly
sex'i·ness
sex'less
sex'tant
sex·tet' or
·tette'
sex'ton
sex·tu'ple
·pled ·pling
sex·tu'plet
sex'u·al
sex·u·al'i·ty
sex'u·al·ly
sex'y
·i·er ·i·est
shab'bi·ly
shab'bi·ness
shab'by
·bi·er ·bi·est
shack'le
·led ·ling
shade
shad'ed
shad'ing
shad'i·ness
shad'ow
shad'ow·y
shad'y
·i·er ·i·est
shaft
shag
shagged
shag'ging
shag'gi·ness
shag'gy
·gi·er ·gi·est
shak'a·ble or
shake'a·ble
shake
shook shak'en
shak'ing

Shake'speare'
Shake·spear'e·an
or ·i·an
shake'-up'
shak'i·ly
shak'i·ness
shak'y
·i·er ·i·est
shal'low
sha·lom'
sham
shammed
sham'ming
sham'ble
·bled ·bling
shame
shamed
sham'ing
shame'faced'
shame'ful
shame'ful·ly
shame'less
sham·poo'
·pooed' ·poo'ing
shang'hai
·haied ·hai·ing
shank
shan'tung'
shan'ty
·ties
shape
shaped shap'ing
shape'less
shape'li·ness
shape'ly
·li·er ·li·est
share
shared shar'ing
share'crop'per
share'hold'er
shark'skin'
sharp'en·er
sharp'-eyed'
sharp'shoot'er
sharp'-sight'ed
sharp'-tongued'
sharp'-wit'ted
shat'ter
shat'ter·proof'
shave
shaved, shaved
or shav'en,
shav'ing
shawl
sheaf
sheaves
shear
sheared, sheared
or shorn,
shear'ing
(cut; see sheer)
shears
sheath
(a case; dress)
sheathe
sheathed
sheath'ing
(put into a sheath)

sheave
sheaved
sheav'ing
shed
shed shed'ding
sheen
sheep'ish·ly
sheep'skin'
sheep'walk'
sheer
(thin; steep;
see shear)
sheet'ing
sheik or sheikh
shelf
shelves
shell
shel·lac' or ·lack'
·lacked'
·lack'ing
shell'fish'
shell'-like'
shell'proof'
shel'ter
shelve
shelved
shelv'ing
she·nan'i·gan
shep'herd
sher'bet
sher'iff
sher'ry
·ries
shib'bo·leth
shield
shift'i·ly
shift'i·ness
shift'less
shift'y
·i·er ·i·est
shil·le'lagh or
shil·la'lah
shil'ly-shal'ly
·lied ·ly·ing
shim
shimmed
shim'ming
shim'mer·y
shim'my
·mies
·mied ·my·ing
shin
shinned
shin'ning
shine
shone or shined
shin'ing
shin'gle
·gled ·gling
shin'i·ness
shin'y
·i·er ·i·est
ship
shipped
ship'ping
ship'board'
ship'mate'
ship'ment

ship'own'er
ship'pa·ble
ship'per
ship'shape'
ship'wreck'
ship'wright'
ship'yard'
shirk'er
shirr'ing
shirt'waist'
shiv'a·ree'
·reed' ·ree'ing
shiv'er
shoal
shock'ing
shock'proof'
shod'di·ly
shod'di·ness
shod'dy
·di·er ·di·est
shoe
shod or shoed,
shod or shoed
or shod'den,
shoe'ing
shoe'horn'
shoe'lace'
shoe'mak'er
sho'er
shoe'shine'
shoe'string'
shoe tree
shoo
shooed shoo'ing
shoot
shot shoot'ing
shop
shopped
shop'ping
shop'keep'er
shop'lift'er
shop'per
shop'talk'
shop'worn'
Shor'an or
shor'-
shore'line'
shore'ward
shor'ing
short'age
short'bread'
short'cake'
short'change'
short'-cir'cuit'
short'com'ing
short'cut'
short'en
short'en·ing
short'hand'
short'-hand'ed
short'horn'
short'-lived'
short'-range'
short'sight'ed
short'stop'
short'-tem'pered
short'-term'
short'-waist'ed

short'wave'
short'-wind'ed
shot'gun'
should
shoul'der
should'n't
shov'el
·eled or ·elled
·el·ing or ·el·ling
shov'el·ful'
·fuls'
show
showed, shown
or showed,
show'ing
show'boat'
show'case'
show'down'
show'er
show'i·ly
show'i·ness
show'man
show'off'
show'piece'
show'place'
show'room'
show'y
·i·er ·i·est
shrap'nel
shred
shred'ded or
shred
shred'ding
shrewd
shriek
shrill'ness
shril'ly
shrine
shrink
shrank or shrunk,
shrunk or
shrunk'en,
shrink'ing
shrink'age
shriv'el
·eled or ·elled
·el·ing or ·el·ling
shroud
shrub'ber·y
shrug
shrugged
shrug'ging
shuck
shud'der
shuf'fle
·fled ·fling
shuf'fle·board'
shun
shunned
shun'ning
shunt
shut
shut shut'ting
shut'down'
shut'-in'
shut'-off'
shut'out'
shut'ter

shut'tle	sig'nal·ly	si'mul·cast'	sitz bath	sky'-dive'	slen'der
·tled ·tling	sig'na·to'ry	·cast' or ·cast'ed	six'fold'	-dived' -div'ing	slen'der·ize'
shut'tle·cock'	·ries	·cast'ing	six'pen·ny	sky'-high'	·ized' ·iz'ing
shy	sig'na·ture	si'mul·ta'ne·ous	six'teenth'	sky'lark'	sleuth
shy'er or shi'er	sign'board'	sin	sixth	sky'light'	slew or slue
shy'est or shi'est	sig'net	sinned sin'ning	six'ti·eth	sky'line'	(a lot; see slue)
shies	sig·nif'i·cance	sin·cere'	six'ty	sky'rock'et	slice
shied shy'ing	sig·nif'i·cant	·cer'er ·cer'est	·ties	sky'scrap'er	sliced slic'ing
Si'a·mese'	sig·ni·fi·ca'tion	sin·cere'ly	siz'a·ble or	sky'ward	slick'er
sib'i·lance	sig'ni·fy'	sin·cer'i·ty	size'·	sky'ways'	slide
sib'i·lant	·fied' ·fy'ing	sine	size	sky'writ'ing	slid slid'ing
sib'ling	sign'post'	(ratio; see sign)	sized siz'ing	slack'en	slide rule
sick'bed'	si'lage	si'ne·cure'	siz'zle	slack'er	slight
sick'en	si'lence	sin'ew·y	·zled ·zling	slake	(frail; see
sick'le	·lenced ·lenc·ing	sin'ful	skate	slaked slak'ing	sleight)
sick'li·ness	si'lenc·er	sing	skat'ed skat'ing	sla'lom	slim
sick'ly	si'lent	sang sung	skein	slam	slim'mer
·li·er ·li·est	si'lex	sing'ing	skel'e·ton	slammed	slim'mest
sick'room'	sil'hou·ette'	singe	skep'tic	slam'ming	slimmed
side	·et'ted ·et'ting	singed	skep'ti·cal	slan'der	slim'ming
sid'ed sid'ing	sil'i·ca	singe'ing	skep'ti·cal·ly	slan'der·ous	slim'i·ness
side'arm'	sil'i·cate	sin'gle	skep'ti·cism	slang'y	slim'ness
side arms	si·li'ceous	·gled ·gling	sketch'book'	·i·er ·i·est	slim'y
side'board'	sil'i·cone'	sin'gle-breast'ed	sketch'i·ly	slant'wise'	sling
side'burns'	sil'i·co'sis	sin'gle-hand'ed	sketch'i·ness	slap	slung sling'ing
side'car'	silk'en	sin'gle-space'	sketch'y	slapped	sling'shot'
side'light'	silk'i·ness	sin'gle·ton	·i·er ·i·est	slap'ping	slink
side'line'	silk'-screen'	sin'gly	skew'er	slap'dash'	slunk slink'ing
side'long'	silk'worm'	sing'song'	ski	slap'stick'	slip
si·de're·al	silk'y	sin'gu·lar	skis or ski	slash	slipped slip'ping
side'sad'dle	·i·er ·i·est	sin'gu·lar'i·ty	skied ski'ing	slate	slip'cov'er
side'show'	sil'li·ness	sin'gu·lar·ize'	skid	slat'ed slat'ing	slip'knot'
side'slip'	sil'ly	·ized' ·iz'ing	skid'ded	slat'tern	slip'-on'
side'split'ting	·lies, ·li·er ·li·est	sin'is·ter	skid'ding	slaugh'ter	slip'page
side'step' v.	si'lo	sink	ski'er	slave	slip'per·i·ness
side'stroke'	·los, ·loed ·lo·ing	sank or sunk,	skil'let	slaved slav'ing	slip'per·y
side'swipe'	sil'ver	sunk sink'ing	skill'ful	slav'er	·i·er ·i·est
side'track'	sil'ver·fish'	sin'ner	skim	slav'er·y	slip'shod'
side'walk'	silver plate	sin'u·ous	skimmed	slav'ish·ly	slip'stream'
side'ways'	sil'ver·smith'	si'nus	skim'ming	slay	slip'-up'
side'wise'	sil'ver-tongued'	si'nus·i'tis	skimp'i·ly	slew slain	slit
sid'ing	sil'ver·ware'	sip	skimp'i·ness	slay'ing	slit slit'ting
si'dle	sil'ver·y	sipped sip'ping	skimp'y	(kill; see sleigh)	slith'er
·dled ·dling	sim'i·an	si'phon	·i·er ·i·est	slea'zi·ness	sliv'er
siege	sim'i·lar	sire	skin	slea'zy	sli'vo·vitz'
si·en'na	sim·i·lar'i·ty	sired sir'ing	skinned	·zi·er ·zi·est	slob'ber
si·er'ra	·ties	si'ren	skin'ning	sled	sloe
si·es'ta	sim'i·le'	sir'loin	skin'-deep'	sled'ded	(fruit; see slow)
sieve	si·mil'i·tude'	si·roc'co	skin'flint'	sled'ding	sloe'-eyed'
sieved siev'ing	sim'mer	·cos	skin'ni·ness	sledge	slog
sift'er	si'mon-pure'	si'sal	skin'ny	sledged	slogged
sigh	sim'per	sis'ter·hood'	·ni·er ·ni·est	sledg'ing	slog'ging
sight	sim'ple	sis'ter-in-law'	skip	sleek'ly	slo'gan
(view; see	·pler ·plest	sis'ters-in-law'	skipped	sleep	sloop
cite, site)	sim'ple-mind'ed	sis'ter·li·ness	skip'ping	slept sleep'ing	slop
sight'less	sim'ple·ton	sis'ter·ly	ski'plane'	sleep'i·ly	slopped
sight'ly	sim·plic'i·ty	sit	skip'per	sleep'i·ness	slop'ping
·li·er ·li·est	·ties	sat sit'ting	skir'mish	sleep'less	slope
sight'see'ing	sim'pli·fi·ca'tion	si·tar'	skit'tish	sleep'walk'ing	sloped slop'ing
sight'se'er	sim'pli·fi'er	sit'-down'	skul·dug'ger·y	sleep'y	slop'pi·ly
sign	sim'pli·fy'	site	or skull·	·i·er ·i·est	slop'pi·ness
(signal; see sine)	·fied' ·fy'ing	(place; see sight)	skulk	sleet	slop'py
sig'nal	sim'ply	sit'-in'	skull	sleeve'less	·pi·er ·pi·est
·naled or ·nalled	sim'u·lant	sit'ter	(head; see scull)	sleigh	slosh
·nal·ing or	sim'u·late'	sit'u·ate'	skull'cap'	(snow vehicle;	slot
·nal·ling	·lat'ed ·lat'ing	·at'ed ·at'ing	sky	see slay)	slot'ted slot'ting
sig'nal·ize'	sim·u·la'tion	sit·u·a'tion	skies	sleight	sloth'ful
·ized' ·iz'ing	sim'u·la'tor	sit'-up' or sit'up'	sky'cap'	(skill; see slight)	

slouch'y
·i·er ·i·est
slough
slov'en·li·ness
slov'en·ly
·li·er ·li·est
slow
(not fast; see
sloe)
slow'-wit'ted
sludge
sludg'y
·i·er ·i·est
slue or slew
slued or slewed
slu'ing or
slew'ing
(turn; see slew)
slug
slugged
slug'ging
slug'gard
slug'gish
sluice
sluiced sluic'ing
slum
slummed
slum'ming
slum'ber
slum'ber·ous
slump
slur
slurred
slur'ring
slush'y
·i·er ·i·est
slut'tish
sly
sli'er or sly'er
sli'est or sly'est
sly'ly or sli'ly
smack
small'-mind'ed
small'pox'
small'-scale'
smart
smash'up'
smat'ter·ing
smear'i·ness
smear'y
·i·er ·i·est
smell
smelled or smelt
smell'ing
smell'i·ness
smell'y
·i·er ·i·est
smidg'en
smile
smiled smil'ing
smirch
smirk
smite
smote, smit'ten
or smote,
smit'ing
smock'ing
smog

smog'gy
·gi·er ·gi·est
smok'a·ble or
smoke'a·ble
smoke
smoked
smok'ing
smok'er
smoke screen
smoke'stack'
smok'i·ness
smok'y
·i·er ·i·est
smol'der
smooth
smooth'bore'
smooth'-faced'
smooth'-shav'en
smooth'-spo'ken
smor'gas·bord'
smoth'er
smudge
smudged
smudg'ing
smudg'i·ness
smudg'y
·i·er ·i·est
smug
smug'ger
smug'gest
smug'gle
·gled ·gling
smut'ty
·ti·er ·ti·est
snack bar
snaf'fle
·fled ·fling
sna·fu'
snag
snagged
snag'ging
snail'-paced'
snake
snaked snak'ing
snak'y
·i·er ·i·est
snap
snapped
snap'ping
snap'drag'on
snap'pish
snap'shot'
snare
snared snar'ing
snarl'y
·i·er ·i·est
snatch
sneak'i·ly
sneak'i·ness
sneak'y
·i·er ·i·est
sneer'ing·ly
sneeze
sneezed
sneez'ing
snick'er
snif'fle
·fled ·fling

snif'ter
snip
snipped
snip'ping
snipe
sniped snip'ing
sniv'el
·eled or ·elled
·el·ing or
·el·ling
snob'ber·y
snob'bish
snoop'er·scope'
snore
snored snor'ing
snor'kel
snout
snow'ball'
snow'-blind'
snow'bound'
snow'drift'
snow'fall'
snow'flake'
snow line
snow'mo·bile'
·biled ·bil'ing
snow'plow'
snow'shoe'
·shoed'
·shoe'ing
snow'storm'
snow'-white'
snow'y
·i·er ·i·est
snub
snubbed
snub'bing
snub'-nosed'
snuff'ers
snuf'fle
·fled ·fling
snug
snug'ger
snug'gest
snug'gle
·gled ·gling
soak'ers
soap'box'
soap'suds'
soap'y
·i·er ·i·est
soar
(fly; see sore)
sob
sobbed
sob'bing
so'ber-mind'ed
so·bri'e·ty
so'bri·quet'
so'-called'
soc'cer
so'cia·bil'i·ty
so'cia·ble
so'cia·bly
so'cial
so'cial·ism
so'cial·ite'
so'cial·i·za'tion

so'cial·ize'
·ized' iz'ing
so·ci'e·tal
so·ci'e·tal·ly
so·ci'e·ty
·ties
so'ci·o·cul'tu·ral
so'ci·o·e'co·
nom'ic
so'ci·o·gram'
so'ci·o·log'i·cal
so'ci·ol'o·gist
so'ci·ol'o·gy
so'ci·o·path'
so'ci·o·po·lit'i·cal
sock'et
sock'eye'
sod
sod'ded sod'ding
so·dal'i·ty
·ties
sod'den·ness
sod'om·y
soft'ball'
soft'-boiled'
soft'-cov'er
soft'en·er
soft'heart'ed
soft'-shell'
soft'-spo'ken
soft'ware'
sog'gi·ness
sog'gy
·gi·er ·gi·est
soil
soi·ree' or ·rée'
so'journ
sol'ace
·aced ·ac·ing
so'lar
so·lar'i·um
·lar'i·a
sol'der
(metal alloy)
sol'dier
(man in an army)
sole
soled sol'ing
(bottom surface;
only; see soul)
sol'e·cism
sole'ly
sol'emn
so·lem'ni·fy'
·fied' ·fy'ing
so·lem'ni·ty
·ties
sol'em·nize'
·nized' ·niz'ing
so'le·noid'
sole'plate'
so·lic'it
so·lic'i·ta'tion
so·lic'i·tor
so·lic'i·tous
so·lic'i·tude'
sol'id
sol'i·dar'i·ty

so·lid'i·fi·ca'tion
so·lid'i·fy'
·fied' ·fy'ing
sol'id-state'
so·lil'o·quize'
·quized' ·quiz'ing
so·lil'o·quy
·quies
sol'i·taire'
sol'i·tar'y
sol'i·tude'
so'lo
·los
sol'stice
sol'u·bil'i·ty
sol'u·ble
sol'ute
so·lu'tion
solv'a·bil'i·ty
solv'a·ble
solve
solved
solv'ing
sol'ven·cy
sol'vent
som'ber
som·bre'ro
·ros
some'bod'y
some'day'
some'how'
some'one'
som'er·sault'
some'thing
some'time'
some'times'
some'what'
some'where'
som·nam'bu·late'
·lat'ed ·lat'ing
som'no·lent
so'nar
so·na'ta
sonde
song'ster
son'ic
son'-in-law'
sons'-in-law'
son'net
son'net·eer'
so·nor'i·ty
so·no'rous
soon'er
soothe
soothed
sooth'ing
sooth'say'er
soot'i·ness
soot'y
·i·er ·i·est
sop
sopped
sop'ping
soph'ism
soph'ist
so·phis'ti·cal

so·phis'ti·cate'
·cat'ed ·cat'ing
so·phis'ti·ca'tion
soph'is·try
·tries
soph'o·more'
soph'o·mor'ic
sop'o·rif'ic
so·pra'no
·nos or ·ni
sor'cer·er
sor'cer·y
·ies
sor'did
sore
(painful; see
soar)
sore'ly
sor'ghum
so·ror'i·ty
·ties
sor'rel
sor'ri·ly
sor'ri·ness
sor'row
sor'row·ful
sor'ry
·ri·er ·ri·est
sor'tie
so'-so'
sou·brette'
souf·flé'
soul
(spirit; see sole)
soul'ful
soul'-search'ing
sound'proof'
soup'çon'
source'book'
sour'dough'
sour'ness
sou'sa·phone'
souse
soused sous'ing
South Car'o·li'na
South Da·ko'ta
south'east'
south'east'er·ly
south'east'ern
south'east'ward
south'er·ly
south'ern
south'ern·er
south'ern·most'
south'ward
south'west'
south'west'er·ly
south'west'ern
south'west'ward
sou've·nir'
sov'er·eign
sov'er·eign·ty
·ties
so'vi·et
sow
sowed, sown or
sowed, sow'ing
(plant; see sew)

soy'bean'
space
  spaced spac'ing
space'craft'
  ·craft'
space'flight'
space'man
space'port'
space'ship'
space'suit'
space'walk'
spa'cious
spack'le
  ·led ·ling
spade
  spad'ed
  spad'ing
spade'work'
spa·ghet'ti
span
  spanned
  span'ning
span'dex
span'drel
span'gle
  ·gled ·gling
span'iel
span'sule
spar
  sparred
  spar'ring
spare
  spared spar'ing
spare'ribs'
spar'kle
  ·kled ·kling
spar'kler
spar'row
sparse'ly
spasm
spas·mod'ic
spas·mod'i·cal·ly
spas'tic
spa'tial
spat'ter
spat'u·la
spawn
spay
speak
  spoke spo'ken
  speak'ing
speak'er
spear'head'
spear'mint'
spe'cial
spe'cial·ist
spe'cial·ize'
  ·ized' ·iz'ing
spe'cial·ly
spe'cial·ty
  ·ties
spe'cie
  (coin money)
spe'cies
  ·cies
  (kind)
spec·i·fi'a·ble
spe·cif'ic

spe·cif'i·cal·ly
spec'i·fi·ca'tion
spec'i·fy'
  ·fied' ·fy'ing
spec'i·men
spe'cious
speck'le
  ·led ·ling
spec'ta·cle
spec'ta·cled
spec·tac'u·lar
spec'ta·tor
spec'ter
spec'tral
spec'tro·scope'
spec·tros'co·py
spec'trum
  ·tra or ·trums
spec'u·late'
  ·lat'ed ·lat'ing
spec·u·la'tion
spec'u·la·tive
spec'u·la·tor
speech'less
speed
  sped or speed'ed
  speed'ing
speed'boat'
speed'i·ly
speed'i·ness
speed·om'e·ter
speed'up'
speed'y
  ·i·er ·i·est
spe'le·ol'o·gy
spell
  spelled or spelt
  spell'ing
  (name the letters)
spell
  spelled spell'ing
  (work in place of)
spell'bind'
  ·bound' ·bind'ing
spell'down'
spe·lunk'er
spend
  spent spend'ing
spend'thrift'
sper'ma·ce'ti
spew
sphere
spher'i·cal
sphe'roid
sphinx
  sphinx'es or
  sphin'ges
spice
  spiced spic'ing
spic'i·ness
spick'-and-span'
spic'y
  ·i·er ·i·est
spi'der
spi'er
spig'ot
spike
  spiked spik'ing

spill
  spilled or spilt
  spill'ing
spin
  spun spin'ning
spin'ach
spi'nal
spin'dle
  ·dled ·dling
spin'dly
  ·dli·er dli·est
spin'drift'
spine'less
spin'et
spin'ner
spin'off'
spin'ster
spin'y
  ·i·er ·i·est
spi'ral
  ·raled or ·ralled
  ·ral·ing or
  ·ral·ling
spir'it·less
spir'it·u·al
spir'it·u·ous
spit
  spit'ted
  spit'ting
  (impale)
spit
  spit or spat
  spit'ting
  (eject saliva)
spite
  spit'ed
  spit'ing
spite'ful
spit'fire'
spit'tle
spit·toon'
spitz
splash'down'
splat'ter
splay'foot'
  ·feet'
spleen'ful
splen'did
splen'dor
sple·net'ic
splice
  spliced
  splic'ing
splin'ter
split
  split split'ting
split'-lev'el
split'-up'
splotch
splurge
  splurged
  splurg'ing
splut'ter
spoil
  spoiled or spoilt
  spoil'ing
spoil'age
spoil'sport'

spoke
  spoked spok'ing
spoke'shave'
spokes'man
spo'li·a'tion
sponge
  sponged
  spong'ing
sponge'cake'
spon'gi·ness
spon'gy
  ·gi·er ·gi·est
spon'sor
spon·ta·ne'i·ty
  ·ties
spon·ta'ne·ous
spoon'er·ism
spoon'-feed'
  -fed' -feed'ing
spoon'ful'
  ·fuls'
spo·rad'ic
sport'ing
spor'tive
sports'man
sports'wear'
spot
  spot'ted
  spot'ting
spot'-check'
spot'light'
spot'ti·ness
spot'ty
  ·ti·er ·ti·est
spout'less
sprain
sprawl
spray
spread
  spread'ing
sprig
  sprigged
  sprig'ging
spright'li·ness
spright'ly
  ·li·er ·li·est
spring
  sprang or
  sprung, sprung,
  spring'ing
spring'board'
spring'i·ness
spring'time'
spring'y
  ·i·er ·i·est
sprin'kle
  ·kled ·kling
sprin'kler
sprint'er
spritz
sprock'et
sprout
spruce
  spruc'er
  spruc'est
  spruced
  spruc'ing

spry
  spri'er or spry'er
  spri'est or
  spry'est
spry'ly
spry'ness
spume
  spumed
  spum'ing
spu·mo'ni or ·ne
spur
  spurred
  spur'ring
spu'ri·ous
spurn
spurt
sput'nik
sput'ter
spu'tum
spy
  spies
  spied spy'ing
spy'glass'
squab'ble
  ·bled ·bling
squab'bler
squad'ron
squal'id
squall
squal'or
squan'der
square
  squared
  squar'ing
square'-rigged'
squar'ish
squash'i·ness
squash'y
  ·i·er ·i·est
squat
  squat'ted
  squat'ting
squawk
squeak'i·ly
squeak'y
  ·i·er ·i·est
squeal'er
squeam'ish
squee'gee
  ·geed ·gee·ing
squeez'a·ble
squeeze
  squeezed
  squeez'ing
squelch
squig'gle
  ·gled ·gling
squint'-eyed'
squire
  squired
  squir'ing
squirm'y
  ·i·er ·i·est
squir'rel
squirt
stab
  stabbed
  stab'bing

sta·bil'i·ty
sta'bi·li·za'tion
sta'bi·lize'
  ·lized' ·liz'ing
sta'bi·liz'er
sta'ble
  ·bled ·bling
sta'bly
stac·ca'to
  ·tos
stack'up'
sta'di·um
  ·di·a or di·ums
staff
  staffs or staves
  (stick; music)
  staffs
  (people)
stage
  staged
  stag'ing
stage'craft'
stage'hand'
stage'-struck'
stag'ger
stag'nan·cy
stag'nant
stag'nate
  ·nat·ed ·nat·ing
stag·na'tion
stag'y
  ·i·er ·i·est
staid
  (sober; see stay)
stain'less
stair'case'
stake
  staked
  stak'ing
  (post; share;
  see steak)
stake'hold'er
stake'out'
sta·lac'tite
sta·lag'mite
stale
stal'er stal'est
staled stal'ing
stale'mate'
  ·mat'ed ·mat'ing
stalk'ing-horse'
stall
stal'lion
stal'wart
stam'i·na
stam'mer
stam·pede'
  ·ped'ed ·ped'ing
stance
stan'chion
stand
  stood stand'ing
stand'ard
stand'ard-bear'er
stand'ard·i·
  za'tion
stand'ard·ize'
  ·ized' ·iz'ing

stand'by'
· bys'
stand·ee'
stand'-in'
stand'off'
stand'pat'
stand'point'
stand'still'
stand'-up'
stan'za
staph'y·lo·coc'cus
· coc'ci
sta'ple
· pled ·pling
sta'pler
star
starred
star'ring
star'board
starch'i·ness
starch'y
· i·er ·i·est
star'dom
stare
stared
star'ing
star'gaze'
· gazed ·gaz'ing
stark'-nak'ed
star'let
star'light'
star'lit'
star'ry
· ri·er ·ri·est
star'-span'gled
start'er
star'tle
· tled ·tling
star·va'tion
starve
starved
starv'ing
starve'ling
stat'a·ble
state
stat'ed stat'ing
State'hood'
state'li·ness
state'ly
· li·er ·li·est
state'ment
state'room'
states'man
state'-wide'
stat'ic
stat'i·cal·ly
sta'tion
sta'tion·ar'y
(not moving)
sta'tion·er
sta'tion·er'y
(writing paper)
sta·tis'tic
sta·tis'ti·cal
sta·tis'ti·cal·ly
stat'is·ti'cian
stat'u·ar'y
· ies

stat'ue
stat'u·esque'
stat'u·ette'
stat'ure
sta'tus
sta'tus quo'
stat'ute
stat'u·to'ry
staunch
stave
staved or stove
stav'ing
stay
stayed stay'ing
(stop; see staid)
stead'fast'
stead'i·ly
stead'i·ness
stead'y
· i·er ·i·est
· ied ·y·ing
steak
(meat; see stake)
steal
stole stol'en
steal'ing
stealth'i·ly
stealth'y
· i·er ·i·est
steam'boat'
steam'er
steam'roll'er
steam'ship'
steam shovel
steam'y
· i·er ·i·est
steel mill
steel wool
steel'work'er
steel'yard'
stee'ple
stee'ple·chase'
stee'ple·jack'
steer'age·way'
steers'man
stein
stel'lar
stem
stemmed
stem'ming
stem'-wind'ing
sten'cil
· ciled or ·cilled
· cil·ing or
· cil·ling
ste·nog'ra·pher
sten'o·graph'ic
ste·nog'ra·phy
sten'o·type'
sten'o·typ'ist
sten'o·typ'y
sten·to'ri·an
step
stepped
step'ping
step'broth'er
step'child'
· chil'dren

step'daugh'ter
step'-down'
step'fa'ther
step'lad'der
step'moth'er
step'par'ent
steppe
(treeless plain)
stepped'-up'
step'ping·stone'
step'sis'ter
step'son'
step'-up'
ster'e·o'
ster'e·o·phon'ic
ster'e·op'ti·con
ster'e·o·scope'
ster'e·o·scop'ic
ster'e·o·type'
· typed' ·typ'ing
ster'e·o·typ'ic
ster'ile
ste·ril'i·ty
ster'i·li·za'tion
ster'i·lize'
· lized' ·liz'ing
ster'ling
stern'ness
stern'-wheel'er
stet
stet'ted
stet'ting
steth'o·scope'
ste've·dore'
stew'ard
stew'ard·ess
stick
stuck stick'ing
stick'i·ness
stick'le
· led ·ling
stick'ler
stick'pin'
stick-to'-it·ive·
ness
stick'y
· i·er ·i·est
stiff'en
stiff'-necked'
sti'fle
· fled ·fling
stig'ma
· mas or ·ma·ta
stig'ma·tize'
· tized' ·tiz'ing
stile
(steps; see style)
sti·let'to
· tos or ·toes
still'born'
still life
still'y
stilt'ed
stim'u·lant
stim'u·late'
· lat'ed ·lat'ing
stim'u·la'tion
stim'u·la'tive

stim'u·lus
· li'
sting
stung sting'ing
stin'gi·ly
stin'gi·ness
stin'gy
· gi·er ·gi·est
stink
stank or stunk,
stunk stink'ing
stint'ing·ly
sti'pend
sti·pen'di·ar'y
· ar'ies
stip'ple
· pled ·pling
stip'u·late'
· lat'ed ·lat'ing
stip'u·la'tion
stip'u·la'tor
stir
stirred stir'ring
stir'rup
stitch
stock·ade'
· ad'ed ·ad'ing
stock'bro'ker
stock'hold'er
stock'i·ness
stock'i·nette' or
· net'
stock'ing
stock'pile'
stock'room'
stock'-still'
stock'y
· i·er ·i·est
stock'yard'
stodg'i·ness
stodg'y
· i·er ·i·est
sto'gie or ·gy
· gies
sto'ic
sto'i·cal
sto'i·cism
stoke
stoked stok'ing
stoke'hole'
stok'er
stole
stol'en
(pp. of steal)
stol'id
stol'len
(sweet bread)
stom'ach
stom'ach·ache'
stone
stoned ston'ing
stone'-blind'
stone'cut'ter
stone'-deaf'
stone'ma'son
stone'ware'
stone'work'
ston'i·ly

ston'y
· i·er ·i·est
stoop
(porch; bend;
see stoup)
stop
stopped
stop'ping
stop'cock'
stop'gap'
stop'light'
stop'o'ver
stop'page
stop'per
stop'ple
· pled ·pling
stop'watch'
stor'a·ble
stor'age
store
stored stor'ing
store'house'
store'keep'er
store'room'
storm'bound'
storm door
storm'i·ly
storm'i·ness
storm'y
· i·er ·i·est
sto'ry
· ries
· ried ·ry·ing
sto'ry·tell'er
stoup
(basin; see
stoop)
stout'heart'ed
stove'pipe'
stow'a·way'
stra·bis'mus
strad'dle
· dled ·dling
Strad'i·var'i·us
strafe
strafed straf'ing
strag'gle
· gled ·gling
strag'gler
straight
(not bent;
see strait)
straight'a·way'
straight'edge'
straight'ened
(made straight;
see straitened)
straight'-faced'
straight'for'ward
strain'er
strait
(waterway; see
straight)
strait'ened
(limited; see
straightened)
strait'jack'et
strait'-laced'

strange
strang'er
strang'est
strange'ly
stran'ger
stran'gle
· gled ·gling
stran'gle·hold'
stran'gu·late'
· lat'ed ·lat'ing
stran'gu·la'tion
strap
strapped
strap'ping
strat'a·gem
stra·te'gic
stra·te'gi·cal·ly
strat'e·gist
strat'e·gy
· gies
strat'i·fi·ca'tion
strat'i·fy'
· fied' ·fy'ing
strat'o·sphere'
stra'tum
· ta or ·tums
stra'tus
· ti
straw'ber'ry
· ries
stray
streak'i·ness
streak'y
· i·er ·i·est
stream'line'
· lined' ·lin'ing
street'car'
strength'en
stren'u·ous
strep'to·coc'cal
strep'to·coc'cus
· coc'ci
strep'to·my'cin
stretch'er
stretch'i·ness
stretch'y
· i·er ·i·est
streu'sel
strew
strewed, strewed
or strewn,
strew'ing
stri'ate
· at·ed ·at·ing
stri·a'tion
strict'ly
stric'ture
stride
strode strid'den
strid'ing
stri'dent
strid'u·late'
· lat'ed ·lat'ing
strife
strike
struck, struck or
strick'en,
strik'ing

strike'break·er
string
  strung
  string'ing
strin'gen·cy
  ·cies
strin'gent
string'halt'
string'i·ness
string'y
  ·i·er ·i·est
strip
  stripped
  strip'ping
stripe
  striped
  strip'ing
strip'ling
strip'tease'
strive
  strove *or* strived,
  striv'en *or*
  strived, striv'ing
strobe
stroke
  stroked
  strok'ing
stroll'er
strong'-arm'
strong'box'
strong'hold'
strong'-mind'ed
strong'-willed'
stron'ti·um
strop
  stropped
  strop'ping
struc'tur·al
struc'ture
  ·tured ·tur·ing
stru'del
strug'gle
  ·gled ·gling
strum
  strummed
  strum'ming
strut
  strut'ted
  strut'ting
strych'nine
stub
  stubbed
  stub'bing
stub'ble
stub'bly
  ·bli·er ·bli·est
stub'born
stub'by
  ·bi·er ·bi·est
stuc'co
  ·coes *or* ·cos
  coed ·co·ing
stud
  stud'ded
  stud'ding
stud'book'
stu'dent
stud'horse'

stu'di·o'
  ·os'
stu'di·ous
stud'y
  ies, ·ied ·y·ing
stuff'i·ness
stuff'y
  ·i·er ·i·est
stul'ti·fy'
  ·fied' ·fy'ing
stum'ble
  ·bled ·bling
stun
  stunned
  stun'ning
stu'pe·fac'tion
stu'pe·fy'
  ·fied' ·fy'ing
stu·pen'dous
stu'pid
stu·pid'i·ty
  ·ties
stu'por
stur'di·ly
stur'di·ness
stur'dy
  ·di·er ·di·est
stur'geon
stut'ter
stut'ter·er
sty
  sties
stied sty'ing
  (*pig pen*)
sty *or* stye
  sties
  (*eyelid swelling*)
style
  styled styl'ing
  (*mode;* see stile)
styl'ish
styl'ist
sty·lis'tic
styl'i·za'tion
styl'ize
  ·ized ·iz·ing
sty'lus
  ·lus·es *or* ·li
sty'mie
  ·mied ·mie·ing
styp'tic
sty'rene
Sty'ro·foam'
su'a·ble
sua'sion
suave
suave'ly
suav'i·ty
sub'as·sem'bly
sub'base'ment
sub'com·mit'tee
sub·con'scious
sub·con'tract
sub'cul'ture
sub'cu·ta'ne·ous
sub'di·vide'
sub'di·vi'sion

sub·due'
  ·dued' ·du'ing
sub'gum'
sub'ject
sub·jec'tive
sub'jec·tiv'i·ty
sub·join'der
sub'ju·gate'
  ·gat'ed ·gat'ing
sub'ju·ga'tion
sub'ju·ga'tor
sub·junc'tive
sub'lease'
sub·let'
  ·let' ·let'ting
sub'li·mate'
  ·mat'ed ·mat'ing
sub'li·ma'tion
sub·lime'
  ·limed' ·lim'ing
sub·lim'i·nal
sub·lim'i·ty
sub·mar'gin·al
sub'ma·rine'
sub·merge'
sub·mer'gence
sub·mer'gi·ble
sub·merse'
  ·mersed'
  ·mers'ing
sub·mers'i·ble
sub·mer'sion
sub·mis'sion
sub·mis'sive
sub·mit'
  ·mit'ted
  ·mit'ting
sub·nor'mal
sub'nor·mal'i·ty
sub·or'di·nate'
  ·nat'ed ·nat'ing
sub·or'di·na'tion
sub'or·na'tion
sub'plot'
sub·poe'na
  ·naed ·na·ing
sub ro'sa
sub·scribe'
  ·scribed'
  ·scrib'ing
sub'script
sub·scrip'tion
sub'se·quent
sub·ser'vi·ent
sub·side'
  ·sid'ed ·sid'ing
sub·sid'i·ar'y
  ·ies
sub'si·di·za'tion
sub'si·dize'
  ·dized' ·diz'ing
sub'si·dy
  ·dies
sub·sist'ence
sub'soil'
sub'stance
sub·stand'ard
sub·stan'tial

sub·stan'tial·ly
sub·stan'ti·ate'
  ·at'ed ·at'ing
sub·stan'ti·a'tion
sub'stan·ti'val
sub'stan·tive
sub·sta'tion
sub'sti·tut'a·ble
sub'sti·tute'
  ·tut'ed ·tut'ing
sub'sti·tu'tion
sub·stra'tum
  ·ta *or* ·tums
sub·struc'tur·al
sub'struc'ture
sub'ter·fuge'
sub'ter·ra'ne·an
sub'ti'tle
sub'tle
  ·tler ·tlest
sub'tle·ty
  ·ties
sub'tly
sub·tract'
sub·trac'tion
sub'tra·hend'
sub·trop'i·cal
sub'urb
sub·ur'ban
sub·ur'ban·ite'
sub·ur'bi·a
sub·ver'sion
sub·ver'sive
sub·vert'
sub'way'
suc·ceed'
suc·cess'
suc·cess'ful
suc·cess'ful·ly
suc·ces'sion
suc·ces'sive
suc·ces'sor
suc·cinct'
suc'cor
  (*help;* see sucker)
suc'co·tash'
suc'cu·lence
suc'cu·lent
suc·cumb'
suck'er
  (*one that sucks;*
  see succor)
suck'le
  ·led ·ling
su'crose
suc'tion
sud'den·ly
sud'den·ness
su'dor·if'ic
suds'y
  ·i·er ·i·est
sue
  sued su'ing
suede *or* suède
su'et
suf'fer
suf'fer·ance
suf'fer·ing

suf·fice'
  ·ficed' ·fic'ing
suf·fi'cien·cy
suf·fi'cient
suf'fix
suf'fo·cate'
  ·cat'ed ·cat'ing
suf'fo·ca'tion
suf'frage
suf'fra·gette'
suf'fra·gist
suf·fuse'
  ·fused' ·fus'ing
suf·fu'sion
sug'ar
sug'ar·coat'
sug'ar-cured'
sug'ar·plum'
sug'ar·y
sug·gest'
sug·gest'i·ble
sug·ges'tion
sug·ges'tive
su'i·ci'dal
su'i·cide'
suit
  (*set;* see suite)
suit'a·bil'i·ty
suit'a·ble
suit'a·bly
suit'case'
suite
  (*rooms; furniture;*
  see suit, sweet)
suit'or
su'ki·ya'ki
sul'fa
sul'fur
sulk'y
  ·i·er ·i·est
sul'len
sul'ly
  ·lied ·ly·ing
sul'tan
sul·tan'a
sul'tri·ness
sul'try
  ·tri·er ·tri·est
sum
  summed
  sum'ming
su'mac
sum·mar'i·ly
sum'ma·rize'
  ·rized' ·riz'ing
sum'ma·ry
  ·ries
  (*brief account*)
sum·ma'tion
sum'mer·time'
sum'mer·y
  (*like summer*)
sum'mit
sum'mon
sum'mons
  ·mons·es
sump'tu·ar'y
sump'tu·ous

sun
  sunned sun'ning
sun bath
sun'bathe'
  ·bathed ·bath'ing
sun'bath'er
sun'beam'
sun'burn'
sun'burst'
sun'-cured'
sun'dae
Sun'day
sun'di·al
sun'down'
sun'-dried'
sun'dries
sun'dry
sun'glass·es
sunk'en
sun'lamp'
sun'light'
sun'lit'
sun'ni·ness
sun'ny
  ·ni·er ·ni·est
sun'proof'
sun'rise'
sun'set'
sun'shade'
sun'shine'
sun'spot'
sun'stroke'
sun'tan'
sun'-tanned'
sup
  supped sup'ping
su·perb'
su'per·car'go
  ·goes *or* ·gos
su'per·charge'
su'per·cil'i·ous
su'per·e'go
su'per·fi'cial
su'per·fi'ci·al'i·ty
  ·ties
su'per·fi'cial·ly
su'per·fine'
su'per·flu'i·ty
  ·ties
su·per'flu·ous
su'per·het'er·
  o·dyne'
su'per·hu'man
su'per·im·pose'
su'per·in·duce'
su'per·in·tend'ent
su·pe'ri·or
su·pe'ri·or'i·ty
su·per'la·tive
su'per·man'
su'per·mar'ket
su'per·nat'u·ral
su'per·nu'mer·
  ar'y
  ·ar'ies
su'per·scribe'
su'per·script'
su'per·scrip'tion

su'per·sede'
 sed'ed ·sed'ing
su'per·se'dure
su'per·sen'si·tive
su'per·ses'sion
su'per·son'ic
su'per·sti'tion
su'per·sti'tious
su'per·struc'ture
su'per·vene'
 ·vened'
 ·ven'ing
su'per·ven'tion
su'per·vise'
 ·vised' ·vis'ing
su'per·vi'sion
su'per·vi'sor
su'per·vi'so·ry
su·pine'
sup'per
sup·plant'
sup'ple
sup'ple·ly
sup'ple·ment
sup'ple·men'tal
sup'ple·men'ta·ry
sup'ple·men·
 ta'tion
sup'pli·ant
sup'pli·cant
sup'pli·cate'
 ·cat'ed ·cat'ing
sup'pli·ca'tion
sup·pli'er
sup·ply'
 ·plied' ·ply'ing
 ·plies'
sup·port'
sup·port'ive
sup·pose'
 ·posed' ·pos'ing
sup·pos'ed·ly
sup'po·si'tion
sup·pos'i·to'ry
 ·ries
sup·press'
sup·press'i·ble
sup·pres'sion
sup·pres'sor
sup'pu·rate'
 ·rat'ed ·rat'ing
sup'pu·ra'tion
su·prem'a·cist
su·prem'a·cy
su·preme'ly
sur'charge
sur'cin'gle
sure
 sur'er sur'est
sure'-foot'ed
sure'ly
sur'e·ty
 ·ties
surf
 (waves; see serf)
sur'face
 ·faced ·fac·ing
surf'board'

surf'boat'
surf'-cast'
sur'feit
surf'er
surge
 surged surg'ing
 (sudden rush;
 see serge)
sur'geon
sur'ger·y
 ·ies
sur'gi·cal
sur'gi·cal·ly
sur'li·ness
sur'ly
 ·li·er ·li·est
sur·mise'
 ·mised' ·mis'ing
sur·mount'
sur'name'
 ·named'
 ·nam'ing
sur·pass'
sur'plice
 (cloak)
sur'plus
 (excess)
sur·prise'
 ·prised' ·pris'ing
sur·pris'ing·ly
sur·re'al
sur·re'al·ism
sur·ren'der
sur'rep·ti'tious
sur'rey
 ·reys
sur'ro·gate'
 ·gat'ed ·gat'ing
sur·round'
sur'tax'
sur·veil'lance
sur'vey
 ·veys
sur·vey'or
sur·viv'a·ble
sur·viv'al
sur·vive'
 ·vived' ·viv'ing
sur·vi'vor
sus·cep'ti·bil'i·ty
sus·cep'ti·ble
sus·pect'
sus·pend'
sus·pense'
sus·pen'sion
sus·pen'so·ry
sus·pi'cion
sus·pi'cious
sus·tain'
sus·tain'a·ble
sus'te·nance
sut·tee'
su'ture
 ·tured ·tur·ing
svelte
swab
 swabbed
 swab'bing

swad'dle
 ·dled ·dling
swag'ger
swal'low
swal'low-tailed'
swa'mi
 ·mis
swamp'y
 ·i·er ·i·est
swan's'-down'
swap
 swapped
 swap'ping
sward
 (turf; see sword)
swarm
swarth'y
 ·i·er ·i·est
swash'buck'ler
swas'ti·ka
swat
 swat'ted
 swat'ting
swath n.
 (strip)
swathe v., n.
 swathed
 swath'ing
 (bandage)
sway'backed'
swear
 swore
 sworn
 swear'ing
swear'word'
sweat
 sweat or
 sweat'ed,
 sweat'ing
sweat'band'
sweat'er
sweat shirt
sweat'shop'
sweat'y
 ·i·er ·i·est
sweep
 swept sweep'ing
sweep'stakes'
 ·stakes'
sweet
 (like sugar;
 see suite)
sweet'bread'
sweet corn
sweet'en·er
sweet'heart'
sweet'meat'
swell
 swelled, swelled
 or swol'len,
 swell'ing
swel'ter
swept'back'
swerve
 swerved
 swerv'ing
swift'ness
swill

swim
 swam swum
swim'ming
swim'ming·ly
swim'suit'
swin'dle
 ·dled ·dling
swing
 swung
swing'ing
swing'by'
swin'ish
swipe
 swiped
swip'ing
swirl
switch'board'
switch'man
swiv'el
 ·eled or ·elled
 ·el·ing or ·el·ling
swol'len
sword
 (weapon; see
 sward)
sword'fish'
sword'play'
swords'man
syb'a·rite'
syc'a·more'
syc'o·phant
syc'o·phan'tic
syl·lab'ic
syl·lab'i·fi·ca'tion
syl·lab'i·fy'
 ·fied' ·fy'ing
syl'la·ble
syl'la·bus
 ·bus·es or ·bi'
syl'lo·gism
sylph
syl'van
sym·bi·ot'ic
sym'bol
 (mark; see
 cymbal)
sym·bol'ic
sym'bol·ism
sym'bol·is'tic
sym'bol·ize'
 ·ized' ·iz'ing
sym·met'ri·cal
sym'me·try
 ·tries
sym'pa·thet'ic
sym'pa·thet'i·
 cal·ly
sym'pa·thize'
 ·thized' ·thiz'ing
sym'pa·thy
 ·thies
sym·phon'ic
sym'pho·ny
 ·nies
sym·po'si·um
 ·ums or ·a
symp'tom
symp'to·mat'ic

syn'a·gogue'
syn'chro·mesh'
syn'chro·nism
syn'chro·ni·
 za'tion
syn'chro·nize'
 ·nized' ·niz'ing
syn'chro·nous
syn'chro·tron'
syn'co·pate'
 ·pat'ed ·pat'ing
syn'co·pa'tion
syn'co·pe
syn'cre·tize'
 ·tized' ·tiz'ing
syn'di·cal·ism
syn'di·cate'
 ·cat'ed ·cat'ing
syn'drome
syn·ec'do·che
syn'e·col'o·gy
syn'er·gism
syn'od
syn·od'i·cal
syn'o·nym
syn·on'y·mous
syn·on'y·my
 ·mies
syn·op'sis
 ·ses
syn·op'size
 ·sized ·siz·ing
syn·op'tic
syn·tac'tic
syn·tac'ti·cal·ly
syn'tax
syn'the·sis
 ·ses'
syn'the·size'
 ·sized ·siz'ing
syn·thet'ic
syn·thet'i·cal·ly
syph'i·lis
syph'i·lit'ic
sy·ringe'
 ·ringed' ·ring'ing
syr'up
sys'tem
sys'tem·at'ic
sys'tem·at'i·
 cal·ly
sys'tem·a·tize'
 ·tized' ·tiz'ing
sys·tem'ic

T

tab'ard
tab'by
 ·bies
tab'er·nac'le
ta'ble
 ·bled ·bling
tab'leau
 ·leaux or ·leaus
ta'ble·cloth'

ta'ble d'hôte'
ta'ble-hop'
ta'ble·land'
ta'ble·spoon'ful
 ·fuls
tab'let
ta'ble·ware'
tab'loid
ta·boo' or ·bu'
 ·boos' or ·bus'
 ·booed' or ·bued'
 ·boo'ing or
 ·bu'ing
ta'bor or ·bour
tab'o·ret
tab'u·lar
tab'u·late'
 ·lat'ed ·lat'ing
tab'u·la'tion
tab'u·la'tor
ta·chis'to·scope'
ta·chom'e·ter
tac'it
tac'i·turn'
tac'i·tur'ni·ty
tack'i·ness
tack'le
 ·led ·ling
tack'y
 ·i·er ·i·est
tact'ful
tact'ful·ly
tac'ti·cal
tac·ti'cian
tac'tics
tac'tile
tact'less
tac'tu·al
tad'pole'
taf'fe·ta
taf'fy
tag
 tagged tag'ging
tail'gate'
 ·gat'ed ·gat'ing
tail'less
tail'light'
tai'lor
tai'lor-made'
tail'piece'
tail'race'
tail'spin'
tail wind
taint'ed
tak'a·ble or take'·
take
 took tak'en
tak'ing
take'off'
take'out'
take'o'ver
talc
tal'cum
tale'bear'er
tal'ent·ed
ta'les·man
 (juryman)
tale'tell'er

tal'is·man	ta'pir	taw'dry	tech·ni'cian	tell'er	tense'ly
·mans	(animal; see	·dri·er ·dri·est	tech'ni·col'or	tell'tale'	tense'ness
(good luck charm)	taper)	taw'ny	tech·nique'	tel'pher or ·fer	ten'sile
talk'a·tive	tap'pet	·ni·er ·ni·est	tech·noc'ra·cy	Tel'star'	ten·sil'i·ty
talk'y	tap'room'	tax·a·bil'i·ty	tech·nog'ra·phy	te·mer'i·ty	ten'sion
tal'low	tap'root'	tax'a·ble	tech'no·log'i·cal	tem'per	ten'ta·cle
tal'ly	tar	tax·a'tion	tech·nol'o·gy	tem'per·a	ten'ta·tive
·lies, ·lied ·ly·ing	tarred tar'ring	tax'-de·duct'i·ble	te'di·ous	tem'per·a·ment	ten'ta·tive·ly
Tal'mud	tar'an·tel'la	tax'-ex·empt'	te'di·um	tem'per·a·	ten'ter
tal'on	ta·ran'tu·la	tax'i	tee	men'tal	ten'ter·hook'
tam'a·ble or	tar·boosh'	·is, ·ied	teed tee'ing	tem'per·ance	tenth
tame'·	tar'di·ness	·i·ing or ·y·ing	teem	tem'per·ate	ten·u'i·ty
ta·ma'le	tar'dy	tax'i·cab'	(abound; see	tem'per·a·ture	ten'u·ous
tam'bour	·di·er ·di·est	tax'i·der'mist	team)	tem'pered	ten'ure
tam·bou·rine'	tare	tax'i·der'my	teen'-age'	tem'pest	(time held;
tame	tared tar'ing	tax'i·me'ter	teen'-ag'er	tem·pes'tu·ous	see tenor)
tamed tam'ing	(weight deduction;	tax'i·way'	tee'ter-tot'ter	tem'plate or ·plet	ten·u'ri·al
tam'-o'-shan'ter	see tear)	tax·on'o·my	teethe	tem'ple	te'pee or tee'·
tamp'er n.	tar'get	tax'pay'er	teethed teeth'ing	tem'po	tep'id
tam'per v.	tar'iff	tea bag	tee·to'tal·er	·pos or ·pi	te·pid'i·ty
tam'per·er	tar'nish	teach	tee·to'tal·ism	tem'po·ral	te·qui'la
tam'pi·on	ta'ro	taught teach'ing	Tef'lon	tem'po·rar'i·ly	ter'cen·te'nar·y
tam'pon	·ros	teach'a·ble	teg'u·ment	tem'po·rar'i·ness	·ies
tan	(plant)	teach'er	tel·au'to·graph'	tem'po·rar'y	ter'gi·ver·sate'
tan'ner tan'nest	tar'ot	teach'-in'	tel'e·cast'	tem'po·rize'	·sat'ed ·sat'ing
tanned tan'ning	(playing cards)	tea'cup'	·cast' or ·cast'ed	·rized' ·riz'ing	ter'gi·ver·sa'tor
tan'dem	tar·pau'lin	tea'cup·ful'	·cast'ing	temp·ta'tion	ter'ma·gant
tan'ge·lo'	tar'pon	·fuls'	tel'e·com·mu'·	tempt'er	ter'mi·na·ble
·los'	tar'ra·gon'	teak	ni·ca'tion	tempt'ing	ter'mi·na·bly
tan'gent	tar'ry	tea'ket'tle	tel'e·course'	tempt'ress	ter'mi·nal
tan·gen'tial	·ried ·ry·ing	team	tel'e·gen'ic	tem'pus fu'git	ter'mi·nate'
tan'ge·rine'	tar'tan	(group; see teem)	tel'e·gram'	ten'a·ble	·nat'ed ·nat'ing
tan'gi·ble	tar'tar	team'mate'	tel'e·graph'	te·na'cious	ter'mi·na'tion
tan'gi·bly	tar'tar sauce	team'ster	te·leg'ra·pher	te·nac'i·ty	ter'mi·nol'o·gy
tan'gle	tart'ly	team'work'	tel'e·graph'ic	ten'an·cy	ter'mi·nus
·gled ·gling	task force	tea'pot'	te·leg'ra·phy	·cies	·ni' or ·nus·es
tan'go	task'mas'ter	tear	tel'e·ki·ne'sis	ten'ant	ter'mite
·gos	tas'sel	tore torn	tel'e·me'ter	ten'ant·a·ble	ter'na·ry
tang'y	·seled or ·selled	tear'ing	te·le·o·log'i·cal	ten'ant·ry	terp'si·cho·re'an
·i·er ·i·est	·sel·ing or	(rip; see tare)	te·le·ol'o·gy	·ries	ter'race
tank'age	·sel·ling	tear	tel'e·path'ic	tend'en·cy	·raced ·rac·ing
tank'ard	taste	teared tear'ing	te·lep'a·thy	·cies	ter'ra cot'ta
tank'er	tast'ed tast'ing	(eye fluid;	tel'e·phone'	ten'der	ter'ra fir'ma
tank'ful	taste'ful	see tier)	·phoned'	(soft; offer)	ter·rain'
·fuls	taste'ful·ly	tear'drop'	·phon'ing	tend'er	Ter'ra·my'cin
tan'ner·y	taste'less	tear'ful	tel'e·phon'ic	(one who tends)	ter'ra·pin
·ies	tast'er	tear gas	te·leph'o·ny	ten'der·foot'	ter·rar'i·um
tan'nic	tast'i·ness	tear'i·ness	tel'e·pho'to	·foots' or ·feet'	·i·ums or ·i·a
tan'nin	tast'y	tea'room'	tel'e·pho'to·graph'	ten'der·heart'ed	ter·raz'zo
tan'ta·lize'	·i·er ·i·est	tear'y	tel'e·pho·tog'ra·	ten'der·ize'	ter·res'tri·al
·lized' ·liz'ing	tat'ter·de·mal'ion	·i·er ·i·est	phy	·ized' ·iz'ing	ter'ri·ble
tan'ta·mount'	tat'tered	tease	tel'e·play'	ten'der·iz'er	ter'ri·bly
tan'trum	tat'ter·sall'	teased teas'ing	tel'e·prompt'er	ten'der·loin'	ter'ri·er
tap	tat'tle	tea'sel	tel'e·ran'	ten'don	ter·rif'ic
tapped	·tled ·tling	·seled or ·selled	tel'e·scope'	ten'dril	ter·rif'i·cal·ly
tap'ping	tat'tle·tale'	·sel·ing or	·scoped' ·scop'ing	ten'e·ment	ter'ri·fy'
tape	·toos'	·sel·ling	tel'e·scop'ic	ten'et	·fied' ·fy'ing
taped tap'ing	·tooed' ·too'ing	tea'spoon·ful'	tel'e·thon'	ten'fold'	ter'ri·to'ri·al
tape deck	taught	·fuls'	Tel'e·type'	Ten'nes·see'	ter'ri·to'ri·al'i·ty
ta'per	(trained; see taut)	teat	·typed' ·typ'ing	ten'nis	ter'ri·to'ry
(candle; decrease;	taunt	tea'-ta·ble	tel'e·type'writ'er	ten'on	·ries
see tapir)	taupe	tea'tast'er	tel'e·view'er	ten'or	ter'ror
tape'-re·cord'	taut	tea'time'	tel'e·vise'	(tendency; singer;	ter'ror·ism
tape recorder	(tight; see taught)	tech'nic	·vised' ·vis'ing	see tenure)	ter'ror·ist
tap'es·try	tau·tol'o·gy	tech'ni·cal	tel'e·vi'sion	ten'pins'	ter'ror·is'tic
·tries	·gies	tech'ni·cal'i·ty	tell	tense	ter'ror·i·za'tion
tape'worm'	tav'ern	·ties	told tell'ing	tens'er tens'est	ter'ror·ize'
tap'i·o'ca		tech'ni·cal·ly	tell'a·ble	tensed tens'ing	·ized' ·iz'ing

ter'ry
terse
 ters'er ters'est
terse'ness
ter'ti·ar'y
tes'sel·late'
 ·lat'ed ·lat'ing
tes'sel·la'tion
test'a·ble
tes'ta·ment
tes'ta·men'ta·ry
tes'tate
tes'ta·tor
tes'ti·cle
tes'ti·fi'er
tes'ti·fy'
 ·fied' ·fy'ing
tes'ti·ly
tes'ti·mo'ni·al
tes'ti·mo'ny
 ·nies
tes'ti·ness
tes'ty
 ·ti·er ·ti·est
tet'a·nus
tête'-à-tête'
teth'er
tet'ra·cy'cline
tet'ra·he'dron
 ·drons or ·dra
te·tral'o·gy
 ·gies
Tex'as
text'book'
tex'tile
tex'tu·al
tex'tur·al
tex'ture
than conj., prep.
thank'ful
thank'less
thanks'giv'ing
that
 those
thatch
thaw
the'a·ter or ·tre
the·at'ri·cal
theft
their
 (poss. form of
 they; see there,
 they're)
theirs
 (belonging to
 them; see there's)
the'ism
the·is'tic
the·mat'ic
theme
them·selves'
then
 (at that time)
thence'forth'
the·oc'ra·cy
 ·cies
the·od'o·lite'
the'o·lo'gian

the'o·log'i·cal
the·ol'o·gy
 ·gies
the'o·rem
the'o·ret'i·cal
the'o·ret'i·cal·ly
the'o·re·ti'cian
the'o·rize'
 ·rized' ·riz'ing
the'o·ry
 ·ries
the·os'o·phy
 ·phies
ther'a·peu'tic
ther'a·pist
ther'a·py
 ·pies
there
 (at that place;
 see their, they're)
there'a·bouts'
there·af'ter
there·at'
there·by'
there·for'
 (for it)
there'fore'
 (for that reason)
there·in'
there·in·af'ter
there·in'to
there's
 (there is; see
 theirs)
there'to·fore'
there·up·on'
there·with'
ther'mal
therm'i·on'ics
ther'mo·dy·
 nam'ics
ther·mo·e·lec'·
 tric'i·ty
ther·mom'e·ter
ther'mo·nu'cle·ar
ther'mo·pile'
ther'mo·plas'tic
ther'mos
ther'mo·stat'
ther'mo·stat'i·
 cal·ly
the·sau'rus
 ·ri or ·rus·es
the'sis
 ·ses
they'd
they'll
they're
 (they are; see
 their, there)
they've
thi'a·mine'
thick'en·ing
thick'et
thick'ness
thick'set'
thick'-skinned'
thick'-wit'ted

thief n.
thieves
thieve v.
 thieved thiev'ing
thiev'er·y
 ·ies
thiev'ish·ly
thigh'bone'
thim'ble·ful'
 ·fuls'
thin
 thin'ner
 thin'nest
thinned
thin'ning
thing
think
 thought
 think'ing
thin'-skinned'
third'-class'
third'-rate'
thirst'i·ly
thirst'i·ness
thirst'y
 ·i·er ·i·est
thir'teenth'
thir'ti·eth
thir'ty
 ·ties
this
 these
this'tle·down'
thith'er·to'
thole
thong
tho·rac'ic
tho'rax
 ·rax·es or ·ra·ces
tho'ri·um
thorn'y
 ·i·er ·i·est
thor'ough
thor'ough·bred'
thor'ough·fare'
thor'ough·go'ing
though
thought
thought'ful·ly
thought'ful·ness
thought'less
thou'sand·fold'
thrall'dom
thrash
thread'bare'
thread'i·ness
thread'y
 ·i·er ·i·est
threat'en
3'-D'
three'-deck'er
three'-di·men'·
 sion·al
three'fold'
three'-ply'
three'-quar'ter
three'score'
three'some

three'-way'
three'-wheel'er
thren'o·dy
 ·dies
thresh'er
thresh'old
threw
 (pt. of throw;
 see through)
thrice
thrift'i·ly
thrift'i·ness
thrift'y
 ·i·er ·i·est
thrill'er
thrive
 thrived or throve,
 thrived or
 thriv'en,
 thriv'ing
throat'y
 ·i·er ·i·est
throb
throbbed
throb'bing
throe
 (pang; see throw)
throm·bo'sis
throne
throned
thron'ing
throng
throt'tle
 ·tled ·tling
through
 (from end to end
 of; see threw)
through·out'
throw
 threw thrown
 throw'ing
 (hurl; see throe)
throw'a·way'
throw'back'
thrum
thrummed
thrum'ming
thrust
 thrust thrust'ing
thud
 thud'ded
 thud'ding
thumb'nail'
thumb'screw'
thumb'stall'
thumb'tack'
thump
thun'der·bolt'
thun'der·cloud'
thun'der·head'
thun'der·ous
thun'der·show'er
thun'der·squall'
thun'der·storm'
thun'der·struck'
Thurs'day
thus
thwack

thwart
thyme
 (herb; see time)
thy'mus
thy'roid
ti·ar'a
tib'i·a
tic
 (muscle spasm)
tick
 (click; insect)
tick'er tape
tick'et
tick'ing
tick'le
 ·led ·ling
tick'ler
tick'lish
tick'-tack-toe'
tick'y tack'y
tid'al
tid'bit'
tide'land'
tide'mark'
tide'wa'ter
ti'di·ly
ti'di·ness
ti'dings
ti'dy
 ·di·er ·di·est
 ·died ·dy·ing
tie
 tied ty'ing
tie'back'
tie'-dye'
 -dyed' -dye'ing
tie'-in'
tie'pin'
tier
 (row; see tear)
ti'er
 (one that ties;
 see tie)
tie tack
tie'-up'
ti'ger
ti'ger's eye
tight'en
tight'fist'ed
tight'fit'ting
tight'knit'
tight'-lipped'
tight'rope'
ti'gress
tile
 tiled til'ing
till'a·ble
tilt'-top'
tim'bale
tim'ber
 (wood)
tim'ber·line'
tim'bre
 (quality of sound)
time
 timed tim'ing
 (duration;
 see thyme)

time'card'
time clock
time'-con·sum'ing
time'-hon'ored
time'keep'er
time'less
time'li·ness
time'ly
 ·li·er ·li·est
time'out'
time'piece'
tim'er
time'sav'ing
time'ta·ble
time'-test'ed
time'worn'
time zone
ti·mid'i·ty
tim'id·ly
tim'or·ous
tim'o·thy
tim'pa·ni
tim'pa·nist
tin
 tinned tin'ning
tinc'ture
 ·tured ·tur·ing
tin'der·box'
tin'foil'
tinge
 tinged, tinge'ing
 or ting'ing
tin'gle
 ·gled ·gling
tin'gly
 ·gli·er ·gli·est
ti'ni·ness
tin'ker
tin'ker·er
tin'kle
 ·kled ·kling
tin'ni·ness
tin·ni'tus
tin'ny
 ·ni·er ·ni·est
tin'-plate'
tin'sel
 ·seled or ·selled
 ·sel·ing or
 ·sel·ling
tin'smith'
tin'tin·nab'u·
 la'tion
tin'type'
tin'ware'
ti'ny
 ·ni·er ·ni·est
tip
 tipped tip'ping
tip'-off'
tip'pet
tip'ple
 ·pled ·pling
tip'sy
 ·si·er ·si·est
tip'toe'
 ·toed' ·toe'ing

tip'top'
ti'rade
tire
  tired tir'ing
  (*weary; rubber
  hoop;* see tier)
tired'ly
tire'less
tire'some
tis'sue
ti'tan
tithe
  tithed tith'ing
ti'tian
tit'il·late'
 ·lat'ed ·lat'ing
tit'il·la'tion
ti'tle
 ·tled ·tling
ti'tle·hold'er
tit'mouse'
 ·mice'
tit'ter
tit'u·lar
toad'stool'
toad'y
 ·ies, ·ied ·y·ing
toad'y·ism
to'-and-fro'
toast'mas'ter
to·bac'co
 ·cos
to·bac'co·nist
to·bog'gan
toc·ca'ta
toc'sin
 (*alarm;* see toxin)
to·day'
tod'dle
 ·dled ·dling
tod'dler
tod'dy
 ·dies
to-do'
toe
 toed toe'ing
toe'-dance'
 -danced'
 -danc'ing
toe'hold'
toe'-in'
toe'less
toe'nail'
tof'fee *or* ·fy
to'ga
 gas *or* gae
to·geth'er
tog'gle
 ·gled ·gling
toi'let
toi'let·ry
 ·ries
toil'some
toil'worn'
to'ken
tole
tol'er·a·ble
tol'er·a·bly

tol'er·ance
tol'er·ant
tol'er·ate'
 ·at'ed ·at'ing
tol'er·a'tion
tol'er·a'tor
toll'booth'
toll bridge
toll call
toll'gate'
toll'keep'er
toll road
tom'a·hawk'
to·ma'to
 ·toes
tom'boy'
tomb'stone'
tom'cat'
tom'fool'er·y
to·mor'row
tom'-tom'
ton
 (*weight;* see tun)
ton'al
to·nal'i·ty
 ·ties
tone
 toned ton'ing
tone'-deaf'
tongs
tongue
 tongued
 tongu'ing
tongue'-lash'ing
tongue'-tie'
 -tied' -ty'ing
ton'ic
to·night'
ton'nage
ton·neau'
 ·neaus' *or*
 ·neaux'
ton'sil
ton·sil·lec'to·my
 ·mies
ton'sil·li'tis
ton·so'ri·al
ton'sure
 ·sured ·sur·ing
ton'tine
tool'mak'er
tooth
 teeth
tooth'ache'
tooth'brush'
tooth'paste'
tooth'pick'
tooth'some
top
 topped top'ping
to'paz
top'coat'
top'-drawer'
top'-dress'ing
top'-flight'
top'-heav'y
to'pi·ar'y
top'ic

top'i·cal
top'knot'
top'less
top'-lev'el
top'most'
top'-notch'
to·pog'ra·pher
top'o·graph'i·cal
to·pog'ra·phy
 (*surface features;*
 see typography)
top'ple
 ·pled ·pling
top'sail
top'-se'cret
top'soil'
top'sy-tur'vy
toque
to'rah *or* ·ra
torch'bear'er
torch·ier' *or*
 ·iere'
torch'light'
tor'e·a·dor'
tor'ment
tor·men'tor
tor·na'do
 ·does *or* ·dos
tor·pe'do
 ·does
tor'pid
tor·pid'i·ty
tor'por
torque
tor'rent
tor·ren'tial
tor'rid
tor·rid'i·ty
tor'sion
tor'so
 ·sos *or* ·si
tort
 (*wrongful act*)
torte
 (*cake*)
tor·til'la
tor'toise
tor·to'ni
tor'tu·ous
 (*winding*)
tor'ture
 ·tured ·tur·ing
tor'tur·ous
 (*agonizing*)
toss'up'
to'tal
 ·taled *or* ·talled
 ·tal·ing *or*
 ·tal·ling
to·tal'i·tar'i·an
to·tal'i·ty
to'tal·i·za'tor
to'tal·ly
tote
tot'ed tot'ing
to'tem
tot'ter
touch'back'

touch'down'
tou·ché'
touch'hole'
touch'i·ly
touch'i·ness
touch'stone'
touch'-type'
touch'-typ'ist
touch'y
 ·i·er ·i·est
tough'en
tough'-mind'ed
tou·pee'
tour' de force'
 tours' de force'
tour'ism
tour'ist
tour'ma·line
tour'na·ment
tour'ney
 ·neys
tour'ni·quet
tou'sle
 ·sled ·sling
tow'age
to·ward'
tow'boat'
tow'el
 ·eled *or* ·elled
 ·el·ing *or* ·el·ling
tow'er·ing
tow'head'
tow'line'
town'ship
towns'peo'ple
tow'path'
tow'rope'
tox·e'mi·a
tox'ic
tox'i·cant
tox'i·col'o·gy
tox'in
 (*poison;* see
 tocsin)
trace
 traced trac'ing
trace'a·ble
trac'er
trac'er·y
 ·ies
tra·che'a
 ·ae' *or* ·as
tra·cho'ma
track
 (*trace*)
tract
 (*land; leaflet*)
trac'ta·ble
trac'tile
trac'tion
trac'tor
trad'a·ble *or*
 trade'a·ble
trade
 trad'ed trad'ing
trade'-in'
trade'-last'
trade'mark'

trade name
trades'man
trades'peo'ple
trade wind
tra·di'tion
tra·di'tion·al
tra·duce'
 ·duced' ·duc'ing
traf'fic
 ·ficked ·fick·ing
traf'fick·er
tra·ge'di·an
tra·ge'di·enne'
trag'e·dy
 ·dies
trag'ic
trag'i·cal·ly
trag'i·com'e·dy
 ·dies
trag'i·com'ic
trail'blaz'er
trail'er
train·ee'
train'man
trait
trai'tor
trai'tor·ous
trai'tress
tra·jec'to·ry
 ·ries
tram'mel
 ·meled *or* ·melled
 ·mel·ing *or*
 ·mel·ling
tram'ple
 ·pled ·pling
tram'po·line'
trance
tranced
tranc'ing
tran'quil
 ·quil·er *or* ·quil·ler
 ·quil·est *or*
 ·quil·lest
tran'quil·ize'
 or ·quil·lize'
 ·ized' *or* ·lized'
 ·iz'ing *or* ·liz'ing
tran'quil·iz'er *or*
 ·quil·liz'er
tran·quil'li·ty *or*
 ·quil'i·ty
tran'quil·ly
trans·act'
trans·ac'tion
trans·ac'tor
trans'at·lan'tic
trans·ceiv'er
tran·scend'
tran·scend'ent
tran'scen·den'tal
trans·con·ti·
 nen'tal
tran·scribe'
 ·scribed' ·scrib'in
tran'script'
tran·scrip'tion
tran'sept

trans·fer'
 ·ferred'
 ·fer'ring
trans·fer'a·ble
 or ·fer'ra·ble
trans·fer'al
 or ·fer'ral
trans'fer·ee'
trans·fer'ence
trans·fer'rer
trans·fig'u·ra'tion
trans·fig'ure
trans·fix'
trans·form'
trans'for·ma'tion
trans·form'er
trans·fuse'
trans·fus'i·ble
trans·fu'sion
trans·gress'
trans·gres'sion
trans·gres'sor
tran'sient
tran·sis'tor
tran·sis'tor·ize'
 ·ized' ·iz'ing
trans'it
tran·si'tion
tran·si'tion·al·ly
tran'si·tive
tran'si·to'ry
trans·lat'a·ble
trans·late'
 ·lat'ed ·lat'ing
trans·la'tion
trans·la'tor
trans·lit'er·ate'
 ·at'ed ·at'ing
trans·lit'er·a'tion
trans·lu'cence
trans·lu'cent
trans·mi'grate
 ·grat·ed ·grat·ing
trans'mi·gra'tion
trans·mis'si·ble
trans·mis'sion
trans·mit'
 ·mit'ted
 ·mit'ting
trans·mit'tal
trans·mit'tance
trans·mit'ter
trans·mut'a·ble
trans'mu·ta'tion
trans·mute'
 ·mut'ed
 ·mut'ing
trans'o·ce·an'ic
tran'som
tran·son'ic
trans·pa·cif'ic
trans·par'en·cy
 ·cies
trans·par'ent
tran·spire'
 ·spired' ·spir'ing
trans·plant'
tran·spon'der

trans·port'
trans·por·ta'tion
trans·pos'a·ble
trans·pose'
 ·posed' ·pos'ing
trans'po·si'tion
trans·sex'u·al
trans·ship'
 ·shipped'
 ·ship'ping
tran'stage'
tran'sub·stan'ti·
 ate'
trans·val'ue
trans·ver'sal
trans·verse'
trans·verse'ly
trans·ves'tite
trap
 trapped trap'ping
trap'door'
tra·peze'
tra·pe'zi·um
trap'e·zoid'
trap'per
trap'pings
trap'shoot'ing
trash'i·ness
trash'y
 ·i·er ·i·est
trau'ma
 ·mas or ·ma·ta
trau·mat'ic
trau·mat'i·cal·ly
trav'ail
 (hard work)
trav'el
 ·eled or ·elled
 ·el·ing or ·el·ling
 (journey)
trav'el·er or
 ·el·ler
trav'e·logue' or
 ·log'
trav·ers'a·ble
trav·ers'al
trav·erse'
 ·ersed' ·ers'ing
trav'er·tine'
trav'es·ty
 ·ties
 ·tied ·ty·ing
trawl'er
tray
 (holder; see
 trey)
treach'er·ous
treach'er·y
 ·ies
trea'cle
tread
 trod, trod'den or
 trod, tread'ing
trea'dle
 ·dled ·dling
tread'mill'
trea'son
trea'son·ous

treas'ure
 ·ured ·ur·ing
treas'ur·er
treas'ure-trove'
treas'ur·y
 ·ies
treat'a·ble
trea'tise
treat'ment
trea'ty
 ·ties
tre'ble
 ·bled ·bling
tree
treed
tree'ing
tree'nail'
tree'top'
tre'foil
treil'lage
trek
trekked
trek'king
trel'lis
trem'ble
 ·bled ·bling
tre·men'dous
trem'o·lo'
 ·los'
trem'or
trem'u·lous
trench'ant
trench mouth
trend
trep'i·da'tion
tres'pass
tress'es
tres'tle
tres'tle·work'
trey
 (a three; see
 tray)
tri'a·ble
tri'ad
tri'al
tri·an'gle
tri·an'gu·lar
tri·an'gu·late'
 ·lat'ed ·lat'ing
tri·an'gu·la'tion
trib'al
trib'al·ism
tribes'man
trib'u·la'tion
tri·bu'nal
trib'une
trib'u·tar'y
 ·ies
trib'ute
tri'cen·ten'ni·al
tri'ceps
 ·cep·ses or ·ceps
tri·chi'na
 ·nae
trich'i·no'sis
tri·chot'o·my
tri'chro·mat'ic
trick'er·y

trick'i·ly
trick'i·ness
trick'le
 ·led ·ling
trick'ster
trick'y
 ·i·er ·i·est
tri'col'or
tri'cot
tri'cy·cle
tri'di·men'sion·al
tri·en'ni·al
tri·en'ni·um
 ·ums or ·a
tri'er
tri'fle
 ·fled ·fling
tri·fo'cal
trig'ger
trig'o·no·met'ric
trig'o·nom'e·try
tri·lat'er·al
tri·lin'gual
tril'lion
tril'li·um
tril'o·gy
 ·gies
trim
trimmed
trim'ming
trim'mer
trim'mest
tri·mes'ter
tri·month'ly
trin'i·ty
 ·ties
trin'ket
tri·no'mi·al
tri'o
 ·os
trip
 tripped trip'ping
tri·par'tite
trip'ham'mer
tri'ple
 ·pled ·pling
tri'ple-space'
tri'plet
trip'li·cate'
 ·cat'ed ·cat'ing
tri'ply
tri'pod
trip'per
trip'tych
tri·sect'
triste
tris·tesse'
trite
 trit'er trit'est
trite'ly
trit'u·rate'
 ·rat'ed ·rat'ing
tri'umph
tri·um'phal
tri·um'phant
tri·um'vi·rate
triv'et
triv'i·a

triv'i·al
triv'i·al'i·ty
 ·ties
triv'i·al·ly
tri·week'ly
 ·lies
tro'che
 (lozenge)
tro'chee
 (poetic meter)
trod'den
trof'fer
trog'lo·dyte'
troll
trol'ley
 ·leys
 ·leyed ·ley·ing
trol'lop
trom·bone'
trom·bon'ist
troop
 (of soldiers;
 see troupe)
troop'ship'
tro'phy
 ·phies
trop'ic
trop'i·cal
tro'pism
trop'o·sphere'
trot
 trot'ted trot'ting
trot'ter
trou'ba·dour'
trou'ble
 ·bled ·bling
trou'ble·mak'er
trou'ble-shoot'er
trou'ble·some
trough
trounce
 trounced
 trounc'ing
troupe
 trouped
 troup'ing
 (of actors;
 see troop)
troup'er
trou'sers
trous'seau
 ·seaux or ·seaus
trout
trow'el
 ·eled or ·elled
 ·el·ing or ·el·ling
tru'an·cy
 ·cies
tru'ant
truce
truck farm
truck'le
 ·led ·ling
truc'u·lence
truc'u·lent
trudge
 trudged
 trudg'ing

true
 tru'er tru'est
 trued tru'ing
 or true'ing
true'-blue'
true'-life'
true'love'
truf'fle
tru'ism
tru'ly
trump
trumped'-up'
trump'er·y
 ·ies
trum'pet
trum'pet·er
trun'cate
 ·cat·ed ·cat·ing
trun·ca'tion
trun'cheon
trun'dle
 ·dled ·dling
trunk line
trun'nion
truss
trus·tee'
 ·teed' ·tee'ing
 (manager; see
 trusty)
trus·tee'ship'
trust'ful
trust'ful·ly
trust'i·ness
trust'wor'thy
trust'y
 ·ies, ·i·er ·i·est
 (relied upon;
 see trustee)
truth'ful
truth'ful·ly
truth'ful·ness
try
 tries
 tried try'ing
try'out'
tryst
tset'se fly
T'-shirt'
tsim'mes
tsor'is
T square
tsu·na'mi
tub
 tubbed tub'bing
tu'ba
 ·bas or ·bae
tub'ba·ble
tub'bi·ness
tub'by
 ·bi·er ·bi·est
tube
 tubed tub'ing
tu'ber
tu'ber·cle
tu·ber'cu·lar
tu·ber'cu·lin
tu·ber'cu·lo'sis
tu·ber'cu·lous

tube'rose'
 (plant)
tu'ber·ous
 (having tubers)
tu'bu·lar
tuck'er
Tu'dor
Tues'day
tuft'ed
tug
 tugged tug'ging
tug'boat'
tu·i'tion
tu·la·re'mi·a
tu'lip
tulle
tum'ble
 ·bled ·bling
tum'ble·down'
tum'bler
tum'ble·weed'
tum'brel
tu'me·fy'
 ·fied' ·fy'ing
tu·mes'cence
tu·mes'cent
tu'mid
tu'mor
tu'mor·ous
tu'mult
tu·mul'tu·ous
tun
 tunned tun'ning
 (cask; see ton)
tun'a·ble
 or tune'·
tun'dra
tune
 tuned tun'ing
tune'ful
tune'less
tun'er
tune'up' or
 tune'-up'
tung'sten
tu'nic
tun'nel
 ·neled or ·nelled
 ·nel·ing or
 ·nel·ling
tu'pe·lo'
 ·los'
tur'ban
 (headdress)
tur'bid
tur'bine
 (engine)
tur'bo·jet'
tur'bo·prop'
tur'bu·lence
tur'bu·lent
tu·reen'
turf
tur'gid
tur'key
tur'mer·ic
tur'moil
turn'a·bout'

turn'a·round'
turn'buck·le
turn'coat'
turn'down'
tur'nip
turn'key'
 ·keys'
turn'off'
turn'out'
turn'o·ver
turn'pike'
turn'stile'
turn'ta·ble
tur'pen·tine'
tur'pi·tude'
tur'quoise
tur'ret
tur'tle
tur'tle·dove'
tur'tle·neck'
tus'sle
 ·sled ·sling
tu'te·lage
tu'te·lar'y
tu'tor
tu·to'ri·al
tut'ti-frut'ti
tu'tu
tux·e'do
 ·dos
TV
 TVs or TV's
twang
tweak
tweed
tweed'y
 ·i·er ·i·est
tweeze
 tweezed
 tweez'ing
tweez'ers
twelfth
twelve'fold'
twen'ti·eth
twen'ty
 ·ties
twen'ty·fold'
twice'-told'
twid'dle
 ·dled ·dling
twi'light'
twi'lit
twill
twine
 twined twin'ing
twin'-en'gined
twinge
 twinged
 twing'ing
twi'-night'
twin'kle
 ·kled ·kling
twirl'er
twist'er
twitch
twit'ter
two'-by-four'
two'-edged'

two'-faced'
two'-fist'ed
two'fold'
two'-hand'ed
two'-leg'ged
two'-piece'
two'-ply'
two'-sid'ed
two'some
two'-way'
ty·coon'
tym·pan'ic
typ'a·ble or type'·
typ'al
type
 typed typ'ing
type'bar'
type'cast'
 ·cast' ·cast'ing
 (in acting)
type'-cast'
 -cast' -cast'ing
 (in printing)
type'script'
type'set'
 ·set' ·set'ting
type'set'ter
type'write'
 ·wrote' ·writ'ten
 ·writ'ing
type'writ'er
ty'phoid
ty·phoon'
ty'phus
typ'i·cal
typ'i·cal·ly
typ'i·fy'
 ·fied' ·fy'ing
typ'ist
ty·pog'ra·pher
ty·po·graph'i·cal
ty·pog'ra·phy
 (setting of type;
 see topography)
ty·pol'o·gy
ty·ran'ni·cal
tyr'an·nize'
 ·nized' ·niz'ing
tyr'an·nous
tyr'an·ny
 ·nies
ty'rant
ty'ro
 ·ros
ty'ro·thri'cin

U

u·biq'ui·tous
u·biq'ui·ty
ud'der
 (milk gland;
 see utter)
u·fol'o·gist
ug'li
 (fruit)

ug'li·ness
ug'ly
 ·li·er ·li·est
u'kase
u'ku·le'le
ul'cer
ul'cer·ate'
 ·at'ed ·at'ing
ul'cer·ous
ul'ster
ul·te'ri·or
ul'ti·mate
ul'ti·mate·ly
ul'ti·ma'tum
 ·tums or ·ta
ul'tra
ul'tra·con·serv'·
 a·tive
ul'tra·ism
ul'tra·ma·rine'
ul'tra·mi'cro·
 scope'
ul'tra·mod'ern
ul'tra·na'tion·al·
 ism
ul'tra·son'ic
ul'tra·sound'
ul'tra·vi'o·let
ul'u·late'
 ·lat'ed ·lat'ing
um'ber
um·bil'i·cal
um·bil'i·cus
 ·ci·
um'bra
 ·brae or ·bras
um'brage
um·bra'geous
um·brel'la
u'mi·ak' or ·ack'
um'laut
um'pire
 ·pired ·pir·ing
un·a'ble
un·a'bridged'
un·ac·count'a·ble
un·ac·count'ed-
 for'
un·ac·cus'tomed
un·af·fect'ed
un'-A·mer'i·can
u'na·nim'i·ty
u·nan'i·mous
un·apt'
un·armed'
un·as·sum'ing
un·at·tached'
un·a·void'a·ble
un·a·ware'
un·a·wares'
un·bal'anced
un·bear'a·ble
un·beat'a·ble
un·be·com'ing
un·be·known'
un·be·lief'
un·be·liev'a·ble
un·be·liev'er

un·bend'
 bent' or bend'ed,
 bend'ing
un·bi'ased or
 ·assed
un·bid'den
un·bolt'ed
un·bos'om
un·bound'ed
un·bri'dled
un·bro'ken
un·buck'le
un·but'ton
un·called'-for'
un·can'ni·ly
un·can'ni·ness
un·can'ny
un·cared'-for'
un·cer·e·mo'ni·
 ous
un·cer'tain
un·cer'tain·ty
 ·ties
un·char'i·ta·ble
un·chris'tian
un'ci·al
un·civ'il
un·civ'i·lized'
un·clad'
un·class'i·fied
un'cle
un·clothe'
 ·clothed' or
 ·clad', ·cloth'ing
un·com'fort·a·ble
un·com'pro·
 mis'ing
un'con·cerned'
un'con·di'tion·al
un'con·scion·a·
 ble
un'con·scious
un'con·sti·
 tu'tion·al
un·cou'ple
un·couth'
unc'tion
unc'tu·ous
un·daunt'ed
un·de·cid'ed
un·de·ni'a·ble
un·der·age'
un'der·age
un'der·brush'
un'der·buy'
 ·bought' ·buy'ing
un'der·car'riage
un'der·class'man
un'der·clothes'
un'der·coat'
un·der·cov'er
un'der·cur'rent
un'der·cut'
un·der·de·vel'·
 oped
un'der·do'
 ·did' ·done'
 ·do'ing

un'der·dog'
un'der·em·ployed'
un·der·es'ti·mate'
un'der·fired'
un'der·foot'
un'der·gar'ment
un'der·glaze'
un'der·go'
 ·went' ·gone'
 ·go'ing
un'der·grad'u·ate
un'der·ground'
un'der·growth'
un'der·hand'
un'der·hand'ed
un'der·hung'
un'der·lay'
 ·laid' ·lay'ing
un'der·lie'
 ·lay' ·lain'
 ·ly'ing
un'der·line'
un'der·ling
un'der·lin'ing
un·der·mine'
un'der·neath'
un'der·nour'ish
un'der·pants'
un'der·part'
un'der·pass'
un'der·pay'
 ·paid' ·pay'ing
un'der·pin'ning
un'der·play'
un'der·priv'i·
 leged
un'der·proof'
un'der·rate'
un'der·score'
un'der·sea'
un'der·sec're·
 tar'y
 ·ies
un'der·sell'
 ·sold' ·sell'ing
un'der·sexed'
un'der·shirt'
un'der·shot'
un'der·side'
un'der·signed'
un'der·sized'
un'der·staffed'
un'der·stand'
 ·stood' ·stand'ing
un'der·stand'a·
 ble
un·der·stand'a·bly
un'der·state'ment
un'der·stud'y
 ·ies, ·ied ·y·ing
un'der·take'
 ·took' ·tak'en
 ·tak'ing
un'der·tak'ing
un'der·tone'
un'der·tow'
un'der·val'ue
un'der·wa'ter

un'der·wear'
un'der·weight'
un'der·world'
un'der·write'
 ·wrote' ·writ'ten
 ·writ'ing
un·do'
 ·did' ·done'
 ·do'ing
un·doubt'ed·ly
un·dress'
un·due'
un'du·lant
un'du·late'
 ·lat'ed ·lat'ing
un·du'ly
un·dy'ing
un·earned'
un·earth'
un·eas'y
un'em·ploy'a·ble
un·e'qualed
 or ·qualled
un'e·quiv'o·cal·ly
un·err'ing
un·es·sen'tial
un·e'ven·ness
un·e'vent'ful·ly
un'ex·cep'tion·
 a·ble
un'ex·cep'tion·al
un'ex·pect'ed
un·faith'ful
un'fa·mil'iar
un·feel'ing
un·feigned'
un'for·get'ta·ble
un·for'tu·nate
un·found'ed
un·freeze'
 ·froze' ·froz'en
 ·freez'ing
un·frock'
un·furl'
un·gain'ly
un·god'ly
un'guent
un'gu·late
un·hand'
un·heard'-of'
un·hoped'-for'
un·horse'
 ·horsed'
 ·hors'ing
u'ni·cam'er·al
u'ni·cel'lu·lar
u'ni·corn'
u'ni·cy'cle
u'ni·fi'a·ble
u'ni·fi·ca'tion
u'ni·form'
u'ni·form'i·ty
u'ni·fy'
 ·fied' ·fy'ing
u'ni·lat'er·al
un·im·peach'a·ble
un'in·hib'it·ed

un·in·tel'li·gi·ble
un'ion
un'ion·ize'
·ized' ·iz'ing
u·nique'
u'ni·son
u'nit
U·ni·tar'i·an
u·nite'
·nit'ed ·nit'ing
u'nit·ize'
·ized' ·iz'ing
u'ni·ty
·ties
u'ni·ver'sal
u'ni·ver·sal'i·ty
u'ni·ver'sal·ly
u'ni·verse'
u'ni·ver'si·ty
·ties
un·kempt'
un·known'
un·lade'
·lad'ed, ·lad'ed
or ·lad'en,
·lad'ing
un·law'ful
un·less'
un·let'tered
un·like'li·hood'
un·like'ly
un·lim'it·ed
un·list'ed
un·looked'-for'
un·loose'
·loosed' ·loos'ing
un·loos'en
un·luck'y
un·make'
·made' ·mak'ing
un·man'
·manned'
·man'ning
un·men'tion·a·ble
un·mer'ci·ful
un'mis·tak'a·ble
un·mit'i·gat'ed
un·nat'u·ral
un·nec'es·sar'y
un·nerve'
·nerved'
·nerv'ing
un·num'bered
un·oc'cu·pied'
un·or'gan·ized'
un·paid'-for'
un·par'al·leled'
un·pleas'ant
un·prec'e·dent'ed
un·prej'u·diced
un·prin'ci·pled
un·qual'i·fied
un·ques'tion·a·
bly
un'quote'
un·rav'el
·eled or ·elled
·el·ing or ·el·ling

un're·al·is'tic
un·rea'son·a·ble
un're·gen'er·ate
un·rest'
un·rul'i·ness
un·rul'y
·i·er ·i·est
un·said'
un·sa'vor·i·ness
un·sa'vor·y
un·scathed'
un·scru'pu·lous
un·seat'
un·seem'ly
un·shod'
un·sight'li·ness
un·sight'ly
un·speak'a·ble
un·stead'y
un·strung'
un·sung'
un·tan'gle
·gled ·gling
un·ten'a·ble
un·think'a·ble
un·thought'-of'
un·ti'dy
un·tie'
·tied' ·ty'ing or
·tie'ing
un·til'
un·time'ly
un·told'
un·touch'a·ble
un·to'ward
un·truth'ful
un·tu'tored
un·u'su·al
un·veil'ing
un·want'ed
(not wanted;
see unwonted)
un·war'y
un·whole'some
un·wield'i·ness
un·wield'y
un·wit'ting·ly
un·wont'ed
(not usual;
see unwanted)
un·wor'thy
un·writ'ten
un·zip'
up'-and-com'ing
up'-and-down'
up'beat'
up·braid'
up'bring'ing
up'coun'try
up·date'
up·end'
up'grade'
up·heav'al
up'hill'
up·hold'
·held' ·hold'ing
up·hol'ster
up·hol'ster·er

up·hol'ster·y
·ies
up'keep'
up'land
up·lift'
up·on'
up'per-case'
·cased' -cas'ing
up'per·class'man
up'per·most'
up'right'
up'ris'ing
up'roar'
up·roar'i·ous
up·root'
up·set'
·set' ·set'ting
up'shot'
up'stage'
·staged'
·stag'ing
up'stairs'
up·stand'ing
up'start'
up'state'
up'stream'
up'swept'
up'swing'
up'take'
up'thrust'
up'-tight' or
up'tight'
up'-to-date'
up'town'
up·turn'
up'ward
u·ra'ni·um
ur'ban
(of the city)
ur·bane'
(socially poised)
ur'ban·ism
ur·ban'i·ty
·ties
ur'ban·i·za'tion
ur'ban·ize'
·ized' ·iz'ing
ur'chin
u·re'mi·a
u·re'ter
u·re'thra
·thrae or ·thras
urge
urged urg'ing
ur'gen·cy
·cies
ur'gent
u'ri·nal
u'ri·nal'y·sis
·ses
u'ri·nar'y
u'ri·nate'
·nat'ed ·nat'ing
u'rine
urn
u'ro·log'i·cal
u·rol'o·gy
u·ros'co·py

us'a·ble or use'·
us'age
use
used us'ing
use'ful
use'less
us'er
ush'er
ush'er·ette'
u'su·al
u'su·al·ly
u'su·fruct'
u'su·rer
u·su'ri·ous
u·surp'
u'sur·pa'tion
u'su·ry
·ries
U'tah
u·ten'sil
u'ter·ine
u'ter·us
·ter·i'
u·til'i·tar'i·an
u·til'i·ty
·ties
u'ti·liz'a·ble
u'ti·li·za'tion
u'ti·lize'
·lized' ·liz'ing
ut'most'
u·to'pi·a
ut'ter
(speak; see udder)
ut'ter·ance
U'-turn'
ux·o'ri·ous

V

va'can·cy
·cies
va'cant
va'cate
·cat·ed ·cat·ing
va·ca'tion
vac'ci·nate'
·nat'ed ·nat'ing
vac'ci·na'tion
vac·cine'
vac'il·late'
·lat'ed ·lat'ing
vac'il·la'tion
vac'il·la'tor
va·cu'i·ty
·ties
vac'u·ous
vac'u·um
·ums or ·a
vag'a·bond'
va·gar'y
·ies
va·gi'na
·nas or ·nae
va'gran·cy
·cies

va'grant
vague
vague'ly
vain
(futile; conceited;
see vane, vein)
vain'glo'ri·ous
vain'glo'ry
val'ance
(drapery; see
valence)
vale
(valley; see veil)
val'e·dic'tion
val'e·dic·to'ri·an
val'e·dic'to·ry
·ries
va'lence
(term in chemis-
try; see valance)
val'en·tine'
val'et
val'iant
val'id
val'i·date'
·dat'ed ·dat'ing
val'i·da'tion
va·lid'i·ty
va·lise'
val'ley
·leys
val'or
val'or·i·za'tion
val'u·a·ble
val'u·a'tion
val'ue
·ued ·u·ing
val'ue·less
valve
val'vu·lar
vam'pire
van'dal
van'dal·ism
van'dal·ize'
·ized' ·iz'ing
Van·dyke'
vane
(blade; see
vain, vein)
van'guard'
va·nil'la
van'ish
van'i·ty
·ties
van'quish
van'tage
vap'id
va'por
va'por·i·za'tion
va'por·ize'
·ized' ·iz'ing
va'por·iz'er
va'por·ous
va·que'ro
·ros
var'i·a·ble
var'i·a·bly
var'i·ance

var'i·ant
var'i·a'tion
var'i·col'ored
var'i·cose'
var'ied
var'i·e·gate'
·gat'ed ·gat'ing
var'i·e·ga'tion
va·ri'e·tal
va·ri'e·ty
·ties
var'i·o'rum
var'i·ous
var'nish
var'si·ty
·ties
var'y
·ied ·y·ing
(change; see very)
vas'cu·lar
vas de'fe·rens'
vas'e·line'
vas'sal
(a subordinate;
see vessel)
vast'ness
vat
vat'ted vat'ting
vat'-dyed'
vaude'ville
vault'ing
vaunt
vec'tor
vec·to'ri·al
V'-E' Day
veer
veg'e·ta·ble
veg'e·tar'i·an
veg'e·tate'
·tat'ed ·tat'ing
veg'e·ta'tion
veg'e·ta'tive
ve'he·mence
ve'he·ment
ve'hi·cle
ve·hic'u·lar
veil
(screen; see vale)
vein
(blood vessel;
streak; see
vain, vane)
Vel'cro
vel'lum
ve·loc'i·pede'
ve·loc'i·ty
·ties
ve·lour' or ·lours'
·lours'
ve·lure'
vel'vet
vel'vet·een'
vel'vet·y
ve'nal
(corrupt; see
venial)
ve·nal'i·ty
·ties

vend·ee'
ven·det'ta
ven'dor *or*
vend'er
ve·neer'
ven'er·a·ble
ven'er·ate'
· at'ed · at'ing
ven'er·a'tion
ve·ne're·al
Ve·ne'tian
venge'ance
venge'ful
ve'ni·al
(*pardonable;* see
venal)
ven'i·son
ven'om·ous
ve'nous
ven'ti·late'
· lat'ed · lat'ing
ven'ti·la'tion
ven'ti·la'tor
ven'tri·cle
ven·tril'o·quist
ven'ture
· tured · tur·ing
ven'ture·some
ven'tur·ous
ven'ue
ve·ra'cious
(*truthful;* see
voracious)
ve·rac'i·ty
ve·ran'da *or* ·dah
ver'bal
ver'bal·i·za'tion
ver'bal·ize'
· ized' · iz'ing
ver'bal·ly
ver·ba'tim
ver·be'na
ver'bi·age
ver·bose'
ver·bos'i·ty
ver'dant
ver'dict
ver'di·gris'
ver'dure
verge
verged verg'ing
ver'i·fi'a·ble
ver'i·fi·ca'tion
ver'i·fy'
· fied' · fy'ing
ver'i·ly
ver'i·si·mil'i·tude'
ver'i·ta·ble
ver'i·ta·bly
ver'i·ty
· ties
ver'mi·cel'li
ver'mi·cide'
ver·mic'u·lar
ver·mic'u·lite'
ver'mi·form'
ver'mi·fuge'
ver·mil'ion

ver'min
Ver·mont'
ver·mouth'
ver·nac'u·lar
ver'nal
ver'ni·er
ver'sa·tile
ver'sa·tile·ly
ver'sa·til'i·ty
versed
ver'si·fi·ca'tion
ver'si·fy'
· fied' · fy'ing
ver'sion
ver'sus
ver'te·bra
· brae' *or* · bras
ver'te·bral
ver'te·brate
ver'tex
· tex·es *or* · ti·ces'
ver'ti·cal
ver·tig'i·nous
ver'ti·go'
verve
ver'y
· i · er · i · est
(*complete; exceed-*
ingly; see vary)
ves'i·cant
ves'i·cate'
· cat'ed · cat'ing
ves'i·cle
ves'per
ves'sel
(*container; ship;*
see vassal)
ves'tal
ves'ti·bule
ves'tige
ves·tig'i·al
vest'ment
vest'-pock'et
ves'try
· tries
vet'er·an
vet'er·i·nar'i·an
vet'er·i·nar'y
· ies
ve'to
· toes
· toed · to·ing
vex·a'tion
vex·a'tious
vi'a·bil'i·ty
vi'a·ble
vi'a·duct'
vi'al
(*bottle;* see
vile, viol)
vi'and
vi'brant
vi'bra·phone'
vi'brate
· brat·ed · brat·ing
vi·bra'tion
vi·bra'to
· tos

vi'bra'tor
vi'bra·to'ry
vic'ar
vic'ar·age
vi·car'i·al
vi·car'i·ous
vice
(*evil conduct;*
flaw; see vise)
vice'-chair'man
vice'-chan'cel·lor
vice'-con'sul
vice'-pres'i·dent
vice'roy
vi'ce ver'sa
vi'chy·ssoise'
vi·cin'i·ty
· ties
vi'cious
vi·cis'si·tude'
vic'tim
vic'tim·ize'
· ized' · iz'ing
vic'tor
vic·to'ri·a
vic·to'ri·ous
vic'to·ry
· ries
vi·cu'ña
vid'e·o'
vid'i·con
vie
vied vy'ing
view'point'
vig'il
vig'i·lance
vig'i·lant
vig'i·lan'te
vi·gnette'
vig'or
vig'or·ous
vile
(*evil; offensive;*
see vial, viol)
vile'ly
vil'i·fi·ca'tion
vil'i·fy'
· fied' · fy'ing
vil'la
vil'lage
vil'lag·er
vil'lain
(*scoundrel;*
see villein)
vil'lain·ous
vil'lain·y
· ies
vil'lein
(*serf;* see
villain)
vin'ai·grette'
vin'ci·ble
vin'di·cate'
· cat'ed · cat'ing
vin'di·ca'tion
vin'di·ca'tive
vin'di·ca'tor
vin·dic'tive

vin'e·gar
vin'er·y
· ies
vine'yard
vin'i·cul'ture
vi'nous
vin'tage
vint'ner
vi'nyl
vi'ol
(*instrument;*
see vial, vile)
vi·o'la
vi'o·la·ble
vi'o·late'
· lat'ed · lat'ing
vi'o·la'tion
vi'o·la'tor
vi'o·lence
vi'o·lent
vi'o·let
vi'o·lin'
vi'o·lin'ist
vi'o·lon·cel'lo
· los
VIP *or* V.I.P.
vi'per
vi·ra'go
· goes *or* · gos
vi'ral
vir'gin
vir'gin·al
Vir·gin'ia
vir·gin'i·ty
vir'gule
vir'ile
vi·ril'i·ty
vi·rol'o·gy
vir·tu'
vir'tu·al
vir'tu·al·ly
vir'tue
vir·tu·os'i·ty
vir·tu·o'so
· sos *or* · si
vir'tu·ous
vir'u·lence
vir'u·lent
vi'rus
vi'sa
vis'age
vis'-à-vis'
vis'cer·a
vis'cid
vis·cos'i·ty
vis'count
vis'count·ess
vis'cous
vise
vised vis'ing
(*clamp;* see vice)
vis'i·bil'i·ty
vis'i·ble
vis'i·bly
vi'sion
vi'sion·ar'y
· ies
vis'it

vis'it·ant
vis·it·a'tion
vis'i·tor
vis'or
vis'ta
vis'u·al
vis'u·al·ize'
· ized' · iz'ing
vi'ta
· tae
vi'tal
vi·tal'i·ty
· ties
vi'tal·ize'
· ized' · iz'ing
vi'ta·min
vi'ti·a·ble
vi'ti·ate'
· at'ed · at'ing
vit'i·a'tion
vi'ti·a'tor
vit're·ous
vit'ri·fy'
· fied' · fy'ing
vit'ri·ol
vit'ri·ol'ic
vi·tu'per·ate'
· at'ed · at'ing
vi·tu'per·a'tion
vi·va'cious
vi·vac'i·ty
viv'id
viv'i·fy'
· fied' · fy'ing
vi·vip'a·rous
viv'i·sect'
viv'i·sec'tion
vix'en
V'-J' Day
V'-neck'
vo·cab'u·lar'y
· ies
vo'cal cord
vo'cal·ist
vo'cal·ize'
· ized' · iz'ing
vo·ca'tion
vo·cif'er·ate'
· at'ed · at'ing
vo·cif'er·ous
vo'cod'er
vod'ka
vogue
voice'less
voice'print'
void'a·ble
voi·là'
voile
vol'a·tile
vol'a·til'i·ty
vol·can'ic
vol·ca'no
· noes *or* ·nos
vol'i·tant
vo·li'tion
vol'ley
· leys
· leyed · ley·ing

vol'ley·ball'
volt'age
vol·ta'ic
vol·tam'e·ter
volt'me'ter
vol·u·bil'i·ty
vol'u·ble
vol'u·bly
vol'ume
vo·lu'mi·nous
vol·un·tar'i·ly
vol'un·tar'y
vol'un·teer'
vo·lup'tu·ar'y
· ies
vo·lup'tu·ous
vo·lute'
vo·lu'tion
vom'it
voo'doo
· doos
vo·ra'cious
(*greedy;* see
veracious)
vo·rac'i·ty
vor'tex
· tex·es *or* ·ti·ces'
vot'a·ble *or* vote'·
vo'ta·ry
· ries
vote
vot'ed vot'ing
vo'tive
vouch'er
vouch·safe'
· safed' · saf'ing
vow
vow'el
voy'age
· aged · ag·ing
voy'ag·er
vo·yeur'
vroom
vul'can·i·za'tion
vul'can·ize'
· ized' · iz'ing
vul'gar
vul·gar'i·an
vul'gar·ism
vul·gar'i·ty
· ties
vul'gar·ize'
· ized' · iz'ing
vul'ner·a·bil'i·ty
vul'ner·a·ble
vul'ner·a·bly
vul'ture
vul'tur·ous
vul'va
vy'ing

W

wad
wad'ded
wad'ding

wad'dle
· dled · dling
wade
wad'ed
wad'ing
wa'fer
waf'fle
waft
wag
wagged
wag'ging
wage
waged wag'ing
wa'ger
wag'ger·y
· ies
wag'gish
wag'gle
· gled · gling
Wag·ne'ri·an
wag'on·load'
wa·hi'ne
waif
wail
(cry; see wale, whale)
wain'scot
· scot·ed or
· scot·ted
· scot·ing or
· scot·ting
wain'wright'
waist'band'
waist'coat
waist'-high'
waist'line'
wait'er
wait'ress
waive
waived waiv'ing
(give up; see wave)
waiv'er
(a relinquishing; see waver)
wake
woke or waked,
waked or wok'·
en, wak'ing
wake'ful
wak'en
wale
waled wal'ing
(ridge; see wail, whale)
walk
walk'a·way'
walk'ie-talk'ie
walk'-in'
walk'-on'
walk'out'
walk'-through'
walk'-up'
walk'way'
wall'board'
wall'et
wall'eyed'
wall'flow'er

wal'lop·ing
wal'low
wall'pa·per
wall'-to-wall'
wal'nut
wal'rus
waltz
wam'pum
wan
wan'ner
wan'nest
wan'der
(stray; see wonder)
wan'der·lust'
wane
waned wan'ing
wan'gle
· gled · gling
want'ing
wan'ton
(unjustifiable; see won ton)
war
warred war'ring
war'ble
· bled · bling
ward
war'den
ward'robe'
ward'room'
ware'house'
· housed
· hous'ing
war'fare'
war'head'
war'i·ly
war'i·ness
war'like'
war'lock'
warm'blood'ed
warmed'-o'ver
warm'heart'ed
war'mon·ger
warmth
warm'-up'
warn'ing
warp
war'path'
warped
war'plane'
war'rant
war'ran·ty
· ties
war'ren
war'ri·or
war'ship'
wart
war'time'
war'y
· i·er · i·est
wash'a·ble
wash'-and-wear'
wash'board'
wash'bowl'
wash'cloth'
washed'-out'
washed'-up'

wash'er
wash'er·wom'an
Wash'ing·ton
wash'out'
wash'room'
wash'stand'
wash'tub'
was'n't
wasp'ish
was'sail
wast'age
waste
wast'ed
wast'ing
waste'bas'ket
waste'ful
waste'land'
waste'pa'per
waste pipe
wast'rel
watch'band'
watch'case'
watch'dog'
watch fire
watch'ful
watch'mak'er
watch'man
watch'tow'er
watch'word'
wa'ter·borne'
wa'ter·col'or
wa'ter-cooled'
water cooler
wa'ter·course'
wa'ter·craft'
wa'ter·cress'
wa'ter·cy'cle
wa'tered
wa'ter·fall'
wa'ter·front'
water glass
water hole
wa'ter·i·ness
wa'ter·less
wa'ter·line'
wa'ter·logged'
wa'ter·mark'
wa'ter·mel'on
water pipe
water power
wa'ter·proof'
wa'ter-re·pel'lent
wa'ter-re·sist'ant
wa'ter·scape'
wa'ter·shed'
wa'ter·side'
wa'ter·ski'
-skied' -ski'ing
wa'ter-ski'er
water skis
wa'ter·soak'
wa'ter-sol'u·ble
wa'ter·spout'
wa'ter·tight'
water tower
wa'ter·way'
water wheel
water wings

wa'ter·works'
wa'ter·worn'
wa'ter·y
watt'age
watt'-hour'
wat'tle
· tled · tling
watt'me'ter
wave
waved wav'ing
(curving motion; see waive)
wave'length'
wav'er
(one that waves; see waiver)
wa'ver
(falter; see waiver)
wav'i·ness
wav'y
· i·er · i·est
wax
wax'en
wax'i·ness
wax'work'
wax'y
· i·er · i·est
way
(route; manner; see weigh, whey)
way'bill'
way'far·er
way'far'ing
way'lay'
laid' lay'ing
way'side'
way'ward
weak'en
weak'-kneed'
weak'ling
weak'ly
· li·er · li·est
weak'-mind'ed
weak'ness
weal
(ridge; welfare; see wheal, wheel)
wealth'i·ness
wealth'y
· i·er · i·est
wean
weap'on
wear
wore worn
wear'ing
wear'a·ble
wea'ri·ly
wea'ri·ness
wea'ri·some
wea'ry
· ri·er · ri·est
· ried · ry·ing
wea'sel
weath'er
(atmospheric conditions; see whether)

weath'er-beat'en
weath'er-bound'
weath'er·cock'
weath'er·man'
weath'er·proof'
weath'er·strip'
· stripped'
· strip'ping
weather vane
weave
wove, wov'en or
wove, weav'ing
(interlace)
weave
weaved
weav'ing
(move in and out as in traffic)
weav'er
web
webbed
web'bing
web'foot'
· feet'
web'-foot'ed
wed
wed'ded,
wed'ded or
wed, wed'ding
we'd
wedge
wedged
wedg'ing
Wedg'wood'
wed'lock
Wednes'day
wee
we'er we'est
weed'i·ness
week'day'
week'end' or
week'-end'
week'ly
· lies
weep
wept weep'ing
weep'i·ness
weep'y
· i·er · i·est
wee'vil
weigh
weighed
weigh'ing
(measure weight of; see way, whey)
weight'i·ness
weight'less
weight'y
· i·er · i·est
weir
(dam; see we're)
weird
wel'come
· comed · com·ing
weld'er
wel'fare'
well'-ad·vised'
well'-ap·point'ed

well'-bal'anced
well'-be·haved'
well'-be'ing
well'-be·loved'
well'born'
well'-bred'
well'-chos'en
well'-con·tent'
well'-dis·posed'
well'do'ing
well'-done'
well'-fa'vored
well'-fed'
well'-found'ed
well'-groomed'
well'-ground'ed
well'-han'dled
well'head'
well'-in·formed'
well'-in·ten'·
tioned
well'-knit'
well'-known'
well'-made'
well'-man'nered
well'-mean'ing
well'-meant'
well'-nigh'
well'-off'
well'-or'dered
well'-pre·served'
well'-read'
well'-round'ed
well'-spo'ken
well'spring'
well'-thought'-of'
well'-timed'
well'-to-do'
well'-turned'
well'-wish'er
well'-worn'
we'll
Welsh rabbit
or rarebit
welt'er
welt'er·weight'
we're
(we are; see weir)
weren't
were'wolf'
· wolves'
wes'kit
west'er·ly
· lies
west'ern·er
west'ern·ize'
· ized' · iz'ing
west'-north'west'
west'-south'west'
West Vir·gin'ia
west'ward
wet
wet'ter wet'test
wet or wet'ted
wet'ting
(moistened; see whet)

wet'back'
wet'ta·ble
whale
  whaled whal'ing
  (fishlike mammal;
  see wail, wale)
whale'boat'
whale'bone'
whal'er
wharf
  wharves or
  wharfs
wharf'age
wharf'in·ger
what·ev'er
what'not'
what'so·ev'er
wheal
  (pimple; see
  weal, wheel)
wheat
whee'dle
  dled ·dling
wheel
  (disk for turning;
  see weal, wheal)
wheel'bar'row
wheel'base'
wheel'chair'
wheel'house'
wheel'wright'
wheeze
  wheezed
  wheez'ing
wheez'y
  ·i·er ·i·est
whelp
when
whence
when·ev'er
where
where'a·bouts'
where·as'
where·by'
where'fore'
where·in'
where·of'
where·up·on'
wher·ev'er
where·with'
where'with·al'
wher'ry
  ·ries, ·ried ·ry·ing
whet
  whet'ted
  whet'ting
  (sharpen; see wet)
wheth'er
  (if; see weather)
whet'stone'
whey
  (thin part of milk;
  see way, weigh)
which·ev'er
whiff
while
  whiled whil'ing
  (time; see wile)

whim
whim'per
whim'si·cal
whim'sy
  ·sies
whine
  whined whin'ing
  (cry; see wine)
whin'i·ness
whin'ny
  ·nies
  ·nied ·ny·ing
  (neigh)
whin'y
  ·i·er ·i·est
  (complaining)
whip
  whipped
  whip'ping
whip'cord'
whip'lash'
whip'pet
whip'poor·will'
whip'saw'
whip'stitch'
whip'stock'
whir or whirr
  whirred
  whir'ring
whirl
whirl'pool'
whirl'wind'
whisk broom
whisk'er
whis'key
  ·keys or ·kies
whis'per
whis'tle
  ·tled ·tling
whis'tler
whit
  (bit; see wit)
white
  whit'ed whit'ing
white'cap'
white'-col'lar
white'-haired'
white'-hot'
white'-liv'ered
whit'en·er
white'ness
whit'en·ing
white room
white'wall'
white'wash'
whith'er
  (where; see
  wither)
whit'ing
whit'tle
  ·tled ·tling
whiz or whizz
  whizzed
whiz'zing
who·ev'er
whole'heart'ed
whole'sale'
  ·saled ·sal'ing

whole'sal'er
whole'some
whole'-wheat'
whol'ly
  (completely; see
  holey, holy)
whom·ev'er
whom'so·ev'er
whoop'ee
whop'per
whore
whorl
who's
  (who is; who has)
whose
  (poss. of who)
who'so·ev'er
why
wick'ed
wick'er·work'
wick'et
wide'-an'gle
wide'-a·wake'
wide'-eyed'
wid'en
wide'-o'pen
wide'spread'
wid'get
wid'ow
wid'ow·er
width
wield
wield'y
  ·i·er ·i·est
wie'ner
wife
  wives
wife'ly
wig'gle
  ·gled ·gling
wig'gly
wig'let
wig'wam
wild'cat'
  ·cat'ted ·cat'ting
wil'de·beest'
wil'der·ness
wild'-eyed'
wild'fire'
wild'life'
wile
  wiled wil'ing
  (trick; see while)
wil'i·ness
will'ful or wil'·
  will'ing·ness
will'-o'-the-wisp'
wil'low·y
will'pow'er
wil'ly-nil'ly
wi'ly
  ·li·er ·li·est
wim'ple
  ·pled ·pling
win
  won win'ning
wince
  winced winc'ing

wind
  wound wind'ing
wind'blown'
wind'-borne'
wind'break'er
wind'burn'
wind'fall'
wind'i·ness
wind'lass
  (winch)
wind'less
  (without wind)
wind'mill'
win'dow
win'dow·pane'
win'dow·shop'
wind'row'
wind'shield'
wind'storm'
wind'-swept'
wind'up'
wind'ward
wind'y
  ·i·er ·i·est
wine
  wined win'ing
  (drink; see whine)
wine cellar
wine'-col'ored
wine'glass'
wine'grow'er
wine press
win'er·y
  ·ies
Wine'sap'
wine'skin'
wing chair
wing'span'
wing'spread'
win'ner
win'now
win'some
win'ter
win'ter·green'
win'ter·ize'
  ·ized' ·iz'ing
win'ter·time'
win'try
  ·tri·er ·tri·est
wipe
  wiped wip'ing
wire
  wired wir'ing
wire'draw'
  ·drew' ·drawn'
  ·draw'ing
wire'hair'
wire'-haired'
wire'less
Wire'pho'to
wire'pull'er
wire'tap'
wire'work'
wir'i·ness
wir'y
  ·i·er ·i·est
Wis·con'sin
wis'dom

wise
  wis'er wis'est
wise'ly
wish'bone'
wish'ful
wisp
wist'ful
wit
  (sense; see whit)
witch'craft'
witch'er·y
  ·ies
with·draw'
  ·drew' ·drawn'
with·draw'al
with'er
  (wilt; see whither)
with·hold'
  ·held' ·hold'ing
with·in'
with·out'
with·stand'
  ·stood'
  ·stand'ing
wit'less
wit'ness
wit'ti·cism
wit'ti·ness
wit'ty
  ·ti·er ·ti·est
wiz'ard
wiz'ard·ry
wiz'ened
wob'ble
  ·bled ·bling
woe'be·gone'
woe'ful
wolf
  wolves
wolf'hound'
wom'an
wom'en
wom'an·hood'
wom'an·kind'
wom'an·li·ness
wom'an·ly
womb
wom'en·folk'
won'der
  (marvel; see
  wander)
won'der·ful
won'der·land'
won'der·work'
won'der·work'er
won'drous
wont
  (accustomed)
won't
  (will not)
won' ton'
  (food; see wanton)
wood'carv'ing
wood'chuck'
wood'craft'
wood'cut'
wood'ed

wood'land'
wood'peck'er
wood'pile'
wood pulp
wood'shed'
woods'man
wood'sy
  ·si·er ·si·est
wood'wind'
wood'work'
wood'y
  ·i·er ·i·est
woof'er
wool'en
wool'gath'er·ing
wool'grow'er
wool'lies or
wool'ies
wool'li·ness or
wool'i·ness
wool'ly or
wool'y
  ·li·er or ·i·er
  ·li·est or ·i·est
Worces'ter·shire'
word'age
word'book'
word'i·ly
word'i·ness
word'less
word'-of-mouth'
word'play'
wood'y
  ·i·er ·i·est
work
  worked or
  wrought
  work'ing
work'a·ble
work'a·day'
work'bench'
work'book'
work'day'
work'house'
work'ing·man'
work'load'
work'man·like'
work'man·ship'
work'out'
work'room'
work'shop'
work'ta·ble
work'week'
world'li·ness
world'ly
  ·li·er ·li·est
world'ly-wise'
world'-shak'ing
world'-wea'ry
world'wide'
worm'-eat'en
worm gear
worm'hole'
worm'i·ness
worm wheel
worm'wood'
worm'y
  ·i·er ·i·est

worn'-out'
wor'ri·er
wor'ri·ment
wor'ri·some
wor'ry
·ries
·ried ·ry·ing
wor'ry·wart'
worse
wors'en
wor'ship
·shiped *or*
·shipped
·ship·ing *or*
·ship·ping
wor'ship·er *or*
wor'ship·per
wor'ship·ful
worst
wor'sted
wor'thi·ly
wor'thi·ness
worth'less
worth'while'
wor'thy
·thi·er ·thi·est
would
would'-be'
wound
wrack
wraith
wran'gle
·gled ·gling
wran'gler
wrap
wrapped *or*
wrapt
wrap'ping
(*cover;* see rap)
wrap'a·round'
wrap'per
wrath'ful
wreak
(*inflict;* see reek)

wreath *n.*
wreathe *v.*
wreathed
wreath'ing
wreck'age
wreck'er
wrench
wres'tle
·tled ·tling
wres'tler
wretch
(*miserable person;* see retch)
wretch'ed
wrig'gle
·gled ·gling
wring
wrung wring'ing
(*twist;* see ring)
wrin'kle
·kled ·kling
wrin'kly
·kli·er ·kli·est
wrist'band'
wrist'let
wrist pin
wrist'watch'
writ
write
wrote writ'ten
writ'ing
(*inscribe;* see
right, rite)
write'-in'
write'-off'
writ'er
write'-up'
writhe
writhed
writh'ing
wrong'do·er
wrong'do·ing
wrong'ful

wrote
(*pt. of write;*
see rote)
wrought
wrought'-up'
wrung
(*pt. and pp. of
wring;* see rung)
wry
wried wry'ing
wri'er wri'est
(*twisted;* see rye)
wry'ly
Wy·o'ming

X

x
x-ed *or* x'd
x-ing *or* x'ing
xan'thous
xe'bec
xen'o·pho'bi·a
xe·rog'ra·phy
xe·roph'i·lous
Xe'rox
Xmas
X'-ray' *or*
X ray
xy'lo·phone'
xy'lo·phon'ist

Y

yacht
yachts'man
Yan'kee

yard'age
yard'arm'
yard'mas'ter
yard'stick'
yarn'-dyed'
yawl
yawn
yea
year'book'
year'ling
year'long'
year'ly
yearn
year'-round'
yeast
yel'low
yelp
yen
yenned yen'ning
yeo'man
yes
yessed yes'sing
ye·shi'va
yes'ter·day
yes'ter·year'
yet
yew
(*tree;* see ewe)
Yid'dish
yield
yip'pie
yo'del
·deled *or* ·delled
·del·ing *or*
·del·ling
yo'del·er *or*
yo'del·ler
yo'ga
yo'gi
·gis
yo'gurt
yoke
yoked yok'ing
(*harness*)

yolk
(*of an egg*)
Yom Kip'pur
yon'der
you'd
you'll
young'ster
your
(*poss. of* you)
you're
(*you are*)
yours
your·self'
·selves'
youth'ful
you've
yowl
yo'-yo'
yule log
yule'tide'

Z

zai'ba·tsu'
·tsu'
za'ni·ness
za'ny
·nies, ·ni·er
·ni·est
zeal
zeal'ot
zeal'ous
ze'bra
ze'brass'
ze'bu
Zeit'geist'
Zen
ze'nith
ze'o·lite'

ze'o·lit'ic
zeph'yr
zep'pe·lin
ze'ro
·ros *or* ·roes
·roed ·ro·ing
zest'ful·ly
zest'ful·ness
zig'zag'
·zagged'
·zag'ging
zinc
zincked *or* zinced
zinck'ing *or*
zinc'ing
zin'ni·a
Zi'on·ism
zip
zipped zip'ping
ZIP Code
zip'per
zir'con
zith'er
zo'di·ac'
zo·di'a·cal
zom'bie
zon'al
zone
zoned zon'ing
zoo
zo'o·ge·og'ra·phy
zo'o·log'i·cal
zo·ol'o·gist
zo·ol'o·gy
zoom lens
zoy'si·a
zuc·chet'to
·tos
zuc·chi'ni
·ni *or* ·nis
zwie'back
zy'gote
zy·mol'o·gy
zy'mur·gy

15

Forms of Address

revised by Joyce Gold

The proper form of address is essential for creating a positive initial impression, whether in a letter, on the telephone, or in person. The chart on the following pages is arranged alphabetically by the title of the person being addressed. Where pertinent, the plural form is also given for situations in which more than one person with the same title is addressed.

A few general guidelines:

Military officers retain their highest rank when they retire and this rank should be used when they are addressed.

Titles such as Reverend and Honorable are used with the full name on the envelope address, but they are not used in the salutation.

When the title Esquire is used, it is abbreviated after the full name, and no other title is used before the name—for example, John Smith, Esq.

For titles not on the chart, the common procedure to be used when addressing the person is to use the title and the surname—for example, Chief Smith.

Person Being Addressed	Envelope Address	Business Salutation	Social Salutation	In Speaking
Abbot	The Right Reverend (full name), (address of church)	Right Reverend Abbot:	Dear Father Abbot:	Abbot (surname)
Ambassador (United States)	The Honorable (full name), The Ambassador of the United States, Embassy of the United States of America (city and country)	Sir (or Madam):	Dear Mr. (or Madam) Ambassador:	Mr. Ambassador (or Madam Ambassador) Mr. (or Mrs., Ms., or Miss) (surname) or Sir (or Madam)
Ambassador (Foreign)	His (or Her) Excellency (full name), Ambassador of (country), Washington, D.C.	Excellency:	Dear Mr. (or Madam) Ambassador:	Excellency or Mr. Ambassador (or Madam Ambassador) or Sir (or Madam)
Apostolic Delegate	His Excellency, The Most Reverend (full name), Archbishop of (name of church), The Apostolic Delegate, (address of church)	Your Excellency:	Dear Archbishop:	Your Excellency or Archbishop (surname)
Archbishop (Roman Catholic)	The Most Reverend (full name), Archbishop of (city), (city and state, etc.)	Your Excellency: or Most Reverend Sir:	Dear Archbishop (surname):	Your Excellency or Archbishop (surname)
Assemblyman (see Representative)				
Attorney General	The Honorable (full name), Attorney General, Washington, DC 20503	Sir:	Dear Mr. Attorney General:	Mr. Attorney General or Mr. (surname)
Bishop (Methodist)	Bishop (full name), (city and state, etc.)	Dear Bishop (surname):	Dear Bishop (surname):	Bishop (surname)
Bishop (Protestant Episcopal)	The Right Reverend (full name), Bishop of (diocese), (city and state, etc.)	Right Reverend Sir:	Dear Bishop (surname):	Bishop (surname)

Person Being Addressed	Envelope Address	Business Salutation	Social Salutation	In Speaking
Bishop (Roman Catholic)	The Most Reverend (full name), (church), (city and state, etc.)	Most Reverend Sir:	Dear Bishop (surname):	Bishop (surname)
Brother (of a religious order)	Brother (religious name) plus initials of his order, (address, city, and state)	Dear Brother:	Dear Brother (religious name):	Brother (religious name)
Cabinet Officer of the United States	The Honorable (full name), (title), Washington, D.C.	Sir (*or* Madam): *or:* Dear Sir (*or* Dear Madam):	Dear Mr. (*or* Madam) Secretary: *or* Dear Mr. (*or* Mrs. or Ms. or Miss) (surname):	Mr. (*or* Madam) Secretary *or* Sir (*or* Madam) *or* Mr. (*or* Mrs. or Ms. or Miss) (surname)
Cardinal (Roman Catholic)	His Eminence (given name) Cardinal (surname), Archbishop of (city, etc.), (city and state, etc.)	Your Eminence:	Dear Cardinal (surname):	Your Eminence *or* Cardinal (surname)
Clergyman, Protestant (without degree)	The Reverend (full name), (address of his church)	Dear Sir:	Dear Mr. (surname):	Mr. (surname) *or* The Reverend (full name)
Clergyman, Protestant (with degree)	The Reverend (full name), D.D. (LL.D., if held), (address of his church)	Dear Sir:	Dear Dr. (surname):	Dr. (surname) *or* The Reverend Dr. (full name)
Clergyman, Lutheran	The Reverend (full name), (address of his church)	Dear Sir:	Dear Pastor (surname):	Pastor *or* Pastor (surname)
Commissioner	The Honorable (full name), Commissioner, (city, state)	Dear Mr. (*or* Madam) Commissioner:	Dear Mr. (*or* Madam) Commissioner or Mr. (*or* Mrs. or Miss or Ms.) (surname)	Mr. (*or* Mrs. or Miss or Ms.) (surname)
Common Form (Man)	Mr. (full name), (address, city, and state)	Dear Mr. (surname): *or* My Dear Sir: *in plural*, Gentlemen:	Dear Mr. (surname): *in plural*, Dear Messrs. (surname):	Mr. (surname)

	Address	Formal Salutation	Informal Salutation	Spoken Address
Common Form (Woman)	Mrs. (*or* Miss *or* Ms.) (full name), (address, city, and state)		Dear Mrs. (*or* Miss *or* Ms.) (surname): *or* Dear Madam: *in plural,* Mesdames:	Miss (*or* Mrs. *or* Ms.) (surname)
Congressman (see Representative)				
Consul (United States or other)	(full name), Esquire, American (or other) Consul, (city and country, or state)	Sir (*or* Madam): *or* Dear Sir (*or* Dear Madam):	Dear Mr. (*or* Mrs. *or* Ms. *or* Miss) (surname):	Mr. (*or* Mrs. *or* Ms. *or* Miss) (surname)
Doctor (of Philosophy, Medicine, Divinity, Dentistry, etc.)	(full name), Ph.D., M.D., D.D., D.D.S., etc., *or* Dr. (full name), (address, city, and state)	Dear Dr. (surname): *or* Dear Sir (*or* Dear Madam):	Dear Dr. (surname):	Dr. (surname)
Former President	The Honorable (full name), (address, city, and state)	Sir:	Dear Mr. (surname):	Mr. (surname) *or* Sir
Governor (of a state)	The Honorable (*or in some states* His *or* Her Excellency) (full name), Governor of (state), (capital city and state)	Sir (*or* Madam):	Dear Governor (surname):	Governor (surname) *or* Sir (*or* Madam)
Judge (see also Supreme Court)	The Honorable (full name), Justice (name of court), (city and state)	Sir (*or* Madam):	Dear Judge (surname):	Judge (surname)
Lawyer	(Full name), Esq. (office address) *or* Mr. (*or* Mrs. *or* Miss *or* Ms.) (surname)	Dear Sir (*or* Madam):	Dear Mr. (*or* Mrs. *or* Miss *or* Ms.) (surname):	Mr. (*or* Mrs. *or* Miss *or* Ms.) (surname)
Mayor	His (*or* Her) Honor, The Mayor, City Hall (city and state)	Sir (*or* Madam):	Dear Mr. (*or* Madam) Mayor:	Mr. (*or* Madam) Mayor *or* Mayor (surname)
Military Enlisted Personnel (American)—Army, Navy, Coast Guard, Air Force, Marine Corps	(title of rank), (full name), (address)	Sir (*or* Madam): *or* Dear Sir (*or* Dear Madam):	Dear Private (*or* Airman, *or* Seaman) (surname)	Private (*or* Airman, *or* Seaman) (surname)

Person Being Addressed	Envelope Address	Business Salutation	Social Salutation	In Speaking
Military Officer (American)—Army, Navy, Coast Guard, Air Force, Marine Corps	(title of rank), (full name), (address)	Sir (*or* Madam): *or* Dear Sir (*or* Dear Madam):	Dear General (*or* Admiral, Colonel, Major, Captain, etc.) (surname):	General (*or* Colonel, *or* Admiral, Major, Captain, etc.) (surname)
Minister of a Foreign Country	The Honorable (full name), The Minister of (Country), Washington, D.C.	Sir:	Dear Mr. Minister:	Mr. Minister *or* Mr. (surname)
Minister Plenipotentiary of the United States	The Honorable (full name), The Minister of the United States, American Legation, (city, country)	Sir *or* Madam:	Dear Mr. (*or* Madam) Minister:	Mr. (*or* Madam) Minister *or* Mr. (surname) *or* Mrs. *or* Miss *or* Ms. (surname)
Minister (Protestant)	The Reverend (full name plus D.D. if applicable), (address, city, and state)	Dear Sir (*or* Dear Madam): *or* Sir (*or* Madam):	Dear Mr. (*or* Mrs. *or* Ms. *or* Miss *or* Dr.) (surname):	Mr. (*or* Mrs. *or* Ms. *or* Miss *or* Dr. *or, if a Lutheran*, Pastor) (surname)
Monsignor (Roman Catholic)	The Right Reverend Monsignor (surname), (church), (city and state)	Right Reverend and Monsignor (surname):	Dear Monsignor (surname):	Monsignor (surname)
Naval Enlisted Personnel (American)	(title of rank), (full name), (address)	Sir (*or* Madam): *or* Dear Sir (*or* Dear Madam):	Dear Seaman (*or* Quartermaster, etc.) (surname):	Seaman (*or* Quartermaster, etc.) (surname)
Naval Officer (American)	(title of rank), (full name), (address)	Sir (*or* Madam): *or* Dear Sir (*or* Dear Madam):	Dear Admiral (*or* Commodore, Captain, etc.) (surname):	Admiral (*or* Commodore, Captain, etc.) (surname)
Patriarch (Eastern Orthodox Church)	His Beatitude the Patriarch of (name of church), (address of his church)	Most Reverend Lord:	Your Beatitude *or* Most Reverend Lord:	Your Beatitude *or* Most Reverend Lord

	Envelope and Inside Address	Formal Salutation	Less Formal Salutation	Spoken Address
Pope	His Holiness the Pope, Vatican City, Italy	Your Holiness:	Your Holiness: *or* Most Holy Father:	Your Holiness (*or* Most Holy Father)
Premier	His (*or* Her) Excellency (full name), Premier of (country), (city, country)	Excellency:	Dear Mr. (*or* Madame) Premier:	Your Excellency *or* Mr. (*or* Mrs. *or* Miss *or* Ms.) (surname)
President (of the United States)	The President, The White House, Washington, D.C. 20500	Sir: *or* Mr. President:	Dear Mr. President: *or* Dear President (surname):	Mr. President *or* Sir
Priest (Episcopal)	The Reverend (full name) *or* (if with degree) The Reverend Dr. (full name), (address of his church)	Dear Mr. (surname): *or* Dear Dr. (surname):	Dear Mr. (surname): *or* Dear Dr. (surname): *or* Dear Father (surname):	Mr. (surname) *or* Father (surname) *or* Dr. (surname)
Priest (Roman Catholic)	The Reverend (full name plus initials of his order), (address, city, and state)	Reverend Father:	Dear Father (surname):	Father (surname) *or* Father
Prime Minister	His (*or* Her) Excellency (full name), Prime Minister of (country), (city, country)	Excellency:	Dear Mr. (*or* Madame) Prime Minister:	Mr. (*or* Madame) Prime Minister *or* Mr. (*or* Mrs. *or* Miss *or* Ms.) (surname)
Professor	Professor (*or* Dr. if Ph.D.) (full name), Department of (Mathematics, History, etc.), (name of university or college), (address, city, and state)	Dear Sir (*or* Dear Madam):	Dear Professor (surname): *or* Dear Dr. (surname):	Professor (*or* Dr. *or* Mr.) (surname). In certain universities (e.g., Harvard) all faculty members are orally addressed as Mr. (*or* Mrs. *or* Ms. *or* Miss) (surname)
Rabbi	Rabbi (full name plus D.D. if applicable), (address, city, and state)	Dear Sir (*or* Madam):	Dear Rabbi (*or* Dr.) (surname):	Rabbi (*or* Dr.) (surname)

Person Being Addressed	Envelope Address	Business Salutation	Social Salutation	In Speaking
Representative (of a state legislature)	The Honorable (full name), Member of Assembly (or other name of the legislature), (capital city and state)	Sir (*or* Madam):	Dear Mr. (*or* Mrs. *or* Ms. *or* Miss) (surname):	Mr. (*or* Mrs. *or* Ms. *or* Miss) (surname)
Representative (of the United States Congress)	The Honorable (full name), United States House of Representatives, Washington, D.C. 20515	Sir (*or* Madam):	Dear Mr. (*or* Mrs. *or* Ms. *or* Miss) (surname)	Mr. (*or* Mrs. *or* Ms. *or* Miss) (surname)
Senator (of a state legislature)	The Honorable (full name), The Senate of (state), (capital city and state)	Sir (*or* Madam):	Dear Senator (surname):	Senator (surname) *or* Mr. (*or* Madam) Senator
Senator (of the United States)	The Honorable (full name), United States Senate, Washington, D.C. 20510	Sir (*or* Madam):	Dear Senator (surname):	Senator (surname) *or* Mr. (*or* Madam) Senator
Sister (of a religious order)	Sister (religious name plus initials of her order), (address, city, and state)	Dear Sister:	Dear Sister (religious name):	Sister (religious name)
Supreme Court (of a state) (Associate Justice)	The Honorable (full name), Associate Justice of the Supreme Court of (state), (address)	Sir (*or* Madam):	Dear Justice (surname):	Mr. (*or* Madam) Justice (surname) *or* Judge (surname)
Supreme Court (of a state) (Chief Justice)	The Honorable (full name), Chief Justice of the Supreme Court of (state), (address)	Sir (*or* Madam):	Dear Mr. (*or* Madam) Chief Justice:	Mr. (*or* Madam) Chief Justice *or* Chief Justice (surname) *or* Judge (surname)
Supreme Court (of the United States) (Associate Justice)	Mr. Justice (surname), The Supreme Court, Washington, D.C. 20543	Sir (*or* Madam):	Dear Mr. (*or* Madam) Justice (surname):	Mr. (*or* Madam) Justice *or* Mr. (*or* Madam) Justice (surname) *or* Sir (*or* Madam)

Supreme Court (of the United States) (Chief Justice)	The Chief Justice, The Supreme Court, Washington, D.C. 20543	Sir:	Dear Mr. Chief Justice:	Mr. Chief Justice *or* Sir
United Nations Delegate (other than U.S.)	His (*or* Her) Excellency, (country) Representative to the United Nations, United Nations, New York 10017	Sir (*or* Madam): *or* Your Excellency:	Dear Mr. (*or* Madam) Ambassador: *or* Dear Mr. (*or* Ms. *or* Miss *or* Mrs.) (surname):	Your Excellency
United Nations Delegate (United States)	The Honorable (full name), United States Permanent Representative to the United Nations, United Nations, New York 10017	Sir (*or* Madam):	Dear Mr. (*or* Madam) Ambassador *or* Dear Mr. (*or* Ms. *or* Miss *or* Mrs.) (surname):	Mr. Ambassador (*or* Madam Ambassador)
United Nations Secretary-General	His Excellency (full name), Secretary-General of the United Nations, United Nations, New York 10017	Sir *or* Your Excellency:	Dear Mr. Secretary-General:	Your Excellency *or* Secretary-General (surname)
University Chancellor	Dr. (full name), Chancellor, (address of university)	Sir (*or* Madam):	Dear Dr. (surname):	Dr. (surname)
University or College Chaplain	The Reverend (full name), Chaplain, (address of school)	Dear Sir (*or* Madam):	Dear Chaplain (surname): *or* Dear Mr. (*or* Mrs. *or* Miss *or* Ms.) (surname): *or* Dear Father (surname):	Chaplain (surname) *or* Mr. (*or* Mrs. *or* Miss *or* Ms.) (surname) *or* Father (surname)
University or College Dean	Dean (full name) *or* Dr. (full name) Dean, (address of school)	Sir (*or* Madam):	Dear Dr. (surname): *or* Dear Dean (surname):	Dean (surname) *or* Dr. (surname)
University or College President	Dr. (full name) *or* President (full name) (address of school)	Sir (*or* Madam):	Dear President (surname): *or* Dear Dr. (surname):	Dr. (surname)

503

Person Being Addressed	Envelope Address	Business Salutation	Social Salutation	In Speaking
Vice President (of the United States)	The Vice President, United States Senate, Washington, D.C. 20510	Sir:	Dear Mr. Vice President:	Mr. Vice President *or* Sir
Warrant Officer	Warrant Officer (*or* Chief Warrant Officer) (full name), (address)	Sir (*or* Madam): *or* Dear Sir (*or* Dear Madam):	Dear Mr. (*or* Mrs. *or* Ms. *or* Miss) (surname):	Mr. (*or* Mrs. *or* Ms. *or* Miss) (surname)

Legal Information

General Legal Principles

by William W. Cook
revised by Naomi Dornfeld Platt

This overview of general legal principles can trace its sources and heritage to the great law givers: Moses, Solon, and Justinian; to the *Code of Hammurabi* and to the *Magna Carta*; and to the common law as it developed throughout English history. The common law is the basis of our legal system and, where it has not been changed by constitutional provisions or statutes, is in force and effect throughout this country. The laws of the state of Louisiana, which have their antecedents in the *Napoleonic Code,* are the exception.

The Constitution of the United States is the supreme law of the land. It creates the basic framework of our government and provides for and protects the fundamental rights of each citizen and of society as a whole. Congress is conferred with authority to pass legislation to govern in accordance with its constitutional mandate. But the Constitution reserves to the individual states: *The powers not delegated to the United States . . . nor prohibited by it to the states. . . .* Each state, therefore, has its own constitution and laws, which are markedly varied and diverse.

We have in effect 51 different "legal systems" or jurisdictions: one for the federal government and one for each of the 50 states. In addition, the states confer upon their townships and municipalities the authority to pass laws, regulations, and ordinances. Both the federal and state governments confer upon agencies the power to enact rules and regulations affecting, among other things, trade and commerce. This vastly increases the total number of legal systems that govern, regulate, and control almost every aspect of our lives.

The laws passed by the respective legislatures are codified. Federal laws can be found in the *United States Code* and state laws in the respective statutes· of each state. In addition, rules and regulations passed by various agencies can be found in registers such as the *Code of Federal Regulations*. The laws passed by municipalities may be found in *Administrative Codes*. The common law is found in the published legal decisions of each court.

This overview of general legal principles is not meant to be, nor is it a substitute for, competent legal advice. Because of the marked diversity of our legal systems, legal advice must be sought from attorneys licensed in the jurisdiction where the activity, matter, or event arises and occurs.

This chapter discusses briefly criminal law, civil law, the uniform commercial code, and the forms of doing business and the service relationships involved.

CRIMINAL LAW

One of the major divisions of U.S. law is that between criminal law and civil law. The underlying purpose of criminal laws is to ensure that members of society have their constitutional rights of life, liberty, and the pursuit of happiness. To this end, criminal laws provide for the punishment of antisocial behavior. Essentially, a crime is an offense against society as a whole.

Traditionally, crimes have been punished by either a fine or imprisonment or both. Courts today are also increasingly ordering offenders to make restitution to their victims, that is, to "pay back" or compensate the victim for the loss that has been sustained. A court may, for example, punish by imprisonment one who has embezzled funds from an employer. It may also order the offender to return the embezzled funds to the rightful owner.

Generally, to be a crime, the act must be committed intentionally, although negligence, if it is sufficiently wanton and willful, may be criminal. Crimes are also classified according to their seriousness.

Levels of Crimes

There are two basic levels of crimes: felonies and misdemeanors.

Felony

Felonies are serious crimes. They can be either violent, such as homicide, arson, rape, robbery, and assault, or nonviolent, such as embezzlement, extortion, larceny, bribery, insurance fraud, and tax fraud. Felonies are usually punishable by one or more years' imprisonment and/or a fine and, in some cases, by death.

The violent crimes (homicide, rape, robbery, arson, and assault) are committed directly against the person or his/her property by use of physical force. This endangers not only the victim's life but also the lives of others who may be injured or killed during the commission of such a crime. For example, in the case of arson (the destruction, by burning, of another person's real property), tenants in a building and not just the owner may be killed in the fire.

Nonviolent, or *white collar*, crimes are committed directly against the property of an individual, business, corporation, or government without the element of physical force. These crimes are committed by stealth, concealment, and deception.

Misdemeanors

All other crimes, less serious by their nature, are considered misdemeanors. They are usually punishable by imprisonment of less than one year and/or a fine. Examples include lesser degrees of both violent and nonviolent crimes. To determine if a crime is a misdemeanor or a felony, distinctions are made as to the amount of money involved, the extent of force used, and intent. What constitutes a crime—the definition of an act as a felony or misdemeanor—varies from state to state.

Violations

Most states and the federal government make distinctions between crimes (felonies and misdemeanors) and violations. A violation is not a crime. It is an infraction of some rule or regulation promulgated by a federal, state, or city government or regulatory agency. Such an infraction is usually punishable by a fine. Examples include traffic violations (speeding, parking, red light, and stop sign infractions); disturbing the peace; violations of Health Department no-smoking prohibitions; and Building Department construction code violations.

In our complex society, almost every phase of business is regulated, to some degree, by federal, state, and/or municipal regulatory agencies. Any breach of their regulations may constitute a violation.

Criminals and Jurisdiction

Crimes and violations may be committed by individuals and corporations. As will be subsequently discussed, the corporation is legally similar in many ways to a person. A corporation cannot, of course, do or be subject to things that are peculiar to persons. A corporation cannot, for example, commit perjury or be imprisoned. Corporate offenses can therefore be punished only by fines. A careful distinction should be made concerning a criminal offense by an individual within a corporation and an offense by the corporation itself. A corporate officer *could* commit perjury or be imprisoned for an offense committed in that officer's own right.

Other forms of doing business such as the proprietorship (one person doing business) or the partnership (two or more persons doing business jointly) cannot commit a criminal offense in the same way as a corporation.

Crimes fall under either federal or state jurisdiction. Jurisdiction is simply the power of a given type of court to hear and decide a case. A crime that crosses state lines is subject to federal jurisdiction. A federal statute—the Dyer Act, for example—prohibits transporting a vehicle known to be stolen across state lines. Crimes committed on federal property, such as a military reservation, also fall under federal jurisdiction.

THE CIVIL LAW

The civil law includes the remainder of the law after criminal law. The civil law has many branches, but the principal ones include the law of torts, contracts, real and personal property, estates and trusts, and domestic relations. Civil law exists to resolve conflicts between parties rather than between an offender and society. A civilly injured party is entitled to receive some type of compensation for the injury, and the party responsible for the injury cannot be fined or imprisoned for the act. "Injury" as used here refers not only to physical injury but to other types such as monetary damage.

The Law of Torts

A *tort* is any wrong or damage, except breach of contract, for which a civil action, usually for monetary damages, can be brought by one person against another. (As a rule, the attorney fees of the injured party cannot be recovered.)

The monetary damages that can be recovered in any tort action consist of the following:

actual out-of-pocket expenses incurred as a direct result of the tort, such as medical bills, hospital bills, nursing bills, loss of earnings, cost of hiring replacement vehicles (in the case of loss of use of a vehicle resulting from an automobile accident);

anticipated out-of-pocket expenses for medical, hospital, and nursing services, and anticipated loss of earnings resulting from any permanent injury or loss sustained; and

compensation for pain, suffering, and mental anguish sustained as a result of the tort.

Categories of Torts

Torts fall into two main categories: intentional torts and negligence.

Intentional torts. Many intentional torts may be crimes as well. Assault and battery afford an example of this. If A commits battery upon B and damages B's teeth, it will do B little good if A is criminally fined or imprisoned. But B can sue A for battery—a tort—and receive monetary damages from A not only for the dental bills and other out-of-pocket expenses B incurred as a result of the battery but also for pain, suffering, and mental anguish.

Several other intentional torts include fraud and deceit, libel and slander, the invasion of another's privacy, the maintenance of a nuisance, and antitrust violations. All of these may be committed by a business entity. Fraud and deceit, for example, involve the intentional misrepresentation of a material fact that leads another party to act upon it to his detriment and resulting damage. Such an offense could easily arise in a sales situation. But a salesperson's mere commendation of a product is not necessarily fraudulent or deceitful. A reference to a used car for sale as "a real cream puff" is a sales practice known as "puffing." Puffing is not a tort and can be best defined as *judicious exaggeration*.

Two or more persons can conspire to commit an intentional tort. In such a situation, the tortfeasors are jointly and severally liable to the injured party for the damages that party sustained. There can be *conspiracy to defraud* by false representation; to obtain delivery of goods on false credit; or to induce a breach of an existing contract, as, for example, when a merchant's competitors cause the merchant's wholesaler not to deliver the goods for the price stated in the contract between the merchant and the wholesaler.

Businesses that are involved with mass communications, such as newspapers, magazines, and the broadcast media, are apt without utmost care to commit the tort of libel or slander. The damage suffered by a victim is essentially to the person's reputation as the result of a false statement or imputation. Thus, both *libel* (written statement) and *slander* (oral statement) are included in the broad term *defamation*. The constitutional guarantee of "freedom of speech" does not protect the tortfeasor who intentionally and knowingly defames the reputation of another.

The tort of *invasion of privacy* stems from the right of the individual to be left alone and like other rights is not an absolute one. Because it is an individual right, it cannot be claimed by a corporation, institution, or business. Damages for intrusion into an individual's privacy might consist of humiliation or shame, mental distress, or outrage by a person of ordinary sensibilities.

Nuisance consists of using one's property in such an unreasonable way as to damage another. The doctrine is really a limitation on the use of property. Many businesses, as a part of a manufacturing process, could cause damage to adjacent property owners. The process could, for example, discharge noxious fumes, which the business should take every precaution to prevent. Environmental pollution may be a public nuisance, and courts could order it abated or stopped. Nuisance can be a private one as well, and the victim may be entitled to damages for the injury sustained. Public nuisance can be criminally prosecuted.

Antitrust violations involve the activities of an unlawful monopoly or combination that injure another. While state antitrust statutes provide for the recovery of actual damages by an injured party, the federal statute, the Sherman Act, provides for treble, or three times, the actual damages.

Negligence. Negligence is an unintentional tort for which a person can receive a monetary judgment for damages. In all negligence actions, the standard of care that an individual must exercise is *due care under the circumstances*. A person is negligent when he or she fails to exercise that degree of care that a reasonably prudent person would have exercised under the same circumstances. Negligence may arise from an act of omission (the failure to do an act a reasonably prudent person would have done under the same circumstances) or an act of commission (the doing of an act that a reasonably prudent person would not have done under the same circumstances). The negligent act—the wrong—must be the proximate cause of the injuries sustained.

In many instances, the law will infer negligence when injury results from inherently or abnormally dangerous activities, such as blasting with explosives. In such a situation, strict liability is imposed upon the person using the explosives. Breach of the duty to use due care need not be proved, but the injury must have been directly caused by the blast.

The law of negligence is very complex and is based upon the legal duty to use care. At the same time, the prevention of an action for negligence is largely a matter of common sense. It cannot, therefore, be overemphasized that all employees of a given business should be alert to the existence of negligent practices.

Frequently, the victim of negligence will have contributed to the cause of injury. Under the doctrine of *contributory negligence*, the victim would be barred from recovering damages. Today, most states have enacted comparative negligence statutes that allow recovery of damages from the negligent party less the proportion of the victim's contribution of negligence to the accident. The doctrine of comparative negligence is most commonly invoked in motor vehicle negligence cases.

The owner of property owes varying degrees of care to different classes of people who come upon the premises. Owners owe the highest degree of care to invitees on the property. Invitees are those who enter another's property and whose presence is of some interest or advantage to the owner. Customers in stores and shops and guests in hotels and restaurants would be considered invitees. To them the owner owes the care of keeping the premises reasonably safe.

The Law of Contracts

Contracts may be oral or written, express or implied. They include all agreements or promises to buy and sell personal property and real property; to perform services; to agree to do or not to do specified acts; to lease property—real or personal; to mortgage or otherwise encumber real or personal property; and to include all dealings and relationships between persons, including marriage, that are not classified as torts or crimes.

Requirements for a Contract

A contract is formed when the following three requirements are met:

1. There are at least two parties with legal capacity to enter into the agreement. Legal capacity means that the parties are adults (usually over the age of eighteen years) and are not under any mental or physical disability that diminishes or impairs their capacity to enter into an agreement. If a party lacks legal capacity, the contract is voidable—that is, it can be disaffirmed and set aside by the legal representative of such person (in the case of infancy, the guardian; in the case of incompetency, the committee; in the case of physical disability, the conservator) or by the person when the disability is removed (as when an infant attains the age of eighteen years). If the contract is not disaffirmed, it is fully enforceable.

2. There must be mutual assent to the terms of the agreement—that is, *a meeting of the minds* on all essential terms. This is the finality of the negotiations between the parties. It encompasses, and is the end result of, the offers, counteroffers, and acceptances of the offers made by the parties.

3. Consideration is the final requirement. It is a *quid pro quo*, an exchange of value, for the mutual promises of the parties. Consideration may consist of money, services, a product, a promise not to do something (a forbearance), a promise to do something, or simply love and affection. In some situations, where the promise is in writing and signed by the promisor, consideration is not required in order to have a valid, enforceable contract. The New York General Obligations Law provides that a written signed promise to change or modify, or to discharge in whole or in part, any contract, obligation, lease, mortgage, or other security interest in personal or real property shall not be invalid because of lack of consideration.

Purpose of the Contract

The purpose for which the contract is entered into must be one that is not void by statute or rules of common law. Generally, any agreement entered into to commit a criminal act or any act that is against the public policy of the state is void and unenforceable. If, for example, an agreement is entered into in New York State to rent a store as a gambling casino, such agreement is void on its face (gambling in New York is a crime), and the Court will not enforce the contract on behalf of either party.

Breach of Contract

When a party fails to perform what he or she has agreed to do, such party will have *breached* the contract, and an action can be maintained by the *damaged* or injured party for specific performance of the contract or for monetary damages sustained as a result of the breach. An action for *specific performance* compels the breaching party to perform his or her promises in accordance with the contract's terms and provisions. Usually, courts grant relief for specific performance because of the uniqueness of the subject matter of the contract and the fact that monetary damages would be inadequate compensation to the injured party. The equitable relief of specific performance has been traditionally granted by the courts in cases where a seller of real property (each parcel of real property is considered unique) wrongfully refuses to tender a deed to a purchaser who is ready, willing, and able to purchase the property in accordance with the terms of the contract of sale.

An action for breach of contract may be maintained when proof of the following elements exists:

1. formation of the contract between the plaintiff and the defendant;
2. performance by the plaintiff;
3. defendant's failure to perform;
4. resulting damages to the plaintiff.

Usually the monetary damage sustained is the difference between the contract price the plaintiff would have paid if the breach had not occurred and the higher cost that the plaintiff actually paid to a third party because of the defendant's breach.

Implied and Written Contracts

Every day, each of us enters into many contracts. Most of these contracts are oral and many are implied from our actions. These contracts include buying a newspaper, riding public transportation, eating in restaurants, buying items in department stores, and hiring gardeners, electricians, plumbers, painters, doctors, or dentists. The *consideration* for the products and services we buy and use is a specified sum of money. The specification of the cost of the item or service and/or its display or availability for use is the *offer*. Our taking of the item or use of the service is the acceptance of the offer, thereby giving rise to our duty to pay the consideration.

However, certain agreements are not valid or enforceable unless they are in writing; in fact, these agreements are void, as against the public policy of their terms and conditions. These contracts or agreements, which must be in writing, are specified in the *Statute of Frauds*, whose antecedents date back to seventeenth-century England. Today, all states have a Statute of Frauds in one form or another. Generally, the following contracts or agreements must be in writing or else they are void:

> all contracts concerning the sale of real property or an estate or interest in real property;
>
> all deeds to real property;
>
> all mortgages, liens, easements, or other encumbrances affecting real property;
>
> all leases of real property for a term of one year or more;
>
> a promise to answer for the debt or obligation of another;
>
> any agreement that is not to be performed within one year of the date of the promise;
>
> the sale of personal property of a value of $500 or more, unless there has been partial performance by the seller or purchaser.

Personal Property

The law relating to the *sale* of personal property is largely contained in Article 2 of the Uniform Commercial Code, which will be discussed as a separate topic. Inherent in the ownership of property is the right to transfer or dispose of it. A sale is but one medium through which this may be done. The owner of property may transfer property by will (a bequest) or by making a gift of it. It is difficult to formulate a precise definition of personal property. Clearly the term includes objects other than real property, which consists of land and the buildings on it.

Types of Personal Property

Personal property is frequently classified as corporeal or incorporeal.

Corporeal personal property. The term *corporeal personal property* refers to personal property that is tangible and includes goods that are also referred to as *chattels*. Another distinction of corporeal personal property is that it is visible and movable.

Incorporeal personal property. Incorporeal personal property involves "rights" rather than tangible objects. Examples of such rights include patents, copyrights, and trademarks. A patent is a grant to the inventor to use, sell, or allow others to use the invention exclusively for a period of 17 years. A copyright is a grant giving an author an exclusive right to possess, publish, or sell the production of his or her intellect. Formerly a copyright was a grant for 28 years with the right to renew it for another 28 years. Today, however, for copyrights granted during and after 1978, there is a single period consisting of the lifetime of the author plus 50 years. A trademark, which is the property of a business, is a sign, mark, name, or symbol that identifies it or its product. Trademarks may be registered for a period of 20 years and may be renewed at the end of each 20-year period. Other examples of incorporeal personal property include mortgages on both real estate and chattels; leases of apartments, offices, and stores; promissory notes; stock certificates; bonds; bank accounts; and even court judgments.

Title

Title to or ownership of corporeal personal property (chattels) may be established by exclusive possession of the chattel, a bill of sale, or a certificate of title (as in the case of an automobile).

Title to or ownership of incorporeal personal property is established by the document itself: the stock certificate, the lease, the mortgage, the bond, the certificate of deposit, or the bankbook. All of these documents name the owner—the mortgagee, lessee, promisee, stockholder, payee, or judgment creditor, as the case may be, on the face of the instrument.

Single or Joint Ownership

Personal property can be owned by a single person, by two or more persons as *tenants in common* where each person owns an undivided equal interest in the property, or as *joint tenants with rights of survivorship* where two or more persons own an undivided equal interest in the property. On the death of one such tenant, the surviving tenant or tenants own the deceased tenant's share.

Ownership vs Possession

The ownership of personal property should be distinguished from the possession of it. Frequently the owner of personal property will deliver it to another for some purpose, such as safekeeping or repair. When this happens, the possession by one other than the owner is known as a *bailment*. The one in possession (the bailee) has responsibilities for the property to the owner (the bailor). The bailee is responsible for using ordinary care as to the bailed property and returning or disposing of the property at the direction of the bailor. A bailment comes into being upon agreement of the parties and delivery of the property to the bailee.

A bailment does not exist when a party merely rents space for the safekeeping of personal property. A bank, for example, is not a bailee of goods kept in a safety-deposit box because it cannot enter the box without the owner's key. Similarly, a "park and lock" parking lot is not a bailee; but when a vehicle owner leaves the key to the vehicle with the parking lot operator, a bailment does exist. In the latter case the lot operator would be responsible if the owner's vehicle was damaged while stored.

Sometimes the law will infer what is known as a constructive bailment. A person who finds lost property is a constructive bailee who owes the owner the standard of ordinary care for it.

Real Property

Real property consists of land and all improvements (structures and buildings with appurtenant fixtures), if any, situated on the land. Fixtures are items of personal property that are affixed to the structure or building and are thereby considered part of the real property. They would include sinks, cabinets, lighting fixtures (but not lamps), spigots, etc. They do not include furniture. Each parcel of real property is unique. As we have previously seen, it is for this reason that specific performance can be obtained if a seller breaches a contract of sale.

Types of Real Property Estates

When a person owns (has title to) real property, he or she in effect owns an *estate* in real property. There are two types of real property estates: *freehold* and *leasehold*.

Freehold estate. A freehold estate is either a *fee* (sometimes referred to as a *fee simple* or *fee simple absolute*) or a *life estate*. A *fee* is the highest degree of ownership that can be had in real property, being diminished only by encumbrances (such as mortgage liens and easements for electric, gas, water, and rights-of-way). In a *life estate*, the holder of the estate owns the property during his lifetime. As an example, A, the owner of a fee, grants the fee to B for the life of B. During B's lifetime, B has all of the incidents of ownership, including absolute possession. B could sell his estate to C, who, of course, would own it only as long as B lives; B could mortgage the estate or lease it to another. In effect, B could do anything with the property that the grantor, A, could do. On B's death, however, the title to the estate would revert back to the grantor or any person the grantor designated as remainderman (the person who takes the estate on the death of the life tenant). The interest in the fee of C or any other party would terminate on the death of the life tenant.

Leasehold estate. A leasehold estate entitles the party to exclusive possession and use of the real property—the land and any and all improvements thereon—for a specified term. To have a leasehold estate, the land must be leased. If the land is not included in the lease, an estate in real property would not be created; such a lease would be incorporeal personal property. Therefore, a lease of a portion of a structure or building for a store or an apartment does not create a leasehold estate, but the lease of vacant or improved land for any specified term would create such an estate.

Tenancy

The manner in which an estate in real property, freehold or leasehold, is owned (how title is held) is called a *tenancy*. Generally there are four tenancies: in severalty; in common; joint with rights of survivorship; and by the entireties.

Tenancy in severalty. A misnomer, tenancy in severalty is individual ownership; one person owns the estate.

Tenancy in common. Tenancy in common is a form of joint ownership, whereby each individual tenant owns an equal undivided portion of the whole estate. In the case of the death of one tenant, his or her undivided equal share will be distributed in accordance with his or her last will and testament or by the laws of descent and distribution in case of intestacy. If two or more names are listed on a deed as the grantees with nothing else following their names, the law in most jurisdictions assumes that such a transfer is a tenancy in common.

Joint tenancy with rights of survivorship. This is another form of joint ownership between two or more persons. It differs from a tenancy in common in that, upon the death of one tenant, that tenant's undivided equal interest in the property will become the property of the surviving tenant or tenants. If it is the intention to create such a tenancy, the words "as joint tenants with rights of survivorship" must be placed after the names of the grantees on the deed. Otherwise, a tenancy in common will be created.

Tenancy by the entireties. Tenancy by the entireties is a joint tenancy with rights of survivorship between a husband and wife. After the names of the grantees, the words *his wife* or the Latin abbreviation *ux* are placed to designate the creation of this tenancy.

Transfer of Real Property

The transfer of real property is called *alienation of title*. The "ownership" of the estate is evidenced by a document called a *deed*. Property is transferred by delivery of a deed from the grantor, the current owner of the estate, to the grantee, the person to whom the estate is being transferred. A grantor can transfer all or a portion of the estate owned. The most common form of transfer is by sale of property where, for example, A conveys to B his fee in a one-family house for an agreed-upon price. The delivery of the deed to B by A transfers the ownership. Property can also be transferred by deed of gift (no consideration required), by last will and testament, by the laws of descent and distribution (which will be discussed in the next section), and by mortgage foreclosure.

Almost every jurisdiction has recording laws that require that every deed, mortgage, easement, or other encumbrance affecting real property be recorded. Usually, such document is recorded in the county clerk's office of the county in which the property is located.

Leases

When the owner of an estate in real property rents a portion of the property—for example, as an apartment or store—to a person for a period of time, a contract, called a *lease*, is created. The owner, in this situation, becomes the *lessor*, or landlord. The person to whom the premises are rented is called the *lessee*, or *tenant*. The description of the premises leased is called the *demised premises*. The length of the lease is called the *term*. The *rental* is the sum of money that the tenant will pay to the landlord, usually monthly, for the possession and use of the premises.

A lease, as indicated before, is personal property and not an estate in real property. If the lease is for a term that is less than one year, it can be oral. If it is for a term of one year or more, most jurisdictions require it to be in writing in order to satisfy the requirements of the Statute of Frauds. Some jurisdictions will permit a lease for a term of three years or more to be recorded.

When a lease is for a fixed term, it is called a *tenancy for years*. This is true even if the term is for less than a year; the name is a misnomer. The essential characteristic is that the term is a fixed period of time, whether it be five months or five years.

When a lease is from one period to another, such as week to week or month to month, it is called a *periodic tenancy*. Such a lease may be oral or written. At the end of each period, a new lease is created, unless the landlord or tenant terminates the agreement. Usually periodic oral tenancies can be terminated by either the landlord or tenant giving proper *notice* to the other party. On a month-to-month tenancy, thirty-day notice is required. On a week-to-week tenancy, seven-day notice is required.

At the end of the term of the lease, the tenant is required to turn over possession of the premises to the landlord. When a tenant remains in possession of the premises after the term has expired without entering into a new agreement with the landlord, the tenant becomes a *holdover* and can be dispossessed.

Estates and Trusts

Distribution of an Estate by a Will

Estate law provides for the transfer of property at the time of death. Such a transfer may be by will or without a will. The maker of a will, a *testator*, provides his or her representative after death, the *executor*, with instructions for the distribution of property. In the absence of a will, distribution will be made as stipulated by law. It is certainly advisable for most people to make a will, not only so that their wishes may be effected but also because a will might be most advantageous to the relatives of the testator.

The basic requirement for a will is the *intent*, sometimes called the *donative intent*, of the maker. A will has no force until death and may be revoked or changed at any time by the testator. It creates no rights or benefits in others during the life of the maker. No special form is necessary for a will, although the maker must know and understand the contents of it. Anyone who is "sound of mind" can make a will. Through the years there has been great controversy about what a sound mind really is. Because a will is a solemn document, the law requires with rare exceptions that it be written and signed by the testator. Signing must be attested to or witnessed in all states, although the number of witnesses required varies.

Upon the death of the testator, a probate court in the appropriate jurisdiction appoints an executor, usually the person so named in the will. The court is not bound in this respect, however, since the person named may be unavailable or unqualified at the time of probate. Following appointment, the executor distributes the property according to the will and under the supervision of the court. Finally, the executor must account to the court for the distribution.

Distribution of an Estate without a Will

When a person dies without a will, his or her property is distributed according to the various state statutes of descent and distribution. Such statutes provide for distribution to various classes of relationship. The most preferred class of persons are the lineal descendents who are in a direct line of the decedent, such as children and grandchildren or parents and grandparents. A second relationship is that by affinity or marriage, and the third class consists of collateral relatives such as brothers and sisters and cousins. In default of the above classes, the decedent's estate goes to the "next of kin."

A person who dies without a will is said to be *intestate*. Distribution is made by an administrator rather than an executor, and the probate procedure is similar in many ways to that under a will.

Trusts

A trust is a relationship between two or more parties in which one party, a *trustee*, holds property for the enjoyment of the person creating the trust, the trustor or settler, or a third party. The reasons for the creation of trusts are endless; but a trust once created must be for an active purpose. The decision to have a second party manage one's property would be a valid reason for establishing a trust.

Any legally competent person can create a trust and must manifest an intent to do so. The trust instrument must reasonably describe the property that is entrusted, and the duties of the trustee must be clear. If a trust is to be revocable, that is, subject to cancellation by the trustor or another, this should be so stated in the instrument. Otherwise it will be irrevocable.

A trustor may also be the trustee, but in such a case he or she cannot be a beneficiary or person who is to enjoy the benefits of the trust. Trusts must, of course, have a lawful purpose. As the term implies, the trustee has a fiduciary responsibility and must act in good faith.

THE UNIFORM COMMERCIAL CODE

The basic document governing the conduct of business is the Uniform Commercial Code (UCC). It covers the sale of goods; commercial paper; bank deposits and collections; letters of credit; bulk transfers; warehouse receipts, bills of lading, and other documents of title; investment securities; and secured transactions.

The UCC is, in effect, a codification of many of the commonlaw rules with respect to the law of contracts, personal property, and bills and notes. It does not cover the law of real property. The UCC, in one form or another and with minor variations, has been adopted by every state.

Sales

Article 2 of the UCC contains the basic law of sales. It is sometimes referred to as "the buyer's law," because it sets out remedies for the breach of sales contracts and defines various types of warranties for goods that are sold. But it also contains remedies for abuses suffered by the seller and delineates the responsibility for goods that are in the possession of a bailee such as a trucker or railroad.

When one considers the sheer number of sales transactions that occur each day and the fact that many of them are not cash transactions, it is apparent that both buyers and sellers need the protection of the law to clearly define their respective rights and responsibilities. The article on sales should, therefore, be considered in the light of the article on secured transactions. A secured transaction is simply one in which the seller maintains a right in that which is sold until the full purchase price has been paid.

Article 2 applies specifically to the sale of "goods" that are movable and identifiable. The term excludes money that is used to pay for the goods. Even more specifically, Article 2 governs contracts for the sale of goods and recognizes different types of buyers and sellers. A "merchant," for example, is one who has special occupational skills and knowledge of the particular type of goods sold. A merchant is charged with a higher standard of care in dealing than one who is not a merchant.

Contract for the Sale of Goods

As noted, Article 2 basically governs *contracts* for the sale of goods. Most of the casual retail transactions that occur daily would thus be excluded. The Statute of Frauds in Article 2 further limits those transactions that must be covered by a written sales contract. Generally, a sales contract that provides for a price of $500 or more must be in writing. A special situation exists in Article 2 as to merchants. If a merchant receives a letter of confirmation of a transaction that is not written, he or she must, if desired, repudiate or reject the transaction within ten days just as though he or she had signed the writing. This provision cures a previous evil in which a party could repudiate a contract by simply ignoring a confirming letter. It is imperative that a buyer or seller who is in the "merchant" class closely monitor incoming mail. The secretary may therefore be instrumental in preventing an unwanted contract by default.

It should be emphasized that the requirement of the Statute of Frauds that certain contracts be in writing does not necessarily mean the existence of what most people consider a formal contract. The reason for the rule is evidentiary in the sense that as an agreement becomes more important, there is a greater need for written evidence of it. In the case of Article 2, $500 is the criterion that invokes the Statute.

A writing under the Statute must meet several requirements, however. It must be signed, although this may be done by printing, stamping, typewriting, or even initials if it is the intent of the party to authenticate the writing. The terms of the writing should give assurance that there is or was a transaction and state the quantity of goods involved. The writing may be a single one or consist of several writings such as the exchange of letters, bills of sale, or even telegrams. Lesser documents such as cash register receipts usually do not satisfy the signature requirement.

There are situations in which a transaction is taken out of the Statute of Frauds even though the price is greater than $500. If, for example, the goods are delivered by the seller and accepted by the buyer, the contract will be enforceable without a writing. Delivery and acceptance of only a part of the goods will render a contract enforceable only as to that part.

Once a valid contract, written or oral, exists, each of the parties has certain rights and responsibilities. It may seem too obvious, but the essential two acts of performance are that the seller deliver the goods and that the buyer pay for them. Such a simplistic statement raises a variety of questions. Where, for example, is delivery to be made? How is payment to be made? While goods are in transit, who bears the risk of their destruction? What if the goods are not exactly of the quantity and quality ordered? Normally it is advisable to have specific provisions in the contract that answer these questions. But in practice such specific provisions are frequently omitted, because customary practices in dealing are followed.

Delivery of Goods

The UCC, Article 2, does provide some answers. Unless otherwise stated, the place of delivery is the seller's place of business or, if there is none, the seller's residence. Or, if both parties know that the goods are at a location other than the seller's place of business, that location is the place of delivery. Such a situation might exist where the seller's goods are stored in another's warehouse.

Article 2 stipulates, unless otherwise stated, that the time for delivery is a *reasonable* time. In the event that a contract was breached on this basis, the court would decide what a reasonable time would have been. The type of goods would, of course, have a bearing upon the decision and even the hour of delivery must be reasonable. Without agreement to the contrary, a buyer is entitled to have all goods delivered at the same time.

If a contract states that the place of delivery of goods is that of the buyer, the seller must so deliver them and may do so through a carrier such as a trucking company or railroad. When the goods are turned over to the carrier, the carrier signs a bill of lading that lists goods, weight, etc. A *bill of lading* is a document by which the carrier acknowledges receipt of goods and agrees to transport them to the designated place of delivery. Generally, risk for the destruction of goods rests with the seller until time of delivery.

Acceptance or Rejection of Goods

When the goods are delivered, the buyer has the right to inspect them to ensure that they comply with the contract. The time and place for inspection are described as reasonable ones by the UCC. And sometimes because of the complexity and nature of goods, the right of inspection extends to using the goods. Such is the case of a purchaser of an automobile since a visual inspection alone might not be sufficient to discover a defect.

If upon inspection the buyer determines that goods do not conform to the terms of the contract, they may be rejected or accepted. And the buyer may also elect to accept any commercial unit or units and reject the rest. If the buyer rejects all or part of the tendered goods, he or she must promptly notify the seller and hold them with reasonable care for a period of time sufficient for the seller to remove them. The buyer cannot, of course, use the goods after rejection.

Payment for Goods

Once the buyer has accepted goods, he or she must tender payment to the seller. Any method of payment is sufficient if it is in the ordinary course of business. The seller can demand payment in legal tender (money). When this is done, the buyer must be given a reasonable extension of time to procure it. Payment by check is conditional upon its being honored on due presentment.

Warranties

The UCC sets out three kinds of warranties, the breach of which may create liability upon the seller. The most obvious warranty is an express one and need not be created by the words *warrant* or *guarantee*. Any affirmation of fact or promise by the seller may create an *express warranty* and may be determined by whether or not it is a basis for the bargain between the seller and buyer. A seller's mere "puffing" of a product—that is, an opinion or commendation of goods—does not create an express warranty. Since an express warranty is an affirmative statement, it cannot be excluded or modified as can implied warranties.

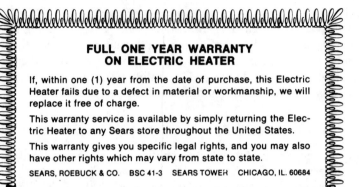

**FULL ONE YEAR WARRANTY
ON ELECTRIC HEATER**

If, within one (1) year from the date of purchase, this Electric Heater fails due to a defect in material or workmanship, we will replace it free of charge.

This warranty service is available by simply returning the Electric Heater to any Sears store throughout the United States.

This warranty gives you specific legal rights, and you may also have other rights which may vary from state to state.

SEARS, ROEBUCK & CO.   BSC 41-3   SEARS TOWER   CHICAGO, IL. 60684

Two types of *implied warranties* exist under the UCC. The first is the *warranty of merchantability*. For such a warranty to exist, the seller must be a merchant for a particular purpose as defined by the Code. Very generally, for the criteria are complex, goods are merchantable as they compare with the quality of other brands on the market and conform within variations permitted by the agreement. The reason for this warranty is that because of the merchant's special skill and knowledge, he or she is held to a higher standard for the quality of goods sold. And the UCC specifically includes the sale of food or drink for value in the warranty of merchantability.

A second implied warranty is that of *fitness* for a particular purpose. This warranty arises where the seller knows the purpose for which the goods are bought and that the buyer is relying on the seller's skill or judgment to furnish the appropriate goods.

Implied warranties may be modified or excluded. A warranty of fitness must be in writing and conspicuous. A warranty of merchantability must mention merchantability; and, if in writing, it too must be conspicuous. If a buyer examines or refuses to examine goods before entering a contract and such examination should have revealed a defect, there can be no implied warranty.

All warranties may extend to the family or those in the household of a buyer or even guests if they could reasonably expect to use or consume the product.

Secured Transactions

In recent years credit buying has become an American way of life. The practice is not new, however, although expansion of it has largely occurred in the consumer sector. Credit buying usually consists of a person's buying something and paying for it with a commitment against future income. The real estate mortgage is a form of credit buying and has its roots in antiquity.

The problem with a credit sale is that a seller parts with property to a buyer who may default on his or her promise to pay for the goods or who subsequently sells them to a third party. Article 9 of the UCC provides an orderly system that not only allows the seller's interest in goods sold on credit to be retained but also gives notice of this interest to subsequent buyers. This system is similar in many ways to the mortgage system used in real estate.

Security Interests

Article 9 of the UCC essentially covers personal property and fixtures. Because personal property is movable and real estate is not, considerable differences also exist between Article 9 security interests and the real estate mortgage. What, then, is a security interest? It is simply an interest that, once established, secures the payment or performance of an obligation. Security interests are not limited only to a buyer–seller sales situation. A may lend B money to buy an automobile. When B has purchased the automobile, A may have a security interest in it to secure the loan to B. In this situation A would be called a lender, B would be called a debtor, and the automobile would be called collateral.

A security interest is said by the UCC to "attach" at a certain time. In essence, this means that it becomes effective. When three requirements have been met and coexist, a security interest is said to attach. There must first be agreement between the lender and debtor that it attach; the secured party must have given value; and the debtor must have rights in the collateral. In the example in the above paragraph, attachment would not occur at the time of the loan but at the time B had an interest in the collateral, that is, the automobile.

The medium for agreement is a document called a *security agreement*. It must reasonably identify the collateral and be signed by the debtor. Although the secured party does not have to sign the security agreement, such is the usual practice.

Once a security agreement has attached, the lender (or creditor) has enforceable rights in the collateral and is thus protected against the default of the debtor. The secured party is also *usually* protected against subsequent purchasers of the collateral and other creditors.

Financing Statement

In the case of certain types of goods, the secured party must take one more step in order to have a fully protected interest. This procedure is known as "perfecting" the security interest and consists of filing a document called a financing statement with an appropriate agency. The place for filing varies from state to state, but typically it is with, say, the UCC Division in the Office of the Secretary of State. Here financing statements are filed and indexed under the name of the debtor.

The purpose behind the filing process is to give notice to another party considering extending credit to the debtor that there is a preexisting security interest in collateral. If, for example, A lends B $10,000 and takes a security interest in B's manufacturing equipment, A will file a financing statement to protect his or her interest. B might try to obtain another loan from C against the same collateral. If C checks with the place for filing, it will be apparent that there is another security interest in B's equipment and C will be well advised not to extend a loan to B. If C does so anyway or fails to check for a previously filed security interest, C's interest will be subordinate to that of A.

Financing statements may be filed on very simple forms that are supplied by the Secretary of State. They must include the names and addresses of both the creditor and debtor and be signed by the latter. The description of collateral need not be as specific as in the security agreement because, as noted, the purpose is only to give notice to one considering a subsequent loan or extension of credit that a security interest already exists. Addresses are given so that a prospective creditor may further investigate the matter.

Security interests may be filed before attachment, in which case perfection does not occur until attachment. If, for example, B borrows from A to buy equipment that will become the collateral in which A will have a security interest, A may file at the time of making the loan. The interest cannot attach until B purchases the equipment, and thus it is not perfected until that time.

A security interest is a perfected one if the creditor has the collateral in possession. The reason for this is that a prospective creditor is automatically put on notice of the security interest of a secured party.

Article 9 of the UCC generally classifies goods as consumer goods, equipment, farm products, and inventory. In the case of consumer goods, a security interest need not be perfected by filing, a rule largely based upon expediency. As a practical matter it would be nearly impossible to file the extremely large number of secured transactions in consumer goods. The burden of filing would be particularly heavy on retail merchants who typically sell their goods on installment contracts. Such a burden outweighs the interest of the possible creditor of the consumer. Consumer goods are defined by the

UNIFORM COMMERCIAL CODE — FINANCING STATEMENT — FORM UCC-2

INSTRUCTIONS
1. This form is designed to avoid double typing when filing with more than one office. Place this form over UCC-1.
2. PLEASE TYPE this form. Fold only along perforation for mailing.
3. Send all 3 copies with interleaved carbon paper to the filing officer. Enclose filing fee.
4. If the space provided for any item(s) on the form is inadequate the item(s) should be continued on additional sheets, preferably 5" x 8" or 8" x 10". Only one copy of such additional sheets need be presented to the filing officer with a set of three copies of the financing statement. Long schedules of collateral, indentures, etc., may be on any size paper that is convenient for the secured party.
5. If collateral is crops or goods which are or are to become fixtures, describe generally the real estate and give name of record owner.
6. When a copy of the security agreement is used as a financing statement, it is requested that it be accompanied by a completed but unsigned set of these forms, without extra fee.
7. At the time of original filing, filing officer will return third copy as an acknowledgment. At a later date, secured party may date and sign the termination legend and use third copy as a Termination Statement.

This FINANCING STATEMENT is presented to a filing officer for filing pursuant to the Uniform Commercial Code.

1 Debtor(s) (Last Name First) and address(es)	2 Secured Party(ies) and address(es)	3 Maturity date (if any): For Filing Officer (Date, Time, Number, and Filing Office)

4 This financing statement covers the following types (or items) of property:

Check ☒ if covered: ☐ Proceeds of Collateral are also covered   ☐ Products of Collateral are also covered   No. of additional sheets presented:

Filed with: _ _ _ _ _ _ _ _ _

This instrument prepared by _ _ _ _ _ _ _

By: _ _ _ _ _ _ _ _ _ _ _ _ _   By: _ _ _ _ _ _ _ _ _ _ _
        Signature(s) of Debtor(s)   Signature(s) of Secured Party(ies)

Filing Officer Copy — Alphabetical   STANDARD FORM · UNIFORM COMMERCIAL CODE · FORM UCC-2
                Approved by The Secretary of State

The Ohio Legal Blank Co., Cleveland
Publishers and Dealers Since 1883

Standard financing statement of the Uniform Commercial Code

UCC as goods ". . . used or bought primarily for personal, family, or household purposes."

It has been noted that Article 9 covers secured transactions in fixtures as well as all other kinds of personal property. The place of filing a security interest in fixtures is usually the place of filing for the real property to which an item is affixed. This would usually be in a county office such as a Registry of Deeds. Filing may therefore be either local (in a county office) or central (in the Secretary of State's Office). The UCC does not, unfortunately, define fixtures. Thus a secured party must rely on individual state interpretations. If there is any doubt, the secured party should file *both* locally and centrally.

The system for secured transactions here described results in degrees of security for the creditor. Depending on the degree of security, the UCC establishes priorities among conflicting interests in the same collateral for nonfixtures and fixtures, respectively. Under these provisions a perfected security interest has priority over an unperfected interest, and the first party to perfect has priority over a party who perfects subsequently. If A advanced credit to B on January 1st and took a security interest in B's equipment but did not file a financing statement, and if on February 1st C executed the same transaction taking a security interest in the same equipment and did file a financing statement, C's interest would have priority over that of A. Even if A filed on March 1st, C's claim would be paramount. If B became insolvent on April 1st, C's rights in B's equipment would allow C to take it in satisfaction of the debt and A's rights would be defeated.

The secretary will often be the person in a business responsible for the documentation of a secured transaction. It should be apparent that the secretary must be alert to the need for timeliness and correct procedure in satisfying the requirements of Article 9. Procrastination in filing a financing statement, for example, might leave the business unprotected in the event of a buyer's or borrower's default. The secretary should live by the maxim that "when in doubt, file!"

Bulk Sales or Transfers

It is not, happily, a common occurrence, but a merchant could transfer the majority of his or her materials, supplies, or inventory to another with the purpose of defeating creditors' claims. Article 6 of the Uniform Commercial Code regulates just such transactions and serves to protect the creditors in a bulk transaction. For example, A, a merchant hounded by creditors, says to his friend B, "B, I'm tired of this business. I'll sell you my stock at a good price." B accepts and pays A in cash for his stock. A leaves the area. What recourse do the creditors of A have?

Article 6 of the UCC deals with the matter between the bulk tranferee, B in the sample above, and the creditors of the transferor, A. First the transfer must be a "bulk" transfer. Article 6, Sec. 102 refers to a transfer not in the ordinary course of the transferor's business of ". . . a major part of the materials, supplies, merchandise, or other inventory." Article 6 does not proscribe bulk transfers; it merely dictates that certain procedures be followed, and the responsibility for so doing is largely on the transferee. In effect, an illegal or procedurally incorrect transfer is treated as no transfer at all with respect to the creditors.

The correct procedure is relatively simple. The transferee must require the transferor to supply him or her with a list of the transferor's property, that is, a schedule of the property transferred in bulk. The transferor is also required to furnish a list of his or her creditors. Next, the transferee must notify the creditors of the sale within ten days before either taking possession of the goods or paying for them. Finally, the transferee must maintain the list of creditors and schedule of property for six months and allow inspection or copying of them by the creditors.

Clearly, Article 6 is designed to prevent surprise or "midnight" sales that leave the creditor without protection. Since the very nature of a fraudulent bulk sale involves the absence of a transferor, the responsibility for compliance with Article 6 falls on the transferee. The creditors cannot be held responsible since they are not parties to the transaction nor do they ordinarily have knowledge of it.

Section 6-106 of the UCC requires that a bulk transferee apply the proceeds of the transferred goods to the creditors of the transferor as properly listed. Without correct procedure in the sale, creditors have a claim on the goods as though there had been no sale or transfer.

The law of bulk transactions logically follows that of secured transactions. It should again be noted that Article 6 does not invalidate a bulk transfer. It only provides protection to the creditors of the transferor and does not in any way affect the seller–buyer relationship in a bulk transfer.

Commercial Paper

The law concerning commercial paper was once known as the *law of negotiable instruments*. The latter term was possibly more descriptive than the present one because the negotiability of commercial paper is one of its main characteristics. The law concerning commercial paper is largely contained in Article 3 of the Uniform Commercial Code.

Money is, as it always has been, the principal medium for the exchange of value. But because money has value as it stands, there is always the danger of losing it or having it stolen, and the finder or thief will have little trouble in using it. Commercial paper is in a sense "substitute money," but it acquires value only when signed or endorsed.

Types of Commercial Paper

There are four types of commercial paper: promissory notes, drafts, checks, and certificates of deposit.

Promissory notes. A promissory note is basically a promise by one party to pay another party a certain sum of money either on demand or at a specific time. If the note is payable on demand, it is almost the same as money to the holder of it. If A signs a promissory note in favor of B on demand, B can use it to pay value to C because it can be immediately converted to cash. If a note is for payment on a certain future date, it serves to extend credit and is therefore not

Name of Student: _____

Student No.: _____

PROMISSORY NOTE AND DISCLOSURES

$ _____   Date: _____, 19 ___

    FOR VALUE RECEIVED, the undersigned (which includes all "undersigned" jointly and severally if more than one) promises to pay to the order of _____ . (which includes any holder hereof) at its offices: (i) the Amount Financed shown in item 1 below; (ii) interest on the balance of such Amount Financed from time to time remaining unpaid, at the rate per annum shown in item 3 below, from the date hereof, in accordance with the Payment Schedule shown in item 5 below. All payments shall be applied first to interest accrued to the date upon which payment is made, and the remainder in reduction of the Amount Financed. The undersigned and any guarantor agree that _____ may from time to time grant extensions or renewals for any period. Undersigned will pay reasonable attorney's fees not in excess of 15% of the unpaid balance after default and referral to an attorney. DEFAULT shall result from any of the following events: (a) failure to make a payment as required by this Note; (b) the significant impairment of the prospect of payment or performance, which includes, but is not limited to: death, insolvency, assignment for benefit of creditors, or the commencement of any proceeding under any bankruptcy or insolvency laws by or against undersigned. In the event of default, holder may, at its option, declare the entire unpaid balance of the Amount Financed and accrued interest thereon immediately due and payable without notice or demand, subject, however, to such rights, if any, as undersigned may have to cure a default for failure to make a required payment.

Terms and Disclosures

1. Amount Financed $ _____
2. **FINANCE CHARGE:** $ _____
3. **ANNUAL PERCENTAGE RATE**   _____ %
4. Total of Payments (1+2) $ _____
5. Payment Schedule: This Note is payable in _____ consecutive monthly installments of $ _____ each and one final monthly installment of $ _____, commencing on _____, 19 ___ and on the same date of each month thereafter. If payments are not made when due, one or more additional payments may be necessary to pay in full.

NOTICE TO CONSUMER: 1. Do not sign this Note before you read it. 2. You are entitled to a copy of this Note. 3. You may prepay the unpaid balance at any time without penalty, except for minimum charges as permitted by law.

WITNESS:

_____

_____

                                Address

Typical form of a promissory note (including terms) agreed to by a student and the financial officer of a college. This type of note is essentially an unconditional promise to pay the stipulated sum of money (often in designated installments) by some specified future date to the party named in the document. The note may be secured or unsecured.

Account No.

Date of Issuance ...., 19 ......

FIXED-RATE FIXED TERM CERTIFICATE ACCOUNT

HOME FEDERAL SAVINGS & LOAN ASSOCIATION OF LAKEWOOD ("ASSOCIATION")
LAKEWOOD, OHIO 44107

1. ACCOUNT SUMMARY SECTION

ACCOUNT
HOLDER

Opening Balance	Initial Maturity Date ....
Rate of Earnings % per annum	Extended Maturity Date ....
Frequency of Compounding	Renewal Term ....
Minimum Balance Requirement	Minimum Addition $ ....

$ ....

EARNINGS DISTRIBUTION DATES

Beginning .... and ....
thereafter, with the last distribution on the final maturity date.

2. GENERAL SECTION This certifies that the Accountholder holds a savings account with the Opening Balance and for the initial term expiring on the Initial Maturity Date shown hereon in Home Federal Savings & Loan Association of Lakewood, Lakewood, Ohio.

The Accountholder may, from time to time, with the consent of the Association, make additions to the balance in this account in any amount not less than the Minimum Addition provided for in Section 1. In the event of any such addition, the term of this account shall be extended so that the period from the date of such addition to the Extended Maturity Date (which shall be recorded with the entry as to such addition) shall not be less than the initial term (or Renewal Term, if the addition is made during a Renewal Term).

3. EARNINGS SECTION This account shall receive earnings at the rate and with the Frequency of Compounding as above set forth. Such earnings shall be payable on the Earnings Distribution Dates above set forth, provided the balance in the account is not reduced below the Minimum Balance Requirement. If such balance is reduced below the Minimum Balance Requirement, the Rate of Earnings on the remaining balance shall thereafter be reduced to the rate then paid on regular savings accounts. (See also Section 5).

4. AUTOMATIC RENEWAL This account shall be automatically renewed at the close of business on the Initial Maturity Date or the maturity date of any renewal or extended term unless (1) withdrawn within the 10-day period referred to in Section 5 hereof or (2) at least 15 days prior to any such date, the Association gives written notice to the Accountholder that this account will not be renewed at the Rate of Earnings and or the Renewal Term set forth above. In such event, the account will either be extended for such additional term and at such rate of earnings as set forth in said notice or the account will be converted to a regular savings account and receive earnings at the rate then paid on regular savings accounts.

A form acknowledging that a certain person holds a certificate-of-deposit account in a particular savings and loan association. Certificates of deposit of this kind are usually time deposits; that is, they are payable on or after a stated future date at a stipulated rate of interest. They are also payable on demand or subject to withdrawal, but in either case the rate of interest is reduced. These certificates are transferable and negotiable instruments.

the same thing as money. Parties to a promissory note are the "maker," the one promising to pay, and the "payee," the one to whom the promise is made. Promissory notes must be in writing and signed by the maker. They may be secured by the borrower, who provides some kind of collateral to the lender. When a mortgage on property is given to the lender, the note is known as a mortgage note; in the event of nonpayment, the lender can foreclose on the property for satisfaction.

Drafts. A draft, or bill of exchange, involves three parties. One party orders a second party to pay a third party. For example, A, the drawer, orders B, the drawee, to pay a certain amount of cash to C, the payee. The system presupposes that B is in some way indebted to A. Drafts are the least common form of commercial paper.

Checks. Checks, of course, are very common and are a part of the fabric of modern business. A check is very simply a draft drawn on a bank. Here A, who has deposited money in the bank, orders it on demand to pay an amount to another, C. The bank would be similar to B in the example of a draft above.

Checks have a utilitarian value over money. When cashed by the payee, the check is canceled by the bank and returned to the maker. It thereby serves as a receipt or at least an indication that payment has been made. One of the characteristics of commercial paper is transferability. Thus, A may write a check in favor of C, who, in turn, uses it to pay a debt to D. Transfer is done by C signing it over or "endorsing" it to D. When the check is finally returned to A, C's signature serves as evidence that C has received the face value of the check. It could also serve as evidence of the discharge of the debt of C to D.

Certificates of Deposit. A final type of commercial paper is the certificate of deposit. In recent years the certificate of deposit, or "CD," as it is commonly called, has gained in popularity. There are many forms of these certificates, but what is common to them all is redemption on demand. One popular form is the six-month CD. Usually a minimum amount of money is required, often $10,000. The purchaser is told that the money must be left in the bank for the full term of the certificate. If it is not left for the full period, a reduced interest rate will be applied. The latter situation is often referred to as a "penalty." But CDs of any kind must be redeemable on demand.

Value of Commercial Paper

The law of commercial paper is essentially protective of the rights of the various parties to it. There are problems inherent in a system that allows people to "make" money even if it is only substitute money. The maker of a check, for example, may not have sufficient funds on deposit with the bank to cover it. Another problem, especially with checks, is the possibility of forgery or an intentionally written bad check. The secretary who may receive checks on behalf of the employer should insist on identification of the party writing a check. While many checks are overdrawn through a simple mistake by the drawer and may be eventually satisfied, it may require an unreasonable amount of time to collect on such a debt.

RELATIONSHIPS BETWEEN BUSINESSES AND EMPLOYEES/AGENTS

There are various relationships common to all business entities and the people who assist them. The most common of these relationships include services, such as employment, agency, and the hiring of independent contractors.

Employer–Employee Relations

An employer–employee, or master–servant, relationship exists when one person performs services, for a salary, under the control of and exclusively for the business entity. This relationship is contractual; the employment agreement may be written or oral, express, or implied. Depending on the size of the business entity and in some instances the type of business involved, various statutes, both federal and state, may apply to and control such factors as the minimum amount of wages the employee can receive, the types of insurance coverage that must be provided by the employer (such as worker's compensation and disability insurance), and whether the employer must be an equal opportunity employer. Federal and state law provide that the employer must withhold income taxes and social security contributions from the employee's pay.

Agencies

An agency is created when one person or business entity, the *agent*, acts for and on behalf of another person or business entity; the *principal*. The principal, by an agency agreement, confers upon the agent authority to act in the principal's place and stead with a third party. This authority can be general or limited to do a specific act. Generally, any act that a business entity or individual can legally do can be delegated to the agent.

The relationship between an agent and the principal is said to be a *fiduciary relationship*. This means that the agent owes the highest degree of care and responsibility to the principal. The agent acts for the principal in dealings with a third party or parties. When the agent acts within his or her conferred authority, the principal is bound by the acts of the agent to the third party. If the agent exceeds the authority conferred, the principal is not bound to the agreement entered into by the agent with the third party unless the principal ratifies the agent's unauthorized acts. For example, if the principal retains a down payment on a contract that the agent was not specifically authorized to enter into, then ratification occurs.

The authority given to the agent can be written or oral. Some of the more common forms of agency agreements are *power of attorney* and real estate broker's *listing agreements*. Some states require that certain agency agreements concerning real property must be in writing and recorded.

The agent is not an employee of the principal, but is an independent contractor. That is, the agent solely determines how to perform and execute the limited authority given to him or her by the principal. In fact, the agent may have many principals for whom it performs services, as in the case of building managers, real estate brokers, or manufacturer's representatives. No taxes are withheld from the agent's fee or commission for services rendered. As a separate entity, the agent pays these items. The agent may have employees and may hire other independent contractors to aid him or her in performing the authorized duties or in performing any function necessary for the operation of the agent's business.

Independent Contractors

While agents are independent contractors, not all independent contractors are agents. Any business entity (a sole proprietorship, partnership, or corporation) can contract with another business entity to perform certain acts or services not involving a third party. For example, a corporation may hire a computer consultant to create a data base program, or a building owner may hire a contractor to remodel an apartment. In these situations, no third party is involved, and therefore no agency situation exists.

FORMS OF DOING BUSINESS

There are several types of business entities: individual proprietorships, different types of partnerships, and corporations.

Individual Proprietorship

In a strictly legal sense a proprietor is one who has rights in something—that is, an owner. A proprietor in a business sense, then, is one who owns and operates a business alone. The proprietorship is probably the largest single form of business operation.

The term *proprietorship* gives no indication of size. A proprietor's business may be small, such as a one-chair barber shop, or large, employing thousands of people at many locations. What is common to all proprietorships is the centralization of control and authority in one person, the owner. A proprietor of a business is ultimately responsible for all decisions. For this, he or she reaps the benefits of the business out of net profits.

There are distinct advantages and disadvantages in doing business as a proprietor. With the decision-making process in but one person, there is no need to go through the lengthy process of getting agreement such as is necessary in multi-owned businesses. The greatest disadvantage of the proprietorship is that the owner has unlimited liability. The owner's personal assets, as well as business assets, are accountable and liable for the payment of business debts if the business fails.

Probably the greatest problem of the proprietorship is forming and acquiring capital for the conduct of the business. Where more than one person owns a business, each of the owners contributes or brings something of value into it. Thus by "pooling" assets, the multi-owned business is able to operate on a larger capital amount. Also, while centralized decision-making may be an advantage in one sense, it may be a disadvantage in another sense. The collective skills of, say, a partnership may result in better decisions for the business. A proprietor can overcome the disadvantage of unilateral decision-making by hiring those with special skills to serve in advisory roles, but he or she must also understand that those hired do not have the same proprietary interest as the owner.

No special documentation is needed to form a proprietorship, and a proprietor's earnings out of profits are taxed to the individual. This is to be compared with corporate profits, which are taxed first to the corporation and again as income to the shareholder. A double-taxation structure is therefore avoided by a proprietorship.

If the proprietor operates his or her business under an assumed name, most jurisdictions require that a certificate of doing business be filed in the county clerk's office where the business is located. This certificate shows the name under which the proprietor is doing business and the name and address of the proprietor.

Partnership

A partnership provides for ownership of a business by two or more persons, and there is no limit on the number of partners who may participate. The partners may be equal or unequal (junior partners). This is usually determined by the amount of assets each partner contributes to the partnership business.

A partnership is a voluntary, contractual association. Upon the formation of a partnership, each of the partners brings something of value to it, such as money, other personal or real property, or a skill. Based upon a negotiated agreement, partners usually enter a written partnership agreement that states the proportionate contribution of each partner. Partnership agreements do not necessarily have to be in writing, but they must satisfy the requirement of the Statute of Frauds, which states that contracts that cannot be performed within one year must be in writing.

Any business or profession can form a partnership. The disadvantage of the partnership form of business is that the partnership entity and each and every partner are severally and jointly liable for all partnership debts.

As in the case of a single proprietorship, many states require that a certificate of doing business as partners be filed in the county clerk's office where the partnership maintains its business office. The certificate must show the assumed business name the partnership is using, its principal business address, and the name and address of each partner. When the partnership is dissolved, a certificate of discontinuance of business as partners must also be filed in the appropriate county clerk's office.

Duties and Rights of Partners

As a practical matter, it is sensible for partners to have a written partnership agreement. The agreement should clearly specify the rights, duties, and responsibilities of all concerned.

Each partner is, in addition to being a co-owner, a principal in the conduct of the business. As such, each partner has the authority to do a variety of things on behalf of the business. The scope of a partner's authority includes making contracts that bind the partnership, selling goods (but not other assets) in the regular course of business, making purchases, obtaining loans, purchasing insurance, and hiring employees. In practice, partnerships assign the various areas of authority to individual partners.

A partnership might be formed in this way: Partner A has invented and patented a very superior mousetrap, which he brings into the business as his contribution. In the written agreement it is stated that his contribution is worth $50,000, that he will be in charge of the manufacturing process for the traps, and that he will share in the profits equally with the other partners. Partner B owns a building worth $50,000, which he will contribute and in which the mousetraps will be made. Partner B has an advertising background and it is agreed that he will be in charge of marketing. He, too, will receive a share of the profits. Partner C brings in $50,000 in cash, which will be used as start-up and as operating capital. Partner C is assigned responsibility for the general administration of the business and will also receive a proportionate share of the profits.

This example serves to show how authority might be assigned and thus limited. Partner A might have authority to purchase raw materials and manufacturing equipment and to hire plant workers. Partner B might be given authority to sell the mousetraps on the market and hire salespeople to solicit orders. Partner C would logically have authority to obtain a loan to be used for working capital, to purchase liability insurance, and to hire clerical workers. Such a division of labor is a sensible way to ensure a smoothly functioning cooperative organization. An agreement among partners as to the scope of authority of each is binding between them.

Generally, partners have certain rights in the business. These may be and should be resolved in a written partnership agreement. Without such an agreement, all partners have equal rights. One such right is to manage the business. As noted, it is not very practical for all partners to manage all areas of the business. Also, without agreement to the contrary, all partners have a right to share equally in the profits of the business. Partners do not have a right to be compensated other than by a share of profits. If two partners manage the firm while a third partner is on vacation, they are not entitled to extra compensation for their extra work.

Partners have a right to inspect the books of a firm at any time. The books should be kept at the principal place of business for this purpose.

Terminating a Partnership

Partnerships may be dissolved or terminated in several ways. First, partnerships may be formed by agreement for a specific purpose or for a specific time. Upon the accomplishment of purpose or expiration of time, dissolution occurs. Even before that time *all* partners may agree to dissolution. Where no definite term is specified, a partnership may be dissolved by the express will of one partner only. If by agreement other partners can expel a partner, such expulsion for cause will result in dissolution. Other reasons for dissolution include the death or bankruptcy of any partner or the bankruptcy of the partnership itself.

Upon application of a partner, a court will decree a dissolution in several instances. These include the insanity of a partner or a partner's incapacity to perform his or her part of the partnership contract. A court will also decree dissolution where the conduct of a partner is prejudicial to carrying on the business or where a partner willfully breaches the partnership agreement. Finally, a court will dissolve a partnership that can be continued only at a loss or dissolve it for purely equitable reasons.

Once dissolution has occurred, someone must "wind up" or finally complete the business of the partnership. This may be done by the legal representative of the last remaining partner. Winding up consists generally of satisfying partnership liabilities and distributing the partnership assets to qualifying parties.

Limited Partnership

In most jurisdictions, the creation of a limited partnership is governed by statute. It is a partnership formed by two or more persons having as members one or more general partners and one or more limited partners.

A certificate of limited partnership must be filed in the county where the limited partnership has its main office for business. In many respects, it is similar to a certificate of incorporation, showing among other things the firm name, the purpose of the business to be transacted, its principal office, the duration of the limited partnership, the name and address of each general and limited partner, and the amount of cash or property contributed by each limited partner. Many states require that the limited partnership certificate, or a notice containing the substance of the certificate, be published in newspapers in the county in which the certificate was filed.

While limited partnerships can be formed to carry on any form of business activity, they are often used to form real estate syndicates and general stock brokerage businesses.

The *limited partners*, as such, are not bound by the obligations of the partnership. This is the main difference between a limited partnership and the partnership form of doing business. The limited partner's liability for the entity's debts is limited to the amount of money contributed to or invested into the limited partnership, and such a partner is not liable to creditors. The contribution of the limited partner may be cash or other property but cannot be services.

However, the *general partners*, as in the case of a partnership, are jointly and severally liable for all partnership obligations and debts. Only the general partners can act for and on behalf of the entity. They have the power and right to do anything that partners can do in the partnership form of doing business, provided that such act does not violate the certificate of limited partnership. The contribution of the general partners may be cash, property, or services to be rendered.

Incorporation

Corporations are organized, and thereby incorporated, under the laws of the state in which their principal place of business is located. In the state of incorporation, a corporation is considered to be a *domestic corporation*. If the corporation does business in any other state, it is considered to be a *foreign corporation* doing business in that state. Each foreign corporation is required to file a *certificate of doing business* in each and every state in which it operates. Many corporations, usually corporate giants with millions of stockholders, operate and conduct business not only in all fifty states but also internationally, having satisfied the legal requirements of each country in which they operate.

However, a corporation need not be large. In fact, in most states a corporation can be formed having only one person, who may simultaneously hold all of the corporate offices (president, vice-president, secretary, and treasurer) and comprise the entire board of directors.

Unlike an individual, the corporation's *life* may be perpetual or for a specific term, after which it will cease to exist. In law, a corporation is considered to be an artificial person and is entitled to most of the constitutional protections afforded to a natural person, such as due process of law. In addition, a corporation, as an individual and partnership, can avail itself of the protection of the bankruptcy laws to discharge its debts or reorganize. The corporation also has many of the same duties and obligations of a natural person, such as the payment of income taxes.

Reasons for Incorporation

The reasons for the corporate form of doing business are twofold. First, it permits a person to invest in a company and to share in the profits of it while having liability only to the degree of investment. If, for example, an individual purchases 10 shares of stock in a given company and the shares cost $100 each, he or she has a $1,000 investment. But the value of the shares may increase or decrease if they are traded on a market. If the market value rises to $120, the value of the total investment will be $1,200. If the company fails, the investor will be out of pocket $1,000.

This limitation on liability makes an investment far more attractive. In a proprietorship or partnership, the parties are responsible for all liabilities—even those above and beyond the amount invested.

The second reason for the corporate form follows from the first reason, the feature of limited liability. Because investors naturally want to keep risk at a minimum, they are more willing to invest in corporations. It is therefore easier for the corporation to acquire capital. For a corporation, the pool of investors is virtually without limit. Proprietorships and partnerships do not have such an advantage.

Types of Corporations

Corporations are classified as public, private, and quasi-public. Public corporations exist for some governmental purpose such as a municipality. Private corporations are those that are privately owned and, as will be explained, may be for profit or nonprofit. Quasi-public corporations are those that serve a public need but that are privately owned. Public utilities are an example of quasi-public corporations. They usually are regulated by the government and have territorial protection from competition through a licensing process. Although it may be confusing, private corporations whose stock is publicly traded are known as public corporations in the business community.

The Creation of Corporations

The creation or formation of a corporation, like other business forms, begins with an idea. Someone feels that the idea has commercial value. When a person decides to form a business and it is to be in the corporate form, he or she is known as a *promoter*. Most corporations are formed to make a profit for the owners, but they may also be designated as "not-for-profit," which results in a tax-free status. A corporation may be created for any lawful purpose such as manufacturing a product, selling goods, or providing a service. Schools, hospitals, and religious organizations are examples of nonprofit corporations, and they may not be owned as such by individuals.

Most states allow licensed professionals such as doctors, lawyers, accountants, and dentists to form *professional service corporations* in order to practice their profession for profit. When a professional service corporation is formed, all incorporators must be duly licensed to practice the same profession for which the corporation is being formed. The stock cannot be issued to nor owned by any unlicensed person. When such a corporation is formed, the words *Professional Corporation* or the letters *PC* must appear after the name. However, unlike other corporations, each shareholder of a professional services corporation is personally and fully liable and accountable for any negligent or wrongful act or misconduct committed by him or her or by any person under his/her direct supervision and control while rendering professional services on behalf of such corporation.

Tasks of the promoter. Once a decision has been made to incorporate and the type of corporation has been selected, the promoter begins preparations for eventual incorporation. The promoter has three basic tasks. First, he or she must promote the original idea that gave rise to the decision to form a new business. In effect, promotion of the idea is to get financial backing for the venture. The promoter works under a considerable handicap in that all of his or her efforts are tentative and depend upon eventual incorporation. The promoter cannot sell shares in the corporation until it exists. Instead, he or she procures subscriptions or promises to buy shares when they are available.

The promoter's second task is to perform those acts that will enable the corporation to function once it has come into existence. Such acts might be to acquire a place of business, buy equipment, or hire employees. Again, the promoter is handicapped by the lack of existence of the corporation. If the promoter enters into contracts, he or she is personally bound by them unless the agreement states otherwise. While the promoter cannot bind the corporation, in practice the corporation once formed will agree to become a party in these contracts in order to relieve the promoter of personal liability. If for any reason the corporation is not formed as planned, the promoter remains liable on the contracts he or she has made.

The promoter's third and final task is to carry out the statutory procedure for incorporation. The first step is to prepare and submit a document commonly known as the Articles of Incorporation, usually to the Secretary of State. The articles must include certain information such as the name of the corporation, its purpose, the amount of capital stock to be authorized together with the number of shares into which it is to be divided, the place of business, the duration of existence that many states permit to be perpetual, the names of officers and directors for the first year of operation, the names and addresses of the incorporators and the number of shares for which each has subscribed, and the name and address of an agent or clerk. The latter requirement exists to give one who is suing the corporation a contact for the service of process. There are variations in these requirements from state to state.

Once submitted, the Articles of Incorporation are examined by a government official and, if approved, are returned to the new corporation. Articles may be amended at a later time if, for example, the purpose of the corporation changes. Approved Articles are in essence a contract between the state, the corporation, and the owners (shareholders). They become the document that confers authority upon the corporation.

Powers of a corporation. Once created, the corporation has powers and is required to follow certain procedures. Among the powers of a corporation are those to establish a corporate seal, make bylaws that supplement the Articles of Incorporation, issue stocks and bonds, borrow money, sell or acquire property, and even invest in other corporations.

Possibly one of the most important items of business at the first meeting of a corporation is to make bylaws for the conduct of the business. *Bylaws* are analogous to written partnership agreements. It is usually desirable to keep the Articles of Incorporation both brief and general and to provide specificity in bylaws. Articles should be effective for the life of the corporation and can be changed only upon application to the state. Bylaws can and should be changed when necessary, and this may be done within the corporation by the shareholders. Since the bylaws are a reflection of the will of the owners, they are binding on those who conduct the business of the corporation. Some states allow directors to amend bylaws. If a corporation wishes to retain this power for shareholders only, such must be done in the Articles of Incorporation.

Corporate Organization

The lines of authority in a corporation run from the shareholders who are the owners, to the board of directors, to the officers. Directors are elected by the shareholders and in turn appoint the officers of the corporation. Usually the executive officers consist of a president, one or more vice-presidents, a secretary, and a treasurer. One person could be a shareholder, director, and officer; and some corporations require that directors be shareholders.

Shareholders may make policy indirectly through their power to elect directors. Frequently, too, a power is reserved to make broad policy changes such as the establishment of a pension plan. When a shareholder wishes to change policy, he or she does so by putting a resolution before the other shareholders for vote.

Frequently, because of geographical distribution or for other reasons, shareholders cannot attend meetings. In such an event, the shareholder is entitled to vote through another person, a practice known as "voting by proxy."

Although a few states forbid it, most states provide for a practice known as "cumulative voting." This process provides that each shareholder have a number of votes equal to the number of shares owned multiplied by the number of directors to be elected. Cumulative voting provides that a minority of shareholders can have representation on the board of directors.

Shareholders meet regularly, usually annually. No notice is required, although most corporations not only provide notice of regular meetings but provide forms for proxy votes as well. Special meetings do require notice and are usually called by the board of directors. In some cases special meetings are called by a fixed percentage of the shareholders. Quorum requirements for a valid meeting are based on either a specified percentage of shareholders being present or on a specified percentage of voting stock being represented. Once a quorum has been established, shareholders cannot obstruct the conduct of business by leaving and breaking a quorum.

The board of directors. The management of the corporation is the responsibility of the board of directors. Directors are considered to be fiduciaries or persons who are in a position of special trust by virtue of that position. They owe their allegiance to the corporation in general and specifically to the shareholders. As fiduciaries, directors should be careful to avoid any conflict of interest such as favoritism toward a relative or another business interest. A director should refrain from voting on a matter that might raise a conflict of interest. Similarly, a director should not use information acquired through the office for personal gain if such use is contrary to the interests of the corporation.

The bylaws of most corporations provide for regular board meetings, and directors usually cannot vote by proxy. The reason for requiring that a director be physically present is based on the idea that attendance is meeting a responsibility, whereas a shareholder's voting by proxy is the waiver of a right. As a rule, special meetings may be called by the chairperson, the president, or any two directors; bylaws frequently provide that an executive committee of the board can act on matters between meetings.

Corporate officers. As noted, officers are considered to be agents of the corporation, which, in turn, is the principal. When in this role, officers' conduct is governed by the law of agency. The scope of authority of an officer includes those actions that are consistent with the general purposes of the corporation as delineated in the articles of incorporation and the bylaws.

Officers derive their authority from the board of directors that appoints them. Rarely, officers may be appointed by the shareholders. Logically, directors should have the power of appointment because of their responsibility for management of the corporation and the fact that officers are the agents of management.

Termination of a Corporation

Corporations may be terminated by either voluntary or involuntary actions. Unfortunately, the vast majority of corporate terminations are involuntary, because of the failure of the business.

A corporation may be dissolved by written consent of shareholders, as by a vote on a resolution to dissolve. Such a resolution may be proposed by the board of directors or by shareholders possessing among them 20 percent of the outstanding shares of the corporation. After the voting procedure takes place, the corporation must file a "statement of intent to dissolve" with the Secretary of State and must notify all creditors of the filing. At this time the corporation ceases business and begins the winding-up process.

Insolvency in itself does not automatically terminate a corporation. But insolvency would probably lead to bankruptcy and that, in turn, would lead to a forced sale of the assets of the corporation. So as a practical matter, it could not continue to operate and exist without any assets.

Corporations may terminate because of a consolidation or merger of two or more corporations where it is legal under antitrust legislation. A consolidation occurs when two corporations join to form a third. If, for example, Company A and Company B consolidate to form Company C, A and B cease to exist and their combined assets are those of C. In a merger, A would acquire B and continue as A while B would terminate. There is one other multicorporate relationship, the conglomerate, which does not involve termination. A conglomerate exists when one corporation, a parent company, acquires another corporation that exists for a different purpose. If, for example, an oil company acquired a chain of motels, it would be a conglomerate. Usually corporations become conglomerates to diversify activities or to avoid the antitrust prohibition on consolidations and mergers.

Finally, corporations may be terminated for cause by the government authorizing it or by court decree. The latter method is used when a board of directors becomes so deadlocked that the company can't continue operations.

For the Specialized Secretary

The Medical Secretary

by Lois M. Burns, Ed.D.

A career as a medical secretary offers a challenging and rewarding experience with opportunity for professional and intellectual growth. Because of the ever-increasing need and demand for good medical care, the career of a medical secretary will continue to be available and growing. And, since medical research is ongoing with new diagnostic and treatment methods being developed, the medical secretary will find there is always something new to learn. Good medical care is not possible without the trained medical secretary.

To be successful, the medical secretary must possess good secretarial and English skills, a knowledge of medical terminology, and personal attributes necessary for working with physicians and patients.

To appreciate the importance of the medical secretary, it is essential to know what medical secretaries are, what tasks they perform, what qualifications they must have, where they are employed, what professional certifications they may obtain, and what professional organizations they may join. This chapter touches on all of these topics and then discusses medical communications, medical records, insurance claims processing and accounting procedures, and medical office technology. A brief glossary, which lists prefixes and suffixes commonly used in medical terms, completes the chapter.

WHAT A MEDICAL SECRETARY IS

A medical secretary performs the administrative and secretarial functions required at a particular medical facility and sometimes also performs some clinical functions by assisting the doctor in the examination and treatment of patients. The medical secretary is a trained member of the medical health-care team.

Tasks

The trained and competent medical secretary manages the medical office smoothly and efficiently, thus saving the doctor time and work. Some tasks may be routine. However, there can be no routine in handling patients. Each patient is different, with specific needs.

The specific tasks performed by the medical secretary are varied in scope. In general, they can be grouped as administrative or secretarial duties and clinical duties.

Administrative/Secretarial Duties

handling the telephone
obtaining and recording messages from the answering service
scheduling, canceling, and rescheduling patients' appointments

greeting patients

recording patients' visits

quoting and collecting fees

sending out bills

preparing and processing insurance claim forms

maintaining financial records

ordering and maintaining office supplies and equipment

typing and transcribing dictated and handwritten correspondence
and case histories

composing correspondence

maintaining patients' records

opening, sorting, and distributing mail

handling petty cash

making bank deposits

taking patients' medical histories

assisting patients in understanding the doctor's instructions regarding their prescribed health-care treatment

filing and pulling patients' charts, reports, and records for their
visits

arranging for patients' hospital reservations

Clinical Duties

taking patients' medical histories

measuring patients' vital signs: temperature, pulse, respiration,
blood pressure

sterilizing instruments and equipment

positioning and draping patients for examination

collecting specimens from patients and either sending them to a
laboratory or performing certain diagnostic tests for which one
has been trained

taking electrocardiograms

assisting doctors with the patients' examinations or treatment

keeping medical supply cabinets well stocked

Qualifications

The qualifications for a medical secretary depend on whether the
specific position requires mainly secretarial/administrative tasks, clinical tasks, or both; on the specialty of the physician; and on the nature
and size of the medical facility. A medical secretary/assistant in a

small office may be called on for a wide range of duties, whereas one in a large facility with a large staff and greater specialization may be required to perform only a limited number of specific tasks (e.g., transcribing medical records).

In all situations the medical secretary should have a desire to help people, strong interpersonal skills, and personal characteristics such as patience, poise, tact, consideration, dependability, punctuality, and flexibility. Also important are carefulness, accuracy, and attention to detail, as well as respect for confidentiality. It should go without saying that a well-groomed appearance is also important, since the medical secretary must convey a professional image and create an impression that office procedures and medical attention are efficient.

The medical secretary must be proficient in English pronunciation, spelling, grammar, and punctuation. In addition, a basic understanding of anatomy, medical terminology, and the legal implications of the practice of medicine is essential. Such knowledge is invaluable in transcribing and typing medical correspondence, case histories, laboratory reports, medical abstracts, and manuscripts.

The secretary must also know how to maintain patient records, quote and collect fees, process insurance claims, maintain financial records, and inventory and order office and medical supplies. Familiarity with computers is a plus as more and more medical facilities are using them to assist in patient recordkeeping, patient billing, insurance claims processing, and appointment scheduling. Courteous and efficient use of the telephone is also essential, as is familiarity with filing methods and the use of common office equipment.

If the medical secretary is required to perform some clinical duties, there are additional qualifications, some of which depend on the physician's specialty. The medical secretary must know the name and purpose of the instruments used in the medical practice and their proper care and use. To prevent infection, appliances and instruments used in the examination and treatment of patients must be sterilized. The assistant must be familiar with the methods of sterilization, although many items are now disposable. In assisting with an examination or treatment, the assistant is expected to hand the instruments to the physician as needed, assembling them in order of their use and making sure that all are clean and in working order.

Positioning and draping the patient for examination are important clinical functions of the medical secretary. He or she must know the standard positions for specific types of examinations and treatments. The assistant should also know how to take pulse, respiration, and temperature readings and how to measure blood pressure.

If the secretary/assistant is to perform or assist in any routine laboratory procedures, special training is usually needed. The assistant may be trained to collect and label specimens, prepare slides, and perform specific tests on the specimens or arrange for their delivery to a special laboratory. Absolute accuracy, honesty, and reliability are essential.

Educational Requirements

The minimum educational requirement for a job as a medical secretary is a high school diploma; however, many positions require additional education. Vocational/technical institutes offer three-to-six-month training programs, and many two-year colleges offer an associate's degree program that provides a broad foundation in both clinical and administrative skills. Courses cover medical terminology, medicolegal topics, medical office procedures, medical transcription, medical assisting procedures, keyboarding, business English, accounting, word processing, basic biological sciences, basic laboratory techniques, cardiopulmonary resuscitation (CPR), and human relations.

Places of Employment

The medical secretary may be employed in a doctor's office, a medical clinic, a hospital, a public health facility, a health maintenance organization (HMO), a nursing home, a research center, a laboratory, an insurance company, a pharmaceutical company, a government or private health service agency, a medical transcription service, a business that manufactures medical supplies and equipment, or the medical department of any large business.

Medical Ethics and the Law

Medicine is perhaps the oldest profession to have developed a code to govern its practitioners. These principles of right and wrong are referred to as *medical ethics*. Medical ethics concerns itself with a standard of conduct; *medical etiquette* deals with courtesy, manners, and customs. These two areas complement each other and are often formally set forth in social contracts and codes.

About 400 B.C. Hippocrates, the Greek physician known as the Father of Medicine, devised a brief statement of principles to govern the conduct of physicians toward their patients and the public. The *Oath of Hippocrates* has been taken by physicians for centuries and remains an inspiration to the physicians of today.

The American Medical Association (AMA) formulated its own principles of medical ethics, which were accepted by the medical profession in the United States. They have been revised and updated several times, but their moral intent has never been changed. These principles are not laws but standards. A physician who violates the ethical standards of an association may be censured or have his/her membership in the organization suspended.

While the code and standards and their interpretation are directed toward the physician, the medical secretary is considered an agent of the physician and plays an important role in applying these same standards of conduct.

Law as applied to the practice of medicine holds many responsibilities for both the doctor and the medical team. The law is different in the different states. The *Medical Practice Act* of each state regulates all activities in the health field. Its general principles prescribe who must be licensed to perform various procedures, the requirements for licensure, the duties imposed by licensure, and government regulations. Violation of a law followed by conviction may result in punishment by fine, imprisonment, or revocation of licensure.

Professional liability encompasses all civil liability that a physician can incur as a result of professional acts. However, the *Good Samaritan Acts* protect the physician from liability for civil damages that may occur as a result of emergency care.

Negligence as applied to the medical profession is called *malpractice*. Most patients never consider taking legal action against their physicians. The medical secretary, who must understand the legal implications of the practice of medicine, can play a role in preventing litigation by

establishing good patient rapport

keeping all information confidential

avoiding the transmittal of criticisms of physicians to a patient

avoiding discussion of a patient's condition, diagnosis, or treatment with him or her

keeping complete and accurate records

obtaining proper authorization, releases, and consents

using discretion in telephone and office conversations

notifying the physician if learning that the patient is under treatment by another physician for the same condition

being available to assist the doctor.

The medical secretary must always remember that the relationship between the doctor and the patient is legally considered a contract. All information furnished to a doctor by the patient—information the medical secretary may have access to or be aware of—is considered confidential and may not be divulged to any unauthorized person.

Professional Organizations and Certifications

The professional medical secretary/assistant enjoys an enviable professional status. He or she is eligible to join professional associations and can apply for certification in the medical field.

The American Association of Medical Assistants (AAMA) and the American Association for Medical Transcription (AAMT) provide the opportunity for members to attend local, state, regional, and national meetings and conventions. Members may participate in workshops, learn of educational opportunities in the field, visit exhibits, hear prominent speakers, obtain continuing education units (CEUs), and establish networks.

The AAMA publishes a bimonthly journal, *The Professional Medical Assistant.* The AAMT publishes the *Journal of the AAMT* four times a year and the *AAMT Newsletter* six times a year.

Both the AAMA and the AAMT offer certifying examinations, the successful completion of which leads to certification. Passing the AAMA tests leads to recognition as a Certified Medical Assistant, either Administrative (CMA-A) or Clinical (CMA-C) or both. Passing the AAMT test leads to recognition as a Certified Medical Transcriptionist (CMT).

For more information contact the American Association of Medical Assistants, 20 North Wacker, Suite 1575, Chicago, IL 60606 and the American Association for Medical Transcription, P.O. Box 6187, Modesto, CA 95355.

By joining a professional organization and participating in the activities it offers, the medical secretary will grow personally and professionally and will keep abreast of current trends. Participation in a recognized professional organization indicates to an employer that you are serious about your career and would be an asset to his or her practice. The rewards are limitless.

MEDICAL COMMUNICATIONS

A medical secretary's ability to communicate effectively, both orally and in writing, is essential. Communication with those concerned with health-care delivery may be in person, by telephone, or by letter.

Telephone

Most medical office telephone contacts involve health problems, and the medical secretary should respond compassionately and tactfully in dealing with the patients' problems. The medical secretary is expected to exercise good judgment, courtesy, and calmness when answering patient calls.

The telephone should be answered by the second ring at the latest. When answering a phone in a medical office, it is acceptable to greet the caller with the doctor's name. Most calls involve scheduling appointments, requests to speak with the doctor, or inquiries about laboratory test results or information about a medical condition, medication, or charges and bill payment. Callers often ask to speak with the doctor, although most simply want to schedule an appointment. The medical secretary must screen and handle calls to save the doctor's time for examining and treating patients.

The medical secretary must obtain complete information for each call. Most medical offices use prepared telephone message pads or spiral-bound telephone message books with carbons so copies of messages can be kept. The information noted should include

date and time of call

person called

caller's name

caller's phone number, including area code

action to be taken (return call, wants to see you, will call again, returned your call, urgent)

complete message

name of the person who took the call

Answering Service

Most physicians use an answering service for after-office hours and weekend calls. Some services receive calls automatically if they are not answered by the medical secretary; other services require the medical secretary to inform them when to begin answering, where the doctor can be reached, and when to stop answering. Upon entering the office, the medical secretary checks with the service for messages.

Some medical offices use a recorded message to give patients the regular office hours and a number where the doctor can be reached in an emergency.

Scheduling, Canceling, and
Rescheduling Appointments

The medical office depends on efficient management of the scheduling of appointments for patients and visitors. Appointments scheduled too closely may result in patients waiting unnecessarily, while appointments scheduled too far apart result in the doctor's loss of valuable time.

Patient appointments vary in length depending on the reason for the appointment and the specialty of the doctor. The doctor usually establishes a formula for standard appointments—for example, 30 to 45 minutes for new patients, physical examinations, consultations, and treatments; 15 to 20 minutes for routine follow-ups or injections.

Each patient's full name, telephone number, and reason for the appointment should be recorded in the appointment book beside the time of the appointment. As each patient is seen by the doctor, a check mark should be placed in the appointment book next to the name. Ditto marks should be used to indicate length of appointments, and diagonal lines should be used to indicate when the doctor will not be available for appointments with a brief explanation given.

If there is a medical emergency, the injured or ill patient must see the physician immediately. Waiting patients should be informed of the emergency and assured that the delay will not be lengthy. If the delay will be lengthy, patients who have not arrived at the office should be called and their appointments rescheduled.

Canceled appointments should be noted by a line drawn through the patient's name in the appointment book. This appointment slot then becomes available for another patient. Patients should be discouraged from canceling appointments and, when they must be canceled, should be encouraged to reschedule them.

All appointments that must be canceled should be rescheduled for the first available opening. The appointment book should show a line drawn through the patient's name and a notation beside the name indicating that the appointment has been rescheduled.

Greeting Patients and Visitors

When they enter the office, patients and visitors should be greeted with a cheerful attitude and a friendly smile. The medical secretary's goal should be to make the patient and visitor feel at ease. The patient or visitor should be identified, the name located in the day's schedule, and he or she should be asked to be seated in the waiting room.

Correspondence

Medical secretaries frequently compose routine letters that the physician asks them to compose for his or her signature or letters that explain, clarify, or transmit instructions and information. Correspondence may involve letters of referral and reference; the scheduling, canceling, and rescheduling of appointments; summaries of attending physicians' statements for insurance companies; preparation of instructions for laboratory tests and examinations; billing and insurance inquiries; and the ordering of supplies, equipment, and subscriptions.

The letters must be courteous, concise, complete, accurately typewritten, properly formatted, and proofread. Just as the proper use of the telephone is vital to the medical office, so too is the correspondence leaving the medical office.

RECORDS IN A MEDICAL OFFICE

The records in a physician's office consist of medical records of the patient's health and business records of general correspondence, financial files, insurance information, and so forth.

What a Medical Record Is

A patient's record includes the medical history or chart, medical reports, and correspondence pertaining to each patient. A medical history begins with the patient's first contact with the doctor and continues with subsequent visits, noting the patient's progress and discharge.

A patient's history contains the following information:

chief complaint and date, or reason for initial visit
medical history
personal history
family history
results of examination
diagnosis
prognosis
treatment and medication prescribed
progress reports
discharge summary.

The history is obtained by questioning the patient. (The medical secretary may obtain part of the history before the patient sees the doctor.) Examination results and diagnostic, prognostic, and treatment reports are completed by the doctor, and the medical secretary types them into the medical report either from the doctor's notes or from dictation.

Filing Records

Each medical office has its own filing system, type of records, and filing equipment. Patients' medical records may be arranged alphabetically or numerically. Files that relate to the other areas of the medical office—for example, insurance or financial matters—may be arranged by subject. These filing systems will be briefly discussed.

Patient Files

Offices using alphabetic filing file by the patient's last name, given name, and middle initial. Prefixes such as De, Di, La, Le, Mac, and Mc are considered as an inseparable part of the surname. If two names are identical, then the city or town is used as the indexing unit.

Offices using numeric filing must have a way of assigning each patient a number. Many offices use the social security number for numeric systems.

Business Files

Business files are usually arranged by subject and placed in alphabetical order. The file label identifies the contents of the file. For example, the label may be Financial Statements, Insurance, Licensing, Memberships, Office Equipment Contracts, Office Supplies, or Payroll Records.

Storing Records

The storage of medical records can be centralized or decentralized, depending on the size of the medical facility. Centralized filing systems house files from many departments in one place and are usually overseen by a medical records person trained in records management. Decentralized files are those kept in each department and organized according to its own system.

Medical records must be protected from theft, fire, and water damage. Therefore, they are usually sorted in metal file cabinets, either lateral or vertical. There are lateral files that have drawers that do not open outward, saving aisle space, and folders can be filed either front to back or sideways. Vertical files have drawers that open outward with file folders standing upright and folders filed front to back.

INSURANCE CLAIMS PROCESSING AND ACCOUNTING PROCEDURES

Most people have some form of health-care insurance with benefits varying widely from policy to policy. The patient is responsible for the payment of his or her account and must pay any difference between the charges of the physician or medical provider and the insurance coverage.

Insurance Claims

When a patient with health insurance coverage is treated at a medical facility, either the patient or the medical facility files a claim with the insurance carrier for payment. The carrier reviews the claim and, if the patient is covered, mails a check to the physician or to the patient. Physicians sometimes require payment at the time of their service. The patient then pays the physician at the time of service and files a claim for reimbursement by the insurance company.

Health insurance may be designed for a group of people insured under one policy, or it may be designed to meet the needs of an individual and the individual's dependents. The major health-care coverage plans are Blue Cross and Blue Shield, Health Maintenance Organizations (HMOs), Medicare, Medicaid, and CHAMPUS (Civilian Health and Medical Program of the Uniformed Services). Workers Compensation is an income-maintenance and health-care insurance program established by law in each state to cover work-related occupational diseases, injury, or death.

Some physicians prefer that the medical secretary complete insurance claim forms for patients to reduce the possibility of errors. Other physicians prefer that the patient complete the top of the form and the medical secretary complete the bottom.

Patient Billing

One of the medical secretary's responsibilities may be to maintain the financial records of the office. These accounting duties may include recording patient charges and receiving payments from patients and insurance companies. Patients' billing statements can be computer generated, individually typewritten on statement forms, or photocopied from the patient's ledgers.

In an office in which a majority of the patients pay their bills at the time of service, a statement may be typed, with one or more copies given to the patient and one filed. The statement will show that the full charges have been paid or what balance is due. The patient may use copies of the statement to submit to his or her insurance company for possible reimbursement.

Accounts may also be billed on a monthly basis, with all bills processed at the same time each month. A cyclical billing system in which accounts are billed on a staggered basis during the month may also be used.

When a computer is used for patient billing, a superbill or patient charge slip is usually prepared. The superbill is a one-page preprinted form with a multi-carbon packet. It lists the comprehensive services a patient might receive from a medical facility and the fees for each of these services. The services actually received and their fees are marked off. A superbill eliminates the need for patient ledger cards.

In the ledger card system, each patient has a card that lists chronologically the dates of the doctor's services, a description of each service, the charge for the service, the payment received, and the balance remaining.

Collections

The medical secretary may have to handle collections, since patients do not always pay their accounts on time. A comprehensive collection policy involving letters, telephone calls, or use of collection agencies may be necessary for the doctor to receive payment for services rendered to patients.

Although each facility has its own collection policy, the general practice is to bill the patient. If no response is received after the mailing of two consecutive monthly statements, a third bill is mailed containing a reminder that the bill is overdue and a request for an explanation. There may be a series of follow-up collection letters, each expressing more urgency in settling the account.

Another way to effect collections is for the secretary to telephone the patient to determine why the patient has not paid or answered the collection inquiries. This collection effort requires tact, understanding, confidence, experience, and listening skills. After the telephone call is completed, a note of the conversation should be recorded.

The doctor may also collect on bad accounts by suing the patient and going to court or by using the services of a collection agency. These options are often costly and time-consuming.

MEDICAL OFFICE TECHNOLOGY

Advances in technology continue to provide more ways to handle written communication in the medical office. Because medical facilities have expanded, there is an increase in the volume of paperwork. The increased paperwork and higher production costs have led many medical offices to improve efficiency through the use of sophisticated dictation, word processing, and computer equipment.

Machine Dictation and
Transcription Equipment

The dictation and transcription of correspondence and medical reports can be a large part of a medical secretary's job. Because machine dictation is less time-consuming and often more convenient than in-person dictation, many doctors prefer machine dictation.

Transcription of dictation into typewritten hard copy requires that the secretary have excellent listening skills, be familiar with the transcription equipment, and have a solid background in medical terminology, grammar, punctuation, spelling, and the formats to be used for different types of medical reports.

Word Processing

Word processing is the automated production of documents and correspondence using modern electronic equipment. Electronic type-writers, dedicated word processors, and personal computers may be used. Keyboarding (typing) speeds can range from 150 to over 600 words per minute. Word processing also provides memory for storing,

TABLE 17.1

Prefixes Commonly Used in Medical Terms

A prefix is a word part found at the beginning of a word; it is never used alone. Awareness of what a prefix means often leads to understanding of the full word. For example, postoperative = post (after) operation, or after an operation.

Prefix	Meaning	Prefix	Meaning
a, an	no; not; without	epi	above; upon; on
ab	away from	eso	inward
ad	toward	eu	good
ana	up; apart; excessive	ex	out; away from
ante	before; forward	poly	many
anti	against	post	after; behind
auto	self	pre	before; in front of
bi	two	pro	before
brachy	short	re	back
brady	slow	retro	behind
cata	down	semi	half
con	together; with	sub	under; below
contra	against; opposite	supra	above
de	lack of; down	sym	together; with
dia	complete; through	syn	together; with
dys	bad; painful; difficult	tachy	fast
ec	out; outside	tetra	four
ecto	out; outside	trans	across
em	in	tri	three
en	in; within	ultra	beyond; excess
endo	in; within	uni	one

producing, retrieving, revising, and correcting the documents and correspondence. It greatly improves the efficiency of any office.

Use of Computers

The medical office is being revolutionized by the use of the computer. Initially the computer was used in hospitals for billing and administrative purposes. Today, computers and word processing systems are used in most medical facilities for a wide range of applications, including

TABLE 17.2

Suffixes Commonly Used in Medical Terms

A suffix is a word part found at the end of a word. Knowledge of the meaning of a suffix can often help the secretary figure out the meaning of the entire word. For example, *tendonitis* = *tendon* + *itis* (inflammation), or an inflammation of a tendon.

Suffix	Meaning	Suffix	Meaning
ac	pertaining to	oid	resembling
agia	excessive pain	ole	little, small
al	pertaining to	oma	tumor, mass
algia	pain	opsy	view of
ar	pertaining to	or	one who
ary	pertaining to	osis	abnormal condition
cele	hernia	ous	pertaining to
crine	secrete; separate	pathy	disease
crit	separate	penia	deficiency
cyesis	pregnancy	pexy	fixation; to put in place
cyte	cell	phagia	eating; swallowing
dynia	pain	plasty	surgical repair
eal	pertaining to	pnea	breathing
ectomy	removal; excision	ptosis	drooping; sagging; prolapse
emia	blood	rrhage	bursting forth of blood
er	one who	rrhea	flow; discharge
fusion	to pour	scope	instrument for visual examination
grade	to go	sis	state of; condition
gram	record	spasm	sudden contraction of muscles
graph	instrument for recording	stomy	new opening
ia	condition	therapy	treatment
iac	pertaining to	thorax	pleural cavity; chest
ic	pertaining to	tic	pertaining to
ism	process	tome	instrument to cut
ist	specialist	tomy	process of cutting
itis	inflammation	ule	little; small
logy	study of	uria	urination; urine
megaly	enlargement	us	thing
meter	measure	y	condition; process

patients' records, patients' ledgers, daily logs, insurance form processing, research, electronic appointment scheduling, and the production of graphics.

MEDICAL MINI-GLOSSARY

It is impossible for the medical secretary to become familiar with all medical terms and abbreviations. A medical dictionary, such as *Webster's New World/Stedman's Medical Dictionary*, is a must at all medical secretaries' desks. However, familiarity with prefixes and suffixes commonly used in medical terms greatly helps in understanding the meaning of a word. (See Tables 17.1 and 17.2.) Knowledge of the abbreviations used in medicine is also very important.

The Legal Secretary

by Milton Katz

Although the duties of the legal secretary are similar in most respects to those of other secretaries, there are several important differences deriving from the major concern of a law firm—the practice of law. As a result, the legal secretary must be well versed in the terminology, forms, and procedures of the legal profession. In addition, because of the precise standards set by the law, the legal secretary must be particularly careful to follow correct procedures in exact sequence.

REQUIREMENTS

In addition to those common to all secretaries, the competent legal secretary should possess the following characteristics:

comprehensive background in legal matters
keen interest in the law

thoroughness and high standards

ability to deal with pressure and to work under severe time limitations

interest in people

ability to deal with people who may be in a highly emotional state

respect for confidentiality

strong oral communication skills.

The position of legal secretary is demanding, but it is also rewarding. Because a legal secretary requires training and skills greater than those of the average secretary, pay and fringe benefits are generally superior. In addition, involvement in human drama and a variety of social and economic experiences makes for more interesting work. Although many legal matters deal with such normal actions as the purchase of a house, people in trouble or crisis often turn to the law for help. The legal secretary is a participant in this search for redress and so is offered valuable insight into society's legal framework.

TYPES OF POSITIONS

Many kinds of positions are available to the legal secretary. They include working in a single-attorney office in a partnership, in a large law firm, in the in-house law department of a large corporation, and in the local, state, and federal court systems. In addition, legal practices vary from the general to specialties in real estate law, corporate law, criminal law, tax law, estate planning, marital law, and labor law.

DUTIES

The functions of the legal secretary may be divided into three major areas: dealing with people, managing the law office, and preparing legal instruments and court papers. Since many of the duties of the legal secretary are identical with those of other types of secretaries, when relevant information appears elsewhere in this handbook, the reader will be referred to the appropriate chapter.

Dealing with People

The legal secretary comes in regular contact either personally or by written or phone communication with lawyers, fellow employees, clients and potential clients, and court personnel. Certain principles should guide the secretary's behavior with each of these four types.

The Attorney

In dealing with the attorney she or he works for, the secretary must never be afraid to ask questions when unsure of what should be done. It is far better to ask for an explanation than to make errors. All attorneys would prefer to answer questions than to be presented with a legal paper done incorrectly. Moreover, the more a secretary knows about the attorney's clients, cases, and work habits, the more effective she or he can be in helping the attorney deal with the burden of work.

The secretary should also understand that each attorney adopts an individual approach and that it is the secretary's obligation to conform to the attorney's way. Techniques learned in previous instruction or experience sometimes must be unlearned.

This is certainly true in the sensitive area of formality/informality. There is increasing familiarity today between attorney and secretary. However, the wise secretary understands that individual preferences differ and that some attorneys do not wish to be addressed by their first name. Moreover, in the presence of a client, *always* use Mr., Ms., or Mrs. when talking to or referring to the attorney, no matter how informal the office is customarily.

The secretary must also understand that attorneys often work under pressure and, being human, sometimes erupt. No matter how slight the provocation, the secretary should not take the criticism personally. When the pressure abates, the emotional atmosphere will almost always return to normal.

Finally, the secretary must always respect the confidentiality of legal matters that come to her or his attention. Opinions, information, and anecdotes must never be carried beyond the confines of the office. It is always possible that, for example, a derogatory comment about a client could find its way back to that client and affect the attorney–client relationship, or that a piece of information could reach the opposing counsel and adversely affect the case of the secretary's employer.

Fellow Employees

This verbal "buttoning up" is also desirable in the secretary's relationship with fellow employees—other secretaries, paralegals, law clerks, and receptionists. The completion of work within a certain time span is often crucial in a law office. Too much chitchatting at the expense of work can lead to negative productivity and perhaps even negative office morale. And even here, within the office, the principle of confidentiality must be respected.

In the office, it is essential to know what your duties are and how they differ from those of other employees. Don't infringe on someone else's territory, even with the best of intentions. For example, you may have nothing to do for the moment and see your fellow secretary knee-deep in legal papers; you may think that by going through that secretary's mail, you may be saving her or him time and effort, but your co-worker may be looking forward to a change of pace from the typing and so not appreciate your efforts. By all means help out, but ask first.

Also, if you're relatively new to the office, you can save yourself a good deal of time and trouble by enlisting the help of a veteran. Don't hesitate to ask; most secretaries will be glad to assist.

Clients

Clients come in all varieties, and much of your success in dealing with them will spring from your instinctive reaction to their characters and needs. There are, however, a few principles that apply to your interaction with all clients. First, unless the client specifically requests otherwise, always refer to him or her by surname. Many people resent the easy familiarity of a quick first-name basis.

Also, be patient, courteous, and never sarcastic. Be friendly, but don't get overly involved with the client's problems. Most important, don't give legal advice! Leave that to the attorneys. Even if you think you know the answer, don't offer it. Be sympathetic, but emphasize that your legal knowledge is limited.

Clients may sometimes ask to see their files, or to take from the office some document pertaining to their case. A client has the right to see personal papers, such as the deed to his or her house. Aside from personal papers, however, politely resist such requests, saying you need permission from your employer. It is a good idea to find out in advance what your attorney's policy is in regard to clients' requests to examine their files.

Court Personnel

The secretary will also come in contact with court personnel, most often through phone contact with court clerks. These contacts are usually important, involving requests for information, such as the postponement date of a trial, whether some legal papers were received, or whether certain exhibits need to be attached to papers (e.g., a copy of a lease in a landlord–tenant dispute).

Court personnel are usually busy, so it is important to know beforehand what you are going to say. Have available the name of the case and the case index number. And when receiving information from the court clerk, *write it down*. You may think you'll remember it, but you may be interrupted as soon as you hang up and then find that an important detail has slipped your mind.

Managing the Law Office

Write it down is a good rule to follow at all times in the law office. Other practices experienced legal secretaries have learned to apply relate to key areas of time management, office machines, dictation and legal shorthand, correspondence, filing, books and records, and miscellaneous functions such as taking charge of mail. Our emphasis here will be on legal procedures, but many procedures discussed elsewhere in this handbook will also be helpful. Therefore, for each of the seven areas listed above, a related chapter will be indicated and recommended.

Sometimes the legal secretary may experience a lull, but more often than not she or he will be working under the pressure of time. One technique to help diminish this pressure is to bring a body of work to the attorney as soon as it is completed, rather than wait until the end of the day. Since changes are sometimes necessary, getting the work in early can help avoid the press of correction near departing time.

Another time-saving technique is to attach a client's file to any correspondence from or related to the client that has just arrived in that day's mail. This enables the attorney to have necessary information at his or her disposal while dealing with the communication.

Other time-management techniques include filing material as soon as it is completed; keeping phone conversations to a minimum length, but doing so courteously ("Excuse me, there's a call on another line. I'll get back to you."); and not photocopying or fastening court papers the attorney has dictated until he or she approves, for changes are often made. (See Chapter 11 for additional time-management suggestions.)

Law offices employ the same machines found in other types of offices: computers, word processors, copying machines, dictaphones, fax machines, postage meters, etc. (see Chapter 2). Of these, one that has been most adaptable to the law office is the word processor. It can be used to set up formats for wills, caption boxes, attorney's affirmations, etc. For example, the opening of an attorney's affirmation ("John Jones, being duly sworn, deposes and says") can be placed on a word processing file page, thus avoiding retyping. Also, since all wills contain "boilerplate" (specific material used over and over again), a paragraph such as the one that follows can be set up on a word processing file and copied onto each new will, thus avoiding much unnecessary typing.

> I, (NAME), residing at (ADDRESS, CITY), County of (COUNTY), State of (STATE), do hereby make, publish and declare this to be my Last Will and Testament, hereby revoking any and all Wills and Codicils by me at any time heretofore made.

One kind of office machine peculiar to the law office is the stenotype. Although it is most often used by court reporters, some secretaries who have been schooled in its use and have the machine will use it for taking office dictation. Also, computer data bases such as LEXUS and NEXUS are now used in larger offices to supplement legal research.

For techniques in dictation and shorthand, see Chapter 4. Many legal phrases can be reduced to the stroke of a pen or a letter or two. Familiarity with legal phrases and their meanings will help make a more efficient legal secretary. (A concise glossary of often-used legal terms appears at the end of this chapter.) Use can be made of such books as *The Legal Secretary: Terminology and Transcription* by Dorothy Adams and Margaret Kurtz, published by McGraw-Hill, and *Speedwriting for the Legal Secretary* by Berniece Craft, et al., a paperback published by Bobbs Merrill.

Chapter 5 material dealing with correspondence is pertinent for the legal secretary. It is important to emphasize absolute accuracy in the law office: *Always proofread carefully.* Also, when sending correspondence to a business rather than a home address, ask the attorney if the envelope should be marked PERSONAL & CONFIDENTIAL. Another good policy is to make sure to state the position of the addressee when addressing a letter (e.g., Vice-President, Marketing).

Hints for Correspondence

There are a number of routines involving correspondence that can diminish the secretary's frustrations. These include:

1. When opening mail, stamp the date received immediately on the letter.
2. If a copy of a pleading (answer, bill of particulars, etc.) is received in the mail, save the envelope. Sometimes the date stamp becomes important.
3. Always make a copy of an original for the file. Use a color other than white for the copy; this helps to distinguish office correspondence from letters received from clients or other lawyers.
4. When mailing an original and a copy (either to the same or different recipients), stamp COPY on the copy.

5. When sending out correspondence requesting or requiring a follow-up, make a calendar entry for the follow-up due date.

6. Don't throw out any written matter given to you by the attorney, such as a handwritten version of a letter. Let the attorney do the discarding.

Hints for Filing

Filing is treated more fully in Chapter 8, but the following suggestions apply particularly to the law office.

1. In opening a file, attach correspondence to one side of the manila folder (e.g., the left) and legal papers to the other side (e.g., the right).

2. When naming a file in a court proceeding, always put the client's name first: JONES vs. BROWN when the client is the plaintiff, JONES adv. BROWN when the client is being sued (*adv.* = *adversus*, Latin for *against*).

3. Smaller law firms generally file alphabetically. Large firms most often use a numerical system, with each case receiving a number. When writing concerning a case, always use the file number. (Of course, numerical systems must employ a reference file to trace correspondence without the file number.)

4. For a very large file, as in the handling of an estate, use a red expandable envelope, and within the envelope insert separate manila folders for such areas as CORRESPONDENCE, SURROGATE COURT MATTERS, BANK STATEMENTS, and STOCKS & BONDS.

5. On the outside of the file, in addition to the client's name, place home address and phone and business address and phone. This eliminates the need to go through the file when it is necessary to reach the client.

Miscellaneous

The keeping of books and records in a law office generally follows customary practice elsewhere (see Chapter 9). When there are unusual expenses incurred for a client, such as securing a copy of records from the county clerk or sending mail by express service (at the request of the client), such expenditures should be listed on a disbursement sheet kept in the client's file.

Miscellaneous functions, too, follow customary practice (see Chapter 10). These include such matters as taking care of the mail, arranging for travel, and social amenities.

Preparing Legal Instruments

Along with correspondence, the preparation of legal instruments and court papers (pleadings) generally consumes most of the legal secretary's time. A *legal instrument* is a formal written document such as a deed, contract, affidavit, or will. A legal instrument is not usually related to a court action. A *court paper*, on the other hand, is a statement to the court presenting the claims of the plaintiff or the answer of the defendant.

Preparation of Legal Instruments:

1. Double-space (although long agreements may sometimes be single-spaced, as may citations and land descriptions).
2. CAPITALIZE names of parties involved.
3. When referring to money or numbers, always write out the number and then, in parentheses, put the number in figures, as: *four thousand (4,000).*
4. Enumerate paragraphs (optional with an affidavit).
5. Don't fill in the complete date until there is certainty as to when the instrument will be signed.
6. On a preprinted form (such as a deed), if the signature must be notarized, fill in the acknowledgment for the notary.
7. When sending a paper to a client for a signature, put initials or a check mark lightly in pencil to indicate where the client should sign. Do the same where a notary's signature is required.
8. Type the client's name under the signature line where he or she has to sign (execute).
9. When photocopying an executed paper of several pages (e.g., a will), *don't* remove staples from the original document, since this might suggest tampering.

Types of Legal Instruments

A *deed* is a legal instrument which, when delivered, transfers a present interest in property. Deed forms are generally preprinted and can be readily gotten from a title company.

A *contract* is a legal agreement between two or more people to do something. Some contracts, such as those pertaining to real estate, are available as preprinted forms, obtainable from title companies. Contracts that are not preprinted are usually dictated by the attorney.

An *affidavit* is a written statement made on oath before a notary public or other person authorized to administer oaths. Below is an example of the format for an affidavit. (The first line is typed about ten spaces below the place where it normally would go.)

STATE OF NEW YORK)
) SS. :
COUNTY OF KINGS   )

JOHN JAMES, being duly sworn, deposes and says:

1.
   (Body of affidavit goes here and should be double-spaced. When completed, come down four spaces to the signature line.)

_____
                                JOHN JAMES

Sworn to me before this
1st day of September, 19--

_____
    Notary Public

A *will* is a legal statement of a person's wishes concerning the disposal of his or her property after death. Simple wills are often assemblages of "boilerplate," paragraphs whose format is unvaried from will to will but whose information is individualized to the wishes of the testator (male who has made out the will) or testatrix (female who has made out the will).

The signature line of the testator or testatrix and the several witnesses must always be together on the same page—never separated. In addition, these signatures must never appear on an otherwise blank page; the page must contain some section of the body of the will.

Preparing Court Papers

The various types of court papers can be summarized most easily through an understanding of the sequence of pretrial procedures.

In civil cases, a court action is initiated by the plaintiff's service of a *summons* and *complaint*. A *summons* is an official order to appear in court, to respond as a defendant to a charge. A *complaint* is a formal charge or accusation. It contains the plaintiff's explanation of the reason for the suit. Allegations are enumerated. The complaint ends with a *wherefore clause* asking for a favorable judgment and costs and disbursements in connection with the legal action. Though the summons and complaint can be served separately, most often they are served together.

The defense attorney replies with an *answer*, responding to the plaintiff's charges. The answer sometimes contains a *counterclaim*, clauses that present countercharges against the plaintiff's charges. The answer is sometimes accompanied by a *demand for a bill of particulars*, a request of the plaintiff by the defendant for a detailed list of the amounts of money asked for. The plaintiff responds with a *bill of particulars*.

In order to get the case on the court calendar, a series of papers must be presented, such as a *notice of issue* or a *request for judicial information*. The defendant may present a *demurrer*, a plea for the dismissal of the suit on the grounds that even if the plaintiff's statements are true, they do not sustain the claim because they are insufficient or otherwise legally defective. Also, attorneys frequently make *motions*, requests of the court, such as a request for an order to show cause. During trial, or on appeal, attorneys may file a *brief*, usually at the request of the court. A brief is a concise statement of the main points of the case.

General Procedures to Follow in Preparing Court Papers:

1. Send the original to the court and one copy to each of the attorneys involved, and keep one copy for office files.
2. For most pleadings, follow the sample format shown on the next page (lines are numbered to aid recognition of spatial arrangement):

Sample Pleading Format

```
SUPREME COURT OF THE STATE OF NEW YORK
COUNTY OF KINGS
                                                    X
JOHN JONES,
                              Plaintiff,

          -against-                       ANSWER
                                          Index No.  1234/89
JAMES DOE,
                              Defendant.

                                                    X
```

(NOTE: The above caption box is used for most pleadings. The body of the work, whether a complaint, answer, etc. will be double-spaced. All pleadings will end with a WHEREFORE clause.)

```
DATED:   New York, NY
         Jan. 1, 1989
                                    BROWN & SMITH
                                    Attorneys for Defendant
                                    10 Broad Street
                                    New York, NY 10001
                                    (212) 555-1234

TO:      DAVID JAMES
         Attorney for the Plaintiff
         2 State Street
         Brooklyn, NY 12201
```

The following is an example of a WHEREFORE clause in an answer:

> "WHEREFORE defendant demands judgment dismissing the complaint herein, together with the costs and disbursements of this action and for such other relief as to this court may seem just and proper."

3. Assemble and fasten prepared court papers into a legal back, a preprinted, heavier paper, sometimes in a color such as blue or yellow. The *caption box* on the outside of the legal back must be completed. Part of the inside includes a space for *verification*, a swearing to the truthfulness of the statements made in the pleading. Usually, the verification must be signed by the client and notarized.

4. When a copy is mailed to the opposing attorney, the secretary should complete and mail to the court, along with the original paper, an *affidavit of service*. This states that on a particular date a copy of the paper was mailed to the attorney. Give the attorney's name, state that he or she is attorney for the plaintiff (or defense), and provide the attorney's address. The secretary should sign her or his name on the signature line and have the affidavit notarized.

5. With the papers sent to the court, enclose a stamped self-addressed postcard, following the sample below:

```
X    JONES vs. BROWN            X   (name of action)
X    Index # 123/88             X   (case number)
X    ANSWER                     X   (name of pleading)
X    received and filed         X
X          (stamped & returned  X
X               by court clerk) X
X_____X
```

6. When sending pleadings to the court, with copies that must be returned (for example, for a signature, or for a copy to be conformed), always enclose a stamped self-addressed envelope.

SOURCES OF INFORMATION

The legal secretary must be familiar with sources of information and with the meanings of commonly used legal words and phrases. Three indispensable sources of information for the legal secretary are a dictionary (*Webster's New World Dictionary*, 3rd College Edition), phone directories, and court directories. A zip code listing is also helpful. In addition, the following reference works should be valuable:

> Black, Henry Campbell. *Black's Law Dictionary*, 5th ed. St. Paul, Minn.: West Publishing Company, 1979. (An abridged version was published in 1983.)
>
> Cohen, Morris L. *Legal Research in a Nutshell*, 4th ed. St. Paul, Minn.: West Publishing Company, 1985. (Provides a brief introduction to main areas of legal literature. A more detailed work by Cohen is *How to Find the Law*, 8th ed., 1983, which appears in an abridged version, *Finding the Law*, 1984.)
>
> DeVries, Mary A. *Legal Secretary's Encyclopedic Dictionary*, 3rd ed. Englewood Cliffs, NJ: Prentice-Hall, 1982. (Contains sample forms.)
>
> Miller, Besse May (revised by Mary A. DeVries). *Legal Secretary's Complete Handbook*, 3rd. ed. Englewood Cliffs, NJ: Prentice-Hall, 1981.

Also, two widely used providers of legal forms, both in New York City, are Matthew Bender and Julius Blumberg. In addition, *Sletwold's Manual of Documents and Forms for the Legal Secretary*, 2nd ed., Prentice-Hall, should be helpful.

GLOSSARY OF LEGAL WORDS AND PHRASES

Latin words and phrases are italicized. Terms defined in the preceding text are not included.

alleged so declared, but without proof; presumed

appellant person making an appeal

appellee person against whom the appeal is brought; respondent

attestation certification by oath or signature; testimony

bona fide in or with good faith

certiorari writ issued by a higher court to a lower court requesting the record of a case for review

codicil addition to or modification of a will

contra against

deposition testimony of a witness, made under oath but not in open court, written down to be used when the case comes to trial

docket court calendar

duress unlawful restraint by which a person is forced to perform or refrain from doing an act

et alii (*et al.*) and others

execution completion or validation of a legal instrument, as by signing, sealing, and delivering

fee simple absolute ownership (of land) with unrestricted rights of disposition

felony a major crime, as murder, arson, or rape; results in greater punishment than for a misdemeanor, a minor crime

habeas corpus writ directed to a person having custody of another to produce that person in court

id est (*i.e.*) that is

injunction writ or order from a court prohibiting a person or group from carrying out a given action or ordering a given action to be done

in re in the matter of

intestate without having made a will

jurat statement or certification added to an affidavit, telling when, before whom, and (sometimes) where the affidavit was made

lien the right of a creditor against the property of a debtor for payment of a debt or duty

mandamus writ issued by a superior court commanding that a specified thing be done

mortgagee one who receives a mortgage (creditor)

mortgagor one who mortgages his or her property (debtor)

nolo contendere I will not contest it

non compos mentos not of sound mind

per annum by the year

perjury willful telling of a lie while under lawful oath to tell the truth

plaintiff person who brings a suit into a court of law

postmortem after death

power of attorney written statement legally authorizing a person to act for another *prima facie* at first sight; on the face of it

pro for; in behalf of

quid pro quo one thing in return for another; something for something

retainer type of contract in which a lawyer is employed by a client to perform services when needed

scilicet (*ss.*) to wit; that is to say

stipulation clause in a contract or any agreement; agreement between opposing lawyers in a civil case

subornation crime of inducing another to commit perjury

subpoena written legal order directing a person to appear in court to testify, show records, etc.

supra above

tort wrongful act, injury, or damage (not involving a breach of contract) for which a civil action can be brought

venue county or locality in which a cause of a legal action occurs or a crime is committed; county or locality in which a jury is drawn and a case tried

versus (*vs.*; *v.*) against

writ formal legal document ordering or prohibiting some action, as a writ of *habeas corpus*

The Technical Secretary

by James C. Matthews, Ed.D.

Technology has fostered growth in research in both the public and private sectors. The technical secretary works for scientists, mathematicians, researchers, and others in scientific and technical fields. In addition to basic knowledge of secretarial procedures and skills for information gathering, the technical secretary needs special skills. The secretarial work will involve the formatting and handling of a variety of technical documents, such as scientific reports and abstracts, as well as the deciphering and interpretation of information. The secretary must deal with technical terms and symbols, be able to type or key technical data accurately, proofread, and make decisions with reference to mathematical equations, language symbols, and other technical data.

THE ROLE OF THE
TECHNICAL SECRETARY

The role of the technical secretary in the office is different from that of secretaries in many other categories. Many scientists and researchers work in government-sponsored institutes and projects in both the public and the private sector. In many cases the security of records and personnel is an important factor. The technical secretary working in such areas may be bonded and may have a position involving certain security risks. These factors in themselves make the technical secretary's position more sophisticated.

The technical secretary, in addition to having a knowledge of routine secretarial skills, may be required to be familiar with a variety of electronic equipment and be able to understand and follow sophisticated organizational patterns. In general, the higher the technical level of the work, the greater the number of tasks, functions, and duties the secretary may be responsible for. The overall nature and scope of the job make it technical.

Because many tasks involve documents, inventions, diagrams, and designs that are subject to copyright or patent, confidentiality is most important. The technical secretary must develop an awareness of what is confidential material and should be well prepared never to slip and make a mistake, divulging information. The ability to keep a secret and act on confidential matters ensures professional integrity and stance as a trusted secretary who exhibits expertise in technical as well as general matters.

TYPES OF OFFICES

Career fields for the technical secretary are varied—aerospace, engineering, environmental control, chemistry, life sciences, mathematics, synthetics, and physics, to name just a few. Each field has subsets, and some subdivisions develop into full-blown separate technologies. In addition, fields often change as new technologies emerge, interface, and integrate with others.

Technical secretaries may work in conventional offices, but most work in modern electronic offices.

The Electronic Office

In the broadest sense, automation is a system of production and processing that uses machines to process information. The key is improved equipment that permits the technical secretary to streamline procedures and have several alternatives to do work more efficiently.

The electronic office, also called the automated and/or computerized office, uses new technologies to improve the quality of work and increase productivity. Electronic machines equipped with special elements for scientific and mathematical characters produce documents of high quality—and at a much greater speed than is possible without automation.

In the electronic office, the technical secretary will use personal computers, electronic typewriters, word processors, intelligent copiers, and a number of other machines to prepare technical documents and create technical databases. The technical secretary needs this equipment and should not be intimidated by it.

A Typical Day

A typical day for a technical secretary in an electronic office might include arriving at the office ahead of the scheduled time, deactivating security systems for database files and vaults, and checking messages electronically transmitted on a computer network. Also, he or she might calendar appointments on a managerial workstation and then print a copy for the executives. Other tasks might include "booting up" the systems and keying into specific networks in which formulas and equations may be stored. The next order of business might be to gather supplies and scientific manuals needed for special typing jobs to be handled during the day. For example, if a secretary is typing a scientific abstract of four pages on which a 66-line calculation has to be reduced 50 percent for one of the pages, including a freehand drawing and insertion of mathematical symbols, he or she would need access to special equipment or media, such as graphics and/or desktop publishing software, stencils, templates, and so forth. Access to a copier for reduction of work and a variety of forms rulers may also be required.

You might be working directly with an executive for two to three hours. Your assistant or another office worker may be assigned to handle your desk operations during this period, or perhaps your electronic managerial workstation can answer all calls, etc.

During the course of the day, you might work with a number of different technologies, including telecommunications, photocomposition or phototypesetting, optical character recognition, optical (laser) discs, and image processing. Peripheral devices you might use with electronic equipment include pointing devices and cursor manipulations, such as a mouse, track ball, light pen, cursor disc, electronic pad, and so forth. You manipulate these technologies so they become integrated tools to produce a final-quality product. Here, your technical expertise surpasses those basic skills used in the conventional office.

This hypothetical day in the life of a technical secretary is offered as an example only. Other work periods may include research in specialized libraries in completing data needed for meeting a deadline. You must also develop an ability to work on a "crisis" basis. You must learn to cope and deal with stressful periods; you must always identify positive measures to combat physical and mental intimidation that would hinder success.

The Conventional Office

The conventional office and its basic operations still exist in business, small and large. Conventional office procedures include handling business reports, shorthand and machine dictation including transcription activities, handling telephone duties, processing and distributing mail, making travel arrangements, preparing for meetings, and so forth. A small number of secretaries use manual machines, mostly in small businesses that cannot afford the cost of automated equipment. However, a large number of offices, especially those in technical fields, have or are switching to automation and electronic equipment. The advantages of the electronic office in the preparation of technical reports must be weighed against the cost of the equipment.

The Office of the Future

No doubt you have heard of the "paperless office." Integrated, electronic transmission of data allows information to appear on visual display terminals, screens, and cathode-ray tubes (CRTs). However, a paper product is still needed in a majority of situations. The impact of word processing and personal computers long ago reared the hope of a paperless office and a paperless society. However, the effect of technology has generated more paperwork than ever before. Even though the office of the future has been speculated on as one with no or minimal paper output and handling, efforts are still being made to make this a reality. And, even in the paperless office, security is still a problem because systems can be entered by access sources other than those having rights to the information filed in databases.

Empirical research conducted in the mid-1980s has indicated that the role of the secretary, technical or other, is everchanging and will continue to evolve as the needs of business and industry change. In a survey conducted by Professional Secretaries International (PSI), Inc., secretaries identified more than 50 considerations (statements) as to the secretary's role on or before the year 2020 ("In the Year 2020," *The Secretary*, June/July 1987, p. 18). Among others, these five statements relate to a few technical considerations:

1. Every secretarial desk will have a personal computer or terminal.
2. Personal computer networks will allow worldwide communication.
3. The most important function of the secretary will be managing information systems.
4. Computerized files will have created the paperless office.
5. Technical skills will be more important than interpersonal skills.

Within these perceptual considerations, the level of technical expertise is high. Change is inevitable, and as a technical secretary, you must prepare for change. How? By becoming aware of what, where, and how changes are taking place and how you and your job are being affected. The technical secretary must update his or her knowledge and skills and create a plan, meeting change head-on for career advancement.

PREPARING TECHNICAL REPORTS

A technical report involves visuals; electronically prepared graphics; mathematical, scientific, chemical engineering, and other notations, such as equations; and technical text. The text is somewhat different from the business text used in accounting, banking, investment, insurance, real estate, fashion, advertising, and so forth. Technical text refers to that which is specialized, abstract or theoretical, scientific, and formal, rather than practical. Technical text thus exemplifies an air or sense of technicity, *i.e.,* something meaningful or relevant only to a specialist.

Parts of a Technical Report

A technical report basically includes the following elements: letter or memorandum of transmittal, title page, abstract, table of contents, list of illustrations and tables (or figures), body, appendix, bibliography, index, and distribution list. Theoretically, these parts are similar to the elements of a business report. However, there are differences. Since these reports are technical and scientific in nature, the main element—the body—includes these subsections: introduction, discussion, conclusions, and recommendations.

Letter or memorandum of transmittal. This section includes authorization, a brief background, and the purpose and scope of the report. It may be placed in an envelope and attached to the outside of the report.

Title page. The title page should include, in addition to the title of the report, the name, address, and contract number (if any) of the writer's company. If there is a government or foundation number, it should be listed in a conspicuous place.

Abstract. The abstract culls and summarizes the entire report. It serves as an outline for the report. It should be thorough, highly detailed, and phrased to correlate with corresponding headings in the text. The abstract should be typed double-spaced on a separate sheet of paper.

Body. This is the largest part and main section of the technical report. It follows the general format of the business report. However, there are three distinct subsections that should be included:

1. the introduction, which follows the abstract's statement
2. the discussion, in which the research method is clearly explained step by step
3. conclusions and recommendations, which includes results, a summary, and, if appropriate, implications and/or recommendations for further research or study.

If there is a report number, it should be centered at the top of each page. Allow space for insertions of freehand symbols; if you are working on a first draft, insert symbols and other similar items with a pencil.

Appendix. The sequence may be different depending on the scientific style guide used. Identify each appendix by letter, *i.e.,* Appendix A, Appendix B, etc., each on a separate page. All data that needs to be included in the report but for some reason cannot be placed in the body should be placed in this section.

Bibliography. In general, this section should follow the same format as it does in business reports. However, carefully check format variations depending on the manual used. In some scientific reports, references may be arranged in order of appearance, cross-referenced by the page number.

Index. An index is used only for lengthy reports (over 200 pages). It should include an alphabetical listing of all topics, names, etc., appearing in the complete report.

Distribution list. This is a separate list which provides the names of persons and officers (departments, units, firms) receiving the report.

It should be typed on a separate page. In some cases, this data may be placed on the letter or memorandum of transmittal.

Scientific Manuscripts

A scientific manuscript is a specific type of technical report usually submitted to a professional journal for consideration for publication. Some standard parts in a scholarly writing are: title, by-line and supplemental data (similar to contract data listed on the title page of the basic technical report), abstract, acknowledgments, references, and index. *A word of caution:* You, the secretary, may be asked to verify or complete incomplete references. As a check-and-balance technique, always check every reference for accuracy both in the body and the reference list. For scholarly writing, journals specify a style for references and footnotes. Obtain a copy of the style *first*—before you begin to type/key the report, if possible.

In the acknowledgment section, credit may be given to others who may have assisted: institutions, foundations, and/or individuals in business and industry, including both the private and public, governmental sectors.

FORMATTING TECHNICAL MATERIALS

The technical secretary is expected to deal with varied and detailed material. How you approach these challenges is important for self-development and improvement of technical knowledge and skills. Depending on your responsibilities, your employer's needs, and the nature of the firm, you should try to establish a good rapport at the beginning. There are many sciences; each with its own vocabulary, principles, subject content, and so forth. *Don't hesitate: When in doubt, ask.* Remember, you may be able to save yourself a great deal of trouble if you simply ask *first*.

Formatting technical material is a learning experience in itself. Once mastered, technical material becomes much easier to deal with. The following sections introduce you to some of the basic considerations used in formatting.

Mathematics

Mathematical expressions consist of abbreviations and several types of symbols and signs, including English, Greek, and Roman letters;

signs of operation and relation; and superscripts, subscripts, and primes.

The following are examples of English word abbreviations:

| sin (sine)   exp (exponent)

Greek and Roman letters are used to note kinds of quantities:

| A (alpha)

Superscripts ($a°$), subscripts (h_1), and primes (f') are often used, and the technical secretary must be careful to type or draw freehand every character exactly as the originator wants it. Errors are much more serious than in standard text. For example, an error like "personel computer" is easy to spot when proofreading straight draft copy, but dropping a superscript from an equation may go unnoticed, thus making the equation incorrect.

Numbers and computation signs must also be carefully keyed and proofread for accuracy. Here is an example of an error in a computation sign:

| $3 - 5 = 8$ (Correct: $3 + 5 = 8$)

Signs of operation ($+$, $-$, $\times$, $\div$) indicate specific mathematical operations. These can be carried out in letter symbols such as abc, which means $a \times b \times c$. Here, the multiplication signs are understood.

Typing elements may or may not have the symbol for the root of a quantity. You may draw this: $\sqrt{}$. This symbol is called the radical symbol; $\sqrt{9}$ is read as "the square root of 9."

Signs of relation, in contrast to signs of operation, indicate relationships among terms in expressions:

| $<$ Less than $>$ Greater than

Thus $x < y$ is read as "x is less than y."

Fences are symbols of inclusion; they serve as punctuation marks in mathematics. Fences include the following:

Parentheses (left and right)

Brackets   [ ]

Braces   { }

The conventional order is { [( )] }.

Some electronic typewriters, word processors, and computer keyboards have special elements for these and other symbols. Use of typed, hand-drawn, or rub-on symbols depends on what is available to you. Remember, however, that the finished product must be clear and consistent.

TABLE 19.1

Some Abbreviations Used in Mathematics

Word	Abbreviation
constant	const
sine	sin
cosine	cos
secant	sec
cosecant	csc
tangent	tan
cotangent	cot
logarithm	log

TABLE 19.2

Some Symbols Used in Mathematics

Symbol	Meaning
$\sim$	similar to
∞	infinity, indefinitely great
$\propto$	directly proportional to
Σ	sum of
iff	if and only if
$\neq$	does not equal
$\therefore$	therefore, hence
$\rightarrow$	yields
$\equiv$	identical with
$\perp$	perpendicular to
∂	the partial
$\in$	belongs to
$\notin$	does not belong to
$:$	ratio (is to); divided by
$\int$	integral
π	product; pi
When an experimental design is discussed in research, these symbols are used:	
R	random selection of subjects or treatments
X	variable to be manipulated
C	control variable
O	test
————	a line between levels represents equated groups
Thus:	
$\underline{R\ X\ O_1}$ $R\ C\ O_2$	

Chemistry

The technical secretary may have to type and prepare reports containing chemical symbols and notations.

Style for Names and Symbols of Elements

- The first time the name of an element appears in the text, capitalize the first letter.

    > . . . plus two other elements: Oxygen and Nitrogen . . .

- The first letter of the symbol for an element is always capitalized, but the second letter is not.

    > C   (carbon)
    > Cl (chlorine)
    > Fe (iron)

- Leave no space between a chemical symbol and its index numbers.
- The index number that represents the atomic number of the element is typed as a subscript or as a superscript on the left side of the symbol.

    > $_{50}$Sn or ^{50}Sn

- The index number that represents the ionic charge is typed as a superscript on the right side of the symbol.

    > Fe^3 (iron with an ionic charge of $+3$)

- The index number representing the number of atoms of an element in a molecule of a compound is typed as a subscript on the right side of the element symbol.

    > CO_2 (two atoms of oxygen [O] in the molecule carbon dioxide [CO_2])

Equations and Formulas

The typing of equations and formulas must be accurate and artistic. As mentioned earlier, technical symbols not appearing on your typewriter may be drawn by hand or with a template or typed with interchangeable keys or elements. For word processors and personal computer software programs, check the operator's manual. Software packages can be purchased with a wide variety of symbols for equations and formulas.

General Guidelines for Typing Equations and Formulas

1. The "base" or "center line" is the main line of the equation and should be aligned with the major symbol(s) used:

$$A = \frac{R + b}{E_r}$$

Use the variable line lever, called the ratchet release.

2. Space once before and after major symbols:

$$A = 2$$

3. Do not space in parenthetical expressions:

$$[b-2] \qquad (b-3_p)$$

4. Do not space between a number and a following letter:

$$a^2 + 3ac$$

5. Do not use periods with abbreviations. Leave a space before and after:

$$P = 10 \log$$

6. Use a lower-case o for super- and subscripts unless a zero is specified:

$$X_o$$

7. Use the apostrophe to indicate prime:

$$p'$$

8. Use half-space adjustments for super- and subscripts having letters and numbers superior or posterior below or above the main line:

$$K = \frac{C^{c^q}D}{C_A^m}$$

9. When two or more equations of varying lengths are grouped together, the longest should be centered. Align equal signs:

$$p = p''$$
$$V = p' + abc'$$
$$b = b' + 2(a \times b') + 2$$

10. An equation should not be divided within parentheses, braces, or brackets; within an expression, such as $(a + b)$; or at the end of a page.

11. Use punctuation (, ; .) only when a mark adds to the equation's meaning. Three or four spaces should be allowed between the end of the equation and the mark of punctuation:

$$x = (y + z) = (x + y) = z \quad ;$$
$$(xy)z = x(yz) = xyz \quad .$$

12. Ellipsis (three periods with spaces before and after each) indicates omitted symbols within:

$$a_1 + b_2 \ldots + c = -x$$

DEVELOPING A
TECHNICAL VOCABULARY

TABLE 19.3

Prefixes Commonly Used in Technical Terms

Prefix	Meaning	Example
alco-	relating to alcohols	alcohol
alk-	relating to alkyls	alkylate, alkiodide
alka-	relating to alkanes	alkaloid
anti-	opposed to	antiacid, antienzyme
bi-	double; two; a compound containing two rings	bifurcation, bimetallic, bimodal, binary
cyclo-	relating to a circle	cyclobarbital, cyclometer
hydr-	relating to water; hydrogen	hydraulic, hydroelectric
iso-	equal; denoting an isomer of a compound	isobutyl, isonuclear, isoctane
macr-	large; excessively developed	macroanalysis, macrocyte, macrophysics
micro-	small	microfilm, microorganism, microwave
naphth-	related to naphthalene	naphtha, naphthalia, naphthene
nitr-	pertaining to nitrogen	nitrate, nitric, nitridge
par-, para-	closely related to; beside	paraformaldehyde, parallel, paragenesis
radio-	relating to energy or radiation	radioactive, radioisotope, radiometer
syn-	at the same time; with	syneresis, synergist, synthesize, synthol
therm-	related to heat	thermal, thermodynamics, thermolysis, thermonuclear
turbo-	related to driving a turbine	turbofan, turbogeneration, turbojet, turboprop
ultra-	beyond the limits of; the other side	ultrabasic, ultrasonic, ultraviolet

The technical secretary should become familiar with the technical terms, particularly the frequently used words, of the field in which he or she is working. This section lists prefixes and suffixes used in various fields. Often a knowledge of what the prefix or suffix means will help in figuring out the meaning of the word.

The lists given here are selective. Consult standard references in your specialized field and find out if local business schools, universities, and technical institutes have special courses or other instruments by which you can improve your vocabulary—and your value as a technical secretary.

TABLE 19.4

Suffixes Commonly Used in Technical Terms

Suffix	Meaning	Example
-al	related to; characterized by dehydrogenated alcohols	butanal, ethanal, hormonal, medicinal
-amide	derived from ammonia	capramide, carboxamide, oleamide
-ane	a saturated or completely hydrogenated carbon compound	butane, ethane, methane, propane
-ate	relating to a chemical compound derived from another element that may modify it	butyrate, fractionate, nitrate
-ene	denoting unsaturation; carbon compound with one double bond	benzene, ethene, kerosene, terpene
-ol	may represent a chemical compound containing hydroxyl (alcohols and phenols classified as hydrocarbons noted by the suffix -ol)	ethanol, glycerol, phenol, mannitol
-on	an elementary particle or antiparticle; a unit	electron, meson, photon, proton, neutron
-one	a ketone, frequently used as a solvent	acetone, lactone, pentanone
-mer	belonging to a specific or specified class	isomer, copolymer, elastomer
-scope	viewing with the eye in any way	microscope, telescope
-scopy	viewing; examination	cryoscopy, microscopy, spectroscopy
-yne	unsaturated straight-chain hydrocarbon; presence of one triple bond	alkyne, butyne, pentyne
-yl	a radical containing oxygen	acetyl, butyl, vinyl, ethyl

REFERENCES AND
SOURCES OF INFORMATION

The technical secretary is frequently called on to research information. The research may involve completing bibliographic references and checking specific dates or other facts for the researcher/executive, or it may involve the secretary's own need to understand symbols and technical terms. A skill for searching, retrieving, and analyzing information, either in a traditional manner through encyclopedias, textbooks, and other references or through modern electronic databases and software, is a skill required for the secretary of the 1990s, especially the technical secretary.

Books and Other References

Science encyclopedias such as *Van Nostrand's Scientific Encyclopedia* and *McGraw-Hill's Encyclopedia of Science and Technology* can be valuable references, as can specialized dictionaries (e.g., *Webster's New World/Stedman's Concise Medical Dictionary*) and directories (e.g., *American Medical Directory*). Indexes, such as *Applied Science and Technology Index*, can direct you to specific articles on various subjects.

Other sources of technical information may be found in public and private libraries, the U.S. Government (The Superintendent of Documents, U.S. Government Printing Office, Washington, DC 20442), and independent government agencies (see *U.S. Government Manual*). Agencies include the National Aeronautics and Space Administration and the Civil Aeronautics Board, among others, and public and private organizations and foundations. For specialized libraries, consult *The Directory of Special Libraries and Information Centers*, published by Gale Research Co., Detroit, MI.

For information on the metric system, see *Standard for Metric Practice*, American Society for Testing and Materials. The International System of Units (SI), the metric system, is a standard system for expressing units of measurement throughout the world. The U.S. Customary (English) system (feet, pounds) is now officially defined in SI units. The book listed includes common SI-derived units, the metric system, and conversion charts and is a useful guide.

For scientific journal writing and formatting, consult *The Chicago Manual of Style*, 13th edition (The University of Chicago Press) and *Writing for Technical and Professional Journals* by John H. Mitchell (John Wiley & Sons, Inc.).

Style and symbols notes in mathematics, physics, etc. can be found in *American Institute of Physics Style Manual*, 3rd edition. This book includes common mathematical operations, signs of relation, identification of symbols, and hints on spelling and typesetting.

Symbols in the Greek, Roman, and Latin alphabets—the alphabets sometimes used in technical writing—are found in most major dictionaries.

Software

The technical secretary in the electronic office may also consult electronic databases for information. Among those to consult are:

Research Institute, Inc., New York, NY

Dialog, Lockheed's Information System

Bibliographic Retrieval Services (BRS)

NewsNet

OAG North American & Worldwide Electronic Edition

Cuadra Associates, Inc.'s *Directory of Online Databases* and *DataPro Directory of Online Services*

The Membership Secretary

by Linda Bruce

WHAT A MEMBERSHIP SECRETARY IS

The membership secretary is a critical link in any organization that deals with a membership base, since without a satisfied, supportive, and growing membership constituency, the parent organization cannot continue to exist. The secretary who deals with the members, therefore, must do so in an efficient and pleasant manner, since he or she is most often the first person with whom members come in contact, whether in person, on the telephone, or in writing.

Organizations that most often employ a membership secretary are usually in the nonprofit or service sector and run the gamut from trade and professional associations to educational and arts institutions (including their alumni associations) and charities.

QUALIFICATIONS

There are no specific rules about educational qualifications for a membership secretary. However, a knowledge of personal computers is becoming increasingly desirable as the use of PCs filters down into the nonprofit world.

In addition, strong "people" skills are essential, since the focus of any membership department is servicing the members or potential members of the organization. A parallel function that requires these same skills is the role of liaison between other staff members, elected officials, volunteers, and the public at large.

Equally important are excellent administrative and organizational capabilities, a command of communication skills (both written and oral), and the ability to effectively handle a great amount of detail.

Finally, shorthand is still in demand by some executives, particularly in situations where minutes of meetings are required.

TASKS

There are a number of special tasks that a membership secretary may be asked to perform, depending on the size of the organization. In small organizations, greater flexibility and versatility is required of all staff members, whereas in larger organizations, there are usually enough employees to allow greater specialization.

Telephone Use

Responses to telephone inquiries can take up as much as 50 percent of the membership secretary's working day. The nature of the calls varies greatly, covering such things as general information about the organization, categories of membership and costs involved, membership status questions, services and programs, statistical information, complaints and compliments, and new product and service needs and suggestions. Whether the secretary is the first to answer the telephone in an organization or answers a referral call, he or she must give an impression of friendliness and efficiency.

List Maintenance and Record Keeping

In order to respond intelligently to questions about membership status—i.e., affiliation, disaffiliation, transfers, etc.—the membership secretary is often required to keep such records current. The dates of membership activity, as well as accurate information on the payment of fees or dues, is essential to the smooth fiscal functioning of any organization. Records of contributions, addresses and telephone numbers, names of employers, job titles, and other types of detailed information are also maintained, depending on their intended uses.

Record keeping is increasingly being converted from a manual to a computerized operation as more and more membership database software packages come onto the market. For example, individually addressed letters (as well as labels or envelopes) may be generated on the computer to remind members of an upcoming dues renewal date, with the appropriate membership classification and dues amount inserted in each letter. The computer can also sort these letters by zip code for mailing, alphabetically by last name, or by membership category, affiliation date, or any number of other specific information needs. Letters soliciting annual or special-cause contributions might need to be sorted by dollar ranges based on previous giving, in order to tailor the newest appeal letters; or, lists of names and telephone numbers by geographic areas might be needed to send or phone invitations to regional events.

As can be seen from the few examples given, accurate record keeping is a cornerstone for meaningful and therefore successful mail or telephone communications between an organization and its membership base.

Handling Conventions, Conferences, and Seminars

Many nonprofit organizations hold conventions, annual meetings, conferences, seminars, and committee meetings regularly throughout the year. The membership secretary's involvement in organizing this type of activity depends on the size of the group and varies greatly, as does the extent of computerization.

The secretary may be responsible for the inspection and contracting of meeting sites, registration, setting up of workshops, production of meeting materials and name badges, collection of fees, hotel reservations, and on-site assistance.

Preparing for and assisting at any conventions, conferences, or seminars involves considerable contact with the membership base and requires flexibility and the ability to handle with grace numerous last-minute changes in complex and detailed information. Organizational and administrative talents must be brought into play as well, or disaster is inevitable. These tasks can be very demanding, challenging, and rewarding (when things run smoothly). They can also afford the opportunity for travel, which appeals to many secretaries.

Numerous books are available that provide more detail on planning meetings, site inspections, and meeting setups. Professional organi-

zations for meeting planners (recommended for all membership secretaries involved in planning large meetings) and meeting planners'
trade magazines provide additional information.

Bulk Mailings

Responsibility for numerous mailings to members and nonmembers
alike is another aspect of the membership secretary's job. Such mailings
might consist of an announcement of new services, programs and
conferences/seminars, fundraising efforts, newsletters, and magazine
subscriptions, among other things. They can involve thousands of
single or multiple enclosures.

The membership secretary is often called on not only to affix
postage and get the mail to the post office but also (if possessing these
skills) to assist with the writing, editing, artwork, and reproduction of
the enclosures. If a computer is available for the creation of mailing
labels, the job becomes easier than it would be if names and addresses
needed to be typed or handwritten. The computer will also make the
process of sorting data into categories (such as those mentioned
previously in the "List Maintenance and Record Keeping" section of
this chapter) far more efficient than a manual system.

For large mailing projects, it is often a better use of the secretary's
time to hire and supervise temporary help for manual addressing and
sorting and affixing of postage. Depending on the degree of mechanical/
technical sophistication and budget constraints within an organization,
a great deal of time can also be saved by using computerized postal
scales and meters. Gone are the days of having to carry the meter to
the post office to have additional postage entered. It is now possible
to do everything by telephone and computer, once an account has
been established with a postal meter company.

Alternatively, it is possible to "farm out" the entire job to an
office service bureau or mailing house that will even take the mail to
the post office for you. When an outside firm is used, it is essential
that accurate lists or computer data be provided since there is usually
no "in-house" control of what actually goes out in the mail.

Fundraising

Fundraising is often the lifeblood of a membership-based organization,
and it is critical that the tasks involved be carried out with skill and
effectiveness.

Fundraising is often cyclical in nature—often annual or semiannual. Some organizations may restrict themselves entirely to fundraising by mail, in which case the "Bulk Mailings" section of this
chapter would apply. However, in many organizations fundraising

involves a special event or program. The membership secretary's involvement again depends on the size of the organization and also on the specialized skills or positions of others on the staff and on the interest and initiative of the secretary.

In the "Jack/Jill-of-all-trades" type of secretarial spot, the membership secretary may be called on to exercise all sorts of talents—from conceptualizing the type of event to negotiating contracts for facilities, entertainment, catering, advertising, decorating, speakers, and security. Invitation lists and responses must be tracked, place cards printed and set out, receiving lines and registration organized, and initial and follow-up mailings or phone calls made. A series of checklists based on tasks to be performed, staff assignments, and completion dates is an indispensable tool to ensure that small details do not "fall between the cracks." Indeed, the checklist system should be used for any multi-task areas.

Correspondence, Reports, and Minutes

The underpinnings of any organization's functioning involve the documentation of decisions and actions. This documentation can take many forms, including correspondence typed from shorthand or dictation equipment or rough manuscript. In addition, reports and business plans need to be prepared and minutes of meetings taken. (In some organizations the membership secretary may need to know shorthand to take minutes at meetings.) Depending on demonstrated writing skills and the amount of autonomy given the membership secretary, he or she may be required to do a fair amount of original writing—letters, brief press announcements, etc.

SUMMARY

The work of a membership secretary may be broad or narrow in scope, has the potential of being very challenging, and may draw on a wide range of skills learned over the years. Involvement in any of the tasks mentioned varies not only with the size of the organization but also with the secretary's experience, willingness to learn (not only on the job but also through specialized classes and seminars), and initiative.

The Educational Secretary

by Ardis R. Morton

The educational secretary is one who is employed by any educational system, institution, or organization related to education. Such an institution might be a public, private, or church-affiliated school, a school for blind or hearing-impaired children or adults, a school for physically or mentally handicapped students, a correctional school, or a vocational school. The secretarial/clerical personnel employed by institutions of higher learning (colleges, universities, seminaries, business schools, community colleges, medical schools, etc.) are also termed "educational secretaries." In addition, there are many organizations, such as the National Education Association, the American Association of School Administrators, and others, that employ educational secretaries.

The responsibilities of secretaries on any educational level are as diversified as the levels of education. With the varied responsibilities come different job descriptions and titles. The educational secretary may be known as an administrative assistant, manager, coordinator, executive assistant, or other title reflecting the particular position. Although the school secretaryship probably started out as a clerical job, the technological and information age, coupled with the realization that administrators, teachers, and educational secretaries are partners in education, has brought new emphasis and a great number of responsibilities to this specialized aspect of the secretarial profession.

REQUIREMENTS

The educational secretary is on the "front line" with students, teachers, administrators, coworkers, parents, and the local community and must feel comfortable with this type of position. Frequently called upon to be a confidant, peacemaker, nurse, disciplinarian, and public relations expert, the educational secretary must remain calm and professional at all times. When confronted with myriad requests from several administrators and the need to do several things, the secretary must be able to make priority judgments and complete each task efficiently.

The basic educational requirements for the position of educational secretary vary from job to job. However, the minimum requirement in most educational systems or institutions is a high school diploma in addition to knowledge of basic secretarial and office functions. Many institutions require additional formal education: a business college or other college degree or specific business courses.

As with all secretaries, the educational secretary should be able to take and transcribe dictation and type accurately and quickly. A good knowledge of business English, spelling, arithmetic, and basic recordkeeping is essential, as is the ability to learn established policies and practices and plan and organize work schedules. Familiarity with office machines such as photocopiers, calculators, and word processors is also necessary, and with the increased use of computers at all educational office levels, computer knowhow is an asset.

FACETS OF THE EDUCATIONAL
SECRETARY'S JOB

The educational secretary's job is usually multifaceted regardless of the educational level. Secretaries act as a liaison between school members and others, must develop a trusting working relationship with school administrators, and must handle special functions, such as assisting teachers and/or media experts in preparing teaching materials, maintaining centralized management information, and arranging for substitute teachers.

Public Relations

The educational secretary is often the first contact a caller or visitor has with the educational system. In this role, he or she gives in a very few minutes an impression of the entire school system or administration. The picture can be a masterpiece of organization, cooperation, and efficiency, or it can be a rough sketch of discordance and ineffectiveness. The staff of the school may be outstanding, but if the first contact—the office professional—fails, the school gains a critic, not a friend. Since many school districts and institutions of higher learning depend on taxes and contributions, such poor public relations can result not only in loss of a friend but also in loss of needed funds.

Relationship with Administrators

The secretary's relationship with the executive—the school principal, dean, university president, or other in an executive position—is very important. To create an atmosphere that allows each member of the team to function at full potential, a viable working relationship must be developed. Three important factors in this relationship are consideration, confidence, and communication.

Administrators and secretaries must be considerate and understanding of the goals, strengths, and weaknesses of the other. The educational secretary also needs to know that the administrator has confidence in him or her and trusts his or her ability to keep confidences. Finally, communication is the key to all good working relationships. The administrator must communicate in such a manner that the secretary knows what he or she wants, what is expected, and where authority lies. Conversely, the administrator needs to know in what areas the secretary has expertise and then to allow his or her input into daily work.

Liaison

The importance of communication extends beyond the secretary/ executive relationship: it is important throughout the entire school family (students and staff) and with the surrounding community. The educational secretary serves as a liaison between staff and administrators; between administrators and superiors; between staff, administrators, and the public; and between staff and students. Good human relations skills are essential whether the secretary is communicating the administrator's wishes to the staff and her coworkers or providing the administrator with input from the staff. Always on the front line, the educational secretary must develop and nurture tact.

Special Duties

Media service is a new area in which some educational secretaries work. They are involved in working with the librarian at the local school level, in the ordering of films and library materials at the central level, and in processing library and media materials. They might also be involved in preparing materials for teachers and using laminators, paper cutters, and machines that cut out letters for posters and bulletin boards. Many secretaries assist in the preparation of school newspapers and newsletters that are sent to both students and parents. Included in the realm of media can also be assisting with photography and the preparation of television and video presentations.

Many school systems now have centralized management information systems. Secretaries who work with computers input attendance information for both students and employees, payroll information, enrollment information, and student grades; order classroom and lunchroom supplies; and keep financial records.

One important facet of working in many school districts is the hiring of substitute teachers. In some very large school systems this may be done through a centralized program, where several persons spend evenings calling for substitutes for the schools that need them the following day. However, in many school districts it is the secretary who calls each day for the substitutes using a list of persons eligible and approved for substitute work by the administration.

DUTIES AT DIFFERENT EDUCATIONAL LEVELS

In addition to the human relations skills and special duties referred to earlier, the educational secretary has responsibilities that vary with the level and size of the educational facility in which he or she works.

In Small Elementary Schools

The secretary in the elementary school handles all office responsibilities, unless the school is a large one that has two or more secretaries or other office personnel to assist the secretary. The responsibilities of the elementary school secretary may include that of receptionist, recordkeeper, bookkeeper, stenographer, counselor to both students and staff, office manager, lunch period clerk, attendance clerk, data processing clerk, and many other varied positions. Most importantly, the elementary school secretary must be able to relate to young children, for much of the time will be spent in direct contact with the students. Since the secretary must also deal with the teachers, maintenance personnel, and other people in the school building, he or she must be able to relate well with coworkers and convey the messages of the principal or other administrator effectively.

At Larger Elementary Schools and at the Secondary Level

At larger elementary schools and in secondary schools where there are more personnel in each office, the responsibilities of the secretary are more defined and limited. There may be separate positions such as secretary to the principal, bookkeeper, attendance clerk, guidance secretary, data processor, and receptionist.

In Administrative Positions

Educational secretaries who work in administrative areas may hold positions such as executive secretary (e.g., to the superintendent of the school district), administrative secretary, or technical clerk. Duties vary greatly depending on the specific office in which the secretary is employed. Almost all educational offices have personnel departments in which secretaries work with administrators who hire school employees; human relations departments that handle discrimination cases and affirmative action plans; employee assistance directors, who counsel employees with work-related or personal problems; benefits and retirement directors; and specialists who develop school calendars. Other educational offices handle the development of instructional programs and special education programs, maintenance problems, security, food services and school lunch programs, budgets, computer services, and many other specialized programs peculiar to the individual school district. Staff and organizational planning, tuition reimbursement for courses taken by both educational and support staff, planning of workshops for employees, and adult education programs are also activities that many school districts now have as part of their service to employees.

At Higher Education Levels

Secretaries who work in universities or colleges might be the secretary to the dean, an administrator or director, or the university librarian or may work in the registrar's office. In many instances, secretaries may work with more than one administrator and perhaps several professors in a department. Many secretaries in universities and colleges, and sometimes members of their families, receive free tuition, use of athletic facilities and libraries, and discount tickets to sporting and cultural events.

PROFESSIONAL ORGANIZATIONS AND CERTIFICATION

Membership in a professional organization is important, providing a means for further education and communication. In the United States, the only national professional association for office personnel in educational institutions is the National Association of Educational Office Personnel (NAEOP). (The association is also represented in several foreign countries.) The U.S. NAEOP office is located at 7223 Lee Highway, Suite 301, Falls Church, Virginia 22046.

The NAEOP is dedicated to providing its members with opportunities and stimuli for professional growth. It works for increased recognition of educational office personnel as partners in the education team. Its goals are:

1. to promote the advancement of education by improving the quality of service by educational office personnel to institutions of learning and the profession
2. to provide professional growth opportunities
3. to recognize educational office personnel as members of the education team
4. to elevate the standards of office personnel in education.

The NAEOP has a four-point program: Service, Information, Recognition, and Fellowship. The Association also has a Code of Ethics in which it affirms its belief that an education is the birthright of every person and pledges itself to the preservation of that right. The Code of Ethics includes a commitment to the position, to the profession, and to the community.

Certification

NAEOP has a certification program—the Professional Standards Program. Successful completion of approved programs qualifies a member for a certificate at an appropriate level. The distinction of a Certified Educational Office Employee is awarded to those who meet the established criteria. These certificates are increasingly being recognized by educational administrators in both placement and monetary terms.

Travel Information:
Domestic and Foreign

22

Foreign Currency

(For evaluation in U.S. dollars, check with the foreign exchange department of a bank.)

Afgahnistan: afghani
Albania: lek
Algeria: dinar
Andorra: franc; peseta
Angola: kwanza
Antigua: dollar and barbuda
Argentina: austral
Australia: dollar
Austria: schilling

Bahamas: dollar
Bahrain: dinar
Bangladesh: taka
Barbados: dollar
Belgium: franc
Belize: dollar
Benin: franc
Bhutan: ngultrum
Bolivia: peso boliviano
Botswana: pula
Brazil: cruzeiro
Brunei: dollar
Bulgaria: lev
Burkina Faso: franc
Burma: kyat
Burundi: franc

Cambodia (Kampuchea): riel
Cameroon: franc

Canada: dollar
Cape Verde: escudo
Central African Republic: franc
Chad: franc
Chile: peso
China: yuan
Colombia: peso
Comoros: franc
Congo: franc
Costa Rica: colon
Cuba: peso
Cyprus: pound
Czechoslovakia: koruna

Denmark: krone
Djibouti: franc
Dominica: dollar
Dominican Republic: peso

Ecuador: sucre
Egypt: pound
El Salvador: colon
Equatorial Guinea: ekuele
Ethiopia: birr

Fiji: dollar
Finland: markka
France: franc

Gabon: franc
Gambia: dalasi
Germany (East): mark
Germany (West): deutsche mark
Ghana: cedi
Greece: drachma
Grenada: dollar
Guatemala: quetzal
Guinea: syli
Guinea-Bissau: peso
Guyana: dollar

Haiti: gourde
Honduras: lempira
Hungary: forint

Iceland: krona
India: rupee
Indonesia: rupiah
Iran: rial
Iraq: dinar
Ireland: pound
Israel: shekel
Italy: lira
Ivory Coast: franc

Jamaica: dollar
Japan: yen
Jordan: dinar

Kenya: shilling
Kiribati: dollar
Korea (North and South): won
Kuwait: dinar

Laos: kip
Lebanon: pound
Lesotho: maloti
Liberia: dollar
Libya: dinar
Liechtenstein: franc
Luxembourg: franc

Madagascar: franc

Malawi: kwacha
Malaysia: ringgit
Maldives: rufiyaa
Mali: franc
Malta: pound
Mauritania: ouguiya
Mauritius: rupee
Mexico: peso
Monaco: franc
Mongolia: tugrik
Morocco: dirham
Mozambique: metical

Nauru: dollar
Nepal: rupee
Netherlands: guilder
New Zealand: dollar
Nicaragua: cordoba
Niger: franc
Nigeria: naira
Norway: krone

Oman: rial

Pakistan: rupee
Panama: balboa
Papua New Guinea: kina
Paraguay: guarani
Peru: sol
Philippines: peso
Poland: zloty
Portugal: escudo

Qatar: riyal

Romania: leu
Rwanda: franc

San Marino: lira
São Tomé and Principe: dobra
Saudi Arabia: riyal
Senegal: franc
Seychelles: rupee
Sierra Leone: leone

Singapore: dollar
Solomon Islands: dollar
Somalia: shilling
South Africa: rand
Spain: peseta
Sri Lanka: rupee
St. Kitts and Nevis: dollar
St. Lucia: dollar
St. Vincent: dollar
Sudan: pound
Suriname: guilder
Swaziland: lilangeni
Sweden: krona
Switzerland: franc
Syria: pound

Taiwan: dollar
Tanzania: shilling
Thailand: baht
Togo: franc
Tonga: pa'anga
Trinidad and Tobago: dollar
Tunisia: dinar
Turkey: lira
Tuvalu: dollar

Uganda: shilling
Union of Soviet Socialist
  Republics: ruble
United Arab Emirates: dirham

United Kingdom: pound
  (includes Wales, Scotland,
  Northern Ireland, Channel
  Islands, Isle of Man, Gibraltar,
  Montserrat, Anguilla, Cayman
  Islands, Turks and Caicos
  Islands, Bermuda, Falkland
  Islands, British Antarctic
  Territory, St. Helena, Tristan
  da Cuhna, Ascencion, Hong
  Kong, Pitcairn Island)
Upper Volta: franc
Uruguay: peso

Vanatu: dollar, franc
Vatican City: lira
Venezuela: bolivar
Vietnam: dong

Western Samoa: tala

Yemen (People's Democratic
  Republic of): dinar
Yemen Arab Republic: rial
Yugoslavia: dinar

Zaire: zaire
Zambia: kwacha
Zimbabwe: dollar

23

Dialing Codes

- *Codes for U.S. States and Major Cities*
- *Codes for Canadian Provinces and Major Cities*
- *International Country and City Codes*

CODES FOR U.S. STATES AND MAJOR CITIES

Alabama

All points **205**

Alaska

All points **907**

Arizona

All points **602**

Arkansas

All points **501**

California

Alameda **415**
Alhambra **818**

© NYNEX Information
Resources Company
1987

Altadena **818**
Anaheim **714**
Arcadia **818**
Azusa **818**
Bakersfield **805**
Baldwin Park **818**
Bell Gardens **213**
Bellflower **213**
Belmont **415**
Berkeley **415**
Beverly Hills **213**
Buena Pk. **714**
Burbank (L.A. County) **818**
Burlingame **415**
Campbell **408**
Carmichael **916**
Carson **213**
Castro Valley **415**
Chula Vista **619**
Claremont **714**
Compton **213**
Concord **415**

Corona **714**
Costa Mesa **714**
Covina **818**
Culver City **213**
Cypress **714**
Daly City **415**
Davis **916**
Downey **213**
East Los Angeles **213**
El Cerrito **415**
El Monte **818**
Escondido **619**
Eureka **707**
Fairfield **707**
Fountain Valley **714**
Fremont **415**
Fresno **209**
Fullerton **714**
Gardena **213**
Garden Grove **714**
Glendale **818**
Glendora **818**

Hacienda Heights 818
Hawthorne 213
Hollywood 213
Huntington Beach 714
Huntington Park 213
Inglewood 213
La Habra 213
Lakewood 213
La Mesa 619
La Mirada 714
Lancaster 805
La Puente 818
Lawndale 213
Livermore 415
Lodi 209
Lompoc 805
Long Beach 213
Los Altos 415
Los Angeles 213
Los Gatos 408
Lynwood 213
Manhattan Beach 213
Menlo Park 415
Merced 209
Milpitas 408
Modesto 209
Monrovia 818
Montclair 714
Montebello 213
Monterey 408
Monterey Park 818
Mountain View 415
Napa 707
National City 619
Newark 415
Newport Beach 714
North Highlands 916
Norwalk 213
Novato 415
Oakland 415
Oceanside 619
Ontario 714
Orange 714
Oxnard 805
Pacifica 415
Palm Springs 619
Palo Alto 415
Palos Verdes 213
Paramount 213
Pasadena 818
Petaluma 707
Pico Rivera 213

Pleasant Hill 415
Rancho Cordova 916
Redlands 714
Redondo Beach 213
Redwood City 415
Rialto 714
Richmond 415
Riverside 714
Rosemead 818
Sacramento 916
Salinas 408
San Bernardino 714
San Bruno 415
San Carlos-Belmont 415
San Diego 619
San Francisco 415
San Gabriel 818
San Jose 408
San Leandro 415
San Lorenzo 415
San Luis Obispo 805
San Rafael 415
Santa Ana 714
Santa Barbara 805
Santa Clara 408
Santa Cruz 408
Santa Maria 805
Santa Monica 213
Santa Rosa 707
Seal Beach 213
Seaside 408
Simi Valley 805
South Gate 213
South Pasadena 818
South San Francisco 415
South Whittier 213
Spring Valley 619
Stockton 209
Sunnyvale 408
Temple City 818
Thousand Oaks 805
Torrance 213
Upland 714
Vallejo 707
Ventura 805
Visalia 209
Vista 619
Walnut Creek 415
West Covina 818
West Hollywood 213
Westminister 714
Whittier 213

Colorado

Aspen 303
Colorado Springs 719
Denver 303
Grand Junction 303
Pueblo 719
Vail 303
Woodland Park 719

Connecticut

All points 203

Delaware

All points 302

District of Columbia

Washington, D.C. 202

Florida

Boca Raton 407
Carol City 305
Clearwater 813
Coral Gables 305
Daytona Beach 904
Fort Lauderdale 305
Fort Myers 813
Fort Pierce 407
Gainesville 904
Hallandale 305
Hialeah 305
Jacksonville 904
Kendall 305
Key West 305
Lakeland 813
Lake Worth 407
Melbourne 407
Merritt Island 407
Miami 305
Miami Beach 305
Miramar 305
North Miami 305
North Miami Beach 305
Ocala 904
Orlando 407
Panama City 904
Pensacola 904
Plantation 305
Pompano Beach 305

St. Petersburg **813**
Sarasota **813**
Tallahassee **904**
Tampa **813**
Titusville **407**
West Palm Beach **407**

Georgia

Albany **912**
Athens **404**
Atlanta **404**
Augusta **404**
Columbus **404**
East Point **404**
Fort Benning **404**
Gainesville **404**
Griffin **404**
La Grange **404**
Macon **912**
Marietta **404**
Rome **404**
Savannah **912**
Valdosta **912**
Warner Robins **912**

Hawaii

All points **808**

Idaho

All points **208**

Illinois

Addison **312**
Alton **618**
Arlington Hts. **312**
Aurora **312**
Belleville **618**
Berwyn **312**
Bloomington **309**
Blue Island **312**
Calumet City **312**
Carbondale **618**
Carpentersville **312**
Champaign-Urbana **217**
Chicago **312**
Chicago Hgts. **312**
Cicero **312**
Danville **217**

Decatur **217**
De Kalb **815**
Des Plaines **312**
Dolton **312**
Downers Grove **312**
East St. Louis **618**
Elgin **312**
Elk Grove Village **312**
Elmhurst **312**
Elmwood Park **312**
Evanston **312**
Evergreen Park **312**
Freeport **815**
Galesburg **309**
Granite City **618**
Harvey **312**
Highland Park **312**
Hinsdale **312**
Hoffman Estates **312**
Joliet **815**
Kankakee **815**
La Grange **312**
Lansing **312**
Lombard **312**
Maywood **312**
Melrose Park **312**
Moline **309**
Morton Grove **312**
Mount Prospect **312**
Naperville **312**
Niles **312**
Normal **309**
Northbrook **312**
North Chicago **312**
Oak Lawn **312**
Oak Park **312**
Palatine **312**
Park Forest **312**
Park Ridge **312**
Pekin **309**
Peoria **309**
Rantoul **217**
Rockford **815**
Rock Island **309**
Schaumburg **312**
Skokie **312**
South Holland **312**
Springfield **217**
Urbana **217**
Villa Park **312**
Waukegan **312**

Wheaton **312**
Wilmette **312**

Indiana

Anderson **317**
Bloomington **812**
Columbus **812**
East Chicago **219**
Elkhart **219**
Evansville **812**
Fort Wayne **219**
Gary **219**
Hammond **219**
Highland **219**
Indianapolis **317**
Kokomo **317**
Lafayette **317**
Marion **317**
Merrillville **219**
Michigan City **219**
Mishawaka **219**
Muncie **317**
New Albany **812**
Richmond **317**
South Bend **219**
Terre Haute **812**

Iowa

Ames **515**
Burlington **319**
Cedar Falls **319**
Cedar Rapids **319**
Clinton **319**
Council Bluffs **712**
Davenport **319**
Des Moines **515**
Dubuque **319**
Fort Dodge **515**
Iowa City **319**
Marshalltown **515**
Ottumwa **515**
Sioux City **712**
Waterloo **319**

Kansas

Emporia **316**
Hutchinson **316**
Kansas City **913**
Lawrence **913**

Leavenworth **913**
Manhattan **913**
Overland Park **913**
Salina **913**
Topeka **913**
Wichita **316**

Kentucky

Ashland **606**
Bowling Green **502**
Covington **606**
Fort Knox **502**
Frankfort **502**
Henderson **502**
Lexington **606**
Louisville **502**
Newport **606**
Owensboro **502**
Paducah **502**
Pleasure Ridge Park **502**
Valley Station **502**

Louisiana

Alexandria **318**
Baton Rouge **504**
Bossier City **318**
Gretna **504**
Houma **504**
Kenner **504**
Lafayette **318**
Lake Charles **318**
Marrero **504**
Metairie **504**
Monroe **318**
New Iberia **318**
New Orleans **504**
Scotlandville **504**
Shreveport **318**

Maine

All points **207**

Maryland

All points **301**

Massachusetts

Amherst **413**
Andover **508**
Arlington **617**
Attleboro **508**
Barnstable **508**
Belmont **617**
Beverly **508**
Boston **617**
Braintree **617**
Brookline **617**
Cambridge **617**
Chelmsford **508**
Chelsea **617**
Chicopee **413**
Danvers **508**
Dedham **617**
Everett **617**
Fall River **508**
Fitchburg **508**
Framingham **508**
Gardner **508**
Gloucester **508**
Greenfield **413**
Haverhill **508**
Holyoke **413**
Lawrence **508**
Leominster **508**
Lexington **617**
Longmeadow **413**
Lowell **508**
Lynn **617**
Malden **617**
Marblehead **617**
Marlborough **508**
Medford **617**
Melrose **617**
Methuen **508**
Milton **617**
Nantucket **508**
Needham **617**
New Bedford **508**
Newton **617**
North Adams **413**
Northampton **413**
Norwood **617**
Paxton **508**
Pittsfield **413**
Quincy **617**
Randolph **617**
Reading **617**
Revere **617**
Roxbury **617**
Sandwich **508**
Saugus **617**

Somerville **617**
Springfield **413**
Stoughton **617**
Taunton **508**
Tewksbury **508**
Wakefield **617**
Waltham **617**
Watertown **617**
Wellesley **617**
Westfield **413**
West Springfield **413**
Weymouth **617**
Woburn **617**
Worcester **617**

Michigan

Allen Park **313**
Ann Arbor **313**
Battle Creek **616**
Bay City **517**
Benton Harbor **616**
Birmingham **313**
Dearborn **313**
Detroit **313**
East Detroit **313**
East Lansing **517**
Ferndale **313**
Flint **313**
Garden City **313**
Grand Rapids **616**
Hamtramck **313**
Hazel Park **313**
Highland Park **313**
Holland **616**
Inkster **313**
Jackson **517**
Kalamazoo **616**
Lansing **517**
Livonia **313**
Madison Heights **313**
Marquette **906**
Midland **517**
Monroe **313**
Muskegon **616**
Niles **616**
Oak Park **313**
Pontiac **313**
Portage **616**
Port Huron **313**
Roseville **313**
Royal Oak **313**
Saginaw **517**

St. Clair Shores 313
St. Joseph 616
Southfield 313
Southgate 313
Sterling Heights 313
Taylor 313
Trenton 313
Troy 313
Warren 313
Westland 313
Wyandotte 313
Wyoming 616
Ypsilanti 313

Minnesota

Austin 507
Bloomington 612
Brooklyn Center 612
Columbia Heights 612
Coon Rapids 612
Crystal 612
Duluth 218
Edina 612
Fridley 612
Mankato 507
Minneapolis 612
Minnetonka 612
Moorhead 218
New Hope 612
Rochester 507
Roseville 612
St. Cloud 612
St. Louis Park 612
St. Paul 612
White Bear Lake 612
Winona 507

Mississippi

All points 601

Missouri

Affton 314
Cape Girardeau 314
Columbia 314
Ferguson 314
Florissant 314
Ford Leonard Wood 314
Gladstone 816
Independence 816

Jefferson City 314
Joplin 417
Kansas City 816
Kirkwood 314
Lemay 314
Overland 314
Raytown 816
St. Charles 314
St. Joseph 816
St. Louis 314
Sedalia 816
Springfield 417
University City 314
Webster Groves 314

Montana

All points 406

Nebraska

Fremont 402
Grand Island 308
Hastings 402
Lincoln 402
North Platte 308
Omaha 402

Nevada

All points 702

New Hampshire

All points 603

New Jersey

Asbury Park 201
Atlantic City 609
Barnegat 609
Bayonne 201
Belleville 201
Bellmawr (Camden Co.)
609
Bergenfield 201
Bloomfield 201
Bound Brook 201
Bridgeton 609
Burlington 609
Camden 609
Carteret 201

Cliffside Park 201
Clifton 201
Collingswood 609
Dover 201
Dumont 201
East Orange 201
East Paterson 201
Eatontown 201
Elizabeth 201
Englewood 201
Ewing 609
Fair Lawn 201
Flemington 201
Fort Dix 609
Fort Lee 201
Garfield 201
Glassboro 609
Glen Ridge 201
Gloucester 609
Hackensack 201
Haddonfield 609
Hasbrouck Heights 201
Hawthorne 201
Hoboken 201
Irvington 201
Jersey City 201
Kearny 201
Lakewood 201
Linden 201
Long Branch 201
Madison 201
Maplewood 201
Mendham 201
Metuchen 201
Middlesex 201
Millburn 201
Millville 609
Montclair 201
Morristown 201
Mount Holly 609
Newark 201
Newark Int'l Airport 201
New Brunswick 201
New Milford 201
North Arlington 201
North Plainfield 201
Nutley 201
Old Bridge 201
Orange 201
Paramus 201
Passaic 201
Paterson 201

Perth Amboy **201**
Phillipsburg **201**
Plainfield **201**
Pleasantville **609**
Point Pleasant **201**
Pompton Lakes **201**
Princeton **609**
Rahway **201**
Red Bank **201**
Ridgefield **201**
Ridgewood **201**
Roselle **201**
Rutherford **201**
Sayreville **201**
Somerville **201**
South Amboy **201**
South Orange **201**
South Plainfield **201**
South River **201**
Summit **201**
Teaneck **201**
Trenton **609**
Union City **201**
Verona **201**
Vineland **609**
Weehawken **201**
Westfield **201**
West New York **201**
West Orange **201**
Wildwood **609**
Woodbridge **201**
Woodbury **609**
Wyckoff **201**

New Mexico

All points **505**

New York

Albany & Suburbs **518**
Amagansett **516**
Amityville **516**
Amsterdam **518**
Armonk Village **914**
Auburn **315**
Babylon **516**
Baldwin **516**
Batavia **716**
Bay Shore **516**
Bedford Village **914**
Bellmore **516**

Bethpage **516**
Binghamton **607**
Brentwood **516**
Brewster **914**
Bridgehampton **516**
Bronx **212**
Bronxville **914**
Brooklyn **718**
Brookville **516**
Buffalo & Suburbs **716**
Callicoon **914**
Carmel **914**
Center Moriches **516**
Central Islip **516**
Chappaqua **914**
Cohoes **518**
Cold Spring (Putnam Co.) **914**
Commack **516**
Congers **914**
Copiague **516**
Corning **607**
Cortland **607**
Croton-on-Hudson **914**
Deer Park **516**
Depew **716**
Dobbs Ferry **914**
Dunkirk **716**
Eastchester **914**
East Hampton **516**
East Massapequa **516**
East Meadow **516**
Eastport **516**
Ellenville **914**
Elmira **607**
Elmsford **914**
Elwood **516**
Endicott **607**
Endwell **607**
Fairmount **315**
Fallsburg **914**
Farmingdale **516**
Fire Island **516**
Fishers Island **516**
Floral Park **516**
Franklin Square (Nassau Co.) **516**
Freeport **516**
Fulton **315**
Garden City **516**
Garrison **914**
Geneva **315**

Glen Cove **516**
Glens Falls **518**
Gloversville **518**
Grahamsville **914**
Great Neck **516**
Grossinger **914**
Hamilton **315**
Hampton Bays **516**
Harrison **914**
Hastings-on-Hudson **914**
Haverstraw **914**
Hempstead **516**
Hicksville **516**
Hudson **518**
Huntington **516**
Huntington Sta. **516**
Hurleyville **914**
Irvington **914**
Islip **516**
Ithaca **607**
Jamestown **716**
Jeffersonville **914**
Johnson City **607**
Kenmore **716**
Kennedy Int'l Airport **718**
Kerhonkson **914**
Kiamesha **914**
Kingston **914**
Lackawanna **716**
LaGuardia Airport **718**
Lake Huntington **914**
Lakeland **914**
Lake Success **516**
Larchmont **914**
Levittown **516**
Liberty **914**
Lindenhurst **516**
Livingston Manor **914**
Lockport **716**
Long Beach **516**
Long Island (Nassau & Suffolk Co.) **516**
Lynbrook **516**
Mahopac **914**
Mamaroneck **914**
Manhasset **516**
Manhattan **212**
Massapequa **516**
Massapequa Park **516**
Massena **315**
Merrick **516**
Middletown **914**

Mineola **516**
Montauk Point **516**
Monticello **914**
Mount Kisco **914**
Mount Vernon **914**
Nanuet **914**
Narrowsburg **914**
Nassau County **516**
Newark **315**
Newburgh **914**
New City **914**
New Rochelle **914**
Niagara Falls **716**
North Babylon **516**
North Bellmore **516**
North Massapequa **516**
North Tonawanda **716**
Norwich **607**
Nyack **914**
Oceanside **516**
Olean **716**
Oneida **315**
Oneonta **607**
Ossining **914**
Oswego **315**
Oyster Bay **516**
Patchogue **516**
Pearl River **914**
Peekskill **914**
Pelham **914**
Penn Station **212**
Piermont **914**
Plainview **516**
Plattsburgh **518**
Pleasantville **914**
Port Chester **914**
Port Jefferson **516**
Port Washington **516**
Potsdam **315**
Poughkeepsie **914**
Queens County **718**
Riverhead **516**
Rochester **716**
Rockville Centre **516**
Roosevelt **516**
Rome **315**
Ronkonkoma **516**
Roscoe **607**
Roslyn **516**
Rye **914**
Sag Harbor **516**
Saratoga Springs **518**

Sayville **516**
Scarsdale **914**
Schenectady **518**
Seaford **516**
Shelter Island **516**
Sloatsburg **914**
Smithtown **516**
Southampton **516**
Spring Valley **914**
Staten Island **718**
Stony Point (Rockland
    Co.) **914**
Suffern **914**
Suffolk County **516**
Syracuse & Suburbs **315**
Tarrytown **914**
Ticonderoga **518**
Tonawanda **716**
Troy **518**
Tuckahoe **914**
Uniondale **516**
Utica & Suburbs **315**
Valley Stream **516**
Wantagh **516**
Watertown **315**
Westbury (Nassau Co.)
516
Westchester Co. **914**
Westhampton **516**
West Hempstead **516**
West Islip **516**
Wheatley Hills **516**
White Lake **914**
White Plains **914**
Williamsville **716**
Woodbourne **914**
Woodmere **516**
Woodridge **914**
Woodstock **914**
Wyandanch **516**
Yonkers **914**
Yorktown Heights **914**

North Carolina

Asheville **704**
Burlington **919**
Camp Le Jeune **919**
Chapel Hill **919**
Charlotte **704**
Durham **919**
Fayetteville **919**
Fort Bragg **919**

Gastonia **704**
Goldsboro **919**
Greensboro **919**
Greenville **919**
High Point **919**
Kannapolis **704**
Kinston **919**
Lexington **704**
Raleigh **919**
Rocky Mount **919**
Salisbury **704**
Wilmington **919**
Wilson **919**
Winston-Salem **919**

North Dakota

All points **701**

Ohio

Akron **216**
Alliance **216**
Ashtabula **216**
Athens **614**
Austintown **216**
Barberton **216**
Boardman **216**
Brook Park **216**
Canton **216**
Chillicothe **614**
Cincinnati **513**
Cleveland **216**
Columbus **614**
Cuyahoga Falls **216**
Dayton **513**
East Cleveland **216**
East Liverpool **216**
Elyria **216**
Euclid **216**
Fair Born **513**
Findlay **419**
Garfield Heights **216**
Hamilton **513**
Kent **216**
Ketering **513**
Lakewood **216**
Lancaster **614**
Lima **419**
Lorain **216**
Mansfield **419**
Maple Heights **216**

Marion **614**
Massillon **216**
Mentor **216**
Middletown **513**
Newark **614**
North Olmsted **216**
Norwood **513**
Parma **216**
Parma Heights **216**
Portsmouth **614**
Rocky River **216**
Sandusky **419**
Shaker Heights **216**
South Euclid **216**
Springfield **513**
Steubenville **614**
Toledo **419**
Upper Arlington **614**
Warren **216**
Whitehall **614**
Xenia **513**
Youngstown **216**
Zanesville **614**

Oklahoma

Altus **405**
Bartlesville **918**
Bethany **405**
Dill City **405**
Enid **405**
Lawton **405**
Midwest City **405**
Muskogee **918**
Oklahoma City **405**
Ponca City **405**
Shawnee **405**
Stillwater **405**
Tulsa **918**

Oregon

All points **503**

Pennsylvania

Allentown (Lehigh Co.) **215**
Altoona **814**
Beaver Falls **412**
Bellefonte **814**
Bethel Park **412**
Bethlehem **215**

Bloomsburg **717**
Bradford **814**
Chambersburg **717**
Chester **215**
Columbia **717**
DuBois **814**
Easton **215**
Erie **814**
Greensburg **412**
Harrisburg **717**
Hazelton **717**
Indiana **412**
Johnstown **814**
Lancaster **717**
Lebanon **717**
Levittown **215**
Lock Haven **717**
McKeesport **412**
Monroeville **412**
New Castle **412**
Norristown **215**
Philadelphia **215**
Pittsburgh **412**
Pottstown **215**
Reading **215**
Scranton **717**
Sharon **412**
State College **814**
Stroudsburg **717**
Sunbury **717**
Uniontown (Indiana Co.) **814**
Warren **814**
Washington **412**
Wayne **215**
West Chester **215**
West Mifflin **412**
Wilkes-Barre **717**
Wilkinsburg **412**
Williamsport **717**
York **717**

Puerto Rico

All points **809**

Rhode Island

All points **401**

South Carolina

All points **803**

South Dakota

All points **605**

Tennessee

Chattanooga **615**
Clarksville **615**
Jackson **901**
Johnson City **615**
Kingsport **615**
Knoxville **615**
Memphis **901**
Murfreesboro **615**
Nashville **615**
Oak Ridge **615**

Texas

Abilene **915**
Amarillo **806**
Arlington **817**
Austin **512**
Baytown **713**
Beaumont **409**
Big Spring **915**
Brownsville **512**
Bryan **409**
Corpus Christi **512**
Dallas **214**
Denison **214**
Denton **817**
El Paso **915**
Farmers Branch **214**
Fort Hood **817**
Fort Worth **817**
Galveston **409**
Garland **214**
Grand Prairie **214**
Harlingen **512**
Houston **713**
Hurst **817**
Irving **214**
Killeen **817**
Kingsville **512**
Laredo **512**
Longview **214**
Lubbock **806**
Lufkin **409**
Marshall **214**
McAllen **512**
Mesquite **214**
Midland **915**

Nacogdoches **409**
Odessa **915**
Orange **409**
Paris **214**
Pasadena **713**
Port Arthur **409**
Richardson **214**
San Angelo **915**
San Antonio **512**
Sherman **214**
Temple **817**
Texarkana **214**
Texas City—La Marque **409**
Tyler **214**
Victoria **512**
Waco **817**
Wharton **409**
Wichita Falls **817**

Utah

All points **801**

Vermont

All points **802**

Virgin Islands

All points **803**

Virginia

Alexandria **703**
Annandale **703**
Arlington **703**
Charlottesville **804**
Chesapeake (Norfolk Co.)
  804
Covington **703**
Danville **804**
Hampton **804**
Hopewell **804**
Jefferson **804**
Lynchburg **804**
Newport News **804**
Norfolk **804**
Petersburg **804**
Portsmouth **804**
Richmond **804**
Roanoke **703**
Staunton **703**

Virginia Beach **804**
Woodbridge **703**

Washington

Bellevue **206**
Bellingham **206**
Bremerton **206**
Edmonds **206**
Everett **206**
Fort Lewis **206**
Longview **206**
Olympia **206**
Renton **206**
Richland **509**
Seattle **206**
Spokane **509**
Tacoma **206**
Vancouver **206**
Walla Walla **509**
Yakima **509**

West Virginia

All points **304**

Wisconsin

Appleton **414**
Beloit **608**
Brookfield **414**
Eau Claire **715**
Fond Du Lac **414**
Green Bay **414**
Greenfield **414**
Janesville **608**
Kenosha **414**
La Crosse **608**
Madison **608**
Manitowoc **414**
Menomonee Falls **414**
Milwaukee **414**
Neenah **414**
New Berlin **414**
Oshkosh **414**
Racine **414**
Sheboygan **414**
South Milwaukee **414**
Stevens Point **715**
Superior **715**
Waukesha **414**
Wausau **715**

Wauwatosa **414**
West Allis **414**

Wyoming

All points **307**

CANADA

Alberta

All points **403**

British Columbia

All points **604**

Manitoba

All points **204**

New Brunswick

All points **506**

Newfoundland

All points **709**

Nova Scotia

All points **902**

Ontario

Fort William **807**
London **519**
North Bay **705**
Ottawa **613**
Thunder Bay **807**
Toronto **416**

Prince Edward Island

All points **902**

Quebec

Montreal **514**
Quebec **418**
Sherbrooke **819**

Saskatchewan

All points **306**

INTERNATIONAL COUNTRY AND CITY CODES

The following list provides the telephone area codes for most countries of the world and their major cities as well as the difference in time (TD) between those cities or countries and U.S. Eastern Standard Time (EST). For example, if you wish to place a call to Alexandria, Egypt at 2:00 P.M. EST, you should know that it is 9:00 P.M. Egyptian time and that the country code is 20, followed by the city code of 3.

	TD		TD		TD
Algeria* 213	+6	**Costa Rica* 506**	−1	**German Dem.**	+6
American	−6	**Cyprus 357**	+7	**Rep. 37**	
Samoa* 684				Berlin **2**	
		Czechoslovakia 42	+6	**Germany**	+6
Andorra 33	+6	Prague **2**		**Fed. Rep. of 49**	
All points **628**				Berlin **30**	
		Denmark 45	+6	Frankfurt **69**	
Argentina 54	+2	Aalborg **8**		Munich **89**	
Buenos Aires **1**		Copenhagen **1** or **2**			
Australia 61	+15	**Ecuador 593**	0	**Greece 30**	+7
Melbourne **3**		Cuenca **7**		Athens **1**	
Sydney **2**		Quito **2**		Rhodes **241**	
Austria 43	+6	**Egypt 20**	+7	**Guam* 671**	+15
Vienna **1**		Alexandria **3**			
Bahrain* 973	+8	Port Said **66**		**Guantanamo Bay***	0
		El Salvador* 503	−1	**(U.S. Naval Base**	
Belgium 32	+6			**"Cuba") 53**	
Brussels **2**		**Ethiopia 251**	+8	All points **99**	
Ghent **91**		Addis Ababa **1**		**Guatemala 502**	−1
Belize 501	−1	**Fiji* 679**	+17	Guatemala City **2**	
Belize City*				Antigua **9**	
		Finland 358	+7	**Guyana 592**	+2
Bolivia 591	+1	Helsinki **0**		Georgetown **2**	
Santa Cruz **33**					
		France 33	+6	**Haiti 509**	0
Brazil 55	+2	Marseille **91**		Port au Prince **1**	
Brasilia **61**		Nice **93**			
Rio de Janeiro **21**		Paris **13** or **14** or **16**		**Honduras* 504**	−1
Cameroon* 237	+6	**French**	+1	**Hong Kong 852**	+13
		Antilles* 596		Hong Kong **5**	
Chile 56	+1			Kowloon **3**	
Santiago **2**		**French Antilles**	+1		
		Guadeloupe* 590		**Hungary 36**	+6
Colombia 57	0			Budapest **1**	
Bogotá **1**		**French**	−5		
		Polynesia* 689		**Iceland 354**	+5
				Akureyri **6**	
* City Codes not required.		**Gabon* 241**	+6	Hafnarfjorour **1**	

	TD		TD		TD
India 91	+10.5	**Luxembourg* 352**	+6	**Panama* 507**	0
Bombay 22		**Malawi 265**	+7	**Papua**	+15
New Delhi 11		Domasi 531		**New Guinea***	
Indonesia 62	+12	**Malaysia 60**	+13	675	
Jakarta 21		Kuala Lumpur 3		**Paraguay 595**	+1
Iran 98	+8.5	**Mexico 52**	−1	Asunción 21	
Teheran 21		Mexico City 5		**Peru 51**	0
Iraq 964	+8	Tijuana 66		Arequipa 54	
Baghdad 1		**Monaco 33**	+6	Lima 14	
Ireland 353	+5	All points 93		**Philippines 63**	+13
Dublin 1		**Morocco 212**	+5	Manila 2	
Galway 91		Agadir 8		**Poland 48**	+6
Israel 972	+7	Casablanca*		Warsaw 22	
Haifa 4		**Namibia 264**	+7	**Portugal 351**	+5
Jerusalem 2		Olympia 61		Lisbon 1	
Tel Aviv 3		**Netherlands 31**	+6	**Qatar* 974**	+9
Italy 39	+6	Amsterdam 20		**Romania 40**	+7
Florence 55		The Hague 70		Bucharest 0	
Rome 6		**Netherlands**	+1	**Saipan* 670**	+15
Venice 41		**Antilles 599**		**San Marino 39**	+6
Ivory Coast* 225	+5	**Netherlands**	+1	All points 541	
Japan 81	+14	**Antilles**		**Saudi Arabia 966**	+8
Tokyo 3		**Aruba 297**		Riyadh 1	
Yokohama 45		Aruba 8		**Senegal* 221**	+5
Jordan 962	+7	**New Caledonia***	+16	**Singapore* 65**	+13
Amman 6		687		**South Africa 27**	+7
Kenya 254	+8	**New Zealand 64**	+17	Cape Town 21	
Korea,	+14	Auckland 9		Pretoria 12	
Rep. of 82		Wellington 4		**Spain 34**	+6
Pusan 51		**Nicaragua 505**	−1	Barcelona 3	
Seoul 2		Managua 2		Las Palmas	
Kuwait* 965	+8	**Nigeria 234**	+6	(Canary Is.) 28	
Liberia* 231	+5	Lagos 1		Madrid 1	
Libya 218	+7	**Norway 47**	+6	Seville 54	
Tripoli 21		Bergen 5		**Sri Lanka 94**	+10.5
Liechtenstein 41	+6	Oslo 2		Kandy 8	
All points 75		**Oman* 968**	+9	**Suriname* 597**	+15
		Pakistan 92	+10	**Sweden 46**	+6
* City Codes not required.		Islamabad 51		Göteborg 31	
				Stockholm 8	

		TD
Switzerland 41		+6
Geneva **22**		
Lucerne **41**		
Zurich **1**		
Taiwan 886		+13
Tainan **6**		
Taipei **2**		
Thailand 66		+12
Bangkok **2**		
Tunisia 216		+6
Tunis **1**		

---
* City Codes not required.

		TD
Turkey 90		+8
Istanbul **1**		
Izmir **51**		
United Arab		+9
Emirates 971		
Abu Dhabi **2**		
Al Ain **3**		
Dubai **4**		
Ras Al Khainah **77**		
Sharjah **6**		
Umm Al Quwain **6**		
United Kingdom 44		+5
Belfast **232**		
Cardiss **222**		
Glasgow **41**		

		TD
London **1**		
Uruguay 598		+2
Mercedes **532**		
Montevideo **2**		
Vatican City 39		+6
All points **6**		
Venezuela 58		+1
Caracas **2**		
Maracaibo **61**		
Yemen Arab		+8
Republic 967		
Amran **2**		
Yugoslavia 38		+6
Belgrade **11**		

Distances: Air and Road

24

DISTANCES—AIR AND ROAD

AIR MILEAGE BETWEEN PRINCIPAL CITIES OF THE WORLD

	Berlin	Bombay	Buenos Aires	Calcutta	Capetown	Gibraltar	Honolulu	Istanbul	London	Los Angeles	Manila	Melbourne	Mexico City	Moscow	New York	Oslo	Panama	Paris	Peking	Port Said	Quebec	Reykjavik	Rio de Janeiro	Rome	Seattle	Shanghai	Singapore	Tokyo	Valparaiso	Wellington
Berlin, Ger.	—	3910	7376	4376	5977	1453	7305	1078	574	5782	6128	9919	6037	996	3961	515	5849	542	4567	1747	3583	1479	6144	734	5041	5215	6166	5538	7795	11265
Bombay, Ind.	3910	—	9273	1041	5134	4814	8020	2991	4462	8701	3148	6097	9722	3131	7794	4130	9742	4359	2964	2659	7371	5191	8257	3843	7741	3133	2429	4188	10037	7677
Buenos Aires, Arg.	7376	9273	—	10242	4270	5963	7558	7568	6918	6118	11042	7234	4633	8375	5297	7613	3381	7099	11974	6877	5680	7362	1218	6929	7099	12197	9864	11400	761	6260
Calcutta, Ind.	4376	1041	10242	—	6026	5521	7037	3646	4954	8148	2189	5547	9547	3181	7918	4954	10355	4883	2042	3500	7543	5591	9377	4482	8190	2558	1791	3194	10993	7042
Capetown, S.Afr.	5977	5134	4270	6026	—	5076	11532	5219	6005	9969	7483	5936	8519	6300	7764	6441	7783	5786	8044	5409	7481	7857	3773	5249	10199	8044	6010	9156	5187	7019
Gibraltar	1453	4814	5963	5521	5076	—	8075	1874	1094	5659	6667	9659	5799	2417	3362	1650	4954	959	6004	1909	3300	2047	4575	1034	5659	6395	7224	6916	6623	12060
Honolulu, U.S.A.	7305	8020	7558	7037	11532	8075	—	8104	7226	2557	5293	5513	3781	7037	4964	7152	5278	7442	5070	8824	4857	5383	8190	8022	2677	4941	6726	3850	6634	4708
Istanbul, Turk.	1078	2991	7568	3646	5219	1874	8104	—	1551	6843	5772	8822	7102	1091	5009	1522	6750	1400	4383	717	4590	4000	6389	854	6063	4961	5373	5560	8088	10663
London, Eng.	574	4462	6918	4954	6005	1094	7226	1551	—	5439	6672	10501	5558	1557	3458	722	5278	213	5063	2234	3059	1171	5750	887	4799	5710	6744	5940	7640	11682
Los Angeles, U.S.A.	5782	8701	6118	8148	9969	5659	2557	6843	5439	—	7269	7931	1549	6068	2451	5328	2855	5601	6250	7580	2464	4310	6330	6326	959	6438	8767	5433	5577	6714
Manila, P.I.	6128	3148	11042	2189	7483	6667	5293	5772	6672	7269	—	3941	8829	5131	8498	6688	9577	6677	1767	5461	8150	6457	11254	6457	6635	1151	1480	1866	11650	5162
Melbourne, Austl.	9919	6097	7234	5547	5936	9659	5513	8822	10501	7931	3941	—	8422	8963	9918	9950	8493	10430	5642	8450	10250	10497	8226	9929	8186	5005	3761	5089	6998	1595
Mexico City, Mex.	6037	9722	4633	9547	8519	5799	3781	7102	5558	1549	8829	8422	—	6676	2086	5669	1485	5706	7753	8085	2454	4622	4770	6353	2339	8039	10307	7035	4053	6899
Moscow, U.S.S.R.	996	3131	8375	3181	6300	2417	7037	1091	1557	6068	5131	8963	6676	—	4662	1018	6688	1542	3597	1714	4242	4439	7170	1474	5199	4235	5238	4650	8792	10279
New York, U.S.A.	3961	7794	5297	7918	7764	3362	4964	5009	3458	2451	8498	9918	2086	4662	—	3671	2216	3636	6844	5602	450	2659	4801	4273	2408	7371	9630	6740	5130	8946
Oslo, Nor.	515	4130	7613	4954	6441	1650	7152	1522	722	5328	6688	9950	5669	1018	3671	—	5667	822	4360	2448	3227	1083	6485	1254	4273	5181	6477	5200	7914	10974
Panama, Pan.	5849	9742	3381	10355	7783	4954	5278	6750	5278	2855	9577	8493	1485	6688	2216	5667	—	5350	9040	7231	2576	5125	3289	5698	3614	9630	11687	9097	2943	7433
Paris, Fr.	542	4359	7099	4883	5786	959	7442	1400	213	5601	6677	10430	5706	1542	3636	822	5350	—	5106	1989	3227	1380	5684	682	5020	5754	6671	6034	7750	11791
Peking, Ch.	4567	2964	11974	2042	8044	6004	5070	4383	5063	6250	1767	5642	7753	3597	6844	4360	9040	5106	—	4652	6423	5101	10768	5047	5396	662	2774	1307	11791	6698
Port Said, Eg.	1747	2659	6877	3500	5409	1909	8824	717	2234	7580	5461	8450	8085	1714	5602	2448	7231	1989	4652	—	5250	4584	6423	1317	6759	5088	5088	5752	8088	10249
Quebec, Can.	3583	7371	5680	7543	7481	3300	4857	4590	3059	2464	8150	10250	2454	4242	450	3227	2576	3227	6423	5250	—	2189	5125	4903	2353	6981	9097	6130	5842	9228
Reykjavik, Ice.	1479	5191	7362	5591	7857	2047	5383	4000	1171	4310	6457	10497	4622	4439	2659	1083	5125	1380	5101	4584	2189	—	6118	2056	3614	5132	7160	5550	7225	10724
Rio de Janeiro, Braz.	6144	8257	1218	9377	3773	4575	8190	6389	5750	6330	11254	8226	4770	7170	4801	6485	3289	5684	10768	6423	5125	6118	—	5684	6759	11340	9774	11535	1855	7349
Rome, It.	734	3843	6929	4482	5249	1034	8022	854	887	6326	6457	9929	6353	1474	4273	1254	5698	682	5047	1317	4903	2056	5684	—	5677	5677	6232	6124	6230	11524
Seattle, U.S.A.	5041	7741	7099	8190	10199	5659	2677	6063	4799	959	6635	8186	2339	5199	2408	4273	3614	5020	5396	6759	2353	3614	6759	5677	—	5659	8057	4777	6230	7242
Shanghai, Ch.	5215	3133	12197	2558	8044	6395	4941	4961	5710	6438	1151	5005	8039	4235	7371	5181	9630	5754	662	5088	6981	5132	11340	5677	5659	—	2377	1094	10226	6054
Singapore	6166	2429	9864	1791	6010	7224	6726	5373	6744	8767	1480	3761	10307	5238	9630	6477	11687	6671	2774	5088	9097	7160	9774	6232	8057	2377	—	3304	10635	5292
Tokyo, Jap.	5538	4188	11400	3194	9156	6916	3850	5560	5940	5433	1866	5089	7035	4650	6740	5200	9097	6034	1307	5752	6130	5550	11535	6124	4777	1094	3304	—	10635	5760
Valparaiso, Chile	7795	10037	761	10993	5187	6623	6634	8088	7640	5577	11650	6998	4053	8792	5130	7914	2943	7750	11791	8088	5842	7225	1855	6230	6230	10226	10635	10635	—	5785
Wellington, N.Z.	11265	7677	6260	7042	7019	12060	4708	10663	11682	6714	5162	1595	6899	10279	8946	10974	7433	11791	6698	10249	9228	10724	7349	11524	7242	6054	5292	5760	5785	—

623

AIR MILEAGE BETWEEN PRINCIPAL CITIES OF THE UNITED STATES

	Atlanta	Boston	Buffalo	Charleston	Cheyenne	Chicago	Cleveland	Dallas	Denver	Detroit	Houston	Indianapolis	Jacksonville	Kansas City	Los Angeles	Louisville	Memphis	Miami	Minneapolis	New Orleans	New York	Philadelphia	Phoenix	Pittsburgh	Portland	St. Louis	Salt Lake City	San Francisco	Seattle	Washington
Atlanta, Ga.		937	697	267	1229	587	554	721	1212	596	701	426	285	676	1936	319	337	604	907	424	748	666	1592	521	2172	467	1583	2139	2182	543
Boston, Mass.	937		400	820	1736	851	551	1551	1769	613	1605	807	1017	1251	2596	941	1137	1255	1123	1359	188	271	2300	483	2537	1038	2099	2699	2493	393
Buffalo, N.Y.	697	400		699	1335	454	173	1198	1370	216	1286	435	861	803	2198	532	861	1198	731	1086	292	279	1906	178	2517	723	1699	2300	2117	292
Charleston, S.C.	267	820	699		1486	757	609	981	1474	721	936	681	261	865	2137	533	739	479	1057	773	589	561	1818	455	2423	711	1845	2405	2428	453
Cheyenne, Wyo.	1229	1736	1335	1486		891	1199	726	96	1125	920	1009	1670	537	830	1054	1009	1807	693	1208	1616	1568	736	1420	1116	830	371	967	973	1477
Chicago, Ill.	587	851	454	757	891		308	803	920	238	940	165	864	414	1745	269	482	1188	355	830	713	666	1453	410	1749	262	1260	1858	1737	597
Cleveland, Ohio	554	551	173	609	1199	308		1080	1199	90	1119	263	770	700	2049	311	630	1085	630	924	405	360	1749	115	2020	492	1568	2166	2026	306
Dallas, Tex.	721	1551	1198	981	726	803	1080		663	999	225	763	879	451	1240	726	420	1111	862	443	1374	1299	887	1070	1637	547	999	1483	1681	1185
Denver, Colo.	1212	1769	1370	1474	96	920	1199	663		1227	879	1000	1636	600	831	1038	879	1726	700	1082	1631	1579	602	1302	1009	796	371	949	1021	1494
Detroit, Mich.	596	613	216	721	1125	238	90	999	1227		1105	238	999	630	1983	311	623	1152	528	939	482	443	1671	205	1938	455	1492	2091	1938	396
Houston, Tex.	701	1605	1286	936	920	940	1119	225	879	1105		865	821	644	1374	803	484	968	1056	318	1420	1341	1009	1137	1825	679	1356	1645	1891	1220
Indianapolis, Ind.	426	807	435	681	1009	165	263	763	1000	238	865		763	453	1809	107	384	1024	511	712	646	585	1504	330	1794	231	1356	1949	1872	494
Jacksonville, Fla.	285	1017	861	261	1670	864	770	879	1636	999	821	763		1101	2147	645	644	326	1152	484	831	758	1809	703	2439	781	1837	2374	2455	647
Kansas City, Mo.	676	1251	803	865	537	414	700	451	600	630	644	453	1101		1356	480	369	1420	413	680	1097	1038	1049	781	1494	238	925	1506	1506	945
Los Angeles, Cal.	1936	2596	2198	2137	830	1745	2049	1240	831	1983	1374	1809	2147	1356		1829	1603	2339	1524	1673	2451	2394	357	2136	825	1589	579	347	959	2300
Louisville, Ky.	319	941	532	533	1054	269	311	726	1038	311	803	107	645	480	1829		320	919	605	623	652	582	1508	344	1808	242	1402	1986	1943	476
Memphis, Tenn.	337	1137	861	739	1009	482	630	420	879	623	484	384	644	369	1603	320		872	699	357	957	881	1263	660	1849	240	1250	1802	1867	765
Miami, Fla.	604	1255	1198	479	1807	1188	1085	1111	1726	1152	968	1024	326	1420	2339	919	872		1501	669	1092	1019	1982	1010	2708	1061	2089	2594	2734	923
Minneapolis, Minn.	907	1123	731	1057	693	355	630	862	700	528	1056	511	1152	413	1524	605	699	1501		1056	1018	985	1280	743	1426	466	987	1584	1395	934
New Orleans, La.	424	1359	1086	773	1208	830	924	443	1082	939	318	712	484	680	1673	623	357	669	1056		1182	1089	1316	1070	2063	598	1434	1926	2101	966
New York, N.Y.	748	188	292	589	1616	713	405	1374	1631	482	1420	646	831	1097	2451	652	957	1092	1018	1182		83	2145	317	2445	875	1972	2571	2408	205
Philadelphia, Pa.	666	271	279	561	1568	666	360	1299	1579	443	1341	585	758	1038	2394	582	881	1019	985	1089	83		2083	259	2440	811	1925	2523	2380	123
Phoenix, Ariz.	1592	2300	1906	1818	736	1453	1749	887	602	1671	1009	1504	1809	1049	357	1508	1263	1982	1280	1316	2145	2083		1828	1009	1262	504	653	1114	1983
Pittsburgh, Pa.	521	483	178	455	1420	410	115	1070	1302	205	1137	330	703	781	2136	344	660	1010	743	1070	317	259	1828		2145	575	1668	2264	2138	192
Portland, Ore.	2172	2537	2517	2423	1116	1749	2020	1637	1009	1938	1825	1794	2439	1494	825	1808	1849	2708	1426	2063	2445	2440	1009	2145		1828	636	534	145	2354
St. Louis, Mo.	467	1038	723	711	830	262	492	547	796	455	679	231	781	238	1589	242	240	1061	466	598	875	811	1262	575	1828		1162	1744	1724	712
Salt Lake City, Utah	1583	2099	1699	1845	371	1260	1568	999	371	1492	1356	1356	1837	925	579	1402	1250	2089	987	1434	1972	1925	504	1668	636	1162		600	701	1848
San Francisco, Cal.	2139	2699	2300	2405	967	1858	2166	1483	949	2091	1645	1949	2374	1506	347	1986	1802	2594	1584	1926	2571	2523	653	2264	534	1744	600		678	2442
Seattle, Wash.	2182	2493	2117	2428	973	1737	2026	1681	1021	1938	1891	1872	2455	1506	959	1943	1867	2734	1395	2101	2408	2380	1114	2138	145	1724	701	678		2329
Washington, D.C.	543	393	292	453	1477	597	306	1185	1494	396	1220	494	647	945	2300	476	765	923	934	966	205	123	1983	192	2354	712	1848	2442	2329	

ROAD MILEAGE BETWEEN PRINCIPAL CITIES OF NORTH AMERICA

	Albuquerque	Atlanta	Birmingham	Boston	Chicago	Cleveland	Dallas	Denver	Detroit	Houston	Indianapolis	Kansas City	Los Angeles	Mexico City	Miami	Minneapolis	Montreal	Nashville	New Orleans	New York	Omaha	Philadelphia	Phoenix	Portland	St. Louis	Salt Lake City	San Francisco	Seattle	Toronto	Washington
Albuquerque, N. Mex.		1381	1251	2172	1281	1560	638	417	1525	834	1266	782	807	1414	1938	1190	2087	1218	1134	1979	858	1899	432	1371	1038	604	1115	1440	1847	1824
Atlanta, Ga.	1381		150	1037	674	672	795	1398	699	789	493	798	2182	1768	655	1068	1181	242	479	841	986	741	1793	2601	541	1878	2496	2618	925	608
Birmingham, Ala.	1251	150		1165	642	709	645	1286	724	639	475	697	2032	1618	751	969	1270	196	342	969	898	869	1643	2505	465	1781	2366	2535	950	736
Boston, Mass.	2172	1037	1165		963	628	1748	1949	695	1804	906	1391	2979	2783	1504	1329	318	1088	1507	206	1412	296	2604	3046	1141	2343	3095	2976	539	429
Chicago, Ill.	1281	674	642	963		335	917	996	266	1067	181	499	2054	2367	1329	405	828	446	912	802	459	738	1713	2083	289	1390	2142	2013	492	671
Cleveland, Ohio	1560	672	709	628	335		1159	1321	170	1273	294	779	2367	2251	1386	740	561	528	1045	473	784	459	1992	2418	529	1715	2467	2418	287	346
Dallas, Tex.	638	795	645	1748	917	1159		781	1143	243	865	489	1387	1059	1387	936	1705	660	496	1552	644	1452	1019	2009	630	1242	1753	2078	1369	1319
Denver, Colo.	417	1398	1286	1949	996	1321	781		1253	1019	1058	600	1059	1746	2037	841	1815	1059	1273	1771	537	1691	792	1238	857	513	1235	1307	1479	1616
Detroit, Mich.	1525	699	724	695	266	170	1143	1253		1265	278	716	2311	2243	1352	698	537	537	1058	637	720	573	1957	2399	513	1700	2450	2279	226	506
Houston, Tex.	834	789	639	1804	1067	1273	243	1019	1265		1002	710	1538	1048	1190	1210	1827	769	356	1608	894	1585	1176	2205	779	1438	1912	2274	1491	1375
Indianapolis, Ind.	1266	493	475	906	181	294	865	1058	278	1002		485	2073	1917	1152	592	967	290	838	713	586	633	1746	2259	243	1538	2190	2240	504	558
Kansas City, Mo.	782	798	697	1391	499	779	489	600	716	710	485		1589	1438	1504	447	1305	556	806	1198	201	1214	1086	1845	257	1091	1835	1839	969	1043
Los Angeles, Cal.	807	2182	2032	2979	2054	2367	1387	1059	2311	1538	2073	1589		1917	2687	2025	2873	2025	1883	2786	1595	2706	389	959	1845	715	379	1131	2537	2354
Mexico City, Mex.	1414	1768	1618	2783	2367	2251	1059	1746	2243	1048	1917	1438	1917		2169	2687	3053	2074	1595	2786	1782	2532	1549	3256	1654	1782	2291	3053	2852	2081
Miami, Fla.	1938	655	751	1504	1329	1386	1387	2037	1352	1190	1152	1504	2687	2169		1782	1654	915	883	1308	1683	1207	2342	3256	1308	2587	3053	3273	1638	1076
Minneapolis, Minn.	1190	1068	969	1329	405	740	936	841	698	1210	592	447	2025	2687	1782		1143	826	1214	1207	357	1186	1616	1678	552	1208	2074	1654	897	1075
Montreal, Que.	2087	1181	1270	318	828	561	1705	1815	537	1827	967	1305	2873	3053	1654	1143		1074	1490	378	1207	449	2706	2785	1074	2487	2934	2815	336	579
Nashville, Tenn.	1218	242	196	1088	446	528	660	1059	537	769	290	556	2025	2074	915	826	1074		532	892	673	744	1591	2505	309	1591	2249	2376	754	659
New Orleans, La.	1134	479	342	1507	912	1045	496	1273	1058	356	838	806	1883	1595	883	1214	1490	532		1311	1007	1251	1494	2411	673	1738	2249	2574	1271	1078
New York, N.Y.	1979	841	969	206	802	473	1552	1771	637	1608	713	1198	2786	2786	1308	1207	378	892	1311		1251	100	2411	2885	948	2182	2934	2815	453	233
Omaha, Neb.	858	986	898	1412	459	784	644	537	720	894	586	201	1595	1782	1683	357	1207	673	1007	1251		1290	1251	1654	449	931	1654	1638	942	1116
Philadelphia, Pa.	1899	741	869	296	738	459	1452	1691	573	1585	633	1214	2706	2532	1207	1186	449	744	1251	100	1290		2411	2885	892	2182	2934	2815	453	133
Phoenix, Ariz.	432	1793	1643	2604	1713	1992	1019	792	1957	1176	1746	1086	389	1549	2342	1616	2706	1591	1494	2411	1251	2411		1337	1470	648	752	1438	2183	2256
Portland, Ore.	1371	2601	2505	3046	2083	2418	2009	1238	2399	2205	2259	1845	959	3256	3256	1678	2785	2505	2411	2885	1654	2885	1337		2060	767	636	172	2566	2754
St. Louis, Mo.	1038	541	465	1141	289	529	630	857	513	779	243	257	1845	1654	1308	552	1074	309	673	948	449	892	1470	2060		1337	2089	2081	739	793
Salt Lake City, Utah	604	1878	1781	2343	1390	1715	1242	513	1700	1438	1538	1091	715	1782	2587	1208	2487	1591	1738	2182	931	2182	648	767	1337		752	836	1873	2047
San Francisco, Cal.	1115	2496	2366	3095	2142	2467	1753	1235	2450	1912	2190	1835	379	2291	3053	2074	2934	2249	2249	2934	1654	2934	752	636	2089	752		808	2625	2799
Seattle, Wash.	1440	2618	2535	2976	2013	2418	2078	1307	2279	2274	2240	1839	1131	3053	3273	1654	2815	2376	2574	2815	1638	2815	1438	172	2081	836	808		2496	2684
Toronto, Ont.	1847	925	950	539	492	287	1369	1479	226	1491	504	969	2537	2852	1638	897	336	754	1271	453	942	453	2183	2566	739	1873	2625	2496		456
Washington, D.C.	1824	608	736	429	671	346	1319	1616	506	1375	558	1043	2354	2081	1076	1075	579	659	1078	233	1116	133	2256	2754	793	2047	2799	2684	456	

Time

TIME ZONES IN THE UNITED STATES

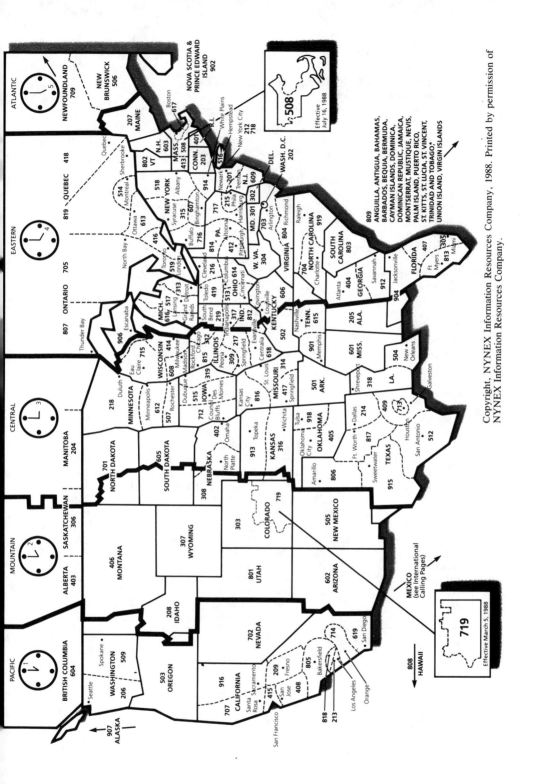

Copyright, NYNEX Information Resources Company, 1988. Printed by permission of NYNEX Information Resources Company.

Standard Times At 12 Noon, Eastern Standard Time
(Selected Areas of the World)

Area	Time	Area	Time
Argentina	2 P.M.	Korea	2 A.M.*
Austria	6 P.M.	Mexico (Mexico City)	11 A.M.
Australia (Sydney)	3 A.M.*	Morocco	5 P.M.
Bangladesh	11 P.M.	Netherlands	6 P.M.
Belgium	6 P.M.	Netherlands Antilles (Aruba,	
Brazil	2 P.M.	Bonaire, Curaçao)	1 P.M.
Burma	11:30 P.M.	New Zealand	
Canada (Toronto)	12 noon	(Auckland)	5 A.M.*
Canada (Vancouver)	9 A.M.	Newfoundland	1:30 P.M.
Chile	1 P.M.	Nigeria	6 P.M.
China (Shanghai)	1 A.M.*	Norway	6 P.M.
Colombia	12 noon	Pakistan	10 P.M.
Costa Rica	11 A.M.	Peru	12 noon
Cuba	12 noon	Philippines	1 A.M.*
Czechoslovakia	6 P.M.	Poland	6 P.M.
Denmark	6 P.M.	Portugal	6 P.M.
Dominican Republic	1 P.M.	Romania	7 P.M.
Egypt	7 P.M.	Senegal	5 P.M.
Ethiopia	8 P.M.	Singapore	12:30 A.M.*
Finland	7 P.M.	South Africa	7 P.M.
France	6 P.M.	Spain	6 P.M.
Germany	6 P.M.	Sweden	6 P.M.
Gibraltar	6 P.M.	Switzerland	6 P.M.
Greece	7 P.M.	Thailand	12 midnight
Haiti	12 noon	Tunisia	6 P.M.
Hong Kong	1 A.M.*	Turkey	7 P.M.
Hungary	6 P.M.	United Kingdom	5 P.M.
India	10:30 P.M.	Uruguay	2 P.M.
Indonesia (Java)	12 midnight	U.S.A. (Chicago)	11 A.M.
Iran	8:30 P.M.	U.S.A. (Salt Lake City)	10 A.M.
Iraq	8 P.M.	U.S.A. (San Francisco)	9 A.M.
Ireland	5 P.M.	U.S.S.R. (Moscow,	
Israel	7 P.M.	Leningrad)	8 P.M.
Italy	6 P.M.	U.S.S.R. (Vladivostok)	3 A.M.*
Ivory Coast	5 P.M.	Venezuela	1 P.M.
Jamaica	12 noon	Vietnam	12 midnight
Japan	2 A.M.*	Zaire (Kinshasa)	6 P.M.

* Morning of the following day

CALENDAR TIME

The early Roman calendar was based on the lunar month of $29\frac{1}{2}$ days and had 354 days. But the solar year (the time it takes the earth to circle the sun) is about $365\frac{1}{4}$ days. The Romans added an extra month from time to time to bring the calendar into agreement with the seasons.

A more consistent calendar was instituted by Julius Caesar in 46 B.C. Its year was 365 days with an extra day added in February every fourth year (leap year). The Julian calendar set the length of a month at 30 or 31 days, except for February.

By 1582, the calendar was again out of phase with the seasons. In October of that year, Pope Gregory XIII dropped ten days from the calendar to correct the error that had accumulated. To keep the error from recurring, the Gregorian calendar has leap year every fourth year except those centesimal years that can be divided by 400. Many countries adopted the new calendar at once, but Great Britain and its American colonies waited until 1752. Sometimes two dates are specified for an early event. "Old Style" means the Julian calendar and "New Style" means the Gregorian calendar.

A year is divided into 12 months, 52 weeks, or 365 days (except a leap year, which has 366 days):

January	31 days	July	31 days	
February	28 days	August	31 days	
	(leap year 29)			
March	31 days	September	30 days	1 week has 7 days
April	30 days	October	31 days	1 day has 24 hours
May	31 days	November	30 days	1 hour has 60 minutes
June	30 days	December	31 days	1 minute has 60 seconds

To compute actual days between two dates, find the number of days between months in the chart below and to that add the difference between the days (after February in a leap year, add one day).

To the Same Date in

From Any Date in	Jan.	Feb.	Mar.	Apr.	May	June	July	Aug.	Sept.	Oct.	Nov.	Dec.
January	365	31	59	90	120	151	181	212	243	273	304	334
February	334	365	28	59	89	120	150	181	212	242	273	303
March	306	337	365	31	61	92	122	153	184	214	245	275
April	275	306	334	365	30	61	91	122	153	183	214	244
May	245	276	304	335	365	31	61	92	123	153	184	214
June	214	245	273	304	334	365	30	61	92	122	153	183
July	184	215	243	274	304	335	365	31	62	92	123	153
August	153	184	212	243	273	304	334	365	31	61	92	122
September	122	153	181	212	242	273	303	334	365	30	61	91
October	92	123	151	182	212	243	273	304	335	365	31	61
November	61	92	120	151	181	212	242	273	304	334	365	30
December	31	62	90	121	151	182	212	243	274	304	335	365

PERPETUAL CALENDAR (A.D. 1–2400)

To find the calendar for any year, first find the Dominical letter for the year in the upper section of the table. Two letters are given for leap year: the first for January and February, the second for other months. In the lower section of table, find the column in which the Dominical letter for the year is in the same line as the month for which the calendar is desired; this column gives the days of the week that are to be used with the month. For example, in the table of Dominical letters we find that the letter for 1960, a leap year, is CB; in the line with July, the letter B occurs in the third column; hence July 4, 1960, is Monday.

DOMINICAL LETTERS

Century				Julian Calendar 0 / 700 / 1400	100 / 800 / 1500+	200 / 900	300 / 1000	400 / 1100	500 / 1200	600 / 1300	Gregorian Calendar 1500‡	1600 / 2000	1700 / 2100	1800 / 2200	1900 / 2300
		Year													
0				DC	ED	FE	GF	AG	BA	CB		BA	C	E	G
1	29	57	85	B	C	D	E	F	G	A	F	G	B	D	F
2	30	58	86	A	B	C	D	E	F	G	E	F	A	C	E
3	31	59	87	G	A	B	C	D	E	F	D	E	G	B	D
4	32	60	88	FE	GF	AG	BA	CB	DC	ED	CB	DC	FE	AG	CB
5	33	61	89	D	E	F	G	A	B	C	A	B	D	F	A
6	34	62	90	C	D	E	F	G	A	B	G	A	C	E	G
7	35	63	91	B	C	D	E	F	G	A	F	G	B	D	F
8	36	64	92	AG	BA	CB	DC	ED	FE	GF	ED	FE	AG	CB	ED
9	37	65	93	F	G	A	B	C	D	E	C	D	F	A	C
10	38	66	94	E	F	G	A	B	C	D	B	C	E	G	B
11	39	67	95	D	E	F	G	A	B	C	A	B	D	F	A
12	40	68	96	CB	DC	ED	FE	GF	AG	BA	GF	AG	CB	ED	GF
13	41	69	97	A	B	C	D	E	F	G	E	F	A	C	E
14	42	70	98	G	A	B	C	D	E	F	D	E	G	B	D
15	43	71	99	F	G	A	B	C	D	E	C	D	F	A	C
16	44	72		ED	FE	GF	AG	BA	CB	DC	—	CB	ED	GF	BA
17	45	73		C	D	E	F	G	A	B	—	A	C	E	G
18	46	74		B	C	D	E	F	G	A	—	G	B	D	F
19	47	75		A	B	C	D	E	F	G	—	F	A	C	E
20	48	76		GF	AG	BA	CB	DC	ED	FE	—	ED	GF	BA	DC
21	49	77		E	F	G	A	B	C	D	—	C	E	G	B
22	50	78		D	E	F	G	A	B	C	—	B	D	F	A
23	51	79		C	D	E	F	G	A	B	—	A	C	E	G
24	52	80		BA	CB	DC	ED	FE	GF	AG	—	GF	BA	DC	FE
25	53	81		G	A	B	C	D	E	F	—	E	G	B	D
26	54	82		F	G	A	B	C	D	E	C	D	F	A	C
27	55	83		E	F	G	A	B	C	D	B	C	E	G	B
28	56	84		DC	ED	FE	GF	AG	BA	CB	AG	BA	DC	FE	AG

Month		Dominical letter						
Jan., Oct.		A	B	C	D	E	F	G
Feb., Mar., Nov.		D	E	F	G	A	B	C
Apr., July		G	A	B	C	D	E	F
May		B	C	D	E	F	G	A
June		E	F	G	A	B	C	D
Aug.		C	D	E	F	G	A	B
Sept., Dec.		F	G	A	B	C	D	E

Day											
1	8	15	22	29	Sun.	Sat.	Fri.	Thurs.	Wed.	Tues.	Mon.
2	9	16	23	30	Mon.	Sun.	Sat.	Fri.	Thurs.	Wed.	Tues.
3	10	17	24	31	Tues.	Mon.	Sun.	Sat.	Fri.	Thurs.	Wed.
4	11	18	25		Wed.	Tues.	Mon.	Sun.	Sat.	Fri.	Thurs.
5	12	19	26		Thurs.	Wed.	Tues.	Mon.	Sun.	Sat.	Fri.
6	13	20	27		Fri.	Thurs.	Wed.	Tues.	Mon.	Sun.	Sat.
7	14	21	28		Sat.	Fri.	Thurs.	Wed.	Tues.	Mon.	Sun.

+ On and before 1582, Oct. 4 only.   ‡ On and after 1582, Oct. 15 only.

This calendar was prepared by G. M. Clemence, U. S. Naval Observatory, and is reprinted from the Smithsonian Physical Tables, Ninth Edition, by permission of the Smithsonian Institution.

26

Foreign Travel Tips

by Linda A. Bruce

- *Business and Banking Hours, Tipping Practices, and Dialing (Area) Codes in Selected Countries*
- *Business and Secretarial Services Overseas*
- *Passport, Visa, and Immunization Requirements*
- *Insurance for International Travel*
- *Money*
- *Medical Help Overseas*
- *Legal Help Overseas*
- *Jet Lag*
- *Average Temperatures by Month in Selected Cities*
- *Holidays in Selected Countries*

Increasing numbers of businesses are involved in business dealings with foreign countries. With this growth in international business has come a great increase in the amount of foreign travel by executives.

The secretary is almost always called on to help organize the executive's trip. The executive needs to know specific regulations concerning passport, visa, and immunization requirements of the country or countries to be visited. A familiarity with the rules concerning the currency of the country and plans on how to handle money—both small amounts for such items as tipping and large amounts for business deals—is very important. Information on the general business practices of the country (e.g., banking hours) as well as an awareness of the culture (e.g., tipping practices, holidays) will also help to make the executive's trip less stressful and possibly more profitable.

TABLE 26.1

Business and Banking Hours, Tipping Practices, and Dialing (Area) Codes in Selected Countries

Country	Business Hours	Banking Hours	Tipping*	Dialing (Area) Code(s)	
Canada	M–F 9:00–5:00	M–F 10:00–3:00	R 15% P Meter + $1.00 T 15–20%	Alberta Brit. Col. Manitoba N. Bruns. Newfound. N. Scotia Ft. Wm. London N. Bay Ottawa Toronto Pr. Ed. Is. Montreal Queb. City Saskatch.	403 604 204 506 709 902 807 519 705 617 416 902 514 418 306
Denmark	M–F 9:00–5:00	M–F 9:30–4:00	R 15% P Kr5/bag T None	Country # Aalborg Copenhagen or 2 Odense	45 8 1 9
England	M–F 9:30–5:30	M–F 9:30–3:30	R 12–15% P 50p/bag T 20p/L fare	Country # Birmingham Bristol Coventry Liverpool London Manchester Sheffield	44 21 272 203 51 1 61 742
France	M–F 9:30–12:30; 2:30–6:00	M–F 9:00–4:00	R included in bill + chg. P F5 T 15–20%	Country # Bordeaux Cannes Le Havre Lyon Marseille Nice Paris	33 55 93 35 78 91 93 1
West Germany	M–F 9:00–4:00	M–F 9:00–1:00 Tu/Th 2:30–6:00	R included in bill + chg. P DM4–5/bag T 5%	Country # Berlin (W) Bonn Cologne Frankfurt Hamburg Hannover Munich Stuttgart	49 30 228 221 611 40 511 89 711

Country	Business Hours	Banking Hours	Tipping*	Dialing (Area) Code(s)
Hong Kong	M–F 9:00–4:30	M–F 9:00–4:30 Sat 9:00–12:30	R included in bill + 5% P HK$1/bag T 10%	Country # 852 Hong Kong 5 Kowloon 3

Italy	M–F 8:30–1:00;
	  4:00–9:00
		M–F 8:30–1:30	R included in
			  bill + 5–10%
			P L800/bag
			T 15%
				Country # 39
				Florence 55
				Milan 2
				Naples 81
				Rome 6
				Venice 41

Japan	M–F 9:00–6:00	M–F 9:00–3:00
		Sat 9:00–12:00
		closed 2nd Sat
			R not custom
			  or included
			P Y250/bag
			T none unless
			  help w/bags
				Country # 81
				Hiroshima 822
				Kyoto 75
				Osaka 6
				Tokyo 3

Mexico	M–F 9:00–2:30; 5:30–8:00	M–Sat 9:00–1:00 Some 2:30–8:00	R 15% P 50p/bag T 50p	Mex. City 905 Tijuana 903

Netherlands	M–F 9:00–5:30	M–F 9:00–4:00	R included in
			  bill
			P fixed rate +
			  15%
			T included +
			  chg.
				Country # 31
				Amsterdam 20
				Rotterdam 10
				The Hague 70

Norway	M–F 8:00–4:00
	Summer 8:00–3:00
		M–F 8:15–3:30	R included
			P Kr5/bag
			T included or
			  round off to
			  nearest Kr
				Country # 47
				Oslo 2

Sweden	M–F 9:00–5:00	M–F 9:30–3:00	R included P Kr3/bag + Kr2/add'l. T 10–15%	Country # 46 Göteborg 31 Malmö 40 Stockholm 8
Switzerland	M–F 9:00–5:30	M–F 9:00–4:15	R included in bill P SF1/bag T 12–15%	Country # 41 Geneva 22 Lucerne 41 Zurich 1

* R = Restaurants; P = Porters; T = Taxi drivers

This chapter provides hints for foreign business travel. However, for any information subject to frequent or last-minute change, be sure to check with local embassies or other organizations that have up-to-the-minute information.

BUSINESS AND SECRETARIAL SERVICES OVERSEAS

If your need for business or secretarial services is occasional and/or short-term, the most convenient procedure to follow might be to investigate whether or not the hotel in which you are staying offers such a service. Many hotels have a completely separate office established to accommodate just such needs on a fee basis. If that is not the case, or if you expect frequent or long-term office requirements, it is possible to rent furnished offices and office/secretarial services in almost any country in the world on a daily, weekly, monthly, or annual basis.

Services that can be expected from such rental companies are:

private office space/conference rooms/showrooms

business mailing address

mail collecting and forwarding service

24-hour telephone answering service

multilingual secretarial services

communication services; photocopy, dictation, telex, facsimile services

safekeeping of documents.

In addition, it is possible that assistance may be provided in making business contacts in the country in which you rent space/services or in obtaining legal and financial advice. Costs, of course, will vary depending on the space or services required.

Following are some companies that might be used:

England

Chesham Executive Centre Adfone Services Ltd., 150 Regent Street, London W1R 5FA, England;
Tel: (44) 734-5351; Telex 261426

Execusuites International, Suite 67, Kent House, 87 Regent Street, London W1R 7HF, England;
Tel: (44) 439-7094; Telex 268048 EXTLDN-G

France

> Borbor International Management Consultants, 21 rue Vernet, 75008 Paris, France;
> Tel: (331) 723-8046; Telex 630602

> International Business Services, 15 Ave. Victor-Hugo, 75116 Paris, France;
> Tel: (331) 502-1800; Telex IBOS 620893F

> Le Satellite, 8 de la rue Copernic, 75116 Paris, France;
> Tel: (331) 727-1559; Telex 620183 LESATEL

Hong Kong

> Far East Executive Services Centre, 5th Floor, 7 Ice House Street, Hong Kong;
> Tel: (852) 5-217461; Telex 72091 FAREX HX

Switzerland

> Master Key Executive Business Centre, Ave. des Mousquines 4, 1005 Lausanne, Switzerland;
> Tel: (41) 21-230249/230875; Telex 25074

> Business Services and Consultants Corp., P.O. Box 5610, CH-8022 Zurich, Switzerland;
> Tel: (41) 211-92-07/12; Telex 813-062 BSCC CH

Other

> World-Wide Business Centres, Inc., 575 Madison Avenue, New York, 10022 (offices in 12 countries overseas);
> Tel: (212) 486-1333; Telex 125864 (Dom/Intl) 237699

PASSPORT, VISA, AND IMMUNIZATION REQUIREMENTS

There are a few countries that do not require a passport, but it is strongly recommended that you obtain and carry one with you at all times in any case. It is impossible to predict what circumstances might arise in your travels that would necessitate your having this important form of identification. Unexpected itinerary changes and the possibility of legal or medical problems are only a couple of the reasons you should never travel abroad without a current passport. Passport applications may be made at almost any U.S. Passport Office.

In addition to a passport, most countries require either an entry permit or a visa. Check with the consulate or embassy of any country you plan to visit for current visa/entry permit requirements. (Your travel agent or library can provide you with the address and telephone number of the nearest embassy or consulate.) These organizations will also tell you what, if any, immunizations are needed. A Certificate of Vaccination, as well as the "shots" themselves, can be obtained at your local board of health.

When having passport/visa photos taken, it is a good idea to get a few extras to take along for unforeseen needs, such as a lost passport or wallet or the need to apply for an additional visa should your itinerary vary from that planned.

INSURANCE FOR INTERNATIONAL TRAVEL

Quite often, your own health and personal property insurance, whether business or personal, will cover you when traveling overseas. It is very important, however, that you check with either your employer or insurance agent to get all the details of coverage, including exceptions, deductibles, maximum limits, and procedures to follow in the event you do need to seek medical assistance or suffer a loss or theft of personal property abroad.

If you are not covered by an existing policy, there are numerous organizations that provide coverage. A few suggestions follow:

Access America, Tel: 800-851-2800 or 800-228-2028, Ext. 26. Special health insurance and other services for travelers; run by Blue Cross-Blue Shield.

Assist Card Corporation of America, 347 Fifth Avenue, New York, NY 10016, Tel: 800-221-4564. Evacuation, medical assistance, and other services for travelers.

Intermedic, 777 Third Avenue, New York, NY 10017, Tel: 212-486-8900. Listing of physicians, fees, and services in other countries.

International Health Service, Georgetown University Hospital, 3800 Reservoir Road, N., Washington, DC 20007, Tel: 202-627-7379. Immunizations and medical treatment before and after trips abroad.

MONEY

Travelers checks are probably the safest and most convenient form in which to carry money while traveling abroad. Travelers checks can be cashed easily in most cities around the world. In case of loss or theft, they can also be replaced when a report is filed with the bank or agency from which the checks were purchased.

Obtaining a small amount of cash in the currency of the country you plan to visit before leaving is very helpful for paying taxis and porters on arrival at your foreign destination, particularly if you arrive at a time when banks are closed. Banks with an international department can usually provide a limited amount of funds in the currencies of the countries you plan to visit. Currency dealers and most international airports and hotels are other sources, but you will usually obtain the best rate of exchange at banks. Although the exchange rate on the "black market" may be tempting, it is extremely inadvisable, foolish, and possibly even dangerous to take this route.

When you expect to need large amounts of cash in a foreign country, it is best to arrange for a line of credit with a U.S. bank before leaving. You can then use this line of credit to obtain funds at associated banks en route.

Some countries have currency restrictions to limit the amount of local currency that may be brought into or taken out of the country. Check with the appropriate consulate or embassy for the latest information in this regard.

MEDICAL HELP OVERSEAS

A few simple first aid items brought in a personal emergency kit can help ease uncomplicated illness. Such things as aspirin or an aspirin substitute, bandages, an antiseptic cream, a thermometer, sunscreen, antihistamines, nasal decongestants, antidiarrheal medication, an extra pair of prescription glasses (or at least the prescription), and sunglasses can all make life much more comfortable. For more disease-prone areas of the world, it is wise to include water purification tablets, antimalarial medicine, and insect repellent.

Before traveling overseas, it is advisable to contact a Travelers' Clinic in the major city nearest you. These clinics offer counseling on travel health, especially in countries in which water or disease problems exist. The clinics receive weekly updates from the Center for Disease Control in Atlanta and the World Health Organization in order to provide this information to their clients. One such clinic is the International Travel Clinic, Johns Hopkins University, Hampton House, 624 N. Broadway, Baltimore, MD (301) 955-8931. As an alternative, the traveler can consult his or her private physician.

Another suggestion is membership in the International Association for Medical Assistance to Travelers (IAMAT), a nonprofit, donation-supported foundation located at 736 Center Street, Lewiston, NY

14092, Tel: 716-754-4883. There is no membership fee, although donations are accepted. Upon joining, you are sent a membership directory of doctors serving in 450 cities worldwide. The physicians have been educated in international medical practices with skills meeting Western standards. They all speak English and are available to members 24 hours a day. A fixed fee is charged for office visits and house or hotel calls, as well as holiday and Sunday visits. You will also receive their Travelers Clinical Record (to be completed by your family doctor and carried with you). In addition, you are supplied with world immunization and malaria risk charts.

Another organization providing personal and medical service for international travelers is International SOS Assistance, Inc., P.O. Box 11568, Philadelphia, PA 19116, Tel: 215-244-1500. If the local medical center is inadequate, the patient will be evacuated to the nearest adequate medical facility for treatment of the illness or injury. After stabilization, the patient will be brought to facilities near home. More details are available by contacting the organization directly.

Most major hotels around the world also have a doctor on call and arrangements with the nearest clinic or hospital to treat guests who become ill.

LEGAL HELP OVERSEAS

Legal difficulties abroad can run the gamut, including suits involving drug trafficking, personal injury, divorce, child custody, nationality, paternity, wills and estates, immigration violations, customs violations, drunk driving, etc. Because of the complicated and varied legal systems in many other parts of the world, it is advisable to consult a law firm with experience in these matters. One such firm is the International Legal Defense Counsel, which has been providing this type of assistance for many years. It is staffed by practiced American attorneys. Their address is 1420 Walnut Street, Suite 315, Philadelphia, PA 19102.

JET LAG

A useful item to obtain before traveling is a wallet-sized card that explains the anti-jet-lag diet. To obtain one, send a stamped, self-addressed envelope to Anti-Jet Lag Diet, Argonne National Laboratory, 9700 South Cass Avenue, Argonne, IL 60439.

Essentially, what is called for is a highly structured diet for four days before embarking on a trip by air. On the first of the four days, a high-protein breakfast and lunch and a high-carbohydrate dinner are recommended. On the second day, only salads, fruits and fruit juices, and light soups are to be consumed. The same cycle followed on days one and two are followed on days three and four. Another suggestion is to eat fairly lightly when in the air. Alcohol should not be taken before or immediately after a time change, due to the lengthened period of adjustment it causes, to say nothing of decision-making and memory difficulties already brought on by jet lag.

If traveling east, it is advisable to try to retire the evening before departure one hour later than normal for each time zone you will be crossing. When traveling west, the opposite is the case: go to bed an hour earlier for every time zone to be crossed, as much as is practical.

Your mood and the need for sleep are affected by exposure to sunlight. For this reason, it is wise to bring a sleeping mask to wear on long trips during which you will be flying during daylight hours. If at all possible, try to eat and sleep according to the local schedule in effect at your destination. When flying east, make your business appointments in the afternoon. When traveling west, early morning appointments are best.

A useful resource containing more detailed information on jet lag and other travel-related health and safety issues is the Traveler's Health and Safety Handbook, available for $5.00 from Agora, 824 E. Baltimore Street, Baltimore, MD 21202, Tel: (301) 324-0515.

TABLE 26.2

Average Temperatures by Month in Selected Cities

	January	February	March	April	May	June	July	August	September	October	November	December
Amsterdam	37	38	41	48	56	61	65	65	59	51	43	38
Berlin	36	32	39	49	55	66	63	61	56	48	37	32
Copenhagen	32	32	34	42	51	59	62	60	54	46	39	34
London	42	42	46	48	56	60	60	62	60	55	44	46
Melbourne	67	67	64	59	54	50	48	51	53	57	61	64
Mexico	53	56	60	64	64	63	74	61	62	58	55	53
Milan	32	37	45	54	62	74	69	71	65	54	43	35
Montreal	12	14	25	41	55	64	74	66	58	46	33	24
Naples	44	46	48	54	66	71	74	74	68	64	53	45
Nice	46	48	51	57	58	68	71	69	69	61	52	48
Oslo	24	24	29	39	60	59	62	60	52	41	32	25
Paris	36	39	44	50	57	62	65	65	60	52	43	38
Rome	43	46	50	55	68	73	77	80	73	67	56	52
Stockholm	27	26	29	38	47	57	62	59	52	66	34	28
Sydney	73	73	69	65	57	53	53	55	59	65	67	70
Tokyo	37	38	44	54	61	68	75	77	71	60	50	41

Holidays in Selected Countries*

Canada

New Year's Day, January 1; Good Friday; Easter Monday; Victoria Day; St. Jean Baptiste (Quebec); Canada Day, July 1; Fed. Gov. Holiday (Quebec), first Monday in August; Labor Day, first Monday in September; Thanksgiving Day, second Monday in October; Veteran's Day, November 11; Christmas Day, December 25; Boxing Day, December 26

Denmark

New Year's Day, January 1; Shrove Tuesday; Holy Thursday; Good Friday; Easter Sunday; Easter Monday; Prayer Day (fourth Friday after Easter); Ascension Day; Whit Monday; Constitution Day (half-day, June 5); Christmas Day, December 25; Second Day of Christmas, December 26

England

New Year's Day, January 1; Good Friday; Easter Monday; Early May Bank Holiday; Spring Holiday (last Monday in May); Queen's Birthday, June 11; Late Summer Holiday (last Monday in August); Christmas Day, December 25; Boxing Day, December 26

France

New Year's Day, January 1; Easter Monday; Labor Day, May 1; Ascension Day; Whitsuntide; Whit Monday; Bastille Day, July 14; Assumption, August 15; All Saints Day, November 1; Veterans Day, November 11; Christmas Day, December 25

Germany (West)

New Year's Day, January 1; Epiphany, January 6; Rose Monday, February 8; Good Friday; Easter Monday; Labor Day; Ascension Day; Whit Monday; Corpus Christi; Day of German Unity, June 17; Repentance Day; Christmas Day, December 25; Boxing Day, December 26

Hong Kong

New Year's Day, January 1; Chinese New Year, February 15–17; Good Friday; Day after Good Friday; Easter Monday; Ching Ming Festival, April 4; Dragon Boat Festival, June 11; Queen's Birthday, June 11; Day after Queen's Birthday, June 12; Public Holiday, August 22; Liberation Day, August 25; Mid-Autumn Festival, September 25; Chung Yeung Festival, October 19; Christmas Holiday, December 25–26

Italy

New Year's Day, January 1; Easter Monday; Liberation Day, April 25; Labor Day, May 1; Assumption, August 15; All Saints Day, November 1; Immaculate Conception, December 8; Christmas Day, December 25; St. Stephen's Day, December 26

Japan

New Year's Day, January 1; Adults' Day, January 15; National Foundation Day, February 11; Vernal Equinox Day, March 20 or 21; Emperor's Day, April 29; Constitution Day, May 3; Children's Day, May 5; Respect for the Aged Day, September 15; Autumnal Equinox, September 23 or 24; Sports Day, October 10; Cultural Day, November 3; Labor Thanksgiving Day, November 23; Government Off Season, December 29–January 3; any holiday that falls on Sunday is celebrated the following day.

Mexico

New Year's Day, January 1; Constitution Day, February 5; Benito Juarez' Birthday, March 21; Holy Thursday; Good Friday; Labor Day, May 1; Anniversary of the Puebla Battle, May 5; Independence Day, September 16; Columbus Day, October 12; All Saints Day, November 1; All Souls Day, November 2; Mexican Revolution Day, November 20; Fiesta of Our Lady of Guadelupe, December 12; Christmas Day, December 25

Netherlands

New Year's Day, January 1; Good Friday; Easter Monday; Queen's Birthday, April 30; Liberation Day, May 5; Ascension; Whit Monday; Christmas Day, December 25; Boxing Day, December 26

Norway

New Year's Day, January 1; Holy Thursday; Good Friday; Easter Monday; Labor Day, May 1; Ascension Day; Constitution Day, May 17; Whit Monday; Christmas Day, December 25; Boxing Day, December 26

Sweden

New Year's Day, January 1; Good Friday; Easter Monday; Ascension Day; Whit Monday; Swedish Flag Day, June 6; Midsummer Day; All Saints' Day, November 1; Christmas Day, December 25; Boxing Day, December 26

Switzerland

New Year's Day, January 1; Berchtoldstag; Good Friday; Easter Sunday; Easter Monday; Labor Day, May 1; Ascension Day, Whitsuntide; Whit Monday; National Day, August 1; Federal Day of Prayers, September 21; Christmas Day, December 25; Boxing Day, December 26

* In some countries, the exact date of a holiday may vary by one or two days because holidays are based on the lunar calendar (determined by the sighting of the moon). Travelers should therefore check with the appropriate embassy before making travel plans.

General Reference

27

Sources of Information

Revised by Joyce Gold

- *Dictionaries*
    - *Desk-Size*
    - *Unabridged*
    - *Biographical*
    - *Foreign Language*
- *Word Books*
    - *Books of Synonyms and Antonyms*
    - *Books of Quotations*
    - *Books on Usage*
- *Style Books and Printing Guides*
- *Encyclopedias*
- *Atlases and Gazetteers*
- *Yearbooks and Almanacs*
- *Books on Parliamentary Procedure*
- *Directories*
    - *Business, Manufacturers, Merchants*
    - *Finance*
    - *Education*
    - *Who's Who*
    - *Foreign Diplomats*
    - *U.S. Government Offices*
    - *U.S. Government Officials*
- *Professional Associations*
- *Indexes*
- *Libraries*
- *Travel Information*
- *Miscellaneous Directories, Guides, and Registers*
    - *Telephone Directories*
    - *City Directories*
- *Publicity Departments*
- *Newspaper Offices*

"The factor to be used in order to convert inches to millimeters? I think it's 25.4, but we'd better look it up."

"You are moving to Cedar Rapids, Iowa? Er . . . just how big a city is it?"

"The number of chemical elements? Well, over a hundred, certainly. The exact number escapes me."

Secretaries, business executives, students—all of us—are often faced with such questions. We "look up" the answers, and that is one form of research.

The subject for research might be the development of the computer, the hybridization of marigolds, the advertising rates for a metropolitan newspaper, the best hotel in Syracuse, New York, or the airline schedule between Nashville and London.

Resourcefulness often brings greater recognition for a researcher than does any other quality. Besides being an important part of general efficiency, it enables one to build up a reputation for knowing virtually everything.

Digging out information is first a matter of knowing *where* to dig. Following are sources of information with which all of us should be acquainted.

DICTIONARIES

A dictionary is indispensable as a quick reference for spelling, hyphenation, and syllabification of words and names. It is also valuable in finding definitions of words and phrases, synonyms, place names, biographical data, the usage of words, and the derivations of words from foreign languages.

Desk-size

The desk dictionary known as a "college edition" is of the size and scope that has proved to be most useful in a business office.

> *Webster's New World Dictionary of American English, Third College Edition*

Unabridged

Some offices and families and most libraries will also have an unabridged dictionary, larger in vocabulary coverage than the "college" editions.

> *Webster's Third New International Dictionary of the English Language* (Merriam-Webster)
>
> *Random House Dictionary of the English Language*

Biographical

Biographical dictionaries contain concise biographies of noted men and women.

> *Webster's Biographical Dictionary*

Foreign Language

Bookstores carry many foreign-language dictionaries.

> French: *Collins-Robert French-English: English-French Dictionary*
> Spanish: *Appleton's Revised Cuyas Dictionary*

WORD BOOKS

Books of Synonyms and Antonyms

Synonyms and antonyms are groups of words with like or opposite meanings, respectively. *Sharp* and *keen* are synonyms, while *sharp* and *dull* are antonyms. Here again, your dictionary is a useful tool, but you may want a more concentrated resource. A *thesaurus* ("treasury" or "storehouse") of synonyms and antonyms is then recommended.

> *Webster's New World Thesaurus*, edited by Charlton Laird
> *Roget's International Thesaurus*
> Funk & Wagnalls *Modern Guide to Synonyms and Related Words*

Books of Quotations

> John Bartlett's *Familiar Quotations*
> Burton Richardson's *The Home Book of Quotations*
> Bergen Evans' *Dictionary of Quotations*
> H. L. Mencken's *New Dictionary of Quotations on Historical Principles*
> *Oxford Dictionary of Quotations*

Books on Usage

> *Webster's New World Guide to Current American Usage* by Bernice Randall (most up-to-date)
> *Elements of Style* by William Strunk and E. B. White (most concise advice on usage)

Dictionary of Modern English Usage by H. W. Fowler (conservative view on usage)

Dictionary of Contemporary American Usage by Bergen and Cornelia Evans (liberal point of view)

The Careful Writer by Theodore M. Bernstein

Modern American Usage by Wilson Follett

English Grammar and Composition by John E. Warriner and Francis Griffith

STYLE BOOKS AND PRINTING GUIDES

Manual of Style, Chicago University Press (guide for the preparation of manuscripts for printing)

United States Government Printing Office *Style Manual*

New York Times Manual of Style and Usage (newspaper and magazine style)

Words into Type by Marjorie E. Skillen, et al.

Ink on Paper by Edmund Arnold

ENCYCLOPEDIAS

A general encyclopedia is a good reference source because it summarizes what otherwise might take hours of reading to discover. Good encyclopedias also contain maps and lists of books on the subjects treated (bibliographies).

Encyclopaedia Britannica (24 volumes; generally considered the finest reference set)

Collier's Encyclopedia (24 volumes)

Encyclopedia Americana (30 volumes)

Columbia Encyclopedia (a good one-volume work)

Van Nostrand's Scientific Encyclopedia (a one-volume source of general scientific information)

McGraw-Hill Encyclopedia of Science and Technology (15 volumes, updated each year with a *Yearbook* supplement)

Encyclopedia of Associations (3 volumes)

ATLASES AND GAZETTEERS

Even the best atlases, or books of maps and geographical data, find it hard to keep up with the rapidly changing boundaries and the formation of new countries in our world today. It is important for the secretary to check the publishing dates of these works before purchase to be sure the information within is up to date. An extensive listing of geographical names is also contained in each of the atlases.

Gazetteers are dictionaries or indexes of geographic names.

Hammond's *Ambassador World Atlas*
Rand McNally *International Atlas*
Columbia Lippincott Gazetteer of the World
Webster's New Geographical Dictionary (Merriam-Webster)

YEARBOOKS AND ALMANACS

Although an almanac was originally and primarily a book of tables with astronomical information, data on tides and sunrise, etc., a number of commercial yearbooks and almanacs of a much broader scope are on the market.

The World Almanac and Book of Facts and *Information Please Almanac* are both handy, inexpensive annual guides that give information and statistical data on scores of subjects of current interest, from sports to state histories.

Facts on File is the most comprehensive of the standard hardcover yearbooks, a semimonthly periodical for which the subscriber receives at the beginning of each year a binder and updated maps along with the cumulative index of the preceding year. Additional titles are listed below.

International Yearbook and Statesman's Who's Who
Statesman's Yearbook
Political Handbook and Atlas of the World
Yearbook of American and Canadian Churches
Yearbook of International Organizations

BOOKS ON PARLIAMENTARY PROCEDURE

A secretary may be required to assist at and record executive meetings in which parliamentary procedures are followed. It is useful to have a reference for settling procedural questions.

Robert's Rules of Order
O. Garfield Jones' *Parliamentary Procedure at a Glance*

DIRECTORIES

Business, Manufacturers, Merchants

A Guide to Business Directories, United States Department of Commerce (Directories listed under type of business and subdivided by local and regional directories)

Poor's Register of Corporations, Directors and Executives (Factual information about executives and directors of large American and Canadian corporations)

Directory of American Firms Operating in Foreign Countries

Thomas' Register of American Manufacturers

Kelley's Directory of Merchants, Manufacturers, and Shippers of the World

American Book Trade Directory

A Directory of Foreign Manufacturers in the United States

National Trade and Professional Associations of the United States and Canada and Labor Unions

International Business Bibliography

Finance

How to Read the Financial News by C. Norman Stabler (Discussion of operation of Wall Street and stock market)

Who's Who in Finance and Industry

Dun and Bradstreet Ratings and Reports

Moody's Manuals (Reports on companies)

Ayer Directory of Publications (Geographical listing of newspapers and magazines, with address, name of editor, frequency of publication, advertising rates, and circulation figures)

Education

Education Directory (Published by the U.S. Office of Education; lists educational institutions, national and state educational officials and associations, county, town, and district superintendents, college presidents, etc.)

Patterson's American Education (One of several lists of schools, colleges, and other educational institutions in the U.S.)

Handbook of Private Schools

American Universities and Colleges, American Council on Education, Washington, D.C. (Lists all universities and colleges in

United States with information such as admission requirements, courses offered, degrees granted, number of departments, professors, students, and physical facilities)

Lovejoy's College Guide (Lists information about universities, colleges, junior colleges, community colleges, and technical institutes

Who's Who

Who's Who in American Art
Who's Who in Art
Who's Who in American Education
Who's Who in Commerce and Industry
Who's Who in Labor
Who's Who in Religion
American Men and Women of Science
American Medical Directory
Who's Who in Insurance
Leaders in Education
The World of Learning
American Men and Women of Science
Who's Who in Finance and Industry
Who's Who Among Black Americans
Who's Who in Computer Education and Research
Who's Who in America
Who's Who (British version)
Who's Who of American Women
International Who's Who
Who's Who in Canada
Who's Who in the World
Who's Who in Electronics
Who's Who in American Law
Dictionary of American Biography
Twentieth Century Authors, a Biographical Dictionary

Foreign Diplomats

Diplomatic List, Department of State (Lists names of foreign diplomatic personnel in Washington with their addresses)

U.S. Government Offices

The United States Government is the largest publisher in the country. The Superintendent of Documents, United States Government Printing Office, Washington, D.C. 20402, has catalogs of available government publications that cover a wide range of subjects. Some of the bulletins and pamphlets are free, but for some of them and for books a charge is made. Write the Superintendent of Documents to receive a monthly listing or to ask which government department or agency may have the specific information you are seeking. Otherwise, address the department or agency itself:

Department of Agriculture, 14th Street and Independence Avenue, SW, Washington, D.C. 20250; (202) 447-2791. For information regarding crops in general and statistics relating to agricultural production, the Forest Service, the combating of injurious insects and animal and plant pests and diseases, soil conservation, food and nutrition service, marketing, and farm prices.

Department of Commerce, 14th Street and Constitution Avenue, NW, Washington, D.C. 20230; (202) 377-4901. For information on the national census, standards of weights and measures, government fisheries, lighthouses, and coast and geodetic surveys. Within the Department of Commerce, address specific inquiries to the Patent and Trademark Office and the National Weather Service.

Department of Defense, The Pentagon, Washington, D.C. 20301; (202) 545-6700. For information regarding the armed forces, the Joint Chiefs of Staff, training academies, and military installations of the United States.

Department of Education, 400 Maryland Avenue, SW, Washington, D.C. 20202; (202) 732-4576. For information on educational programs and opportunities for learning-disabled, mentally retarded, or handicapped students, the Head Start program and vocational rehabilitation, and on special classes for gifted students.

Department of Energy, 1000 Independence Avenue, SW, Washington, D.C. 20585; (202) 586-5806. For information about energy conservation, research, development, and technology; the marketing of federal power; regulation of energy production; and the nuclear weapons program.

Department of Health and Human Services, 200 Independence Avenue, SW, Washington, D.C. 20201; (202) 245-6343. Within the department, address Public Health Services with inquiries about the Center for Disease Control or for the Food and Drug

Administration, the National Health Institutes, and the Alcohol, Drug Abuse, and Mental Health Administration. Address specific inquiries about social security to the Social Security Administration.

Department of Housing and Urban Development, 451 7th Street, SW, Washington, D.C. 20401; (202) 755-6685. For information on urban renewal and public and federal housing.

Department of the Interior, 18th and C Streets, NW, Washington, D.C. 20240; (202) 343-1100. For information about government lands, national parks, national monuments, national forests, the geological survey, reclamation of wastelands, and control of mines. Within the Department of the Interior, address specific inquiries to the U.S. Fish and Wildlife Service and the Bureau of Indian Affairs.

Department of Justice, 10th Street and Constitution Avenue, NW, Washington, D.C. 20530; (202) 633-2007. For information regarding the administration of the system of federal courts, the supervision of federal prisons and the violation of federal law and for inquiries to the Immigration and Naturalization Service, the Antitrust Division, and the Federal Bureau of Investigation.

Department of Labor, 200 Constitution Avenue, NW, Washington, D.C. 20210; (202) 523-7316. For information on the welfare of wage earners' conditions in the United States, minimum wage and other wage-and-hour regulations, and statistics relating to labor and workers' compensation.

Department of State, 2201 C Street, NW, Washington, D.C. 20520; (202) 647-3686. To apply for passports for Americans traveling abroad. For information regarding ambassadors, ministers, consuls, and their staffs; the diplomatic relations of the United States with foreign countries; and activities of American citizens in foreign countries.

Department of Transportation, 400 7th Street, SW, Washington, D.C. 20590; (202) 366-5580. For information about transportation by air, road, and rail as well as programs involving urban mass transportation. Also for information about the St. Lawrence Seaway. Address the U.S. Coast Guard in the Transportation Department with inquiries about smuggling, law enforcement in coastal and other navigable waters of the United States, and assistance to vessels in distress.

Department of the Treasury, 15th Street and Pennsylvania Avenue, Washington, D.C. 20220; (202) 566-2041. For information about minting and coinage, prosecution of counterfeiters, U.S. Savings Bonds, the U.S. Secret Service, and the Bureau of Alcohol,

Tobacco and Firearms. Within the Department of the Treasury, address inquiries about income taxes to the Internal Revenue Service and about duties on imported products to the U.S. Customs Service.

Independent Government Agencies

In addition to the departments, there are nearly sixty independent agencies, commissions, boards, etc. of the federal government. They are listed with addresses in the *United States Government Manual*. Many of them have offices in major cities and some have offices in many smaller cities. Among these agencies are the United States Postal Service, the National Aeronautics and Space Administration, the Federal Trade Commission, the Environmental Protection Agency, the Equal Employment Opportunity Commission, the Civil Aeronautics Board, the Federal Reserve System, and the Veterans Administration.

U.S. Government Officials

Congressional Directory for the Use of the United States Congress (Gives comprehensive information regarding the legislative, judicial, and executive departments of the government, including biographical sketches of members of Congress and lists of members of diplomatic and consular services)

Office of the President of the U.S. 1600 Pennsylvania Avenue, NW, Washington, D.C. 20500; (202) 456-2343

Office of the Vice President of the U.S. Old Executive Office Building, 17th and Pennsylvania Avenue, NW, Washington, D.C. 20500; (202) 456-2326

PROFESSIONAL ASSOCIATIONS

Professional Secretaries International
301 East Armour Boulevard
Kansas City, MO 64111
(816) 531-7010

Professional organization of secretaries. Develops research and educational projects for secretaries.

American Society of Corporate Secretaries
1270 Avenue of the Americas
New York, NY 10020
(212) 765-2620

For corporate secretaries, assistant secretaries, officers and executives of corporations, and others interested in corporate practices and procedures. Maintains a central information and reference service.

Executive Women International
Spring Run Office Plaza
965 E. Van Winkle, Suite #1
Salt Lake City, UT 84117
(801) 263-3296

For women employed as executive secretaries or in administrative positions.

National Association of Legal Secretaries
2250 E. 73rd Street, Suite 550
Tulsa, OK 74136
(918) 493-3540

For legal secretaries and others employed in work of a legal nature in law offices, banks, and courts. Sponsors legal secretarial training courses.

INDEXES

Recourse to the proper indexes will uncover many important newspaper and magazine articles that may answer questions arising in your work. Such indexes list thousands of subjects and the newspapers, periodicals, etc. where articles on those matters can be found. Individual subjects in various fields are indexed in the following reference books.

Cumulative Book Index (Lists all currently published books)
United States Catalogue (Lists all books printed in the U.S., beginning in 1898; superseded by the *Cumulative Book Index*)
Books in Print (Lists current books by title, author, and subject)
Book Review Digest
The New York Times Index (Possibly the most comprehensive index of news, politics, scientific progress, international development, etc.)
Reader's Guide to Periodical Literature
Business Periodical Index
Index to Periodical Articles By and About Negroes
Index Medicus
Bibliography of Medical Reviews (Part of *Index Medicus,* but also published separately)

656 SOURCES OF INFORMATION

Index to Legal Periodicals
Education Index
Applied Science and Technology Index
Social Sciences and Humanities Index
Biological and Agricultural Index

The question will arise as to how many of the reference books listed above should be purchased for home or business use. There can be no general answer. If you find that you must visit or phone the library frequently to get information from certain books, it might be wise to buy them. But a shelf of unused books serves the dubious purpose of decoration. It is more important for you to familiarize yourself with what is available and to know where to look.

If you are asked to get the name of a paper manufacturer in Calcutta, the digest of an article on fire hoses that appeared in *The New York Times* sometime in August 1908, or the rate for sending a telegram to Belgium, just remember that there are many research avenues open and many people and books to help you.

LIBRARIES

The public-library system of the United States has a high standard of helpfulness and courtesy. It is exceptional when a reference librarian is not alert to your requests for information. In any part of the country, the great majority of librarians are not only willing but eager to help.

At libraries you will find books on special subjects, both technical and general, including the reference books listed above. You will also find information on government activities, current events, current biographies, scientific advances, industrial and commercial developments, and many other subjects.

Most libraries have photocopying devices of one kind or another for reproducing printed material. It may be helpful to have a copy of a magazine article or of a page from a reference book to take back to the office. In some library departments permission to reproduce material or assistance from the librarian may be required.

The habit of going to the library for research will uncover many hitherto unsuspected sources of information. In using reference books, always check the date of publication; if a book was published in 1934, the data it contains may have no particular value today.

In making notes for your future use, be sure to cite the year in which the book, magazine, or newspaper was published. In the case of a book, the publisher and the city in which the book was published should be included.

TRAVEL INFORMATION

Travel Agencies

In most cities and towns, full information regarding transportation schedules and rates is on file with airline, bus, railroad, or ship offices or agencies. Travel agencies give efficient service free.

The American Automobile Association (AAA) provides travel information and service to members. It will plan trips, provide maps, report on best routes and road and weather conditions, and recommend hotels and motels.

Departments of Tourism

Each of the fifty states has a Department of Tourism, and many cities also have such a department, separate from or connected with the Chamber of Commerce. Brochures about historical sites, road maps, hotel and motel listings, and calendars of coming events are easily obtainable from these sources.

MISCELLANEOUS DIRECTORIES, GUIDES, AND REGISTERS

Telephone Directories

In the larger cities, telephone directories of other large cities are usually on file at the central telephone offices and in libraries that have comprehensive reference departments. They are valuable not only for the telephone numbers listed, but for the street addresses as well. Telephone companies also publish directories in which entries are made under streets and numbers so that, given a certain address, they can tell whether there is a phone at that place. Although these directories are not available to the general public, they are rented to businesses.

If you had to secure a quantity of dry ice so that you could send a dozen brook trout in first-class condition to a friend or favored customer, the problem of finding a dealer in that unusual article might be difficult without the classified telephone directory. The "Yellow Pages" list the names, addresses, and telephone numbers of business houses, merchants, and professionals according to the specialties. Most big-city directories have indexes.

City Directories

These are intended to give the name, address, and occupation of each resident of the cities for which they are issued. Because Americans move frequently and businesses change names, a certain percentage of the information in each of these is out of date by the time it is published. In the cross index at the back of the book, entries are made by street and number so that by looking up a certain address, one can discover who lives there.

> *Foundations Directory*
>
> *Association Index: a Source-List of Directories and Other Publications Listing Associations*
>
> *Directory of Historical Societies in the United States and Canada*
>
> *Directory of Religious Organizations in the United States*
>
> *Lloyd's Register:* Lloyd's Register of Shipping lists names and factual details of seagoing merchant ships in the world.

Another directory is the *Social Register,* which lists persons socially prominent in larger cities.

PUBLICITY DEPARTMENTS

Large corporations, groups supporting causes, and public institutions such as universities generally maintain departments of public information that handle inquiries regarding their products, services, policies, and plans. It is possible that the information they give out will seek to promote their own interests, but much valuable information may be secured from such sources. Inquiries or requests for photographs should be addressed to the director of public relations of the company or organization. Some businesses have a standard policy of enclosing a self-addressed, stamped envelope when requesting information from a charitable or other nonprofit organization.

NEWSPAPER OFFICES

Newspapers maintain libraries or "morgues" that are sometimes open to the public, or at least to businesses in the community, for reference work. Here are filed thousands of news clippings under alphabetically arranged subject headings. Editors of special departments, such as society, finance, business, sports, etc., keep their own files and are often helpful. Furthermore, most photographic departments of newspapers make prints available for a fee. *The New York Times* has developed a computerized research system available to other newspapers, public libraries, business libraries, and so on.

28

Holidays in the United States

Each state has jurisdiction over holidays that will be observed in that state. They are designated either by the state legislature or by executive proclamation and therefore may be changed with each new state executive or legislature.

There are no national holidays in the United States. The President and Congress designate holidays only for the District of Columbia and for federal employees throughout the nation.

In most states, holidays that fall on Sunday are observed on the following day.

New Year's Day (January 1)—All the states.

Martin Luther King's Birthday (January 15)—Connecticut, Illinois, Louisiana, Maryland, Massachusetts, Michigan, New Jersey, and Ohio. Many groups and institutions in other states also observe this day.

Robert E. Lee's Birthday (third Monday in January)—Mississippi and (as *Lee–Jackson Day*) Virginia: (January 19)—Arkansas, Georgia, Louisiana, North Carolina, and South Carolina.

Inauguration Day (January 20)—District of Columbia (observed every fourth year).

Mardi Gras or *Shrove Tuesday* (last day before Lent; February or early March)—Alabama and Louisiana.

Lincoln's Birthday (February 12)—Alaska, Arizona, California, Colorado, Connecticut, Delaware, Illinois, Indiana, Iowa, Kansas, Maryland, Michigan, Missouri, Montana, Nebraska, New Jersey, New Mexico, New York, Oregon, Pennsylvania, Rhode Island, Tennessee, Utah, Vermont, Washington, and West Virginia.

Washington's Birthday (third Monday in February)—All the states except Florida. In several states the holiday is called *President's Day* or *Washington–Lincoln Day*.

Good Friday (Friday before Easter Sunday)—All the states. It is a legal holiday in Connecticut, Delaware, Hawaii, Indiana, Kentucky, Louisiana, Maryland, New Jersey, North Dakota, and Tennessee. It is a partial holiday in New Mexico and Wisconsin.

Memorial Day (last Monday in May)—All the states except Alabama, Mississippi, and South Carolina; (May 30)—Delaware, Florida, Kentucky, Maryland, New Hampshire, New Mexico, South Dakota, and Vermont.

Independence Day (July 4)—All the states.

Labor Day (first Monday in September)—All the states.

Columbus Day (second Monday in October)—All the states except Alaska, Arkansas, Hawaii, Iowa, Mississippi, Nevada, North Dakota, Oregon, South Carolina, South Dakota, and Washington: (October 12)—Maryland.

General Election Day (first Tuesday after first Monday in November)—Colorado, Delaware, Hawaii, Illinois, Indiana, Kentucky, Louisiana, Michigan, Missouri, Montana, New Hampshire, New Jersey, New York, North Carolina, Pennsylvania, Rhode Island, South Carolina, Tennessee, Virginia, Wisconsin, and Wyoming. It is observed only when Presidential or general elections are held. (Days on which primary elections are held are observed as holidays or partial holidays in some states.)

Veterans Day or *Armistice Day* (November 11)—All the states.

Thanksgiving Day (fourth Thursday in November)—All the states. The day after Thanksgiving Day is observed as a full or partial holiday in several states.

Christmas Day (December 25)—All the states.

29

Signs and Symbols

- *Astronomy*
- *Biology*
- *Commerce and Finance*
- *Computer Systems Flowchart*
- *Mathematics*
- *Medicine and Pharmacy*
- *Weather*
- *Miscellaneous*
- *Proofreader's Marks*

ASTRONOMY

Sun, Moon, Planets, etc.

☉ (1) the sun   (2) Sunday

☾, ☽ (1) the moon   (2) Monday

● new moon

☽, ●,) first quarter

○ full moon

☾, ●, ☾ last quarter

✳, ✺ fixed star

☿ (1) Mercury   (2) Wednesday

♀(1) Venus   (2) Friday

⊕, ⊖, ♁ Earth

♂ (1) Mars   (2) Tuesday

♃ (1) Jupiter   (2) Thursday

♄ (1) Saturn   (2) Saturday

♁, ♅ Uranus

Ψ Neptune
P Pluto
⚳ comet
①, ②, ③, *etc.* asteroids in the order of their discovery
α, β, γ, *etc.*   stars (of a constellation) in the order of their brightness;
the Greek letter is followed by the Latin genitive of
the name of the constellation

Signs of the Zodiac

Spring Signs
1. ♈   Aries (the Ram)
2. ♉   Taurus (the Bull)
3. ♊, □ Gemini (the Twins)

Summer Signs
4. ♋, ⊗ Cancer (the Crab)
5. ♌   Leo (the Lion)
6. ♍   Virgo (the Virgin)

Autumn Signs
7. ♎   Aries (the Ram)
8. ♏   Scorpio (the Scorpion)
9. ♐   Sagittarius (the Archer)

Winter Signs
10. ♑, ♅ Capicorn (the Goat)
11. ♒   Aquarius (the Water Bearer)
12. ♓   Pisces (the Fish)

Aspects and Nodes

☌ conjunction: with reference to bodies having the same longitude,
or right ascension
✳ sextile: being 60° apart in longitude, or right ascension
□ quadrature: being 90° apart in longitude, or right ascension
△ trine: being 120° apart in longitude, or right ascension
☍ opposition: being 180° apart in longitude, or right ascension
☊ ascending node
☋ descending node

Signs and Abbreviations Used in Astronomical Notation

α	mean distance
α, R.A.	right ascension
β	celestial latitude
D	diameter
α	mean distance
δ	declination
Δ	distance
e	eccentricity of orbit
G	universal gravitational constant
h, ^{h}	hours: as, 5h or 5^h
i	inclination to the ecliptic
L, l	mean longitude in orbit
λ	longitude
M	mass
m, ^{m}	minutes of time: as, 5m or 5^m
μ, η	mean daily motion
+	north
Ω	longitude of ascending node
π, ω	longitude of perihelion
q	perihelion distance
R	radius or radius vector
—	south
$\overline{S}$	mean position of satellite
s, ^{s}	seconds of time: as, 16s or 16^s
T	periodic time
φ	geographical latitude
°	degrees of arc
′	minutes of arc
″	seconds of arc

BIOLOGY

○, ☉, ①	annual plant
☉☉, ②	biennial plant
♃	perennial herb
△	evergreen plant
☉	monocarpic plant, which bears fruit but once
♂, ♂	(1) male organism or cell (2) staminate plant or flower
♀	(1) female organism or cell (2) pistillate plant or flower

☿	perfect, or hermaphroditic, plant or flower
○	individual, especially female, organism
□	individual, especially male, organism
♂ ♀	unisexual; having male and female flowers separate
♂ − ♀	monoecious; having male and female flowers on the same plant
♂ : ♀	dioecious; having male and female flowers on different plants
♀ ♂ ♀	polygamous; having hermaphroditic and unisexual flowers on the same or different plants
∞	indefinite number, as of stamens when there are more than twenty
0	lacking or absent, as a part
)	turning or winding to the left
(	turning or winding to the right
×	crossed with: used of a hybrid
P	parental (generation)
F	filial (generation); offspring
F_1, F_2, F_3, *etc.*	offspring of the first, second, third, etc. filial generation
+	possessing a (specified) characteristic
−	lacking a (specified) characteristic
⁎̲	northern hemisphere
⁎	southern hemisphere
|⁎	Old World
⁎|	New World
°, ′, ″	feet, inches, lines
′, ″, ‴	feet, inches, lines (in European usage)

COMMERCE AND FINANCE

$	dollar or dollars: as, $100
¢	cent or cents: as, 13¢
£	pound or pounds sterling: as, £100
/	shilling or shillings: as, 2/6, two shillings and sixpence
@	(1) at: as, 200 @ $1 each (2) to: as, shoes per pr. $30 @ $50
℔	per
%	(1) percent: as, 5% (2) order of
‰	per thousand
a/c	account
B/L	bill of lading
B/S	bill of sale

c/d, C/D   carried down (in bookkeeping)
c/f, C/F   carried forward (in bookkeeping)
c/o   (1) care of   (2) carried over (in bookkeeping)
d/a   days after acceptance
d/s   days after sight
L/C   letter of credit
O/S   out of stock
w/   with
w/o   without
(1) number (before a figure): as, #5 can   (2) pounds (after a
           figure): as, 25#

COMPUTER SYSTEMS FLOWCHART

⬭ terminal: beginning, end, or interruption of a flowchart

◻ input/output: any input/output function, as processing information (input) or printout of processed information (output)

☐ process: any processing function that results in a change in form
   or location of information

○ preparation: instructions to modify a program

◇ decision: choice of alternatives at this point

▥ predefined process: a process that is specified elsewhere, as in
   a subroutine

○ connector: entry from or to another part of the flowchart

▽ offline storage: on perforated or magnetic tape, cards, or paper

◖ online storage: in a storage unit, as a disc, magnetic tape, etc.

↑← flow direction: direction of data flow: arrows not required if
    flow is top to bottom or left to right

→ communication link: transmission of data from one location to
   another by telephone or other telecommunications medium

⊣ annotation: addition of explanatory notes: dotted line extends
   to flowchart symbol

▱ manual input: data input by an online device, usually a keyboard

▽ manual operation: manual offline operation

▱ punched card

▱ punched tape

▱ document

◖ magnetic tape

◖ transmittal tape

○ display

MATHEMATICS

Numeration

Capital letters were sometimes used for the Greek numerals, and lower-case letters are often used for the Roman. In the Roman notation, the value of a character to the right of a larger numeral is added to that of the numeral: as, VI = V + 1 = 6. I, X, and sometimes C are also placed to the left of larger numerals, and when so situated their value is subtracted from that of such numerals: as, IV, that is, V − I = 4. After the sign IↃ for D, when the character Ↄ was repeated, each repetition had the effect of multiplying IↃ by ten: as, IↃↃ, 5,000; IↃↃↃ, 50,000; and the like. In writing numbers twice as great as these, C was placed as many times before the stroke I as the Ↄ was written after it. Sometimes a line was drawn over a numeral to indicate thousands: as, $\overline{C}$ = 100,000.

Arabic	Greek	Roman
0	. . .	. . .
1	α	I
2	β	II
3	γ	III
4	δ	IV *or* IIII
5	ε	V
6	ς	VI
7	ζ	VII
8	η	VIII *or* IIX
9	θ	IX *or* VIIII
10	ι	X
11	ια	XI
12	ιβ	XII
13	ιγ	XIII *or* XIIV
14	ιδ	XIV *or* XIIII
15	ιε	XV
16	ις	XVI
17	ιζ	XVII
18	ιη	XVIII *or* XIIX
19	ιθ	XIX *or* XVIIII
20	κ	XX
30	λ	XXX
40	μ	XL *or* XXXX
50	ν	L
60	ξ	LX
70	ο	LXX

Arabic	Greek	Roman
80	π	LXXX *or* XXC
90	ϑ	XC *or* LXXXX
100	ρ	C
200	σ	CC
300	τ	CCC
400	υ	CD *or* CCCC
500	φ	D *or* IƆ
600	χ	DC *or* IƆC
700	ψ	DCC *or* IƆCC
800	ω	DCCC *or* IƆCCC
900	. . .	CM, DCCCC, *or* ICCCCC
1,000	. . .	M *or* CIƆ
2,000	. . .	MM *or* CIƆCIƆ

Calculation

+   (1) plus, the sign of addition; used also to indicate that figures are only approximately exact, some figures being omitted at the end: as, 2.1557 +   (2) positive

−   (1) minus, the sign of subtraction; used also to indicate that figures have been left off from the end of a number, and that the last figure has been increased by one: as, 2.9378 = 2.94 −   (2) negative

±, ∓   plus or minus: indicating that either of the signs + or − may properly be used; used also to introduce the probable error after a figure obtained by experimentation, etc.

×   multiplied by: $5 \times 4 = 20$; multiplication is also indicated by a centered dot $(5 \cdot 4 = 20)$ or by placing the factors in immediate juxtaposition $(2ab = 2 \times a \times b)$

÷   divided by; division is also indicated by a colon $(x \div y = x : y)$, by a straight line between the dividend and the divisor $(\frac{x}{y})$, or by an oblique line (x/y)

=   is equal to; equals

≠   is not equal to

>   is greater than: as, $x > y$; that is, x is greater than y

<   is less than: as, $x < y$; that is, x is less than y

≮, ≦, ≧   is not less than; is equal to or greater than

≯, ≧, ≦   is not greater than; is equal to or less than

≎   is equivalent to: applied to magnitudes or quantities that are equal in area or volume but are not of the same form

$\equiv$	is identical with
$\cong$	is congruent to
$\sim$	the difference between: used to designate the difference between two quantities without indicating which is the greater: as, $x \sim z$ = the difference between x and z
$\propto$	varies as; is directly proportional to: as, $x \propto y$; that is, x varies as y
$\div$	geometric proportion: as, $\div x : y : : a : b$; that is, the geometric proportion x is to y as a is to b
$:$	is to; the ratio of
$: :$	as; equals: used between ratios
∞	indefinitely great; the symbol for infinity
$!, \llcorner$	the factorial of, or the continued product of numbers from one upward: as, $5! = 5 \times 4 \times 3 \times 2 \times 1$
$\therefore$	therefore
$\because$	since; because
$. . .$	and so on
$\angle$	angle: as, $\angle$XYZ
$\perp$	the perpendicular; is perpendicular to: as, EF $\perp$ MN = EF is perpendicular to MN
$\parallel$	parallel; is parallel to: as, EF $\parallel$ DG
$\bigcirc$	circle; circumference; 360°
$\frown$	arc of a circle
$\odot$	triangle
$\square$	square
$\square$	rectangle
$\square$	parallelogram
$\sqrt{}, \sqrt{}$	radical sign; root, indicating, when used without a figure placed above it, the square root: as, $\sqrt{9} = 3$. When any root other than the square root is meant, a figure (called the *index*) expressing the degree of the required root is placed above the sign: as, $\sqrt[3]{27} = 3$.
$^1, ^2, ^3, \textit{etc.}$	exponents, placed above and to the right of a quantity to indicate that it is raised to the first, second, third, etc. power: as, a^2, $(a + b)^3$
$', '', ''', \textit{etc.}$	prime, double (or second) prime, triple (or third) prime, etc., used to distinguish between different values of the same variable: as, x', x'', x''', etc.

$\overline{}$	vinculum: as, $\overline{x + y}$	These signs indicate that the quantities connected or enclosed by them are to be taken together, as a single quantity.
( )	parentheses: as, $2(x + y)$	
[ ]	brackets: as, $a[2(x + y)]$	
{ }	braces: as, $b + \{2 - a[2(x + y)]\}$	

f, F   function; function of: as, f (a), a function of a

d differential of: as, da

δ variation of: as, δa

$\triangle$ finite difference, or increment

D   differential coefficient, or derivative

$\int$ integral; integral of, indicating that the expression following it is to be integrated: as, $\int f(x)dx$ indicates the indefinite integral of $f(x)$ with respect to x

$\int_a^b$ definite integral, indicating the limits of integration: as, $\int_a^b f(x)dx$ indicates the integral of $f(x)$ with respect to x, between the limits a and b

Σ sum: algebraic sum; when used to indicate the summation of finite differences, it has a sense similar to that of the symbol $\int$

Π the continued product of all terms such as (those indicated)

π pi, the number 3.14159265 + : the ratio of the circumference of a circle to its diameter, of a semicircle to its radius, and of the area of a circle to the square of its radius

e, ϵ the number 2.7182818 + : the base of the Napierian system of logarithms; also, the eccentricity of a conic section

M   the modulus of a system of logarithms, especially of the common system of logarithms, where it is equal to 0.4342944819 +

°   degrees: as, 90°

′   (1) minutes of arc   (2) feet

″   (1) seconds of arc   (2) inches

h hours

m minutes of time

s seconds of time

MEDICINE AND PHARMACY

ĀĀ, Ā, āā   [Gr. *ana*] of each

a.c.   [L. *ante cibum*] before meals

ad   [L.] up to; so as to make: as, *ad*3ij, so as to make two drams

add.   [L. *adde*] let there be added; add

ad lib.   [L. *ad libitum*] at pleasure; as needed or desired

aq.   [L. *aqua*] water

b. (i.) d.   [L. *bis (in) die*] twice daily

c̄.   [L. *cum*] with

coch.   [L. *cochleare*] a spoonful

D.   [L. *dosis*] a dose

dil.   [L. *dilue*] dilute or dissolve

ess.   [L. *essentia*] essence

ft. mist.   [L. *fiat mistura*] let a mixture be made

ft. pulv.   [L. *fiat pulvis*] let a powder be made

gr.   [L. *granum*] a grain

gtt.   [L. *guttae*] drops

guttatim   [L.] drop by drop

H.   [L. *hora*] hour

haust.   [L. *haustus*] a draft

hor. decub.   [L. *hora decubitus*] at bedtime

in d.   [L. *in dies*] daily

lot.   [L. *lotio*] a lotion

M.   [L. *misce*] mix

mac.   [L. *macera*] macerate

O., o.   [L. *octarius*] a pint

p.c.   [L. *post cibum*] after meals

pil.   [L. *pilula(e)*] pill(s)

p.r.n.   [L. *pro re nata*] as circumstances may require

pulv.   [L. *pulvis*] powder

q.(i.)d.   [L. *quater (in) die*] four times daily

q.l.   [L. *quantum libet*] as much as you please

q.s.   [L. *quantum suficit*] as much as will suffice

q.v.   [L. *quantum vis*] as much as you like

℞   [L. *recipe*] take: used at the beginning of a prescription

S, Sig.   [L. *signa*] write: used in prescriptions to indicate the directions to be placed on the label of the medicine

t.(i.)d.   [L. *ter (in) die*] three times daily

tab.   [L. *tabella*] tablet

℥   ounce; ℥i = one ounce; ℥ij = two ounces; ℥ss = half an ounce; ℥iss = one ounce and a half, etc.; *f*℥ = a fluid ounce

ʒ   dram; ʒi = one dram; ʒij = two drams; ʒss = half a dram; ʒiss = one dram and a half, etc.; *f*ʒ = a fluid dram

ϴ   scruple; ϴi = one scruple; ϴij = two scruples; ϴss = half a scruple; ϴiss = one scruple and a half, etc.

♍, ♍   minim

WEATHER

◎   calm

○   clear

●   cloudy

◐   partly cloudy

=   fog

∞   haze

6   tropical storm

•   rain

⚹   rain and snow

△   sleet

∗   snow

℞   thunderstorm

MISCELLANEOUS

&, &ₚ   (the ampersand) and: as, A. B. Smith & Co.

&c.   [L. *et cetera*] and others; and so forth

©   copyright; copyrighted

®   registered trademark

☾   crescent: symbol of Islam

†   cross: symbol of Christianity

✝   Celtic cross: symbol of Protestant Episcopal Church

☦   Russian cross: symbol of Russian Orthodox Church

✛   Greek cross: symbol of Greek Orthodox Church

℞.   response: in religious services, used to mark the part to be uttered by the congregation in answer to the officiant

∗   in Roman Catholic service books, a mark used to divide each verse of a psalm into two parts, indicating where the response begins

℣,V',V   versicle: in religious services, used to mark the part to be uttered by the officiant

✠   (1) a sign of the cross used by the pope, by archbishops, and by bishops, before their names   (2) in religious services, used to mark the places where the sign of the cross is to be made

✡   star of David: symbol of Judaism

🕎   menorah: symbol of Judaism

†   died: used in genealogies, etc.

×   (1) by: used in dimensions, as 8″ × 11″ paper   (2) a mark representing a signature, as on a legal document, made by someone unable to write; the name is added by someone else, e.g.,

> *his*
> *John* × *Doe*
> *mark*

☢   radioactive

PROOFREADER'S MARKS

⊙ Insert period

⌄ Insert comma

:| Insert colon

;| Insert semicolon

! Insert exclamation point

V́ Insert apostrophe or single quotation mark

"/ V́ Insert quotation marks

(/) Insert parentheses

[/] Insert brackets

=| Insert hyphen

tr̃ Insert en dash

im Insert em dash

?| Insert question mark

(?) Query to author

∧ Insert marginal addition

ℓ Delete

ℓ̣ Delete and close up

⌒ Close up

Insert space

⧣ Less space

eq.# Equalize spacing

¶ Paragraph

No *¶* Run in same paragraph

⊏/⊐ Move to left or to right

⊓/⊔ Raise or lower

= Straighten type horizontally

‖ Align type vertically

tr Transpose

stet Let crossed-out words stand

ctr Center

lc Set in lower-case letters

caps Set in capital letters

s.c. Set in small capitals

rom Set in roman type

ital Set in italic type

bf Set in boldface type

(X) Replace imperfect letter

☊ Reverse upside-down letter

↧ Push down space that prints

wf Wrong font (wrong size or style of type)

sp Spell out word or figure

ld in Insert lead, or space, between lines

cl ld Delete lead, or space, between lines

Weights and Measures

U.S. CUSTOMARY AND METRIC MEASUREMENT EQUIVALENTS

Length or Distance

Linear Measure

1 inch	=	2.54 centimeters
12 inches = 1 foot	=	0.3048 meter
3 feet = 1 yard	=	0.9144 meter
5½ yards or 16½ feet = 1 rod	=	5.029 meters
40 rods = 1 furlong	=	201.17 meters
8 furlongs or 1,760 yards or 5,280 feet = 1 (statute) mile	=	1,609.3 meters
3 miles = 1 (land) league	=	4.83 kilometers

Nautical Measure

6 feet = 1 fathom   = 1.829 meters

100 fathoms = 1 cable's length (ordinary)
(In the U.S. Navy 120 fathoms or 720 feet = 1 cable's length; in the British Navy, 608 feet = 1 cable's length.)

10 cables' lengths = 1 nautical mile (6,076.11549 feet, by international agreement)   = 1.852 kilometers

1 nautical mile = 1.1508 statute miles (the length of a minute of longitude at the equator)

3 nautical miles = 1 marine league (3.45 statute miles)   = 5.56 kilometers

60 nautical miles = 1 degree of a great circle of the earth

Area

1 square inch	=	6.452 square centimeters
144 square inches = 1 square foot	= 929	square centimeters
9 square feet = 1 square yard	=	0.8361 square meter
30¼ square yards = 1 square rod	=	25.29 square meters
160 square rods or 4,840 square yards or 43,560 square feet = 1 acre	=	0.4047 hectare
640 acres = 1 square mile	= 259	hectares or 2.59 square kilometers

Volume or Capacity

Cubic Measure

1 cubic inch		= 16.387 cubic centimeters
1,728 cubic inches	= 1 cubic foot =	0.0283 cubic meter
27 cubic feet	= 1 cubic yard =	0.7646 cubic meter

(in units for cordwood, etc.)

16 cubic feet	= 1 cord foot =	0.453 cubic meter
8 cord feet	= 1 cord =	3.625 cubic meters

Dry Measure

1 pint	=	33.60 cubic inches =	0.5505 liter
2 pints	= 1 quart =	67.20 cubic inches =	1.1012 liters
8 quarts	= 1 peck =	537.61 cubic inches =	8.8098 liters
4 pecks	= 1 bushel =	2,150.42 cubic inches =	35.2383 liters

1 British dry quart = 1.032 U.S. dry quarts

According to U.S. government standards, the following are the weights avoirdupois for single bushels of the specified grains: for wheat, 60 pounds; for barley, 48 pounds; for oats, 32 pounds; for rye, 56 pounds; for corn, 56 pounds. Some states have specifications varying from these.

Liquid Measure

1 gill	= 4 fluid ounces =	7.219 cubic inches	= 0.1183 liter

(see next table)

4 gills	= 1 pint	= 28.875 cubic inches	= 0.4732 liter
2 pints	= 1 quart	= 57.75 cubic inches	= 0.9464 liter
4 quarts	= 1 gallon	= 231 cubic inches	= 3.7854 liters

The British imperial gallon (4 imperial quarts) = 277.42 cubic inches = 4.546 liters. The barrel in Great Britain equals 36 imperial gallons; in the United States, usually 31½ gallons.

Apothecaries' Fluid Measure

1 minim		= 0.0038 cubic inch	= 0.0616 milliliter
60 minims	= 1 fluid dram =	0.2256 cubic inch	= 3.6966 milliliters
8 fluid drams	= 1 fluid ounce =	1.8047 cubic inches	= 0.0296 liter
16 fluid ounces	= 1 pint	= 28.875 cubic inches	= 0.4732 liter

See table immediately preceding for quart and gallon equivalents.
The British pint = 20 fluid ounces.

Weight

Avoirdupois Weight

(The grain, equal to 0.0648 gram, is the same in all three tables of weight.)

1 dram or 27.34 grains	=	1.772 grams
16 drams or 437.5 grains = 1 ounce	=	28.3495 grams
16 ounces or 7,000 grains = 1 pound	= 453.59	grams
100 pounds = 1 hundredweight	= 45.36	kilograms
2,000 pounds = 1 ton	= 907.18	kilograms

In Great Britain, 14 pounds (6.35 kilograms) = 1 stone, 112 pounds (50.80 kilograms) = 1 hundredweight, and 2,240 pounds (1,016.05 kilograms) = 1 long ton.

Troy Weight

(The grain, equal to 0.0648 gram, is the same in all three tables of weight.)

3.086 grains = 1 carat	= 200	milligrams
24 grains = 1 pennyweight	= 1.5552 grams	
20 pennyweights or 480 grains = 1 ounce	= 31.1035 grams	
12 ounces or 5,760 grains = 1 pound	= 373.24	grams

Apothecaries' Weight

(The grain, equal to 0.0648 gram, is the same in all three tables of weight.)

20 grains = 1 scruple	= 1.296	grams
3 scruples = 1 dram	= 3.888	grams
8 drams or 480 grains = 1 ounce	= 31.1035 grams	
12 ounces or 5,760 grains = 1 pound	= 373.24	grams

CIRCULAR OR ANGULAR MEASUREMENT

60 seconds(")	= 1 minute(')
60 minutes	= 1 degree(°)
90 degrees	= 1 quadrant or 1 right angle
4 quadrants or 360 degrees	= 1 circle

THE METRIC SYSTEM

Length or Distance

Linear Measure

10 millimeters	= 1 centimeter	=	0.3937 inch
10 centimeters	= 1 decimeter	=	3.937 inches
10 decimeters	= 1 meter	=	39.37 inches or 3.28 feet
10 meters	= 1 decameter	= 393.7	inches
10 decameters	= 1 hectometer	= 328.08	feet
10 hectometers	= 1 kilometer	=	0.621 mile
10 kilometers	= 1 myriameter	=	6.21 miles

Area

Square Measure

100 square millimeters	= 1 square centimeter	=	0.15499 square inch
100 square centimeters	= 1 square decimeter	=	15.499 square inches
100 square decimeters	= 1 square meter	= 1,549.9	square inches or 1.196 square yards
100 square meters	= 1 square decameter	=	119.6 square yards
100 square decameters	= 1 square hectometer	=	2.471 acres
100 square hectometers	= 1 square kilometer	=	0.386 square mile

Land Measure

1 square meter	= 1 centiare	= 1,549.9	square inches
100 centiares	= 1 are	=	119.6 square yards
100 ares	= 1 hectare	=	2.471 acres
100 hectares	= 1 square kilometer	=	0.386 square mile

Volume or Capacity

Volume Measure

1,000 cubic millimeters = 1 cubic centimeter =   .06102 cubic inch
1,000 cubic centimeters = 1 cubic decimeter = 61.02   cubic inches
1,000 cubic decimeters = 1 cubic meter   = 35.314   cubic feet
                            (the unit is called a
                            stere in measuring
                            firewood)

Capacity Measure

10 milliliters = 1 centiliter =   .338   fluid ounce
10 centiliters = 1 deciliter =   3.38   fluid ounces
10 deciliters = 1 liter   =   1.0567 liquid quarts or 0.9081 dry quart
10 liters   = 1 decaliter =   2.64   gallons or 0.284 bushel
10 decaliters = 1 hectoliter = 26.418   gallons or 2.838 bushels
10 hectoliters = 1 kiloliter   = 264.18   gallons or 35.315 cubic feet

---

Weight

Weights

10 milligrams = 1 centigram =   0.1543 grain
10 centigrams = 1 decigram   =   1.5432 grains
10 decigrams   = 1 gram   =   15.432 grains
10 grams   = 1 decagram   =   0.3527 ounce
10 decagrams   = 1 hectogram =   3.5274 ounces
10 hectograms = 1 kilogram   =   2.2046 pounds
10 kilograms   = 1 myriagram =   22.046 pounds
10 myriagrams = 1 quintal   =   220.46   pounds
10 quintals   = 1 metric ton = 2,204.6   pounds

Index

BOOKS FOR JOB HUNTERS

CAREERS / STUDY GUIDES

Airline Pilot
Allied Health Professions
Automobile Technician Certification Tests
Federal Jobs for College Graduates
Federal Jobs in Law Enforcement
Getting Started in Film
How to Pass Clerical Employment Tests
How You Really Get Hired
Law Enforcement Exams Handbook
Make Your Job Interview a Success
Mechanical Aptitude and Spatial Relations Tests
Mid-Career Job Hunting
100 Best Careers for the Year 2000
Passport to Overseas Employment
Postal Exams Handbook
Real Estate License Examinations
Refrigeration License Examinations
Travel Agent

RESUME GUIDES

The Complete Resume Guide
Resumes for Better Jobs
Resumes That Get Jobs
Your Resume: Key to a Better Job

AVAILABLE AT BOOKSTORES EVERYWHERE

PRENTICE HALL